AMERICAN EDUCATION

THE METROPOLITAN EXPERIENCE
1876–1980

AMERICAN EDUCATION

THE METROPOLITAN EXPERIENCE

1876–1980

Lawrence A. Cremin

PERENNIAL LIBRARY

HARPER & ROW, PUBLISHERS, New York
Grand Rapids, Philadelphia, St. Louis, San Francisco
London, Singapore, Sydney, Tokyo, Toronto

A hardcover edition of this book was published in 1988 by Harper & Row, Publishers.

AMERICAN EDUCATION: THE METROPOLITAN EXPERIENCE 1876–1980. Copyright © 1988 by Lawrence A. Cremin. All rights reserved. Printed in the United States of America. No part of this book may be used or reproduced in any manner whatsoever without written permission except in the case of brief quotations embodied in critical articles and reviews. For information address Harper & Row, Publishers, Inc., 10 East 53rd Street, New York, N.Y. 10022.

First PERENNIAL LIBRARY edition published in 1990.

The Library of Congress has cataloged the hardcover edition as follows:

Cremin, Lawrence Arthur, 1925–
    American education, the metropolitan experience, 1876-1980.
Bibliography: p.
Includes index.
1. Education—United States—History—19th century. 2. Education—United States—History—20th century. 3. Education sociology—United States. 4. Urbanization—United States. I. Title.
LA216.C73 1988   370'.973   87-45040
ISBN 0-06-015804-2

ISBN 0-06-091656-7 (pbk.)
90 91 92 93 94 FG 10 9 8 7 6 5 4 3 2 1

For Jody and David

Today, nowhere in the world are there elders who know what the children know, no matter how remote and simple the societies are in which the children live. In the past there were always some elders who knew more than any children in terms of their experience of having grown up within a cultural system. Today there are none.

MARGARET MEAD

CONTENTS

vii

Part IV. A Metropolitan Education

PREFACE

The present work concludes the trilogy begun with *American Education: The Colonial Experience, 1607–1783* (New York: Harper & Row, 1970) and continued with *American Education: The National Experience, 1783–1876* (New York: Harper & Row, 1980). My effort in the three volumes has been to present a comprehensive, scholarly account of the history of American education. The first volume traced the origins of American education to the European Renaissance, depicting the transplantation of educational institutions to the New World as part of the colonizing efforts of the seventeenth and eighteenth centuries, describing the gradual modification of those institutions under novel social and economic circumstances, and explicating the role of those institutions in the movement for independence. The second volume carried the account to 1876, portraying the development of an authentic American vernacular in education that proffered a popular *paideia* compounded of evangelical pieties, democratic hopes, and utilitarian strivings, and indicating the role of that *paideia* in the creation of a unified American society, on the one hand, and in the rending of that society by civil conflict, on the other. The present volume carries the account to 1980, emphasizing the transformation and proliferation of educative institutions as the United States became a metropolitan society and explicating the role of those institutions in the export of American culture and civilization to other regions of the world. More particularly, it explores the ways in which ethnoreligious configurations of education wrought fundamental changes in the nature and character of the American *paideia;* it traces the role of progressive reformism in the unprecedented expansion of the schools and colleges and in the establishment of a host of educationally oriented social service agencies; it describes the rise of the media of popular communication as critically important institutions in the education (and miseducation) of the public; it documents the transformation of libraries, museums, and other cultural agencies from essentially custodial institutions with ancillary educative functions into primarily educational institutions; it traces the transformation of educational endeavors within agriculture, industry, and the military services from informal apprenticeship efforts that affected a few workers over short periods of time into well-organized programs that affected millions of workers over extensive periods of time; and it describes the ways in which missionaries, businessmen, philanthropists, and government officials transplanted American educative institutions overseas, with varying and frequently ironic outcomes. And, in all of these developments, it explicates the myriad ways in which popularization, multitudinousness, and politicization became the leading characteristics of American education, marking some of its most formidable achievements at the same time that they created some of its most intractable problems.

As in the first two volumes, I have defined education broadly, as the deliberate, systematic, and sustained effort to transmit, evoke, or acquire knowledge, values, attitudes, skills, and sensibilities, as well as any learning that results from that effort, direct or indirect, intended or unintended. The definition is intended to call attention to the wide range of situations and institutions in which education has gone forward over the years. I have also paid special heed to the changing configurations of education in twentieth-century America—particularly the increasing significance of schools and colleges and of the media of popular communication—and to the various ways in which different individuals interacted with those configurations. The more general theory underlying all this is set forth in *Public Education* (New York: Basic Books, 1976). As in the earlier volumes, too, I have given substantial attention to ideas about education, not as disembodied notions or as mere rationalizations of existential reality, but rather as moving forces that operate within a social context, that compete for attention, and that profoundly affect what people believe is possible and desirable in the realm of education. Similarly, I have dealt extensively with institutions, though one should bear in mind that, even as educative institutions became more organized, more systematized, and more powerful during the twentieth century, individuals continued to make their way through those institutions with their own agenda, their own perceptions, and their own particular goals. Finally, I have tried steadfastly to avoid the related sins of Whiggishness and anachronism: what happened in the past century of American educational history was neither inexorable nor foreordained; it was the outcome of the particular combinations of people, politics, and chance that mark all of human history.

One or two technical comments about style may be of interest. I have tried to keep footnotes to a minimum, as a rule documenting only quotations (except where they are meant to indicate commonplaces) and direct assertions involving statistics or statutes. Also, given the choice between citing an original source or referring to some more easily accessible accurate reprint, I have ordinarily chosen the latter; thus, Herbert Croly's well-known work *The Promise of American Life* (1909) is quoted, not from the original edition, but rather from the more recent John Harvard Library edition (1965), with its excellent introduction by Arthur M. Schlesinger, Jr. I have discussed most of the secondary and tertiary literature on which the work rests in the bibliographical essay; hence, those interested in the sources for a particular section should read that essay in conjunction with the text and the notes. I should add that I have not tried to be exhaustive in the bibliography—that would have further lengthened an already lengthy book; I have merely tried to enable the reader to retrace my steps and then proceed independently. Particularly in instances where an authoritative synthesis with a competent bibliography is available, for example, Lawrence C. Stedman and Carl F. Kaestle, *An Investigation of Crude Literacy, Reading Performance, and Functional Literacy in the United States, 1880 to 1980* (Madison: Wisconsin Center for Education Research, 1986), I have kept my own citations to a minimum. As in the earlier volumes, I have expanded, modernized, and Americanized all spelling and some punctuation in quoted passages; in the case of titles of written works, I have made only those alterations required to follow modern typographical convention.

The overall project of which the present volume is part originated from an invitation in 1964 by W. Stull Holt, then secretary of the American Historical Association, Francis Keppel, then United States Commissioner of Education, and John Gardner, then president of the Carnegie Corporation of New York, to prepare a comprehensive scholarly history of American education in connection with the centenary of the United States Office of Education in 1967. I agreed at the time to produce the three volumes in seven years; in the end, it has taken twenty-three. The sponsoring organizations have been consistently patient and encouraging, however, especially the Carnegie Corporation, which, under the leadership of Alan Pifer, provided additional funds in 1973 to sustain the effort. It is a pleasure once again to state my gratitude to the Association, the Office (now the Department), and the Corporation for their kindness in furthering the work and at the same time to absolve them of any responsibility for the outcome: characteristically, Messrs. Holt, Keppel, Gardner, and Pifer arranged for all matters of content to rest wholly and finally in my hands.

No one engaged in a work of comprehensive scholarship can fail to be aware of the infinite variety of kindnesses that contribute at every point to the progress of the enterprise. Librarians and archivists at dozens of research centers in the United States and abroad have been patiently generous with their time and expertise; they remain the unsung heroes and heroines of historical inquiry. In addition, I am fortunate to have had the assistance of a number of able associates during the course of the endeavor. Kathryn O'Brien Bordonaro was helpful with the research on Washington Gladden; Mary Ann Dzuback and Sarah Henry Lederman assisted me with several of the educational biographies in Chapter 13, and Mary Ann Dzuback was also extraordinarily helpful in tracking down the sources and checking the footnotes of several of the other chapters. My colleague Ellen Condliffe Lagemann, who collaborated with me in much of the work on the second volume and with whom I have co-taught over the past ten years, contributed invaluably at every point, from the definition of the volume to the substance of its leading arguments; and she also generously read and criticized the final draft. My editor, Cass Canfield, Jr., has been a model of patience and encouragement, following the project with spirited interest from its inception and sharing his wisdom about writing and publishing at every point. And Nancy Fernandez typed the manuscript with intelligence and care. To these and others is owed a good deal of whatever merit the book may possess; responsibility for its shortcomings is most assuredly mine.

The work on the volume began during a summer of residence at the Center for Advanced Study in the Behavioral Sciences in 1980, and has continued since at the Center (during the summers of 1981 and 1983), at the School of Education of Stanford University (during the summers of 1982 and 1984), and at Teachers College, Columbia University. In addition I enjoyed a wonderfully fruitful year during 1984–85 as the Director's Visitor at the Institute for Advanced Study. I am grateful to Gardner Lindzey, Director of the Center, J. Myron Atkin, Dean of the Stanford School of Education during my periods of residence there, and Harry Woolf, Director of the Institute during

1984–85, for their gracious hospitality and many kindnesses. Teachers College has nurtured the project from its beginning, and it is a pleasure to acknowledge the continuing encouragement of the trustees of the college and of my faculty and student colleagues. Through the generosity of the University of Wisconsin, I had the opportunity to present the principal theses of the volume in the 1976 Merle Curti Lectures, which were subsequently published as *Traditions of American Education* (New York: Basic Books, 1977).

My revered mother and father died during the time I was at work on this volume. They had read every word I had ever published and they had saved me from publishing any number of words that should not have been published; and they had shared freely and lovingly their ideas, their appreciations, and their criticisms. I have learned a good deal over the years about the family as educator from my perusal of historical sources and contemporary studies; but I learned at least as much from the ways in which they nurtured, sustained, and taught as parents. I owe them an inestimable debt of gratitude.

Finally, there is my debt to my beloved wife and children, who assisted me from time to time with the work itself and whose devotion and understanding have been, as always, unfailing. Again, my gratitude is unbounded.

L.A.C.

Teachers College, Columbia University
May, 1987

AMERICAN EDUCATION
The Metropolitan Experience
1876–1980

INTRODUCTION

I believe that education is the fundamental method of social progress and reform.

J O H N   D E W E Y

Americans commemorated the centennial of the Republic in 1876 with a curious mixture of pride, pretension, cynicism, and shame. There was no escaping the fact that the country was in the throes of a depression, that its government was ridden by scandal, that its southern states continued under a military occupation, that its army was at war with the Indians, that its newly emancipated blacks were neither enfranchised nor literate, and that some of its most articulate women had chosen the Fourth of July itself to promulgate a Declaration of Rights for Women, demanding justice, equality, and "all the civil and political rights that belong to citizens of the United States." Yet, there was the boost to the national spirit that derived from the great Philadelphia exposition, which was attended by one in five Americans and which confidently proclaimed American industrial preeminence to the world; there was the exhilaration of a flood of centennial rhetoric celebrating the achievement of independence and the triumph of self-government; and there was the more general stocktaking that seemed to leave Grantism behind and set the nation on the road to a moral recovery.[1]

As usual, the preachers saw it all as the continuing manifestation of God's special concern for his chosen people. According to the liberal minister Horace Bushnell, there had been three steps in the

---

1. "Declaration of Rights for Women," in Elizabeth Cady Stanton, Susan B. Anthony, and Matilda Joslyn Gage, eds., *History of Woman Suffrage, 1848–1885* (3 vols.; New York and Rochester: Fowler & Wells and Susan B. Anthony, 1881–1886), III, 34.

evolution of true "nationhood." The first was the Declaration of Independence, which did little more than confirm politically the nation that already existed spiritually. The second was the drafting of the Constitution, which did little more than detail "the constitution already framed by Almighty God in the historic cast of our nation itself." And the third was the testing in the fires of the Civil War of "a sacredly heroic, providentially tragic unity, where God's cherubim stand guard over grudges and hates and remembered jealousies, and the sense of nationality becomes a kind of religion." America was now free to play its millennial role in history, Bushnell announced; it remained for the Republic to demonstrate its loyalty to God's example in its national life and in so doing to "give bent to the world's thoughts" and "command its movements."[2]

However chauvinistic Bushnell's theology, there can be no denying its representativeness. An entire generation of Protestant clergymen lectured the people of the United States on their responsibilities for righteous world leadership at precisely the time the resources were coming available with which to attempt it. And the interaction of aspiration with possibility shaped much of the nation's development during the century that followed. The key to that development was metropolitanization: the United States became a nation of cities at the same time that it became an exporter of culture and civilization to the world. And education, in a bewildering variety of forms and institutions, was profoundly involved in both phenomena.

II

The expansion of the Republic, in territory and population, continued unabated during the years following 1876. The entry of New Mexico and Arizona into the Union in 1912 completed the process of state making within the continental boundaries of the nation, while the admission of Alaska and Hawaii in 1959 indicated that territorial separation would not in and of itself preclude statehood. More important, all twelve of the states admitted after 1876 entered under the principles first laid down in the land ordinances of the 1780's, namely, that new territories wishing to join the Union and meeting certain criteria with respect to population, politics, and culture could do so on the basis of full and equal participation in the polity rather than being held in some lesser colonial status. As a result of the additions,

2. Horace Bushnell, *Building Eras in Religion* [1881] (reprint ed.; New York: Charles Scribner's Sons, 1903), pp. 292, 329.

the nation came to embrace three and a half million square miles of territory, with the distance from New York to Honolulu stretching a third of the way around the world. The United States had become the largest republic in history, and in its very nature called to the fore classical concerns about the relation between size and self-government in the politics of a free society.

The American population continued to diversify as it increased, rising from 46,107,000 in 1876 to 226,546,000 in 1980. The rate of natural increase declined during the latter decades of the nineteenth century, owing to falling birth rates; it remained fairly steady between 1900 and 1925, declined again between 1925 and 1940, rose moderately between 1940 and 1960, and then declined again after 1960. Immigration also waxed and waned, depending upon changing political and economic conditions in the United States and in the world at large; yet some 40,000,000 people entered the country between 1876 and 1980, constituting one of the greatest migrations in history. The principal regions of origin varied over time. Southern, central, and eastern Europe predominated during the period from 1880 to 1924; northwestern and central Europe predominated during the 1930's, 1940's, and 1950's, with many of the immigrants arriving as refugees from totalitarian or war-ravaged countries; Canada, the West Indies, and Latin America predominated during the 1960's; and those regions along with south and southeast Asia predominated during the 1970's, again with many of the immigrants arriving as refugees from totalitarian or war-ravaged countries.

The result of this diverse immigration was an extraordinarily variegated population with respect to race, religion, and ethnicity; and the complex of problems surrounding Americanization and the attainment of citizenship that had surfaced during the earliest years of the Republic persisted throughout the era. What did it mean to be an American and who was eligible for full membership in the American community? The earliest national policies had tended toward birthright citizenship for the native-born and relative ease of naturalization for immigrants. Yet from the beginning there had been ambivalence and confusion on questions of race and gender. American blacks achieved *de jure* citizenship only with the ratification of the Fourteenth Amendment to the United States Constitution in 1868, and in fact they were still striving for a full measure of *de facto* citizenship during the 1970's and 1980's. Native Americans achieved similar *de jure* citizenship through the Citizenship Act of 1924, yet they too were pressing for *de facto* rights during the 1970's and 1980's. And native-born citizens of Japanese ancestry, who had never enjoyed the full measure of their citizenship, actually found themselves confined to relocation camps with presidential and congressional sanction during World War II. Women were covered from the earliest days by citizenship and naturalization policies comparable to those of men, but the rights attaching to their citizenship were at best restricted and confused; they did not achieve the suffrage until the ratification of the Nineteenth Amendment in 1920 and many Americans still felt obliged during the 1970's and 1980's to seek an additional constitutional amendment fully guaranteeing equal rights for women. As for white ethnic immigrants, they too faced the continuing problems of linguistic differences and cultural affirmation—both associated with conceptions of Americanization and requirements for naturalization. Should German or Mexican or Vietnamese immigrants who spoke no English be accepted as citizens? Should such individuals be required to learn English or should public and private agencies be expected to adjust to their diverse linguistic needs? Once such individuals (and their children) had decided to undergo education for citizenship, should they be taught in English or in their native language? Such issues were heatedly debated through much of the twentieth century, serving as surrogates for larger and more fundamental questions about the nature of American identity and the character of the American community.

The urbanization of the United States involved much more than the simple demographic fact that in 1890 some 30 percent of a population of 63 million lived in cities, in 1920 over half of a population of 106 million lived in cities, in 1950 almost two-thirds of a population of 151 million lived in cities, and in 1980 some three-fourths of a population of 227 million lived in cities. Urbanization was inextricably tied to the complex and interrelated phenomena that constituted the industrial, communications, and organizational revolutions of the late nineteenth and twentieth centuries. The national network of railroads that marked the first stage of American industrialization was in many ways a result of vigorous interurban rivalry, initially in the linking of short lines that connected individual cities with their hinterlands and that subsequently became the branches of more comprehensive trunk lines, and later in the efforts of coalitions of cities to obtain transcontinental lines in one region of the country rather than another. Once the national network had been built, the reduced costs of transporting raw materials and finished goods, coupled with the enlarged possibility of markets, spurred the development of large-scale manufacturing of producers' and consumers' goods, which in turn made possible the capital accumulations that created great financial centers such as New York, Boston, Chicago, and San Francisco. With continuing technological advance, especially in the electronics, chemical, and information industries, those centers also became the hubs of new service and knowledge economies, though it should be noted that the continuing development of transportation and communication rendered these new industries more "footloose" because they were less dependent upon steady supplies of heavy raw materials. Moreover, the extraordinary technological advances that gave rise to the electric trolley and elevator, the telephone, and the automobile, the truck, and the bus made possible the expansion of cities to sizes earlier unimaginable, while large-scale bureaucratic organization made possible the management, not only of vast urban services, but also of the corporate modes of production that sustained the urban economy.

One outcome of urbanization was the early emergence of complex interrelationships between central cities and their suburban rings and rural hinterlands, which produced highly specialized mosaics of sub-communities tied together into functional wholes in which traditional distinctions between "urban," "suburban," and "rural" tended to blur and even to disappear. The result, recognizable demographically in its large size and area, was the metropolis. Later, once distinct metropolitan areas themselves entered into complex interrelationships with one another, forming, first, great regional megalopolitan communities, and, ultimately, the network or system of metropolitan and megalopolitan communities that constituted the post–World War II United States. As early as 1880, almost two decades before the political consolidation that created Greater New York, the Bureau of the Census acknowledged the existence of a New York metropolitan district by grouping the data for New York City and its suburbs in one section. Thirty years later, in 1910, the Bureau extended the conception of the metropolitan district to the entire nation, defining such a district as a central city with a population of 200,000 or more along with its suburbs and identifying twenty-five such agglomerations, ranging in size from Portland, Oregon, with an area of 44,000 acres and a population of 215,000, to New York, with an area of 617,000 acres and a population of 6,500,000. Forty years after that, in 1950, the Bureau transformed the concept into the Standard Metropolitan Area (later, the Standard Metropolitan Statistical Area), defining such an area as a county or group of contiguous counties (in New England, a town) with a central city of 50,000 or more and identifying 168 such areas across the country. In 1960, the Census Bureau also created a category called the Standard Consolidated Area (later, the Standard Consolidated Statistical Area) to designate adjoining Standard Metropolitan Areas that had become socially and economically interrelated. And in 1961, the geographer Jean Gottmann published his study entitled *Megalopolis: The Urbanized Northeastern Seaboard of the United States,* surveying the metropolitan region from southern New Hampshire to northern Virginia and from the Atlantic shore to the Appalachian foothills, and suggested that there was an ecological unity about the region that transcended the boundaries of any particular city, even New York. In "Megalopolis," not only had distinctions between city, suburb, and country disappeared, but the distinctions between one city and another had disappeared; for all intents and purposes the various human activities of the region had achieved such scale, flow, and interdependence as to transcend the traditional boundaries of cities, counties, and states. By extension, it was readily discernible that the same phenomena prevailed in the metropolitan regions that extended from Chicago to St. Louis in the Midwest and from San Francisco to San Diego on the West Coast.

Metropolitan areas were most easily defined demographically, as having a certain size and density of population, or in terms of area, though it was always difficult to determine precisely where to draw the boundaries and on what basis. In the end, however, it was in their various kinds of functional coherence that metropolitan areas exerted their most profound influences on the lives of individuals. As early as 1922, the economic historian N. S. B. Gras explicated the various criteria according to which one might define a metropolitan population or area, beginning with the economic (the metropolis as market region) and going on to the political (the metropolis as administrative unit), the religious (the metropolis as ecclesiastical unit), and the intellectual (the metropolis as cultural unit). In 1933, as part of the work of President Herbert Hoover's Committee on Recent Social Trends, the sociologist R. D. McKenzie carried the analysis further, pointing to the acceleration of metropolitanization politically, as a result of the creation of new regional administrative and planning entities; economically, as a result of motor trucks making increasing use of an expanding highway system; and culturally, as a result of radio broadcasting. Both scholars ended their analyses with discussions of the relationships between and among American cities that ultimately formed a national metropolitan community, and both proved prescient in that respect. By the 1970's and 1980's, whether one defined the national metropolitan community politically (a single federal housing program could stimulate suburban growth across the country), economically (the cities of the northeastern megalopolis imported most of the food they consumed from elsewhere in the nation or abroad), or culturally (sixty million Americans could and did simultaneously view the same television program), it was everywhere in evidence. There was no denying significant differences among metropolitan regions: Detroit still produced automobiles; Akron, rubber tires; and Pittsburgh, steel. Washington was still an administrative center, and New York was still a financial capital. Nevertheless, the growing interdependence and commonality of the nation's metropolitan communities were established facts.[3]

The demands of metropolitan civilization upon education were far-reaching. At the very least, they placed added burdens on extant institutions, ranging from the insistence that they provide the social discipline essential to life amidst crowded conditions to the suggestion that they convey every manner of vital specialized knowledge. One result was that statements of educational purpose tended to broaden significantly. Thus, L. Emmett Holt recommended to families a tough-minded, no-nonsense child-rearing regime that would firmly inculcate the lifelong self-denial he deemed requisite for urban living. Washington Gladden summoned the church to extend Christian influence to art, amusement, business, politics, industry, and international relations, indeed to every department of human affairs. John Dewey called upon each school to become an embryonic social community, "active with types of occupations that reflect the life of the larger society, and permeated throughout with the spirit of art, history, and science." And Walter Lippmann demanded nothing less than a new machinery of knowledge, in which bodies of experts imbued with a selfless equanimity would use the searchlight of reason to enlighten public vision. In place of the self-instructed person of virtuous character, abiding patriotism, and prudent wisdom, reformers such as these foresaw the responsible citizen informed by the detached and selfless expert—it was a relationship that would involve every institution in every realm of human affairs and ultimately transform most politics into education. "I believe that education is the fundamental method of social progress and reform," Dewey main-

3. N. S. B. Gras, *An Introduction to Economic History* (New York: Harper & Brothers, 1922), p. 186; and R. D. McKenzie, "The Rise of Metropolitan Communities," in *Recent Social Trends in the United States* (2 vols.; New York: McGraw-Hill Book Company, 1933), I, 443–496.

tained in his pedagogic creed; ". . . all reforms which rest simply upon the enactment of law, or the threatening of certain penalties, or on changes in mechanical or outward arrangements, are transitory and futile." Like Emerson, Dewey envisioned the day when education would largely replace politics; though, far more than Emerson, he recognized that in the process education itself would be politicized.[4]

At the same time that they broadened, statements of educational purpose asserted new demands for highly specialized knowledge and skill. Proponents of every manner of vocational education sought to shift from apprenticeship to schooling as the basis of preparing new practitioners for their specialties—the thrust was at the heart of the movement that culminated in the Smith-Hughes legislation of 1917, establishing programs of federal assistance for the teaching of agriculture, the trades and industries, and home economics in the high schools, and it was also at the heart of the rapid development of professional schools associated with the nation's colleges and universities. New technologies were fashioned for upgrading the skills of those already practicing the various trades and professions—Seaman A. Knapp's work in establishing a system of agricultural extension that would convey the new knowledge being developed in the agricultural colleges and agricultural experiment stations is an excellent example, as is the work of the various so-called corporate schools of the electrical, railroad, gas, and machine industries, established during and after the 1890's to offer everything from simple sales-training programs to postgraduate engineering programs. And a generation of university presidents, imbued with German research ideals, called for a new emphasis on the production of knowledge within the universities—one thinks immediately of Daniel Coit Gilman's celebrated inaugural address at the Johns Hopkins University, remarking the shared responsibilities of colleges, universities, learned societies, technical schools, and museums as institutions of "superior education," but asserting the special obligation of the universities to advance, refine, conserve, and distribute knowledge.[5]

4. L. Emmett Holt, *The Care and Feeding of Children: A Catechism for the Use of Mothers and Children's Nurses* (New York: D. Appleton and Co., 1894); Washington Gladden, *Applied Christianity: The Moral Aspects of Social Questions* (Boston: Houghton, Mifflin and Company, 1886); John Dewey, *The School and Society* [1899], in *John Dewey: The Middle Works, 1899–1924*, edited by Jo Ann Boydston (15 vols.; Carbondale: Southern Illinois University Press, 1976–1983), I, 19; Walter Lippmann, *Public Opinion* (New York: Harcourt, Brace and Company, 1922); and John Dewey, "My Pedagogic Creed" [1897], in *John Dewey: The Early Works, 1892–1898* (5 vols.; Carbondale: Southern Illinois University Press, 1969–1972), V, 93.

5. Daniel Coit Gilman, *University Problems in the United States* (New York: The Century Co., 1898), p. 13.

Yet, however much educators attempted to order and systematize the institutional response to new needs, there was the ubiquitous and incessant education implicit in the very nature of metropolitan life. As had been the case at least since Sir George Buck had described seventeenth-century London as "the third university of England," the sheer multiplicity of models available to the apt learner, from the cunning thief to the skillful politician, and the vast range of cultural and commercial displays expressly intended to attract, from the costumed dancers in ethnic celebrations to the products for sale in downtown department stores, made the metropolis itself a school of incomparable richness. Not everyone was aware of its curriculum and not everyone was prepared to profit from its offerings; but the concentration and coexistence of an extraordinary variety of models and displays did permit an unprecedented exchange of traditions, aspirations, and ways of thinking, believing, and acting. In addition, the central city of the metropolis was a purveyor of education to its hinterland, through the advertisement of goods, the setting of intellectual, artistic, and ethical styles, and the dissemination of information and news. In fact, the very essence of its cosmopolitanism lay in a continuing educational assault upon local idiosyncrasy, with the result that one way of defining the boundaries of a metropolis was to measure the outer limits of that assault.[6]

The metropolitanization of America in the second sense, in which the nation became an exporter of culture and civilization to the world, was intimately bound up with the profound shift in foreign policy that occurred during the decades following the Civil War. From the earliest days of the Republic, there had been a millennial strain in American thought that had made it appear to be the nation's divine obligation to instruct the world in the principles of social justice, at the least by exemplification and where possible by more systematic means. Yet the foreign policy of the United States through much of the nineteenth century had been essentially isolationist, seeking the preservation of the nation's newly won independence, on the one hand, by ruling the Western hemisphere off limits to political penetration by the European powers, and, on the other hand, by declaring the conflicts among the European powers of no interest to the United States (as late as 1901 William McKinley's secretary of state, John Hay, could

6. Sir George Buck, "The Third Universitie of England" [1615], printed as part of an appendix to John Stow and Edward Howes, *The Annales, or Generall Chronicle of England* (London: Thoma[s] Adams, 1615), p. 965.

unabashedly explain American foreign policy as "the Monroe Doctrine and the Golden Rule"). Although the term "empire" had been in general use during that period, it had usually referred to the "manifest destiny" of the United States to expand to the Pacific coast and exercise dominion over the continent (for some, this included Canada and Mexico).[7]

During the 1880's and 1890's, however, the idea of the American "empire" underwent a significant redefinition, coming to refer to the "manifest destiny" of the United States to exert world leadership through a "benevolent" imperialism that would at the same time strengthen and be sustained by an expanding American industry. No longer were new territories to be incorporated into the American "empire" as part of the metropolis itself, however; rather, the metropolis would maintain more traditional relationships with its dependencies: under the protection of the metropolis they would serve as sources of raw materials, markets for manufactured products, and clients for metropolitan education. This reformulated idea of empire was central to the more activist diplomacy of William McKinley and Theodore Roosevelt, and it provided a natural transition to the full-blown participation in world affairs in the interest of collective security espoused by Woodrow Wilson, Franklin Delano Roosevelt, and all the presidents who followed. In the aftermath of World War II, individual American metropolitan and megalopolitan complexes found themselves linked politically, economically, and culturally with their counterparts abroad, precisely as the metropolitan system that the United States itself had become found itself linked politically, economically, and culturally with the nations of the world. Thus, the financial markets of New York were inextricably linked with the financial markets of Zurich and Tokyo; American cigarettes and blue jeans became staple commodities in a hundred countries; and programs of technical assistance to a variety of nations became a continuing element of American foreign policy.

Within this increasingly international milieu, the deliberate and systematic export of American culture and civilization assumed a multitude of forms. Christian missions, for example, underwent a resurgence during the 1880's and 1890's. The Student Volunteer Movement for Foreign Missions, formally organized in 1888, set out to evangelize the world in a single generation; and a plethora of church and interchurch organizations came into being to sponsor, support,

7. *Addresses of John Hay* (New York: The Century Co., 1906), p. 120.

organize, and direct the efforts of a vast army of educators, not only in the strange lands of Africa, Asia, and Latin America, but in England and on the European continent as well. President McKinley revealed the tie between those missionary efforts and national policy when he explained to a number of Methodist friends about his change of heart with respect to acquiring the Philippine Islands: "I am not ashamed to tell you, gentlemen, that I went down on my knees and prayed Almighty God for light and guidance more than one night. And one night late it came to me this way— . . . that there was nothing left for us to do but to take them all, and to educate the Filipinos, and uplift and civilize and Christianize them, and by God's grace do the very best we could by them, as our fellow men for whom Christ had also died." Imperialism as a policy was compounded of many elements, of which evangelicism was merely one, although it was the evangelical dimension that led many proponents of imperialism to believe that it was beneficent. Nevertheless, the fact that evangelicism was an important aspect of imperialism meant that education would inevitably become associated with dollar diplomacy and direct conquest.[8]

Beyond the missions movement, there was the export of cultural products—books, magazines, films, and television programs that instructed directly or that entertained and in the process often instructed indirectly. And beyond cultural products there was the export of entire systems of education. Kenneth James King, for example, has sketched the process whereby the British foreign office exported industrial education on the Hampton-Tuskegee model to the British colonies in Africa; Peter Buck has explicated the transfer of American scientific medicine and medical education to China under the aegis of the Rockefeller Foundation; and W. H. G. Armytage has traced the influence of American ideals and examples on the English educational system itself. And during the years after World War II there were the multifarious programs under national and international auspices in which everything from nursery schools to graduate management education on the American model was exported to countries around the world.[9]

Finally, there was the export of large numbers of people who

8. Charles S. Olcott, *The Life of William McKinley* (2 vols.; Boston: Houghton, Mifflin and Company, 1916), II, 110–111.

9. Kenneth James King, *Pan-Africanism and Education: A Study of Race Philanthropy and Education in the Southern States of America and East Africa* (Oxford: Clarendon Press, 1971); Peter Buck, *American Science and Modern China* (Cambridge: Cambridge University Press, 1980); and W. H. G. Armytage, *The American Influence on English Education* (London: Routledge and Kegan Paul, 1967).

taught by example, by design, and by force—armies of travelers, of technicians, and of occupation. Like the missionaries who preceded and often accompanied them, they frequently carried well-planned curricula that they set out explicitly to teach; and, like the missionaries, too, whether or not they were systematically teaching, they were exemplifying by their every act a civilization whose growing political and economic power bespoke the advantages of emulation. That the civilization, incidentally, was itself still in the process of definition— that its own *paideia* was still in the making—in no way lessened the impact of the teaching; for, as Alexis de Tocqueville had noted earlier in the nation's history, a lack of self-definition is not at all incompatible with a garrulous patriotism—indeed, the one may occasion the other.[10]

Having stressed the shift that metropolitanization occasioned in the balance of trade in products and ideas, one should point out that the traffic was never unidirectional. The United States imported manual training from Russia, the kindergarten from Germany, and the social settlement from England, and it then returned them to Europe in transformed American versions, along with indigenously developed junior high schools, demonstration farms, and children's television programs. However discernibly American some patterns of educational thought and practice became, they were never exclusively American. Indeed, the very concept of an American education in a metropolitan era became problematical, as the extension of ideas and institutions across geographical boundaries accelerated.

III

The movement of education to the core of the American experience, already discernible during the nineteenth century, accelerated during the twentieth. Education not only became an ever more significant American undertaking in its own right, it was increasingly *perceived* as such and assigned an appropriate public value. Precisely for this reason, education became more political, as groups with conflicting ideas of the public interest sought to have their views prevail. One result was that many of the great twentieth-century battles over traditionalism and modernity in religion, politics, and culture were ultimately framed as educational issues and fought out in debates over educational policy and practice. One thinks of the evolution trials of the

10. Alexis de Tocqueville, *Democracy in America,* edited by Phillips Bradley (2 vols.; New York: Alfred A. Knopf, 1946), I, 241–244.

1920's as they affected the churches and the schools, of the debates over popular culture in the 1930's as they affected the federal arts program, and of the loyalty investigations of the 1950's as they affected, not only the colleges and universities, but the entire cultural apparatus of the nation. But these were merely the most publicized crises in a continuing tug-of-war over what should be taught by whom and how in the nation's educating institutions.

Issues of traditionalism and modernity were inseparable, of course, from issues of democracy itself. Should the individualism that Tocqueville found regnant in the 1830's and that many conceived to be synonymous with American liberty remain the dominant motif of church and school teaching, or should it be leavened by the communal emphasis at the heart of Washington Gladden's Social Gospel and John Dewey's social philosophy? Should equality mean the cultivation of the most talented in the nation's colleges and universities, or the nurturance of the average, or the compensatory encouragement of those long discriminated against? Should comity lead the agencies of popular communication to seek the largest general audiences or the greatest number of specialized audiences? What should be the proper balance between popular preference and elite taste in a publicly supported library or museum? Or between local preference and national taste? In sum, how should the legitimate but often unclear and conflicting demands of liberty, equality, and comity be resolved in and through programs of education? And who, in a nation where education had moved to the heart of politics, should do the resolving?

To raise the question of who should make decisions about education was to run headlong into the complexities of metropolitan civilization. Jane Addams, who with Ellen Gates Starr founded Hull House and led its efforts for fully forty years, once observed: "We have learned to say that the good must be extended to all of society before it can be held secure by any one person or any one class; but we have not yet learned to add to that statement, that unless all men and all classes contribute to a good, we cannot even be sure that it is worth having." Her assertion gave voice to the more general pragmatic dictum that decisions needed to be made by those who would suffer the consequences of what was being decided. But a metropolitan society was in its very nature a complicated society, whose affairs were increasingly managed by experts who claimed to be specially equipped by talent, education, and commitment to lead and indeed who commonly had their claims legitimatized by law. In twentieth-century America, it was increasingly professionals who carried on the work of education in churches, schools, colleges, universities, libraries, museums, newspapers, and television stations. Yet in the American system those professionals were almost always subject to the control of boards of laypersons who mediated between them and the external interest groups of the market and the polity who laid ever-increasing claims upon education. Who, then, would decide upon Jane Addams's "good"? The professionals, or the boards of laypeople, or the clienteles being educated? To compound the problem, a metropolitan civilization was increasingly a transnational civilization, whose decisions affected publics beyond the national pale. Who would formulate the "good" in such instances? Given the advances in information technology during the post–World War II era, as symbolized, for example, by the joining of the computer to the instruments of telecommunications, the question became as pressing in education as in politics. Decisions made by American institutions as varied as the United States Information Agency, the Associated Press, and the International Business Machines Corporation exerted worldwide influence; yet, as the controversies surrounding UNESCO's effort during the 1970's and 1980's to create a "new world information and communication order" revealed, there were few established mechanisms whereby those decisions could be made by those who would suffer the consequences of what was being decided and indeed few common bases on which the issues could even be formulated. If education had moved to the heart of the polity, it was the political questions of education that were becoming ever more intractable in the metropolitan world of the 1980's.[11]

Yet political questions had been inescapable from the beginning. Two hundred years after they had made their Revolution, Americans were still in the process of defining what it meant to be an American and hence what they were prepared to teach themselves and their children—they were still in the process of defining an America *paideia*. Given the dynamics of American education, the essence of that process of definition would ultimately be political; given the nature of metropolitan civilization, it would inevitably be transnational; and given the pace of technological and cultural change, it would almost surely be continual. Like the ancient Greeks, who searched through dialogue for a truth that would never be fully or finally discovered, twentieth-century Americans searched through education for a self-definition that would never be fully or finally determined.

11. Jane Addams, *Democracy and Social Ethics* [1902], edited by Anne Firor Scott (Cambridge, Mass.: Harvard University Press, 1964), p. 220.

PART I

THE MORAL COMMONWEALTH

I believe it is fully in the hands of the Christians of the United States, during the next ten or fifteen years, to hasten or retard the coming of Christ's kingdom in the world by hundreds, and perhaps thousands, of years. We of this generation and nation occupy the Gibraltar of the ages which commands the world's future.

JOSIAH STRONG

INTRODUCTION

"We are living in extraordinary times," the Reverend Josiah Strong counseled his fellow Americans in *Our Country* (1885). "There are certain great focal points of history toward which the lines of past progress have converged, and from which have radiated the molding influences of the future. Such was the Incarnation, such was the German Reformation of the sixteenth century, and such are the *closing years of the nineteenth century,* second in importance to that only which must always remain first; viz., the birth of Christ." In Strong's view, the destiny of the United States and of the entire world lay in the hands of contemporary Americans, and whether or not they would seize the opportunity to lead the world to redemption was the central question of the day.[1]

Strong's tract had been commissioned by the American Home Missionary Society as an updating of a fund-raising pamphlet that the Society had been circulating for a generation; and, not surprisingly, its arguments epitomized the commonplaces of contemporary evangelical belief. The United States, Strong maintained, with its incomparable natural resources and its flourishing agricultural, mining, and manufacturing industries, was on the threshold of an unprecedented economic development, with the newly settled regions of the West in the vanguard. Given the historic course of empire, the nation, led by the West, was destined for world leadership. But the fulfillment of that destiny, Strong warned, was threatened by severe perils—the flood of immigrants from central and southeastern Europe, the growing power of the Roman Catholic and Mormon churches, the prevalence of intemperance throughout the land, the challenge of radical socialism and crass materialism. Nowhere were these perils more concentrated or more dangerous than in the nation's

1. Josiah Strong, *Our Country: Its Possible Future and Its Present Crisis* (New York: The Baker & Taylor Co., 1885), p. 1.

burgeoning cities. It was there, in the "storm centers" of contemporary life, that the nation's course would be determined. With the completion of Western settlement, surely to be accomplished within a generation, the permanent outlines of American civilization would be set: a new society, with all the accouterments of modernity, would spring into being, "like Minerva from the head of Jupiter, full-grown and fully equipped." Whether that new society would remain faithful to the ways of the Puritan fathers or succumb to the evils of Mammonism, materialism, intemperance, and irreligion would determine the future of America and ultimately of the world; for it was the God-appointed mission of America, and especially of Anglo-Saxon America, to instruct the world in the truths of Christianity and that mission could be fulfilled only if Americans chose righteousness. The crisis was at hand; the choice was up to each and every individual.[2]

Most of these assertions were readily recognizable from the pre–Civil War evangelical movement: one could hear the voices of Lyman Beecher, Charles Finney, and Horace Bushnell almost as if they were contemporary. But Strong had given the argument a new turn by focusing on the emerging problems of metropolitan America. Americans would still have to choose righteousness and their prime vehicle for achieving righteousness would still be Christian education; but the definition of righteousness and the character of Christian education would now have to be worked out anew in the strange and frightening world of the city. The conversion of America was still the goal; but the conversion of America was now but a first step, for God with infinite wisdom was training Americans for the hour that would soon be at hand, when their institutions, representing "the largest liberty, the purest Christianity, the highest civilization," would spread across the entire earth. The challenge was greater than ever, Strong concluded, but so was the goal—the Kingdom of God, in this world, now; and the great instrument that God had given humankind for achieving the Kingdom was education.[3]

2. *Ibid.*, pp. 128, 158.
3. *Ibid.*, p. 175.

Chapter 1

THE CHALLENGE OF MODERNISM

The first demand that Christianity has to make respecting popular education is that it be directed toward the formation of character rather than the communication of abstract knowledge.

WASHINGTON GLADDEN

American Protestantism faced two profound challenges in its confrontation with the city. Intellectually, it had to make its peace with modernism in culture, and particularly with modern science; socially, it had to determine its stance toward industrial capitalism and the class inequities that arose from capitalism. There were Protestants, of course, who managed to avoid both problems, remaining content with the explanations and assurances of traditional faith; but, as communication increased between the metropolitan centers and rural hamlets of the society, it was more and more difficult to buffer oneself against the controversies associated with intellectual and social change.

Washington Gladden was among the earliest to contend with the challenges of modernism and inequality in a way that seemed persuasive to his contemporaries. Like many Americans of his time, Gladden grew up in the country and then moved to the city. Born in 1836 to the family of a rural Pennsylvania schoolmaster, Gladden was reared on a farm near Owego, New York, where his mother placed him in the care of an uncle after his father's premature death in 1841. He appears to have had a typical rural education, featuring communal reading in the household, attendance at the winter terms of a district school, liberal use of local libraries, and regular participation in church, Sunday school, and other devotional activities—he later reminisced that his first years were "bathed in an atmosphere of piety." He showed early signs of academic precocity and, after a three-year

19

apprenticeship at the Owego *Gazette,* he decided to enroll in the Owego Academy with a view to preparing for the ministry. Eighteen months later he entered Williams College as a sophomore, supplementing the rigorous academic regimen there by teaching school during winter vacations, by serving as college reporter for the *Springfield Republican,* and by helping to edit the *Williams Quarterly.* [1]

After his graduation from Williams in 1859, Gladden taught school for a time in Owego and, more important, began to read theology with Moses Coit Tyler, the newly appointed pastor of the Owego Congregational Church. With Tyler's encouragement, Gladden successfully petitioned the Susquehanna Association of Congregational Ministers for a license to preach and, shortly thereafter, in 1860, accepted a post as assistant to the minister of a church in LeRaysville, Pennsylvania. Within a few months he was called from there to the First Congregational Methodist Church of Brooklyn, where he managed in slightly over a year to build up the congregation, achieve ordination, and then suffer the nervous breakdown that forced him to resign. He was fortunate, though, in receiving an invitation from a church in suburban Morrisania, just north of New York City, where he not only recovered his health but once more revitalized a congregation. In 1866, Gladden moved again, this time to the Congregational Church of North Adams, Massachusetts, where he remained until 1871, when he accepted the religious editorship of the *Independent,* a prestigious Congregational weekly with a circulation of nearly one million. He stayed in that post until 1875, when he felt obliged to resign in a conflict over advertising policy. From 1875 until 1882 he took charge of the North Congregational Church in Springfield, Massachusetts, and then, in 1882, he accepted a call to the First Congregational Church of Columbus, Ohio, where he remained for the rest of his life.

The years between his study with Tyler in Owego and his editorial work with the *Independent* in New York City might best be seen as a period of apprenticeship for Gladden, not merely as a Congregational minister but also as a social thinker. One of the most important elements in the apprenticeship was Gladden's discovery of the writings of Horace Bushnell. As a boy, Gladden had experienced difficulty in achieving the sort of conversion that he had been led to believe would constitute the evidence of God's saving grace; only later, under the

1. Washington Gladden, *Recollections* (Boston: Houghton Mifflin Company, 1909), p. 32.

ministrations of a visiting evangelist, did he come to the conviction that "it was perfectly safe to trust the Heavenly Father's love . . . and walk straight on in the ways of service." Not surprisingly, when Gladden came upon Bushnell's *Christian Nurture,* probably at Williams, he found himself resonating to the arguments there about the child's gentle growth into faith. Later, when he read Bushnell's *God in Christ,* he considered it a revelation, deeming the discussion of Christ as an expression of God's intention to re-engage the world's love to be a deliverance once and for all from the kind of theology in which a wrathful God condemned helpless human beings to eternal damnation. Toward the end of his life, Gladden pronounced Bushnell "the greatest theological genius of the American church in the nineteenth century."[2]

The second important element in Gladden's apprenticeship was his discovery of the social class problem inherent in the developing order of industrial capitalism. North Adams was a manufacturing town, with textile mills, shoe factories, carriage works, and machine shops. Gladden liked to remark the absence of social stratification and class consciousness he perceived in the community. Yet a third of the population was foreign-born, and hundreds of children labored in the mills and factories throughout the year. When growing numbers of those youngsters began to spend their time and wages in so-called corrupting amusements, Gladden urged the local YMCA to create a game room where youngsters might play at chess, checkers, and backgammon, maintaining that wholesome amusements were more moral than the kind of vacuum within which corrupting amusements flourished. Later, when some of the wealthier people of the town began to reveal the telltale signs of luxury, Gladden preached sermons denouncing idleness, extravagance, and display. And, in 1870, when one of the leading shoe manufacturers imported a contingent of Chinese workers to break the hold of the Knights of St. Crispen on the local shoe industry, Gladden urged his congregation to extend the hand of friendship to the despised Orientals. Such preachments were full of sentimentalism, addressing as they did the symptoms rather than the causes of social unrest. What was remarkable about them, however, was Gladden's continuing insistence that the church take the initiative in making its principles prevail in the social life of the community.

Gladden's apprenticeship clearly ended with the publication of

2. *Ibid.,* pp. 38, 167.

two major works in 1876, *Being a Christian: What It Means, and How to Begin* and *Working People and Their Employers*. Both, characteristically, originated in sermons at the North Congregational Church in Springfield; both went through multiple editions; and both found national audiences. *Being a Christian* was a brief treatise on what was involved in embarking upon the Christian life. It rejected ritualism, dogmatism, and sacramentalism in favor of an active, ethical Christianity directed to the affairs of everyday existence. Doubtless recalling Bushnell's preachments about Christian nurture, Gladden noted tersely that to be a Christian "is to believe in Christ, to learn of him, and to follow him. To become a Christian is simply *to begin doing these things.*" *Working People and Their Employers* was an extensive discussion of the moral problems that were coming to the fore with the emergence of the new industrialism. Gladden sketched the emergence of the wage system that was the basis of so much social conflict during the 1870's, lamented the class warfare he saw in the making, condemned socialism while offering qualified approval of the right of working people to organize and strike, and urged the church to take the lead in developing a cooperative system in which profit-sharing and Christian collaboration would prevail throughout American industry. Again, the proposals were full of sentimentalism, but what was remarkable was Gladden's insistence that the church be responsible for Christianizing the industrial order.[3]

Gladden pressed forward with these arguments over the four decades that followed, refining, extending, and enriching them in the process. The simple faith and ethical activism that were at the heart of his Christianity readily lent themselves to his efforts to incorporate the implications of both Darwinism and the higher criticism. Adopting from popularizers like John Fiske and Benjamin Kidd the idea of God as immanent, he was able to conceive of evolution in the natural world as "not only rational, but sublimely religious." And, accepting the idea of revelation as progressive, he was able to conceive of the Bible as an inspired book containing supernatural elements, but scarcely a work of science and certainly not the last word on Christian obligation. Similarly, his commitment to the Christianizing of the industrial order led naturally to a vision of the Kingdom of God on earth, in which science, reason, and Christian values would prevail in the formulation of law, in which the state would take an active role in the achievement of social justice, and in which capital and labor would be

---

3. Washington Gladden, *Being a Christian: What It Means, and How to Begin* (Boston: Congregational Publishing Society, 1876), p. 62.

persuaded to abandon violence and brutality in favor of compulsory arbitration.[4]

In the synthesis of these several convictions lay the core of an emergent social Christianity that embodied a new view both of the person and of education. Gladden saw human brotherhood as a natural extension of divine fatherhood, and it was in the context of that brotherhood and the Christian love it implied that he conceived the nature and duties of the individual. Christian love proclaimed the moral equality of human beings: it dictated decency rather than brutality toward others, opposition to rather than acquiescence in conditions that brutalized others, and cooperation rather than competition in public affairs. Sin in an individual sense was the triumph of selfishness over the dictates of Christian love; sin in a social sense was the toleration of conditions that robbed others of the self-respect that was the essence of moral equality. Indeed, sin itself derived from sinful conditions, so that whether or not an individual sinned in the first place was partly dependent upon the social circumstances within which the individual lived.

Such a view of human nature carried clear implications for education. It projected Gladden to a concern for the stability of the family, as "the oldest of the institutions of society, and the most sacred." And, beyond the *sine qua non* of stability, it led him to see the family as the first and foremost educator of children. "Civilized men live in communities," he maintained, "and the art of living includes the art of living together. The primary school in which this art is learned and practiced is the family. No higher function belongs to the family than that of equipping those who are under its discipline with such an outfit of principles, sentiments, and habits of thought and action as shall enable them to fulfill their duties to the community. . . . Industrial training, intellectual training, moral training,—all these the children ought to receive in the household."[5]

Granting these elemental obligations of the family, Gladden was only too aware, first, that many parents were incapable in view of their own education or circumstance of carrying out these obligations, and second, that even in the case of those who were capable, the demands of modern life were such that schoolteachers needed to complement whatever parents could provide. Hence, Gladden saw public

4. Washington Gladden, *How Much Is Left of the Old Doctrines? A Book for the People* (Boston: Houghton, Mifflin and Company, 1899), p. 42.

5. Washington Gladden, *Working People and Their Employers* (Boston: Lockwood, Brooks, and Company, 1876), p. 94, and *Social Salvation* (Boston: Houghton, Mifflin and Company, 1902), p. 178.

schooling carrying crucial social responsibilities. But it was not merely schooling that concentrated on instruction in the traditional subjects. "The first demand that Christianity has to make respecting popular education," he wrote, "is that it be directed toward the formation of character rather than the communication of abstract knowledge." A second demand, closely related, would be that schooling convey a sound public morality; and a third demand, also closely related, given Gladden's conception of Christianity, would be that schooling convey the industrial skills that would enable all young people to become economically productive and financially self-sufficient. In effect, the goals that Gladden's Christianity posited for schooling were social goals that would enable schools to assist in achieving the Kingdom of God on earth: schools would have to encourage "social sentiments and social aims," Gladden insisted; they would have to nurture strong individuals of cooperative spirit.[6]

Gladden also commented from time to time on the education provided by colleges and universities, public libraries and reading rooms, Chautauquas and extension lectures, YMCAs and Christian Endeavor Societies, and prisons and reform schools. He saw all of them serving the high purpose of teaching sound moral sentiments and convictions. And, beyond that, he proclaimed the virtue and efficacy of social science in enabling public policy to proceed rationally toward the achievement of the good society. The relation between Christianity and social science, he observed, is "the relation of an offspring to its parent. Social science is the child of Christianity. The national and international associations that are so diligently studying the things that make for human welfare in society are as distinctly the products of Christianity as is the American Board of Missions."[7]

Gladden was essentially a preacher, who first proclaimed the doctrines of the new social Christianity—or the Social Gospel, as it came to be called—from the pulpit. True, a steady stream of books and articles flowed from his prolific pen; yet, given the fact that he gave his primary attention to the congregation he served in Columbus throughout most of his mature career, his influence during the years after 1876 remains remarkable. Social Christianity never became a mass movement among the Protestant laity, but it did become a profoundly significant movement among the Protestant clergy and to a lesser degree among the non-Protestant clergy. And its rise to promi-

6. Washington Gladden, *Applied Christianity: Moral Aspects of Social Questions* (Boston: Houghton, Mifflin and Company, 1894), p. 299, and *Social Salvation*, p. 189.
7. Gladden, *Applied Christianity*, p. 214.

nence in clerical thought and affairs tells much about the metropolitan nation that the United States was becoming during the closing decades of the nineteenth century.

For one thing, the social and intellectual problems Gladden was contending with were pervasive, both in the United States and in Great Britain, and others were thinking and writing along similar lines. The English preachers Frederick Denison Maurice and Frederick Robertson, for example, were widely read and quoted by American churchmen seeking affirmation of an immanent God, an embracing church, and a socially conscious faith, and indeed Gladden himself was much influenced by their work. At the same time Americans like Henry Ward Beecher, Theodore T. Munger, William J. Tucker, Josiah Strong, Lyman Abbott, Walter Rauschenbusch, and William S. Rainsford were promulgating a liberal evangelicism highly similar to Gladden's in its reconciliation with evolutionary theory and the higher criticism and in its special concern for urban affairs. Gladden himself was personally familiar with all these men and indeed inspired several of them. The point, however, is that they were Gladden's co-workers in the formulation of social Christianity; and, whatever the extent of his influence on them, the simple fact of their work helped create a more favorable climate for his.

As these men and others sensed their common concerns, they developed an organizational apparatus to further their efforts that was not unlike the evangelical united front of the 1820's and 1830's. They founded new associations like the American Congress of Churches, established in 1884 to promote Christian union and to advance the Kingdom of God through free discussion of the religious, social, and moral questions of the time; and they took over extant associations like the Evangelical Alliance for the United States, which had been established in 1867 to war on free thought and Roman Catholicism but which was redirected in 1886 to rousing the churches to their social responsibilities. They also worked in, with, and through a host of local, state, and regional associations, ranging from the Ethical Culture Society, which included people of Jewish as well as Christian background, to the Brotherhood of the Kingdom, which was formed by but not confined to Baptists. These organizations employed all the public relations techniques familiar to the evangelical movement— they undertook studies, organized conferences, issued manifestoes, founded newspapers and magazines, prepared articles for established periodicals, published books and tracts, supported missionaries, and generally directed the attention of denominational groups and the broader public to social issues. Their efforts served to popularize and broadcast the ideas of social Christianity.

Also paralleling the strategies of the earlier evangelical movement, the proponents of social Christianity made important intellectual alliances with middle-class reform in general and with the emerging organizational apparatus of social science. It is significant that Gladden was one of the founders of the American Economic Association, along with Richard T. Ely, who was himself one of the foremost articulators of social Christianity. Gladden also worked with John Heyl Vincent and others in organizing the American Institute of Christian Sociology at Chautauqua in 1893 and more generally in making the Social Gospel an important theme in the adult education activities of Chautauqua, and he joined with Josiah Strong and others in the work of the League for Social Service and its successor, the American Institute of Social Service. These organizations and their activities, which ran the gamut from research on social problems to campaigns for municipal social services, exemplified the broad collaboration between evangelicism, social science, and reform that, in the first place, augmented the influence of social Christianity by providing additional forums for its propagation and more secular versions of its mission, and, in the second place, advanced a new formulation of the pre–Civil War identification of the American *paideia* as a Protestant *paideia.* When Gladden maintained that social science was the child of Christianity, he was noting an intellectual interpenetration that came to be widely accepted at the turn of the century.

The organizational activities of the 1880's and 1890's, coupled with the popularizing of liberal magazines like Lyman Abbott's *Christian Union* (renamed the *Outlook* in 1893), moved the ideas and issues of social Christianity from *avant-garde* doctrines to familiar commonplaces by the end of the century. When the editors of the *Congregationalist* undertook a comparative study of the topics considered at religious gatherings in 1894 with those that had been considered twenty-five years earlier, they found the concern with the church's relation to social movements to be overwhelming. "Never, perhaps, were the themes of discussion as nearly alike in church assemblies of all denominations as now," they concluded. Similarly, when the editors of *Bibliotheca Sacra* reviewed the subjects of recent religious books in the following year, discussions of sociology, socialism, social reform, and the social aspects of Christianity predominated. True, one could discern greater concern with the Social Gospel among Unitarians, Universalists, Quakers, Methodists, Baptists, and Disciples of

Christ than among Presbyterians or Lutherans; and true, too, one could already perceive a deepening opposition to the Social Gospel in many quarters; but the fact remains that ideas of social Christianity had come to be widely accepted or at least widely acquiesced in. As William R. Hutchison has observed, "liberalism, while still probably in a numerical minority, had attained a voice equal to those of the older and newer conservatisms that opposed it; . . . its dynamism or momentum as a movement . . . was at least as great as that of any opposing faction."[8]

The movements for interdenominational collaboration and indeed for denominational unity in the cause of social Christianity that were symbolized by the American Congress of Churches and the Evangelical Alliance quickened during the 1890's and 1900's. The Open and Institutional Church League, founded in 1894, asserted that the church should "take the leading part in every movement which has for its end the alleviation of human suffering, the elevation of man, and the betterment of the world"; and leaders of the League early proposed bringing the denominations into "federative relations through which they can work out the problems of Christian service in city, country and abroad without the present waste of forces." Similarly, the National Federation of Churches and Christian Workers, organized in 1901, sought cooperation among churches and Christian workers throughout the United States for the more effective promotion of the interests of the Kingdom of God. Through interdenominational deliberative conferences, draft plans for federation, and tireless lobbying within the several denominations, these organizations helped to create the Federal Council of Churches of Christ in America, which was established in 1908 by delegates from thirty-three denominations on a simple doctrinal basis of "the essential oneness of the Christian Churches of America in Jesus Christ as their Divine Lord and Saviour" and with a commitment to Christianizing the social order. While the Council's powers were strictly advisory, it turned at its very first meeting to a draft report on "The Church and Modern Industry" and adopted a statement suggesting that Christians had a responsibility to seek the realization of social ideals, urging that the churches recognize more fully "the great work of social reconstruction," and recommending the creation of a Commission on the Church and Social Service "to cooperate in all practicable ways to

8. "Changes in Religious Thinking," *Congregationalist*, LXXIX (1894), 580; *Bibliotheca Sacra*, LII (1895), 205–207; and William R. Hutchison, *The Modernist Impulse in American Protestantism* (Cambridge, Mass.: Harvard University Press, 1976), p. 113.

promote in the churches the development of the spirit and practice of social service and especially to secure a better understanding and a more natural relationship between workingmen and the Church." These actions presaged a vigorous advocacy from that time forward of liberal social policies generally designed to alleviate the problems associated with rapid industrialization and large-scale urbanization and to improve the lot of workingpeople and their families.[9]

Social Christianity was essentially an evangelical movement and as such it was inherently educational; in the end, the Kingdom of God would be achieved through preaching, persuasion, and application. Given that faith, and given the rapid development of specialization in the emerging metropolitan society, it should not be surprising that the movement gave encouragement to a number of men and women who decided to focus their energies directly upon the problems of teaching and learning, upon the pedagogy of Christian nurture and the psychology of social ethics. Pre-eminent among these during the first decades of the twentieth century was George Albert Coe, the leading figure in what came to be known as the religious education movement and the guiding spirit of the Religious Education Association, which was founded in 1903 for the express purpose of promoting broad programs of religious instruction and which quickly became the pedagogical voice of social Christianity. Born in western New York in 1862 and educated at the University of Rochester and Boston University, Coe had an extraordinarily productive and often controversial career that began at Northwestern University (1891–1909), that continued at Union Theological Seminary in New York City (1909–1922) and at Teachers College, Columbia University (1922–1927), and that then had a lively final phase at Pilgrim Place, a home for ministers and missionaries in Claremont, California, until his death in 1951. Like Gladden, a man who had grown up in the country and moved to the city, and like Gladden, a man who early concluded that being a Christian meant beginning to live as a Christian, Coe taught that to come of age in the new industrial order was immensely complicated, since the education of the streets bombarded the child with evil at precisely the time the child was supposed to be growing in Christian habits and awareness. Hence he saw need for a vigorous,

9. "Platform of the Open and Institutional Church League," in Elias B. Sanford, *Origin and History of the Federal Council of Churches of Christ in America* (Hartford, Conn.: The S. S. Scranton Company, 1916), p. 397; E. B. Sanford, "The Institutional Church and Christian Unity," *ibid.*, p. 403; "Constitution of the National Federation of Churches," *ibid.*, p. 449; "The Constitution of the Federal Council," *ibid.*, p. 464; "The Church and Modern Industry," *ibid.*, pp. 499, 502.

coordinated, intense religious education by the home, the church, the Sunday school, and the public school that would nurture true Christianity at the same time that it encouraged the application of Christian principles to everyday life. Education, Coe observed in 1904, "is the means by which the immature human being is made acquainted with his world and with himself; it is the process by which we reveal to him what constitutes real living. It is therefore the primary means of maintaining in the individual and in the world at large the comforting, joy-giving, all-conquering piety that realizes God as the ever-present basis, law, and end of our life." In effect, Coe began with the process of individual growth into faith that Bushnell had described as Christian nurture, socialized the process, and made it one with the process of redemption. The Christian life, lived within the institutions of society, became a pilgrimage in which the individual participated in the struggle to establish an industrial democracy based on Christian principles. In the end, Coe's theories became little more than Gladden's social Christianity articulated as a progressive philosophy of education.[10]

I I

Washington Gladden could not have been more pleased when Dwight L. Moody and Ira D. Sankey chose Springfield, Massachusetts, for one of their revivals during the early weeks of 1878. As pastor of Springfield's North Congregational Church, Gladden lent every assistance to the enterprise, serving on the local planning committee, introducing a number of Sankey's gospel hymns into the services of his own congregation in anticipation of the revival, counseling converts in the "inquiry room" during the revival itself, and in the end receiving fifty-one new members into the North Church as a direct result of the revival. Gladden himself felt quite warmly toward the two evangelists and actively supported their endeavors; yet much of what they preached during their month in Springfield diverged in fundamental ways from Gladden's own teaching, and indeed would diverge more and more with the passage of time.

Moody and Sankey were at the peak of their powers at the time of the Springfield revival, having been catapulted to world-wide attention during their extraordinary tour of the British Isles between 1873 and 1875 and their subsequent tour of leading American cities. And

10. George A. Coe, *Education in Religion and Morals* (Chicago: Fleming H. Revell Company, 1904), p. 391.

the particular combination of technique and substance that had gone into the making of their triumphant evangelicism, as well as their profound differences with Gladden, reveals much about the complex character of Anglo-American religious life during the first years of the metropolitan era.

Moody and Sankey, again like Gladden, had both grown up in small towns and had then gone on to live their adult lives in large cities. Moody was born in 1837 in Northfield, Massachusetts, the son of a brickmason who unfortunately died shortly after the boy turned four. One of nine children reared by his mother, he attended the Northfield schools until he was thirteen and then worked at various jobs on nearby farms and shops. At the age of seventeen he left Northfield for Boston, where he was a salesman for a time in his uncle's shoe establishment and associated himself with the recently founded YMCA and with the Mount Vernon Congregational Church and its affiliated Sunday school. Two years later he relocated to Chicago, where he continued to work as a shoe salesman and, more important, intensified his participation in the YMCA, joined the Plymouth Congregational Church, and began to teach his own Sunday school classes. His energetic initiative and his singular devotion to whatever he undertook led to success in all these domains, especially the mission work. In 1859 he organized the North Market Sunday School in a rented loft located in one of the run-down districts of the city and made it the center of a remarkable round of evangelical activities—prayer meetings, home visitations, adult literacy classes, and a host of philanthropic and welfare efforts. Together with the YMCA, the school consumed all of Moody's energy and more, and in 1860 he decided to give full time to his religious endeavors.

After serving briefly during the Civil War as a YMCA representative to the military and then as a member of the Christian Commission, Moody returned to Chicago and built upon the foundation of the Sunday School—now removed to its own building on Illinois Street—an independent congregation that came to be known as the Illinois Street Church (after the Chicago fire of 1871, the congregation moved again and became the Chicago Avenue Church). Through his growing responsibilities with the YMCA and his indefatigable labors with the Illinois Street Church, Moody gained city-wide, then regional, and then national and international prominence. It was through networks of Sunday school and YMCA colleagues that his influence first came to be felt more widely through the Midwest, and it was through these same networks that he was able to capitalize personally and intellectually on his first visit to England in 1867. It was also at a YMCA convention in Indianapolis, in 1870, that Moody first made the acquaintance of the man who would be his lifelong associate, Ira D. Sankey.

Born in 1840, Sankey had grown up in a musically inclined Methodist family in western Pennsylvania and had early become acquainted with the standard music of the church. Upon completing his schooling, he had served as a clerk in his father's bank in Newcastle, Pennsylvania, also busying himself in the affairs of the local Methodist church and giving particular attention to the choir and the Sunday school. After a period of service in the Union Army, he had returned to Newcastle, continuing in the bank and assisting his father as local collector of internal revenue. When a local branch of the YMCA was organized in 1867, Sankey became its president, and, like Moody, found himself increasingly active in regional religious affairs through networks of Sunday school and YMCA colleagues, with singing serving as his prime claim to attention. It was as president of the Newcastle YMCA that Sankey attended the convention in Indianapolis, and it was at an impromptu hymn-singing session he had organized that he first came to Moody's attention. Much taken with Sankey's dramatic effect on the audience, Moody acted impulsively, as was his wont, and invited Sankey to join him in his evangelical activities in Chicago. Thus was formed the most remarkable evangelical partnership of the era.

Obviously, Moody and Sankey had each had considerable experience with church affairs before the establishment of their partnership, though neither had had formal theological training and neither had been ordained. However that may be, the particular elements that made for their extraordinary success as a revivalist team were worked out during the 1870's, and especially during the period between 1873 and 1878. The two men employed many of the evangelical "means" that had become commonplace since the days of Charles Grandison Finney. As William G. McLoughlin, Jr., has observed, Moody and Sankey may never have read Finney's *Lectures on Revivals of Religion* (1835), but Finney's principles were such commonplaces by the 1870's that they were widely assumed and observed by preachers and audiences alike. As one commentator put it in describing the New York revival of 1876 for the *Nation*, "The Moody and Sankey services are an old-fashioned revival with the modern improvements."[11]

What, then, were the so-called modern improvements? They were

11. William G. McLoughlin, Jr., *Modern Revivalism: Charles Grandison Finney to Billy Graham* (New York: The Ronald Press Company, 1959), p. 221; and *Nation*, XXII (March 9, 1876), 156.

in part organizational and in part technological. On the organizational side, Moody developed an apparatus of interdenominational cooperation, business support, and expert assistance that made it possible for him to mount city-wide campaigns involving tens of thousands of individuals. Whereas Finney had realized his greatest successes in smaller towns and cities, Moody achieved his triumphs in London, New York, Boston, and Chicago. Before Moody would even contemplate a revival, he insisted that an interdenominational committee of local clergymen be organized to sponsor the event and issue him a formal invitation. In addition, he sought an associated committee of prominent local citizens, including well-to-do businessmen, who would agree to contribute and raise the substantial sums required to underwrite the endeavor. And, through these two committees, he then reached out to the organized civic and religious institutions of the community—the YMCA, the several churches, the larger businesses, and the complex of overlapping community and evangelical associations—for a more extensive group of welcomers, ushers, and assistants, who would help to shepherd the large crowds and lead them efficiently through the planned activities. Finally, since Moody preferred not to use any particular church building but rather to have some large "tabernacle" for his exercises, he required that the local committees arrange for an appropriate local structure to house the revival—in Philadelphia, John Wanamaker contributed the use of a former railroad freight depot which, when renovated, seated eleven thousand; in New York, a committee under the leadership of William E. Dodge, Cornelius Vanderbilt II, and J. P. Morgan arranged for the rental of P. T. Barnum's Hippodrome, which seated just under twelve thousand; in Boston, where no suitable structure could be found, a committee under the leadership of Amos A. Lawrence and Joseph Story sponsored the erection of a new brick building seating more than six thousand.

On the technological side, Moody and Sankey introduced a variety of innovations in format and style. The standard pattern for a campaign ordinarily included three meetings a day on weekdays—a morning inspiration service, a noon prayer meeting, and an evening preaching service; no meetings on Saturdays; and an afternoon and an evening meeting on Sunday—the effort was obviously not to compete in any way with regular local church services. There were also special meetings for particular groups: young men, women, children, businessmen, the unemployed, prostitutes, and drunkards, and special meetings on particular subjects, temperance being a favorite.

Moody's major innovations were the prayer meeting, with its combination of prayers based on requests from those present (and petitions via letter) and testimony concerning the efficacy of prayer; the inquiry room, to which the anxious repaired after the sermon for additional exhortations by Moody and counseling by "personal workers" recruited from the local churches (an obvious succession to the "anxious bench" of Finney's day); and a preaching style featuring a remarkably effective mix of Scriptural passages, anecdotes, parables, testimony, exegesis, and exhortation. Sankey's contribution was to preside over the "singing of the Gospel," surely the most striking innovation of the Moody-Sankey team, via solo renditions of his own and ensemble renditions by choirs and by the congregation at large, all accompanied by Sankey himself at his melodeon (a small reed organ using suction bellows). The music Sankey rendered, borrowed, adapted, and composed featured catchy, repetitive tunes joined to simple harmonies; it was easily learned by large and diverse congregations, who then reveled in responsive singing with Sankey himself and the ever-present choirs.

In the end, this combination of organizational and technological innovation made possible the large-scale exercises in religious sentimentalism that were at the heart of late-nineteenth-century urban revivalism. That said, however, there was a more basic element in the Moody-Sankey revivals, namely, their theological bias, and that bias lay at the heart of the differences with Gladden. Whereas Gladden conceived of the Bible as an inspired but historical document, Moody preached Biblical inerrancy. Whereas Gladden took from Bushnell the doctrine of Christian nurture, Moody preached the necessity of conversion and rebirth. Whereas Gladden viewed the Atonement symbolically, as the "reconciliation through suffering of holiness with love," Moody viewed it literally, maintaining that Christ "died as your substitute and mine, and that is my hope of heaven." Whereas Gladden saw human brotherhood as a natural extension of divine fatherhood, Moody preached the coexistence of two vastly disparate classes of human beings, those who had chosen Christ and those who had not. Whereas Gladden maintained that individual sin derived from sinful social conditions, Moody insisted that sinful social conditions resulted from individual sin. And whereas Gladden espoused a postmillennial doctrine of the realization of the Kingdom of God on earth, Moody preached a premillennial doctrine of Christ's return, bringing in its wake God's awful judgment upon the world. The two men preached God's love and saving grace, and they shared a penchant toward ecumenicism; but their theologies led in profoundly different directions, Gladden's toward modernism, Moody's toward fundamentalism.[12]

The nub of the difference stemmed in large measure from the premillennialism Moody had imbibed during his first visit to England, from a small, lay, pietistic sect known as the Plymouth Brethren. Organized in the 1820's as a dissenting group of "primitive Christians" within the Church of England, the Plymouth Brethren had evolved after midcentury under the leadership of John N. Darby into uncompromising critics of Anglicanism, espousing as their primary doctrines the absolute inerrancy of Scripture, the central role of the conversion experience in salvation, and the imminent bodily return of Christ. Moody had become acquainted with the Brethren through the educational efforts of George Müller (in establishing schools for English orphans) and the Biblical commentaries of C. H. McIntosh. Later, back in Chicago, he was much taken with the preaching of Henry Moorhouse and indeed with Darby himself, who spoke in Chicago under Moody's auspices. Moody never adopted the entire theology of the Brethren; but he did take on their view of the world as a sinking vessel whose doomed passengers could save themselves only by immediate conversion.

Like all the major American revivalists before them, Moody and Sankey were essentially educators: the entire range of activities associated with the tabernacle—those they inherited from Finney's generation and those they introduced on their own—was ultimately intended as a technology of persuasion, in effect, as a pedagogy. And that pedagogy, with its appeal to sentimentalism and its emphasis on evangelical orthodoxy, profoundly affected the entire institutional apparatus of late-nineteenth-century evangelical Protestantism—families and churches, Sunday schools and colleges, YMCAs and YWCAs, publishing houses and overseas missions. Through his sermons, lectures, and prayers, oral and printed, Moody reached tens of thousands; through his various collections of church hymns and gospel songs, Sankey reached millions. Directly and through their disciples, the two revivalists influenced every corner of the evangelical domain with their view of what it meant to live the good life in this world. To be sure, like most of the major American evangelists before them, Moody and Sankey were far more effective in returning to the

12. Gladden, *How Much Is Left of the Old Doctrines?*, p. 194; and D. L. Moody, *Calvary's Cross: A Symposium on the Atonement* (Chicago: Bible Institute Colportage Association, 1900), p. 31.

Protestant fold those who had undergone at least a minimal education in Protestantism than they were in winning new recruits to Christ; but that merely testifies to the inextricable pedagogical relationships between tabernacle and church in the phenomenon of revivalism. Moody and Sankey may have created a new educational institution in the urban tabernacle, but in the end they also reaffirmed the significance of the traditional evangelical configuration of education, with the church at the center.

Granted the pervasiveness of the Moody-Sankey influence, there were a number of quite specific educational contributions on Moody's part that are worthy of note. For one thing, he was first and foremost an enthusiast by temperament, and at various points in his career he focused his attention on one or another of the evangelical institutions, with energizing effect. Thus, he was active throughout the 1860's in the Illinois Sunday school movement, and played a key role in the eventual development of a uniform, graded Sunday school curriculum, not only for the state, but for the nation as a whole. Similarly, as president of the Chicago YMCA during the late 1860's, he led in the rapid development of that organization, placing personal evangelization through prayer meetings at the heart of the Association's program, raising funds for an extensive building plan, and, as representative of the Chicago Association at YMCA conventions, pressing similar priorities upon the national organization. Later, during the 1890's, he turned his attention to college revivals as a vehicle for recruiting missionaries and to the creation of libraries of suitable evangelical literature and the training of colporteurs to sell them.

Beyond these energizing efforts and beyond the educational innovations he introduced with respect to the tabernacle itself, Moody pioneered in the development of at least three major educational strategies that would continue to mark the evangelical configuration—the Bible Institute, the Bible conference, and the Student Volunteer Movement. Moody initially conceived of the Bible Institute as a training school for what he called gap-men who would "stand between the laity and the ministers," Christian workers without seminary degrees and the baggage of Latin and Greek but thoroughly versed in the word and ready to do battle in the cause of Jesus Christ among the unchurched in the great cities of the nation. He actually set out to erect such an institute on the foundation of a school of "Bible work" that his friend and colleague Emma Dryer had conducted in Chicago since 1873, initially in Moody's church and later at the YMCA. In 1886 Moody shared his hopes and plans for the Institute with a group of Chicago friends, including several well-to-do businessmen, and in 1887 the group organized the Chicago Evangelization Society with the express purpose of expanding Dryer's efforts into a full-blown permanent training school. The new Institute formally opened in 1889 with Moody as president (it was a painful birth, during which Dryer was forced out of her own enterprise); and it developed over the next half-century into a major center of orthodox evangelical Christian education under the leadership of three immensely gifted leaders: Reuben A. Torrey, who was the first superintendent; James M. Gray, who served as dean from 1904 to 1923 and as president from 1923 to 1934; and Clarence H. Benson, who inaugurated the Institute's Religious Education Course in 1924. Torrey and Gray exerted national influence in developing a systematic pedagogy for Bible study, while Benson led in the preparation and publication of curriculum materials for orthodox evangelical Sunday schools and in the organization of the Evangelical Teacher Training Association as a kind of orthodox evangelical alternative to the Religious Education Association. Unconstrained by the traditions of degree-granting colleges and seminaries and committed solely to the preparation of competent practitioners of evangelization, the Institute was one of the most innovative educational institutions of the era, pioneering in the use of new technologies such as gospel wagons, correspondence courses, radio broadcasting, and missionary aviation in the traditional cause of proffering the word.[13]

Prophetic and Bible conferences grew up in the United States during the late 1860's and 1870's as exercises in group study and mutual education. They appear to have originated with a group of premillennialists associated with the periodical *Waymarks in the Wilderness,* and, according to one early participant, emphasized "the doctrines of the verbal inspiration of the Bible, the personality of the Holy Spirit, the atonement of sacrifice, the priesthood of Christ, the two natures in the believer, and the personal imminent return of our Lord from heaven." After waxing and waning, they started on a regular basis in 1875 as one- or two-week summer affairs, usually at some resort (and the fact that they met from 1883 to 1897 at Niagara-on-the-Lake, Ontario, led to their being referred to generically as Niagara Conferences). Moody was doubtless aware of the premillennialist conferences, given his longstanding association with the Plymouth Brethren; and indeed he was also aware of the so-called Keswick

13. *Record of Christian Work,* V (February, 1886), 5.

holiness conferences in England, which had concentrated on many of the same themes. In addition, Moody had also had personal familiarity with a variety of conferences in connection with his Sunday school and YMCA work. In any case, he resolved in 1879 to set up a conference the following year in Northfield, where he lived, for the purpose of promoting spiritual renewal through Bible study. The conference was duly held in September, 1880, with some one hundred people in attendance; a second conference was held in August, 1881; and then, after a lapse of three years while Moody was in Great Britain, the Northfield Conference was re-established on a regular annual basis. Moody's conferences continued to revolve around spiritual renewal through Bible study; and the mutual instruction they involved, coupled with the networks of association formed in the process, constituted their prime pedagogical significance. But they had a substantive significance as well, since Moody's regular invitations to English and American premillennialists made the Northfield Conferences a prime vehicle for the dissemination of their ideas through the leadership of the American evangelical community. Once again, as with the Bible Institute, a new educational technology was pressed into the service of doctrinal orthodoxy.[14]

Moody's role in the formation of the Student Volunteer Movement was directly related, on the one hand, to his longstanding association with the YMCA, and, on the other hand, to his sponsorship of the Northfield Conferences. The YMCA had made considerable headway on college and university campuses, and in 1877, largely under the prodding of a Princeton undergraduate named Luther Deloraine Wishard, an intercollegiate YMCA movement had been launched, with a primary interest in recruiting able graduates for service as domestic and foreign missionaries. In 1879 Moody was elected national president of the YMCA, and Wishard, now centrally involved in the youth division of the Association, pressed Moody for permission to organize special conventions for college students. Moody himself had never indicated much interest in college revivals, doubtless owing in part to his own lack of formal schooling. Nevertheless, during his sojourn in Great Britain between 1881 and 1884 he conducted remarkably successful revivals at Edinburgh, Oxford, and Cambridge, and on his return to the United States he conducted equally successful revivals at Harvard, Yale, Dartmouth, and Princeton. Wishard redoubled his efforts in 1885 and persuaded Moody to invite the collegiate members

14. Geo. C. Needham, "Bible Conferences," *Watchword,* XIII (March, 1890), 60.

of the YMCA to the Northfield Conference in 1886 (the conference was actually held at the Mount Hermon School, which Moody had founded in 1881 about five miles from Northfield proper). There is little doubt but that Moody's interest was to inspire the students to serve as Christian workers for the evangelization of American institutions of higher education. Wishard's hope, on the other hand, was to recruit Christian workers for overseas missions. In the end, the results of the 1886 conference surpassed everyone's expectations: before its conclusion a hundred students—subsequently known as the "Mount Hermon Hundred"—pledged themselves to work as foreign missionaries after graduation. By the time of the 1887 conference at Northfield the number had grown to 2,100—1,600 men and 500 women. And in 1888, under the leadership of John R. Mott, head of the Cornell University YMCA, the Student Volunteer Movement was organized, with its goal of "the evangelization of the world in this generation." Yet again, the surge of interest marked the placing of a pedagogical tool, namely, associated study and mutual instruction (doubtless strengthened by Moody's charisma), in the service of an evangelical doctrine, namely, the premillennial belief that Christ's imminent return necessitated the immediate conversion of the heathen. As with the Bible Institute and the Bible conferences, the outcomes would extend considerably beyond Moody's own lifetime.[15]

Moody was in many ways the progenitor of twentieth-century American fundamentalism, though he did not use the term and indeed the term was not current in his time. He himself articulated many of the doctrines that came to be associated with the fundamentalist movement—the inerrancy of Scripture, the centrality of conversion, substitutionary Atonement, and the imminent bodily return of Christ—and he gave welcome at his tabernacles and Bible conferences to many of the other doctrines fundamentalists would embrace. Yet Moody was spiritually ecumenical and temperamentally conciliatory; he was able over the years to maintain warm relationships with people as different as John Nelson Darby and Washington Gladden. During the period following Moody's death in 1899, however, the American religious scene changed markedly. With the steady advance of modernist ideas in the churches and in the culture at large, orthodox evangelicals became more alienated, more fearful, more deter-

15. Arthur T. Pierson, "The Evangelization of the World in This Generation," in Max Wood Moorhead, ed., *The Student Missionary Enterprise: Addresses and Discussions of the Second International Convention of the Student Volunteer Movement for Foreign Missions* [*1894*] (Boston: T. O. Metcalf & Co., 1900), pp. 105–115.

mined to reverse what they perceived as a vast spiritual decline, and consequently more strident in their rhetoric and more aggressive in their political and educational endeavors. A fundamentalist movement grew up, complete with elaborations of doctrine, such as the twelve volumes of *The Fundamentals,* published by Lyman and Milton Stewart between 1910 and 1915; creeds and confessions, such as the Five Points of essential doctrine affirmed by the General Assembly of the Presbyterian Church in 1910; brilliant polemics, such as J. Gresham Machen's *Christianity and Liberalism* (1923); strange alliances, such as the one between the urbane Machen and the folksy Billy Sunday; militant organizations, such as the World's Christian Fundamentals Association, formed by William Bell Riley and others in 1919 as a holding company for insurgent groups seeking to cleanse the several denominations of liberal heresy; and pugnacious periodicals, such as Riley's *Christian Fundamentals in School and Church,* the official organ of the WCFA (it was later renamed the *Christian Fundamentalist*). Moody died believing that Americans were tired of religious controversy. "I hope the motto of the ministers of this country," he said in one of his last sermons, "will be, 'quit your fighting and go to work, and preach the simple gospel.' " But the opposite occurred. During the quarter-century following Moody's death, the ministers chose up sides, so to speak, for a series of battles that were patently about religious doctrine but were also inevitably about cultural and educational policy, or, in more concrete terms, about what kind of America was worth having, what kinds of men and women would constitute that America, and what kinds of educational arrangements would bring such men and women into being.[16]

III

The World's Christian Fundamentals Association came into being in 1919 during a time of pervasive anxiety among Americans concerning the future of the nation. The war had shattered easy assumptions about any world-wide movement toward decency, rationality, and justice in human affairs, or, in theological terms, toward the Kingdom of God on earth. In fact, for many, the unprecedented brutality, destruction, and carnage that had racked the world since 1914 had simply meant that the last days long prophesied by the premillennialists were finally at hand—a view doubtless strengthened by the wave

16. D. L. Moody, *Latest Sermons* (Chicago: Fleming H. Revell Company, 1900), p. 125.

of bitter strikes accompanying the return to a peacetime economy, the intense political controversy surrounding the Treaty of Versailles, and the general fear of imminent revolution that came to be known as the Red Scare. For others, the massive dislocations set in motion by the war and the inevitable loosening of social bonds they occasioned had created a situation of precipitous national decline that demanded prompt and decisive reversal if the country was not to sink irretrievably into a morass of sinfulness and anarchy.

The earliest pronouncements of the WCFA addressed the crisis in ringing theological terms. "The Great Apostasy was spreading like a plague throughout Christendom," declared the organizers of the first meeting. "Thousands of false teachers, many of them occupying high ecclesiastical positions, were bringing in damnable heresies, even denying the Lord that bought them, and bringing upon themselves swift destruction." Those in attendance heard the expected expositions of the true fundamentals and the expected excoriations of erroneous doctrine. In that respect, the WCFA continued in the best tradition of the Bible conferences. But what was new about the discussions of 1919 was, first, the aggressive urgency of the rhetoric—there was no time to lose in combating rampant heresy; second, the sense of possibility that manifested itself, the feeling conveyed to the participants of "widespread revival in, and hunger for, the Word of God"; and third, the focus on organized educational effort that came through a series of carefully prepared committee reports and resolutions.[17]

The last was especially significant, since the committees were expected to function permanently and hence to carry forward the Association's work between meetings. One committee attempted to develop a common creed to which Bible schools and institutes seeking WCFA accreditation might subscribe (thereby providing authorized safe havens for Christians seeking to bypass the increasingly secularized colleges and universities). Another set out to do likewise for the missionary movement. Another set about persuading religious periodicals to publish only material reflecting subscription to the true fundamentals of the faith. And another sought to expand the work of Bible conferences to bring them within reach of a much broader segment of the population. The Association's executive committee applauded these efforts at the same time that it inveighed against attempts by the modernists in the several denominations to achieve intellectual hegemony through denomination-wide periodicals (like

17. *God Hath Spoken: Twenty-Five Addresses Delivered at the World Conference of Christian Fundamentals* (Philadelphia: Bible Conference Committee, 1919), pp. 7, 8.

the recently established *Baptist*) and through interdenominational organizations (like the Federal Council of Churches of Christ); and indeed it went so far as to threaten schism within the denominations if the modernists did not hearken to the call. Finally, the Association adopted as its official organ *Christian Fundamentals in School and Church,* the periodical William Bell Riley had started in 1918 to do battle against secular tendencies in the schools and colleges, thus further strengthening its explicit concern with education.

Some six thousand individuals are reported to have attended the first conference of the WCFA, an impressive as well as an auspicious number. It portended not merely the growing attractiveness of fundamentalist theology to Americans anxious about the future of the nation but also the broadening appeal that marked the emergence of a fundamentalist movement. Very quickly, the rather narrow group of premillennialists who had actually organized the WCFA were joined by conservatives within the several denominations who did not necessarily subscribe to premillennialism but who were more than ready to enlist in a war against modernist tendencies in general and Darwinist doctrines in particular. Riley and the founders of the WCFA made common cause with men like Curtis Lee Laws, editor of the *Watchman-Examiner* and a leader in the effort to purge modernism from the Northern Baptist Convention, and David S. Kennedy, editor of the *Presbyterian* and a leader in a similar effort within the Presbyterian Church of the United States. More important, they made common cause with laymen like William Jennings Bryan, whose irrepressible energy and national reputation lent a panache to the movement that a group of clergymen could never have hoped to achieve on their own. As early as 1920 the WCFA asked Bryan to head up a "Layman's Movement" against modernism and evolution, but Bryan was not prepared to take on the responsibility. A year later, however, the Great Commoner was speaking out so frequently and forcefully against modernism and evolution that he quite literally slipped into the role. Moreover, the movement he found himself leading not only included the WCFA but went far beyond to embrace a broad spectrum of Americans frightened about what they thought was happening to their country and determined to reverse the trend. What had started out as a movement of theological purification had become a great cultural crusade.

Bryan himself in many ways personified the broadening of fundamentalism into a social movement. A midwesterner by birth, who had been educated at Illinois College and had gone on to the practice of law, first in Jacksonville, Illinois, and then in Lincoln, Nebraska, he had served a couple of terms in Congress during the early 1890's, had been the Democratic Party's candidate for president in 1896 and 1900, and had been Woodrow Wilson's secretary of state from 1913 to 1915, when he resigned in protest against what he perceived as Wilson's abandonment of strict neutrality in the *Lusitania* affair. In the course of what was a remarkably influential political career, he had emerged as an immensely popular and much beloved spokesman for ordinary Americans in what they saw as their battle with the "money power" of eastern bankers and businessmen.

One element in Bryan's political charisma was his extraordinary evangelical style. Reared in an intensely religious household, Bryan had been early imbued with a deep sense of piety founded upon a belief in the authority and the infallibility of the Bible, and his education at Illinois College had largely confirmed that teaching. He saw his political efforts as essentially attempts to apply the precepts of Scripture to the problems of government, and indeed he took what was very much a Social Gospel stance in the realm of public affairs, arguing in a piece entitled "Applied Christianity" that he wrote for his weekly newspaper, the *Commoner*, "The teachings of Christ apply to the structure and administration of government as well as to the life and conduct of the individual." Not surprisingly, during the flurry of strikes that marked the immediate postwar era, he called upon the churches to use their influence to effect a reconciliation between capital and labor; and throughout the early 1920's he criticized the churches for their indifference to such issues as economic exploitation and international anarchy.[18]

Progressive on political and economic issues, Bryan remained deeply conservative on intellectual and religious issues. He was no premillennialist, eschewing politics in pessimistic disgust with human sinfulness, and he was no theologian. But he knew the Bible thoroughly and he believed that it set forth the word of God authoritatively and infallibly. And he early fastened upon the writings of Charles Darwin as, on the one hand, corrosive of the teachings of Scripture and, on the other hand, supportive of political conservatism—the idea of the survival of the fittest, Bryan reasoned, was scarcely compatible with the politics of democracy. Equally important, Bryan became convinced, along with many of his fellow Americans, that the schools and colleges were promulgating doctrines of theolog-

18. "Applied Christianity," *Commoner*, May, 1919, p. 12.

ical modernism and evolutionary science that were subversive of Christian belief and contrary to what the great majority of parents wished for their children. The result in his view was an undermining of public morality that jeopardized the future of American civilization.

During the 1920's, Bryan set out to do battle against these tendencies. His efforts proceeded on three fronts. First, he inveighed against modernism and evolution in lectures before church and college audiences and on the Chautauqua circuit, and in articles in the *Commoner* and in syndicated columns published in over a hundred newspapers— through the last alone he reached a weekly audience of over twenty million people. Second, he assumed leadership of the effort to drive modernism from his church, the Presbyterian Church of the United States, initially, by seeking election as Moderator of the church at the 1923 General Assembly, and then, having failed by a narrow margin, by pressing at the Assembly for a resolution to deny financial aid to any Presbyterian school permitting Darwinism or any other evolutionary theory to be taught, an effort that also failed. And third, he enlisted in the campaign to obtain legislation in the several states prohibiting the teaching of Darwinism in state-supported schools and colleges. In all these efforts, Bryan joined with others, with individuals such as Clarence E. Macartney of the Presbyterian Church, who won election as Moderator in 1924 and promptly appointed Bryan Vice-Moderator, and with organizations such as the Anti-evolution League, founded in 1923 by the same William Bell Riley who had founded the World's Christian Fundamentals Association. His very presence provided the leadership that for all intents and purposes transformed a loosely knit congeries of disparate individuals and groups into a genuine social movement.

Bryan, too, galvanized the so-called modernists into active concern. "Early in the year 1922," wrote Henry Fairfield Osborn, the president of the American Museum of Natural History, "I was suddenly aroused from my reposeful researches in paleontology by an article in the *New York Times* of February 26, by William Jennings Bryan, entitled 'God and Evolution.' The force of the article lay in his clever citation of the wide differences of opinion existing among evolutionists as to the *causes* of evolution. . . . It struck me immediately that Bryan's article was far more able and convincing than any previous utterance of his or of any other fundamentalist, and that there should not be a moment's delay in replying to it." Osborn dutifully replied in the *Times,* in an essay affirming his belief in the Bible as an infallible source of spiritual and moral knowledge, in scientific inquiry as the most dependable source of natural knowledge, and in the need for both kinds of knowledge if one was to have "the whole truth and nothing but the truth." In swift profusion, churchmen, theologians, philosophers, and scientists added their replies, seeking to formulate the modernist brief. One of the best was a tract entitled *The Faith of Modernism* by Shailer Mathews, dean of the University of Chicago Divinity School. Modernism, Mathews urged, was neither a denomination nor a theology; it was rather "the use of scientific, historical, social method in understanding and applying evangelical Christianity to the needs of living persons." Modernists were Christians who accepted the results of scientific inquiry as data with which to think religiously; modernists were Christians who adopted the methods of historical and literary science in the study of the Bible and religion; modernists were Christians who believed that the Christian religion would help people meet social as well as individual needs; and modernists were Christians persuaded that the spiritual and moral needs of the world could ultimately be met because Christian attitudes and faiths were entirely consistent with the realities of the world. The connection of Mathews's arguments with the theological developments set in motion by Washington Gladden was unmistakable; indeed, Gladden was as much a progenitor of modernism as Dwight Moody was of fundamentalism.[19]

As the analyses on both sides multiplied, so did the caricatures. For the modernist, the cartoon version of the fundamentalist too often emerged as an ignorant rural bigot proffering crabbed values, antiquated beliefs, and prejudiced opinions. For the fundamentalist, the counter cartoon of the modernist was of an overeducated urban fool (bearing many academic degrees, including the A.S.S.) proffering libertine values, immoral beliefs, and subversive ideas. And each was increasingly certain that the other was busily imposing the cartoon version of his philosophy on young people across the country, to the ultimate ruin of the nation.

The skirmishes between the fundamentalists and the modernists were ubiquitous during the 1920's—in the churches and organized denominations, in the schools and colleges, and in a number of state legislatures. But it was the Scopes trial of 1925 that became the decisive battle of the war. The events leading to the trial and the facts of the trial itself are well-known. Proposals to bar the teaching of evolu-

19. Henry Fairfield Osborn, *Evolution and Religion in Education: Polemics of the Fundamentalist Controversy of 1922 to 1926* (New York: Charles Scribner's Sons, 1926), pp. 3–4, 42; and Shailer Mathews, *The Faith of Modernism* (New York: The Macmillan Company, 1924), p. 35.

tion in public schools and colleges began to be introduced into state legislatures as early as 1921; and, as the fundamentalist crusade gained momentum, the agitation for such laws intensified. In states such as Kentucky, North Carolina, and Texas, political battles of unprecedented bitterness were fought, but in the end the fundamentalists' efforts failed. In other states, however, legislation of one sort or another was enacted. In Oklahoma, a law prohibiting the use in public schools of any book presenting the Darwinist theory of creation was passed in 1923. In Florida, the legislature that same year passed a joint resolution declaring it improper and subversive for any instructor in any public institution to teach atheism, agnosticism, Darwinism, or any other hypothesis linking man in blood relationship to other forms of life. And in Tennessee, the legislature in 1925 enacted the Butler Bill (named for John Washington Butler, the Macon County farmer who introduced the measure into the assembly), making it unlawful for any teacher in any of the state's public schools or universities "to teach any theory that denies the story of the Divine Creation of man as taught in the Bible, and to teach instead that man has descended from a lower order of animals," and imposing a fine of between $100 and $500 on any teacher found guilty of violating this prohibition.[20]

Governor Austin Peay signed the Butler Bill into law on March 21, 1925—there is evidence that he regarded passage of the bill as essentially a symbolic gesture. The American Civil Liberties Union in New York promptly decided to challenge the constitutionality of the statute by financing a test case, assuming that some teacher willing to cooperate could be found. A Dayton, Tennessee, mining engineer named George W. Rappelyea persuaded John Thomas Scopes, a twenty-four-year-old science teacher and football coach at Dayton High School, to become the instrument of the test case. Scopes had been teaching biology from George William Hunter's *A Civic Biology* (1914), the text officially prescribed by the state textbook commission, and Hunter's book set forth the doctrine of evolution; Scopes was thereby in violation of the law. Rappelyea pressed charges, and Scopes was duly arrested on May 7 and charged in a preliminary hearing on May 10. Three days later, William Jennings Bryan announced in Pittsburgh that, if the local prosecutors agreed, he would accept an invitation from the World's Christian Fundamentals Association to represent the Association as associate counsel in the case (the

20. *Public Acts of the State of Tennessee, 1925,* chap. xxvii, House Bill 185, Sec. 1, pp. 50–51.

prosecutors were delighted). The very next day, it was announced that John Randolph Neal, the former dean of the law school at the University of Tennessee and the man Austin Peay had defeated for the governorship, would serve as counsel for Scopes, to be joined, among others, by Arthur Garfield Hays of the ACLU and by Clarence Darrow of Chicago and Dudley Field Malone of New York—Darrow, a brilliantly skeptical, nationally known trial lawyer with a longstanding amateur interest in science, Malone, a vivacious member of New York's Greenwich Village intelligentsia and a highly successful divorce lawyer. Thereby was the stage set for one of the dramatic encounters of the decade.

The trial began on an oppressively hot July 10 in the Dayton courthouse amidst a carnival spirit that had been building for weeks. Judge John T. Raulston, who also served as a lay preacher in the Methodist Episcopal Church, presided over a jammed courtroom, which included not only the principals but more than a hundred reporters from various parts of the United States and abroad. The task of Tennessee Attorney General A. T. Stewart, who headed the prosecution, was simple—to prove that Scopes had actually taught the doctrines of evolution and had thereby violated the statute. The commitment of the defense attorneys, however, was more complicated. Legally, it was to establish that the Butler Law was unconstitutional by demonstrating that it abridged freedom of religion by making the Bible the test of truth, that it was unreasonable in light of modern scientific knowledge, and that it was insufficiently definite because of time-honored disagreements over what the Bible actually meant. But more generally, it was to instruct the public on the meaning of evolution, to demonstrate to the public that evolution was not necessarily incompatible with religion, and to persuade the public that education proceeded best unhampered by restrictive legislation. To that end, the defense was prepared to parade before the court a succession of distinguished scholars and scientists, whose testimony would establish the unreasonableness of the statute. And, well aware of the intention of the defense, the prosecution was prepared to introduce its expert witnesses as well.

For all the build-up, the trial itself proved disappointing. A good deal of time during the first five days was devoted, first, to legal wrangling, and second, to establishing the fact of Scopes's having taught the doctrines of evolution from Hunter's text. On the sixth day, Judge Raulston ruled that the testimony of the distinguished scholars and scientists would be neither necessary nor relevant to the case, thereby precluding the principal effort of the defense. On the seventh day, however, there was an unexpected climax, when the defense called Bryan himself to the stand and neither the court nor Bryan objected—both, indeed, relished the opportunity. Darrow's questioning was merciless. Did Jonah really remain in the whale's belly for three days? Bryan believed he did. Did the great flood really occur in 4004 B.C.? Bryan wasn't certain. Was the earth really created in six days? "Not six days of twenty-four hours," Bryan responded; and the audience in the courtroom gasped. When Stewart, in an effort to relieve the pressure, then asked, "What is the purpose of this examination?" Darrow replied, "We have the purpose of preventing bigots and ignoramuses from controlling the education of the United States and you know it, and that is all." The questioning proceeded, with Bryan first dazed and then defeated as he was deserted even by his supporters in the audience. On the eighth day, Judge Raulston charged the jury, which, after nine minutes of deliberation, returned a verdict of guilty. The judge then imposed a fine on Scopes of $100. On appeal, the Supreme Court of Tennessee upheld the Butler Act but reversed the judgment of the lower court because of a state constitutional mandate that any fine of more than $50 had to be imposed by a jury and not a judge. The court also added, by way of conclusion, "We see nothing to be gained by prolonging the life of this bizarre case. On the contrary, we think the peace and dignity of the state, which all criminal prosecutions are brought to redress, will be the better conserved by the entry of a nolle prosequi [a declaration that the case will not be further prosecuted] herein. Such a course is suggested to the Attorney General." Thus was a further constitutional test precluded.[21]

Bryan's humiliation at the Scopes trial and his sudden death less than a week later left the movement he had helped to shape leaderless. Several men, notably William Bell Riley, who had founded the WCFA, George F. Washburn, who had founded the Bible Crusaders of America, Paul W. Rood, who had founded the Bryan Bible League, and Gerald Winrod, who had founded the Defenders of the Christian Faith, reached for Bryan's mantle, but none succeeded; and, although political efforts to repress evolutionary doctrine through legislation continued for another few years, the movement in the large splintered, leaving it to individual groups and institutions to carry on the crusade. Fundamentalism departed from the headlines as a national

21. *Southwestern Reporter*, CCLXXXIX (1927), 367.

concern, but it in no way died as an intellectual force; rather, it carried on powerfully through the very educational institutions that Moody's generation had created—the tabernacle, the Bible conference, and, most important, the Bible school.

Two additional aspects of the Scopes trial bear comment. First, given the locale of Dayton, given the millions of words of commentary written by those who were present and by those who were not, and given the post-trial literary caricatures wrought by H. L. Mencken and Sinclair Lewis on the modernist side and by Glenn Gates Cole and Luther Little on the fundamentalist side, the fundamentalist-modernist controversy was transformed into a war of the country against the city, of the South and Midwest against the Northeast, of provincialism against cosmopolitanism, of rural reaction against urban progressivism. As with all caricatures, there was a grain of truth to the portrayal, inasmuch as the antievolution crusade at least, while not confined to the more agrarian South and Midwest, did make its greatest headway there, and inasmuch as fundamentalism, while it did embrace an older Baconian view of science, did disdain more recent scientific developments. That said, however, fundamentalism was as much an urban as a rural phenomenon; indeed, some of the main sources of fundamentalist leadership and support lay in Chicago, Minneapolis, Los Angeles, and New York. Moreover, modernists could be quite as provincial and reactionary in some of their social views as the fundamentalists they caricatured—consider, as but one example, the position on Nordic racial superiority of the same Henry Fairfield Osborn who was moved to answer Bryan in the *New York Times*. In the end, the very definitions of provincialism and cosmopolitanism were being altered by the relentless advance of metropolitanization. Whereas in the 1880's rural hamlets and even urban neighborhoods could retain something of the character of "island communities," to use Robert H. Wiebe's apt phrase, the incessant geographical mobility of the era, accelerated as it was by World War I, coupled with rapid advances in transportation, communication, and public schooling, rendered insularity more difficult to maintain. In fact, one reason for the eruption of fundamentalist political agitation in the 1920's may have been the breakdown of insularity: fundamentalists were finding it harder and harder to avoid the challenges of intellectual novelty.[22]

Finally, there remains the fascinating dilemma posed by the Scopes trial with respect to the popularization of schooling, namely,

22. Robert H. Wiebe, *The Search for Order, 1877–1920* (New York: Hill and Wang, 1967), chap. i.

the rights of parents and communities to determine the character of the education given their children. Bryan, the consummate democrat, believed in the universal application of majority rule. In response to the charge that the Butler Law was unconstitutional, he asserted that a minority of intellectuals had no right to use the courts to impose its view on a majority of laymen. "The majority is not trying to establish a religion or teach it—it is trying to protect itself from the effort of an insolent minority to force irreligion upon the children under the guise of teaching science," he contended in the final statement he prepared for the trial but did not deliver (it was made public shortly after his death). "What right has a little irresponsible oligarchy of self-styled 'intellectuals' to demand control of the schools of the United States, in which twenty-five millions of children are being educated at an annual expense of nearly two billions of dollars?" But was the truth a matter to be determined by the voters or by an elected legislature or by a jury randomly selected from the community at large? John Scopes contended that he was merely teaching from Hunter's *A Civic Biology* views that were generally accepted throughout the scientific community, and the experts whom the defense had brought to Dayton were prepared to support him in that view. Who was better able to attest the truths to be taught in a popular education system, professional experts or representative parents and laypeople, and at what level of community—local, state, or national—were such truths to be determined? And, beyond that, did tax-supported schools have the right to teach children truths that controverted the beliefs of their parents? The issues were not resolved at Dayton, and they continued to divide the American people over the next half-century.[23]

IV

A young Detroit minister named Reinhold Niebuhr followed the Scopes trial with a mixture of dismay and disdain. He believed a new civilization was coming into being, and he lamented the fact that it was a civilization in which workingpeople were exploited and businessmen posing as progressive Christians derived wealth from that exploitation. He saw the modernists, in seeking to adjust religion to science, developing a religion so devoid of faith as to be worthless—worse yet, it ended up serving the interests of the exploiters. And he saw the

23. "Mr. Bryan's Last Statement," in Leslie H. Allen, ed., *Bryan and Darrow at Dayton: The Record and Documents of the "Bible-Evolution Trial"* (New York: Arthur Lee & Company, 1925), p. 173.

fundamentalists returning to a religion so out of touch with the new civilization as to be irrelevant—indeed, in its irrelevancy it, too, ended up serving the interests of the exploiters. Moreover, he believed the crusades of the twenties had only hardened positions on both sides. "If we must choose between types of fanaticism," he observed in his notebook, "is there any particular reason why we should prefer the fanatics who destroy a vital culture in the name of freedom and reason to those who try to strangle a new culture at birth in the name of authority and dogma? The latter type of fanaticism is bound to end in futility. The growth of reason cannot be stopped by dogma. But the former type is dangerous because it easily enervates a rational culture with ennui and despair." The observation presaged Niebuhr's life-long critique of American religion and education.[24]

Niebuhr had come to Detroit in 1915 at the age of twenty-three to take over a recently formed Evangelical congregation of eighteen families. He had spent his earliest years in Wright City and St. Charles, Missouri, and Lincoln, Illinois, the son of a German-born Evangelical minister, and had gone on from Lincoln High School to Elmhurst College, a small, denominational institution that did not grant the bachelor's degree but did offer scholarships to ministers' sons, and then to Eden Theological Seminary, the training school of the Evangelical Synod, which his father had also attended. The elder Niebuhr had died suddenly in 1913 while his son was still at Eden, and the younger Niebuhr had been invited to assume his father's pulpit in Lincoln; but he had resolved instead to continue his education at the Yale Divinity School, where he had completed the work for the B.D. and M.A. degrees. There he had imbibed a good deal of the characteristic theological liberalism of the era, and indeed had been offered an assistant rectorship at a good salary at the First Church of Meriden, Connecticut; but he had decided instead to answer the call of the mission board of his own denomination and accept the Detroit appointment.

Niebuhr arrived in Detroit committed to the doctrines of the Social Gospel. His faith in those doctrines and indeed his confidence in his own ability were soon shaken amid the diurnal affairs of a growing urban congregation. His notebook of those years reveals a deepening immersion in the labor conflicts of the Ford Motor Company, a growing skepticism concerning traditional notions of steady progress toward the Kingdom of God on earth, particularly as Woodrow Wilson's

---

24. Reinhold Niebuhr, *Leaves from the Notebook of a Tamed Cynic* [*1929*] (reprint ed.; Hamden, Conn.: The Shoe String Press, 1956), p. 162.

high-minded war aims were dashed in the negotiations at Versailles and in Washington, and a progressive disenchantment with what he perceived to be the blandness and the moral pretentiousness of theological modernism and especially its apparent impotence in the face of the intractable racial, ethnic, and class problems of an industrial city like Detroit. As a consequence, there issued from his pulpit and his pen a steady flow of commentary critical of the Social Gospel, culminating in the publication, in 1927, of his first book, *Does Civilization Need Religion?* There he sounded the theme that would continue to preoccupy him in his writing, namely, the need of the church, if it would be an instrument of human redemption, to divorce itself from the corrupt moral temper of the world at the same time that it tried to accommodate itself to the changing intellectual needs of that world. Whereas he thought modernism had sought a convergence of religion and culture and had in the process become corrupt and conservative, he himself sought a tension between religion and culture that would reassert the dualism between God and the world and in the process reestablish prophecy as the basis of a religiously inspired moral idealism.

Niebuhr left Detroit in 1928 to join the faculty of Union Theological Seminary in New York City and remained there until his death in 1971. During those years he developed and refined his theological views and articulated them in a plethora of lectures, sermons, articles, and books that found an increasingly receptive international audience. Ironically, the same Niebuhr who had left Yale without continuing to work for a doctorate because he desired "relevance rather than scholarship" achieved his influence by drawing upon the imposing scholarship of post–World War I European neo-orthodoxy (and especially the scholarship of the Swiss theologian Karl Barth), by adding his own considerable knowledge of the history of theology, and by making that scholarship relevant to the situation of metropolitan America.[25]

Two books in particular, works profoundly different in character and style, marked the development of Niebuhr's thought. *Moral Man and Immoral Society,* which appeared in 1932 at the depth of the worldwide Depression and of the despair associated with it, proclaimed Niebuhr's decisive rejection of religious modernism and of the naive faith in science, reason, intelligence, and popular education he saw

25. "Reminiscences of Reinhold Niebuhr" (Oral History Collection, Columbia University Library, New York City), p. 16. By permission of the Oral History Collection, Columbia University Library.

associated with it. The stated purpose of the book was to distinguish between the morality of individuals and the morality of collectives, whether races, classes, or nations. The stated thrust of the book was against "the moralists, both religious and secular, who imagine that the egoism of individuals is being progressively checked by the development of rationality or the growth of a religiously inspired goodwill and that nothing but the continuance of this process is necessary to establish social harmony between all the human societies and collectives." Interestingly, the thinker Niebuhr chose to exemplify those moralists was not Shailer Mathews or some other contemporary proponent of liberal Christianity, but John Dewey, who was rather the proponent of a thoroughgoing naturalism (Dewey's Terry Lectures at Yale would appear in 1934 under the title *A Common Faith*). Niebuhr mocked Dewey's belief that the principal barriers to the solution of the world's problems were outmoded traditions and shopworn intellectual systems and that the great hope for solutions to those problems lay in a courageous human intelligence. Utter sentimentalism, Niebuhr retorted; what Dewey and his ilk failed to recognize was the brutal character of all human collectives, the easy subservience of human reason to prejudice and passion, and the consequent irrational egoism that made social conflict inevitable in human history. What was Niebuhr's alternative? It was to stop confusing the morality of individuals, which needed to be based upon the highest ideals of love and altruism, with the morality of collectives, which could at best seek justice, or a reasonable balance of power and interests. The Kingdom of God could not be achieved within human history, Niebuhr concluded; to dispel that illusion would at least make possible the achievement of a decent minimum of social justice.[26]

Moral Man and Immoral Society was a work of criticism, clearly rooted in Niebuhr's developing idea of what might constitute a more truly Christian theory of the nature of man in relation to God. He eventually explicated that theory in his 1939 Gifford Lectures at the University of Edinburgh, which were subsequently published as *The Nature and Destiny of Man* (1941, 1943). There, Niebuhr described human beings as having three levels of existence—as part of nature, as reasoning creatures who could order and systematize knowledge, and as spiritual beings with a capacity for self-transcendence. The problem with modern individuals, Niebuhr explained, was that they had failed to recognize in their self-consciousness as spiritual beings

26. Reinhold Niebuhr, *Moral Man and Immoral Society* [1932] (reprint ed.; New York: Charles Scribner's Sons, 1960), p. xii.

that every attempt to apply reason to the solution of individual and social problems was inevitably tinged with evil as well as good, with selfishness as well as altruism. Indeed, he continued, the contradiction held the essence of sin, namely, the fact that, at every level of human achievement, the good was potentially corrupted by egoism and thereby turned to destructiveness. In seeking the perfection of humankind and of human society, modern individuals had fallen into self-glorification and had in the process committed the sin of pride.

Niebuhr went on to explain the Christian view of redemption, namely, that God through Christ had extended to human beings the saving grace that enabled them to overcome the sinful elements in their achievements. He called Christ's sacrificial love in his death upon the cross *agape;* it was perfect love, in contrast to human love, which even at its most altruistic was invariably tinged with sinful egoism. *Agape* transcended "all particular norms of justice and mutuality in history," rising above history and seeking conformity to divine love rather than harmony with other human interests. Given the argument of *The Nature and Destiny of Man,* one could extend the earlier thesis of *Moral Man and Immoral Society* to mean that sin, or self-centered pride, existed in every individual and collectivity; that power was required for individuals and groups to protect themselves in the social arena; that reason would help people recognize the demands of justice, or the balancing of interests; that justice, when supplemented by love, was a worthy human aspiration but that love was an emotion of individuals rather than collectivities; and that in the end even individual love is tinged with egoism unless suffused by *agape.* [27]

One other theme in *Moral Man and Immoral Society* was further developed during the 1930's and early 1940's, namely, the need for a philosophy that would bind people together in common cause. Having rejected what he saw as the fanaticism of fundamentalism and the sentimentalism of liberalism, Niebuhr was left with the problem of what faiths might undergird society's collectivities and govern their relations. "Contending factions in a social struggle require morale," he observed in *Moral Man and Immoral Society;* "and morale is created by the right dogmas, symbols and emotionally potent oversimplifications." Whence the "right dogmas, symbols and emotionally potent oversimplifications" for the United States? Niebuhr returned to the problem in *An Interpretation of Christian Ethics* (1935). Rejecting again the "devitalized and secularized religion" of modernism that had

27. Reinhold Niebuhr, *The Nature and Destiny of Man: A Christian Interpretation* (2 vols.; New York: Charles Scribner's Sons, 1941–43), II, 98–99, 74.

robbed Christian myth of its motivating power, Niebuhr called for a revival of the transcendent myth of prophetic Christianity. Incorporating, on the one hand, a true recognition of the problem of evil and, on the other hand, a transcendent system of values, such a myth would at least be able to avoid the sinful element he saw in such secular religions as Communism. And in *The Children of Light and the Children of Darkness* (1944), he further specified the discussion with respect to contemporary America. American democracy, he observed, was a "bourgeois ideology" developed by "the children of light," who foolishly believed that self-interest could be brought under the discipline of a higher law. It was a worthy faith, he granted, but it needed to be disciplined by "the children of darkness," who were wise, though evil, because they understood the power of self-interest. Beyond that, the faith would have to be redeemed by a Christian faith that could comprehend the fragmentary and broken character of all historic achievements. In sum, "The children of light must be armed with the wisdom of the children of darkness but remain free from their malice. They must know the power of self-interest in human society without giving it moral justification. They must have this wisdom in order that they may beguile, deflect, harness and restrain self-interest, individual and collective, for the sake of community." Years later, after World War II had cast the United States decisively into the forefront of world affairs, Niebuhr extended the analysis to the world at large, maintaining in *The Structure of Nations and Empires* (1959) that the essential difference between the American and the Communist empires was that the former would be governed by a sense of justice stemming from the Christian religion while the latter would be governed by a sense of self-righteousness stemming from the Communist religion. Americans could know the power of self-interest in human society, he concluded, without according it moral justification.[28]

Niebuhr once responded to the inquiry of a doctoral student who wanted to study his views on human nature and education, that he had not explicated his ideas on the ends and means of education and had neither the interest nor the competence to speak on matters of educational methodology. He was overly modest on two counts: on the

28. Niebuhr, *Moral Man and Immoral Society*, p. xv; *An Interpretation of Christian Ethics* (New York: Harper & Brothers, 1935), p. 10; *The Children of Light and the Children of Darkness: A Vindication of Democracy and a Critique of Its Traditional Defense* (New York: Charles Scribner's Sons, 1944), pp. 1, 41; and *The Structure of Nations and Empires: A Study of the Recurring Patterns and Problems of the Political Order in Relation to the Unique Problems of the Nuclear Age* (New York: Charles Scribner's Sons, 1959).

significance of his published commentaries on education and on the extent to which his more general works were pregnant with educational meaning. Niebuhr wrote no systematic treatise on education, which is doubtless what he had in mind when he responded to the student's inquiry. But he did publish a number of articles on education and he did allude to education at a number of points in his books. Most of the articles dated from the 1950's and 1960's and dealt largely with formal education in the schools and colleges. A substantial piece for the Religious Education Association in 1953 dealt tersely and pointedly with the teaching of religion in the public schools. Contending that America was "at once the most religious and the most irreligious of modern industrial or technically efficient nations," he urged a dramatic increase in church-sponsored released-time instruction in the public schools, essentially after the fashion of the European countries. Yet he went on to admit, with characteristic Niebuhrian irony, that such instruction could not hope to preserve "the religious vitalities which are not transmitted by formal education but by the contagion of individual and collective commitment." Presumably that contagion could occur only within the context of the several religious communities themselves, through the exemplarity and modeling that would take place in the daily living of the good life. An essay in the Harvard magazine *Confluence* in 1957, subsequently republished as a chapter of *Pious and Secular America* (1958), called on the colleges and universities to stand up against the utilitarianism he saw dominating the larger society and to convey through a revitalized humanistic curriculum "an appreciation of forms of art and science, of imagination and comprehension of life's dimensions" that "do not promise an immediate increment of obvious success." And an essay in *Daedalus* in 1959 called for instruction at every level of the formal education system that would prepare young Americans for a world in which the United States stood as a major power, in which competitive coexistence with the Communist bloc would be a major fact of life, and in which that competitive coexistence would take place on the edge of the abyss of nuclear war.[29]

29. For the response to the inquiry, see Timothy Wayne Rieman, "A Comparative Study of the Understanding of Man in the Writings of Reinhold Niebuhr and John Dewey and Some Implications for Education" (doctoral thesis, Northwestern University, 1959), pp. 8–9; Reinhold Niebuhr, "Religion and Education," *Religious Education*, XLVIII (1953), 371–373; *Pious and Secular America* (New York: Charles Scribner's Sons, 1958), pp. 34, 38; and "Education and the World Scene," in Brand Blanshard, ed., *Education in the Age of Science* (New York: Basic Books, 1959), p. 129.

One senses in these articles the call for instruction in the "curriculum" first laid out in *Moral Man and Immoral Society*—instruction leading to an individual life ideally governed by Christian love within a world ideally governed by justice. Indeed that call holds the clue to the larger relevance of Niebuhr's theology for American education. Both explicitly and implicitly, his works addressed themselves to the diurnal teaching and learning that went forward in families and churches, schools and colleges, and the cultural agencies of the larger society. The indictment of the shallowness of theological modernism in family, church, and Sunday school in *Does Civilization Need Religion?* and *Leaves from the Notebook of a Tamed Cynic;* the attack on pragmatic philosophies in *Moral Man and Immoral Society;* the skepticism about the benefits of popular schooling in *The Irony of American History* (1952); the contempt for the "vulgarities of mass communications" in *Pious and Secular America*—these were merely the explicit elements of the fundamental critique of American education that ran throughout the Niebuhr canon. In effect, Niebuhr was arguing that the correspondence between a Protestant Christian *paideia* and an American *paideia* that the nineteenth-century evangelical Protestants had effected had become too much American and too little Christian; his solution was nothing less than the re-Christianizing of the American *paideia* in a form suitable to a metropolitan world.[30]

As for the implicit aspects of Niebuhr's educational effort, eager disciples moved to work out more explicit formulations. To cite but two, H. Shelton Smith of Duke University, who, like Niebuhr, had started out as a partisan of the Social Gospel, undertook during the 1930's a searching re-examination of the theological and educational underpinnings of what he referred to as "progressive religious education"—religious education as typified by the work of George Albert Coe. Publishing the fruits of his analysis in a treatise entitled *Faith and Nurture* (1941), Smith maintained that "progressive religious education" had gradually evolved into a new religious faith that had come to dominate the entire curriculum of the public school—Smith called it "the religion of humanistic experimentalism"—and he argued that the alternative view of the world embodied in Niebuhr's neo-orthodoxy would be much more in keeping with the teachings of America's three traditional faiths. "What kind of religion shall the public schools teach," Smith asked, "the religion of the churches or the religion of humanistic experimentalism?

30. Niebuhr, *Pious and Secular America*, pp. 38, 34.

Sooner or later this must become the focal point of a crucial battle. On the outcome largely hangs the fate of democratic culture in America." If the liberals in Smith's view seemed entranced with the optimistic faith of Horace Bushnell, one could hear in his own dire query the mordant warnings of Bushnell's pessimistic contemporary Lyman Beecher![31]

Three years after the appearance of Smith's treatise, a young Canadian minister named James D. Smart joined the staff of the Board of Christian Education of the Presbyterian Church of the United States, charged with the development of a new religious education curriculum that would take proper account of the Niebuhrian critique. The materials Smart and his colleagues produced—storybooks, textbooks, lesson plans, and periodicals for both children and teachers— not only dramatically altered the teaching of the Presbyterian Church and its associated educational institutions, but also profoundly influenced similar efforts within the Congregational, Episcopalian, and Evangelical and Reformed churches. In 1954 Smart published *The Teaching Ministry of the Church,* a treatise that, like Smith's, sharply criticized the liberally oriented programs of the religious education movement and proposed in their place a neo-orthodox program that would go forward not only in churches and homes but in the public schools as well. Secular schoolteachers had long suffused their instruction with secular views of man and society, Smart charged; Christian educators would have to substitute teaching suffused with Christian conviction.

Efforts such as Smith's and Smart's wrought considerable change in church programs, as Protestantism in general moved in the direction of more orthodox formulations; but they bore little fruit in public school programs. Rather, they tended indirectly to weaken the political coalition that had traditionally supported the public school, a coalition in which Protestants had played such a central role. By charging that any nonsectarian compromise with respect to the teaching of moral values ultimately took on the character of an alternative religion, they made accommodation in this crucial area of public school curricula more difficult at precisely the time when pluralism was becoming more powerful in American religious and cultural affairs.

31. H. Shelton Smith, "Christian Education," in Arnold S. Nash, ed., *Protestant Thought in the Twentieth Century: Whence and Whither?* (New York: The Macmillan Company, 1951), p. 225 and *passim;* and H. Shelton Smith, *Faith and Nurture* (New York: Charles Scribner's Sons, 1941), p. viii.

V

America, Niebuhr had argued, was at the same time the most religious and the most secular of modern industrial nations. Niebuhr's
disciple Will Herberg elaborated the paradox into a powerfully persuasive analysis of the religious situation in post–World War II
America. Herberg had grown up in New York City and had had his
formal education in the public schools and at the College of the City
of New York. But his most intense education had come in the Herberg household, where his immigrant parents had taught him,
among other things, Latin, Greek, French, German, and Russian by
the time he was a teenager, and within the precincts of the Communist Party, which he had joined in 1926 at the age of seventeen. A
young man of profound learning and considerable independence of
mind, Herberg had endured the twists and turns of party policy during the late 1920's, had aligned himself with the deviant Lovestone
faction during the 1930's, and had finally suffered disenchantment
as a result of the Nazi-Soviet nonaggression pact of 1939, the Soviet
invasion of Finland in 1939, and, more generally, his own growing
awareness of Stalinist terrorism. It was at that point, as Herberg
related it, that his encounter with Niebuhr's writings changed his
thinking and his life, permitting him to rekindle "the commitment
and understanding that alone had made life livable." In place of
Marxism, Herberg turned to orthodox Judaism, producing in 1951 a
treatise drawing upon the thought of Niebuhr and of Martin Buber
entitled *Judaism and Modern Man* and in 1955 a treatise drawing upon
the thought of Niebuhr and Max Weber entitled *Protestant-Catholic-
Jew.* It was the latter treatise that seemed to contemporaries so co-
gent in explaining the religious situation in which they found themselves.[32]

Herberg began his analysis with his own version of Niebuhr's
paradox. The American people were experiencing an unmistakable
religious revival, as church membership and church attendance burgeoned; yet the American community was also marked by a growing
secular tendency, a tendency to think and live in terms of intellectual
outlooks ever more remote from the religious beliefs simultaneously
professed. "It is this secularism of a religious people," Herberg maintained, "this religiousness in a secularist framework, that constitutes

32. Will Herberg, "Christian Apologist to the Secular World," *Union Seminary Quarterly
Review,* XI (May, 1956), 12.

the problem posed by the contemporary religious situation in America."[33]

Herberg's explanation for the apparent paradox lay in his concept of the "triple melting pot." Citing sociological data to the effect that Americans were tending to marry more frequently across ethnic than across religious lines, Herberg turned for an explanation to an aphorism of the late historian Marcus Lee Hansen. In the process of Americanization, Hansen noted, what the second generation wanted to forget, the third generation wanted to remember. Put otherwise, what the children of immigrants wanted to leave behind them in their effort to adapt to American ways, the grandchildren of immigrants were attempting to find again in their quest for identity within American society, and they seemed increasingly to be finding what they were looking for in religious beliefs and customs. Yet, granted that, the very process of Americanization had at the same time made Americans more secular in their commitment to a "common religion" called the American Way of Life. "If the American Way of Life had to be defined in one word," Herberg elucidated, " 'democracy' would undoubtedly be the word, but democracy in a peculiarly American sense. On its political side it means the Constitution; on its economic side, 'free enterprise'; on its social side, an equalitarianism which is not only compatible with but indeed actually implies vigorous economic competition and high mobility. Spiritually, the American Way of Life is best expressed in a certain kind of 'idealism' which has come to be recognized as characteristically American. It is a faith that has its symbols and its rituals, its holidays and its liturgy, its saints and its sancta; and it is a faith that every American, to the degree that he is an American, knows and understands."[34]

In the interaction of the three historic faiths of America (Protestantism, Catholicism, and Judaism) with the common faith of America (the American Way of Life), Herberg continued, there had been a continual, reciprocal shaping and reshaping, with the result that by the 1950's the three historic faiths had all emerged in uniquely American versions, and obversely, the American Way of Life had come to be expressed and lived in three diverse but coequal versions. A few ideologists, Herberg remarked, almost in passing, had gone on to

33. Will Herberg, *Protestant-Catholic-Jew: An Essay in American Religious Sociology* (Garden City, N.Y.: Doubleday & Company, 1955), p. 15.
34. M. L. Hansen, *The Problem of the Third Generation Immigrant* (Rock Island, Ill.: Augustana Historical Society, 1938), pp. 9–10; and Herberg, *Protestant-Catholic-Jew*, pp. 18, 91–92.

"erect 'democracy' into a super-faith above and embracing the three recognized religions," but the great mass of Americans had not followed them. For most Americans, the common faith of America operated implicitly rather than explicitly, and made no pretensions to override or supplant the recognized religions. As for the theologians within the historic faiths, Herberg concluded, such a super-faith could be nothing but "a particularly insidious kind of idolatry."[35]

Herberg's picture of three great religious communities, equally legitimate and American and equally committed to a common set of moral ideals and spiritual values, incorporated a radically altered formulation of the American *paideia*. Whereas the achievement of nineteenth-century evangelical Protestantism had been to effect a correspondence between a Protestant *paideia* and an American *paideia*, Herberg was arguing that the American *paideia* was and indeed ought to be plural, that it appeared in at least three different but coequal versions, and that in the end it was transmitted through the educational configurations of the three great religious communities. And, in keeping with his radically altered formulation, Herberg in 1957 proposed that public money be used to support religious schools as well as public schools—as a matter of justice as well as prudence.[36]

The issue, of course, went far beyond religious schools. Within the broad confines of all three of the great religious communities, modernist, conservative, and orthodox theorists alike proffered plans for configurations of educative institutions that included, beyond the churches and synagogues themselves, day-care centers, full-time denominational elementary and secondary schools, weekday religious schools, Sabbath schools, youth groups, summer camps, postsecondary institutions, men's and women's clubs, and senior citizens' facilities. And, what was remarkable about the educational theorizing that emanated from the three communities during the post–World War II era was its rather striking combination of theological continuity and pedagogical breadth. There were modest shifts in theological substance and style to be sure. The new Evangelicals, for example, carried forward the doctrine of Biblical inerrancy, but tended to make their peace with modern science; Roman Catholics displayed a manifestly greater receptivity to theological and social modernism after the Second Vatican Council called by Pope John XXIII, though that receptivity declined somewhat during the papacies of Paul VI, John Paul I, and John Paul II; and religious commentators in general tended to

35. Herberg, *Protestant-Catholic-Jew*, pp. 101, 102.
36. Will Herberg, "Justice for Religious Schools," *America*, XCVIII (1957–58), 193.

display a spirit of mutual regard that clearly flowed from the ecumenical movement of the 1960's. But these developments were less significant educationally than the essential fact of the persistence within each of the three historic religious communities of streams of modernist, conservative, and orthodox thought.

However much Herberg saw the religious communities themselves revitalized by the processes of Americanization, there were equally significant theological developments that emanated, not from the three historic faiths, but from what Herberg had referred to as the common religion of Americans. Flowing from the work of Dietrich Bonhoeffer and other European theologians, a strong secularizing current entered American religious thought, proclaiming a "world come of age," "a post-Christian society," and indeed, "the death of God." The secularizing current cut across the three historic faiths and the three great religious communities, reached outside traditional ecclesiastical structures, and sought to "demythologize" everything from the interpretation of Scripture to traditional theological argument. Of course, as Herberg himself pointed out, secular thought in and of itself was scarcely new in the United States in the 1950's. John Dewey's *A Common Faith* had set forth the substantive and methodological bases for a secular religion, distinguishing between religions per se and the religious quality of experience and maintaining that "any activity pursued in behalf of an ideal and against obstacles and in spite of threats of personal loss because of conviction of its general and enduring value is religious in quality." Horace Kallen's *Secularism Is the Will of God* and Philip H. Phenix's *Intelligible Religion,* both published in 1954, argued in similar veins, Kallen out of a lifelong dedication to religious pluralism, Phenix out of a Tillichian view of religion as "ultimate concern." Further, J. Paul Williams during the early 1950's urged that the public schools teach democracy as a religious dogma and indoctrinate youngsters in a code compounded of the Bill of Rights, the Four Freedoms, the ethical portions of the Ten Commandments, and the doctrines of majority rule and minority rights; V. T. Thayer urged that the public schools teach similar values, but divorced from any necessary connection to religious dogma or creed; and Philip H. Phenix argued that religious values were invariably taught via the diurnal life of any school, whatever the decision to include formal religious instruction in the curriculum. The astute Catholic theologian John Courtney Murray was well aware of these arguments, and in 1958 published a variant of Will Herberg's analysis entitled "America's Four Conspiracies," in which he maintained that the secular religion of Americans was not an implicit set of common values expressed diversely through the three great religious communities but rather a fourth religion standing alongside the historic three, with its own theological and educational apparatus centered in the public schools. For Murray, a true commitment to democratic pluralism required that the schools of all four "conspiracies"—Murray used the term in its root meaning to refer to a group of like-minded individuals acting in concert—be supported by public funds; the unity required for the well-ordered operation of civil society, he judged, would derive from "the unity of an orderly conversation." However interesting this line of theological development from the 1930's to the 1950's, Herberg was probably correct in noting that the formal secularist position was at best a minority view representing a logical argument carried to its intellectual conclusion.[37]

What marked the 1960's was the development of theological argument that took the phenomenon of secularization seriously; and the result was a transformation in theological thought that had profound significance for education. In 1965 a young Harvard professor named Harvey Cox published a slender paperback volume entitled *The Secular City*. The reception was extraordinary. The book went through multiple printings, selling over a quarter-million copies in a year. It was translated into Finnish, German, Korean, Dutch, French, and Swedish, and it elicited a flood of commentary, ranging from dithyrambic praise to disdainful criticism. "Hands down," the *Christian Century* reported in 1966, "Protestantism's most discussed book last year was Harvey Cox's affirmative evaluation of the modern megalopolis."[38]

Cox had grown up in Pennsylvania and had attended the University of Pennsylvania and then the Yale Divinity School, after which he had gone on to the directorship of religious activities at Oberlin College and ordination as a minister of the American Baptist Church. He had served for a time with the American Baptist Home Missionary Society and had then accepted professorships, first at Andover New-

---

37. John Dewey, *A Common Faith* (New Haven: Yale University Press, 1934), p. 27; Horace Kallen, *Secularism Is the Will of God: An Essay on the Social Philosophy of Democracy and Religion* (New York: Twayne Publishers, 1954); Philip H. Phenix, *Intelligible Religion* (New York: Harper & Brothers, 1954); J. Paul Williams, *What Americans Believe and How They Worship* (New York: Harper & Brothers, 1952), pp. 373–374; V. T. Thayer, *Religion in Public Education* (New York: The Viking Press, 1947), chap. ix, and *The Attack upon the American Secular School* (Boston: The Beacon Press, 1951), chap. x; Philip H. Phenix, *Religious Concerns in Contemporary Education: A Study of Reciprocal Relations* (New York: Bureau of Publications, Teachers College, Columbia University, 1959); and John Courtney Murray, "America's Four Conspiracies," in John Cogley, ed., *Religion in America: Original Essays on Religion in a Free Society* (New York: Meridian Books, 1958), p. 41.

38. *Christian Century*, LXXXIII (January 5, 1966), 2.

ton Theological Seminary in Massachusetts, and then at the Harvard Divinity School. Having worked with a variety of youth programs, Cox had been invited to prepare a set of notes for the 1965 conferences of the National Student Christian Federation. He decided to use the occasion to challenge a popular misconception about the relation of theological reflection to practical life. "I had noticed," he observed, "that many serious people in the heady and demanding world of day-to-day decision making in our urban civilization suspect that theology is something for the cloister or for the groves of academe. . . . I strongly differ with this view of the place and purpose of theology." Cox's mission was to make theology relevant to the metropolis. The result was *The Secular City*. [39]

The book announced itself as a celebration of a new epoch in human history. The great metropolis, in Cox's view, had introduced a new social situation and a new ideal of human character; it demanded a new theology. The new social situation was one of anonymity and mobility—modern men and women had been freed from the constraints of traditional social relationships legitimatized by outmoded myths, and as a consequence had been empowered by circumstance to create their own worlds sustained by their own meanings. The new ideal of character was pragmatic to the core. Secular men and women had no occasion to lament the loss of ancient metaphysical explanations of the world. The problems that preoccupied them were essentially functional and operational; rather than looking to the muses and the gods for solutions to these problems, they looked to themselves and their fellow human beings. The new theology that was demanded was a theology of social change. It needed to view the metropolis as God's newest creation in history, indeed as the Kingdom of God in the process of realizing itself. It needed to conceive of the church as Christians organized into a social, political, and cultural *avant-garde* constantly reformulating the meanings, myths, and symbols that sustained, explained, and enriched the diurnal life of the metropolis. And it needed to envision human beings as facing a situation of vastly increased freedom and responsibility, one marked by new possibilities not previously present, fraught, on the one hand, with risk and, on the other, with the opportunity for unprecedented maturity—in sum, a "dangerous liberation."[40]

39. Harvey Cox, "Afterword," in Daniel Callahan, ed., *The Secular City Debate* (New York: The Macmillan Company, 1966), p. 179.

40. Harvey Cox, *The Secular City: Secularization and Urbanization in Historical Perspective* (New York: The Macmillan Company, 1965), p. 167.

The educational implications of the argument were profound. As Cox described them in an essay for *Religious Education* in 1966, they pointed to the need to shake men and women free from inherited outlooks and closed religious systems and to encourage a radically pluralistic consciousness of the world. They pointed to the need as well to nurture men and women of secular mentality, prepared to accept responsibility for fashioning the values and images of culture and for shaping the institutions of their society, equipped to imagine unheard of and untested ideas, and ready to bear the chaos and unceasing readjustment that would be demanded in the kind of society that was coming into being. "No doubt this new urban man displays a different personality from Bunyan's stolid Pilgrim, plodding single-mindedly toward the light above the gate," Cox concluded. "But does the Puritan pilgrim provide us with our only model of Christian personality? Perhaps what we need more than anything else now is a vast variety of Christian identity models, none of which needs to be accepted *in toto*, all of which help, by their very diversity, to extirpate the notion that to be a Christian carries with it a prefabricated personality type."[41]

Following the University of Chicago theologian Gibson Winter, whose treatise *The New Creation as Metropolis* (1963) anticipated much of Cox's argument in *The Secular City*, Cox envisioned the church as servant and healer of the city. And, in that role, he saw the church taking the leadership in exorcising the demon racism, of freeing white people from their prejudice and black people from their "slave mentality." To face the reality of the secular city in America was to confront the ugliness of the urban ghetto—Cox knew the problem at first hand, having moved his family to the Roxbury area of Boston so that they might understand the problems of the black community more compassionately. But theology had to do more than that, he once remarked. "It needs a laboratory to help us find out how to relate our thoughts to concrete action." And, to that end, the theology of the secular city was inevitably intertwined with what came to be known as black theology, whether of the version preached by Martin Luther King, Jr., who envisioned that "one day every Negro in this country, every colored person in the world, will be judged on the basis of the content of his character rather than the color of his skin, and every man will respect the dignity and worth of human personality," or in

41. Harvey Cox, "Secularization and the Secular Mentality: A New Challenge to Christian Education," *Religious Education*, LXI (1966), 86–87. Interestingly, Philip H. Phenix criticized Cox's analysis for not being secular enough; see "Myth and Mystery in the Secular City," *ibid.*, 87–90.

the version of Union Theological Seminary's James M. Cone, who maintained that black theology was "oriented in a single direction: the bringing to bear of the spirit of black self-determination upon the consciousness of black people." And that inextricable tie created a special imperative for education, insofar as it pointed to a mission of social and cultural liberation from poverty, exploitation, and second-class humanity, a mission that began with blacks but extended out to embrace every oppressed, abused, and humiliated minority in American society—and in the world.[42]

Finally, Cox viewed the secular city as a global city, whose life and problems spilled easily over the borders of nations and continents. "Future historians will record the twentieth century as that century in which the whole world became one immense city," he observed. "We know already that America is an urban civilization. . . . But America is not the pacesetter in urbanization. Overseas the transformation is even more jarring and accelerated. In fact, the most portentous phenomenon of our time is the urbanization of the non-Western world." Cox saw the issues in the larger world of cities as essentially the same as the issues of American cities, only multiplied a thousand times. But he continually stressed the fact that "the polymorphic tone of secularization in different places calls for a decidedly different strategy on the part of the Christians who live in these areas." He even included in *The Secular City* a chapter on New Delhi, Rome, Prague, and Boston, seeking thereby to exemplify the vastly differing missions Christians would have to undertake in India (and the Third World), Western Europe, Eastern Europe, and the United States.[43]

"Theology," Cox once remarked, "is now in a position to bring to the global struggle for human liberation a fund of images and hopes without which men might settle for less than they really deserve. It can reawaken a society that has been drugged by menial goals and vicious values. It can help us understand man better and fire his imagination more compassionately." It was precisely such an effort that the World Council of Churches embarked upon during the late 1960's, through a division that came to be known as the Program Unit on Education and Renewal. Under the joint leadership of an American Presbyterian, William B. Kennedy, and a Brazilian Roman Catholic, Paulo Freire, the Unit, working closely with international organizations like the World Student Christian Federation, the YMCA and the YWCA, and

42. *Contemporary Authors*, LXXVII–LXXX, 101; Martin Luther King, Jr., *The Trumpet of Conscience* (New York: Harper & Row, 1968), p. 77; and James M. Cone, *Black Theology and Black Power* (New York: The Seabury Press, 1969), p. 129.

43. Harvey G. Cox, "The Coming World City" [1965], in *On Not Leaving It to the Snake* (New York: The Macmillan Company, 1969), p. 96.

the Lutheran World Federation and with the educational arms of regional ecumenical councils around the world, developed two themes for its literature and its activities, one called "seeing education whole" and the other called "conscientization." Both grew out of a series of consultations on the World Educational Crisis and the Church, in Bergen, The Netherlands; Greenwich, Connecticut; and Lima, Peru; and both, interestingly, emerged from the protests of Third World educators against initial proposals that the Unit concentrate on planning the enlargement and improvement of national school systems.[44]

The theme "seeing education whole" pointed to the insistence of Latin American educators that education in general and schooling in particular were inevitably involved in politics, that they served either as instruments of domination or as instruments of transformation, and that unless the question of purpose was explored fundamentally and in a true political context churches and schools alike tended to be instruments of domination. As John Westerhoff III reported concerning the Lima consultation, when the Minister of Education of the revolutionary Peruvian government asserted that "Education is only a key in the process of social transformation. It is not the only thing necessary, nor is it the first thing that must be done. Educational reform must be part of a global policy of structural, socio-economic transformation," he was wildly applauded by four hundred Protestant, Roman Catholic, and Orthodox delegates from seventy-seven countries. The Roman Catholic educator Ivan Illich, who headed the Center for Intercultural Documentation in Cuernavaca, Mexico, carried the logic even further in his address at the Lima conference, contending that formal schooling in its very nature was an instrument of domination, preparing youngsters for their places in a hierarchical, technocratic, consumption-oriented social order at the same time that it blinded them to the possibilities for learning from the people and the life around them. "Seeing education whole," then, meant not only an examination of the process of education in all the situations and institutions within which it proceeded but also a critical analysis of education in its social, historical, economic, and political context.[45]

Conscientization, as Freire defined it, was the key to what he considered to be a truly liberating education. There could be no such thing as a neutral education, Freire maintained, education either lib-

44. *Contemporary Authors*, LXXVII–LXXX, 101.
45. William B. Kennedy, "Education for Liberation and Community," *Religious Education*, LXX (1975), 5–44; John Westerhoff III, "The Church and Education Debate," *ibid.*, LXVII (1972), 51–52; and Ivan Illich, "Education as an Idol," *ibid.*, LXVI (1971), 414–419.

erated or dominated, it either humanized or dehumanized, and the problem of humanization was man's central problem and education's inescapable concern. Traditional education, and schooling in particular, Freire charged, were based on a "banking" model, in which students were the depositories and the teacher, the depositor. What was deposited was a motionless, static, compartmentalized, and predictable reality. In contrast, he proposed an education rooted in true dialogue, the goal of which would be to "name the world" in order to transform it. Because he saw dialogue as a process of exchange among equals that could not exist apart from a profound love for the world and for one's fellow human beings, he believed dialogue could not be an instrument of domination. And by conscientization he meant the process of learning, through dialogue, that would enable people to perceive the social, political, and economic contradictions of their particular political, economic, and cultural situations and to take action against the oppressive elements of those situations. It was a process by which people would become aware of and sensitive to their objective worlds and liberated and empowered to act upon them.[46]

Ivan Illich and Paulo Freire developed their educational ideas while working with the Latin American poor and then obtained an international hearing for those ideas through the World Council of Churches. In consequence, the world city exercised a return influence upon the American city, and the theology and pedagogy of liberation, as set forth in Illich's *Deschooling Society* (1971) and *Celebration of Awareness* (1970) and in Freire's *Pedagogy of the Oppressed* (1970), all three of which circulated widely in the United States, informed not only the efforts of newly self-conscious minorities but also the broader attempts of schoolpeople, church educators, youth workers, and adult educators, leading them to infuse their teaching with a new vitality and self-consciousness.

Cox concluded *The Secular City* with a question Dietrich Bonhoeffer had asked from his prison cell in Germany in 1944: "How do we speak in a secular fashion of God?" Cox also drew a clue from Bonhoeffer in working toward an answer: In the last analysis, Bonhoeffer observed, the word "God" means nothing, the name "God" means everything; hence to speak of God in a secular fashion is to "name" in a particular historical context, the context of the new metropolitan world that was coming into being. That way of speaking, Cox suggested, had yet to be created, but the painful process of developing

46. Paulo Freire, *Pedagogy of the Oppressed*, translated by Myra Bergman Ramos (New York: Herder and Herder, 1970), p. 27.

it needed to go forward. "The Exodus," Cox perorated, "marked for the Jews a turning point of such elemental power that a new divine name was needed to replace the titles that had grown out of their previous experience. Our transition today from the age of Christendom to the new era of urban secularity will be no less shaking. Rather than clinging stubbornly to antiquated appellations or anxiously synthesizing new ones, perhaps, like Moses, we must simply take up the work of liberating the captives, confident that we will be granted a new name by events in the future."[47]

Cox's analysis pointed to at least one line of contemporary argument that had an inextricable tie to the secular city, namely, the formulation of a civil, or public, religion. Will Herberg had seen the civil religion of Americans as "an organic structure of ideas, values, and beliefs that constitutes a faith common to Americans as Americans, and is genuinely operative in their lives; a faith that markedly influences, and is influenced by, the professed religions of America." Sidney Mead, a contemporary historian of religion, conceived of it as the religion of the Republic, a prophetic religion, the ideas and aspirations of which "stand in constant judgment over the passing shenanigans of the people, reminding them of the standards by which their current practices and those of their nation are ever being judged and found wanting." The United States, Mead suggested, was "a nation with the soul of a church." Robert Bellah, a sociologist of religion, saw it as an elaborate and well-institutionalized faith that stood alongside the historic faiths and had a seriousness and integrity all its own. "Behind the civil religion at every point lie Biblical archetypes: Exodus, Chosen People, Promised Land, New Jerusalem, Sacrificial Death and Rebirth. But it is also genuinely American and genuinely new. It has its own prophets and its own martyrs, its own sacred events and sacred places, its own solemn rituals and symbols. It is concerned that America be a society as perfectly in accord with the will of God as men can make it, and a light to all the nations." Indeed, Bellah hoped that the destiny of the American civil religion was to be transformed into a genuine global religion, reflective of the finest values of the world city. Finally, John F. Wilson, another historian of religion, saw the civil religion as a public religion, rooted in the history of the Republic, that could actually itself serve as a "revitalization movement" in American civilization during the final years of the century.[48]

47. Cox, *The Secular City*, pp. 241, 268.
48. Will Herberg, "America's Civil Religion: What It Is and Whence It Comes," in Russell E. Richey and Donald G. Jones, eds., *American Civil Religion* (New York: Harper &

In the end, it was Wilson, in his 1979 treatise *Public Religion in American Culture,* who turned most directly to the question of the social institutions that might best sustain public religion in America—in a discussion, incidentally, that called to mind Alexis de Tocqueville's 1835 discussion of the sources of democracy in America. Wilson considered first the question of whether the public school system functioned as the church of the public religion in America, in effect, as the church of democracy; and he concluded that, although the public schools fell far short of constituting such a church, they were patently *among* the institutions that might function to sustain a public religion. Wilson then went on to cite the law, the communications industry, and, most important, a plethora of voluntary associations, from the Rainbow Girls to the American Legion, that gave support to the commitments and the ideologies associated with public religion.[49]

Whatever the merits of the argument, and the idea of a civil or public religion was intensely controversial during the 1970's, it carried a set of implications that marked a new direction in American social and educational thought. Whereas Will Herberg's formulation had conceived of the American *paideia* as plural and existing in three different but coequal versions taught by the Protestant, Catholic, and Jewish communities, the proponents of a civil or public religion were really formulating an American *paideia* to which the historic faiths had contributed but which had come to enjoy an existence independent of those historic faiths. It was a secularized *paideia* that would have to be defined and redefined in a continuing process, not unlike the process proposed by Dewey in *A Common Faith* and by Cox in *The Secular City.* And it was a *paideia* by which the quality of life in American society would be continually judged (in Bellah's formulation) and continually revitalized (in Wilson's). In sum, it embodied a new conception of national mission to set alongside those that had been carried forward from the past.

Row, 1974), pp. 77–78; Sidney Mead, *The Nation with the Soul of a Church* (New York: Harper & Row, 1975), p. 65; Robert N. Bellah, "Civil Religion in America," in William G. McLoughlin and Robert N. Bellah, eds., *Religion in America* (Boston: Houghton Mifflin Company, 1968), p. 20; and John F. Wilson, *Public Religion in American Culture* (Philadelphia: Temple University Press, 1979), pp. 169–175. As Mead points out, the phrase "a nation with the soul of a church" was coined by G. K. Chesterton in response to his question, "What is America?" See Raymond T. Bond, ed., *The Man Who Was Chesterton* (Garden City, N.Y.: Doubleday & Company, 1960), p. 131.

49. Wilson, *Public Religion,* chap. vi.

Chapter 2

METROPOLITAN MISSIONS

Modern missions have everywhere heralded an educational revival.

JAMES S. DENNIS

Josiah Strong was first and foremost an activist. His place in history has rested principally on his authorship of *Our Country,* but it is for his works as an organizer that he should really be remembered. Strong was thirty-eight years old when *Our Country* first appeared in 1885 and the energetic pastor of the Vine Street Church in Cincinnati. He had grown up in Ohio, the son of an old New England family, and had attended Western Reserve College and then prepared for the ministry at Lane Theological Seminary. Ordained in 1871, he had served as a home missionary in Cheyenne, Wyoming, as the chaplain of Western Reserve College, as pastor of the First Congregational Church in Sandusky, Ohio, and as secretary of the Ohio Home Missionary Society—it was in the last role that he had collected the data and formulated the ideas that became the substance of *Our Country.* The volume was a remarkable success and instantly projected Strong onto the national scene. Not surprisingly, when the leaders of the Evangelical Alliance for the United States decided in 1886 to redirect the efforts of the organization toward a reawakening of the churches to their social responsibilities, they looked to Strong as the man who could best accomplish the "enlarged and aggressive work," and elected him to the newly created general secretaryship of the Alliance.[1]

The Alliance was an international, interdenominational organization that had been established in London in 1846 to war against free

1. Evangelical Alliance for the United States, Minutes (Union Theological Seminary Library, New York City), III (April 1, 1886), 16.

thought and Roman Catholicism (the American branch had been founded in 1867 under the leadership of William E. Dodge). It was also a quintessential expression of the united evangelical front that had played such an important role in Protestant educational affairs during the pre–Civil War era. Under Strong's leadership, it became equally a symbol of the adaptation of that earlier effort to the needs of the metropolitan America that was coming into being. As general secretary of the American Alliance, Strong developed the characteristic agenda of evangelical Protestantism during the Progressive era— the reaching out of awakened churches to the unchurched poor; the application of Christian principles to the solution of urban social problems; the cooperation of churches with one another and with students of the new social sciences in the work of social planning and reform; and, through collaborative endeavor, the extension of Christian principles throughout the world. By 1898 Strong's program of collaboration was consistently exceeding the bounds that the trustees of the Alliance had seen as appropriate to that organization; and, after an amicable parting, Strong was forced to continue his efforts through the newly founded League for Social Service, which subsequently became the American Institute of Social Service. But, whatever the organizational context of his work, Strong's efforts from 1886 until his death in 1916 were for all intents and purposes the living embodiment of the Protestant program for metropolitan America.

Strong's skills as an activist were extraordinary. He wrote clearly and persuasively, and his books and articles—most of them programmatic in character—were widely read and commented upon. Equally important, he collaborated broadly in working toward his goals—with politicians such as Theodore Roosevelt and Woodrow Wilson, with businessmen such as Andrew Carnegie and William E. Dodge, with journalists such as Albert Shaw and Walter Hines Page, with leaders of women's education such as Grace Hoadley Dodge and Alice Freeman Palmer, with social scientists such as E. A. Ross and William D. P. Bliss, with social settlement workers such as Jane Addams and Graham Taylor, and with religious leaders as diverse as James Cardinal Gibbons and Isaac Mayer Wise. Interestingly, like his spiritual forebears of the united evangelical front, he pictured America facing a crisis of unprecedented severity and saw the solution in a vast church-led program of education and reform. From the local hamlet to the world at large, a profound readjustment in social relations was required. Evangelical Protestantism would lead the way in America, and a Christian America would lead the way among nations.

II

It was the city that, in the words of H. Paul Douglass, precipitated for the church "the greatest inner revolution it has ever known." The exponential growth and diversification of urban populations after 1876 created dilemmas for downtown churches that were new and frightening. A church could follow its congregation uptown and leave the poor and transient who filled its traditional neighborhood to their own devices or it could choose to remain in its traditional neighborhood and cope with the novelty and uncertainty of poverty and cultural difference. Many moved, and those that remained suffered decline and alienation unless they changed dramatically. One result was the institutional church, probably the best-known symbol of Progressive Christianity. Of the numerous examples that might be cited, St. George's Episcopal Church in New York City is one of the most revealing.[2]

A prosperous evangelical institution on Stuyvesant Square, St. George's had slipped into decline during the 1870's as its parishioners had left the neighborhood, to be replaced by older immigrants moving up from the Tompkins Square area south of Fourteenth Street and by newly arrived immigrants from Europe. The church was quite literally facing collapse when the Reverend William S. Rainsford assumed the rectorship in January, 1883. A native of Ireland and scion of an old Anglo-Irish Evangelical family, Rainsford had been educated at Cambridge and had done mission work in the East End of London, where he had become aware, on the one hand, of the terrible suffering of the urban poor, and, on the other hand, of the efforts of a number of evangelical groups to alleviate that suffering through various types of social services. He brought with him to St. George's an abiding commitment to social justice and a firm resolve to minister to the needs of the church's new parishioners. The story is told that in his interview with the vestry of St. George's he insisted upon "a truly democratic church," with all pews free, all committees to be appointed by him, and an annual discretionary fund of $10,000 available to the rector for evangelistic work. Apparently, after an embarrassing silence, vestryman J. P. Morgan glanced around at the tense faces of his colleagues, looked back at Rainsford, and then said, "Done."[3]

2. H. Paul Douglass, "Religion—The Protestant Faiths," in Harold E. Stearns, ed., *America Now: An Inquiry into Civilization in the United States* (New York: Charles Scribner's Sons, 1938), p. 514.

3. W. S. Rainsford, *The Story of a Varied Life: An Autobiography* (Garden City, N.Y.: Doubleday, Page & Company, 1922), pp. 200, 201.

Under Rainsford's leadership, St. George's became the testing ground for a series of innovations that rapidly transformed the program and structure of the church as well as the life and character of the parish. He began by declaring St. George's to be a free church, open to all comers; and he sought through the preaching of an expansive evangelical message and the introduction of an extensive program of educational and recreational activities to make the church not only free but inviting. With the aid of a number of assistant rectors and deaconesses (in effect, lay sisters), he arranged for the church to be open throughout the year from 8 A.M. to 5 P.M. daily. He obtained funds for an adjunct building called Memorial House and created there a "palace of delight," where young people might read, dance, play games, or listen to music (the dancing scandalized some members of the congregation). He organized a trade school where boys might learn carpentry, printing, mechanical drawing, electrical and metal work, and applied design. "The public schools of New York are lamentably behind the times," he charged; "and what the Church should do is to set an example of a higher standard for growing boys and girls." He renovated the Sunday school, arranging the curriculum as a series of graded lessons, choosing as teachers men and women as warm in their personalities as they were informed about Scripture, and then instructing and inspiring the teachers at an annual training conference. He established a circulating library. He organized a Battalion Club for boys between the ages of fourteen and eighteen, with a program of military exercises, a rifle range, and a summer camp at Eaton's Neck on Long Island; a Girls' Friendly Society, with a program of basket weaving, cooking, sewing, dressmaking, calisthenics, and reading; a Men's Club with a billiard room, a common room, and a gymnasium; and a Women's Society, with a varied program revolving largely around matters relating to child rearing. Finally, he established a program of relief for the needy, with a grocery department, a clinic, a summer camp, and an emergency fund for the impoverished.[4]

Rainsford would have insisted that the enlarged social mission of St. George's was in no way a substitute for its spiritual mission but merely a more effective fulfillment of it. And his parishioners felt likewise, increasing from the handful that Rainsford found when he arrived in 1883 to some four thousand during the 1890's and includ-

4. George Hodges and John Reichert, *The Administration of an Institutional Church: A Detailed Account of the Operation of St. George's Parish in the City of New York* (New York: Harper & Brothers, 1906), p. 16; Rainsford, *Story of a Varied Life*, p. 251.

ing not only J. P. Morgan, who continued to serve as senior warden, but also W. L. Bull, president of the New York Stock Exchange, and a number of other millionaires.

By 1899 there were more than a dozen institutional churches in New York City alone, most of them Episcopal (the Episcopalians were the largest formal denomination in the city at the time), but some of them Baptist, Presbyterian, Congregational, and Unitarian. That same year, Russell H. Conwell, who presided over an institutional church in Philadelphia, actually tried to compile a comprehensive list of such churches across the country and was able to identify 173 of them, while admitting that a considerable number might well have escaped his notice. And by 1908 Josiah Strong could assert in an influential article in *The New Encyclopedia of Social Reform* that there were few urban churches that had not in one form or another introduced activities that might be described as institutional.[5]

Beyond the broadening of their programs, institutional church ministers tended to broaden the social concern of their preaching. Rainsford, for example, not only devoted sermon after sermon to municipal issues, he also immersed himself generally in the public affairs of the city and in 1897 actually campaigned vigorously for the Citizens Union ticket. His friend R. Heber Newton, rector of All Souls Episcopal Church, was an outspoken supporter of Henry George, as were Walter Rauschenbusch, who was pastor of the Second German Baptist Church from 1886 to 1897, and James Otis Sargent Huntington, who was vicar of the Holy Cross Mission from 1881 to 1889. Similarly, a variety of Boston ministers, ranging from the Congregational Charles A. Bockinson to the Universalist George L. Perin, preached on good government, industrial issues, and social policy while leading institutional churches in that city. In fact, as Arthur Mann has pointed out, by the last years of the century modernist conceptions of God, human nature, and society quite literally dominated Boston preaching, at least in the Episcopal, Congregational, Unitarian, Universalist, and Methodist congregations.[6]

When Rainsford published his autobiography in 1922, he put forth three rules for the guidance of those who would engage the churches in social work: first, they should select the activities with special refer-

5. Russell H. Conwell, "The Church of the Future," *Our Day*, XIX (1899), 205; and Josiah Strong, "Institutional Churches," in William D. P. Bliss and Rudolph M. Binder, eds., *The New Encyclopedia of Social Reform* (New York: Funk & Wagnalls Company, 1908), pp. 629–631.

6. Arthur Mann, *Yankee Reformers in the Urban Age* (Cambridge, Mass.: Harvard University Press, 1954), chap. iv.

ence to the particular needs of their surrounding communities; second, they should try to exemplify positive possibilities rather than merely attacking social evils; and third, they should select their activities with a view to educating their surrounding communities to the need for such activities and, once successful in that education, they should turn the activities over to other agencies. That Rainsford saw the institutional church as essentially educational in emphasis, both in its program and in its politics, is patent. But one might also note that by the time Rainsford wrote his autobiography, the thrust of social Christianity was beginning to wane in favor of more formal and circumscribed definitions of the role of the church, while public and undenominational quasi-public institutions were beginning to assume responsibility for many of the social activities that the institutional churches had pioneered a quarter-century earlier. The surveys of the 1930's revealed that at most some 4 percent of American churches had explicitly committed themselves to institutional programs directed toward the disadvantaged, while some 13 percent had chosen to sponsor partial welfare programs. That said, it was also clear that, beyond their ubiquitous Sunday school programs (in fact, there were more Sunday schools than there were churches), churches and especially urban churches had come to see educational and recreational social programs for young people and adults as among their core activities and that, in addition to their own locally sponsored efforts, they had come to depend on organizations like Christian Endeavor, the YMCA, and the YWCA to assist them in those domains. Later, when the conception of the church as a community center re-emerged in the burgeoning suburbs of post–World War II America, the expanded social programs of an earlier era provided a solid foundation on which to build.[7]

The institutional church was one of several manifestations of the religious revolution of the 1880's and 1890's set in motion by the burgeoning of cities. Another was the social settlement. Arising from many of the same intellectual sources as the institutional church and responding to many of the same social problems, the settlement developed many of the same programs. But in time it assumed its own form and in the process became one of the characteristic educative institutions of Progressive and post–Progressive America.

The settlement had its origins in the social Christianity of Victo-

7. H. Paul Douglass and Edmund deS. Brunner, *The Protestant Church as a Social Institution* (New York: Harper & Brothers, 1935), pp. 143, 190, 146–152.

rian England, and notably in the intellectual ferment stimulated by the writings of Frederick Denison Maurice and Charles Kingsley. Moved by the Maurice-Kingsley charge that the social fabric was being torn apart by the class conflict set in motion by industrialization, a generation of English intellectuals clustered around the writer John Ruskin, the poet William Morris, the housing reformer Octavia Hill, the social activist Edward Denison, the historian Arnold Toynbee, and the clergyman Samuel A. Barnett set out to restore the organic unity of social life. Denison and Toynbee in particular pioneered in what was to become the characteristic settlement attack on the problem by seeking lodging among the urban poor and attempting to teach workingpeople at the same time that they learned from them as Christians. Both were frail young men: Denison died in 1870 at the age of thirty-two and Toynbee in 1883 at the age of thirty-one. Equally committed, Barnett was left to carry on the cause. In 1872 he accepted the vicarage of St. Jude's parish in the notorious Whitechapel district of London. He renovated the parish school, arranging for evening as well as day sessions; he reorganized the poor relief of the parish, connecting the effort to that of the recently organized Charity Organization Society; and he arranged summer outings in the country for the children of the parish. Most important, perhaps, he reached out to the professors and students at Oxford and Cambridge who had responded to the idea of the new social Christianity and interested them in the plight of the poor. In 1883, the very year Rainsford was beginning his reformist ministry at St. George's Church in New York City, Barnett read two papers to the students at Oxford and Cambridge, "Our Great Towns and Social Reform" and "Settlements of University Men in Great Towns," asserting that it was the responsibility of the educated to bridge the gap that industrialism had created between rich and poor by taking up residence among the poor and making their residences—or "settlements," as Barnett called them—crossroads of education. The university intellectuals would bring culture to the workingpeople; they would in turn receive from the workingpeople an education in the hard realities of industrial life. In the process, the bonds of society would be reformed and neighborhoods regenerated. "Many have been the schemes of reform I have known," Barnett insisted, "but, out of eleven years' experience, I would say that none touches the root of the evil which does not *bring helper and helped into friendly relations.* Vain will be higher education, music, art, or even the Gospel, unless they come clothed in the life of brother men—'it took the Life to make God known.' " Years later, Robert A. Woods and

Albert J. Kennedy referred to the second paper, read at St. Jude's College, Oxford, as "the charter of the settlements."[8]

Barnett was not merely imaginative, he was persuasive. A handful of Oxford and Cambridge men harkened to his call and took up residence in a building adjoining St. Jude's that they named Toynbee Hall. On Christmas Eve 1884, the residents first slept there, and the first permanent settlement, as well as the spiritual mother house of the social settlement movement, was in operation.

The earliest American settlement was founded by Stanton Coit at 46 Forsyth Street on New York City's Lower East Side. A graduate of Amherst College and a disciple of Felix Adler, founder of the Ethical Culture Society, Coit lived at Toynbee Hall for several months at the beginning of 1886 and decided to launch a similar venture in New York. Allying himself with a graduate of Union Theological Seminary named Charles Stover and an English Socialist named Edward King, Coit established what came to be known as the Neighborhood Guild (subsequently renamed the University Settlement) later that year. In 1887 a group of Smith College alumnae led by Vida Dutton Scudder took the initial steps that eventuated in the founding of the College Settlements Association. And in 1889 Jane Addams and Ellen Gates Starr founded Hull House in Chicago. In those instances too, the ties to the thinking of English social Christianity and the model of Toynbee Hall were unmistakable. By 1891 there were six settlements in the United States; by 1900 there were over a hundred; by 1910 there were over four hundred. The settlement had become an established feature of American urban life.

Of the early settlements, Hull House was surely the best known, owing largely to the brilliant intellectual advocacy of Jane Addams. Addams had been born and educated at Cedarville, Illinois, and had then gone on to Rockford (Illinois) Female Seminary, an institution with a record of turning out high-minded Christian missionaries. At Rockford she encountered the writings of John Ruskin and at Rockford, too, she decided she would study medicine and prepare for a career. She attended the Woman's Medical College of Pennsylvania for a time, but withdrew after a year because of ill health. There followed a period of vocational uncertainty, until in 1888 she resolved, with her Rockford classmate Ellen Gates Starr, to found a

8. S. A. Barnett, "Settlements of University Men in Great Towns," in Canon S. A. Barnett and Mrs. S. A. Barnett, *Practicable Socialism*, New Series (London: Longmans, Green and Co., 1915), pp. 104–105; and Robert A. Woods and Albert J. Kennedy, *The Settlement Horizon: A National Estimate* (New York: Russell Sage Foundation, 1922), p. 26.

social settlement. The following year they moved into the old, broken-down Hull mansion on the corner of Polk and Halsted streets in Chicago, invited their neighbors to visit, and declared Hull House open and established.

Several features of the Hull House venture during its early years shed light upon the settlement movement as a whole. The first concerns the motivation of the founders. Addams and Starr had both attended Rockford Seminary and had both been religious seekers. Addams, having been baptized into the Presbyterian Church in Cedarville in 1888, soon moved beyond the intensity of her early religious commitments; while Starr, having undergone a series of religious decisions that had led her from the Unitarianism of her family to Episcopalianism in 1884, ultimately joined the Roman Catholic Church and lived the last years of her life as a Benedictine oblate in Suffern, New York. However that may be, religious humanitarianism was surely one among the complex of motives that led the two young women to found Hull House.

Beyond that, it is not incidental that Addams and Starr were both college-educated women. Three-fifths of all settlement residents between 1889 and 1914 were women and almost nine-tenths of them had been to college. John P. Rousmaniere has sketched in some detail the ways in which the colleges, and particularly the women's colleges, nurtured a conception of the educated woman as intellectually disciplined and sufficiently committed to social service to eschew marriage and charity work and to substitute in their place the intense mutual association in the cause of cultural sharing that was at the heart of the social settlement. This shift in the conception of the role of the educated woman was also a factor in the founding of Hull House.[9]

Finally, there was the essentially pragmatic effort to combine social action with social inquiry that in large measure accounts for the experimental character of the Hull House program. When Addams and Starr launched the venture, they were familiar with the program of Toynbee Hall, which Addams had visited in the spring of 1888. And the Hull House program emulated the emphasis at Toynbee Hall on bringing the advantages of a collegiate education to workingpeople through picture exhibitions, university extension classes, and special lectures, as well as engaging in political activities on behalf of public libraries, parks, playgrounds, and schools. Thus, at Hull House as at Toynbee Hall, there were college extension courses, a summer school, a student association, a reading room, picture exhibitions, and Sunday concerts; but there were also a Paderewski Club of young pianists, a Jane Club for young workingwomen, a Phalanx Club for young typographers, various men's and women's clubs and a Nineteenth Ward Improvement Club, cooking and sewing classes, a free kindergarten and day nursery, a public dispensary, and, possibly most interesting of all, a Labor Museum explicitly intended to convey to the immigrant young a respect for the arts and traditions their parents had brought with them from Europe. Beyond the effort to bridge the gap between handwork and headwork, the Museum was intended to inculcate ethnic pride upon the immigrants and thereby to bespeak a commitment to plural values on the part of the Hull House residents.

In addition to the extraordinary program of activities they developed, Addams, Starr, and their colleagues committed themselves to gathering the data about life in the slum that they hoped would stimulate larger reform campaigns in the community. They shared the Progressive assumption that the truth, once revealed, would serve as the basis for remedial public action. Hull House residents therefore used the methods of the newly emerging social sciences to mount a number of pioneering social surveys—Florence Kelley's and Alzina P. Stevens's studies of wage-earning children, Isabel Eaton's studies of cloakmakers' earnings and expenditures, and Julia Lathrop's studies of Cook County charities, which, along with a number of other papers, were collected and published in 1895 as *Hull-House Maps and Papers*. Progressive assumptions and social science methods were also evident in Kelley's extraordinary effectiveness in the politics of social reform. As Kathryn Kish Sklar has pointed out, by "collectivising talents and energies," the largely female, college-educated communities that constituted most of the social settlements enabled particular women residents like Kelley to participate in the political arena with an efficacy that would not have been possible a generation earlier.[10]

That said, there was a curious ambivalence on the part of the settlement workers that Addams herself noted. After 1900, she observed, the young men and women who came to the settlement wanted less and less to do something about social disorder and more and more to investigate it. The rapid development and professionalization of the social sciences in their own right obviously had something to do with the shift, as did the success of muckraking journalists in popularizing the injustices of life in the slum. After 1900, too,

10. Kathryn Kish Sklar, "Hull House in the 1890s: A Community of Women Reformers," *Signs*, X (1984–85), 660.

settlement work itself became increasingly professionalized as the National Conference of Charities and Correction collaborated with institutions like the University of Chicago School of Social Service to define the role of the social worker and the kind of education seen as required for the successful performance of the role. Yet the settlement won for itself a permanent place in the life of American cities. One after another, its innovative programs were taken into the public sphere, beginning with the gradual transfer of its children's programs to the public school during the first quarter of the twentieth century and culminating during the 1930's in the transfer of its dispensaries and its relief programs to public welfare authorities. But, however much its purposes changed with time, the settlement always managed to find new opportunities with new clienteles, giving particular attention to youth during the 1960's and to so-called senior citizens during the 1970's.[11]

The slums of London's East End gave birth to yet another movement during the 1860's and 1870's that profoundly affected education, namely, the Salvation Army. The Army was the creation of William and Catherine Booth, evangelists who had started out as Methodist New Connection preachers (Catherine had carried out a public ministry though she had never been ordained) but who had left that formal affiliation in 1865 to work among the poor in Whitechapel. Their original notion was to supplement the efforts of the existing churches through a combination of preaching and social service, the latter including home visitation, distribution of Bibles and tracts, mothers' meetings, evening classes in reading, writing, and arithmetic, Sunday schools, reading rooms, and poor relief; in less than a year, however, the East London Christian Mission, which they established as the site and organizational structure for their efforts, became itself a place of worship. As the Booths won converts, they developed their own version of the traditional Methodist class, though with a difference: their classes were organized as additional mission stations and the several stations, though originally managed via traditional conference methods, were increasingly organized hierarchically under a quasi-military pattern of centralized autocratic control. In 1878, with fifty mission stations and eighty-six evangelists, the organization was renamed the Salvation Army, with William Booth as general (an abbreviation of general superintendent), with his evangelists as captains,

11. University Settlement Society of New York, *Twenty-Fifth Annual Report, 1911*, pp. 21–22.

with new converts as soldiers, and with stations as corps (Catherine Booth served as an active preacher within the Army and contributed significantly to the development of its characteristic religious beliefs and practices).

The Army expanded rapidly under Booth's charismatic leadership, first through Great Britain and then overseas. The first Salvationists came to the United States in 1879, and in 1880 Booth sent Commander S. Scott Railton, one of his most trusted aides, and seven women as an "invasion force" to evangelize America. Railton and his associates set up corps in New York and Brooklyn and then went on to establish a national headquarters in Philadelphia, since New York had proven inhospitable to the Army's traditional open air meetings. From there, Railton himself went on to found a post in St. Louis. When General Booth called Railton back to England in 1881 and sent Major Thomas E. Moore to replace him, additional corps were established not only in the Middle Atlantic and Midwestern states but in Canada as well. Despite significant schisms in the ranks—in 1884, Major Moore established the Salvation Army of America in violation of General Booth's authority; and in 1896, General Booth's son Ballington, who had been sent to head the American branch in 1887, resigned from the Army with his wife, Maud, and started the Volunteers of America—the Army in America grew rapidly. By 1904, when General Booth's daughter Evangeline assumed command of the Army in the United States, there were 741 corps and outposts throughout the country, and some 2,564 officers and cadets; by 1934, when Evangeline Booth left to assume command of the world-wide Army, the number of corps and outposts had more than doubled, to 1,640, while the number of officers and cadets had grown to 4,477.

The reasons for this growth were complex, but at the least they involved the simplified theology of the Army and the variety of techniques used to reach the unconverted. The theology was an amalgam of the basic principles common to most evangelical denominations of the time—belief in the Trinity, the Bible as the word of God, original sin, the immortality of the soul, and salvation for all who willed it. While baptism and communion were practiced for a time as sacraments, even those were soon abandoned as ineffectual and unnecessary. As for the techniques, the Army used those that would attract the attention of the unreached and the unchurched. Open air meetings and parades were standard techniques, along with brass bands, bass drums, and tambourines. Singing, hand clapping, and feet tapping were common elements in Army services. And a simple declaration of belief in Christ was assumed to set sinners on the road to salvation. As one historian of the Army in America remarked, at the Army's hallelujah meetings the denizens of the slum could "lose themselves in the glory of a new world that was theirs if they but confessed their sins and sought forgiveness through Christ. The meetings offered entertainment, escape, security, fellowship, and absolution from sin—all wrapped in the one package 'salvation.' " When the simplified theology and the attractive techniques were joined to a quasi-military discipline that permitted the efficient deployment of core personnel, the result was an unusually effective organization.[12]

But there was more to the attractiveness of the Salvation Army than that. Jane Addams once reproved the members of the National Conference of Charities and Corrections for the somewhat patronizing attitude even the most committed among them frequently adopted toward their clients, as if the clients were in the end undeserving of their assistance. The charge was never brought against the Salvation Army's social efforts. Indeed, the quiet, unassuming contributions of the Salvationists in every domain of social service became the most eloquent testimony to the truth of the message they preached and thereby enhanced their credibility among the poor. And that eloquence provides the clue to their effectiveness as educators. For, not only in their crèches for very young children and their evening schools for working children but also in their rescue homes for prostitutes, where cooking, sewing, and housekeeping were taught, and in their houses of industry for prisoners, where the trades were taught, they conveyed knowledge, taught skills, redirected aspirations, and changed behavior—and with a friendliness, sympathy, and forgiveness that enhanced profoundly the effectiveness of the pedagogy.

Several aspects of the Army's educational efforts are worthy of comment. For one thing, the Salvationists' approach to their ministry to the poor was remarkably similar in certain respects to that of the settlement workers. Indeed, Vida Dutton Scudder, one of the founders of the College Settlements Association, reported that she had actually been impelled to join General Booth's Army while she was studying at Oxford in 1884. What is more, the standard histories of the Army record the establishment of settlement houses under its auspices as early as 1904, when Evangeline Booth made the creation of settlements a high priority of her administration. And, more than

12. Herbert A. Wisbey, Jr., *Soldiers Without Swords: The History of the Salvation Army in the United States* (New York: The Macmillan Company, 1955), p. 36.

a decade before the Army formally organized its settlements, pairs of Salvationist "slum sisters" in New York, Boston, Philadelphia, Chicago, and Cleveland were renting rooms in slum districts and providing every conceivable assistance to their neighbors. They visited the sick, looked after children, counseled women on housekeeping, and taught the virtues of temperance, while "ceaselessly preaching the religion of Jesus Christ to the outcasts of society." Their mission may have had less of a cultural emphasis than that of the settlement workers, but not less of an educational emphasis.[13]

Also, like the settlement workers, Salvationists were frequently women and frequently young. The Army's position with respect to women was a principled equality. From the earliest writings of Catherine Booth in the 1850's defending her own right to teach and preach, the Army had welcomed women to its ranks and encouraged them to advance through the ranks on an equal basis. Salvationist women tended to come from less established families and did not generally bring the college education that was characteristic of settlement workers; but they brought extraordinary ability and qualities of leadership that were amply demonstrated in the Army's activities. Salvationists also tended to be young; indeed, Herbert A. Wisbey, Jr., has referred to the Army in America as in some respects a "youth movement," with many of the early officers responsible for its extraordinary growth actually teenagers holding positions of responsibility beyond their years. Interestingly, too, black Americans were represented among the Salvationists beyond what chance might have predicted; and, once again, this was the result of a principled effort by Major Moore, Ballington and Maud Booth, the Booth-Tuckers (leaders between 1896 and 1904), and Evangeline Booth, not only to minister to blacks but also to recruit black ministers.[14]

Finally, and again like the settlement workers, the Salvationists protested vigorously against social abuses like sweatshops, slum housing, and child labor and put forward their own social programs as examples of what might be truly possible if society was ever to commit itself to living by Christian principles. And they, too, saw many of their programs, from crèches and kindergartens to rescue homes and houses of industry, eventually taken up by public authorities and administered by professional social workers. Yet they continued their

---

13. Vida Dutton Scudder, *On Journey* (New York: E. P. Dutton & Co., 1937), p. 84; and General [William] Booth, *In Darkest England and the Way Out* (London: International Headquarters of the Salvation Army [1890]), p. 159.

14. Wisbey, *Soldiers Without Swords*, p. 35.

ministry to the poor and benighted, believing that the public programs never went far enough, never reached all in need, and never exhausted the possibilities of Christian charity and decency.

The similarities in these programs of the institutional churches, the social settlements, and the Salvation Army (and indeed of a host of turn-of-the-century social service operations) are striking. Deriving from quite different religious orientations—the institutional churches from Social Gospel theory, the social settlements from a more diffuse Christian humanitarianism, and the Salvation Army from a more orthodox evangelicism—they manifested a common commitment to an outreach toward the poor and unchurched, to a more latitudinarian view of religious mission, and to an educational approach to social service that joined diverse curricula to reformist pedagogies. All saw themselves as pioneering educational programs desperately needed by the poor but unavailable in the public schools; and all participated in efforts to persuade public authorities to assume continuing responsibility for their pilot efforts. More fundamentally, all shared a commitment to the crucial role of education in rebuilding communities rent by the forces of industrialization. Proceeding from their various orientations, they taught a similar solution to the urban problems of the early twentieth century, namely, that those problems would be solved only as people committed to Christian values managed to bridge the growing gap between social classes through a love for their fellow human beings that would rebuild the bonds of community on a new, just, and permanent basis.

III

The various organizations that had constituted the evangelical united front during the pre–Civil War era continued their work with greater or less intensity through the remainder of the nineteenth century and into the twentieth. The power of the American Education Society waned considerably, particularly after 1874, when it merged with the Society for the Promotion of Collegiate and Theological Education in the West. The power of the American Sunday-School Union (which began to call itself the International Sunday School Union during the 1870's in recognition of its Canadian affiliates) grew steadily, particularly after reforms introduced during the 1870's led to the creation of a uniform curriculum that had virtually every Sunday school in the country teaching essentially the same Biblical materials on any given Sunday of the year. Several of the organizations combined their efforts to mount the great missionary effort involved in the education of Southern blacks during and after Reconstruction; while others joined in organizations like the Evangelical Alliance during the 1880's to mount a concerted attack on the problems of the city. Suffice it to say that interdenominational and paradenominational social action persisted as a characteristic American phenomenon during the metropolitan era, and indeed quickened, as new modes of organization developed and as the purview of Christian concern expanded.

The organization of the Federal Council of Churches of Christ in America in 1908 transformed the situation. The work of the individual denominations continued, of course, as did the work of innumerable lay and clerical interdenominational and paradenominational organizations. But the very existence of the Council, representing thirty-three denominations and committed to securing "a larger combined influence for the churches of Christ in all matters affecting the moral and social condition of the people, so as to promote the application of the law of Christ in every relation of human life," was bound to affect education profoundly. For one thing, the Council at its very first meeting enthusiastically adopted the so-called social creed of the churches, declaring that churches must stand for "equal rights and complete justice for all men in all stations of life" and committing them, among other goals, to the conciliation and arbitration of industrial disputes, the abolition of child labor, a living wage as a minimum in every industry, a shorter workday, the regulation of working conditions for women, and the suppression of the "sweating system" in manufacturing. While the adoption of the creed bound no church member or congregation to do anything, it inevitably shaped the teaching of many. It articulated what was a growing consensus among many Christian leaders and defined a new domain of Christian concern, namely, the economy; and, in so doing, it further disseminated and popularized the teachings of social Christianity.[15]

Second, the Council sought to assist participating denominations in rendering service to their members and in reaching out to the unchurched. The plan of federation precluded any authority on the part of the Council to draw up common creeds, modes of worship, or forms of ecclesiastical governance. But the Council did lend support to such causes as temperance, Sabbath observance, missionary activ-

15. "The Constitution of the Federal Council," in Elias B. Sanford, *Federal Council of Churches of Christ in America: Report of the First Meeting of the Federal Council, Philadelphia, 1908* (New York: The Revell Press, 1909), p. 513; and "The Church and Modern Industry," *ibid.*, pp. 235–239.

ity, and world peace, and it did advance interdenominational collaboration in such matters as the sensible location of churches and the development of curricula for weekday religious instruction. Beyond that, both the Council and its successor organization, the National Council of Churches, facilitated the participation of American churches in such international organizations as the Church Peace Union, the World Alliance for Promoting International Friendship Through the Churches, and the World Council of Churches.

Finally, the Council became an important forum for debate on educational policy within and among the denominations. For example, the Council's Commission on Christian Education, founded in 1912, and later the International Council of Religious Education, which incorporated the work of the Commission in 1929, not only served as vehicles through which the associated denominations would resist what they perceived as secular tendencies in education, they also attempted to coordinate denominational and interdenominational efforts with those of organizations like the YMCA, the YWCA, the Epworth League, and the Christian Endeavor Society. Similarly, the Federal Council's Department of National Religious Radio took the lead during the 1930's in organizing and producing programs on behalf of the so-called mainline Protestant denominations, presenting over the networks such noted preachers as S. Parkes Cadman, Harry Emerson Fosdick, Ralph W. Sockman, J. Sutherland Bonnell, and David H. C. Read, while the National Council's Broadcasting and Film Commission did likewise during the 1950's and early 1960's with such television programs as "Thy Kingdom Come" and "Frontiers of Faith."

Given the unremitting activities of these myriad organizations, what became of the configuration of Protestant educative institutions maintained during the pre–Civil War era by the united evangelical front? For one thing, all the institutions in the earlier configuration stayed very much within the purview of organized Protestantism. The family remained an object of concern, both directly, in the continuing flood of counsel on child rearing and child nurture that issued from the denominational publishing houses, and indirectly, in the continuing assumption of Sunday school curriculum developers that parents would assist in the work of Christian formation and education. The Sunday school remained one of the critical elements in the configuration; indeed, it became, next to the church itself, the prime instrument of Protestant systematic nurture. The public school was seen as an important point of entry for Protestant teaching, both through programs for the inculcation of "moral and spiritual values" and through special arrangements for released time or shared time religious instruction. The denominational colleges remained important in their own right, as did religiously oriented youth programs at colleges of every sort and variety. And the religious press continued to issue a steady stream of didactic material, from children's hymnals like Ira David Sankey's *Winnowed Songs for Sunday Schools* (1890) to adult inspirational works like Charles Sheldon's *In His Steps* (1897).

There were major shifts in emphasis, however, that are important to note. Whereas the religious press continued to publish materials on family nurture and whereas the Sunday school movement continued to assume the existence of family nurture, child-centered approaches came to predominate and were significantly popularized by the parent-education movement of the 1920's. Beyond that, with the steady development of public high schools and of well-organized youth service agencies, parents felt less of a primary responsibility for home nurture and increasingly counted on the churches, the schools, and organized youth programs for the proper formation of their children—the so-called Middletown studies of Muncie, Indiana, by Robert and Helen Lynd dramatically portrayed this development. Yet the public schools were also changing, as the growing heterogeneity of their clientele rendered them ever more undenominational or religiously neutral in orientation (much the same was happening with the Protestant colleges). As a result, Protestant concern focused increasingly on two formal institutions for the nurture of young people, namely, Sunday schools and youth organizations, notably the YMCA and the YWCA.

The Sunday school had been a centerpiece of the evangelical configuration of education at least since the second quarter of the nineteenth century, owing largely to the efforts of the American Sunday-School Union. From the time of its founding in 1824, the ASSU had prodded localities from Pennsylvania to Oregon to establish Sunday schools, assisting in the process by rounding up sponsors, providing start-up funds, locating and training teachers, publishing and providing instructional materials, and in general stimulating enthusiasm where there had been none and restoring enthusiasm where it had waned. Often, a pioneer community could boast a Sunday school before it had a public school; often, too, when a public school finally did come into being, it was merely an extension and elaboration of a Sunday school. Generally undenominational but of course Protestant, open to children of every social class (though not necessarily used by children of every social class), and taught by laypeople of varying persuasions, the Sunday school testified eloquently to the success of the united evangelical front in its program to win America for Christ. By the end of the Civil War, however, the ASSU and its mission had run into trouble. A leading officer of the Union had purloined some $88,000 of the organization's funds during the 1850's; the war itself had slowed receipts, scattered members, and destroyed many of the buildings and libraries the Union had subsidized; and Emancipation had increased its burdens and responsibilities along with its opportunities. The time was ripe for renewal, and that renewal began at the Illinois State Sabbath Union convention of 1866.

The prime mover was Dwight L. Moody. In collaboration with William Reynolds, a Peoria businessman Moody had come to know as a colleague on the United States Christian Commission, and Benjamin F. Jacobs, a Chicago real estate dealer with whom Moody had worked in the YMCA, Moody decided to "capture" the Illinois Union and "try to make it a power in the state." The three men achieved their goal; and in 1872, in collaboration with John Heyl Vincent, a Methodist preacher who had turned his attention to Sunday school work, they went on to gain control of the national Union, by then styled the International Sunday School Union.[16]

It was Vincent who gave the group its program. A cleric who conceived of the church as a giant school with many departments—the pastor in the pulpit and the parents in the home constituted a faculty whose business it was to instruct the young—he determined after a visit to the Holy Land in 1862–63 to breathe new life into the American Sunday school through two related efforts. First, he concluded that Sunday school teachers, like public school teachers, needed training for their work, so he created the Union Sunday-School Institute for the Northwest, a regional, interdenominational convention at which Sunday school teachers could meet for a day or two to hear lectures by authorities on the Bible, on pedagogy, and on the practical side of Sunday school work, and to exchange ideas on how to make Sunday schools more effective. And second, he decided that a rationally ordered curriculum was needed, so he set out to construct one, with the Bible as the textbook. Each Sunday school class each week would have a particular passage from Scripture called the Golden

16. Andrew H. Mills, "A Hundred Years of Sunday School History in Illinois, 1818–1918," *Transactions of the Illinois State Historical Society for the Year 1918* (Springfield: Illinois State Journal Company, 1919), p. 104.

Text, along with a topical outline, readings to be done at home (note the assumption of active parental cooperation), graded questions, and illustrations and notes. The vehicle for Vincent's curriculum making was the *Chicago Sunday School Teacher,* which later became the *National Sunday School Teacher* (Vincent was succeeded in the editorship by Edward Eggleston, whose lessons were so attractive that circulation doubled in a year); the lessons, appropriately organized, became a system of instruction.

What Moody, Reynolds, and Jacobs accomplished was simply to persuade the Illinois convention of 1866 to adopt a single uniform curriculum for the state's Sunday schools and to sponsor institutes to train teachers to teach that curriculum, and then convince the International Sunday School Union convention of 1872 to do the same for the nation as a whole. The "Babel of courses" that had been taught since the 1820's and 1830's would be replaced by a single system. For the next half-century, uniform Sunday school lessons under the aegis of the Union were the rule in the United States, and a complex of county, state, and national institutes undertook the work of regularly training the teachers. Indeed, thanks again to Vincent's imaginativeness, the annual Methodist Sunday School Institute that met at Fair Point on Chautauqua Lake in New York gradually expanded its work over the years to become a great national adult education enterprise, comprising a system of local study groups called Chautauqua Literary and Scientific Circles, regional gatherings lasting from a week to a month that mixed lectures, concerts, courses, and recreational activities, and a publishing enterprise that issued books, pamphlets, magazines, and study guides. In addition, the Union itself organized a special school for training Sunday school teachers and field workers at Lake Geneva, Wisconsin, in 1912.

Two countertendencies soon arose to challenge the uniform system, one, denominational, the other, pedagogical. Denominationalism, which was never dormant, began seriously to challenge the work of the Union when, during the 1890's, the churches themselves began to revive their commitment to the religious education of children. In part, this derived from theological differences—the ISSU, for example, was comparatively unresponsive to Biblical criticism, and, given that the Bible was its textbook and that Biblical criticism was increasingly accepted by some groups, that unresponsiveness was bound to occasion conflict. In part, too, it derived from the sense on the part of many churches that denominational boards of education, closely allied with the several denominations, could do a more integral job of Christian education than the independent ISSU—Vincent himself, after all, for all his influence on the Sunday school movement at large, was general agent and then corresponding secretary of the Sunday School Union of the Methodist Episcopal Church. Finally, the denominational boards tended to consist of ministers and professional educators, while the leadership of the ISSU tended to include a mix of ministers and laypeople. In 1910, the denominational thrust was given organizational form with the establishment of the Sunday School Council of Evangelical Denominations. In comparison with the ISSU, the new Council was patently interdenominational rather than undenominational.

The pedagogical thrust against uniform lessons came from those who believed, first, that uniform lessons of any kind ignored the most fundamental principle of modern education, namely, the need for individualized instruction, second, that the concentration on the Bible as textbook ignored a host of other possible sources of religious knowledge and commitment, and third, that the concentration on the Sunday school assigned it the impossible role of producing committed Christians in a society where many other institutions were daily educating and miseducating with respect to Christian principles. While many of these critics were associated with the denominational boards of education, they met on common ground in the Religious Education Association.

The three-way tension here, between the approaches of the ISSU, the Council of Evangelical Denominations, and the REA, began to be resolved organizationally with the creation of the International Sunday School Council of Religious Education (later the International Council of Religious Education) in 1922. Under the aegis of the new Council's International Lesson Committee, a group under the leadership of William Clayton Bower and Paul H. Vieth produced a series of curriculum guides that pointed to a radically new conception of Sunday school education. In place of uniform, ordered, Bible-based lessons designed to stimulate conversion and church membership, the new guides spoke of the goal of Christian character traits (cooperation, goodwill, honesty, dependability, faith, forgiveness), the domains in which persons would ideally display these traits (vocational activities, citizenship activities, recreational activities), and the experiences (Bower and Vieth called them "enterprises") that might lead to the display of those traits in those domains. The progressive oriented curricula that emerged were a world apart from the uniform lessons of the ISSU, as evidenced by enterprises that ranged from the proper care of pets on the part of young children to appropriate dating behavior on the part of adolescents, and source materials as various as the Bible, Johanna Spyri's *Heidi* books, and Booker T. Washington's *Up from Slavery.* [17]

For all the collaboration of the 1920's and 1930's, however, the theological controversies would not down. During the 1940's, profoundly influenced by Niebuhrian neo-orthodoxy, the Presbyterian Church in the United States, under the leadership of James D. Smart, produced the Christian Faith and Life curriculum, which was rooted much more firmly in the life of Jesus and the substance of the Bible, which aimed much more vigorously at the goal of Christian discipleship, and which drew for source material upon an entirely new set of well-written and richly illustrated books—for example, Norman F. Langford's life of Christ entitled *The King Nobody Wanted* (1948) and Paul Sevier Minear's account of early Christianity entitled *The Choice: A Story of Christian Faith* (1948). The new curriculum re-emphasized the responsibility of parents and the household in the process of Christian nurture, with the Sunday school as a helpful supplement, and it clearly appealed to the demand in many quarters for a "return to theology" in Sunday school instruction. Yet it by no means quieted the doctrinal and pedagogical controversies that had divided Sunday school educators since the beginning of the century. The result was a continuing cacophony of voices and programs, marked by a persistent tension between efforts at interdenominational cooperation, for example, the "Christian Education, Shared Approaches" curricula produced during the 1960's and 1970's by ten denominations collaborating in what was called the Joint Educational Development, and the efforts of particular denominations to preserve particular theological identities, for example, the efforts of the Presbyterian Church (U.S.A.) during the 1980's. Given that tension, probably the most interesting ecumenical effort of the post–World War II era was the publication in 1960 of a children's pamphlet entitled *Jesus, Friend of Children Everywhere* in sixty-two languages by the World Council of Christian Education and Sunday School Association—an effort surely indicative of the transnational character of "the secular city" portrayed by Harvey Cox. Several million copies of the pamphlet circulated in 115 countries, and a follow-up pamphlet entitled *Stories Jesus Heard* appeared in 1962. But even that effort was terminated for

17. Paul H. Vieth, *Report to the Sub-Committee on International Curriculum of the International Sunday School Lesson Committee* (Cleveland: International Council of Religious Education, 1927).

lack of funds and support, and no ecumenical effort of similar scale was mounted during the succeeding two decades.

Like the Sunday school movement, the Young Men's Christian Association also experienced a renewal during the years following the Civil War. Established during the 1850's in Boston, New York, Philadelphia, Chicago, and a number of other cities as a loosely joined network of local organizations, each conducting its own evangelical activities, the Association had played a leading role in the great urban revivals of 1857 and 1858 but had subsequently suffered losses of members and of funds during the war years. Then, under the leadership of Robert Ross McBurney in New York and Dwight L. Moody in Chicago, the YMCA experienced a renaissance during the late 1860's and 1870's. New branches were organized; new buildings were erected; paid directors (called secretaries) were recruited and training facilities were established to prepare them for their duties (one such facility, established in Massachusetts in 1885, became Springfield College); and a series of annual conventions was organized that lent an increasingly national—and then international—character to the work.

Most important, however, the Association began to develop a rich and varied program explicitly intended to appeal to the young men who constituted the membership. The religious and rescue activities of the early days continued to go forward; members preached on street corners in the slum districts of their cities; they distributed tracts in boardinghouses, hospitals, and jails; they conducted Bible classes and prayer sessions for businessmen; and they trained Sunday school teachers for their work with children and adults (Moody's friend Benjamin F. Jacobs actually experimented with the first ISSU uniform lessons at the Chicago YMCA). But, along with these characteristic evangelical activities, the Association also began to conduct a more formal program of education that soon rivaled its more traditional religious efforts.

From its earliest days, the YMCA had sponsored libraries and lecture series, along with its evangelical activities. By the 1890's, however, libraries and lecture series under public auspices were beginning to be fairly common in the larger cities; and, in place of those activities, the Association began to introduce regular evening classes for study and improvement—in fact, the classes were increasingly referred to as "a college of the people." The initial offerings most often included courses in elementary school subjects for younger boys who had been required to leave school in order to undertake full-time work, courses in English and in American citizenship for immigrants, and courses in industrial subjects for those wishing vocational preparation. The Association also organized counseling centers to provide guidance with respect to needed skills and employment opportunities, and, later on, summer camps and vacation schools where a mix of study and recreation might be pursued. Moreover, as programs proliferated, the YMCA created the special role of education secretary for those who organized, oversaw, and coordinated the work. By 1913, the Association enrolled some 73,000 students in courses that ran the gamut from accounting to public speaking to wireless telegraphy.[18]

The Association also pioneered in two other areas, namely, physical training and student personnel work. Not surprisingly, physical training had evoked a good deal of ambivalence during the Association's early days. On the one hand, YMCA programs proved most attractive when they were rooted in the interests of young men; hence, sports and athletics were soon on the agenda. On the other hand, the Association's leaders shared the traditional evangelical suspicion of amusements. By the 1890's, however, such ambivalence had been left far behind as the Association warmly embraced physical training as an integral part of its program. The leading figure in the shift was a physician named Luther Halsey Gulick. The son of a missionary father, Gulick's interest in physical training had derived in substantial measure from his efforts to contend with his own health problems. He was early attracted to YMCA work and actually taught physical education at the YMCA Training School at Springfield from 1886 to 1903 at the same time that he served as secretary of the physical training department of the YMCA International Committee. Those activities in and of themselves would have been the basis of considerable influence. But Gulick also developed a philosophy of education that placed physical training at the very heart of the Association's concerns. That philosophy was symbolized by the triangle that became the Association's hallmark during and after the 1890's. As Gulick himself explained:

Of the fundamental principles which lie at the basis of the work of the Young Men's Christian Association, among the most important are unity and symmetry, the unity of man's nature and the need of symmetry in development, unity of the whole and symmetry of the parts. The best results are secured only when each part of man receives its due development, not merely

18. YMCA of the City of New York, *Annual Report, 1900*, p. 22; and Alan Eddy Hugg, "Informal Adult Education in the Y.M.C.A.: A Historical Study" (doctoral thesis, Columbia University, 1950), p. 118.

body, mind, and spirit being symmetrically developed, but each developed symmetrically with reference to the others.

The concept, of course, was scarcely new—Pestalozzian educators throughout the nineteenth century had spoken of the harmonious development of head, heart, and hand. But the concept did provide a framework within which Gulick for all intents and purposes Christianized the gymnasium. In collaboration with Robert J. Roberts, a YMCA worker who invented "body building" (an ordered series of exercises that fell halfway between light gymnastics and heavy exercise, exercises that would be "safe, easy, short, beneficial and pleasing"), Gulick designed a physical education curriculum, first for the Training School at Springfield, and then for the Association as a whole (as part of the development, he inspired his student James Naismith to design the game of basketball, as the perfect gymnasium activity—easy to learn, playable indoors and out, relatively free of roughness, and conducive to all-around development). By the time Gulick died in 1918, physical training, with its accouterment of gymnasiums, swim tanks, athletic leagues, and national and international competitions, had come to occupy a permanent place on the YMCA agenda.[19]

The YMCA's personnel work took the form of student associations organized on college and university campuses. The first such associations had been established at the University of Michigan and the University of Virginia as part of the revival movement of the late 1850's. The Michigan association had looked much like the university Christian associations of the time, while the Virginia association had more closely resembled the urban evangelical associations that had initially constituted the YMCA—it conducted a program that included Sunday school teaching, the distribution of tracts, the organization of prayer meetings, and the collection of funds for benevolent projects. Other student associations had been established at the University of Rochester, Washington College, the College of the City of New York, Olivet College, Howard University, and Cornell University during the 1860's; and in 1870 the Association's annual convention took formal note of the development for the first time by expressing the hope that "Christian Associations may be planted wherever practicable in our academies, colleges, and universities." Thereafter, under the vigorous promotion of Robert Weidensall, the Association's first field sec-

19. Luther Halsey Gulick, "Unity and Symmetry," *Triangle*, V (1891), 39, and "Robert J. Roberts and His Work," in R. J. Roberts, *Home Dumb Bell Drill* (Springfield, Mass.: Triangle Pub. Co., 1894), p. 6.

retary, and Luther Deloraine Wishard, the Association's first student secretary, the number of student associations burgeoned. They became centers of traditional evangelistic work on their several campuses and, during the 1880's and after, centers for the recruitment of foreign missionaries and for the international exchange of students. Beyond that, they became important vehicles for the teaching of social Christianity (called social evangelism) and, as a result of that teaching, for the development of social service programs, interracial activities, and, more generally, personal counseling and intergroup development activities. Finally, they provided some of the earliest opportunities for a wide range of extracurricular programs in colleges and universities, programs that were eventually taken up by the institutions themselves.[20]

In all of this, the Association and its affiliates continued to be symbols of Christian ecumenicism and promoters of Christian unity—though within patent limits. Despite flurries of effort from time to time, the YMCA never really appealed to young men of working-class background; but it did increasingly welcome Roman Catholics (despite the strictures of their bishops not to join) as well as the full range of Protestants, from the most orthodox to the most liberal. Indeed, as the Association's outreach broadened and its programs expanded, it became more and more a quasi-public institution, on campuses as well as in local communities, with the result that by the 1950's and 1960's the question was often raised as to whether the C in YMCA should be cast in lower-case type or dispensed with entirely. The very success of the Association's ecumenicism called into question whether it had a distinctive religious role to play.

The Young Women's Christian Association also began in Boston, New York, and a number of other cities during the 1850's as a loosely joined network of local organizations. It sponsored many of the same evangelical activities as the YMCA and there was talk of providing young workingwomen with many of the same sorts of services offered men by the YMCA. But from the beginning there were profound differences between the YWCA and the YMCA that continued to mark their respective histories over the years. For one thing, the women who organized the early YWCAs tended to be daughters of well-to-do families, generally without occupational skills and seeking in the YWCA an outlet for philanthropic and organizational aspirations. For another, the YWCA remained evangelically committed much longer

20. *Proceedings of the Fifteenth Annual Convention of the Young Men's Christian Associations of the United States and British Provinces, June, 1870*, p. 64.

and more insistently than the YMCA. And finally, the YWCA remained a divided and loosely joined confederation of local organizations much longer than the YMCA, and indeed it was only through the efforts of Grace Hoadley Dodge during the first decade of the twentieth century that the YWCA established a National Board with headquarters in New York City that began to promote centralization and unification on a nationwide basis.

The differences notwithstanding, the YWCA did mount a widening program of educational activities that was much like that of the YMCA in its emphasis on formal classes (not only in the sewing, needlework, dressmaking, and homemaking traditionally deemed appropriate for women but also in telegraphy, bookkeeping, secretarial work, interior decorating, and commercial art, and other occupations that had long been closed to women); in its inclusion of a national training school for secretaries (in New York City); in its sponsorship of student associations on college and university campuses, and in its recruitment through those associations of young women for overseas missionary service; and in its growing emphasis on social service programs during the 1920's and 1930's. One found less of an emphasis on physical training than in the YMCA, but more of a concern with the sort of training that would equip women to enter formerly inaccessible vocations (and, later, with the sort of training that would equip them to enter formerly inaccessible positions of leadership). In the end, in broadening its outreach and expanding its programs the YWCA encountered precisely the same problem as the YMCA, namely, to determine whether it was indeed still Christian and to define what, if any, special role it had to play in the communities it claimed to serve.

As American Protestantism organized on an ever more ecumenical basis in a bewildering variety of institutions, the assumption came to be widely held that the intellectual conflicts that had rent Christianity since the Reformation could now be fought out within those institutions or simply avoided altogether. Thus, the Federal Council issued continuing restatements in the most general terms of the doctrines of evangelical Protestantism, while providing a forum for continuing debate concerning the bearing of social Christianity on such matters as wages and hours, working conditions, child labor, collective bargaining, and the ownership of private property. Similarly, the various lesson committees of the International Sunday School Union worked tirelessly to resolve continuing issues of theology and pedagogy through Sunday school materials that would appeal to the widest possible range of denominations. The YMCA actually went so far as to rule out all debate over "public affairs" (by which the Association meant controversial affairs); while the YWCA preoccupied itself with defining the minimum substance of the Christian commitment that the Association had a right to expect of its members.

For the more orthodox evangelicals of premillennialist persuasion, however, the real debate had long been closed off, and the Council, the Sunday School Union, and the YMCA and YWCA had been captured by the modernists. In effect, the organization of the World's Christian Fundamentals Association in 1919 represented a secession from what was seen as a closed network of modernist institutions and the creation of an alternative network through which fundamentalists hoped to achieve a proper voice. In many respects, that new network was simply an alternative configuration of Protestant education. "Men about the country have been asking, '*Why This Conference?*'" William Bell Riley perorated in his opening remarks to the WCFA gathering.

The answer is at hand. This Conference is called to oppose the false teaching of the hour, and by a renewed emphasis upon God's Revelation, to confirm the faith of the people. This Conference is called to reveal to the world a new fellowship, a fellowship that is bringing into closer and closer union men from the various denominations who hold to the certain deity of Jesus Christ and to the utter authority of the Bible. The Conference is called to back up those magazines and newspapers that have steadfastly espoused and propagated God's eternal truths; to strengthen and extend those colleges, Bible schools and theological seminaries that are remaining loyal to the great fundamentals of the divine revelation.[21]

At the heart of the fundamentalist configuration of education was the Bible institute, which became one of the most influential types of Christian school of the twentieth century. The first of these was the Reverend A. B. Simpson's Missionary Training Institute, founded in New York City in 1882 (it subsequently moved to Nyack, New York); the largest and best known was the Moody Bible Institute, founded in Chicago in 1886. By 1919, some two dozen such schools were in operation, under sponsorship that varied from a single charismatic evangelist to an established denomination. Generally precollegiate in level, practical in orientation, low in cost, and flexible with respect to entry and exit requirements, the institutes were centers of piety and

21. *God Hath Spoken* (Philadelphia: Bible Conference Committee, 1919), p. 45.

sound doctrine at which men and women of all ages could prepare themselves for every conceivable kind of Christian work—as home and foreign missionaries, Bible and Sunday school teachers, youth workers, church musicians, pastors and pastor's assistants, and lay evangelists. While Bible courses were invariably at the heart of the curriculum, there were ancillary courses in Christian evidences, apologetics, and personal ethics and a host of opportunities for practical experience in street preaching, social work, and pedagogy. In addition, there were correspondence courses of every sort and variety. And, beyond the requirements of the formal educational programs, there was the intense informal educative experience of communal Christian living. Students met in prayer meetings, shared accounts of spiritual pilgrimages, underwent the regimen of personal and religious discipline, mounted collaborative evangelical efforts, and formed lasting personal and professional friendships. Also, beyond both the formal and informal education of the institutes, there were the innumerable activities of evangelism itself—the organization of Bible conferences, the publication of newspapers, pamphlets, and magazines as well as tracts and textbooks of every sort, the conduct of radio broadcasts, and the pursuit of home and foreign missionary work. If ever an institution involved its students in the continuing business of learning by doing, it was the early-twentieth-century Bible institute.

In some instances, a Bible institute became a configuration of education in its own right. In the hands of a charismatic leader such as William Bell Riley, who presided over the Northwest Bible and Missionary Training School in Minneapolis, or James M. Gray, who presided over the Moody Bible Institute in Chicago, or Reuben A. Torrey, who presided over the Bible Institute of Los Angeles, a Bible institute would serve as the hub of a complex of institutions that might include a tabernacle, a Sunday school, a young people's missionary organization, adult Bible study classes, a publishing apparatus, and a broadcasting station. It would also house organizations designed to bring like-minded tabernacles, Sunday schools, young people's missionary organizations, Bible study classes, and publishing companies into fruitful association.

What Riley attempted to do through the World's Christian Fundamentals Association was to organize these complexes, along with the orthodox sectors of the several denominations, into an association that would enhance and enlarge their educative efforts. He and his colleagues agreed on the substance of a fundamentalist creed. They heard reports from committees, including a Committee on Correlation of Bible Schools (James Gray's effort to organize, standardize, and accredit Bible institutes), a Committee on Correlation of Colleges, Seminaries, and Academies ("it is the duty of Christian people not only to have no fellowship with the infidel, atheistic education . . . , but to work out institutions which endeavor to be faithful to the Word of God and the persons, teaching and works of our Lord Jesus Christ"), a Committee on Correlation of Religious Magazines and Periodicals (essentially a public relations effort *cum* "list of sound books"), a Committee on Correlation of Bible Conferences, and a Committee on Correlation of Interdenominational Foreign Missionary Societies. They excoriated the Federal Council of Churches of Christ in America and its affiliated organizations, and they promised to work to reverse the "Great Apostasy" spreading like a plague throughout Christendom. For all these high aspirations, however, the effort did not succeed. The WCFA was soon embroiled in the antievolution crusade of the 1920's; the fundamentalist movement fragmented into a host of competing organizations, each, incidentally, built around the charismatic efforts of a particular evangelist (as the WCFA was built around Riley's); Riley ultimately ran out of energy and money; and the WCFA declined into insignificance during the early 1930's. In the end, the organized battle against the Great Apostasy had made little progress beyond the initial declaration of war.[22]

But the Bible institutes and their paraphernalia of associated educative institutions persisted, multiplied, and indeed, flourished. Without the heavy overheads associated with large physical plants and full-time tenured faculties, they weathered the Depression better than many of the traditional schools and colleges, and indeed some achieved accreditation by the secular accrediting associations. In addition, their efforts were complemented by those of like-minded denominations (Churches of Christ, Southern Baptists, Evangelical Free Church), like-minded organizations (Youth for Christ, New England Fellowship, Christian War Veterans of America), and like-minded publishers (Union Gospel Press, *Sunday School Times*, Scripture Press). When a National Association of Evangelicals was organized in 1942, with Harold J. Ockenga as president and J. Elwin Wright as field secretary, these institutions were not only extant but in many instances vigorous, and the NAE was able to accomplish many of the goals that had eluded the WCFA a quarter-century earlier. It

22. *Ibid.*, p. 20.

"rescued" broadcasting from the modernists by setting up the National Religious Broadcaster in 1944; it rescued the Sunday school movement by organizing the National Sunday School Association in 1945; it rescued foreign missions by organizing the Evangelical Foreign Missions Association in 1945; and it rescued the youth movement by backing Youth for Christ and the Inter-Varsity Christian Fellowship and by organizing the NAE Commission on Youth in 1946. In one domain, however, the "rescue" was of a different character. Whereas virtually all the Protestant denominations affiliated with the Federal Council continued to support public schooling for their children and to seek complementary formal religious education via Sunday schools, weekday afternoon classes, or both (along with the religious education offered by home, church, and youth organization), the NAE in 1947 sponsored the creation of the National Association of Christian Schools for the express purpose of promoting the establishment of Christian day schools across the country. The NAE made slow but steady headway during the 1950's and 1960's, and then its efforts gained momentum during the 1970's, when, in response to perceived inadequacies in the public schools, many of them associated with modernist tendencies in intellectual as well as moral matters, evangelical day schools began to multiply. In fact, those institutions became the most rapidly growing segment of American schooling at a time when public schooling in general was marked by declining enrollments and widespread disenchantment on the part of the public at large.

IV

Throughout the 1870's and 1880's, home missions remained the dominant concern of the evangelical movement. The Sunday School Union, working in collaboration with the Bible Society and the Tract Society, saw its task as the nurture and conversion of the entire American people; while a host of institutions from the Salvation Army to the YMCA directed their particular attention to the churched and unchurched masses of the cities, where it was widely assumed the battle for the soul of America would be won or lost. Yet foreign missions had been a concern of the evangelical movement at least since 1810, when the American Board of Commissioners for Foreign Missions had been organized; and it was in the domain of foreign missions that there occurred a burst of renewed enthusiasm during the 1880's that dramatically extended the influence of American education.

The foreign mission movement was compounded of many elements: denominational sponsors like the American Board of Commissioners for Foreign Missions (essentially Congregationalist after 1870), the American Baptist Missionary Union, the Missionary Society of the Methodist Episcopal Church, and the Board of Foreign Missions of the Presbyterian Church in the U.S.A.; quasi-independent and interdenominational sponsors like the Christian and Missionary Alliance and the Student Volunteer Movement; and auxiliary support agencies like the Missionary Education Movement and the Laymen's Missionary Movement. In addition, of course, there were the umbrella organizations that evangelical Protestants managed to develop with such zest and efficiency during the years before World War I, like the Foreign Missions Conference of North America and the International Missionary Union. Of all these, though, none was more representative of the transnational thrust of American evangelical Protestantism than the Student Volunteer Movement, which dominated the foreign missions enterprise during its most influential era.

Dwight L. Moody's role in the "student missionary uprising" of the 1880's has already been alluded to. The pledges of the "Mount Hermon Hundred" in 1886 marked the beginning of a surge that continued unabated over the next thirty years. Yet Moody's role in this, as in so many other domains, was to energize and reinforce developments that were already under way. In this instance, the effort had originated with a group of Princeton undergraduates, led by R. W. Van Kirk and Robert P. Wilder, who had organized themselves in 1883 as the Princeton Foreign Missionary Society. Stirred by the example of the Inter-Seminary Missionary Alliance, an organization of theological students inspired by Adoniram Judson Gordon, a well-known Boston Congregationalist who, like Moody, preached a vividly present Christ and a passionate commitment to Christian service, and encouraged by Princeton's president, James McCosh, they met weekly in the home of Wilder's father, the Reverend Royal G. Wilder. The elder Wilder had been a member of the Brethren Society, a secret organization to encourage foreign missions, during his student days at the Andover Theological Seminary in the 1840's; he had worked for thirty years as a missionary in India; and he had then returned to the United States to found the *Missionary Review,* which he edited from his home in Princeton. "The question," he was fond of remarking to the young men, "is not why *should* you go, but, if you are a true servant of Christ, why should you *not* go where the need is greater than in the homeland." The influence of Royal Wilder and of Robert Wilder's younger sister Grace, who as a student at Mount Holyoke College (Mary Lyon's "Puritan convent") had led the Mount Holyoke Missionary Association, was compelling. The students framed a declaration stating, "We are willing and desirous, God permitting, to be foreign missionaries"; and most of them then proceeded to take the pledge and go on to careers as foreign missionaries. More important, however, when Luther Wishard persuaded Moody to invite the collegiate members of the YMCA to the Northfield Conference in 1886, it was Wilder (there as a delegate from Princeton) who teamed with Wishard and with the Reverend Arthur T. Pierson (a Presbyterian clergyman who had just completed a premillennialist treatise on *The Crisis of Missions* [1886]), first, to persuade Moody to devote some time at the conference to the problem of foreign missions, and second, to persuade as many of the students as possible to volunteer. And, in the end, it was the Princeton Society's pledge that the Northfield volunteers signed.[23]

What followed the 1886 conference was a remarkable organizational effort. Wilder and a fellow Princetonian, John N. Forman, spent the 1886–87 year visiting 162 colleges and universities in the United States and Canada and persuading 2,106 students to sign declarations. A second College Students' Summer School for Bible Study at Northfield in 1887 brought 269 delegates from 82 colleges, 42 YMCA secretaries from across the country, and 130 other visitors, many of them from abroad, and further stimulated the effort by publishing "An Appeal to the Churches," which concluded, "The whole world can be evangelized in the present generation." Wilder and Forman made no additional visits during 1887–88, Wilder having begun his graduate studies at Union Theological Seminary in New York and Forman having gone off to India as a missionary; yet 600 additional declarations were forwarded from the colleges and universities they had canvassed. A third Student Conference at Northfield in the summer of 1888 brought formal organization. The Student Volunteer Movement for Foreign Missions was established, with its Executive Committee drawn from the YMCA, the YWCA, and the Inter-Seminary Missionary Alliance. Wishard started it and Wilder sat on the Executive Committee, while two youthful volunteers who had been

23. John R. Mott, *Five Decades and a Forward View* (New York: Harper & Brothers, 1939), p. 1; Robert P. Wilder, *The Student Volunteer Movement for Foreign Missions: Some Personal Reminiscences of Its Origin and Early History* (New York: Student Volunteer Movement for Foreign Missions, 1935), p. 10; and Arthur C. Cole, *A Hundred Years of Mount Holyoke College: The Evolution of an Educational Ideal* (New Haven: Yale University Press, 1940), chap. vi.

recruited during the first two years of the effort, John R. Mott and Robert Speer, served respectively as chairman and traveling secretary. In retrospect, there was no more able group of educational leaders to be found in contemporary America. For the next three decades, the SVM was an unqualified success. It sent more than 8,000 volunteers under various denominational auspices to India, the Middle East, southeast Asia, China, Japan, Africa, and Latin America—in all, they probably constituted well over half the total number of foreign missionaries sent abroad under North American Protestant auspices during the period. It helped sponsor and sustain those volunteers in activities as varied as preaching, teaching, community service, medicine, and agriculture. It made itself one of the most influential activities of the YMCA and the YWCA. It managed to work closely and amiably over the years with all the major Protestant mission boards. And it became one of the foremost promoters of international, interfaith missionary cooperation, as evidenced by its role in the founding of the World's Student Christian Federation in 1895.[24]

What were the elements in the SVM's success? For one thing, the volunteers were very much the products of the education created by the evangelical united front during the middle third of the nineteenth century. They tended to come from families where one or both parents were church members (among 6,200 volunteers in 1891, more than three-quarters were of Presbyterian, Methodist, Congregationalist, or Baptist background), families that would tend to follow Horace Bushnell's principles of Christian nurture, using the apparatus of church activity, Sunday schools, and evangelical clubs, camps, youth groups, and publications. But, beyond that, as part of the select group among evangelical young people who went on to higher education, they tended to come from the denominational colleges and theological schools that were seen as the nurseries of a pious evangelical leadership. In addition to active YMCA and YWCA student groups, such institutions tended to have returned missionaries as members of their faculties and even, in the case of some of the more orthodox Bible schools or theological seminaries, special courses or training programs for prospective missionaries. Not surprisingly, some schools pointedly committed themselves to educating for foreign missionary service and judged their success by the number of their graduates who went out to the field—Denison and Yale were such institu-

24. Wilder, *Student Volunteer Movement*, p. 37.

tions among the men's colleges, Mount Holyoke and Rockford among the women's colleges, and Oberlin and Grinnell among the coeducational colleges.

The conversion experience was central in the lives of those who had heard the call. The experience frequently occurred during the college years and could almost always be dated fairly precisely. It was an experience, too, that frequently led to the surrender of material ambitions, the dedication of one's life to the service of God, and the tendency to gravitate toward the company of like-minded individuals. Even at this point, however, it was difficult to distinguish between those who would serve God as foreign missionaries and those who would serve as ministers, YMCA or YWCA secretaries, home missionaries, or denominational functionaries (for the large number of women who volunteered, the choices were considerably narrower). The ultimate differentiating factor was the conviction that the need was greatest abroad, that the spiritual ignorance of the unevangelized masses in China or India or Africa was more compelling than that of the American urban poor. Finally, once the declaration and the decision had been made, there was the possibility of specialized training for service, in a missionary program, divinity school, medical school, normal school, nursing school, or agricultural school. Robert P. Wilder made his declaration and then prepared for service at Union Theological Seminary; Rosetta Sherwood Hall, who served as a medical missionary in Korea for almost forty years, made her decision while a district schoolteacher in New York and then went on to the Woman's Medical College of Pennsylvania; and Kenneth Scott Latourette made his declaration as an undergraduate at McMinnville College (later Linfield College)—a declaration about which he confessed a good deal of ambivalence—and then went on to take a doctorate in history at Yale to prepare himself for the work. The Moody Bible Institute actually made missionary study a required subject in 1904, doubtless responding to the fact that some 12 percent of the Institute's graduates during the first decade were serving as missionaries in foreign lands and that students were coming from all over the world to prepare for missionary careers.

Given the number of women who pledged themselves to service as foreign missionaries and who eventually went abroad, it is well to note that, although they underwent many of the same educational experiences as men en route to making their commitments, they remained restricted in their participation in at least three respects. First, even though "woman's work" in the mission field was widely assumed to comprise medical work, educational work, and evangelical country work, women were as often as not denied access to specialized professional training in medicine and divinity, and thereby relegated to service in professions such as schoolteaching or nursing, or even to service as laypersons. Second, if they went abroad as the wives of missionaries, they were more often than not unpaid and barred from a significant role in decision making. And third, if they went as spinsters or widows, they were treated as second-class citizens and rarely permitted any role in decision making. Even when the American Board decided in 1894 that women should have an equal voice and vote at meetings in the field, the prerogative was restricted to questions touching their own work.

There is a myth to the effect that Afro-Americans were uninterested in foreign missions, owing largely to their segregation and impoverishment within American society and their resultant preoccupation with their own socioeconomic welfare. Yet scores of Afro-American missionaries did go abroad during the decades following 1890, most of them to Africa, and the education preparing them for their vocations bore a striking resemblance to the education of their white counterparts. They grew up in relatively comfortable circumstances amid deeply religious families. They attended schools and colleges like Fisk University, Howard University, Atlanta University, and Hampton Institute, where a combination of official evangelical piety and the inspiration of missionary-oriented professors led many to heed the call. And, while a greater percentage were recruited directly by their sponsoring denominations than was the case with their white counterparts, the organizational apparatus of the SVM and of the YMCA-YWCA student associations did play a modest role—one of the earliest YMCA student associations had been the one founded at Howard.

Once recruited, the young missionary-to-be became part of a special educational effort intended to keep the fires of commitment burning brightly and to provide sustenance for the commitment in the form of community support and understanding. Mott himself once wrote that the fivefold purpose of the SVM was to lead students to a thorough consideration of the claims of foreign missions upon them, to foster this purpose by guiding students who became volunteers in their study and activity for missions until they came under the direction of the several mission boards, to unite volunteers in a common, organized, aggressive movement, to recruit a sufficient number of volunteers to meet the needs of the mission boards, and to maintain an intelligent, sympathetic, and active interest in foreign missions on the part of those students who remained at home. In pursuit of these goals, the SVM encouraged those who had made declarations to form volunteer bands, which in turn held weekly meetings for the study of missions at which all who expressed interest were welcome—the SVM provided textbooks and syllabi for the work. By 1910 there were more than two thousand such groups with some 25,000 students enrolled. In addition, the SVM sent representatives to the churches and especially to their youth organizations—the Epworth Leagues, the Christian Endeavor Societies, and the Baptist Young People's Unions—with the request that they form missionary committees to propagandize for missions, pray for them, and gather funds for them. In 1902 the work was formally organized into the Young People's Missionary Movement (later, the Missionary Education Movement), which soon involved thousands of young men and women in its courses, its Sunday school programs, its summer conferences, and its public exhibitions. And in 1907, the Laymen's Missionary Movement was organized, with a view to enlisting experienced businessmen in the cause, not merely as contributors and fund raisers, but as public proponents and spokesmen for the movement.

Once abroad, the missionaries, no matter what their particular roles and responsibilities, were inevitably and inextricably involved in the business of evangelicism. As Mott and his associates never tired of reiterating, "the evangelization of the world in this generation" did not mean the immediate conversion of the world or even the immediate saturation of the world with Christian ideas; it rather meant giving all people the opportunity to know Jesus Christ as their Saviour and to become his real disciples—in essence, it meant popularizing education by making knowledge of the Gospel accessible to all. The missionaries were expected to teach constantly, ubiquitously, and variously. The ministers were to teach the Bible, and with it a language (English, until they became sophisticated enough to have the Scriptures rendered in the native tongue), a symbolism, a social structure, a value system, and a moral code. The physicians and the nurses were to teach cleanliness and the efficacy of science, quite apart from the Gospel messages conveyed on the walls of hospital wards and dispensary waiting rooms. The agronomists were to teach the uses of fertilizer and the advantages of Western diets. The missionaries' wives were to teach the virtues of wearing clothes and the unvirtues of nakedness. And all, especially when they resided and worked in groups set apart in physical or psychological compounds, were to teach the values and manners of a wider culture deemed superior and worthy of adoption by the heathen.[25]

Beyond all this, however, the missionaries were expected to become centrally involved in schooling; and the schools they actually conducted were invariably American schools and in the end American enclaves within the context of the host society. Their explicit purpose was evangelization: their goal was to nurture Christian converts and to train up a native clergy to minister to the converts. But, particularly in the era before World War I, there was no ability to distinguish the Christian from the American, with the result that as often as not the missionary schools, while intending to nurture Christian converts and train up Christian ministers, actually nurtured American converts and trained up American ministers—and later physicians, nurses, teachers, agronomists, and scholars. The graduates of the schools were well prepared to live in American compounds; but they were ill prepared to continue normally within their own society, except as agents of further evangelization and, with it, of social transformation.

"Modern missions have everywhere heralded an educational revival," the Reverend James S. Dennis proclaimed in his sociological study of foreign missions entitled *Christian Missions and Social Progress*, and then went on to detail the remarkable range of formal educational institutions established around the world by missionaries in general and by American missionaries in particular. Dennis catalogued literally thousands of primary schools, hundreds of boarding schools, high schools, and industrial training schools, and scores of colleges, universities, theological schools, nursing schools, and medical schools. If the Chinese situation may be taken as an example—by the time of Dennis' survey it was the leading field of SVM missionaries and, with India, one of the two leading fields of American missionaries generally—Dennis could note with satisfaction a dozen collegiate-level institutions claiming to offer general collegiate-level instruction. Like many of the underfinanced American denominational colleges of the day, they tended to be small evangelical establishments with severely limited curricula and mixes of secondary and postsecondary students. Also, like many of their American counterparts, particularly those for Afro-Americans, several had industrial training departments. Dennis

25. John R. Mott, *The Evangelization of the World in This Generation* (New York: Student Volunteer Movement for Foreign Missions, 1900), p. 5. The watchword itself appears to have originated with Arthur T. Pierson; see "The Evangelization of the World in This Generation," in Max Wood Moorhead, ed., *The Student Missionary Enterprise: Addresses and Discussions of the Second International Convention of the Student Volunteer Movement for Foreign Missions* [1894] (Boston: T. O. Metcalf & Co., 1900), pp. 105–115.

went on to list some ninety boarding schools, high schools, and seminaries—essentially secondary schools, many with primary departments—under American auspices (the vast majority had fewer than fifty students in attendance). For all intents and purposes, they tended to be secondary-level versions of the colleges—nurseries of evangelical piety and severely restricted in the program they offered. Finally, Dennis included a listing of theological schools, medical schools, and nursing schools, most of them exceedingly small, enrolling fewer than twenty-five students.[26]

This complex of institutions expanded and proliferated rapidly over the next three decades. By 1925 the colleges enrolled some 3,500 students, the middle schools, some 26,000 students, and the primary schools some 250,000 students. Moreover, the schools had been upgraded and had added programs in agriculture, journalism, sociology, and social work. Yet, whatever their size and quality, they were all essentially American in character, placing emphasis on the English language, English literature, and Western history, along with American science and mathematics and the ever-present work in Bible study and Christian apologetics. In their very nature, their curricula were in opposition to Mandarin culture with its historic emphasis on the Chinese language and Chinese letters, Chinese history, and Confucian philosophy.

The Chinese on their side responded with ambivalence. On the one hand, they were eager for the instruction provided by the Christian schools and colleges, seeing their offerings as the key to a reformed China that would take its appropriate place in the modern world. John R. Mott recognized this when he wrote in 1911, "It is Western education that the Chinese are clamoring for, and will have." As Mott saw it, "If the Church can give it to them, plus Christianity, they will take it; otherwise they will get it elsewhere, without Christianity—and that speedily." On the other hand, the Chinese could not but recognize that the missionaries were foreigners, teaching values and ways corrosive of their traditional institutions. For the more conservative Chinese in positions of power, the corrosion was reason enough for hostility. For the more radical Chinese, the idea of foreigners wielding such power was anathema. The result was a growing

26. James S. Dennis, *Christian Missions and Social Progress: A Sociological Study of Foreign Missions* (3 vols.; New York: Fleming H. Revell Company, 1897–1906), III, 7, and *Centennial Survey of Foreign Missions: A Statistical Supplement to "Christian Missions and Social Progress," Being a Conspectus of the Achievements and Results of Evangelical Missions in All Lands at the Close of the Nineteenth Century* (New York: Fleming H. Revell Company, 1902), pp. 69–70, 75–76, 88–92, 109, 113, 119.

antiforeignism that developed hand in hand with Chinese nationalism. The Chinese wanted the Western schools and colleges—and
churches and hospitals—but on their own terms and under their own
control. As Mott observed, they wanted the science without the Christianity.[27]

The missionaries themselves, not surprisingly, responded with an
ambivalence of their own. Some of the more conservative among
them asked insistently whether evangelization required the support
and operation of vast and expensive systems of schooling and medical
services, particularly as inquiries during the 1920's revealed the weaknesses of many of the programs. Others with more liberal views
granted the justice of the Chinese criticisms and supported the Chinese in their efforts to gain control of their own institutions, a position
that brought them into sharp conflict, not only with their conservative
colleagues in the missionary community, but also with their fellow
Americans in the diplomatic and business communities who were
eager to preserve the special privileges they had long enjoyed under
the so-called special treaties negotiated during the nineteenth century. Later, in 1932, the Laymen's Foreign Missions Inquiry under the
leadership of Professor William Ernest Hocking of Harvard University issued a report sharply criticizing many of the missionary activities
for their low standards and misdirected insensitivity to local needs
and strongly recommending that Christian missionaries make common cause with indigenous religions instead of seeking to supplant
them. The report was severely attacked by missionary groups in the
United States and abroad, but the divisions and the uncertainties it
introduced into the missionary enterprise were lasting.

Within this context, American interest in foreign missions waned
considerably. The Student Volunteer Movement peaked shortly after
World War I. Mott stepped down from the leadership of the SVM in
1920, believing that the prospects of the movement had never been
brighter. "We stand on the threshold of the greatest opportunity
which North American students have ever confronted," he assured
some seven thousand enthusiastic delegates to the Des Moines, Iowa,
convention of the SVM in 1919. The assurance was destined to be
ironic. In 1920 and 1921, the SVM sent the largest numbers of volunteers abroad in its history, but there was a decline thereafter, doubtless owing to the disillusionment that followed in the wake of Wilsonian idealism, to the skepticism that suffused American higher

27. John R. Mott, *The Decisive Hour of Christian Missions* (New York: Student Volunteer
Movement for Foreign Missions, 1910), pp. 64, 47–48.

education during the 1920's, and, later, to the economic constraints caused by the Depression. Interestingly, there was a resurgence of interest after World War II; but, characteristically, it derived not so much from the so-called mainline Protestant denominations associated with the Federal Council of Churches of Christ in America and later the National Council of Churches as from fundamentalist and evangelical groups like the Christian and Missionary Alliance. It is significant that the Moody Bible Institute could claim in 1960 to have trained fully 8 percent of all the Protestant foreign missionaries from the United States.[28]

What in retrospect was the outcome of the missionary effort, particularly in the domain of education? Wherever the missionaries went, as in China, American education in general, and American schooling in particular, exerted a transforming effect. The world was neither evangelized nor converted in one generation—or in two or three; but Christianity was widely propagated and appeared stubbornly to persist amid every manner of social and ideological upheaval. The influence of American education, however, went far beyond evangelization: it served in its own right as a force for change. It proffered Western values, Western learning, Western science, and Western technology to peoples immersed in traditional cultures and it consciously as well as unconsciously asserted the superior worth of modern ways—it was undeniably a venture in cultural imperialism. Those who accepted its teaching became by virtue of that acceptance change agents in their own societies; they also became new elites, who took from American education that which they saw as useful and turned it to their own ends. Many parts of the world were transformed as a result, though the transformations were scarcely those initially envisioned by the missionaries.

In addition, it is important to recognize the effect of the foreign missionary effort upon American education at home. From the beginning of the revivals of the 1880's and 1890's, mission enthusiasts had proclaimed the importance of missions abroad for the vitality of Christianity at home. "Missions are an absolute necessity," wrote Henry Van Dyke of Princeton in 1896, "not only for the conversion of the heathen, but also, and much more, for the preservation of the Church." As with the effects abroad, however, mission enthusiasts

28. John R. Mott, "The World Opportunity," in Burton St. John, ed., *North American Students and World Advance: Addresses Delivered at the Eighth International Convention of the Student Volunteer Movement for Foreign Missions, Des Moines, Iowa, December 31, 1919 to January 4, 1920* (New York: Student Volunteer Movement for Foreign Missions, 1920), p. 17.

could not have predicted what the impact of foreign missions at home would actually be. In education, it was prodigious. For one thing, the missionaries became the leading interpreters in the United States of the lands in which they had served. They returned as experts, not only to college and university faculties, but also to influential positions in diplomacy, journalism, and letters. With respect to China, one thinks of Kenneth Scott Latourette, who returned from Yale-in-China to profess the history of Christianity with such distinction at Yale that he won election to the presidency of the American Historical Association, or of John Leighton Stuart, the former president of Yenching University, who was the last American ambassador to mainland China before the Communist victory in 1949, or of Henry R. Luce, who grew up in a missionary family in China and whose policies with respect to *Time*'s reporting of Far Eastern affairs during the 1950's and 1960's exerted incalculable influence on American foreign policy. Furthermore, the ablest graduates of the Chinese colleges and universities came to the United States in large numbers to continue their studies at American colleges and universities and then, once returned, became the key figures in developing special relationships between Chinese and American institutions of higher learning—again, using the Chinese example, one thinks of the association of Nanking University with Cornell, or of Yenching with Princeton and Harvard, or of Ginling College for Women with Smith. The result was a movement toward the internationalizing of American education, and, with it, of American thought that coincided with America's burgeoning international role during and after World War II. But it was an internationalizing that frequently reflected the special perspective of the missionary, especially the relentless concern for saving heathen peoples. It was a perspective, too, that played a part in the enthusiasm that marked the Peace Corps and other post–World War II aid programs, as well as the ideological fervor that marked the Vietnam war during the 1960's and 1970's.[29]

V

Josiah Strong's agenda for the Evangelical Alliance during the later 1880's ultimately became the agenda of evangelical Protestantism during the Progressive era. Strong and his associates spoke in theological terms of achieving the Kingdom of God on earth; their undeni-

29. Henry Van Dyke, "The Necessity and the Needs of Foreign Missions," *Outlook*, LIII (1895–96), 201.

able goal in practice remained the goal of the evangelical united front during the pre–Civil War era, namely, the Christianizing, first of America, and eventually of the world. "The Alliance is called of God to a sublime opportunity," Strong affirmed in one of his early reports to the board. "To save our American civilization and thoroughly season it with the salt of Christianity is to give a Christian civilization to the world." For Strong, the American *paideia,* insofar as it incorporated the social, intellectual, and moral aspirations of the American people, could be none other than a Protestant *paideia*—that was God's charge to his chosen people and the nation's responsibility to God. And, in the minds of most evangelical Protestants as well as any number of non-Protestants, the American *paideia* was inseparable and ultimately indistinguishable from a Protestant *paideia.* In fact, one way to characterize the educational efforts of the full range of Protestant evangelical institutions during the Progressive era—the churches themselves, the Federal Council and its associated interchurch bodies, the ISSU, the YMCA, and the YWCA—would be to say that they devoted themselves to rendering and keeping the American *paideia* indistinguishable from a Protestant *paideia.* [30]

For a time, the goal seemed possible of achievement. The institutional churches, stimulated by the precepts of social Christianity, reached out to the urban poor with significant successes; Protestant churchmen joined Progressive politicians and social scientists to form the leadership of many of the newer urban reform movements; the Federal Council and its affiliates propelled the several denominations into engagement with the world of affairs; the standardized lessons of the ISSU were taught in Sunday schools across the country; the number of YMCAs and YWCAs increased, as did the number of their student chapters at colleges and universities; and the Student Volunteer Movement fired the imagination of significant numbers of able college and university graduates. When the United States entered World War I on the side of the Allies, evangelical Protestants overwhelmingly supported the effort, seeing it in Wilsonian terms as a "great crusade" to "make the world safe for democracy." With the signing of the Armistice, evangelical Protestants looked forward to a glorious era of even greater accomplishment. An Interchurch World Movement was planned to raise unprecedented amounts of money to launch a final crusade for the Christianization of the world. Never was American evangelical Protestantism more hopeful or more confident.

30. Evangelical Alliance for the United States, *Report of the Committee on National Conferences to the Board of Managers of the Evangelical Alliance for the United States* [December 21, 1886], p. 2.

The crusade, however, died aborning; and indeed its failure marked the beginning of an unexpected decline in the influence of American Protestantism—Robert T. Handy has referred to it as the "spiritual depression" of the 1920's. The churches suffered declines in membership, attendance, and contributions, declines that accelerated during the economic depression of the 1930's. A corresponding decline in activities, budgets, and vitality was experienced by the major interdenominational organizations. The Sunday school movement became, on the one hand, increasingly secular (recall the ethical rather than religious emphasis of the materials and "enterprises" that constituted the curricula of the International Council of Religious Education during the 1920's), and, on the other hand, increasingly fragmented (recall the dissatisfactions that led eventually to the production of the Christian Faith and Life curriculum during the late 1930's and 1940's). The YMCA and the YWCA and their college affiliates lost the interest of the young, as local associations turned more and more to the delivery of social, recreational, and educational services and as those services were in turn taken over by public and collegiate authorities; and, in a closely related development, the Student Volunteer Movement failed to recruit young Americans for missionary service overseas in anywhere near the numbers that had early responded to its appeals. In effect, the configuration of evangelical educative institutions that had maintained an undenominational Protestant hegemony over American culture for more than a century suddenly suffered a massive decline in power, vitality, morale, and influence.[31]

The immediate sources of the decline doubtless lay in the widespread disenchantment that followed in the wake of World War I, the same disenchantment that affected the entire panoply of reform movements in American society. But there were other sources of the decline that had long been in the making, among them, the more general influence of Darwinism and the higher criticism, the gradual secularization of the public schools and of the colleges and universities (including many of those founded and sustained by the several denominations), and the inevitable blurring of the evangelical message that came as interdenominational movements increasingly turned to undenominational social reform and social service as their primary activities. In addition, the massive immigration of the years after 1880 had brought large numbers of Roman Catholics and Jews

31. Robert T. Handy, "The American Religious Depression, 1925–1935," *Church History*, XXIX (1960), 3–16, and *A Christian America: Protestant Hopes and Historical Realities* (New York: Oxford University Press, 1971), pp. 200–203.

to the United States, with the result that there were ever more significant challenges to Protestant hegemony from ever more powerful non-Protestant organizations. Particularly as the Roman Catholic Church consolidated its power in the great metropolitan areas under such leaders as George Cardinal Mundelein of Chicago, Denis Cardinal Dougherty of Philadelphia, William Cardinal O'Connell of Boston, and Patrick Cardinal Hayes of New York during the 1920's and 1930's, at precisely the time Protestantism found itself increasingly fragmented theologically and ideologically, Roman Catholics felt able to contend that they articulated American aspirations at least as well as evangelical Protestants and perhaps better. Given the equal participation and equal sacrifice of men and women of all three of the major faiths in World War II, it was but a short step to Will Herberg's suggestion in *Protestant-Catholic-Jew* (1955) that the American *paideia* was not singular but plural and that it manifested itself in at least three coequal forms—a Protestant *paideia,* a Roman Catholic *paideia,* and a Jewish *paideia*—each ideally represented institutionally by its own configuration of educative institutions.

By the time Herberg's book appeared, American Protestantism was on the verge of what William G. McLoughlin would call the "Fourth Great Awakening." That awakening was destined to be vastly different from its predecessors. Evangelical Protestantism would flourish during the 1960's, 1970's, and 1980's and would characteristically lay claim to the obligation to Christianize American civilization; and indeed the movement would achieve many significant victories. But those victories would be widely perceived as victories for evangelical Protestantism rather than for a Christianized Americanism. American demography and American education had rendered any larger notion of a Christianized America at the least outmoded and in the main beside the point.[32]

32. William G. McLoughlin, *Revivals, Awakenings, and Reform: An Essay on Religion and Social Change in America, 1607–1977* (Chicago: University of Chicago Press, 1978).

Chapter 3

PATTERNS OF DIVERSITY

The symphony of America must be written by the various nationalities which keep their individual and characteristic note, and which sound this note in harmony with their sister nationalities. Then it will be a symphony of color, of picturesqueness, of character, of distinction—not the harmony of the Melting Pot, but rather the harmony of sturdiness and loyalty and joyous struggle.

JUDAH L. MAGNES

The evangelical united front continued its efforts during the years following 1876 to define an American *paideia,* a core of affirmations and aspirations that would characterize the divine mission of the United States at home and throughout the world. Precisely as Lyman Beecher had attempted to articulate such a *paideia* for the great Ohio Valley campaign of the 1830's and 1840's, Josiah Strong sought to articulate one for the great urban and international campaigns of the 1880's and 1890's. Strong and like-minded evangelicals viewed Protestantism and Americanism as inseparable and interchangeable; and they saw the institutional apparatus they had developed—the Evangelical Alliance, the Federal Council of Churches of Christ in America, the International Sunday School Union, the YMCA and the YWCA, the Student Volunteer Movement, and a host of similar organizations—as a technology whereby such a *paideia* would be continually defined and disseminated.

For a time the effort appeared to succeed admirably, with statement after statement from the leaders of interdenominational Protestantism announcing the imminent achievement of the Kingdom of God on earth. Then, during the 1920's and 1930's, the effort seemed to falter. The several organizations attempted to be ever more encompassing and inclusive, seeing in ecumenicism a strategy for containing and resolving disagreements. But they were confronted, on the one hand, by the retreat of the neo-orthodox, who argued that only individuals, not societies, acted morally, and, on the other hand, by the secession of the fundamentalists, who argued during the 1920's and 1930's that it was not God's business to make politics moral (and that in the end God's judgment would in any case visit appropriate punishment upon politicians for their transgressions) and who then argued during the 1940's and 1950's that it was the obligation of true believers to use politics to maintain a truly Christian society (the tension and alternation between evangelism and sectarianism was scarcely new to American religion in the twentieth century). By the 1960's and 1970's, what was left of the institutional apparatus of the evangelical united front had abdicated the responsibility of defining an American *paideia,* preferring to preach the virtues of a plural Americanism, while the fundamentalists (by then called evangelicals) had fashioned a technology of their own to define an Americanism of their own and indeed to pit it aggressively against alternative versions, particularly of the modernist variety. The result was a series of bitter educational conflicts—over school textbooks, as in Kanawha County, West Virginia, in 1972, over family policy, as in the ill-fated White House Conferences on the Family during the Carter administration, and over the content of television broadcasting, as in the threatened boycotts of networks and advertisers during the late 1970's and early 1980's.

Moreover, as a counterpoint to the efforts of the evangelical united front, a variety of ethnoreligious groups during the years following 1876 formulated alternative *paideias* of their own, which they initially claimed were entirely consistent with the American *paideia* and which they later claimed to be variant American *paideias* in their own right. Irish Catholics in Chicago, German Lutherans in Wisconsin, Russian Mennonites in Kansas, and Sioux practitioners of the Ghost Dance religion in the Black Hills formed alternative moral communities that defined and taught alternative visions of the good life in America and, with them, alternative versions of Americanism.

Whereas in the first third of the twentieth century it was fashionable to talk of America as a "melting pot," however much intellectuals like John Dewey, Jane Addams, and Horace Kallen might have dissented from the metaphor, it became increasingly fashionable during the second third of the century to talk of a "mosaic," and in so doing to indicate that the parts could contribute to the whole without losing their particularities. Both metaphors had a quality of staticness about them, however, and thereby missed the extent to which ethnoreligious moral communities, through the educative processes whereby they sought to perpetuate themselves, were constantly redefining not only themselves but the larger community of which they were part. Timothy Smith suggested in an address commemorating the bicentennial of the Republic in 1976 that the metaphor of the "kaleidoscope" might be more appropriate than either the "melting pot" or the "mosaic." Insofar as Smith's metaphor conveyed the dynamism and variegation of American life and education, its superiority to the others was undeniable, however much its acceptance by many of his contemporaries might have been problematical at the least.[1]

II

Afro-Americans by the 1870's had formed their own counterparts of the traditional Protestant denominations and were functioning very much as an ethnoreligious community in their own right. The dynamics by which black Protestant churches had come into being had varied from denomination to denomination. Some denominations had forced Afro-Americans to found their own churches by direct acts of discrimination. Others had encouraged the process with financial assistance and paternal oversight. Others had left the Afro-Americans in control of traditional structures at the same time that white members had moved elsewhere. Still others had acquiesced more or less reluctantly in Afro-American demands for self-determination. Whatever the initiatives and whatever the responses, the Afro-Americans made the most of their opportunities. During the last third of the nineteenth century, their churches became not only some of the earliest formal institutions that they themselves actually owned and controlled but also their most important single agencies of social and economic cooperation, their principal arenas of political activity, and their most significant instruments of education.

During the era before the Civil War, free blacks had established their own independent Baptist churches as well as the African Methodist Episcopal Church, founded in Philadelphia in 1815, and the African Methodist Episcopal Zion Church, founded in New York in 1821. In addition, and on a much smaller scale, they had also established Episcopal, Presbyterian, and Congregationalist churches. After Emancipation and Appomattox, they established the Colored Methodist Episcopal Church, founded in Jackson, Tennessee, in 1870, and

1. Timothy L. Smith, "Religion and Ethnicity in America," *American Historical Review*, LXXXIII (1978), 1185.

the National Baptist Convention, founded in Atlanta in 1895 (twelve years later, the NBC split in a dispute over the control of property and of the National Baptist Publishing Board in Nashville; the new organizations were called, respectively, the National Baptist Convention of the U.S.A., Inc. and the National Baptist Convention). Other smaller organizations were established, like the African Union First Colored Methodist Protestant Church, Inc., in 1866, and the Church of Christ (Holiness) USA, in 1894, and it should be borne in mind, too, that significant numbers of Afro-Americans remained within the traditional, predominantly white denominations, notably the Methodist Church, the Protestant Episcopal Church, and the Roman Catholic Church. But the salient fact is that by the end of the nineteenth century Afro-Americans had for all intents and purposes won control of their religious institutions.

The Afro-American churches exerted their educative influence profoundly and pervasively. As the chief institutions of the Afro-American community wholly within the control of that community, and as institutions commonly led by strong individuals who had won their positions through demonstrated leadership abilities (however variously defined), the churches wielded vast authority over the diurnal affairs of their communicants, sternly enforcing social codes such as monogamy and temperance and vigorously promoting personal values such as industry, thrift, and reliability. Ministers made full use of the traditional instruments of church discipline, from public chastisement to outright expulsion, and of the traditional modes of formal teaching, from the sermon to the Sunday school lesson. In effect, the congregations of the Afro-American churches became self-organized, highly disciplined educative communities led by powerful and frequently charismatic preacher-teachers.

Beyond the education proffered by the churches themselves—and many churches actually served during the week as day schools—there was the elaborate system of denominational schools and colleges for blacks that had begun to grow up during Reconstruction. The product was a vast missionary effort led by the American Missionary Association (Congregationalist), the Freedmen's Aid Society of the Methodist Episcopal Church, the American Baptist Home Mission Society, and the missionary arms of the Presbyterian Church, North, the Protestant Episcopal Church, and the Society of Friends; the institutions were essentially mission schools, seen by their predominantly white sponsors and teachers as key instruments for the redemption of the South through the regeneration of the former slaves. By 1895 there were twenty-seven such colleges, along with Wilberforce University, Lincoln University, and Berea College, which had been founded before the Civil War, and sixty-two secondary schools. They stood alongside Atlanta, Howard, and Leland universities, which were conducted under independent auspices, and thirteen predominantly black land-grant institutions, most of them founded under the provisions of the so-called Second Morrill Act of 1890, permitting states to divide federal funds in support of agricultural and mechanic arts colleges between separate institutions for white and black students. At least until the Great Migration of the early twentieth century, these institutions, located primarily in the border states and the South, provided most of the formal schooling beyond training for minimal literacy available to most black Americans.

Granted the differences among the denominational institutions— Meharry Medical College was obviously specialized, as were Gammon Theological Seminary and Richmond Theological Seminary; Berea College was racially integrated while Spelman Seminary was solely for women—they were similar in crucial aspects that profoundly affected the formal education of the first generation of post-Emancipation southern black leaders. For one thing, as missionary institutions they shared in the world-wide phenomenon of missionaries bringing what they deemed to be a superior morality and culture to the newly converted heathen. Indeed, in the minds of the dedicated whites who came South to evangelize them, the emancipated slaves were not very different from the Chinese heathen. It is not surprising, therefore, that the missionary schools and colleges of the American South during the 1890's bore a striking resemblance to the missionary schools and colleges that Americans were conducting in India, China, and Africa. They conveyed a characteristic combination of moral and academic instruction, skill training for a developing agricultural economy in the early phases of industrialization, and acculturation to the larger American society as viewed from the vantage point of the missionaries. The institutions were small and underfinanced; the vast majority of the students, even in the self-styled colleges and universities, worked at the elementary- or secondary-school levels; and even among those who enrolled in the collegiate courses only a small percentage graduated. And, while there were instances like Bennett College in Greensboro, North Carolina, and Biddle University in Charlotte, North Carolina, that by the 1890's had all-black faculties led by black presidents, most of the institutions had predominantly white faculties led by white presidents.

James M. McPherson has pointed incisively to the puritan strain that ran through most of the denominational colleges. Like the evangelical institutions of the 1840's and 1850's—for example, Oberlin College in Ohio or Knox College in Illinois, which sent so many of their graduates to the southern evangelical crusade—they were self-contained moral communities dedicated to the formation of a leadership class of black teachers and preachers. "We have texts of scripture, prayers and singing every evening after supper before rising from the table, & a prayer meeting every other thing," observed the wife of an Atlanta University faculty member in 1875. "Rather an excess of a good thing but it helps to keep the pupils occupied & in order & keeps a strong religious influence around them which is important as of course much of their usefulness will depend upon their religious training." Beyond the explicit pieties and devotions, there were strictly enforced codes of behavior proscribing liquor and tobacco, regulating relations between the sexes, and generally overseeing the diurnal comings and goings of the students. The assumption behind the effort was not unlike the assumption behind John R. Mott's contemporary effort to win China for Christ—a class of people given to dependency, carelessness, infidelity, and hedonism needed to be converted to true Christian behavior, and, with it, civilization. As W. E. B. Du Bois remarked in 1891, when opposing a federal election bill to enforce black voting rights in the South, "A good many of our people . . . are not fit for the responsibility of republican government. When you have the right sort of black voters you will need no election laws. The battle of my people must be a moral one, not a legal or a physical one."[2]

When Du Bois published his study of *The College-Bred Negro* in 1900, it was clear that in certain respects the hopes of the missionaries were being realized. Of 1,252 living black college graduates who reported their occupations, 54 percent were teachers and 17 percent were clergymen. The colleges, and doubtless the secondary schools with them, were indeed training up a representative leadership class for the Afro-American community. Moreover, when the respondents were queried as to what would be the best solution to the race problem in the years ahead, again and again they referred to the missionary virtues of hard work, education, self-discipline, and character. The puritan curriculum had fashioned the puritan leadership the mission-

2. James M. McPherson, "The New Puritanism: Values and Goals of Freedmen's Education in America," in Lawrence Stone, ed., *The University in Society* (2 vols.; Princeton: Princeton University Press, 1974), II, 611–639; the quotations are given at 622–623 and 628.

aries had envisioned—or at least partly envisioned. For, as with missionary efforts elsewhere, the outcomes began to go quite beyond the intentions of the sponsors as the new black leadership increasingly used education for its own purposes.[3]

In the first place, blocked as they were in access to the polls and to public office, Afro-American leaders demanded power at least in the institutions that had prepared them and in which they would prepare their successors, namely, the churches, the colleges, and the schools. True, they already led the denominations that enrolled the greatest numbers of their fellow blacks, the American Baptist Convention and the several black Methodist churches; and true, too, they controlled the dozen institutions like Wilberforce University and Livingstone College that their own denominations had established. But the last decade of the nineteenth century and the first decades of the twentieth saw widespread demands for black bishops where there were significant numbers of black communicants in predominantly white churches and for black presidents and principals and black faculty members in predominantly black colleges and schools. It was a protracted and often bitter struggle. And as late as 1915, when Thomas Jesse Jones made his survey of black schools under the joint auspices of the Phelps-Stokes Fund and the United States Bureau of Education, while the schools and colleges conducted under Northern Baptist and Methodist auspices had predominantly black faculties, most of the Methodist schools had white principals and all the Methodist colleges had white presidents; on the other hand, the schools and colleges conducted by the American Missionary Association still had predominantly white faculties and most had white principals and presidents. It would be another quarter-century before the received missionary leadership of the nineteenth and early twentieth centuries would be replaced by a leadership drawn from the Afro-American community itself.[4]

Beyond their reach for control, Afro-American leaders scrutinized the curriculum itself and proffered both criticisms and programs of reform based on clearly articulated visions of the future of the Afro-American community. There was, of course, the spirited controversy between Booker T. Washington of Tuskegee and W. E. B. Du Bois of Atlanta. What is often forgotten is that each in his own right was a

3. W. E. B. Du Bois, ed., *The College-Bred Negro* (Atlanta: Atlanta University Press, 1900), pp. 63–64, 91, 93.

4. [Thomas Jesse Jones], *Negro Education: A Study of the Private and Higher Schools for Colored People in the United States* (2 vols.; U.S., Bureau of Education, Bulletin, 1916, No. 36; Washington, D.C.: Government Printing Office, 1917).

critic of missionary education. Washington, educated at Hampton Institute and then at Wayland Seminary, a small theological school in Washington, D.C., sponsored by the American Baptist Home Missionary Society, developed the program of industrial education at Tuskegee during the 1880's as a criticism of what he perceived to be the overly academic education of some of the denominational colleges and as a reform effort to enable Afro-Americans to achieve self-respect and economic independence. Du Bois, educated at Harvard, sharply attacked Washington's arguments and programs, contending that only academic and professional education of the highest quality could prepare the "talented tenth" for adequate leadership of the Afro-American community. "He advocates common-school and industrial training, and depreciates institutions of higher learning," Du Bois wrote of Washington in his classic attack on industrial education in *The Souls of Black Folk* (1903); "but neither the Negro common-schools, nor Tuskegee itself, could remain open a day were it not for teachers trained in Negro colleges, or trained by their graduates." No educational system for blacks or whites, Du Bois insisted, could rest on any basis other than that of well-equipped colleges and universities that would "train the best of the Negro youth as teachers, professional men, and leaders." Economic independence without full civil and political equality could never lead to true self-respect; and industrial education alone would never lead to civil and political equality.[5]

Three decades later, Carter Woodson, an alumnus of Berea College who had gone on to do graduate work at the University of Chicago and at Harvard, excoriated both the Washington and the Du Bois positions, attacking the proponents of industrial education for their unreality in preparing young blacks for jobs that had been rendered obsolete by industrial development or for jobs from which they were barred by racial discrimination, and attacking the proponents of literary education for their unreality in believing that the same studies of letters and the classics that prepared whites for leadership would also prepare blacks. In effect, Woodson charged, the "educated Negro" had been taught "to admire the Hebrew, the Greek, the Latin and the Teuton and to despise the African." He had been robbed of his Afro-American heritage and alienated from the deepest values of the Afro-American community. As such, he was ill equipped even to understand his fellow Afro-Americans, much less to lead them by instill-

5. W. E. Burghardt Du Bois, *The Souls of Black Folk: Essays and Sketches* [1903] (reprint ed.; New York: The Blue Heron Press, 1953), pp. 52, 54.

ing in them the pride that would enable them to participate fully in American life.[6]

In 1964, E. Franklin Frazier, the distinguished black sociologist who had been educated at Howard University and had then gone on to graduate study at the University of Chicago, delivered his ironic criticism of the Afro-American church. Its very power and pervasiveness, developed during Reconstruction and after as a device for preparing the emancipated slave community for citizenship, was now hampering the assimilation of Afro-Americans into the larger American community, he claimed. Lower-class blacks were seeking solace in the emotionalism of the Pentecostal sects or in the utopianism of Holiness cults like the Father Divine Peace Mission Movement or in separatist movements like the Moorish Science Temple of America. Middle-class blacks, on the other hand, were finding themselves unsatisfactorily limited by the traditional black Baptist and Methodist churches and seeking upward mobility through membership in the Presbyterian, Congregationalist, Episcopal, or Roman Catholic churches. The singular role of the black church in Afro-American life, Frazier counseled, had derived from the restricted rights to participation of Afro-Americans in American society. The more they won those rights, however, the more the walls of segregation came tumbling down, the more traditional black churches headed by traditional black preachers would have to give way to new forms that would propel blacks into an integrated American community at the same time that they provided them with a continuing experiential education in democratic processes.[7]

During the eight decades between the establishment of Tuskegee and Frazier's critique, the Afro-American community had changed radically. Demographically, the great migrations of the late nineteenth and twentieth centuries had made it more national and more urban. At the end of the Civil War over 92 percent of American blacks lived in the South and the overwhelming majority of those lived in rural areas. Beginning in the 1890's a vast redistribution occurred, from the South to other regions, principally the northeastern and northcentral states, and from the country to the city. By 1980 slightly under half the Afro-American population lived outside the South, and

6. Carter Godwin Woodson, *The Mis-education of the Negro* (Washington, D.C.: The Associated Publishers, 1933), p. 1.

7. E. Franklin Frazier, *The Negro Church in America* (Liverpool: Liverpool University Press, 1964).

three out of every four Afro-Americans lived in urban and suburban regions, with the largest concentrations in New York, Chicago, Philadelphia, Detroit, Washington, and Los Angeles, and with significant concentrations as well in Baltimore, New Orleans, Atlanta, Birmingham, and Memphis. Socially, the great migrations had been as profoundly disruptive for the Afro-Americans as immigration had been for the European-Americans, with the result that they were thrown anew upon the resources of their churches, still in many instances the only institutions over which they retained full control. The impact of this upon the churches was to render them even more sensitive to the emerging needs of their urban parishioners. More than ever, the church was not only a refuge but also a community welfare institution and, in time, a nursery of social action programs. In effect, the institutional church assumed new and particular relevance in the Afro-American community. Educationally, the great migrations had also had profound consequences. They opened up opportunity for schooling in institutions other than the underfinanced public and denominational schools and colleges of the South, with the result that, despite the egregious inequities of schooling in the urban ghettos, a more cosmopolitan education had gradually become available to potential black leaders. The church remained central in the configuration of institutions educating blacks; but increasingly there were more and more varied opportunities for teaching and learning elsewhere as well.

Given the historic role of the black churches, then, and their apt responses to demographic and social changes, it is not surprising that they provided one chief source of the civil rights leadership of the 1960's. Many individual churches and church organizations were involved, but surely Martin Luther King, Jr., and his Southern Christian Leadership Conference were the pre-eminent examples. King was the product of the historic configuration of black education: boyhood in the home of the Reverend Martin Luther King, Sr., and in the elder King's church, the Ebenezer Baptist Church of Atlanta; and undergraduate training at Morehouse College, where the president, the Reverend Benjamin Mays, became the younger King's mentor, model, and counselor. Having decided on a career as a pastor-teacher, Martin went from Morehouse to Crozer Theological Seminary in Pennsylvania, where he discovered, in turn, Thoreau's idea of civil disobedience, Gandhi's idea of passive resistance, and Walter Rauschenbusch's conception of the Social Gospel. Continuing with his studies at Boston University, King fashioned these ideas into his own philosophy of social action, which he then put into effect as pastor of the Dexter Avenue Baptist Church in Montgomery. (King's option of choosing Crozer and then Boston University exemplified the fact that middle-class southern blacks were no longer confined to predominantly black educational institutions in the South; they had increasing access to predominantly white institutions in the North.) The Montgomery bus boycott of 1955–56 gave him the opportunity for leadership; and, following the doctrines of passive resistance increasingly known to leaders of the black community as a result of the conferences, lectures, and workshops sponsored by institutions like the Highlander Folk School in Tennessee, he triumphed. The Southern Christian Leadership Conference, which he organized in 1957 to provide the "spiritual" counterpart of the NAACP's "legal" strategy (as well as a more popular counterpart of the NAACP's elite character), subsequently furnished the base for his civil rights activity, initially in the South and soon in the nation at large and throughout the world. To the very moment of his assassination on April 4, 1968, he provided a leadership that transformed what had been intended during the early twentieth century as an education for accommodation into an education for change and liberation, his vision being of an integrated society in which Afro-Americans would participate on a completely equal basis. And, given his vision, the triumph of his leadership ultimately lay in its active acceptance by people of all races, in the United States and elsewhere. There were those who dissented, of course. There were the younger separatists of the Student Nonviolent Coordinating Committee, who believed that only through disciplined autonomy could blacks achieve the power they needed to claim their legitimate rights in the American political and social structure. And there was the charismatic Malcolm X, whose odyssey was particularly interesting because it led through another characteristic configuration of black education—boyhood in the home of the Garveyite son of a Baptist minister, a brief period in an all-white school in Michigan, apprentice training in the Harlem underworld, and then conversion to the Nation of Islam in a Massachusetts prison, as well as the use of his training to create an education for black liberation through a separatist Afro-American Muslim community, connected spiritually and politically with the emerging African states and insulated socially and ideologically from the "devilishness" of white America.

Finally, given the new situation in which the historically black schools and colleges found themselves, it is not surprising that, like the black churches, they too underwent transformation. Particularly after the decision of the United States Supreme Court in the case of *Brown v. Board of Education* in 1954, Afro-Americans North and South alike had increasing (though never assured) access to integrated institutions; and, with the expansion of public higher education across the country, black students found themselves with attractive alternatives to the older denominational black colleges. Those colleges, on their side, found themselves in a tense and difficult situation between two worlds. On the one hand, like the black churches, they had served their clienteles best in segregated situations—their very strength derived from racial segregation; with the decline of racial segregation in higher education, that strength waned, however well their special experience enabled them to deal with the particular needs and problems of young black men and women. On the other hand, not only underfinanced but underenrolled, they found themselves wanting in academic comparison with predominantly white and integrated institutions. By 1980 some had faltered and foundered; some had converted themselves into public, multiracial institutions; and some were transforming themselves into first-rate academic centers that, like all other American institutions of higher education, would always bear the marks of their distinctive historical experience.

III

The overwhelming majority of black Americans in the 1870's and 1880's had been born in the United States. Mostly former slaves or the children of former slaves, their place in American society was redefined by emancipation but the redefinition was immeasurably complicated by the stark fact of continuing racial discrimination. The black churches played a crucial role in sustaining and nurturing black Americans during the period of their ironclad segregation and in providing them with leadership in their massive drive to secure their civil rights during the years following World War II. Roman Catholics faced a fundamentally different situation. Their community was the product of a continuing migration from Europe and Central and South America and had begun with small numbers of French Catholics during the colonial period, continued with much larger numbers of Irish and German Catholics during the second third of the nineteenth century, and then revived with even larger numbers of southern and eastern European Catholics during the years after Reconstruction. In 1880 they constituted the largest single church in the nation, with 6,259,000 communicants out of a total population of

50,155,783, and their growth thereafter was steady and rapid, particularly during the first years of the twentieth century, so that by 1910 their numbers had increased to 16,363,000 and by 1920, to 19,828,-000.[8]

Some German and Czech Catholics chose to farm and settled in rural communities of the Midwest. Most Catholics, however, concentrated in the cities of the East and Midwest. The Irish preferred New York, Boston, and Philadelphia. The Germans headed for the cities embraced within the triangle defined by Cincinnati, Milwaukee, and St. Louis. The Italians, Poles, Lithuanians, Slovaks, Croats, Slovenes, Ukrainians, and Hungarians, who constituted the bulk of those who came between 1880 and 1920, flocked to the Pennsylvania coal fields and the industrial cities of the Midwest. The Mexicans gravitated to the cities and towns of the Southwest, notably of Texas and California, while small numbers of French Canadians located in the northern communities of Maine, Vermont, Massachusetts, New Hampshire, New York, and Michigan. All told, they made for an extraordinarily variegated American Catholic community.

As a community, they inherited certain traditions and policies that derived from the Catholic accommodation to the pre–Civil War social and cultural situation. For one thing, the evangelical united front had campaigned systematically against Catholic influence from the 1830's on: Lyman Beecher had warned against the forces of darkness incarnate in the clergy and parishioners of the Roman Catholic Church in his campaign to save the West for Christ, and Josiah Strong had warned against these same forces in his campaign to save the cities for Christ. In the process, Beecher and Strong had sought to define not only Protestantism but also Americanism in contradistinction to Catholicism. One result was that Catholics in turn had banded together for mutual sustenance and protection, their neighborhoods—frequently parishes—constituting oases of familiarity in the desert of Protestant hostility. In addition, they had assertively proclaimed their own true Americanism, contending in the process that Americanism came in plural forms and not in the single pattern of a Protestant *paideia.* Another result was that Catholics had developed their own alternative configurations of education in order to preserve their faith

8. I have used the statistics presented in Gerald Shaughnessy, *Has the Immigrant Kept the Faith: A Study of Immigration and Catholic Growth in the United States, 1790–1920* (New York: The Macmillan Company, 1925) rather than those presented in U.S. Department of Commerce, Bureau of the Census, *Historical Statistics of the United States, Colonial Times to 1970* (2 vols.; Washington, D.C.: Government Printing Office, 1975), I, 391–392. Shaughnessy, whose estimates tend to be larger, discusses the differences in chap. xii.

against the onslaught of Protestant evangelism: their parishes supported, not only churches with their ancillary educational programs, but also newspapers, magazines, social clubs, cultural societies, youth organizations, and, pre-eminently, parochial schools. Growing out of the great school wars in New York and other cities during the 1840's and 1850's, American Catholics, in an accommodation to the American scene unique in world-wide Roman Catholicism, had developed a large, privately supported parallel system of elementary and secondary schooling for their children. The decision had been repeatedly supported and confirmed by the American hierarchy, culminating in the decree of the Third Plenary Council of Baltimore in 1884 making it mandatory that, within two years of the promulgation of the Council, a parochial school be erected near each Catholic church (unless one was already in operation) and that parents send their children to Catholic schools unless released from that obligation by the ordinary of the diocese. That decree, along with other decrees of the Council encouraging Catholic high schools, academies, and colleges, providing for diocesan boards of education, and arranging for the establishment of a Catholic University of America, for all intents and purposes established a Catholic school system in the United States. From the 1880's to the middle 1960's, it was the formal goal of the Church to have every Catholic child in a Catholic school.

One other accommodation to the American scene also marked the practices of this quintessentially immigrant church, namely, the national parish. Whereas the French had dominated the Roman Catholic Church and its hierarchy in America during the late eighteenth and early nineteenth centuries, the Irish had rapidly replaced them in positions of leadership during the 1840's, with the result that American Catholicism increasingly took on an Irish cast. When the German Catholics confronted that situation in New York, Philadelphia, Cleveland, Chicago, and Milwaukee, during the 1840's and 1850's, they insistently demanded their own German parishes, led by German-speaking priests sympathetic to their desire for hymns, sermons, and paraliturgical church services in the German vernacular, and for parish schools that would make the German language and literature a central feature of their curriculum. Put otherwise, they viewed the American, English-speaking church as an Irish church and saw justice in their insistence upon their own German church. By the 1860's an accommodation had been worked out in all five cities in which the bishops, after considerable prodding, agreed to create or legitimatize

German parishes staffed by German priests, either recruited from Europe or drawn from the German community in the United States. Later, when significant numbers of Poles, Italians, Slovaks, and others arrived in these cities, they found the extant Irish and German churches as unsatisfactory as the Germans had found the Irish churches, and they in turn demanded and won their own parishes and schools. As a result, for all the formality of its hierarchical organization, the Roman Catholic Church in the United States was a plural, ethnically defined community church, and its educational programs inevitably reflected the tensions inherent in that pluralism.

Given those tensions, three internal conflicts that racked the Catholic Church in America in the last decades of the nineteenth century and first decades of the twentieth had especially profound consequences for education: the conflict over pluralism, the conflict over Americanism, and the conflict over modernism. The conflict over pluralism erupted in specific form when Peter Paul Cahensly, a deputy in the German Reichstag who was also secretary of the St. Raphael Society, a group that looked after the interests of German emigrants in other countries, began to press in Rome for the appointment of American Catholic clergymen on the basis of the ethnic composition of the American Catholic population. On behalf of St. Raphael Societies in Germany, Austria, Italy, Belgium, and Switzerland, Cahensly presented a memorial to Pope Leo XIII in 1891 calling for the creation of ethnic parishes in the United States and the appointment of "priests of the same nationality to which the faithful belong," for the establishment of parochial schools in which the mother tongue of the faithful as well as the language of the adopted country would be taught, and for the appointment of bishops of sufficiently varied ethnicity so that "in the assemblies of bishops, every immigrant race would be represented, and its interests and needs would be protected." James Cardinal Gibbons, the acknowledged leader of the American hierarchy, vigorously protested the memorial and the concerns it engendered in Rome, contending that the whole affair was an unjustified interference in American church affairs by meddlesome European gentlemen. The immediate issue of church governance was settled in 1892 when Gibbons received a letter from the Papal Secretary of State, Cardinal Mariano Rampolla del Tindaro, informing him that the St. Raphael Societies' memorial had been rejected, though the letter did encourage the American bishops to pay special heed to immigrant needs. But the implicit issue of education remained. In

1889 the Massachusetts legislature had considered a bill requiring children from eight to fourteen to attend schools offering an "English education," and in 1890 the Wisconsin legislature had enacted the so-called Bennett Law, requiring the use of English in the teaching of certain subjects. The threat of the first and the actuality of the second had dramatized to American Catholics and non-Catholics alike the issue of ethnic parish schools and indeed had divided Catholics as to appropriate responses. Even so, the pressure for ethnic parishes and schools persisted; and, after Poles began to form Polish national churches in the 1890's and Lithuanians began to form Lithuanian national churches after 1900, the Church hierarchy found it politic to pay special heed to immigrant needs by appointing ethnic priests and bishops.[9]

The conflict over Americanization raised many of the same issues. Gibbons's generation of Catholic churchmen—he was archbishop of Baltimore from 1877 until his death in 1921—was particularly intent upon working out an American Catholicism in which Catholic policy and polity would be uniquely adapted to American conditions and, in the end, expressive of one version of Americanism. In the domain of education, this meant supporting the hopes and plans of Gibbons's friend and close associate Archbishop John Ireland of St. Paul, Minnesota. Born in Kilkenny, Ireland, in 1838, the son of a carpenter, and educated at the Séminaire de Meximieux and then the Scholasticat à Monthel in France, Ireland went on to become the quintessential spokesman for an American Catholic church. He worked closely with John J. Keane and John Lancaster Spalding in vigorously espousing proposals for a national Catholic university at the Third Plenary Council in 1884 and then at Rome, and he steadfastly supported the Catholic University of America after it was established in Washington in 1889, with Keane as rector. He sharply opposed the vicar general of the Milwaukee diocese in 1886 when that official urged the appointment of German priests and bishops, and he vigorously attacked the memorial of the St. Raphael Societies in 1891, seeing the arguments of the Cahenslyites as foreign attempts to undermine the Americanism of the American church. And he took the lead in planning for an American Catholic school system, playing a central role in the development of the education decrees of the Third Plenary Council and

9. The complete text of the St. Raphael Societies' memorial is given in Colman J. Barry, *The Catholic Church and the German Americans* (Milwaukee: The Bruce Publishing Company, 1953), pp. 313–315.

then in the formulation of the compromise associated with the so-called Faribault and Stillwater Plans during the 1890s.

As a framer of the education decrees, Ireland was a staunch supporter of the parochial schools. Yet he saw no conflict between that position and a genuine interest in the public schools. "I am the friend and the advocate of the state school," he told the delegates to the convention of the National Educational Association at St. Paul in 1890. "In the circumstances of the present time," he continued, "I uphold the parish school. I do sincerely wish that the need of it did not exist. I would have all schools for the children of the people state schools." The following year he went on to arrange for the parochial schools of Faribault and Stillwater (two towns within the Archdiocese of St. Paul) to be turned over to the local public school boards and converted into public schools, taught by the same teachers who had taught before the transfer and attended by the same pupils. Under the plan each town would have two public schools, the public school that had existed before and the "Catholic school," and the only difference between the two would be that nuns would teach the usual public-school curriculum to the students in the "Catholic school" during regular school hours and then give religious instruction after school hours. An ingenious accommodation, it resembled a variety of arrangements that had been tried earlier and elsewhere—in Lowell, Massachusetts, during the 1840's and in Poughkeepsie and various other towns of New York during the 1870's and 1880's; nevertheless, it drew fire from several sources. Within the Catholic Church it was attacked by Germans, who wanted parochial schools stressing the German language and literature, and by conservatives, who saw the accommodation as a patent violation of canon law as well as a clear abrogation of the various requirements of the Third Plenary Council that Ireland had led in promulgating. Outside the Catholic Church it was attacked by those who saw it as a patent violation of the constitutional principle requiring the separation of church and state as well as a crass scheme for getting the taxpayers to pay for parochial schools. With respect to the criticisms from within the Church, Gibbons and Ireland actually petitioned the Sacred Congregation of the Propaganda in Rome for approval of the arrangements, and a letter from that body on April 21, 1892, ruled that Ireland's plan could be allowed in view of the circumstances, but that the decrees of the Council of Baltimore on parochial schools remained firmly in force.

With respect to the criticism from without, the matter shortly became moot, since the arrangements in Faribault and Stillwater were soon cancelled in the heat of political controversy.[10]

Interestingly, the Minnesota experience stimulated an extraordinary debate between the Reverend Thomas Bouquillon, a Belgian theologian who held the chair of moral sciences at the Catholic University of America, and a spate of critics, including the Reverend Rene I. Holaind, the professor of ethics at the Jesuit Scholasticate at Woodstock, Maryland, and the Reverend Salvatore M. Brandi, an editor of the Jesuit review *Civiltà Cattolica* in Rome. Bouquillon took the position that the state shared rights in education with parents and the church, a view that had been espoused by the lay Catholic convert Orestes Brownson during the 1850's and by the Reverend Isaac T. Hecker, editor of the *Catholic World,* during the 1870's. Holaind and Brandi contended that the state had no such right, shared or otherwise, and that to grant such rights to the state was contrary to Catholic doctrine. There were those who tried to have Bouquillon's views condemned in Rome; but Ireland vigorously defended them before the same cardinals of the Sacred Congregation of the Propaganda who were considering the validity of his own experiments at Faribault and Stillwater, and in the end Bouquillon was neither condemned nor rebuked.

Finally, there were the conflicts over modernism, which included those surrounding Ireland's experiments and Bouquillon's arguments concerning the state's right to educate but went far beyond to include the nature and authority of Biblical criticism, the structure and content of clerical training, the role of the Church in social reform, and, more generally, the reconciliation of Catholic doctrine with secular culture. Of particular importance were the debates over the education of women, which raged throughout the 1890's, with liberals like Isaac T. Hecker arguing that women had the right to any position whose duties and functions they had the intelligence and competence to fulfill and that Catholic education had the responsibility to give meaning to that right, while conservatives maintained that women could find all the satisfaction they needed in the life of the Catholic home along with the other opportunities the Church had traditionally afforded for appropriate service, and that Catholic edu-

10. John Ireland, "State Schools and Parish Schools," in National Educational Association, *Proceedings and Addresses,* 1890, p. 179. A translation of the Propaganda's decision is given in Daniel F. Reilly, *The School Controversy (1891–1893)* (Washington, D.C.: The Catholic University of America Press, 1943), pp. 160–162.

cation had the obligation to prepare them for the calling the Creator
had patently intended them for, namely, that of wives and mothers.

However significant these national (and international) debates
were for the education conveyed by the Catholic Church, it is also
necessary, given the variegated character of the American Catholic
community, to consider what happened in particular localities. The
experience of Chicago is instructive. Originally settled in the 1820's,
it had become a city of 503,185 by 1880, and it grew rapidly over the
next thirty years by roughly a half-million inhabitants per decade. Of
these, substantial proportions were immigrants, with the result that
in 1910 some 77 percent of Chicago's inhabitants were newcomers or
the children of newcomers. Just as the Catholic Church was quintessentially the church of the immigrant, so was Chicago quintessentially
the city of the immigrant.

Following the national pattern, the earliest Catholic inhabitants of
the city were principally of French background, but the situation
changed radically during the late 1830's and 1840's with a large influx
of Irish as well as German Catholics. By 1880, though the Irish remained a minority within the city as a whole and indeed in most of
the localities where they had settled, they came to dominate the ecclesiastical administration of the Chicago diocese, which had been
created in 1844, and they had also formed highly visible and assertively cohesive ethnoreligious communities within the neighborhoods
in which they lived. It was for the maintenance of that cohesion that
they had also formed a characteristically ethnoreligious configuration
of education.

At the heart of this configuration was the parish church presided
over by a priest of Irish background who was often a prestigious,
indefatigable, and ubiquitous participant in the communal life of his
parish, providing food and fuel to the needy, finding jobs for the
unemployed, acting as a mediator in labor disputes, and generally
serving as counselor, arbiter, and friend in the diurnal lives of young
and old alike. Closely tied to the local church were a variety of organizations intended to address the social, economic, and cultural needs
of the parishioners—a St. Vincent de Paul Society to assist the poor,
a Catholic Total Abstinence Union to promote the cause of temperance, a branch of the Ancient Order of Hibernians or the Irish National League to promulgate the doctrines of Irish nationalism, a local
Democratic club to assist in the election of Irish-Catholic officials and
the subsequent delivery of political patronage, a union of hod carriers
and an association of policemen to look after the interests of Irish

workingmen. Also central to the configuration was a parochial school, probably staffed by nuns of the Irish Sisters of Mercy; and providing it with cultural substance were Catholic publishers who supplied the books, magazines, newspapers, and pamphlets from which the children were taught and through which the adults received and articulated the ideas that defined their community and its members. However various the origins of Chicago's Irish Catholics, this configuration knit them together into a community; it insulated them against the hostility of the dominant Protestant majority at the same time that it nurtured in them the self-confidence to venture forth into the community. What is more, in developing their own particular *paideia,* Irish Catholics in the United States erected a church that was less Irish and more Catholic than the church they had known in Ireland, adapting it to the conditions of life they found in America and especially to the demands of Protestant hostility.

As with the German Catholics in New York, Philadelphia, Milwaukee, and Cleveland, German Catholics in Chicago established their own churches and schools as early as 1846. Moreover, with the active cooperation of the Irish-born bishop, William Quarter, the Germans developed their own traditions and organizations rooted in the German language and culture and created their own German counterparts of the Irish configurations of education to perpetuate those traditions and organizations. Language was at the heart of the effort—"language saves faith" was an aphorism heard again and again in German-American Catholic communities; music became more central in church services; *Unterstützung-Vereine* (mutual benefit societies) stood in place of Irish nationalist organizations and German orders of nuns in place of Irish Sisters of Mercy. Later, as Polish, Bohemian, and French Catholics arrived in significant numbers during the 1880's, they found the German as well as the American (Irish) churches and schools unsatisfying and proceeded to found their own. By the time Rome formally recognized the existence of ethnic parishes in the United States in 1887, Chicago boasted thirty-five territorial parishes, that is, parishes organized with respect to geographical areas but essentially Irish in character, as well as eighteen German, six Polish, five Bohemian, and two French parishes. Still later, when the Lithuanians and the Italians arrived in significant numbers during the 1890's and after 1900, they in turn found the Polish, Bohemian, and French churches and schools unsatisfactory. Thus, when the Lithuanians organized their own parish but had to employ Polish nuns for their schools, there being no Lithuanian teachers available, some fifteen hundred Lithuanian parishioners complained to the diocese about "Polish sisters, incompetent to speak the Lithuanian language . . . who through ignorance convert our children into Poles." Further, when Lithuanian young women began joining the religious order of the Polish teachers, their Lithuanian priests objected and urged them either to form a special Lithuanian unit of the order or to join the Sisters of St. Casimir, an order explicitly formed to conduct parish schools for Lithuanian-Americans.[11]

There was another side to the process of ethnic succession, however, as assimilation began to affect the behavior of the older groups. As early as the 1880's, second-generation German Catholics began to attend the Irish territorial churches and to send their children to Irish parochial schools where English was the language of instruction, and German parishes, in turn, began to report not only the loss of parishioners to other churches but also the desire of second-generation German parishioners to have services conducted in English. Over time, that phenomenon also repeated itself, though the rapidity with which it occurred varied from group to group. It was a phenomenon that in general enabled George Cardinal Mundelein to move forward toward a consolidation of parishes (and schools) during the 1920's and 1930's based on predominantly territorial parishes that would have been politically impossible—or at least vulnerable to major schisms—a generation earlier.

In addition to the acceptance of English as a common language, another important influence for assimilation stemmed from several of the colleges and universities founded in the diocese. Catholic secondary schools tended to be sponsored by the several ethnic groups, as were the general academies, seminaries, and normal schools organized to prepare the various ethnic orders of teaching sisters and brothers (some of these later evolved into collegiate institutions). And some of the colleges derived from similar sources—St. Procopius College, for example, was founded to help preserve the ethnic heritage of Czech Catholics, and St. Stanislaus College to do likewise for Polish Catholics. But the larger Catholic institutions of higher education in Chicago, Loyola and DePaul universities, were explicitly intended to cater to students from various ethnic groups, and indeed DePaul early established a branch at the Academy of Our Lady for the School Sisters of Notre Dame (French) and at St. Casimir's Convent

11. Barry discusses the sources of the slogan "language saves faith" in *The Catholic Church and the German Americans,* pp. 10–11; the complaint of the Lithuanian parishioners is given in James W. Sanders, *The Education of an Urban Minority: Catholics in Chicago, 1833–1965* (New York: Oxford University Press, 1977), p. 30.

(Lithuanian), providing the sisters with their first systematic exposure to ideas from beyond their own ethnoreligious traditions.

The years from the end of World War I to the middle 1960's were an era of great expansion and prosperity for the American Catholic Church. The great "consolidating bishops"—George W. Mundelein of Chicago, William H. O'Connell of Boston, Denis J. Dougherty of Philadelphia, Patrick J. Hayes of New York—vigorously developed the church itself, and especially its organizational structures and financial support, and with it the configuration of education intended to nurture and perpetuate its beliefs. In developing education they supported earlier bases for assimilation by moving beyond a patchwork of ethnoreligious institutions to build what they saw as a more uniformly American Catholic education, with American Catholic schools, colleges, and universities at its center, and with a network of American Catholic educational and cultural organizations and institutions serving it—Catholic scouting societies and youth organizations, Catholic poetry societies and scholarly organizations, Catholic book clubs and theater guilds, and Catholic magazines and newspapers. In the process, owing in part to social and demographic changes within the Catholic community, not least the movement of significant numbers of Catholics into the middle class, they were also able to transform the variegated pluralism and parochialism of loosely joined ethnoreligious institutions into a large, comprehensive, and more integrated educational system, connected at many points with other systems of American education and culture but nevertheless studiedly set apart from it. By 1960, a Catholic population of 42,000,000 was supporting more than 13,000 Catholic elementary and secondary schools that enrolled more than 5,600,000 students as well as almost 400 colleges and universities that varied in size and character from small undergraduate institutions intended solely to meet the needs of teaching orders of nuns and brothers to large universities like Notre Dame, Fordham, and the Catholic University of America. Yet, by 1960, though the system obviously had its boosters, it was eliciting fundamental questions from the very individuals one might consider to have been its most distinguished products. The Catholic historian John Tracy Ellis, for example, pointed to the absence of a love of learning for its own sake in the Catholic community, and to a pervasive overemphasis on moralism in Catholic schools and colleges as contrasted with intellectual development; and a chorus of Catholic sociologists pointed to the failure of American lay Catholics to distinguish themselves in the world of scholarship. In somewhat the same fashion as the predominantly black colleges and universities, the

Catholic colleges and universities were playing an important role in making education available to the children of a minority community in a somewhat protected environment; but, according to some of the most prominent graduates of those Catholic colleges and universities, they were doing so at a price of the intellectual and academic achievement of the community and its young people.[12]

However impressive the development and vitality of the Catholic configuration of education during the 1960's, and however eloquent its testimony to the unremitting effort of the Catholic community to nurture its deepest values in its young, the entire system was shaken to its foundations by the forces set in motion by the Second Vatican Council in Rome (1962–1965). The very character of the Catholic Church in America, from its liturgy to its social organizations, was called into question, as were the assumptions and purposes of Catholic education. The number of seminarians, nuns, and teaching brothers peaked during the mid-1960's and then began to fall off, while the Catholic community at large continued to expand—to 50,450,000 in 1980. And the whole enterprise of parochial elementary and secondary schools and of Catholic colleges and universities and of separate Catholic intellectual and cultural organizations began to be challenged—explicitly in debates over their necessity, as well as implicitly in the failure of the system to attract the financial support, the teaching personnel (underpaid nuns and brothers had supported it for years with the contributions of their time and effort), and the clientele it required. The precise outcome was not yet discernible in the early 1980's, though what was clear was that the isolation of Roman Catholic education from other parts of the American educational system was a thing of the past and that Roman Catholic education would be much more cosmopolitan during the years ahead and much more closely related to other parts of the American education system.[13]

Granted this, there was a demographic fact of enormous significance that also had to be taken into consideration, the effect of which was less predictable, namely, the drastic change in the social composition of the American Catholic community occasioned by the influx during the 1970's and 1980's of large numbers of Hispanic Catholics and, to a lesser extent, large numbers of South Asian Catholics.

12. John Tracy Ellis, "American Catholics and the Intellectual Life," *Thought*, XXX (1955), 351–388; John J. Kane, *Catholic-Protestant Conflicts in America* (Chicago: Henry Regnery Company, 1955); and Thomas F. O'Dea, *American Catholic Dilemma: An Inquiry into the Intellectual Life* (New York: Sheed and Ward, 1958).

13. The statistic for the Roman Catholic population in 1980 is from U.S. Department of Commerce, Bureau of the Census, *Statistical Abstract of the United States: 1985* (Washington, D.C.: Government Printing Office, 1984), p. 51.

Whether these new groups would prove as eager to have their own
parishes and to perpetuate their own traditions as the Polish and
Lithuanian Catholics had been earlier in the century, and whether
they would resort to the same sort of ethnoreligious configurations of
education, remained to be seen. Certainly an energetic effort to do so
was much within the Catholic tradition; and yet both the Catholic
education system and the public education system of the 1980's were
much more responsive than in an earlier era to the needs and wishes
of particular ethnoreligious subcommunities.

IV

If a combination of scorn by the dominant white Protestant majority
and group pride fostered concern for community survival among
American blacks and Catholics—the French Canadians called it *survivance,* or the preservation of religion, language, and custom—a similar
combination evoked a profound ambivalence on the part of American
Jews. On the one hand, they were powerfully attracted by the possibility and prospect of rapid and complete assimilation to the larger
society; on the other hand, they too sought to preserve the particularities of their ethnoreligious heritage, especially when rebuffed, subtly
or otherwise, by the larger society. Indeed, even when they were not
rebuffed, many Jews sought at least to remember that heritage. To
recall the formulation of the historian Marcus Lee Hansen, what the
second generation tried to forget, the third generation tried to remember. And, when the catastrophe of the European Holocaust occurred in the 1930's and 1940's, the wish to remember became even
more powerful.[14]

There were some 230,000 Jews in the United States in 1880, most
of them immigrants who had come from Germany during the 1840's
and 1850's or the children of those immigrants. Driven from the
hamlets and market towns of Bavaria, Baden, Württemberg, and
Posen by repressive legislation and economic depression, they had
spread out across the United States, settling not only in New York and
Philadelphia but as far north as Rochester, as far west as San Francisco, and as far south as Atlanta, Mobile, and New Orleans. Beginning as peddlers and petty entrepreneurs—roles they had played for
generations in Europe—they had managed a remarkably rapid rise

14. Mason Wade, "The French Parish and *Survivance* in Nineteenth-Century New England," *Catholic Historical Review,* XXXVI (1950), 163–189; and Marcus L. Hansen, *The
Problem of the Third Generation Immigrant* (Rock Island, Ill.: Augustana Historical Society,
1938), pp. 9–10.

into the middle class and an astonishingly rapid acculturation to American ways. And, having already embarked upon the religious reforms associated with the Emancipation of the Jews in Europe, they had wrought profound changes in their synagogues and other social and educational institutions. Whereas the synagogue in Europe had been at the heart of the Jewish community but only one key institution of that community, the synagogue in the United States became the community, or at least the community became its congregation. Whereas the synagogue in Europe had been well supplied with learned rabbis who had received a lengthy and thorough education in the sacred texts of Judaism, notably Torah (the first five books of the Old Testament) and Talmud (the ancient tracts expositing the meaning of Torah), the synagogue in the United States was often without a rabbi and managed by the lay leaders of the congregation. Even when there was a rabbi he would as often as not incline toward the sorts of doctrinal and liturgical reform that would appear to make Judaism more compatible with American ways. Finally, whereas the synagogue in Europe had led the Jewish community in its provision for education and welfare, the synagogue in the United States ended up ambivalent with respect to the issues of public versus Jewish schools and of independent versus synagogue-related welfare institutions.[15]

By 1880 American Jews had transformed their synagogue into a characteristically American institution: their rabbis were by then beginning to be trained at the Hebrew Union College in Cincinnati, founded by Isaac Mayer Wise in 1875; their synagogues had become temples and their worship had been reformed to the point where it strongly resembled the liberal Protestantism of the day, with organs, choirs, hymn singing, sermons, and responsive reading in English. Although there were a few Sephardic congregations adhering to a more traditional orthodoxy, American Judaism was for the most part Reform Judaism—the religion of Jews who wanted and indeed expected to be accepted by their non-Jewish countrymen. Jewish children attended the public schools; and, to the extent permitted by the dominant Protestant majority—ironically, the more Jews assimilated, the more they were perceived as parvenus and discriminated against—Jewish adults took part in the diurnal affairs of their communities.

15. The population statistic is from Sidney Goldstein, "Jews in the United States: Perspectives from Demography," in Milton Himmelfarb and David Singer, eds., *American Jewish Year Book, 1981* (Philadelphia: The Jewish Publication Society of America, 1980), p. 9.

This situation was dramatically changed by the arrival of large numbers of Jews from eastern Europe. Between 1881 and 1914, some two million of them arrived, principally from Russia, the Austro-Hungarian Empire, and Romania. Driven from their ancient ghettos by pogroms, severe economic dislocation, and relentless political and economic discrimination, they came eagerly and permanently to the United States, bearing visions of a *goldeneh medina* ("golden land") gleaned from the Hebrew and Yiddish press. Unlike their German predecessors, they did not distribute themselves throughout the United States; rather, they congregated mainly on New York's Lower East Side, Chicago's West Side, Philadelphia's Downtown, and Boston's North End. And, unlike their German predecessors, they did not begin with peddling and move rapidly to proprietorship; rather, they used their experience in the clothing and construction industries, as artisans, and as bakers, butchers, and petty purveyors to the Jewish community to become a skilled working class in the rapidly industrializing cities. Whereas in 1880 some one-sixth of the 230,000 American Jews were of East European background, by 1920 some five-sixths of 4,000,000 American Jews were of East European background.

Two dynamics early affected the education of the East European Jews: first, the transplantation of their own configurations of institutions from the European *shtetl* (small town), which was itself undergoing transformation at the end of the nineteenth century; and second, the creation of new configurations for them by the established American Jews of German background. The new immigrants were first and foremost poor, and they crowded into older neighborhoods among groups of their countrymen—the Russians with Russians, the Hungarians with Hungarians, the Romanians with Romanians. There they sought to reproduce the Jewish communities they had known in Europe. They organized synagogues, though there was a persistent shortage of learned rabbis. They organized mutual benefit societies called *Landsmannschaften* with compatriots from their European towns and regions of origin, which undertook to provide a range of services from funerals to recreation. And they founded special organizations to sponsor hospitals, orphanages, and old-age homes. They provided for heders and Talmud Torah schools that concentrated on the Hebrew language and the sacred texts and for yeshivas that provided advanced education for those who wished to become scholars or rabbis. They also sustained a host of labor, Zionist, socialist, and cultural organizations designed to propagate every manner of philosophy and to further every manner of cause, along with a vigorous

Yiddish press and a lively Yiddish theatre. The problem was that in Europe the life of the *shtetl* went on within a relatively enclosed, encompassing environment; insofar as it reflected an attempt to live purposefully and self-consciously according to Jewish law, that life was itself educative. Ritual, celebration, ceremonial; rabbinical supervision and community oversight; religious law and doctrinal regulation—all constituted the coherent, segregated, relentlessly formative experience of the sectarian community. Of course, in Europe, the life and education of the *shtetl* were already breaking down by the late nineteenth century in the wake of political oppression, economic upheaval, and the intellectual challenge of Jewish Enlightenment (known as the Haskala movement). But in the ghettos of New York, Chicago, and Philadelphia, the life and education of the *shtetl* were even more difficult—indeed, they were impossible—to maintain. There was no lack of religious or intellectual intensity among the East European Jews—quite the opposite; the breakdown came in traditional mechanisms for sustaining and perpetuating the structure, the authority, and the function of the Jewish community. In the absence of rabbis, the authority of the synagogue in diurnal affairs as well as in its more specific province of religious affairs diminished; in the absence of a discernibly structured Jewish community, defined partly in contradistinction to some equally discernible structured non-Jewish community (as in traditional Europe), communal support for education waned; and in the absence of communal support for education, the transmission of Jewish customs and traditions became less effective.

Beyond that, as traditional communal ties weakened, social pathology flourished; and awareness of that social pathology, coupled with the religious traditionalism and intellectual radicalism that marked the East European Jews, appalled and frightened the more well-to-do, assimilated Jews of German background. In some measure, they were concerned out of genuine philanthropic interest; but in much greater measure they were concerned lest a new, more "alien" image of Judaism affect their own position in American society. And a combination of the two led them, first, to join in efforts to restrict the immigration of East European Jews, and, when that failed, to undertake a major educational effort of their own, addressed to their perception of the principal need of the East European Jews, namely, Americanization.

The effort in New York City, which included by far the largest number of Jews, was exemplary. As early as 1864, the Jewish community there discovered that Christian missionaries had opened a school on the Lower East Side and were using the offer to teach Hebrew as a lure to convert Jewish children to Christianity. Outraged, a dozen congregations of moderate Reform and Orthodox Jews banded together to open an all-day Hebrew free school nearby as a countermeasure. The school accomplished its purpose and flourished in its own right; and the sponsors, organized as the Hebrew Free School Association, opened a number of branches in other Jewish neighborhoods of the city, which, reflecting assimilationist aspirations, were structured as afternoon schools offering a Hebrew program supplementary to the standard curriculum of the public schools. The work waned during the 1870's—the original all-day school was closed in 1872 and the afternoon schools experienced large turnovers in student population; but the Association proved a ready vehicle during the 1880's for a heightened educational effort among the East European Jews that offered training in courtesy, cleanliness, and American ways along with Jewish history, Jewish religion, and the Hebrew language.

In addition, the Young Men's Hebrew Association, founded in the 1870's as a Jewish counterpart to the YMCA but essentially as a social, recreational, and cultural organization rather than a missionary organization, began to turn its attention to outreach programs intended to bridge the gap between immigrant parents and their children, both of whom were undergoing the stress of Americanization, though in different ways and at different rates. And charitable organizations like the Baron de Hirsch Fund turned their resources to sponsoring English classes for working adults and a Hebrew Technical School for boys. By far the most ambitious effort, however, was the Educational Alliance, founded in 1889 by the joint effort of the Hebrew Free School Association, the YMHA, and the Aguilar Free Library. Organized for all intents and purposes as a German Jewish social settlement for an East European Jewish clientele, and supported generously by the American Jewish community of German background, the Alliance mounted a large, comprehensive program of social and educational activities, including kindergartens, Hebrew classes for boys and girls that combined Americanization efforts with Jewish studies, singing societies, social clubs, reading rooms, art exhibits, lecture programs, English and naturalization classes, physical education activities, and, after 1899, the remarkable Breadwinners' College started by Thomas Davidson. To encourage thrift, the Alliance sponsored a branch of the Penny Provident Fund; to promote health, it established Surprise Lake Camp for boys; to assist with family problems, it held parents' meetings where mothers and fathers could discuss the problems of rearing children in the novel American environment; and to advance an Americanized version of Judaism, it established a School of Religious Work and a People's Synagogue.

Finally, and most significantly, the German-American Jews assisted in the revitalization of the Jewish Theological Seminary of America. The Seminary had been established in 1886 under the leadership of Sabato Morais as a counter-Reform institution, with the intention of propounding a historical Judaism, one sensitive to the need for change but insistent upon finding its guiding principles within the historical experience of the Jewish people. The hope was doubtless to create and lead some sort of union of immigrant and native Orthodox congregations, but the effort did not succeed. When Morais died in 1897, many of the congregations affiliated with the Seminary went over to the Reform movement and the prospects for the survival of the institution seemed dim. What happened, though, was that Cyrus Adler, a former student of Morais who had gone on to become Professor of Semitics at the Johns Hopkins University and then to be assistant secretary of the Smithsonian Institution, had noticed that many of the rabbinical candidates at the Seminary had come from East European Jewish families. Aware of the concerns and fears of the German-American Jews, Adler approached Jacob Schiff, a wealthy Reform Jew, with the intriguing argument that the Seminary could play a unique role in Americanizing the new immigrants by winning their upcoming leaders to an American version of Orthodox Judaism. Schiff was persuaded, and, with other wealthy friends in the Reform movement such as Daniel and Simon Guggenheim, Leonard Lewisohn, Mayer Sulzberger, and Louis Marshall, raised a half-million dollars for the revival of the Seminary. The infusion of money made possible the attraction of Solomon Schechter, an East European Jewish scholar of impeccable credentials, to the presidency of the Seminary. A man of extraordinarily broad interests within the field of Judaica, Schechter was able to mediate between the Orthodox and Reform communities, and, with a brilliant faculty recruited from Europe and the United States, to lay the foundation of twentieth-century Conservative Judaism in America. In addition, again, with funds supplied by Jacob Schiff, he organized a Teachers Institute at the Seminary in 1909, under the principalship of Mordecai Kaplan. Favorably disposed toward Zionism (in contrast to the anti-Zionism of Schiff and other donors), Schechter and Kaplan made sure that the

Institute conducted its classes in modern Hebrew and in the process trained a generation of teachers for American Jewish education of Zionist persuasion, who were as committed to the perpetuation of Jewish culture as they were to the transmission of Jewish religion. Moreover, because the Institute established links with Teachers College, Columbia University, its students were able to study the new progressive pedagogy of John Dewey and William Heard Kilpatrick at the same time that they immersed themselves in the study of Jewish religion and culture.

It was an extraordinary educational apparatus, then, that the older American Jewish community of German background created for the Americanization of the East European immigrant Jews. But the response of the clients was ambivalent at best. Faced with the continuing effects of dissolution within their own traditional institutions, they were not ready unequivocally to embrace the community that was proffered to them. All the proffered facilities were utilized, but for the immigrants' own purposes; and, even given such utilization, the vast majority of the immigrants remained untouched. Their children attended the public schools and read in the public libraries, and they were as likely to be enrolled in an afternoon Talmud Torah school as they were in a program of the Educational Alliance. The adults read the Yiddish press avidly and were probably instructed more effectively by the *Bintelbriefe* (letters to the editor) in the Yiddish newspapers than they were in the evening classes of the YMHA. And, although the Jewish Theological Seminary continued to draw the majority of its candidates from Jewish families of East European background, the Orthodox community remained skeptical of Schechter's program and used the Rabbi Isaac Elchanan Theological Seminary, founded in 1896, to prepare native-born Orthodox rabbis. In a word, the effort of American Jews of German origin to Americanize their East European co-religionists was in no way a failure; but its effects were limited and did not align precisely with initial expectations.

It was perhaps the sense in all quarters, then, that some larger collaborative community needed to be wrought for the benefit of American Judaism that led to one of the most interesting of the twentieth-century experiments in American Jewish education, the Kehillah (*kehillah* is the Hebrew word for "community"). The Kehillah was established amidst a growing debate during the first years of the twentieth century over the meaning of Americanization, a debate in which the production of Israel Zangwill's play *The Melting Pot* proved a watershed (the play, dedicated to Theodore Roosevelt, opened in Washington, D.C., on October 5, 1908, and ran in New York in 1909).

Given the American Jewish community's historic ambivalence about assimilation vis-à-vis group maintenance, the debate had special meaning for Jewish life and education. On the one hand, there were those who believed with Zangwill's protagonist David Quixano, that America was "God's Crucible, the great Melting-Pot where all the races of Europe are melting and re-forming." On the other hand, there were those who believed with Judah Magnes, the young rabbi of Temple Emanu-El, perhaps the leading institution of Reform Judaism, that America was not a melting pot but rather a "symphony" in which nationalities kept their "individual and characteristic note" and sounded that note "in harmony with their sister nationalities." Obviously, the two views led to differing conceptions of what Jewish communal and educational life should be.[16]

Divided though it may have been on that question, the Jewish community was united in its sense of outrage at a charge of New York City's police commissioner in 1908 that 50 percent of the criminal class in the city were Jews; and that outrage provided the immediate spur to the founding of the Kehillah. An alliance of "uptown" (German) and "downtown" (East European) Jews formed a Jewish council and forced the commissioner to retract. That having been accomplished, Magnes persuaded the informal council that it would be advantageous to form a unified Jewish community (Kehillah) in New York City to further the cause of Judaism in the city and to represent Jews in its affairs. A convention early in 1909 called the organization into existence and by spring it was functioning with offices in the United Hebrew Charities Building on Second Avenue and 21st Street. With Magnes as leader, the organization committed itself to a twofold program that was characteristic of the Progressive era: the creation of an informed Jewish public opinion through annual conventions and the mounting of a scientific research program that would lead to the establishment of Kehillah policy. Efforts to implement the program were undertaken by bureaus on education, social morals (to combat crime), industry (to mediate industrial disputes), and philanthropic institutions (to coordinate philanthropic effort), and later by a School for Jewish Communal Work and a Board of Orthodox Rabbis.

The work in education was begun with a major survey of Jewish schools in the city under the leadership of Mordecai Kaplan and Bernard Cronson, a public school principal in the city. The report, completed in 1910, concluded that the demand for Jewish schooling in the city was small, that the resources for satisfying the demand were

16. Israel Zangwill, *The Melting-Pot* (New York: The Macmillan Company, 1909), p. 33; and Judah Magnes, "The Melting Pot," *Emanu-El Pulpit*, III, No. 1 (Oct. 9, 1909), 9, 10.

inadequate, and that even when the demand was being satisfied the effort was unsystematic and haphazard. The report identified six classes of schools: Talmud Torahs, schools for poor boys which met afternoons and Sundays and were supported by membership fees and contributions; institutional schools, conducted by orphanages and charitable organizations; congregational schools, which met three or four times a week and were attended by the children of synagogue members; Sunday schools, also attended principally by the children of synagogue members (with the exception of a few mission Sunday schools for the poor); heders, or Hebrew schools conducted on a private basis by independent teachers; and private tutorial instruction. The report estimated that at best some 42,000 of the 200,000 Jewish children of school age in the city were actually receiving some form of Jewish schooling and recommended a "central organization" that would spark the religious awakening in the adult Jewish community that was seen as a necessary precondition for greater educational effort and that would then lead to the preparation and certification of competent teachers and the creation of effective curricula and materials.[17]

One direct outcome of the report—clearly calculated by the authors—was the establishment of the Kehillah's Bureau of Education under the leadership of Samson Benderly, head of the Baltimore Hebrew Free School. A Palestinian who had been educated at the American College in Beirut, Benderly had come to the United States to complete his medical studies, only to abandon medicine for Jewish education shortly after his graduation. An articulate proponent of Jewish education in the progressive mode, Benderly early and decisively committed the Bureau to a system of reformed supplementary schools that would complement the public schooling he believed to be the essential basis for the education of American Jews. Armed with a $50,000 contribution from Schiff, Benderly set out to develop modernized versions of the Talmud Torah school, emphasizing the Hebrew language, led by the sorts of teachers Mordecai Kaplan and his colleagues were preparing at the Teachers Institute, and utilizing scientifically prepared and standardized curricula and textbooks. In the initial issue of the *Jewish Teacher* in 1916, which was subsidized by the Bureau, Benderly's protégé Alexander M. Dushkin, who had imbibed progressive educational ideas at Teachers College, made expli-

17. Mordecai M. Kaplan and Bernard Cronson, "Report of Committee on Jewish Education of the Kehillah (Jewish Community) Presented at Its First Annual Convention, New York, February 27, 1910," *Jewish Education*, XX (Summer, 1949), 115–116.

cit the intellectual foundation of Benderly's approach. Paraphrasing John Dewey's more general argument in *The School and Society* (1899), Dushkin wrote:

The home and the synagogue, the communal life and the forces of social control, look to the Jewish school for their vitalization and strengthening. The burden of the world's work is being redistributed, and the school, both the secular and the religious, must be ready to undertake many functions not hitherto assigned to them.[18]

Benderly's program was ambitious and costly; but in its vision of an American Jewish community rooted in a new combination of public and Jewish schooling, it proved unable to retain the support of two crucially important constituencies, the wealthy donors of the Reform community, who became increasingly suspicious of the Zionist proclivities of Benderly and of the Teachers Institute, and the Orthodox rabbis, who became increasingly suspicious of Benderly's modernist philosophy. In the end, the Bureau could not support its program. Sponsorship of its work passed to the Federation for the Support of Jewish Philanthropic Societies, which was much more decisively in the control of the "uptown" Jews and which espoused a much more asymmetric concept of Jewish community that was essentially reflective of differences in social class. As a result, it lost the interest of the East European Jews. Many elements of its program, however, were subsequently embodied in the work of the Central Jewish Institute, which was created by Congregation Kehilath Jeshurun under the leadership of Mordecai Kaplan, its rabbi, and which followed Kaplan, Benderly, and its first director, Isaac B. Berkson, in providing a strong supplementary school program rooted in Hebrew and intended to transmit the culture, religion, and history of the Jewish people, and complemented by a wide range of clubs for children, youth, and parents. In addition, the Institute in 1919 pioneered the first Jewish educational camp in the United States, Camp Cejwin, as an institution for providing young people with a total immersion in Jewish living during the summer months. It was a device that other Jewish groups, including the Teachers Institute, would use extensively during the years ahead.

The years from 1920 to 1980 were a period of extraordinary mobility for American Jews—social mobility, in that they moved rapidly into the middle class, pursuing careers as proprietors, businesspersons, and professionals, and geographical mobility, in that they left

18. *Jewish Teacher*, I (1916), 1.

the ghettos of New York, Chicago, and Philadelphia and moved, initially, to better neighborhoods within the cities where they had settled, and subsequently, to the suburbs. The period was also one of remarkable transformation in American Judaism itself. For a time during the 1930's, the movement for Jewish community centers flourished, representing the interest of a highly mobile Jewish population in having suitable settings for social, recreational, and sometimes religious activities as they made their way in American society. But the more enduringly significant movement was toward Conservative Judaism as propounded by the Jewish Theological Seminary. In a sense, the argument Cyrus Adler, who succeeded Schechter in the presidency of the Seminary in 1915, put to Jacob Schiff had proved prophetic: the East European Jews not only responded to the middle-of-the-road program of the Seminary, they used it to transform American Jewish religious life. By the 1950's, the formerly dominant Reform movement had yielded leadership to the rapidly burgeoning Conservative movement. Along with a revival of ultra-Orthodoxy among some post–World War II refugees from Europe, this shift represented a sea change in the American Jewish community. The reasons for the shift were complex—the experience of the European Holocaust, the creation of the State of Israel in 1948, the movement of Jews to the suburbs, with their more homogeneous class structures, and the more general post–World War II religious revival in the United States were all involved. However that may be, the shift was pronounced and undeniable and affected all aspects of American Jewish life.

The educational consequences of the shift were among the more profound. American Jews continued to rely heavily on the secular schools and liberal arts colleges for their education—beyond Yeshiva University, only Brandeis University, founded in 1946, was tied to the Jewish community and it was founded as a nonsectarian institution. But there was a revival during the 1950's of both Jewish supplementary schooling and Jewish all-day schooling, most of it associated with congregations, on a scale that could not have been predicted in 1945. And beyond this joint effort that bespoke a configuration of home, synagogue, and school, there was a rise, too, in the number of educational camps—not only the Ramah camps associated with the Jewish Theological Seminary, but the camps for Living Judaism of the Union of American Hebrew Congregations (Reform), the Yiddish camps of the Jewish labor movement, the Hebrew camps of the Zionist movement, and the less ideological camps of the YMHA-YWHA movement. As much as any educational institution, the religious camp, with its deliberate immersion of youngsters in an intentional community over a significant part of the year, recognized the new twentieth-century phenomenon of adolescence and tried to deal with it educationally in comprehensive terms.

V

A number of studies undertaken during the early 1960's, toward the end of the post–World War II religious revival, found, occasionally to the surprise of the scholars that undertook them, that for all the relentlessly acculturating and homogenizing influences of metropolitan American society and education, ethnoreligiosity remained a prime influence in American life. Gerhard Lenski found in Detroit that the four major religious groups—white Protestants, black Protestants, Roman Catholics, and Jews—continued to sense particular identities at the same time that they perceived themselves as Americans; and Nathan Glazer and Daniel Patrick Moynihan found in New York City that the five major ethnic groups—the blacks, the Puerto Ricans, the Jews, the Italians, and the Irish—even after they had lost their distinctive languages, customs, and cultures, continued to be recreated by new experiences in America. They were not survivals of an acculturation process that had failed to work; they were new social forms.[19]

In fact, what Lenski and Glazer and Moynihan were confirming was the kaleidoscopic process Timothy Smith had described as a fundamental dynamic of twentieth-century American society. The evangelical united front of the Protestants continued during the period after 1876 to define an American *paideia* that it hoped, through missionary activity, to teach, first to America, and then to the world. But the effort failed, partly because of failures of consensus within the ranks of the united front and partly because its educational efforts were met by the educational efforts of other groups. Meanwhile, black Protestants and Roman Catholics and Jews and indeed a host of other ethnoreligious communities, from Native American peyote cultists to Syrian Moslems and Chinese Buddhists, mounted their own educational efforts, partly in response to Protestant missions but partly independent of

19. Gerhard Lenski, *The Religious Factor: A Sociological Study of Religion's Impact on Politics, Economics, and Family Life* (Garden City, N.Y.: Doubleday & Company, 1961); and Nathan Glazer and Daniel Patrick Moynihan, *Beyond the Melting Pot: The Negroes, Puerto Ricans, Jews, Italians, and Irish of New York City* (Cambridge, Mass.: The M.I.T. Press and Harvard University Press, 1963).

them. And they created through their efforts alternative American *paideias*, both for themselves and for the American community as a whole. Moreover, the efforts of these various communities proceeded in the context of efforts mounted by a vast array of public, quasi-public, and independent educative enterprises that saw themselves as secular American even though inevitably—and sometimes quite intentionally—they drew upon one or more of the ethnoreligious traditions; and these efforts also spawned their own versions of an American *paideia.* The discordant education that had characterized black, Native American, and immigrant communities during the nineteenth century—an education in which at least two conflicting configurations of education sought to inculcate in the same individuals quite different sets of values and attitudes via quite different pedagogies—became even more complicated, as social diversity increased and as so-called Americanization programs were launched with the intention of assimilating one or another of the myriad ethnoreligious minorities more fully into the dominant American community. The dynamics of discordant education were manifest in Native American resistance to federal assimilation programs and in Amish resistance to state and local assimilation programs; and they were manifest, too, in the efforts of ethnoreligious institutions like the immigrant press, with its columns of advice to newcomers intended to ease their adjustment to a more cosmopolitan America.[20]

The outcome of this extraordinarily complex education was a variegation characteristic of metropolitan American society. Americans in the 1980's shared much in common with one another; but there was much, too, that they shared only with smaller subgroups. The configurations of education of the various ethnoreligious communities had helped to create this complex situation. They had helped make a more cosmopolitan American culture accessible at the same time that they had preserved certain ethnoreligious traditions, in the process strengthening both the cosmopolitanism and the particularity suggested by the metaphor of a "kaleidoscope." The process, not of "melting," but of affiliating a heterogeneous population would have persisted even if there had not been continuing immigration to the United States after World War II. But with the "new, new" immigration of the 1970's and 1980's, it was a process that would surely continue to work transforming influences on American life and thought.

20. Timothy L. Smith, "Religion and Ethnicity in America," *American Historical Review,* LXXXIII (1978), 1185.

Part II

THE PROGRESSIVE NATION

By law and punishment, by social agitation and discussion, society can regulate and form itself in a more or less haphazard and chance way. But through education society can formulate its own purposes, can organize its own means and resources, and thus shape itself with definiteness and economy in the direction in which it wishes to move.

JOHN DEWEY

INTRODUCTION

Post–Civil War Americans inherited a commitment to popular education that was extraordinary for its time, even among the industrializing nations of the West. It was a commitment that Alexis de Tocqueville had noted in his *Democracy in America* (1835, 1840), when he remarked the special combination of popular schooling, a free press, and widespread participation in voluntary associations that played such a central role in maintaining what he called the American "character of mind." And it was a commitment that the British scholar-diplomat James Bryce noted a half-century later in *The American Commonwealth* (1888), when he commented at length on the beneficial effects of universal schooling and of a powerful press in creating the informed public opinion that lent a special stability to public affairs. In fact, the commitment had become sufficiently well established by the 1880's so that most of the utopian writers of the time made popular education a prominent feature of the perfect societies they portrayed in their visions of the future. Thus, to take but the leading example, Edward Bellamy in *Looking Backward* (1888) depicted a mythical Boston in which all children were entitled by right as human beings and future citizens to the finest possible care and nurture, in which advanced liberal and technical education as well as elementary and secondary schooling were available to the entire populace, in which newspapers had become "a more perfect expression of public opinion" than ever before, and in which normal retirement at the age of forty-five left "the residue of life" to men and women for the pursuit of individual "improvement or recreation" according to their tastes.[1]

1. Alexis de Tocqueville, *Democracy in America,* edited by Phillips Bradley (2 vols.; New York: Alfred A. Knopf, 1945), I, 299; James Bryce, *The American Commonwealth* (3 vols.; London: Macmillan and Co., 1888), III, 35–42, 52–53; and Edward Bellamy, *Looking Backward 2000–1887,* edited by John L. Thomas (Cambridge, Mass.: Harvard University Press, 1967), pp. 202, 217.

From the time of its development during the 1830's and 1840's, the American commitment to popular education had embraced at least two complementary elements. The first maintained that universal education was a *sine qua non* of republican government, that in its absence liberty would soon become license, and universal suffrage a tyranny of the majority. As the oft-quoted Jeffersonian aphorism phrased it, "If a nation expects to be ignorant and free, in a state of civilization, it expects what never was and never will be." The second element was both more subtle and more characteristically American. It held that certain long-term reforms in society were better achieved through education than through politics, indeed, that education was a form of politics insofar as it altered traditional relationships among individuals and groups. Thus, Horace Mann liked to argue that, "As 'the child is father to the man,' so may the training of the schoolroom expand into the institutions and fortunes of the state"; Robert Dale Owen tried to persuade the New York workingmen that a system of public boarding schools would alter and equalize relations among the social classes; and Horace Greeley saw the *Tribune* as an instrument for educating his countrymen in the principles of free soil, free labor, and free men.[2]

Both of the elements relating education to politics effloresced during the Progressive era. Public schooling expanded upward and was made compulsory; and quasi-familial institutions of every sort, from the day nursery to the reform school, were enlisted in the cause of "child saving," that is, in the "rescue" of dependent and delinquent youngsters. And progressive tracts were filled with millennial bursts of secular enthusiasm for particular educative institutions. The young philosopher John Dewey saw the school as shaping the society "in the direction in which it wishes to move" and the teacher as "the prophet of the true God and the usherer in of the true kingdom of God"; and the young director D. W. Griffith saw film as developing a universal language that would ultimately bring understanding among peoples and peace to the world.[3]

As education came increasingly to be seen as the principal engine of an "intentionally progressive" society—the phrase was Dewey's—interest groups with divergent views of what that society ought to look like staked their claims upon education and in the process politicized education. The Farmers' Alliances distributed free copies of *Looking Backward* as a consciousness-raising device for their members. The National Association of Manufacturers and the American Federation of Labor argued over the role of vocational training in public schools and the organization

2. Thomas Jefferson to Colonel Charles Yancey, January 6, 1816, in *The Writings of Thomas Jefferson*, edited by Paul Leicester Ford (10 vols.; New York: G. P. Putnam's Sons, 1891–1899), X, 4; and Massachusetts, *Twelfth Annual Report of the Board of Education, Together with the Twelfth Annual Report of the Secretary of the Board [1848]*, p. 84.

3. John Dewey, "My Pedagogic Creed" [1897], in *John Dewey: The Early Works, 1882–1898* (5 vols.; Carbondale: Southern Illinois University Press, 1969–1972), V, 94, 95.

of public schooling to deliver vocational training. And the General Federation of Women's Clubs campaigned for a federal agency that would care as much about child rearing as the Department of Agriculture cared about pig rearing. If education was to be principal engine of an intentionally progressive society, then the politics of education would have significance far beyond the control of schools, or child-saving institutions, or communications organizations; in the end, it would hold the key to the achievement of the most fundamental political aspirations—in effect, the key to the American *paideia*. [4]

Progressivism waxed and waned during the half-century following World War I, assuming forms as varied as the technological voluntarism of Herbert Hoover during the 1920's, the pragmatic reformism of Franklin Delano Roosevelt during the 1930's, and the crusading liberalism of Lyndon B. Johnson during the 1960's. And the role of government, particularly at the federal level, expanded steadily through conservative as well as progressive administrations. But the notion of education as holding the key to the achievement of the nation's most fundamental political aspirations—of racial integration or social equality or economic productivity—continued constant, indeed, no longer a characteristic progressive idea but increasingly a characteristic American idea, held with the same depth of commitment that had attached to religious belief during an earlier era in American history. As American education went, so would go the American people and the American nation.

4. John Dewey, *Democracy and Education* [1916], in *John Dewey: The Middle Works, 1899–1924*, edited by Jo Ann Boydston (15 vols.; Carbondale: Southern Illinois University Press, 1976–1983), IX, 331.

Chapter 4

MODES OF PROGRESSIVISM

Dare the school build a new social order?

GEORGE S. COUNTS

Sometime around the middle of January, 1866, seven residents of St. Louis, Missouri, gathered at the downtown office of a lawyer named Britton Armstrong Hill for the purpose of organizing a society for the promotion of speculative philosophy and its application. The group adopted a constitution at a meeting on January 26; and a week later the St. Louis Philosophical Society came formally into existence. The influence of the new society on American life and thought would be prodigious, its influence on American education incalculable.

In time the society added associates from St. Louis and auxiliaries from other parts of the United States and abroad; but from the beginning two men were the moving forces in the venture—Henry Conrad Brokmeyer, a politician whose highest aspiration was to render Hegel's *Logic* into comprehensible English, and William Torrey Harris, a principal in the St. Louis public school system who thought Brokmeyer's translation so important to the future of America that he subsidized it out of his own pocket. Given the differences of background and temperament between the two men, their close association over the years was remarkable. They had met in 1858, when Brokmeyer was twenty-nine years of age and Harris twenty-three. Brokmeyer had fled his native Prussia some thirteen years earlier in rebellion against Prussian militarism, arriving in New York with twenty-five cents in his pocket and three words of English at his disposal. He remained for a time in New York and then decided to move westward, working successively as a bootblack, currier, tanner, shoemaker, and ironmonger, and alternating between formal education at such institutions as Georgetown College in Kentucky and Brown University in Rhode Island, and self-education in literature and philosophy. It was probably during a period as a recluse in the woods of Warren County, Missouri, between 1854 and 1856, that he came to see in Hegel's writing the solution, not only to his personal quest for meaning, but also to the future of American civilization. From that time forward, though he later mounted a highly successful political career in which he rose to the lieutenant governorship (and for a time in 1876–77, the acting governorship) of Missouri, Brokmeyer lived and breathed the philosophy of Hegel.

Harris had grown up in North Killingly, Connecticut, and had enrolled in Yale College hoping to study the "three 'moderns'— modern science, modern literature, and modern history." He had found none of these at Yale, but he had encountered A. Bronson Alcott in New Haven during the winter of 1857 and had found Alcott's "conversations" sufficiently persuasive to exchange the phrenology he had adopted as his personal philosophy for the sort of idealism Alcott preached. Bitterly disappointed in Yale, he had left the college during his junior year and gone to St. Louis, where he had eked out a living as a teacher of shorthand while continuing his education in philosophy along the lines suggested in Goethe's *Wilhelm Meister*, with emphasis upon the writings of Kant, Fichte, Schelling, and Hegel. When a teaching position in the public school system came open, Harris accepted it and thereby began a career that would soon lead him to the superintendency of schools and to national prominence in educational affairs. The young Brokmeyer, consumed with Hegel, met the young Harris, converted to the German gospel of culture, in St. Louis in 1858. It is said that their first conversation lasted most of the night. Out of it grew the so-called St. Louis movement in philosophy.[1]

Having found in Harris an eager disciple, Brokmeyer set out to introduce him and a small group of similarly interested friends to the mysteries of German philosophy. Harris and the others, in turn, contributed the modest funds that enabled Brokmeyer to work on his translation of Hegel's *Logic*. The Civil War interrupted the idyll; Brokmeyer went off to serve in the militia and Harris remained in the public school system. But the collaboration resumed when Brokmeyer returned to St. Louis in 1862 and won election to the legislature as a "War Democrat," thereby launching the political career that would

1. William T. Harris, "How I Was Educated," in *The "How I Was Educated" Papers* (New York: D. Appleton and Company, 1896), p. 50.

carry him to the acting governorship. Four years later, the two friends took the lead in organizing the St. Louis Philosophical Society. They also founded the *Journal of Speculative Philosophy,* the first American periodical wholly devoted to philosophy, and in 1868 Harris succeeded Ira Divoll as superintendent, remaining in that post until 1880, when he resigned and moved East to help organize the Concord School of Philosophy with A. Bronson Alcott and Ralph Waldo Emerson. He was appointed United States Commissioner of Education by President Benjamin Harrison in 1889 and served through the Cleveland, McKinley, and Roosevelt administrations, resigning in 1906 to devote himself fully to his literary and philosophical activities. He died in 1909.

At the outset, one might ask two questions concerning the origins and influence of the Philosophical Society: why St. Louis? and why Hegel? St. Louis had remained a Union bastion within a slave state during the Civil War, owing to a coalition of New Englanders and recently arrived Germans; and one result was that it had begun to develop industrially as a supplier to the Union armies in the West. Stimulated by the wartime economy, the city came into its own during the late 1860's, with a vision of itself as the coming "Capital of the Nation" and indeed as the "Future Great City of the World." The vision lasted until the census of 1880 revealed that Chicago, St. Louis' arch-competitor, had already won the race for population and riches. However that may be, the St. Louis Philosophical Society flourished during the years when the grand vision was at its brightest. Its members truly believed they were thinking through the future of America.[2]

Hegel, of course, had himself proclaimed America to be the land of the future, where the burden of the world's history would be revealed. But in that sentiment he was merely concurring in a view widely held among contemporary educated Europeans. More important, Hegel offered the young enthusiasts of the St. Louis Philosophical Society a method for attacking two problems that were central in the experience of their generation, the relation of the individual to the emerging American community and the relation of various subcommunities to that emerging American community. The Hegelian dialectic was a continuing process in which thesis spawned antithesis in a confrontation that would be resolved by synthesis, which would then in turn become thesis. With respect to the individual, the dialectic

2. The quotations are taken from Denton J. Snider's discussion of the "Great Illusion of St. Louis" in chapter 2 of *The St. Louis Movement in Philosophy, Literature, Education, Psychology, with Chapters of Autobiography* (St. Louis: Sigma Publishing Company, 1920), pp. 84, 104.

explained the process by which the self was defined in continuing relationship to that which was non-self, namely, other selves organized in institutions such as the family, the church, the school, the workplace, the city, the state, the nation, and the world. The outcome of the dialectic was a self increasingly aware, increasingly free, and increasingly in a relationship with the most universal non-self of all, God. With respect to subcommunities, the dialectic offered the process whereby the South and the North could unite to become the regenerated nation, in which capital and labor could unite to form a productive industrial economy, and competing ethnic, religious, and political interests could unite to fashion, first, the Future Great City of the World, and then, God's Chosen Nation. For the members of the St. Louis Philosophical Society, Hegel's philosophy was not some abstruse import appreciated for its aesthetic beauty; it was an intellectual system burningly relevant to the most important problems of their individual and collective lives.[3]

For all his dedication, Brokmeyer had little direct influence on American life and thought—his translation of the *Logic* was never published and he spent the last years of his life in relative seclusion. His greatest achievement was the inspiration and colleagueship he provided to Harris. Harris' influence, on the other hand, was prodigious. Beyond his inestimable contribution to American thought through the *Journal of Speculative Philosophy,* he was far and away the leading American educator of his time.

Harris nowhere set forth his philosophy of education in systematic form. Probably the closest he came to it was the series of five lectures he delivered at the Johns Hopkins University during January, 1893; but even those lectures were published only in outline. Rather, Harris explicated his views in hundreds of articles, addresses, pamphlets, reports, and prefaces published over the four decades of his active professional life. He wrote one book-length treatise, *Psychologic Foundations of Education* (1898), but, characteristically, limited the discussion there to precisely what the title implied, his psychology and its bearing on education. That said, however, his writings taken as a whole conveyed a thoroughly coherent complex of ideas that bespoke a philosophy both carefully developed and fully worked through.

As a Hegelian, Harris was pre-eminently concerned with institutions and their relationships, to one another and to transcendent ideals. Not surprisingly, he defined education as the process by which

3. G. W. F. Hegel, *Lectures on the Philosophy of History,* translated from the third German edition by J. Sibree (London: Henry G. Bohn, 1857), p. 90.

the individual comes into possession of the wisdom derived from the experience of the race. Education in his view proceeded through the five cardinal institutions—family, school, civil society, state, and church. He saw family nurture, lasting from birth through the age of five or six, as the earliest education. When the child outgrew the narrow circle of family life and became curious about the world outside the family, the school took over; its task was to initiate the child into the technicalities of communication and to proffer the ideas that underlay civilization. After schooling came the education implicit in the pursuit of one's special vocation, and, contemporaneously, the education implicit in the laws as laid down and enforced by the state. Finally, there was the education conveyed by the church, that spiritual education that ultimately determined the degree of development of all the other modes of education.

The aim of education for Harris was self-activity. "A material body or a mechanical body of any kind can be modeled or formed or modified externally into some desirable shape," Harris explained in the pedagogical creed he prepared in 1897. "But this external molding is not education. Education implies as an essential condition the activity of a self." For Harris, schools played a unique role with respect to self-activity. He believed that families, churches, and civic institutions *trained:* the outcomes of their education were unconscious habits and ungrounded inclinations taught ceaselessly over the years via oral instruction. He believed, by contrast, that schools *instructed:* they taught the techniques of study via the printed word and thereby enabled individuals to develop self-activity, and, through self-activity, individuality.[4]

Harris's concept of self-activity was marked by Hegelian paradox: individuals needed first to immerse themselves in the collectivity in order eventually to achieve individuality. The paradox had profound bearing on Harris's view of schooling. For one thing, it moved the school to the heart of the educative process in the urban, industrial society that was coming into being. Schools would be charged with providing the discipline and the rationality essential to the self-active individuals who would constitute a free society. Put otherwise, schools had a dual responsibility for developing the will and the intellect. With respect to the will, Harris saw American children as more precocious and earlier independent of familial influence than European children; hence, it fell to the schools to inculcate the self-restraint that made

4. W. T. Harris, "My Pedagogical Creed," *School Journal*, LIV (1897), 813–814.

training in rationality possible. "The child subdues his likes and dislikes, adopts habits of regularity, punctuality, silence, and industry," Harris continued in the pedagogical creed.[5]

Discipline made possible attention; attention made possible instruction; and instruction was the gateway to intellect. The key to instruction was the course of study. Children would begin their ascent to individuality in the kindergarten, where, using the Froebelian gifts and occupations, they would undertake the understanding and conquest of nature through the manipulation of means and instrumentalities and through participation in play and games. Building on this preliminary education, the school would provide the five "windows of the soul, which open out upon the five great divisions of the life of man." Two of the "windows," arithmetic and geography, related to man's comprehension of and conquest over nature; three of the "windows," history, language, and literature, related to the comprehension of human life. As Harris detailed the curricular implications of his analysis, five coordinate groups of studies emerged: mathematics and physics; biology, including botany; literature and art; grammar and the scientific study of language, leading to logic and psychology; and history, including sociology and politics. He believed each of these coordinate groups should be represented at every level of schooling, from the primary grades through the college, by topics appropriate to the age and previous training of the pupils.[6]

Harris deeply believed that the school would be the "great instrumentality to lift all classes of people into a participation in civilized life." He therefore advocated the kind of school that would provide a general, cultural, humanistic education for all young people, an education that would nurture their character and intellect as human beings rather than their particular abilities as workers. He early declared his commitment to coeducation, arguing that the entry of women into productive employment outside the home made it as important for them as for men to be initiated, via the same course of study, into the same modes of intelligence. He insisted, in addition, that women were capable of such education. Albeit with less of a commitment to equality, he also promoted the schooling of black Americans. He sincerely believed that the problem of the emancipated blacks of the South would ultimately be solved by education, but he consistently acquiesced in "separate but equal" schools for

5. *Ibid.*, 814.
6. W. T. Harris, *Psychologic Foundations of Education: An Attempt to Show the Genesis of the Higher Faculties of the Mind* (New York: D. Appleton and Company, 1898), pp. 322, 340.

blacks and in a curriculum for black schools that would combine industrial with intellectual education.[7]

Given Harris's idea of the inextricable tie between rationality and print, he placed great emphasis on textbooks in the education of self-active individuals. "Erudition cannot be gained by oral instruction," he counseled. "All the information that could be given orally by the best of teachers, in a course of ten years, would not suffice to exhaust a single topic, and it would be a very poor substitute for the power a pupil would obtain by mastering one single text-book for himself." Harris argued along similar lines concerning the newspaper. In his view, the three leading characteristics of modern civilization were the railroad, the newspaper, and the common school. The railroad had brought wealth to the United States; the common school and the newspaper had brought a self-active citizenry. The newspaper in concert with the telegraph would conquer ignorance, bigotry, and sectarianism; it would transform the ordinary individual into a cosmopolitan citizen of the world.[8]

Finally, there was the library, which made books and newspapers readily accessible to the average individual. In Harris's view, it would serve many of the purposes of the university in Europe, but in a different way—it would make possible a democratic culture created by self-active individuals. "We do not isolate our cultural class from the rest," Harris liked to point out.

It is our idea to have culture open to every one in all occupations of life. Elihu Burritt may learn fifty languages at the anvil. Benjamin Franklin may study Locke, make experiments in electricity, master the art of diplomacy. These are self-taught men, and the self-taught man is our type;—not the man who wastes his life experimenting to learn what is already known and published, but the man who *reads* and informs himself on all themes, and digests his knowledge into practice as he goes along. A culture for its own sake is a noble aspiration, and it is well to have it advocated at all times. But a culture that belongs to a class that rests like an upper layer upon the mass below, who in turn have to dig and spin for them, is not the American ideal—not at all, even if we do not produce men who devote their whole lives to the dative case, or to the Greek particles. And yet it is the faith of Americans that they will be able to accomplish all that any other civilization can do, besides adding thereto a culture in free individuality to an extent hitherto unattained.[9]

7. Harris, "My Pedagogical Creed," 815; *Twenty-fifth Annual Report of the Board of Directors of the St. Louis Public Schools, 1879* (St. Louis: G. I. Jones and Company, 1880), p. 74; and W. T. Harris, "The Education of the Negro," *Atlantic Monthly*, LXIX (1892), 736.
8. William T. Harris, *The Theory of Education* (Syracuse, N.Y.: C. W. Bardeen, 1893), p. 32.
9. *Ibid.*, pp. 34–35.

In effect, Harris constructed an educational philosophy that he hoped would create a truly democratic community in the emerging urban, industrial America of his day. The philosophy was abstruse in its Hegelian formulations; it was formal and institutional in its neat assignments of specific tasks to families, churches, schools, and work-places; it was austere in its relentless emphasis on obedience, disci-pline, and self-restraint; and it was ultimately conservative in its tend-ency to accept the existing order as a definition of the true America. Yet there was a radical nobility about Harris's insistence that men and women of all classes were educable and that, properly schooled, they would create a popular culture worthy of the finest aspirations of the founders of the Republic. And there was a timeliness about his insis-tence upon using the instruments of the new industrial civilization to humanize and control that civilization. Harris's signal achievement was to persuade his generation that such an education was attainable. As the best-known schoolman of his time, first in St. Louis and then in Washington, as an indefatigable participant in the organizational affairs of the emerging teaching profession, and as a prolific lecturer and writer, he put forth America's first systematic philosophy of schooling at precisely the time when schooling was moving to the center of the American configuration of education. His philosophy would be superseded even before he left the office of U.S. Commis-sioner of Education in 1906; but, in its vision of education as the most effective means of addressing the nation's social, political, and tech-nological problems, it encouraged the more deliberately (and increas-ingly scientifically) instrumental conceptions of education that would come to mark progressive thought.

II

In the spring of 1881, a twenty-one-year-old schoolteacher named John Dewey sent William T. Harris an article for the *Journal of Specula-tive Philosophy* entitled "The Metaphysical Assumptions of Material-ism." In the letter accompanying the manuscript, Dewey put a sober question to Harris. "I suppose you must be troubled with many inqui-ries of this sort," he wrote, "yet if it would not be too much to ask, I should be glad to know your opinion on it, even if you make no use of it. An opinion as to whether you considered it to show ability enough of any kind to warrant my putting much of my time on that sort of subject would be thankfully received, and, as I am a young man in doubt as to how to employ my reading hours, might be of much advantage." Harris was inordinately slow in responding—he was still shuttling back and forth between St. Louis and Concord during the early part of 1881—but his reply when it finally arrived the following autumn was warmly favorable. Indeed, he published not only "The Metaphysical Assumptions of Materialism" but also another article Dewey had sent him entitled "The Pantheism of Spinoza." Meanwhile, Dewey, who was teaching that year at a small academy in Charlotte, Vermont, was advancing his own systematic study of various philosophical classics under the tutelage of his former professor at the University of Vermont, H. A. P. Torrey. Harris's warm response, coupled with encouragement from Torrey, proved decisive. The young schoolteacher, hitherto uncertain not only about his "reading hours" but also about what to do with his life, determined to make a career in philosophy.[7]

Dewey had been born in Burlington, Vermont, in 1859 to a tobacconist's family. He had attended the public schools, had joined the First Congregational Church at the age of eleven, and had subsequently gone on to the University of Vermont, where he had read omnivorously in the library at the same time that he had pursued a fairly standard liberal arts curriculum with an emphasis in philosophy under Torrey, who was professor of intellectual and moral philosophy, and Matthew Buckham, who was president of the university. Uncertain as to a proper vocation, he had taught school between 1879 and 1881 at Oil City, Pennsylvania, where his cousin, Affia Wilson, was principal of the high school. There he had continued on his own the philosophical studies he had begun as a student at the university and there, too, he had undergone what he described as a "mystic experience" in response to insistent self-questioning as to whether he actually meant business when he prayed—years later he reported the outcome in a conversation with Max Eastman as "What the hell are you worrying about, anyway? Everything that's here is here, and you can just lie back on it."[8]

Dewey's decision to make a career in philosophy was at the least a courageous one, not unlike Emerson's search for a vocation after his resignation from the pastorship of Boston's Second Church in 1832. Most of the men who professed philosophy during the years following the Civil War were ordained clergymen who used their classes to purvey a mix of official piety and the prevailing Scottish common-

7. John Dewey to William Torrey Harris, May 17, 1881 (University of Southern California Archives). By permission of the University of Southern California.
8. Max Eastman, "John Dewey," *Atlantic,* CLXVIII (1941), 673.

sense realism. Torrey and Buckham were much in the mold, though Torrey tried to combine his Scottish realism with a measure of Kantianism that rendered his teaching at best eclectic. Be that as it may, the notion of an academic career in philosophy was ill defined during the 1880's, especially for a young man like Dewey, who had no intention of studying for the ministry but who rather envisioned the kind of secular academic appointment that was beginning to appear at some of the better universities.

Appropriately, given his aspiration, Dewey applied for graduate study at the recently founded Johns Hopkins University. At Johns Hopkins, he encountered Charles Sanders Peirce teaching logic, G. Stanley Hall teaching experimental psychology, and George Sylvester Morris teaching the history of philosophy—an extraordinary trio by any lights. He judged Peirce's logic a bit too mathematical for his taste; he was profoundly influenced by Hall's empiricism, though the influence did not become manifest for some years; and he was wholly won over by Morris, who immersed him in German philosophy, particularly the works of Kant and Hegel. Dewey completed the work for the doctorate in 1884 with a dissertation entitled "The Psychology of Kant" (there is no extant copy, but it is likely that his 1884 essay "Kant and Philosophic Method" conveys the main line of his argument) and with sufficient distinction for Morris to recommend him for an instructorship at the University of Michigan, to which Morris himself had gone as professor in 1883.

Dewey spent the years from 1884 to 1894 at Michigan, with the exception of a single academic year, 1888–89, at the University of Minnesota. During this period his work was marked by a gradual movement from the Hegelian idealism he had imbibed at Johns Hopkins to the more characteristic experimentalism of his later years. Yet Hegelianism left a permanent mark on his thinking, especially as it propelled him away from such historic philosophical dualisms as those of individual and community, body and mind, and ideal and actuality, and toward a monism that he saw as "an immense release, a liberation." It was during the Michigan years, too, that Dewey began to manifest the social concerns that would mark his career for the rest of his life. Three individuals played a critical role in this development. The first was Alice Chipman, a young woman of marked independence and social sensibility, who became Dewey's wife in 1886. The other two were Franklin and Corydon Ford, two brothers who enlisted Dewey in a somewhat grandiose scheme to bring philosophy into the service of public affairs via a newspaper to be called *Thought News* that was intended to awaken the American people to the fundamental issues of the day and lead them toward an intelligent participation in politics. The adventure itself died aborning, but the four years of planning, plotting, and discussion that surrounded the venture left their indelible mark on Dewey's thought: from the late 1880's on, the democratic commitment was a leitmotif of his philosophy. In fact, his scientifically based experimentalism charged by that democratic commitment took on something of the character of a secular evangelicism.[9]

Dewey once remarked in an autobiographical sketch that on the whole the forces that had influenced him had come from people and from situations rather than from books. The one exception, he went on to point out, had been William James's *Principles of Psychology*. Its appearance in 1890, propounding an evolutionary view of human behavior and a behavioral view of human cognition, at precisely the time Dewey was attempting to work out a more empirically grounded psychology, proved a revelation to Dewey. James's approach, Dewey observed, "worked its way more and more into all my ideas and acted as a ferment to transform old beliefs." One notes the transformation in comparing Dewey's *Psychology* (1887) with "The Reflex Arc Concept in Psychology" (1896). In the former, he attempted to join the empiricism of Hermann von Helmholtz, Gustav Fechner, and Wilhelm Wundt, an empiricism presumably learned from Hall, to the neo-Hegelianism of Morris; in the latter, he set forth the doctrine of human behavior as the behavior of organisms acting holistically and purposefully within situations, and in so doing announced the basic outlines of the new experimentalism.[10]

It was during Dewey's tenure at the University of Chicago between 1894 and 1904 that his new experimentalism came into full flower. The situation there was ripe for the development of an actively oriented, empirically based, socially concerned philosophy. Chicago had emerged as the pre-eminent midwestern city after the disastrous fire of 1871. By 1890 its population had passed a million, making it second only to New York City in size. The University of Chicago had opened in 1892 under the energetic leadership of William Rainey Harper, succored by a substantial endowment from John D. Rockefeller and by the frank aspiration of becoming the Harvard of the West. Arriving in 1894 with a decade of academic experience behind him, with the sort of personal and intellectual autonomy that derives from

9. John Dewey, "From Absolutism to Experimentalism," in George P. Adams and Wm. Pepperell Montague, eds., *Contemporary American Philosophy: Personal Statements* (New York: The Macmillan Company, 1930), p. 19.

10. *Ibid.*, pp. 22, 23–24.

the quest for one's own philosophical position, and with a growing national reputation as a psychologist, Dewey was in a superb position to take full advantage of the opportunities offered by the city and the university, and he did so with verve. He had come to know Jane Addams while he was still at Michigan, and his relocation to Chicago enabled him to participate actively in the affairs of Hull House. Through Hull House and through his membership in the Civic Federation of Chicago, he doubtless became aware of the social problems of the city and active in the politics of reform. Whatever his hopes had been for his philosophy to "make a difference" in Ann Arbor, they began to be realized in Chicago.

It was in the life of the university that Dewey found many of his most fruitful associations. Harper had initially recruited him as head of the department of philosophy, which, at the time of his arrival, included the university's work in psychology and pedagogy as well. Subsequently, on Dewey's recommendation, the work in pedagogy was organized under a separate department of education, and Dewey became head of that department as well. The opportunity to preside over the development of work in philosophy, psychology, and pedagogy was a propitious one for Dewey. It enabled him to collaborate closely with James H. Tufts, George H. Mead, and James Rowland Angell in the departments he chaired, as well as with Albion Small and W. I. Thomas in sociology, Edward W. Bemis and Thorstein Veblen in political economy, and Frederick Starr in anthropology. Like Dewey, all were able scholars who saw themselves as liberals committed to the cause of reform. Dewey's position at the university also enabled him to collaborate with his wife, Alice Chipman Dewey, in founding a Laboratory School in 1896, intended to test not only his pedagogical theories but also his philosophical and psychological theories, the assumption being that the consequences of an actively oriented, empirically based, socially concerned philosophy would reveal themselves most directly in education. The work of the Laboratory School symbolized the significance of education in Dewey's philosophy. As Dewey himself put it, his involvement in the education of the young "fused with and brought together what might otherwise have been separate interests—that in psychology and that in social institutions and social life." The school was to be the medium through which Dewey's philosophy would "make a difference"; and, through the school, society would be reformed.[11]

11. *Ibid.*, p. 22.

Not surprisingly, the Chicago years saw an outpouring of writings on education. "Interest in Relation to Training the Will" (1896) sharply criticized the Herbartian notion of interest stemming invariably from effort and proposed instead a doctrine that saw interest giving birth to effort and effort deepening interest. "Ethical Principles Underlying Education" (1897) propounded a concept of moral education that located morality within the choices children faced within the diurnal experience of the school rather than as a separate subject to be taught at a particular time. "My Pedagogic Creed" (1897) set forth a brief but comprehensive philosophy of education, defining education as the participation of the individual in the consciousness of the race, viewing the school as a social institution designed to immerse children in an embryonic social life especially organized to nurture intellectual, moral, and aesthetic development, maintaining that the subject matter of the school curriculum was nothing more or less than the accumulated experience of the race, and arguing that education was the fundamental method of social progress and reform. *The Educational Situation* (1902) considered the school system as a whole, from the elementary grades through the university, and made the case for a rethinking of the curriculum that would bring about a unification of the newer studies (drawing, music, nature study, manual training) with the older (the three R's), of studies preparing for life with studies preparing for more systematic inquiry, and of cultural studies and vocational studies. And "Democracy in Education" (1903) spoke to the need to release teachers and students alike from the kind of undesirable suppression of individuality that constrained intelligence, initiative, and independence.

The greatest of Dewey's educational writings of the Chicago period, however, was *The School and Society,* which derived from three lectures he delivered to the parents of students in the Laboratory School. In the years following its publication in 1899, it became Dewey's most widely read book—it was translated into more than a dozen foreign languages. The first lecture, entitled "The School and Social Progress," traced the profound educational changes that had followed in the wake of industrialism, notably, the decline of the small, close-knit, face-to-face rural community with its implicit "training in habits of order and of industry, and in the idea of responsibility," and sketched the modifications in schooling that were already in progress in the effort to take account of those changes—the introduction into the curriculum of new subjects like nature study and of active occupations like weaving; the relegation of the "merely symbolic" to a secondary position; the working out of new relationships between teachers and pupils as a substitute for the old discipline. The lecture concluded with a peroration that later became a manifesto of the progressive school movement:

It remains but to organize all these factors, to appreciate them in their fullness of meaning, and to put the ideas and ideals involved into complete, uncompromising possession of our school system. To do this means to make each one of our schools an embryonic community life, active with types of occupations that reflect the life of the larger society, and permeated throughout with the spirit of art, history, and science. When the school introduces and trains each child of society into membership within such a little community, saturating him with the spirit of service and providing him with the instruments of effective self-direction, we shall have the deepest and best guarantee of a larger society that is worthy, lovely, and harmonious.

The second lecture, entitled "The School and the Life of the Child," pointed to the changes that would be required if teachers were to take account of children's natural tendencies (Dewey called them instincts)—their wish to converse, to construct things, to inquire, and to express themselves artistically—and to seize upon these natural tendencies in guiding children toward true culture (which Dewey defined as "the growth of the imagination in flexibility, in scope, and in sympathy, till the life which the individual lives is informed with the life of nature and society"). The third lecture, entitled "Waste in Education," advocated a unity in the education of children that would derive from harmonious collaboration among homes, schools, libraries, museums, and universities.[12]

Dewey left the University of Chicago in 1904 after a series of conflicts with President Harper growing out of the incorporation of the Chicago Institute and its practice school into the University (the Institute had been founded in 1899 as a vehicle to advance the work of Colonel Francis W. Parker, a distinguished educator well known to Dewey, but Parker unfortunately had died in 1902) and the role of Mrs. Dewey in the management of the Institute's practice school and the Laboratory School after they were merged. Columbia University's philosophy department was expanding at the time, and, through the joint efforts of the department chairman, Dewey's old friend James McKeen Cattell, and President Nicholas Murray Butler, an appointment was arranged at Columbia (with a joint appointment at Teachers

12. John Dewey, *The School and Society* [1899], in *John Dewey: The Middle Works*, I, 7, 19–20, 38.

College, Columbia's affiliated faculty of education). Dewey took up his duties at Columbia in 1905 and remained there for the rest of his life, as professor from 1905 to 1930, as professor emeritus in residence from 1930 to 1939, and as professor emeritus until his death in 1952.

It was during the years at Columbia that Dewey achieved world renown as America's most distinguished and influential philosopher. A series of major publications over three decades provided more mature and elaborate statements of his experimentalism. The *Ethics* (with James H. Tufts, 1908) developed a conception of the moral life with specific reference to a variety of contemporary social, political, and economic issues—morality, as Dewey had argued in "Ethical Issues Underlying Education" (1897), was not some separate, encapsulated domain of human affairs. *How We Think* (1910) elaborated the idea of thought as problem solving—the concept of intelligence at the heart of Dewey's instrumentalism—and examined the bearing of that idea on the practice of education; while *Logic: The Theory of Inquiry* (1938) explored the bearing of instrumentalist doctrines on traditional formulations of logic. *Human Nature and Conduct* (1922) extended the conception of the moral life propounded in the *Ethics* and set forth the social view of individuality that Dewey had developed at Chicago with George H. Mead. *Experience and Nature* (1925) set forth his experimentalist naturalism in systematic philosophical form; while *The Quest for Certainty* (1929) set forth his instrumentalism in systematic philosophic form—operational thinking was "the naturalization of intelligence." *The Public and Its Problems* (1927) sketched a political theory based on a view of democracy as a way of involving ever expanding, mutually influential associations. *Art as Experience* (1934) related acts of artistic creation and aesthetic appreciation to the more general theory of experience that had been set forth in earlier works; while *A Common Faith* (1934) related traditional ideas of the transcendent, the holy, and the sublime to that same general theory.[13]

It was also during the years at Columbia that Dewey achieved renown as America's pre-eminent philosopher of education. His ideas, particularly as presented in *The School and Society,* became increasingly influential in educational reform circles during the first decade of the century, and the spirited discipleship of Randolph Bourne in the *New Republic* between 1914 and 1917 made those ideas commonplaces among progressive intellectuals. In addition, Dewey

13. John Dewey, *The Quest for Certainty: A Study of the Relation of Knowledge and Action* (New York: Minton, Balch & Company, 1929), p. 195.

published *Schools of To-Morrow* in 1915 (with his daughter Evelyn), presenting portraits of innovative schools along with his commentary on the theory underlying their efforts and their place in the larger movement of educational reform, and *Democracy and Education* in 1916. The latter was Dewey's magnum opus on education, setting forth his conception of democracy as not merely a political system but a form of social life, and of education as a social process nurturing the continuing social, intellectual, and aesthetic growth of individuals and, through that growth on the part of individuals, the continuing renewal and regeneration of society. "The devotion of democracy to education is a familiar fact," Dewey wrote in a now-famous passage.

The superficial explanation is that a government resting upon popular suffrage cannot be successful unless those who elect and who obey their governors are educated. Since a democratic society repudiates the principle of external authority, it must find a substitute in voluntary disposition and interest; these can be created only by education. But there is a deeper explanation. A democracy is more than a form of government; it is primarily a mode of associated living, of conjoint communicated experience. The extension in space of the number of individuals who participate in an interest so that each has to refer his own action to that of others, and to consider the action of others to give point and direction to his own, is equivalent to the breaking down of those barriers of class, race, and national territory which kept men from perceiving the full import of their activity. These more numerous and more varied points of contact denote a greater diversity of stimuli to which an individual has to respond; they consequently put a premium on variation in his action. They secure a liberation of powers which remain suppressed as long as the incitations to action are partial, as they must be in a group which in its exclusiveness shuts out many interests.

Given that conception of democracy, a type of education was required that would nurture in individuals "a personal interest in social relationships and control, and the habits of mind which secure social changes without introducing disorder."[14]

Prepared primarily as a textbook for public school teachers and administrators, *Democracy and Education* went on to detail the bearing of these ideas on the daily work of schooling—on the aims and aspirations of the enterprise, on the methods of study and instruction, and on the subject matter of the curriculum. While Dewey was explicitly aware that in one sense all institutions educate, insofar as they affect the conscious experience of those who participate in their activities,

14. John Dewey, *Democracy and Education* [1916], in *John Dewey: The Middle Works*, IX, 93, 105.

it was the deliberate agencies of education, the schools, and the explicit substance of instruction, the subjects of the curriculum, that he saw as the distinctive educative tools of a modern industrial society. Thus, following the reasoning of *The School and Society,* Dewey, like Harris before him, threw the weight of his argument onto schooling. Further, even more than Harris, he saw the school as the pre-eminent lever of reform for an intentionally progressive society. One should note, however, that Dewey's vision was in no way intended to contradict the extraordinarily broad view of education he himself assumed. The Platonic view of the good society as one that in the very character of its daily life nurtures good people was fundamental to his thought. That notwithstanding, there can be no denying that his specialized writings on education, notably *The School and Society* and *Democracy and Education,* encouraged educators to focus upon the school. Moreover, as Dewey himself once remarked, although *Democracy and Education* was for many years the work in which his more general philosophy was most fully expounded—he actually defined philosophy there as "the general theory of education"—philosophers did not so perceive the book and hence did not turn to it. In consequence, much that was essential to Dewey's thought, including much that was vital to his view of the relation between schooling and education and between education and politics, was overlooked.[15]

Beyond his writings on education, which were read by an ever broadening public in a variety of styles of rhetoric, from polemical political tracts to abstruse philosophical essays (and in a variety of foreign languages), Dewey extended his influence through direct participation in organizations such as the American Federation of Teachers, the American Association of University Professors, and the Progressive Education Association, through educational missions to countries as different as Mexico, Turkey, China, Japan, and the Soviet Union, and, indirectly, through the writings and activities of disciples such as Sidney Hook, William Heard Kilpatrick, Boyd H. Bode, John L. Childs, Robert Bruce Raup, and Harold Taylor in the United States, Hu Shih, Ch'en Ho-Ch'n, and Tsuin-Chen in China, J. J. Findley in England, and Stanislav Shatskii and Albert P. Pinkevitch in the Soviet Union. As one might suspect, too, reformers of every sort and variety clothed themselves in the mantle of his philosophy, so that a good deal of his effort in education after 1920 was spent criticizing self-styled disciples—his speech as honorary president of the Progres-

15. *Ibid.,* 338; and Dewey, "From Absolutism to Experimentalism," in Adams and Montague, eds., *Contemporary American Philosophy,* pp. 22–23.

sive Education Association in 1928 was of that genre, as was his mordant treatise *Experience and Education* in 1938, and indeed, as was the very last essay he published before his death, the introduction he wrote for Elsie Ripley Clapp's *The Use of Resources in Education* (1952).

The difficulty was not merely the classic problem of Plato vis-à-vis the Platonists or of Marx vis-à-vis the Marxists. It was rather a three-fold difficulty unique to Dewey. First, as the faculty of the University of Paris recognized when he was granted an honorary degree in 1930 with a citation describing him as "the most profound, most complete expression of American genius," Dewey synthesized in his thought so much that was characteristic of his time and place that a wide range of reformers who had read at best partially in Dewey—if at all—considered themselves Deweyans in education. Second, Dewey wrote about education over a long and fruitful career out of a variety of particular concerns and perspectives in a style that was occasionally less than crystal clear, so that from the beginning there were differences over what Dewey actually meant about this or that issue in education. And, finally, Dewey's progressive philosophy of education was so successful as to have become pervasive during the years after World War II. He himself had once expressed the hope that the adjective would eventually be dropped from the phrase "progressive education" and that progressive education would simply be good education. For better or for worse, that was essentially what happened. The fact that Dewey's arch critic of the 1930's and 1940's, Mortimer Adler, could actually publish a manifesto in 1982 entitled *The Paideia Proposal,* in which he suggested that his own philosophy was merely an extension of what Dewey might have proposed had he still been alive, was symptomatic of the phenomenon. One was reminded of Voltaire's great aphorism about history being a device for playing tricks on the dead.[16]

III

Jane Addams and John Dewey had probably become acquainted during the winter of 1891–92. It had been slightly over two years since Addams and her college classmate Ellen Gates Starr had founded

16. *New York Times,* November 9, 1930, p. 12; and Mortimer Adler, *The Paideia Proposal: An Educational Manifesto* (New York: The Macmillan Publishing Co., 1982), pp. v, 3–7. Adler's colleague at the University of Chicago, Allan Bloom, was more direct in distinguishing between Dewey's modernism and his own antimodernism in *The Closing of the American Mind: How Higher Education Has Failed Democracy and Impoverished the Souls of Today's Students* (New York: Simon and Schuster, 1987).

Hull House on the South Side of Chicago, and already the old, two-storied brick mansion had become something of a Mecca for those interested in progressive causes. Dewey, then thirty-two, was at the peak of his enthusiasm for the Ford brothers' schemes of social reform; Addams, a year younger, had thrown herself wholeheartedly into her plan to enter into "reciprocal relation" with her neighbors on South Halsted Street. Dewey apparently visited the settlement for a few days and then, on his return to Ann Arbor, wrote Addams, "My indebtedness to you for giving me an insight into matters there is great. While I did not see much of any particular thing I think I got a pretty good idea of the general spirit and method. Every day I stayed there only added to my conviction that you had taken the right way." Later, when he accepted the professorship of philosophy at the University of Chicago, he returned regularly to Hull House, to lecture, to observe, and to join the residents for dinner, and, after 1897, when a board of trustees was created, to serve as a trustee. He and Addams would remain good friends until her death in 1935.[17]

The work of Addams and her associates at Hull House has already been described as one of the more interesting expressions of social Christianity during the last years of the nineteenth century and first years of the twentieth. Settlement activities tended to be pragmatic, experimental, and studiedly informal, ranging from clubs for the promotion of various social and ethnic causes to investigations into neighborhood conditions that led to programs of social reform. Addams often noted the purposefully unsystematic character of such activities, explaining that the settlement was "an institution attempting to learn from life itself." Yet there was a common theme that ran through them all, namely, the commitment to mutual education on the part of residents and clients. Addams understood that commitment from the beginning, with the result that the ideas she formulated in developing and reflecting upon the Hull House program became one of the prime sources of reformist educational theory during the Progressive era.[18]

Characteristically, those ideas began as criticisms of contemporary educational practice. The settlement, Addams once remarked, was a protest against a restricted view of education. In the case of young

17. John Dewey to Jane Addams, January 27, 1892 (Rockford College Archives), by permission of Rockford College; and Jane Addams, "The Subjective Necessity for Social Settlements," in Christopher Lasch, ed., *The Social Thought of Jane Addams* (Indianapolis: The Bobbs-Merrill Company, 1965), p. 29.

18. Jane Addams, *The Second Twenty Years at Hull-House* (New York: Macmillan Company, 1930), p. 408.

children, this meant an enthusiastic embrace of Pestalozzian and Froebelian ideals, with their emphasis on self-expression as a central pedagogical device, on the harmonious development of head, heart, and hand as a goal of the curriculum, and on a close collaboration between home and school in the nurturance of youngsters. In the case of boys and girls, it meant a vigorous attempt to reconnect the schools with the families and neighborhoods from which they drew their students. In the case of young men and women about to go to work, it meant a concerted effort to give them some sense of the history and nature of a modern urban, industrial society, so that, wherever they ended up as workers, they would have a conception of the whole and of their own particular parts in it—she gave much of *The Spirit of Youth and the City Streets* (1909), which she always claimed was her favorite book, to this need for workers to have a sense of context that would give meaning to their lives. Finally, in the case of adults, it meant the abandonment of the formal lectures associated with university extension courses and the substitution of vital discussions of contemporary social issues. "A settlement soon discovers that simple people are interested in large and vital subjects," Addams noted in *Twenty Years at Hull-House;* and she cited instance after instance of the residents themselves managing to offer more successful courses than the university specialists they had recruited to teach them. Simple people did not want to hear about simple things, she liked to remark; they wanted to hear about great things, simply told.[19]

The settlement was a protest against a restricted view of education. But it was also the living embodiment of an alternative view of education, one that centered in reformed conceptions of the uses of knowledge, the meaning of culture, and the nature of community. Addams returned again and again to these themes in her writings. "The ideal and developed settlement," she observed in an 1899 article, "would attempt to test the value of human knowledge by action, and realization, quite as the complete and ideal university would concern itself with the discovery of knowledge in all its branches. The settlement stands for application as opposed to research; for emotion as opposed to abstraction, for universal interest as opposed to specialization." She was careful to point out that in emphasizing the application of knowledge she was not merely voicing the traditional American concern with the cash value of ideas. Rather, she had in mind "an application to a given neighborhood of the solace of literature, of the

19. Jane Addams, *Twenty Years at Hull-House* (New York: The Macmillan Company, 1910), pp. 428, 431.

uplift of the imagination, and of the historic consciousness which gives its possessor a sense of connection with the men of the past who have thought and acted, an application of the stern mandates of science, not only to the conditions of sewers and the care of alleys, but to the methods of life and thought; the application of the metaphysic not only to the speculations of the philosopher, but to the events of the passing moment; the application of the moral code to the material life, the transforming of the economic relation into an ethical relation until the sense that religion itself embraces all relations, including the ungodly industrial relation, has become the common property." And she cautioned, too, that in its concern for application, emotion, and universal interest, the settlement was neither a minor adjunct to the university nor a poor imitation of the church. It was rather an educative agency in its own right, with its own unique calling, its own characteristic pedagogy, and its own special relationships with its clientele. Its force was centrifugal. Instead of drawing educational functions unto itself, it reached out into the community to help organize social relations in such a way that the community itself would become educative and conduct, in Addams's apt phrase, a "means of propaganda."[20]

Addams's conception of culture was implicit in her idea of the settlement as "an attempt to express the meaning of life in terms of life itself." She began at Hull House with ideas she had gleaned from Thomas Carlyle, John Ruskin, and Matthew Arnold, of culture as something apart from the diurnal life, of culture as "the best which has been thought and said in the world"; and she conceived of the settlement as an effort to share the cultivation that the residents had acquired in their homes and at their colleges with the impoverished immigrants of the slum. She soon altered her view, as she came increasingly to find culture among the very immigrants she had initially thought brutish and uncultivated. In a 1908 address to the National Education Association, she defined culture as "a knowledge of those things which have been long cherished by men, the things which men have loved because thru [sic] generations they have softened and interpreted life, and have endowed it with meaning." She came to believe that one could find culture in the vibrant life of the immigrant community as well as in the refined life of the upper middle class, that one could find it in the amusements of parks and playgrounds as well

20. Jane Addams, "A Function of the Social Settlement," in Ellen Condliffe Lagemann, ed., *Jane Addams on Education* (New York: Teachers College Press, 1985), pp. 78, 83; and Jane Addams, "Tolstoy and Gandhi," *Christian Century*, XLVIII (1931), 1485–1488.

as in the instruction of classrooms, and that one could find it in manufacturing and commercial processes as well as in the activities associated with leisure. In effect, the Labor Museum at Hull House was her way of concretizing those beliefs. There was an element of romanticism in such arguments, of course, of the sort associated with the so-called arts and crafts movement, with its assumption that once workingpeople understood the sources of industrial art and process they would work "in gladness and not in woe." But they did broaden, expand, and in the process democratize the concept of culture and the sources from which it was seen to derive.[21]

Addams's conception of community was similarly connected to her ideas concerning the application of knowledge and the meaning of culture. "Intellectual life requires for its expansion and manifestation the influences and assimilation of the interests and affections of others," she observed in *Twenty Years at Hull-House*. "Mazzini, the greatest of all democrats, who broke his heart over the condition of the South European peasantry, said: 'Education is not merely a necessity of true life by which the individual renews his vital force in the vital force of humanity; it is a Holy Communion with generations dead and living, by which he fecundates all his faculties.'" The theme, of course, was at the heart of the Christian communalism that inspired the establishment of settlements in England and the United States. And the writings of Mazzini and of Tolstoy could be quoted at length on the subject of universal brotherhood and the need to create social relations that advanced universal brotherhood (though there are the well-known passages in *Twenty Years at Hull-House* in which Addams recounts her rejection of Tolstoy's preachments on "bread labor" for all who would be part of human brotherhood). Most important, perhaps, Addams's conception of community, like her conception of culture, was expansive and inclusive. She saw political and economic problems as essentially social problems, and she saw problems of poverty, prostitution, and crime as problems of warped social relations. Similarly, her idea of "socialized education" bespoke her belief that social relations could be made right if culture could be disseminated through the community and if men and women could be empowered to act upon the insights they derived from culture. "The educational activities of a settlement," she wrote in the concluding

21. Addams, "A Function of the Social Settlement," in Lagemann, ed., *Jane Addams on Education*, p. 78; Matthew Arnold, *Culture and Anarchy* [1869], edited by J. Dover Wilson (Cambridge: Cambridge University Press, 1969), p. 6; Jane Addams, "The Public School and the Immigrant Child," in Lagemann, ed., *Jane Addams on Education*, p. 137; Ellen Gates Starr, "Art and Labor," in *Hull-House Maps and Papers* (New York: Thomas Y. Crowell & Co., 1895), p. 178.

sentence of *Twenty Years at Hull-House,* "as well as its philanthropic, civic, and social undertakings, are but different manifestations of the attempt to socialize democracy, as is the very existence of the settlement itself." In a socialized democracy, the community itself would become educative in the diurnal business of contending with public issues and solving public problems. And out of the process would come a continually evolving definition of the common good.[22]

There has been a tendency among scholars to see John Dewey as the quintessential progressive theorist of education and Jane Addams as the quintessential progressive activist in education, with Dewey as the mentor and Addams as the disciple. The interpretation is incorrect on several counts. For one thing, by their own admission each learned much from the other, with Addams quoting Dewey again and again in her writings and Dewey acknowledging that his faith in democracy as a guiding force in education took on sharper and deeper meaning because of Addams and the work she did at Hull House. More fundamentally, however, it is important to see Jane Addams as a theorist of education in her own right. Dewey and Addams both shared a conception of "socialized democracy" that was common among reform-oriented Progressives during the quarter-century before World War I; and they both were well aware that in the end life itself educates. But whereas Dewey turned to a reconstructed school and a reconstructed university as levers of social change, Addams assigned what was at best a limited role to schools and universities in the cause of social reform and turned instead to settlements and similar institutions as educational forces that would energize the community to become itself the most potent of all educative forces. Dewey argued similar views during the 1930's, in works such as *Liberalism and Social Action* and *Freedom and Culture,* but by then he had become associated in the minds of educators and of the public at large with reformed schooling. Addams, on the other hand, continued to inspire community educators, not only in her own time but in the late 1930's and then again in the 1960's and 1970's, when concepts of community education went hand in hand with concepts of political reform and social reconstruction. By recognizing both as theorists of education, one recaptures the diverse emphases that flowed from the progressive commitment to education as an instrument of social and political reform.[23]

22. Addams, *Twenty Years at Hull-House,* pp. 427, 276–277, 453.
23. Jane Addams, "A Toast to John Dewey," *Survey,* LXIII (1929), 203–204; and Jane M. Dewey, ed., "Biography of John Dewey," in Paul Arthur Schilpp, ed., *The Philosophy of John Dewey* (2d ed.; New York: Tudor Publishing Company, 1951), p. 30.

IV

Walter Lippmann was a generation younger than John Dewey and Jane Addams, but as a self-styled socialist, progressive, philosopher, and intellectual, he came early upon their ideas and made many of them his own. He probably encountered Dewey's writings as a student of philosophy at Harvard between 1906 and 1910, under the tutelage of William James, George Santayana, and the English social scientist Graham Wallas. And he gave every evidence of a thorough and generally favorable acquaintance with Jane Addams's writings by the time he published *A Preface to Politics* in 1913. By 1916, he was prepared to say of Dewey's *Democracy and Education:* "It is an abundant book which will light the future for every one who lives with it. It is rich in that wisdom which democracies need, the common wisdom which must lie beneath the diverse activities of all the professions. It is a great book because it expresses more deeply and more comprehensively than any other that could be named the best hope of liberal men." From the bright young *enfant terrible* of the *New Republic,* that was high praise indeed. More important, Lippmann's early response to Dewey in the *New Republic* marked the beginning of a dialogue between the two men that would continue, with profit to the public, for the remainder of their lives.[24]

Born in New York City in 1889, Lippmann had grown up as the only son of a comfortable, middle-class German-Jewish family that had been able to give him every advantage. He had attended the fashionable Sachs School and had then gone on to Harvard, where he had not only performed brilliantly in his courses but had also played a central role in student affairs as organizer and president of the Socialist Club. In fact, Lippmann's discovery of socialism at Harvard—socialism of the Fabian variety—may well have been the most important element in his education there, for it projected him into politics and journalism, which remained the two dominant interests of his life, and it planted in his mind the idea of a selfless group of enlightened intellectuals who would lead the masses to a better world via radical but nonviolent revolution based on education.

Like Dewey and Addams, Lippmann spent several years searching for a proper vocation. He moved ahead rapidly at Harvard, so that by 1909–10 he had finished most of his undergraduate courses and was working on a master's degree in philosophy and serving as Santayana's assistant. However much he enjoyed the experience, and

24. *New Republic,* VII (1916), 231.

however much he was drawn to Santayana, he did not complete the work for the graduate degree and decided instead to work—first, as a cub reporter on the *Boston Commons,* a reformist weekly published by his friend Ralph Albertson, and then, as an assistant to Lincoln Steffens, the editor of *Everybody's Magazine.* During both stints, he also wrote articles and editorials as a free-lance for various socialist periodicals. Then, in 1912, he signed on as an assistant to the newly elected Socialist mayor of Schenectady, New York, but soon grew impatient with the insistent demands of politics and returned to New York City. There, his friend Alfred Knopf urged him to write a book, and he repaired to the Maine woods to do so. The result was *A Preface to Politics* (1913), a series of forthright essays that sounded many of the theses that would mark Lippmann's characteristically "realist" criticism over the years—the need to channel popular passions rather than to repress them, the importance of science as the essential discipline of intellect and therefore of democracy, and the promise of a partnership between intellectuals, who would illuminate the great issues of the day with objective data, and statesmen, who, armed with objective data, would satisfy public wants and make social movements conscious of themselves.

On the basis of *A Preface to Politics,* Herbert Croly, whose book *The Promise of American Life* (1909) had been projected to national attention by the enthusiastic embrace of Theodore Roosevelt, invited Lippmann to join himself, Walter Weyl, Francis Hackett, and others in editing a new magazine devoted to "constructive nationalism" that would be called the *New Republic.* Lippmann accepted and in so doing found his vocation. The magazine quickly succeeded in attracting a devoted audience, and Lippmann reveled in carrying on a kind of personal journalism in dialogue with that audience. Later, during the 1920's, he would be director of the editorial page of the New York *World;* and, after that, when the *World* expired in 1931, he would launch the column "Today and Tomorrow" that he would carry on regularly for thirty-six years and that would ultimately run in more than two hundred newspapers. There had been personal journalists before, Horace Greeley, for example, or Henry J. Raymond or Charles A. Dana, but none had ever before made the regular column a vehicle of public education on a scale approaching Lippmann's. And none, either, had ever been so consistently close to the great political personalities of his day.

It was during the years of World War I and the immediate postwar period that Lippmann became preoccupied with the problems that he dealt with in the book that was destined to become a classic of educational theory, *Public Opinion* (1922). The ideas and events that went into the making of that book form an important chapter in the evolution of American progressivism. The young Lippmann had taken two significant themes from his teacher Graham Wallas: one, the concept of the "great society," so large in numbers of people and complex in its interrelationships as to provide an invisible environment that men and women could never know at first hand; the other, the concept of human nature in politics, the passions, prejudices, and irrationalities that seemed to make a mockery of such formal political notions as rational choice, national will, and the general good. He had explicated and expanded these themes in *A Preface to Politics* and its sequel, *Drift and Mastery* (1914), and in his articles and editorials for the *New Republic,* and he had used them as important context for his understanding of the events associated with World War I. But it was not until he saw service, first, as an officer in the propaganda division of the U.S. Army, and then, as a policy adviser to President Woodrow Wilson and Colonel Edward House in the framing of the peace treaty, that he recognized the implications of these themes for his own vocation of journalism. He set forth these implications in a pair of articles for the *Atlantic Monthly* in 1919 that subsequently became the body of a book called *Liberty and the News* (1920). What Lippmann argued, essentially, was that men and women in "the great society" perceived public issues and made up their minds on those public issues, not on the basis of firsthand acquaintance with the facts, but rather on the basis of the information they had at hand, most of which came from news carried by the press; that the mechanism of the "news supply" had developed "without plan" and that there was no point at which one could "fix responsibility for truth"; and that, until journalists were better educated and held to a higher standard of "truth," men and women would inevitably end up the victims of agitation and propaganda. "A useful definition of liberty is obtainable only by seeking the principle of liberty in the main business of human life, that is to say, in the process by which men educate their response and learn to control their environment," Lippmann maintained. "In this view liberty is the name we give to measures by which we protect and increase the veracity of the information upon which we act."[25]

Liberty and the News raised many more problems than it solved; and

25. Walter Lippmann, *Liberty and the News* (New York: Harcourt, Brace and Howe, 1920), pp. 41, 68.

it whetted Lippmann's appetite for further inquiry. Having made an informal agreement with Alfred Harcourt to give him first look at any manuscript that resulted, Lippmann took leave from the *New Republic*, severed other regular commitments, and repaired to his summer home on Long Island to undertake a major development of his ideas. The result was *Public Opinion* (1922), which changed the way Americans thought about their larger education via the press. Lippmann's argument there was essentially an expansion of his thesis in *Liberty and the News* joined to a more concrete and elaborate proposal for reform. The world people have to deal with politically, he began, is "out of reach, out of sight, out of mind." What individuals substitute for that world is a series of pictures in their heads, derived from propaganda, public relations, and information purveyed by scores of political, economic, and social interest groups via printed media, especially newspapers proffering news. News, Lippmann continued, must be clearly distinguished from truth. The function of news is "to signalize an event"; news is the end product of a selective process through which interest groups purvey, censors excise, reporters report, and editors choose. Readers read the highly selective end product and form opinions on the basis of it; their collective opinions are public opinion. And yet, Lippmann continued, the function of truth is "to bring to light the hidden facts, to set them into relation with each other, and to make a picture of reality on which men can act." Truth is the result of organized intelligence, systematically applied. It can be discovered and determined only by disinterested experts long steeped in the substance of their expertise, experts who are not partisan to any economic, political, or social interest, experts who are committed solely to the search for truth. The only way truth would ever become available to the public, Lippmann concluded, would be for the federal government to develop "intelligence sections" parallel to the various departments represented in the cabinet, sections staffed by bodies of tenured experts, rendered by tenure and liberal retirement provisions free from the temptations of power, inspired by a selfless equanimity, and devoted to the process of developing and organizing reliable knowledge. Detached from interests and committed to objectivity, they would produce the data that would guide policy makers in formulating their proposals. The result would be a disengagement of intellectuals from politicians, and then a rejoining of the two on a new basis that would provide a firmer foundation for the functioning of good government. Such intelligence sections would also disseminate information broadly to the public at large, providing it too with a firmer foundation for the formulation of individual opinions, and hence of public opinion.[26]

Recognizing that he was calling for nothing less than the re-education of the public in its ways of getting and using information, Lippmann also propounded a new role for the school. "As a working model of the social system becomes available to the teacher, he can use it to make the pupil acutely aware of how his mind works on unfamiliar facts," Lippmann argued. What teachers could do incomparably well would be to make students aware of propaganda and equip them to examine the sources of information. In the process, they could also make students more deeply sensitive to their own subjectivism at the same time that they taught them to be more consistently rational, objective, and intelligent in forming their own views of the world.[27]

Public Opinion was generally well received by the critics. Charles E. Merriam of the University of Chicago proclaimed it "brilliant" and "indispensable"; while Merriam's colleague Robert E. Park observed that no other work had come so near to providing "a text for the social psychological interpretation of politics." The *Springfield Republican* praised the book for its "intellectual integrity and penetration of a high order"; and the *Yale Review* referred to it as a "pioneering work." Probably no one wrote a more searching analysis of the book, however, than Lippmann's friend John Dewey. Dewey was lavish in his praise of *Public Opinion*. "To read the book is an experience in illumination . . . ," he wrote. "The figures of the scene are so composed and so stand out, the manner of presentation is so objective and projective, that one finishes the book almost without realizing that it is perhaps the most effective indictment of democracy as currently conceived ever penned." Dewey summarized the work astutely, explicating Lippmann's indictment and setting forth the remedies he proposed. But it was on the matter of establishing organizations of disinterested experts who would advise policy makers and inform the public on public affairs that Dewey took issue with Lippmann. In effect, Dewey saw the enlightenment of public opinion as far more important than the enlightenment of public officials. In fact, he saw the enlightenment of public opinion as of the essence in the maintenance of democracy. "Mr. Lippmann," Dewey observed, "has thrown

26. Walter Lippmann, *Public Opinion* (New York: Harcourt, Brace and Company, 1922), pp. 29, 358, 386.
27. *Ibid.*, p. 408.

into clearer relief than any other writer the fundamental difficulty of democracy. But the difficulty is so fundamental that it can be met, it seems to me, only by a solution more fundamental than he has dared to give. When necessity drives, invention and accomplishment may amazingly respond. Democracy demands a more thoroughgoing education than the education of officials, administrators and directors of industry. Because this fundamental general education is at once so necessary and difficult of achievement, the enterprise of democracy is so challenging. To sidetrack it to the task of enlightenment of administrators and executives is to miss something of its range and its challenge." Whereas Lippmann was prepared to stake the future of democracy on an educated leadership, Dewey insisted that only an educated community would suffice.[28]

Lippmann drew the difference even more sharply in *The Phantom Public* (1925), which he put forward as "A Sequel to 'Public Opinion.' " There he distinguished pointedly between "insiders," who actually carried on the business of government, and "outsiders," who could at best make judgments about the work of insiders from time to time. "Only the insider can make decisions, not because he is inherently a better man but because he is so placed that he can understand and can act. The outsider is necessarily ignorant, usually irrelevant and often meddlesome, because he is trying to navigate the ship from dry land." In the end, all outsiders could really do was to monitor the work of insiders and act occasionally to take the part of one group of interests against another or to adjust the relationship among all the interests, in the process defining the public interest. Assuming the distinction, Lippmann argued for an education for citizenship clearly different from an education for public officials, an education that could provide public opinion "with its own usable canons of judgment." Once again, Dewey was full of praise for the profundity of Lippmann's analysis but critical of the sharp distinctions between insiders and outsiders and the education appropriate to each. The great society had created new problems for democracy, Dewey observed, but Lippmann's solutions were at best palliatives. "I do not for a moment suppose that these remarks militate against the great value of Mr. Lippmann's discussion," Dewey wrote at the end of his review in the *New Republic*. "But perhaps they suggest the need of

28. *International Journal of Ethics*, XXXIII (1923), 211; *American Journal of Sociology*, XXVIII (1922), 234; *Springfield Republican*, May 7, 1922, p. 15a; *Yale Review*, XII (1923), 419; and John Dewey, "Review of Walter Lippmann, *Public Opinion*" [*New Republic*, 1922], in *John Dewey: The Middle Works*, XIII, 337–344.

further analysis, which should take account primarily of the inherent problems and dangers the Great Society has brought with it, with respect to which the weakness of democracy seems symptomatic rather than causal."[29]

Dewey himself undertook that "further analysis" in *The Public and Its Problems* (1927). Beginning with the reality of the great society, Dewey saw the key problem of democracy in the twentieth century as the transformation of the great society into a great community. And for the educational dynamic that would bring the great community into being, he returned to his formulation in *Democracy and Education,* of democracy as a mode of associated living, of conjoint, communicated experience. "Popular government," he argued, alluding to Tocqueville, "is educative as other modes of political regulation are not. It forces a recognition that there are common interests, even though the recognition of *what* they are is confused; and the need it enforces of discussion and publicity brings about some clarification of what they are. The man who wears the shoe knows best that it pinches and where it pinches, even if the expert shoemaker is the best judge of how the trouble is to be remedied." It was this experiential process of public education that Dewey counted on to render "outsiders" capable of judgment and hence capable of self-government. A free and responsible press, informed by social scientists, could vastly improve the quality of that public education and thereby hasten the emergence of a true public. Dewey was prepared to trust that public with the ultimate power of government far more readily than any restricted class of experts. It may have been that Lippmann had spent more time with those experts and was more inclined to trust them; whatever the reason, he and Dewey never came together on that fundamental educational and political issue.[30]

Lippmann returned to the problems of education from time to time in his writings after 1925, most frequently to lament the foolishness of ill-informed popular majorities in imposing unwise restrictions on the schools (as in *American Inquisitors* [1928], where he dramatized the issues in the Scopes trial between ignorant majorities and informed experts) or to condemn the wrongheadedness of modernists who removed the solid substance of traditional studies from the school curriculum (as in *Essays in the Public Philosophy* [1955], where he

29. Walter Lippmann, *The Phantom Public: A Sequel to "Public Opinion"* (New York: The Macmillan Company, 1925), pp. 150, 151; *New Republic,* XLV (1925), 54.
30. John Dewey, *The Public and Its Problems* (2d ed.; Chicago: Gateway Books, 1946), p. 207.

attacked the "Jacobin heresy" he believed to be at the heart of popular schooling). But it was his writings on the press during the 1920's that propounded a fresh analysis of the problem of popular education. It was an analysis that leaders of free and unfree governments around the globe would turn to their own uses, at the same time that educators tended to ignore it, believing that by manipulating the school curriculum they could ultimately change the world.[31]

V

Dewey once remarked that, whereas his earlier educational writings dealt with society in general, his later educational writings dealt with particular societies at particular places and times. Certainly that particularity marked his writings on Chinese, Turkish, Mexican, and Russian education during the 1920's, and it increasingly marked his writings on American education during the 1930's. Addressing himself to the problems of a nation "divided against itself"—a nation whose material culture was "verging upon the collective and corporate" but whose moral culture was "still saturated with ideal [sic] and values of an individualism derived from the prescientific, pretechnological age"—Dewey became both more specific and more concrete in the proposals he advanced and the policies he endorsed. The result was that he moved to the forefront of one of the most vigorous, and in many ways illuminating, debates over the ends and means of education in the nation's history, namely, the debate carried in the pages of a monthly called the *Social Frontier* during the years between 1934 and 1939.[32]

The *Social Frontier* was a characteristic product of the Depression, though its roots lay in the extraordinary group of educational theorists who had earlier gathered around Dewey and his student William Heard Kilpatrick at Teachers College, Columbia University, during the 1920's. The group included Harold Rugg, George S. Counts, John L. Childs, R. Bruce Raup, Goodwin Watson, Edmund deS. Brunner, Jesse Newlon, Harold F. Clark, and F. Ernest Johnson. Sharing a common orientation derived from the sort of analysis Dewey had undertaken in *Democracy and Education,* they had begun in 1927 systematically to analyze the sweeping changes in American education

31. Walter Lippmann, *American Inquisitors: A Commentary on Dayton and Chicago* (New York: The Macmillan Company, 1928), and *Essays in the Public Philosophy* (Boston: Little, Brown and Company, 1955), pp. 73–78.
32. John Dewey, *Individualism Old and New* (New York: Menton, Balch & Company, 1930), pp. 9, 74.

brought on by the rapid industrialization of American society. When the Depression struck, they saw themselves uniquely equipped—and uniquely responsible—for working out a social and educational agenda that would address itself to the needs of an America in crisis. The announcement of their effort came in George S. Counts's *Dare the School Build a New Social Order?* (1932); the more elaborate presentation of their proposals came in a symposium under Kilpatrick's editorship entitled *The Educational Frontier* (1933); and the extended effort to sharpen and refine their proposals in discussion came in the *Social Frontier*.

Counts had come to Teachers College in 1927, having established himself during the previous decade as an incisive student of American and Russian education. His pamphlet *Dare the School Build a New Social Order?* electrified the teaching profession. Counts argued, contrary to most of the conventional wisdom of the time, that the country was in the throes of a crisis brought on by the failure of capitalism to organize and maintain production; that fundamental changes in the economic system were imperative and that teachers needed to take the lead in planning for a courageous and intelligent reconstruction of economic institutions in the interest of a more just and equitable distribution of the nation's wealth; and that, even though the school was merely one formative agency among many and far from the strongest, teachers had an obligation to think through a vision of the American future and then systematically indoctrinate their students in that vision. "That the teachers should deliberately reach for power and then make the most of their conquest is my firm conviction," Counts announced. "To the extent that they are permitted to fashion the curriculum and the procedures of the school they will definitely and positively influence the social attitudes, ideals, and behavior of the coming generation. . . . It is my observation that the men and women who have affected the course of human events are those who have not hesitated to use the power that has come to them. Representing as they do, not the interests of the moment or of any special class, but rather the common and abiding interests of the people, teachers are under heavy social obligation to protect and further those interests. In this they occupy a relatively unique position in society." Counts was no fool; he was only too aware, as he noted, that "ruling classes never surrender their privileges voluntarily." Yet he had early imbibed both the optimism and the evangelism of the Kansas frontier. "The age is pregnant with possibilities," he assured. "There lies within our grasp the most humane, the most beautiful, the most majestic civilization ever fashioned by any people." Years later, when asked how on reflection he might have written the pamphlet differently, he replied, "I might have placed it more in the context of history."[33]

The Educational Frontier was less stirring, less imaginative, and on the whole less hopeful. Prepared as a yearbook of the National Society of College Teachers of Education by Kilpatrick, Dewey, Childs, and Raup of Teachers College, Boyd H. Bode and H. Gordon Hullfish of Ohio State University, and V. T. Thayer of the Ethical Culture Schools, it had the strengths and weaknesses of a collaborative volume: the authors clearly shared an orientation, but they just as clearly differed on certain significant matters. Like Counts (and like Dewey in *Individualism Old and New*), the authors pointed to the disjunction between the corporatism of the material world wrought by science and technology and the individualism of the moral world inherited from an older agrarian society. Like Counts, too, they called upon teachers to take the lead in planning a social and economic reconstruction of American society suitable to the times and to adapt every aspect of schooling to that reconstruction. Unlike Counts, however, the authors were unwilling explicitly to recommend indoctrination. Moreover, they were far less sanguine about the school making much of a difference in the business of social reconstruction until the larger social ambience within which the school carried on its work had been altered. Thus, Raup called upon teachers to enter the political lists and struggle for a better life in order to create a more hospitable and productive world in which to educate. "When the type of character desired by the school is so dependent for support upon conditions in the whole culture," he maintained, "and this support is not forthcoming, the educator's responsibility moves out into society to agitate and work for that support."[34]

The Educational Frontier appeared in the spring of 1933. During the months that followed, the spirit of inquiry it both incarnated and urged quickened at the same time that the sense of crisis engendered by the Depression deepened. Sometime during the 1933–34 academic year, apparently under the prodding of two graduate students at Teachers College, Mordecai Grossman and Norman Woelfel, it was decided to start a journal called the *Social Frontier* that would carry the

33. George S. Counts, *Dare the School Build a New Social Order?* (New York: The John Day Company, 1932), pp. 28–29, 51, 35. Counts's reflection on the pamphlet in the early 1950's was made in a conversation with the author.

34. William H. Kilpatrick, ed., *The Educational Frontier* (New York: The Century Co., 1933), p. 100.

analysis forward, with Kilpatrick as chairman of a national board of directors and Counts as editor. The first issue appeared in October, 1934, proclaiming that American society, along with world society, was passing through an age of transition in which individualism was giving way to closer integration in social and economic life and in which collective planning and control were required; that education would inevitably play a vital role in the social and economic reconstruction that was needed; and that it was the intention of the editors to open their pages to all who might be interested in helping education to discharge its full responsibility.

The journal created a considerable stir during its first few years, though its circulation never rose much above five thousand. It ran lengthy symposia on the morality of indoctrination, with participants as varied as F. J. Sheed, a leading Roman Catholic publisher, and Earl Browder, the general secretary of the Communist Party of the United States, and on the situation of American youth, with participants ranging from Merle Curti, a historian at Smith College, to Gil Green, the secretary of the Young Communist League. It ran a major discussion of the role of social class in American society and education, with Theodore Brameld of Adelphi College setting forth a Marxist view and with Bode, Dewey, Childs, Raup, and Rugg responding from varying non-Marxist perspectives. And it invited a series of social commentators from the Socialist Norman Thomas to the anarchist Harry Kelly to outline their several visions of the new American commonwealth. John Dewey and William Heard Kilpatrick wrote regular columns for the journal, and the list of sometime contributors included such contemporary luminaries as Charles Beard, Lewis Mumford, Sidney Hook, William F. Ogburn, Robert M. Hutchins, Mortimer Adler, and Henry Pratt Fairchild. The journal commented not only on the work of the schools and colleges but also on the educational activities and potential of the press, the cinema, the churches, unions and employers, and the Civilian Conservation Corps. And it covered a wider range of social commentary in its book review columns than any comparable journal. Despite the journal's liveliness, however, it had trouble holding its audience. Its subscription list shrank markedly in 1936 and by the spring of 1937 it was on the verge of bankruptcy. Counts, Grossman, and Woelfel resigned from their editorial responsibilities that year, and Kilpatrick assumed the leadership for a time, to be followed by George Hartmann, a social psychologist on the faculty of Teachers College. In 1939, the Progressive Education Association undertook sponsorship of the journal, under a new name, *Frontiers of Democracy,* and in a new format. There was much talk about continuity of mission, but the times, the issues, and the editors had changed. In effect, the original journal had died.

For all the differences among those who came to be known as the "frontier thinkers," it was their common view of the crisis in American society and of the crucial role of education in the resolution of that crisis that *The Educational Frontier* and the *Social Frontier* ultimately conveyed. And that common view, not surprisingly, attracted its share of sharp criticism from at least two sources, the radical left and the humanist right. In 1937, Zalmen Slesinger, a young Palestinian Jew who had studied at the University of California, New York University, Dropsie College, and then Teachers College, published the doctoral dissertation he had written under the tutelage of Childs, Counts, Kilpatrick, Raup, and Isaac L. Kandel entitled *Education and the Class Struggle: A Critical Examination of the Liberal Educator's Program for Social Reconstruction.* In it, he undertook a detailed analysis of the views of the "frontier thinkers" from a Marxist-Leninist perspective. The failure of the liberal program, Slesinger contended, derived from the failure of the liberals to comprehend the class structure of American society and hence their naive belief that a fundamental reconstruction of society could be effected by democratic means, with the schools playing a role. Arguing that the real need was for the total destruction of the class economy and its replacement by a collectivist system, Slesinger called for the organization and radicalization by revolutionary intellectuals of every major segment of the society—professionals, small businessmen, writers, artists, teachers, workingpeople, farmers, students, and the unemployed. In contrast with the "frontier thinkers," Slesinger had little faith that schools could contribute much to social reconstruction. "In view of the class character of our society," he concluded, "we must be skeptical about the importance of the school system as an instrument in effecting a revolutionary change within the present order."[35]

Dewey reviewed Slesinger's book for the *Nation* shortly after its appearance. He was gracious in his appreciation of Slesinger's fairness and objectivity in presenting the liberals' arguments, but direct in drawing the differences between Slesinger and the liberals. The important point, Dewey argued, "is the contrast set up between democratic processes and those of class conflict. Mr. Slesinger's book is

---

35. Zalmen Slesinger, *Education and the Class Struggle: A Critical Examination of the Liberal Educator's Program for Social Reconstruction* (New York: Covici-Friede, Publishers, 1937), p. 294.

noteworthy for the rigidity and completeness with which he presents an absolute 'either-or' position. He leaves no option save that between individuals as individuals and economic classes set over against one another in total opposition. There is no place left for social interplay and modification of one group by another." The inconsistency that resulted, in Dewey's view, was the exaggerated power and potential that Slesinger assigned to revolutionary intellectuals. Dewey did not see how, in the sort of class-based society portrayed by Slesinger, intellectuals would have any more power as educators than the schoolteachers of whom Slesinger despaired.[36]

On the humanist right, no voice was more sharply critical of the "frontier thinkers" than that of Robert M. Hutchins. A precocious and articulate educator, trained as a lawyer at the Yale Law School, he had become secretary of Yale University in 1923 (at the age of twenty-four), dean of the Yale Law School in 1928, and president of the University of Chicago in 1929. As early as 1935, he had begun to criticize the ideas of the "frontier thinkers." "In all educational endeavor the basic question is, What are we trying to do?" he told the Pittsburgh Teachers Association in April of that year. "At present a group of able educators in New York are attempting to convince us that what we should be doing is preparing our pupils to bring about a new era of collectivism." And a month later, he carried the argument forward in an address to the Modern Forum of Los Angeles: "Lately a new school of progressive educators and sociologists has arisen," he announced. "They appreciate the inadequacy of a curriculum composed of lots of information about the contemporary scene. They propose one, instead, composed of lots of information about the scene they think the pupil will face when he emerges from school—a scene not contemporary but future. They have gone so far as to say that they know what kind of scene the pupil is going to face: it is one dominated by what they call 'collectivism.' " Making free use of irony and mordant humor, Hutchins excoriated those who would cut education loose from its traditional moorings.[37]

Then, in 1936, *The Higher Learning in America* appeared, presenting a systematic exposition of what Hutchins conceived those traditional moorings to be. Sharply criticizing the utilitarianism, the present-mindedness, and the sentimental humanitarianism of American education, he made the case for a general schooling of all people rooted

36. *Nation,* CXLIV (1937), 413.
37. Robert Maynard Hutchins, *No Friendly Voice* (Chicago: University of Chicago Press, 1936), pp. 113, 129.

in the classic disciplines of grammar, rhetoric, logic, and mathematics and in the careful study of the great books of the Western world, and for a highly selective university devoted wholly to the achievement of wisdom through the cultivation of the intellect. He summed up his argument in a pair of paragraphs that were widely seen by contemporaries as epitomizing his position:

> One purpose of education is to draw out the elements of our common human nature. These elements are the same in any time or place. The notion of educating a man to live in any particular time or place, to adjust him to any particular environment, is therefore foreign to a true conception of education.
>
> Education implies teaching. Teaching implies knowledge. Knowledge is truth. Truth is everywhere the same. Hence education should be everywhere the same. I do not overlook the possibility of differences in organization, in administration, in local habits and customs. These are details. I suggest that the heart of any course of study designed for the whole pupil will be, if education is rightly understood, the same at any time, in any place, under any political, social, or economic conditions.[38]

Hutchins's criticisms of the "frontier thinkers" took issue with many of the traditional values of American education as well as with the quintessentially progressive efforts of Dewey and others to adapt educational agenda to the particular needs of a particular society at a particular time. Not surprisingly, therefore, they elicited a sharp rejoinder from Dewey, who commented mordantly on *The Higher Learning* in the *Social Frontier.* Observing that Hutchins's commitment to a highly selective university teaching traditional studies and perennial truths was ill suited to a democratic society requiring fundamental reconstruction, Dewey argued that "escape from present evil contemporary social tendencies may require something more than escape. It may demand study of social needs and social potentialities of enduring time span. President Hutchins's discussion is noteworthy for complete absence of any reference to this alternative method of educational reconstruction. It is conceivable that educational reconstruction cannot be accomplished without a social reconstruction in which higher education has a part to play." Beyond that, Dewey leveled the charge of authoritarianism against Hutchins's insistence on perennial truths and first principles. "Any scheme based on the existence of ultimate first principles, with their dependent hierarchy of subsidiary principles, does not escape authoritarianism by calling the principles

---

38. Robert Maynard Hutchins, *The Higher Learning in America* (New Haven: Yale University Press, 1936), p. 166.

'truths,' " Dewey suggested, somewhat nastily. "I would not intimate that the author has any sympathy with fascism. But basically his idea as to the proper course to be taken is akin to the distrust of freedom and consequent appeal to *some* fixed authority that is now overrunning the world." The controversy thus joined between progressive liberalism and the humanist right heated up again with the appearance of Hutchins's *Education for Freedom* (1943), where he reargued his case for a school that would war on the dominant materialism, sentimentalism, and anti-intellectualism of American life through a curriculum "concerned first of all with ideas, with principles, with the abiding and the permanent." Dewey responded with the charge that Hutchins's persistent attempt to separate vocational from liberal education was an inheritance from an "earlier class structure of human relations." It was, Dewey maintained, a "denial of democracy."[39]

Several points might be made about the complex of ideas advanced by the "frontier thinkers" and the main lines of criticism those ideas evoked. For one thing, it was very much an academic discussion that never enjoyed wide currency among school and college teachers, or among the writers, artists, journalists, youth workers, and churchpeople who were also seen as professionals engaged in education, or indeed among laypeople interested in education. It was in no way an insignificant discussion, but it was, in the end, an uninfluential discussion. Beyond that, it is important to note that both the "frontier thinkers" and their critics tended to conceive of the American system of education as a national system, despite the reality of a hundred thousand school districts, a thousand colleges and universities, almost two hundred thousand churches and synagogues, and countless newspapers, magazines, and other periodicals. Moreover, they saw themselves as addressing national policy issues in education, despite the relatively minor federal presence that even the expanded programs of the New Deal had created. As a result, there was all too little connection with the pressing immediacies of school taxes and budgets that were drawing public attention in localities across the country.

One might also note that there was a continuing stream of humanist criticism of Deweyan ideas about education from the 1930's onward. Hutchins himself commented on education throughout the 1950's and 1960's, to be joined from time to time by such kindred intellectuals as Jacques Maritain, Arthur E. Bestor, Jr., and Mortimer Adler. Interestingly, however, there was no such continuity of Marxist

39. *Social Frontier*, III (1936–37), 104; and John Dewey, *Problems of Men* (New York: Philosophical Library, 1946), p. 32.

criticism. Some who were Marxist critics during the 1930's—Theodore Brameld is a case in point—moved into the liberal camp during the 1940's and 1950's; others—one thinks of John DeBoer at the University of Illinois—maintained their position in lonely isolation. And, when a new Marxist critique of the liberal position in education appeared during the 1960's and 1970's, in the work of scholars such as Michael B. Katz, Samuel Bowles, Herbert Gintis, Martin Carnoy, and Michael W. Apple, it made few acknowledgments to the work of the 1930's, deriving instead from the Marxism of revisionists like Antonio Gramsci, Jürgen Habermas, and E. P. Thompson, a Marxism that tended to view education much more as an independent variable in the cause of social reconstruction.

Finally, it is important to note several things about the evolution of Dewey's own thinking. In the first place, he maintained a fairly consistent position throughout, despite the shifts and differences among his disciples. To Counts's query, Dare the school build a new social order? Dewey responded that whether or not teachers dared to make the attempt they probably could not succeed in any case. Given the multiplicity of political and educational institutions in a modern industrial society, the best the school could do would be to form the understanding and the dispositions necessary for movement in the direction of a changed social order. And to Raup's invitation to teachers to enter the political lists, Dewey responded that his advocacy of education assisting in social reconstruction in no way implied that the school ought to throw itself into the political arena and support one political cause or party rather than another. More important, however, Dewey continued to develop the democratic ideas he had set forth in *The Public and Its Problems* in contradistinction to the elitism of Lippmann. In *Liberalism and Social Action* (1935), which he dedicated to the memory of Jane Addams, he reiterated the thesis that "the first object of a renascent liberalism is education, I mean that its task is to aid in producing the habits of mind and character, the intellectual and moral patterns, that are somewhat near even with the actual movement of events." Later, in his Felix Adler Lecture entitled "Democracy and Education in the World of Today" (1938), he restated his belief in the fundamental education provided by participation in democratic politics. "Democracy is itself an educational principle," he maintained, "an educational measure and policy. There is nothing novel about saying that even an election campaign has a greater value in educating the citizens of the country who take part in it than it has in its immediate external results." And in *Freedom and Culture* (1939), he developed at length his argument that any judgment of the worth of a society must depend ultimately on the extent to which its activities and institutions provide opportunities for the release, the enlargement, and the fruition of the potentialities of its members, or, alternatively, for their continuing self-education. In the end, for all his faith in the value of scientific expertise, Dewey never failed to emphasize that only as scientific expertise could be made available to all men and women, in ways that seemed relevant to their day-to-day existence, would it translate into the valid public opinion that must ideally guide the affairs of a truly democratic society.[40]

VI

Whether one referred to it as progressivism or, as Dewey did in his later writings, liberalism, that stream of American thought in which education was seen as a mechanism to be adapted to the changing needs and problems of American society inevitably had to contend with the problems of inequality. Blacks could not vote in many parts of the country and enjoyed access to what was at best an inferior education. Women were barred from the suffrage until 1920 and from the opportunity for many kinds of higher, professional, and technical education until well after that date. Native Americans and Asians were barred from citizenship entirely or permitted uncertain access to citizenship and education. And, for all these groups as well as for citizens of Irish, Italian, Polish, Hispanic, Jewish, and Roman Catholic background, the educational opportunities implicit in the free pursuit of a vocation were variously restricted. Not surprisingly, therefore, since there could be no inclusive politics and education of the sort advocated by Dewey and Addams so long as patterns of discrimination based on race, gender, ethnicity, and religion persisted in the United States, the "American dilemma" described by the Swedish economist Gunnar Myrdal in 1944, in his classic treatise on "the Negro problem," became a problem that progressives of necessity had to attack. As Myrdal noted, Americans did indeed believe in the ideals of "liberty, equality, justice, and fair opportunity for everybody"; yet they also believed in the inferiority of certain groups and, depending upon circumstances and self-interest, acted on both sets of beliefs. In conse-

40. John Dewey, "Education and Social Change," *Social Frontier*, III (1936–37), 236, 237, "Can Education Share in Social Reconstruction?" *ibid.*, I (1934–35), 11–12, *Liberalism and Social Action* (New York: G. P. Putnam's Sons, 1935), p. 61, *Problems of Men*, p. 34, and *Freedom and Culture* (New York: G. P. Putnam's Sons, 1939), p. 125.

quence, for the many Americans who continued to subscribe to the basic tenets of progressive thought, finding ways to reconcile creed and deed became the leading political and educational issue of the post–World War II era.[41]

The effort proceeded on many fronts and involved many tactics and strategies; but surely the exemplary leadership came via the black struggle for equality. The political side of that struggle dated, of course, from the pre–Civil War Abolitionist movement, but it began anew in 1909 with the National Negro Conference that led to the establishment of the National Association for the Advancement of Colored People. Convened as a result of a "Call" from sixty distinguished citizens "to discuss means for securing political and civil equality for the Negro"—Dewey and Addams were among the sponsors—and organized by a coalition of white and black activists including a significant number of settlement workers, trade unionists, and suffragists, the Association moved aggressively against the evils of the "new slavery" that had emerged with the rise of Jim Crowism in the 1890's—disfranchisement, discrimination, and the sufferance of police brutality and mob violence. And its agenda early included the problem of inequality in education. The NAACP lobbied for a program of federal aid to the schools and colleges that would be explicitly divided between Negro and white institutions; it protested against the expansion of school segregation in the North in the wake of the Great Migration of the World War I era; and it investigated numerous instances of discrimination in graduate and professional education. Yet education tended to give way to more immediate concerns of life and liberty during the first quarter-century of the Association's work, and not until the 1930's did it again become a central element in the NAACP's program. The shift of the 1930's, which the Association took quite explicitly, really marked the beginning of the civil rights revolution of the 1950's and 1960's.[42]

What was the nature of the shift? Essentially, it was a decision on the part of Walter White, secretary of the NAACP, and his associates to mount a large-scale campaign in the courts to achieve political and civil equality for American blacks. In planning the campaign, the association turned to a brilliant legal strategist named Nathan Ross Margold, who urged a pointed attack on the Plessy doctrine in the

41. Gunnar Myrdal, *An American Dilemma: The Negro Problem and Modern Democracy* (New York: Harper & Brothers, 1944), p, xlviii.

42. " 'The Call': A Lincoln Emancipation Conference," in Charles Flint Kellogg, *NAACP: A History of the National Association for the Advancement of Colored People*, Volume I (1909–1920) (Baltimore: Johns Hopkins University Press, 1967) I, Appendix A.

field of education, which held that states providing separate but equal facilities for the races did not violate the Fourteenth Amendment to the Constitution. The attack Margold urged would question, not state policies mandating segregation, but rather whether states that mandated segregation were really providing the equal protection of the laws, as required by the Fourteenth Amendment. Seeing in the Margold recommendations a strategy for bypassing legislatures and governors committed to the maintenance of segregation, the NAACP turned to Charles W. Houston, dean of the Howard University Law School, to lead the effort.

The choice could not have been more felicitous. Howard University, under the able leadership of Mordecai W. Johnson, who had assumed the presidency in 1926, was in the process of becoming a first-class center for the training of a new black leadership. During his initial ten years as president, Johnson had managed to obtain legislation in Congress authorizing increased annual appropriations for Howard; he had brought the philosopher Alain Locke, who had been summarily fired by his predecessor, J. Stanley Durkee, back to Howard; and he had succeeded in attracting to the university such promising scholars as E. Franklin Frazier in sociology, Ralph Bunche in political science, and Charles R. Drew in medicine. He had also chosen Houston, who had been trained in the law at Harvard and who had been graduated with honors, to develop the university's law school. By the mid-1930's, Johnson was well launched on the effort Locke and others had advised, to transform Howard into a center of black culture and of militant concern for ameliorating the plight of American blacks. Howard was thus a logical center of support for the NAACP's campaign.

Of the generation of students that imbibed the reformist atmosphere of Howard during the early Johnson era, two in particular were destined to play important roles in the NAACP's effort—Thurgood Marshall, who attended the law school from 1930 to 1933, and Kenneth B. Clark, who was an undergraduate from 1932 to 1936 and who then went on to complete a doctorate in psychology at Columbia University. Marshall became the legal strategist who would lead the Association's team to victory in the celebrated case of *Brown v. Board of Education* (1954); Clark became the social scientist who would gather and interpret the data that proved crucial to Marshall's successful pleading of the case.

Richard Kluger has written a brilliantly detailed history of the legal developments that culminated in *Brown v. Board of Education*. What is of special interest here is the complex of ideas about education that in the end proved persuasive to the United States Supreme Court and that, through the Court's opinions, became the law of the land. Essentially, that complex of ideas evolved in a succession of suits mounted by the NAACP. The Association's campaign began with the case of *Missouri ex rel. Gaines v. Canada* (1938), in which the United States Supreme Court held that when a state chose to provide legal training it had a duty to furnish that training "to the residents of the state upon the basis of an equality of right." Tuition assistance that would enable black students to attend law school in other states would not suffice.[43]

The campaign continued in the case of *Alston v. School Board of the City of Norfolk* (1940), where the United States Supreme Court upheld the judgment of the Federal Circuit Court of Appeals for the Fourth District that a disparate salary schedule for equally qualified and similarly assigned black and white teachers violated the due process and equal protection clauses of the Fourteenth Amendment; in the case of *Sipuel v. Oklahoma Board of Regents* (1948), where the Court held that the state must provide opportunity for legal education to blacks as well as whites and must do so for one race as soon as for the other; in the case of *Sweatt v. Painter* (1950), where the Court held that a separate law school for black residents of Texas did not provide a legal education substantially equal to that afforded other races at the University of Texas Law School; and in the case of *McLaurin v. Oklahoma State Regents* (1950), where the Court held that a black student pursuing graduate work in education under rules and regulations intended to segregate him from other students was not enjoying the equal protection of the laws.[44]

Marshall, as director-counsel of the Association's Legal Defense and Educational Fund, had led the NAACP's legal staff in all of those cases except Gaines. With the Supreme Court's judgments in the Sweatt and McLaurin cases, he concluded that the time was ripe for an all-out assault on the Plessy doctrine itself. Having exploited the Margold strategy to the fullest, he recognized in the Sweatt and McLaurin holdings the implication that, on principle, segregated facilities were in their very nature unequal. And at that point he and his colleagues made a crucial decision: having introduced the testi-

43. Richard Kluger, *Simple Justice: A History of "Brown v. Board of Education" and Black America's Struggle for Equality* (New York: Alfred A. Knopf, 1975); and *Missouri ex rel. Gaines v. Canada*, 305 U.S. 349 (1938).

44. *Alston v. School Board of the City of Norfolk*, 311 U.S. 693 (1940); *Sipuel v. Board of Regents of the University of Oklahoma*, 332 U.S. 631 (1948); *Sweatt v. Painter et al.*, 339 U.S. 629 (1950); and *McLaurin v. Oklahoma State Regents*, 339 U.S. 637 (1950).

mony of distinguished social scientists like Robert Redfield of the University of Chicago and Charles Thompson of Howard University into argument in the Sweatt case, with apparent success, they would now turn to social scientists on a much broader scale, seeking to document the inherent harm—and hence the inherent inequality—of racial segregation. In addition to legal scholars, a large number of sociologists, anthropologists, psychologists, psychiatrists, historians, political scientists, and educators were recruited; in the effort that followed, none was more assiduous than Kenneth Clark in marshaling the data and indicating their relevance to the legal issues. Working with his wife and colleague, Mamie Phipps Clark, he summed up the results of their own experiments using dolls as the basis of projective tests on children to determine how they felt about themselves and others of the same and different races; he repeated those experiments in districts where suits were being brought; he gathered together the results of kindred experiments by other psychologists; he helped prepare the major brief of social science materials used in several suits brought to overturn the Plessy doctrine; he testified in three of the four cases that the Supreme Court grouped together in the decision that became known as *Brown v. Board of Education*, and he recruited other social scientists to do likewise. And, given his commitment to the integrity of social science, after the Brown decision had been handed down, he also published analyses and criticisms of the social science data and conclusions that had played a role in the findings. When the Court announced its decision on May 17, 1954, it was clear that Marshall's strategy had proved successful and that the data and arguments furnished by Clark and the other social scientists had been crucial to that success. The Court, in a unanimous opinion, held that education was the most important function of state and local governments; that it was the very foundation of good citizenship and "a principal instrument in awakening the child to cultural values, in preparing him for later professional training, and in helping him to adjust normally to his environment"; that, according to modern authority (social science), the segregation of children in public schools on the basis of race was patently detrimental to black children and indeed deprived them of equal opportunity; and that therefore the Plessy doctrine was no longer tenable. "We conclude that in the field of public education the doctrine of 'separate but equal' has no place," the Court affirmed. "Separate educational facilities are inherently unequal."[45]

45. *Brown v. Board of Education of Topeka*, 347 U.S. 495 (1954).

When the Court decided to separate the question of remedies from the question of rights and principles, Marshall, Clark, and their colleagues again gathered the social science findings on the question. Clark summed up what he saw as five requisites for the accomplishment of efficient desegregation with a minimum of racial disturbance: (1) a clear and unequivocal statement of policy by prestigious authorities; (2) firm enforcement of the changed policy by authorities and persistence in the face of initial resistance; (3) a willingness to deal with violations and attempted violations by a resort to law and strong enforcement; (4) a refusal by authorities to tolerate subterfuge; and (5) an appeal to the individuals concerned in terms of their religious principles of brotherhood and their devotion to American principles of fair play and equal justice (what Myrdal had called the "American creed"). In short, Clark was for firmness in executing the policy laid down by the Court. Marshall, though sensitive to the arguments in favor of gradualism that came from some of his colleagues, was inclined to agree with Clark. In the end, however, the Court opted for insisting that districts with racially segregated schools proceed to desegregate "with all deliberate speed" (a phrase that had come to Chief Justice Warren, who wrote the opinion, through Associate Justice Frankfurter, who had himself taken it from the late Justice Holmes) and for leaving the matter of enforcing compliance in the hands of the federal district courts.[46]

Although the Court had spoken unanimously on the constitutional issues, the actual process of desegregation was thus allowed to move ahead more slowly than Marshall, Clark, and others had thought wise. Nevertheless, equal education remained a central strategy and indeed a central priority of advocates of black civil rights. Marshall continued, as director-counsel of the Legal Defense and Educational Fund, to press for implementation of the Court's decision, until President John F. Kennedy appointed him to the Second Circuit Court of Appeals in 1961; while Clark turned his energies to the effort to achieve a substantially equal education for the children of New York City. He called attention to the long-standing problem of school zoning that imposed racial segregation on a large number of the city's schools and proposed a reorganization of the system that would group primary and middle schools into educational complexes explicitly designed and located to draw students from a wide variety of neighborhoods. But, more fundamentally, he fought against the low expectations and poor teaching that had for years been reflected in the poor performance of

46. *Brown v. Board of Education of Topeka*, 349 U.S. 301 (1955).

black schoolchildren on standard tests of achievement. Through an organization he founded called Harlem Youth Opportunities Unlimited (HARYOU), he formulated a wide-ranging program—again, based on the best social science evidence available—that would not only provide compensatory instruction for children who were falling behind in the basic school subjects but also involve them and their parents in actually making and carrying out the policies that would prevail with respect to their education. It was a program calling for blacks and whites to work collaboratively in the development of truly integrated public schools, and it was a program that insisted on the full participation of the parents and other citizens who would be involved. In effect, it was precisely the sort of a program of inclusive politics and education that Dewey and Addams had proposed. In its New York City version, Clark's program foundered on the shoals of political preference and patronage, but he set it forth in more general terms in a moving treatise called *Dark Ghetto: Dilemmas of Social Power*, which attracted a national audience. Clark made clear in that work his awareness that the problem of the ghetto was essentially "a problem of power—a confrontation and conflict between the power required for change and the power resistant to change." But he also made clear his profound belief that the transformation of ghetto schools from separate and unequal institutions into truly integrated and equal institutions could play a key role in mobilizing and enhancing the power required for change. Like his progressive forebears and liberal contemporaries, he placed education at the heart of his strategy for change, and of his campaign to eradicate the "dark ghetto" from the lives and minds of Americans.[47]

Louis H. Pollak once noted that, apart from the waging and winning of the Civil War and of the two world wars, the *Brown* decision was "probably the most important American governmental act of any kind since the Emancipation Proclamation." Given that apt appraisal, it is important to note that the strategy Walter White and his associates adopted for the NAACP in the early 1930's turned on the courts and in characteristic progressive fashion concentrated on the issue of education. For all intents and purposes, the sequence of case law developed from *Gaines* to *Brown* constituted a national policy for equality in education. There would be endless debate, particularly after the publication in 1966 of the study by James S. Coleman and his colleagues entitled *Equality of Educational Opportunity*, over whether

47. Kenneth B. Clark, *Dark Ghetto: Dilemmas of Social Power* (New York: Harper & Row, 1965), p. 199.

equality meant equality of opportunity or equality of result, and whether equality of opportunity meant identity of opportunity or differences in opportunity based on circumstance and need. But there could be no denying that democracy as it pertained to education during the 1960's and 1970's increasingly meant equality—or equity, as the term emerged in the debate over what equality meant.[48]

Moreover, because the NAACP strategy had achieved important gains for blacks, other groups seeking equal treatment under the law adopted similar strategies, with education continually at the fore. When the National Organization for Women was founded by Betty Friedan and others in 1966, for example, a legal committee was one of the first units established at the organizing conference, and its purpose was to assist with appeals in two pending sex discrimination cases under Title VII (the Equal Employment Opportunity Section) of the Civil Rights Act of 1964. The unit soon became the NOW Legal Defense and Education Fund. The Native American Rights Fund, the Puerto Rican Legal Defense and Education Fund, and the Mexican American Legal Defense and Education Fund appeared in the 1970's, financed largely but not solely by grants from the Ford Foundation, the Carnegie Corporation of New York, the Field Foundation, and the Rockefeller Brothers Fund. And organizations such as the American Jewish Congress, the National Catholic Welfare Conference, and a host of ethnic benevolent and fraternal associations turned to combinations of court action and "consciousness raising" in the effort to win equality in education for their members. Like the NAACP Legal Defense and Educational Fund, all these groups used social science data in support of their efforts; and, though many a legal conflict saw social science experts testifying on both sides of the question, the combination of law and social science quickly became a permanent feature of litigation involving education. Beyond that, even though such efforts created what came to be known as special interest groups, the fact is that they also created the publics Dewey called for in *The Public and Its Problems*. And, as these publics became articulate and interacted with one another, there emerged in the domain of educational policy making a process of rebuilding the eclipsed public that Dewey was seeking as the answer to the phantom public alleged by Lippmann. To paraphrase the Court in *Brown*, education was indeed the most important domain of state and local politics, and increasingly, because of *Brown*, a central domain of national politics.

48. Louis H. Pollak, ed., *The Constitution and the Supreme Court: A Documentary History* (2 vols.; Cleveland: The World Publishing Company, 1966), II, 266.

Finally, and perhaps most important, *Brown* changed the way Americans thought about education. The founders of the Republic, following the ancient Greeks and Romans they read so avidly, deeply believed that the law educates. Insofar as it was consciously made, they thought, and therefore deliberately set norms and standards of conduct, the law surely regulated and ultimately shaped values, attitudes, and beliefs. One need not deny the widespread failure of compliance with the letter and spirit of *Brown* during the 1960's and 1970's to affirm that *Brown* educated: it was pivotal in moving Americans toward an ever greater awareness of the dilemma Myrdal had illuminated and, on the part of many, an ever greater commitment to resolve the dilemma. Prejudice, discrimination, and inequality surely did not disappear; but as the courts—and then legislatures and executives—followed the implications of *Brown* into various domains of American life, the belief in equality that was at the heart of the American creed was strengthened and the prejudice that was at the heart of discrimination was weakened. Perhaps even more important, the belief on the part of many in the redemptive powers of the school was also strengthened—the Court in its own way had taken up the progressive call to enlist education in general and the school in particular in the solving of social problems. Further, as the *Brown* doctrine increasingly affected employment, housing, travel, and recreation, the society at large became a more receptive context for the sorts of schools the Court envisioned. That the Court's vision remained unrealized a generation later did not dull the luster of that vision or the larger impact of that vision on American life and thought.

VII

If Kenneth Clark offered Americans a compelling vision of the role of racially integrated schooling in the development of a democratic society, his longtime friend Margaret Mead offered them profound insight into the role of education in the mastery of cultural change. An anthropologist who achieved international recognition, Mead used her scientific studies to illuminate a score of the world's foremost problems, from the dehumanizing effects of large cities to the high rate of failure among technical assistance programs. More important here, she applied and adapted progressive thinking about education to the needs of a metropolitan world.

Following her graduation from Barnard College in 1923, Mead became a student of the Columbia anthropologist Franz Boas, who had committed his career to demonstrating an essential unity of the human race that manifested itself through diverse cultures. Believing that his theory could best be confirmed by studies of isolated "primitive" societies that had not yet been "spoiled" by "civilization," he sent Mead as a young woman of twenty-four to study Samoa, with a view to illuminating the problem of adolescence in human development. She lived among the Samoans for nine months, and then returned to the United States to write *Coming of Age in Samoa* (1928), a book that described the relatively tension-free transition to adulthood of Samoan young men and women and the processes by which they took their places in a society where the sorts of jealousy, conflict, and emotional upset that were common to contemporary America were comparatively absent. And, in a concluding chapter, Mead drew the moral for American education. Samoan society was free of tensions, she explained, because the child was reared by many kin and fictive kin and not merely the mother and father of a nuclear family; because the child was early assigned real responsibility appropriate to his or her age; and because the child did not face the extraordinary range of choices that were open to American children. American society could not imitate Samoan society, she cautioned, but it could design an education appropriate to its own culture—an education for choice in which people were taught "how to think, not what to think." Such an education, Mead maintained, would at least reduce some of the anxiety suffered by young people.[49]

Two years after the work in Samoa, Mead returned to the South Seas with her husband, Reo Fortune, and settled in a village called Meri to study the culture of the Manus. Described in *Growing Up in New Guinea* (1930), Manus culture was profoundly different from the culture of the Samoans. A materialistic, competitive, puritan people— Mead thought they were much like Americans—the Manus also allowed their children a good deal of freedom. But they kept their children much more insulated from the adult world than the Samoans, and then, at the point of marriage, they used the bride price as a device for inducting the young adults into the "realities" of life. Once again, Mead concluded the work with a final section on education. "Human nature," she argued, is "the rawest, most undifferentiated of raw material, which must be moulded into shape by its society, which will have no form worthy of recognition unless it is shaped and formed by cultural tradition." In the end, the education of "simple," "homo-

49. Margaret Mead, *Coming of Age in Samoa: A Psychological Study of Primitive Youth for Western Civilization* (New York: William Morrow & Company, 1928), p. 246.

geneous" societies was everywhere the same. "Whatever the method adopted, whether the young are disciplined, lectured, consciously taught, permitted to run wild or ever antagonized by the adult world—the result is the same. The little Manus becomes the big Manus, the little Indian, the big Indian. When it is a question of passing on the sum total of a simple tradition, the only conclusion which it is possible to draw from the diverse primitive material is that any method will do." In Mead's view, the bearing of all this on American educational theory was unmistakable. Neither the school nor any other institution could ever change the social order. In fact, the only way deliberately to change the social order would be for a large body of adults consciously to set out to make the change; and even then the change would come slowly and in the end be slight.[50]

Mead returned once more to New Guinea in the early 1930's, again with Reo Fortune, this time to study the temperamental characteristics associated with sex roles. They lived for various periods of time among three societies, the mountain-dwelling Arapesh, the river-dwelling Mundugumor, and the lake-dwelling Tchambuli, and Mead published the results of her research in *Sex and Temperament in Three Primitive Societies* (1935). Although the book did not focus as explicitly upon education as Mead's earlier works, its discussion of gender differences across cultures and of the degree to which sex role differences were "socially produced" illuminated important aspects of the larger process of socialization.[51]

All of Mead's work over the next four decades grew out of the insights and orientations she derived from these early studies, and all of it bore profoundly on education, from her investigations into ways of changing food habits during the 1940's to her investigations into the sources of community initiative during the 1960's. But three of her lines of inquiry in particular pertained to problems of education in the post–World War II era—her analysis of the nature of schooling, her examination of social change and cultural transformation, and her effort to define a more humane, peaceful, and durable metropolitan world. Her analysis of schooling had begun, of course, with the South Seas studies, but it continued to be a central concern throughout her career. In 1950, in her Inglis Lecture at Harvard University, she discussed "The School in American Culture," pointing to the "series of

50. Margaret Mead, *Growing Up in New Guinea: A Comparative Study of Primitive Education* (New York: William Morrow & Company, 1930), pp. 212, 260.

51. Margaret Mead, *Sex and Temperament in Three Primitive Societies* (New York: William Morrow & Company, 1935), p. 310.

images" comprised in any consideration of schooling in the United States—the one-room rural school, known as "the little red schoolhouse," the independent school or academy for the children of the privileged, and the city school with its masses of immigrant children. Drawing upon her earlier formulations, she noted that the first was constructed on the model of the parent passing on a relatively stable tradition to the young, that the second was constructed on the model of a grandparent passing on an even more stable tradition to the young, and that the third was constructed on the model of a parent passing on a series of coping skills for a society that was changing. The problem with all three, Mead went on to argue, was that the world was changing too rapidly for any of the models to succeed. What was needed was a "whole new institution of in-service training" for teachers that would put them in touch with the realities of social change and ready them for "a totally new kind of teaching—a teaching of a readiness to use unknown ways to solve unknown problems."[52]

Eight years later, in a widely read essay for the *Harvard Business Review* entitled "Why Is Education Obsolete?" she for all intents and purposes gave up on the school as a critically important institution in the intelligent management of social change. "No one will live all his life in the world into which he was born," she argued, "and no one will die in the world in which he worked in his maturity." In such a world, what she called "the *vertical* transmission of the tried and true by the old, mature, and experienced teacher to the young" was doomed to obsolescence. In place of that, she pointed to the "*lateral* transmission of knowledge"—"a sharing of knowledge by the informed with the uninformed, whatever their ages." Having made the distinction, she urged a redefinition of primary and secondary education. Primary education would refer to "the stage of education in which all children are taught what they need to know in order to be fully human in the world in which they are growing up—including the basic skills of reading and writing and a basic knowledge of numbers, money, geography, transportation and communication, the law, and the nations of the world." Secondary education would refer to "an education that is based on primary education and that can be obtained in any amount and at any period during the individual's whole lifetime." In *Culture and Commitment* (1970), she developed the argument into a full-fledged thesis on the relation between the generations. There were three kinds of cultures in the world, she argued: "post-

52. Margaret Mead, *The School in American Culture* (Cambridge, Mass.: Harvard University Press, 1951), pp. 7, 36, 40.

figurative cultures," in which the present repeats the past and in which adults are therefore able to pass a tradition on to children; "cofigurative cultures," in which the present is the guide to future expectations and in which adults and children teach one another; and "prefigurative cultures," in which adults have to learn from children about experiences they, the adults, have never had. The undeniable fact for Mead was that the late-twentieth-century world had become a world of prefigurative cultures in which all were equally "immigrants in time" and the past held no models for the future. In such a world, she reasoned, tradition would best be transmitted in such a way as to function instrumentally rather than coercively; it was the young who represented what was to come and the young who would therefore have to lead the way to the future.[53]

The same concern with the rapidity of social change dominated Mead's analysis of the problem of cultural transformation. During the early stages of President Harry S. Truman's Point Four programs, which were intended to provide American know-how in the form of technological knowledge, skills, and equipment to the poorer nations of the world, Mead warned insistently that cultures were integral and that there was no way to export technology without exporting the cultural values that supported technology and in which technology was embedded, and no way to receive it without undergoing the profound changes it would surely set in motion across the entire society. As a way of reinforcing these arguments, she returned to Peri (among the Manus) in 1953, with a view to studying the effects of World War II on the Manus culture. The Australians had evacuated the territory at the beginning of the war; the Japanese had come for a time and occupied Peri; and the Americans had driven out the Japanese and made the Admiralty Islands (of which Peri was a part) a major staging ground for the war in the Pacific. In the process, the Manus had discovered American technology, American medical care, American modes of interpersonal relations, and American values and attitudes. In addition, a local leader named Paliau had appeared on the scene and taken it upon himself to organize a "New Way" for the Manus that ended up touching every aspect of Manus culture, from the clothing people wore to the modes by which orphans and widows

53. Margaret Mead, "Thinking Ahead: Why Is Education Obsolete?" *Harvard Business Review*, XXXVI (No. 6, November–December, 1958), 34, 23, 36, 166–167, and *Culture and Commitment: A Study of the Generation Gap* (Garden City, N.Y.: Doubleday & Company, 1970), pp. 1, 25, 51, 56.

were cared for. By 1953, Mead found the primitive society she had studied in the 1920's transformed by radical social change. In light of this, she cautioned in *New Lives for Old: Cultural Transformation—Manus, 1928–1953* (1956) against simplistic notions of sharing technology with the poor nations and in the process transforming them into modern states. Culture, circumstance, and leadership would interact at every point to spell success or failure.

Mead's studies of cultural transformation led naturally to an even more broadly defined educational concern, with the result that studies of international communication became her primary interest during the last years of her life. By the mid-1960's she was convinced that the foreign aid programs of the industrial nations had failed. With all the good will in the world, the effort to share industrialism as a panacea—to disseminate literacy, medical care, automation, large-scale organization, mechanization, world-wide trade, and urbanization—had not turned out as expected. More people were suffering, aggrieved, and unhappy, she argued, than ever before in history. Why had the grand design failed? Mead's answer was that people had been ignored. Cities had been planned and built for people who found them overwhelming and uninhabitable; technology had been exported and adopted with no concern for the "human component"; and world-wide forces had been set in motion by nation-states that assumed that nation-states were God's permanent plan for the universe.[54]

However intolerable these arrangements might have been in a preatomic age, Mead found them even more intolerable in an age in which the failure of international communication could easily lead to the obliteration of mankind. What were her solutions? Cities built to "human scale," along the lines suggested by her friend and colleague Constantinos A. Doxiadis; technology developed with a "human component" in consultation with those who would use it and be party to its effects; an international "City of Man" that gave full recognition to the easy movement of people and ideas across the earth and that achieved a new balance between the aspirations of human beings and the limitations of the earth. To those who talked about "Spaceship Earth" and the "Global Village," Mead replied that human society at the end of the twentieth century was neither a spaceship nor a village: a spaceship was primarily technological, a masterpiece of engineering but a poor model for a human community; and a village was a commu-

54. Margaret Mead and Ken Hyman, *World Enough: Rethinking the Future* (Boston: Little, Brown and Company, 1975), pp. 210–211.

nity where people knew one another on a face-to-face basis, which was scarcely the world of the 1970's. Mead rather preferred the metaphor of a small island, whose residents must share sufficiently in a system of values to be able to solve common problems.[55]

It was on the shared values of a shared culture to which all people of the world would contribute that Mead ultimately rested her hopes. In a 1965 essay entitled "The Future as a Basis for Establishing a Shared Culture," which she wrote for a symposium on science and culture, she set forth her vision of a "worldwide shared culture," in which a common world language built on a system of glyphs—graphic representations of such ideas as "male," "female," "poison," "stop," "go"—would serve as the basis of international communication, in which a common core of knowledge would be gathered from the peoples of the world, and a common commitment would be made to education in multigenerational groups that would continue over a lifetime. In the end, she concluded, an inclusive transnational politics and education was the only answer to the world's problems.[56]

Mead touched an immense variety of people during her long and varied career. She published more than a score of books; she was an inveterate conference goer and crossed disciplinary boundaries to participate in organizations as diverse as the American Academy of Arts and Sciences, the American Association for the Advancement of Science (of which she was president), the World Society of Ekistics (of which she was also president), the National Council of Churches, and UNESCO; and she aired her views regularly in a number of popular magazines, especially *Redbook*. Her publications appeared in many formats, from technical anthropological monographs to combinations of photographs and text to films; and, given a lucid and pungent style, even her technical monographs reached large audiences. She also advised the United States government on a series of projects, from ways of getting people to eat more nutritious foods during World War II, to ways of dealing with the Russians during the 1950's, to ways of achieving more equitable treatment of women during the 1960's. And she lectured around the world, directly to audiences of thousands and via radio and television to audiences of millions. Her influence on the discussion of child rearing in the United States was prodigious; while her influence on ideas about schooling, though more limited, was significant. More important, she offered Americans a vastly enlarged

55. *Ibid.*, pp. 50, 211, 42; and Rhoda Metraux, ed., *Margaret Mead: Some Personal Views* (New York: Walker and Company, 1979), p. 103.
56. *Daedalus*, XCIV (1965), 143, 155.

domain to consider when they thought about education. Like Kenneth B. Clark, she symbolized the growing influence of social scientists in the discussion of educational affairs and the formulation of educational policies; like John Dewey, Jane Addams, and Walter Lippmann, she quite literally changed the ways in which people conceived of education itself.

Chapter 5

PROGRESSIVE SCHOOL MOVEMENTS

I shall never be content until the beneficent influence of the University reaches every family in the state. This is my ideal of the state university.

CHARLES VAN HISE

Two views of redemption through education vied for the loyalties of Southerners during the elections of 1876. One was a legacy of Reconstruction, which held that the best way to regenerate the miscreant South would be through the wide dissemination of northern values and culture, primarily through common schools. As the president of Illinois Normal University had put it in 1865, it was up to the teacher to finish the work that the soldier had begun. It was this view in one form or another that had motivated the hundreds of men and women who had gone south during the 1860's to teach the freedmen, initially under the auspices of the various missionary and freedmen's aid associations and eventually under the auspices of the Freedmen's Bureau. It was this view that had motivated the Massachusetts financier George Peabody to establish a philanthropic trust in 1867 "for the promotion and encouragement of intellectual, moral, or industrial education among the young of the more destitute portions of the southern and southwestern states of our Union; my purpose being that the benefits shall be distributed among the entire population without other distinction than their needs and the opportunities of usefulness to them." And indeed it was this view in its most resolute form that had motivated the Radical Republicans in Congress in their effort to impose federal requirements for common schools on the seceded southern states.[1]

1. J. L. M. Curry, *A Brief Sketch of George Peabody, and a History of the Peabody Education Fund Through Thirty Years* (Cambridge, Mass.: University Press, 1898), p. 20; and Richard Ed-

212

The last effort, which was led by Senator Charles Sumner of Massachusetts from 1867 until his death in 1874, is of special interest; although it did not succeed, it represented the Radical view of redemption through education at its most determined. Sumner had been the moving force in the 1840's in arguing that racially segregated schools violated the Massachusetts constitution because they were inherently unequal. When his suit in the case of *Roberts v. City of Boston* (1849) failed in the Massachusetts Supreme Court—Chief Justice Lemuel Shaw ruled that separate schools were legal so long as they were equal—Sumner had persuaded his friends in the Massachusetts legislature to outlaw racial segregation in the public schools by statute. Hence it was no surprise when Sumner, as a United States senator, tried in 1867 to attach amendments to the Second and Third Reconstruction bills that would require racially mixed schools in states re-entering the Union. During the early 1870's, in collaboration with such like-minded colleagues in the House of Representatives as George F. Hoar of Massachusetts and Legrand W. Perce of Mississippi, he sought national subsidies for state common school systems, through either the proceeds of federal land sales or direct taxation, with the provision that no federal funds go to states maintaining segregated schools. More important, however, Sumner and his colleagues tried to obtain a more stringent version of the Civil Rights Act of 1866 that would prohibit discrimination in common carriers, theaters, inns, restaurants, and schools on the basis of race, color, or previous condition of servitude. All these measures failed—in the end the much weaker Civil Rights Act of 1875, passed after Sumner's death and with no provision relating to education, was the only outcome and even that was declared unconstitutional by the United States Supreme Court in 1883. More significant for what it did not accomplish than for what it did, the effort dramatically demonstrated the fervor with which some Americans—southerners as well as northerners—would have redeemed the South.

Ultimately, of course, the issue of redemption through schooling would be fought out in the states themselves. In general, the constitutions promulgated by the former Confederate states before the Reconstruction Acts of 1867 paid little heed to education, while the several southern legislatures either ignored education or assumed that it would be for whites only. With the passage of the First Reconstruction Act on March 2, 1867, however, the situation changed dras-

<hr>

wards, "Normal Schools in the United States," in National Teachers' Association, *Proceedings and Lectures, 1865,* p. 276.

tically. The former Confederate states were organized into five military districts, each under the control of a general, who was entrusted with supervising the election of delegates to state conventions that would draft constitutions and establish governments, with the proviso that all adult males who had not been disfranchised for participation in the rebellion, regardless of color, would be eligible to vote for delegates. Of the constitutions that were promulgated in the wake of the Reconstruction acts, all carried more or less general provisions mandating schools for all children, but only two, those of South Carolina and Louisiana, explicitly prohibited racial segregation in public schools. And even in those two states, it was only the university that experienced any significant desegregation in the former and mainly the schools of New Orleans that experienced any significant desegregation in the latter.

The New Orleans experiment was interesting for its time, since in its scale it was unique for the South and unusual for the country as a whole. It appears to have been made possible by a determined Radical state superintendent of schools named Thomas W. Conway, working in an unusually cosmopolitan city. What the school authorities did was simply to require that black children be admitted to white or mixed schools wherever they applied. There were court suits, injunctions, boycotts, and evasions of every sort and variety, but by the end of 1870 even the staunchest opponents of desegregation were ready to admit that all legal remedies had been exhausted. Whereas the white children were withdrawn during the first stages of desegregation, they eventually returned in increasing numbers, so that by 1875 there were 26,000 children in the schools, of whom 21,000 were white and 5,000 black. Of these, it is likely that several thousand of the white children and between five hundred and a thousand of the black children actually attended racially mixed schools.

Whatever the failures of Radical hopes for mixed schools, the Reconstruction governments did achieve notable progress in the establishment of tax-supported common school systems. Indeed, it was during Reconstruction that the common school system was finally extended to the South; and, although it was extended in the form of a racially segregated system, the fact is that racially segregated schools had already become the rule in most of the northern and western states, so that the South ended up merely partaking of a national pattern. The Reconstruction governments also managed to reopen the state universities of the South, though on occasion, as in the case of the University of North Carolina and the University of South Carolina, political efforts to desegregate student bodies and to control professorial appointments led to the shutting down of instruction. However that may be, by the mid-1870's the idea of redeeming the South through education had borne fruit in expanded opportunities for both white and black children to obtain at least enough formal schooling to become literate and therefore able responsibly to carry out the duties of citizenship.

It was in response to this initial view of redemption that an alternative view arose, namely, the redemption of the South from the northern blight of universal schooling, and especially mixed schooling (however nonexistent that was in most places). The so-called Redeemers of the early 1870's campaigned on a platform of returning the South to its traditional leadership and of returning southern education to its traditional format. And, what with the relaxation of Radical ardor in the North and the quarrel among Radical factions in the South, their campaigns were soon successful. Virginia, North Carolina, Georgia, and Tennessee (which had never been subject to Radical Reconstruction) fell back into the hands of the new Redeemers in 1870; Texas, in 1873; Alabama and Arkansas, in 1874; and Mississippi, in 1875. By 1876 the conflict persisted only in Florida, South Carolina, and Louisiana; and in the elections of that year, which were marked by widespread violence and intimidation against black voters, those states, too, yielded.

As the former states of the Confederacy returned, one by one, to home rule, they instituted—or reinstituted—segregated schools with a vengeance and mercilessly slashed the budgets of schools for blacks and poor whites. Those states that did not enact legal requirements for segregation simply practiced it—South Carolina and Louisiana (New Orleans excepted) actually operated dual school systems well into the 1890's in violation of their own constitutions. And, once segregation had become the rule, it was easier to slash educational expenditures for black schools without doing so for white schools. Thus, General Wade Hampton in South Carolina successfully campaigned for the governorship on a platform of "free men, free ballots, free schools," pledging amicable relations between blacks and whites and hoping thereby to win the black vote. Once in office, however, he could not control his fellow Democrats; and, when he went off to the United States Senate in 1879, funds for black schools were brutally cut. In Louisiana, General Francis T. Nicholls also extended the hand of fellowship to black voters, promising a new era of racial good feelings; but once in office—put there, incidentally, largely as a part of the Compromise of 1877—he displayed none of Hampton's reticence about savaging appropriations for black schools. His successors in the governorship, Louis A. Wiltz and Samuel D. McEnery, spoke of their regimes as taxpayers' governments and simply cut all appropriations to all schools. By 1890, the former states of the Confederacy lagged far behind the national average in their support of public schools, and even farther behind in their support of black public schools, with Louisiana at the bottom. Not surprisingly, the same states also led the nation in rates of white and black illiteracy, with Louisiana in the lead. The Radical Redeemers of 1868 may have failed to achieve their ideals of universal schooling during their brief tenure in office; the home-rule Redeemers of the 1870's and 1880's revoked the ideals. There were half-hearted attempts in Congress throughout the 1880's, in the form of the bills introduced by Senator Henry W. Blair of New Hampshire, to reverse the deterioration through a general program of federal aid to state common school systems, based on rates of illiteracy of persons over ten years of age as given in the federal census, and requiring that the funds be distributed to white and black schools in equal proportion; but, despite Senate approval of such bills in 1884, 1886, and 1888, they never reached the floor of the House, doubtless owing to continuing Southern suspicion and resentment of congressionally initiated common school programs. As for the universities, they fared little better under the home-rule Redeemers, suffering chronically constricted budgets and chronically crass political and religious interference in their affairs. And, when the occasional nod was given to higher education for blacks, the constriction and the crassness were, if possible, more egregious. When Louisiana founded Southern University "for the education of persons of color," by allowance of the Constitution of 1879, the legislature made a small appropriation for operations but neglected to provide any funds for construction. When the trustees finally managed to erect a single building, they had to put up future faculty salary funds as collateral for a loan. As late as 1898, only ten students were enrolled in courses beyond the secondary-school level.[2]

Such was the situation when the great progressive school revival of the 1890's began in the South. The movement was doubtless made possible by the economic recovery of the 1880's, deriving from the

2. "Free Men, Free Ballots, Free Schools—The Pledges of General Wade Hampton, Democratic Candidate for Governor, to the Colored People of South Carolina, 1867–1876," in U.S., Congress, House of Representatives, 44th Congress, 2d sess., Miscellaneous Document 31, Part I, *Recent Elections in South Carolina*, pp. 306–310.

opening of federal lands in the South to unrestricted cash sale after 1876, from the accelerated industrialization fueled by a large influx of Northern and English capital, and by the rapid development of commerce in the wake of railroad expansion. And it was surely given initial impetus by developments in the several states associated with business and professional interest in visions of a new South. In North Carolina, for example, a group of young lawyers, doctors, teachers, and businessmen that styled itself the Watauga Club—as one member remarked, to have called it the Progressive Club would have been like waving a red flag—pressed insistently for a system of industrial education in the state that would aid the cause of economic development, while a group of professional teachers led by Edwin A. Alderman and Charles D. McIver seized the opportunity of a state-supported teacher-institute program to mount a statewide campaign for school improvement. In Florida, a similar movement sparked by a similar coalition of businessmen, professionals, and educators pushed through legislation in the 1880's raising taxes for common schools, providing for the creation of county high schools, and establishing normal colleges for the training of teachers. In South Carolina, a farmers' movement led by "Pitchfork" Ben Tillman demanded an expanded program of agricultural and industrial education for the state and was instrumental in creating the Winthrop Normal and Industrial College at Rock Hill and in the allocation of South Carolina's Morrill Act funds to that college. And in Georgia, a genuine citizens' movement in Clarke County (of which Athens was part) collaborated with S. D. Bradwell in developing a normal school under Bradwell's presidency that attracted hundreds of students from throughout the state. These efforts, however, remained sporadic and fluctuant until the late 1890's, when, as part of the larger progressive movement building throughout the nation, yet another effort was launched to redeem the South through education, one that synthesized the earlier versions into a crusade through which the South would be saved by separate and unequal schools.

The story of this third great crusade has been told in rich detail in Charles William Dabney's *Universal Education in the South* (1936), though from the point of view of someone much involved in the effort. The prime movers were a combination of northern businessmen, churchmen, professionals, and philanthropists led by Robert Curtis Ogden, a wealthy New York businessman who managed John Wanamaker's department store in that city and who was a longtime friend of Samuel Chapman Armstrong and Armstrong's colleagues in the development of Hampton Institute, and a group of southern counterparts, led by McIver, Alderman, Governor Charles B. Aycock of North Carolina, the Reverend Edgar Gardner Murphy, an Alabama churchman who had founded the National Child Labor Committee, and the redoubtable Jabez Lamar Monroe Curry of Alabama, who had succeeded Barnas Sears in 1881 as general agent of the Peabody Education Fund. The initial vehicle of the effort was the Conference for Education in the South, a loose network of Christian ministers and educators who began to gather annually at Capon Springs, West Virginia, in the summer of 1898. Ogden used the meetings of the conference beginning in 1899 to introduce a coterie of northern progressives to the educational problems of the South, among them, John D. Rockefeller, Jr., V. Everit Macy, Frank Nelson Doubleday, Albert Shaw, George Foster Peabody, and James Earl Russell. What became known as "the gospel" of the effort was a series of essays by Walter Hines Page, one of the original members of the Watauga Club in North Carolina, who had gone on to a distinguished publishing career in New York, as editor of the *Forum* and the *World's Work* and as a partner in Doubleday, Page and Company. Written and delivered as lectures between 1897 and 1902 and published as *The Rebuilding of Old Commonwealths* (1902), the essays argued that the traditional educators of the South, the "stump" and the "pulpit," had fastened an aristocratic education on the region, leaving "the forgotten man" at the bottom of the social structure in ignorance, that a public school system generously supported by public sentiment and generously maintained by both state and local taxation was "the only effective means to develop the forgotten man, and even more surely the only means to develop the forgotten woman," and that such a public school system, were it to train "both the hands and the mind of every child," would add immeasurably to the wealth of the region and the strength of its communities. "I believe," Page perorated in evangelical tones reminiscent of John Dewey's pedagogical creed, "in the perpetual regeneration of society, in the immortality of democracy, and in growth everlasting." The vehicle of the effort was the Southern Education Board, founded at the 1901 Conference for Education in the South to conduct "a campaign of education for free schools for all the people" by supplying literature to the newspaper and periodical press, by participation in educational meetings, and by correspondence through a Bureau of Information and Advice on Legislation and School Organization. Ogden was named president, McIver (who was then president of North Carolina State Normal and Industrial

College for Women at Greensboro) secretary, and George Foster Peabody treasurer. Curry, who was by then agent for the Slater Fund (organized in 1882 by John F. Slater, a New England cotton manufacturer, "for the uplifting of the lately emancipated population of the Southern States and their posterity by conferring on them the blessings of Christian Education") as well as the Peabody Fund, was appointed supervising director of the work of the Board, with Charles William Dabney (then president of the University of Tennessee at Knoxville) as director of the Bureau of Information and Investigation. And the fuel for the vehicle came initially from gifts from Ogden and Peabody and eventually from grants from the General Education Board, organized by John D. Rockefeller in 1902 as a general holding board for Rockefeller philanthropy in education and with a membership substantially overlapping that of the Southern Education Board.[3]

In some respects, the campaign mounted by the Southern Education Board bore striking resemblances to the one mounted by the "friends of education" in the decades before the Civil War. As in the earlier instance, the formal legal movement toward revived public school systems differed from state to state and proceeded in varying time frames. North Carolina's Governor Aycock had been elected in 1898 on an education platform, so that there would have been progress there apart from the work of the Southern Education Board; but the work of the Board accelerated the effort. The problem in that state was to persuade local districts and counties to raise their taxes for schools, and so, in addition to forming an Association for the Promotion of Public Education in North Carolina that organized local conferences and stimulated publicity in local newspapers, both the state legislature and the General Education Board made available small amounts of matching and loan funds in the hope of arousing local effort. Virginia had scheduled a state constitutional convention in 1902 and, with the pro–public school forces in control of the committee on education, the constitution that emerged modernized and professionalized the basic structure of school administration in the state and established minima as well as maxima of school taxation. Subsequently, under the stimulus of a Cooperative Education Association, organized explicitly to collaborate with the Southern Education Board, a program of stimulus for local effort similar to that in North

3. Walter H. Page, *The Rebuilding of Old Commonwealths, Being Essays Towards the Training of the Forgotten Man in the Southern States* (New York: Doubleday, Page & Company, 1902), pp. 31, 102; Charles William Dabney, *Universal Education in the South* (2 vols.; Chapel Hill: University of North Carolina Press, 1936), II, 539, 433.

Carolina was undertaken by the legislature. South Carolina, on the other hand, experienced a very different development. There, the several campaigns mounted by the Southern Education Board proved abortive. There was no "education governor," and the forces representing the mill owners and the railroad interests in the legislature again and again defeated legislation aiming at common school improvement. In Kentucky, under the leadership of Madeline McDowell Breckenridge, doyenne of an old Kentucky blue-blood family, a whirlwind campaign was mounted in 1908 that pushed such a large assortment of pro-school and university laws through the legislature that the session was widely referred to as the "education legislature." Tennessee experienced a similar whirlwind campaign in 1908, under the leadership of Philander P. Claxton, head of the newly established Department of Education at the University of Tennessee. And in Texas, a Conference for Education organized in 1907 was able to arouse sufficient public interest to obtain constitutional amendments in 1908 and 1909 raising the permissible rates of local school taxation and broadening the permissible uses of local tax funds. In Georgia, a campaign of 1902 and 1903 managed to get a constitutional amendment permitting the levying of local taxes for education ratified by popular vote, but subsequent efforts to induce the counties to levy the taxes met again and again with failure. It was some years before increased state appropriations for common schools, and, after 1912, for a state system of public high schools, initiated an educational renaissance in Georgia.

If there were similarities between the earlier and later common school movements, there were also profound differences. The campaign in the South was explicitly for separate and unequal schools for white and black children. In North Carolina, the so-called education governor, Charles B. Aycock, ran on a platform of black disfranchisement as well as educational development, and his idea of educational development meant universal education only for the white children of North Carolina. In Virginia, the chairman of the committee on education at the Virginia constitutional convention of 1902 granted that blacks had a right to learn to read the Bible but not much more; and one of his fellow members on the committee expressed horror at the realization that there were already 2,500 schoolhouses for blacks in the state turning out literate black voters and counseled against any extension of the effort. In South Carolina, one of the chief reasons school reform repeatedly failed was the fear that blacks would be the principal beneficiaries. And in Georgia, one of the main reasons legislation providing for a comprehensive system of public high schools won assent was that it was explicitly designed for whites only. While school appropriations rose in every one of the Southern states between 1900 and 1930 as a result of the efforts of the Southern Education Board, the gap between appropriations for white and black schools only widened.

Also, in contrast to the informal networks of association and publicity that marked the pre–Civil War national campaign, the Southern campaign was centrally organized, financed, and sponsored by the Southern Education Board and a consortium of philanthropic foundations. The coalition was prudent enough to seek local leadership in each of the Southern states; but its leading agents such as Curry and Dabney and later Claxton were indefatigable in the business of organizing and propagandizing. In the process, the informal techniques of Mann's generation became the formal techniques of Dabney's. Equally important was the role of the Peabody and Slater funds and then of the General Education Board, the Jeanes Fund (organized in 1907 by Anna T. Jeanes, a wealthy Quaker philanthropist, for the improvement of black rural schools), the Phelps-Stokes Fund (organized in 1911 under the will of Caroline Phelps Stokes, *inter alia,* "for educational purposes in the education of negroes both in Africa and the United States, North American Indians, and needy and deserving white students"), and the Julius Rosenwald Fund (begun on an experimental basis in 1912 by Julius Rosenwald, an Illinois industrialist, to aid the erection of black rural schools, and established on a permanent basis in 1917). The trustees of these philanthropies were for all intents and purposes an interlocking directorate, and the policies they set, especially those acquiescing in segregated schooling and espousing Booker T. Washington's mode of industrial education as the chief element in more advanced schooling for blacks, exerted a decisive influence on state education policies throughout the South. However prudently the Southern Education Board sought indigenous local leadership in the several states to carry forward its campaign, it enforced common policies throughout the region, using philanthropic funds as its lever.[4]

The foundations also played an important role in exporting black education on the Southern model to other parts of the world, especially Africa. For example, the Phelps-Stokes Fund took the initiative in financing the study of black education undertaken by the Welsh-

4. James Hardy Dillard, *et al., Twenty Year Report of the Phelps-Stokes Fund, 1911–1931* (New York: Phelps-Stokes Fund, 1932), p. 4.

born minister-sociologist Thomas Jesse Jones between 1912 and 1917. Jones had worked for a time as director of the research department and lecturer in sociology at Hampton Institute and had there imbibed the Hampton-Tuskegee philosophy of education for self-reliance, with industrial training at its core. His two-volume report, *Negro Education* (1917), had won him the Grant Squires Prize of Columbia University for the best "original investigation of a sociological character carried on during the five years preceding the award" as well as an international reputation as America's leading authority on black education. Jones had gone on from that assignment—in his capacity as educational director of the Phelps-Stokes Fund—to serve as chairman of two Phelps-Stokes African education commissions. A first, organized in collaboration with the British Colonial Office and a number of North American and European mission societies, had studied the countries of West, South, and Equatorial Africa between 1920 and 1921; and a second, organized in collaboration with the British Colonial Office, several mission societies, and the International Education Board (organized in 1923 as a Rockefeller philanthropy for promoting scientific investigation of foreign countries and aiding institutions crippled by World War I), had studied the countries of East Africa in 1924. The thrust of the two reports was conveyed by a revealing paragraph in the report of the second commission:

Probably the most important single task of the Commission to East Africa was to try to find the types of education best fitted to meet the twofold needs of the Negro masses and of the Negro leaders of Africa in the near future. In general, the members of the Commission are convinced that all education must be of a character to draw out the powers of the Native African and to fit him to meet the specific problems and needs of his individual and community life. In this connection, they have been profoundly impressed by the ideals of education developed by General Armstrong at the Hampton Institute in Virginia, immediately after the Civil War. He saw that book learning of the old type was entirely inadequate; that the plow, the anvil, the hammer, the broom, the frying pan and the needle must be used to supplement the customary instruction. In other words, that education must be vitally related to the needs of the people as they took up their work as freemen on the plantations and in the towns of the South. He saw that the training in agriculture, in industry and in home economics could not only be made to subserve a useful end, but that the processes used in acquiring skill as a farmer, as a mechanic, or as a cook—to use a few specific illustrations—have large educational value, both mental and moral. Armstrong's theories of education have been developed at Hampton, Tuskegee and scores of other institutions in America, and are beginning to take first root in Africa.

The two reports had direct and enduring effect on British colonial policy in Africa, on the policies of American foundations engaged in international philanthropy, and on the educational outlook of many Africans themselves. Beyond that, they provided a more general model—W. E. B. Du Bois would have said an antimodel—of how developing countries with nonwhite populations could profit from the experience of the American South. William F. Russell, the dean of the internationally influential Teachers College at Columbia University, followed the logic of the reports when he claimed that the South could teach not only the United States about education but the rest of the world as well. The region provided for Russell "examples of the best that is found in American education."[5]

II

The program of the Southern Education Board for the social and economic regeneration of the South was scarcely original, despite the special conditions of the region at the turn of the century. Rather, it was part of a larger national program for the reform of schooling that had been in the making for a generation. That program was compounded of at least four elements, all of which were seen by contemporaries as modernizing efforts and all of which were increasingly dubbed "progressive" by the 1890's: the effort to render schools more individually and socially useful by introducing vocational instruction into the curriculum; the effort to turn schools into social centers; the effort to remove the schools from politics; and the effort to make schooling scientific.

The effort to vocationalize schooling could, of course, be traced in various forms back to Benjamin Franklin and earlier, but it took on a distinctively modern cast at the Philadelphia Centennial Exposition in 1876. A number of American educators, notably President John D. Runkle of the Massachusetts Institute of Technology and Professor Calvin M. Woodward of Washington University, had been searching for a method by which they could offer the instruction in "industrial" subjects that they considered vital for citizens of an industrializing society. They found that method in a display at the Russian exhibit

5. Thomas Jesse Jones, *Education in Africa: A Study of West, South, and Equatorial Africa by the African Education Commission, under the Auspices of the Phelps-Stokes Fund and Foreign Mission Societies of North America and Europe* (New York: Phelps-Stokes Fund, 1922), p. xiii, and *Education in East Africa: A Study of East, Central and South Africa by the Second African Education Commission under the Auspices of the Phelps-Stokes Fund, in Cooperation with the International Education Board* (New York: Phelps-Stokes Fund, 1925), p. xvii; and Teachers College, *Report of the Dean for the Year Ending June 30, 1929* (New York: Teachers College, Columbia University, 1929), p. 18.

at the Centennial that illustrated the work of Victor Della Vos, director of the Moscow Imperial Technical School. When the school had been founded in 1868, its curriculum had embodied the traditional approach to technical education: classroom work in mathematics, physics, and engineering had been complemented by on-the-job training in construction shops (explicitly built for the purpose), where the goal was to produce salable goods. What Della Vos had set out to do was to design *instruction* shops that would prepare the students for their apprenticeships in the *construction* shops; and it was in formulating a curriculum for the instruction shops that he and his associates had come upon the radically new pedagogical idea that one could analyze the skills required for each of the trades, organize them in order of ascending difficulty, and then teach them according to a program that combined drawings, models, and tools into a series of graded exercises by which the student could, under supervision, progress to a requisite standard of skill. The method had been sufficiently successful at the Moscow Imperial Technical School for the construction shops to have disappeared. What the Russians displayed at the Centennial were the drawings, models, and tools illustrating Della Vos's method.

So far as Runkle and Woodward were concerned, Della Vos's innovations were a revelation—in Runkle's view they held "the philosophical key to all industrial education." Both men became enthusiastic proponents of the new "manual training," as the tool work was called, not only as efficient instruction for those contemplating work in industry, but also as requisite instruction for all children, since all needed to understand the character of the new industrial society. They encountered opposition, to be sure, from men such as William T. Harris, who saw manual training as a survival of Rousseauism, insofar as it failed to distinguish between the lower and the higher faculties of human beings. But, more important, they won devotees among both professionals and laymen who saw in Della Vos's innovations possibilities for making the school, on the one hand, more attractive to the new clienteles that were entering and remaining in increasing numbers, and, on the other hand, more pertinent to the needs of a rapidly industrializing economy.[6]

The effort to turn schools into social centers originated in the urban reform movements of the 1880's and 1890's, as exemplified

6. John D. Runkle, "The Manual Element in Education," in Massachusetts, Board of Education, *Forty-First Annual Report, 1876–77* (Boston: Albert J. Wright, State Printer, 1878), p. 188.

initially by the educational programs the Reverend William S. Rainsford introduced at St. George's Episcopal Church in New York City
and somewhat later by the educational programs Jane Addams and
Ellen Gates Starr introduced at Hull House in Chicago. Using a variety of strategies, from kindergartens to boys' woodworking and girls'
sewing clubs to adult civics and vocational training classes, these
programs incarnated, not only an expanded idea of schooling that the
reformers believed more appropriate for the impoverished immigrants of the urban slums, but also a community-building force that
the reformers saw as vital to the regeneration of neighborhoods. A
rural version of the effort also grew up under the leadership of men
such as Liberty Hyde Bailey of Cornell University and Henry Wallace
of *Wallace's Farmer* that pressed for boys' corn and girls' canning clubs
and adult education programs addressed to improving agricultural
yields and rationalizing family farms. As fully developed, the effort
called for nothing less than a radical redirection of school programs
to concentrate on the social and economic life of the local community,
the hope being that in the city such programs would prepare trained
workers for the new industrial order and in the country they would
prepare men and women ready and able to remain on the farm, and
that in the nation at large they would empower citizens to play a
greater part in the shaping of their own destinies.

The effort to remove the schools from politics was essentially an
urban phenomenon that derived from the expansion of city school
systems during the 1880's and the recognition on the part of city
politicians of growing opportunities for patronage and plunder in the
management of school affairs. As cities expanded through immigration and annexation, school boards grew in size, with representatives
of new wards and districts joining those of the old. As John D. Philbrick remarked in an 1885 survey of *City School Systems in the United
States,* "Everywhere there are unscrupulous politicians who do not
hesitate to improve every opportunity to sacrifice the interests of the
schools to the purposes of the political machine." Political bosses like
Christopher Augustine Buckley of San Francisco and Hugh McLaughlin of Brooklyn were as adept in their control of school elections as
they were of general elections, and as eager to obtain school contracts
for supporters as they were general contracts. Of course, one reason
such machine politicians were able to exercise control over extended
periods of time was that they were able to obtain contracts and other
favors for patrons, so that the immigrant, working-class constituencies that provided the votes for the machines felt well served. Never-

theless, to the upper middle-class reformers of the Gilded Age, performing favors was a form of graft. In consequence, they concluded
that the only way to save the schools from machine control was to
consolidate wards and districts into a single city school system, place
a small board of the "best" people in control of it, insulating their
selection and their work from the electoral process, and then encourage the board to operate the schools in nonpartisan ways, after the
fashion of civil service reform. Their reform strategy, of course, meant
that along with nonpartisanship would come professionalism, the development of a group of expert administrators who would run the
schools on behalf of nonpartisan boards. It was an effort born of
urban problems, but not confined to urban areas. Rural reformers
also took up the cry for nonpartisan boards that would employ professional experts to run the schools with maximum efficiency, economy,
and effectiveness.[7]

Finally, there was the effort to make schooling scientific, to use the
latest authoritative knowledge flowing from philosophy, psychology,
and pedagogy in the development of more humane and effective
instructional methods and more efficient and economical administrative techniques. An extensive body of findings from the work of such
European scholars as Wilhelm Preyer, Wilhelm Wundt, and Herbert
Spencer made their way across the Atlantic, to be adapted and further
enriched by the work of such American scholars as William T. Harris,
William James, G. Stanley Hall, and John Dewey. As taught in the state
normal schools and university departments of education, those
findings appeared to buttress the traditional American faith in the
efficacy of education and encouraged teachers and administrators to
dream of a profession of education that would apply an emerging
science of education in solving the burgeoning problems of education, with only limitless gains in store for the children to be served.

The several efforts described here tended to be nascent, episodic,
and disconnected during the 1870's and 1880's. They flowed together
during the 1890's into a national school reform movement that was
one element of the broader Progressive movement in American political and social affairs. One of the earliest portrayals of the school
reform movement came in Joseph Mayer Rice's book *The Public-School
System of the United States* (1893). The origin of the work is interesting
for the light it throws on the emergence of the movement as a movement. Rice was a young New York pediatrician whose interest in

7. John D. Philbrick, *City School Systems in the United States* (U.S., Bureau of Education,
Circular of Information No. 1; Washington, D.C.: Government Printing Office, 1885), pp.
15–16.

prophylaxis had caused him to raise some searching questions about the city's schools—questions that led him to spend the period between 1888 and 1890 studying pedagogy at Jena and Leipzig. He returned with some very definite answers about the need for a "science of education" that almost surely stemmed from the lectures of Wilhelm Wundt. As a means of publicizing his ideas, he prepared a piece for the *Forum*, a magazine that his father, Isaac L. Rice, had had a hand in launching and that the energetic young southerner Walter Hines Page was editing. Page published the article in the December, 1891, issue, and also invited Rice, on behalf of the *Forum*, to undertake a firsthand appraisal of American public school system. Rice agreed and spent the first half of 1892 visiting classrooms, talking with teachers and students, attending school board meetings, and interviewing parents in some thirty-six cities. His findings were published in successive issues of the *Forum*, from October, 1892, through June, 1893, and then as *The Public-School System of the United States*. The result was quite literally a sensation. In city after city, Rice found rote learning, mindless teaching, administrative ineptitude, political chicanery, and public apathy. But he also found some encouraging departures from the rule. In Minneapolis, teachers were dealing sensibly and sympathetically with children from the poorest immigrant homes. In Indianapolis, the several subjects of the curriculum were being taught in ways that encouraged children to see the relationships of one subject to another. In LaPorte, Indiana, children were being taught to collaborate instead of compete in the classroom. And at the Cook County Normal School, under the inspiration of the principal, Colonel Francis W. Parker, teachers were making extraordinarily imaginative use of maps, drawings, models, stuffed animals, and the like in the work of literature, the sciences, and the arts. On the basis of these examples, Rice issued a call to action. All citizens could have the advantages of the "progressive school" for their children, he maintained. Led by an aroused public, school systems would have to be "absolutely divorced from politics in every sense of the word"; scientific supervision would have to be introduced; and teachers would have to be encouraged systematically to improve their performance. "The general educational spirit of the country is progressive," Rice concluded; it remained only for the public in local communities to seize the initiative.[8]

The appearance of *The Public-School System of the United States* was significant on several counts. For one thing, Rice was an astute if

8. J. M. Rice, *The Public-School System of the United States* (New York: The Century Company, 1893), p. 320.

partisan observer, and his descriptions conveyed a vivid picture of urban public schools in the 1890's. Beyond that, he was one of the first to perceive the problems he encountered as national in scope and one of the first to weave the various strands of contemporary school reform into a single program. In a sense, the progressive movement in American schooling began with Rice because he saw it as a movement. It was this growing self-consciousness more than anything else that set the progressive movement of the nineties apart from its sources in the preceding decade. The movement was essentially pluralistic and occasionally even contradictory, bringing together the proponents of child-centered pedagogy with the partisans of socially oriented schooling, espousing equal treatment of blacks and whites, as interpreted by the National Association for the Advancement of Colored People, at the same time that it acquiesced in unequal treatment of blacks and whites, as interpreted by the General Education Board. It embraced an extraordinary variety of people and groups—businessmen like Robert C. Ogden and labor leaders like Samuel Gompers, social settlement workers like Jane Addams and Social Gospel ministers like Washington Gladden, academic scholars like Richard T. Ely and philanthropic foundation leaders like Wallace Buttrick, political conservatives like Charles W. Eliot and democratic socialists like John Dewey, farmer organizations like the Grange and businessmen's organizations like the National Association of Manufacturers. It created a fascinating range of political and social coalitions in different regions at different times. One such coalition was the group of northern philanthropists and southern reformers that constituted the Southern Education Board and its associated political networks in the former states of the Confederacy. Another was the assemblage of businessmen, labor leaders, farmer representatives, and academic protagonists of vocational education that organized the National Society for the Promotion of Industrial Education in 1906 and ultimately pushed the Smith-Hughes vocational education act through the Congress in 1917. Another was the group of private school leaders, philanthropists, and university professors of education that founded the Progressive Education Association in 1919. And yet another was the loosely knit group of religious leaders, social workers, educators, and government bureaucrats that undertook to solve the "youth problem" through the high schools in the 1930's.

Granted the remarkable variegation of the movement, there were certain themes that were consistently in the forefront of progressive school reform efforts and others that were dominant for a time and then receded. Among the former were, first, a broadening of the program and function of the school to include a direct concern for health, vocation, and the quality of family and community life; second, the application in the classroom of more humane, more active, and more rational pedagogical techniques derived from research in philosophy, psychology, and the social sciences; third, the tailoring of instruction more directly to the different kinds and classes of children who were being brought within the purview of the school (for some, this meant teaching a common curriculum in very different ways; for others, it meant teaching differentiated curricula); and finally, the use of more systematically organized and rational approaches to the administration and management of the schools. During the period before World War I the movement tended to concentrate on the broadening and recasting of public elementary-school curricula; the establishment of specialized public vocational and agricultural secondary schools; the rationalization of school governance, administration, and instruction; and the professionalizing of teaching and administration. During the 1920's the movement added a particular focus on a select group of pedagogically innovative independent schools catering principally to middle-class children; and during the 1930's it added yet another focus on the special problems of youth and in particular the problems of secondary schooling for young men and women who had no intention of proceeding on to college.

The strategies of the progressive school reformers tended to reflect the political structure of American education. Campaigns for federal legislation and appropriations, of the sort that eventuated in the passage of the Smith-Hughes Act, were the exception rather than the rule. The federal government did not become extensively involved in education before World War II. The United States Bureau of Education remained a small and relatively powerless agency during the first decades of the twentieth century, which at best provided commissioners of education with a "bully pulpit" during their times in office; but several of the incumbents, notably Philander P. Claxton (1911–1921) and John W. Studebaker (1934–1948), did use that pulpit to advantage in preaching progressive school reform across the country. That notwithstanding, it was the Bureau of Indian Affairs that oversaw the most significant program of schooling then under federal auspices; and, interestingly, that program was dominated during the period from 1887 through the early 1930's by the progressive goal of Americanization (the term "assimilation" was used) and from the mid-1930's on by the then equally progressive goal of biculturalism. In marked contrast to these minimal federal ventures, campaigns for state legislation and appropriations supportive of progressive school programs were common, as were campaigns for local regulations in cities and towns, the substance ranging from requirements affecting the size, structure, powers, and prerogatives of boards of education to requirements mandating that this or that subject be taught. Although the localism of American schooling was thus evident in the dynamics of the movement, the various techniques of propaganda, coalition building, and informal exchange used by the "friends of education" during the 1840's and 1850's, as refined, systematized, and increasingly centralized and professionalized by state, regional, and national associations, were commonly employed across the nation, and were certainly the principal devices in reaching teachers, administrators, and local school board members. The growth of state departments of education and their ever closer links with public and private teacher-training institutions also provided influential agencies for conveying messages of reform to classroom teachers; while the rapid development of the school survey and the curriculum revision exercise as devices for assessing what was actually going on, provided ready vehicles for the dissemination and implementation of progressive policies.

Progressive school reform did not go unchallenged during the half-century between the 1890's and the 1940's—there were articulate and influential conservative critics ranging from William C. Bagley and Isaac L. Kandel at Teachers College, Columbia University, to Robert M. Hutchins and Mortimer Adler at the University of Chicago, to John D. Redden and Francis A. Ryan at Fordham University; but it was surely the prevailing philosophy of American education during that era, especially in the councils of professional schoolpeople. And in the end the congeries of reform efforts that constituted the movement wrought major transformations in the nature and character of American schooling. School systems expanded, as ever larger percentages of the population attended kindergartens, on the one hand, and high schools, on the other—kindergarten enrollments increased sevenfold between 1900 and 1940, and high school enrollments increased tenfold, though the number of five-year-olds grew by less than 20 percent in that same period, and the number of youngsters between the ages of fourteen and seventeen, by less than 60 percent. There was a continuing enlargement and reorganization of curricula at all levels, particularly at the secondary level, where there were vastly extended opportunities for work in trades, commerce, agriculture, home economics, physical education, and the arts (though arts programs of all sorts and at all levels were severely cut back during the Depression); and there was a concomitant expansion in the range and variety of extracurricular activities such as athletics, clubs, and student government and of noninstructional services such as vaccinations, health examinations, meals, and vocational and psychological counseling. There were dramatic changes in the materials of instruction: textbooks became more colorful and attractive, and supplementary devices like flash cards, workbooks, simulated newspapers, slides, film strips, and phonograph records appeared in growing numbers of classrooms. There was more variation in the grouping of students, increasingly on the basis of intelligence, aptitude, and achievement tests, and more tracking of students within schools and among schools. Discipline became less harsh as encouragement and reward began to replace punishment, and as castigation and correction began to replace chastisement. School architecture was modified to include assembly rooms, gymnasiums, swimming pools, playgrounds, athletic fields, laboratories, shops, kitchens, clinics, cafeterias, and lounges; and school buildings were used for an increasing variety of purposes by an increasing range of age groups. And, through it all, systematization moved relentlessly forward, as state departments of education became more powerful and more prescriptive; as school districts consolidated and grew larger, more complex, and more bureaucratic; and as administrative hierarchies developed to manage the system.

Beyond these large general changes, several additional phenomena are worthy of note. First, whatever the increases in the number and percentage of Americans attending school, differentiation within and among schools also increased. Recall that the southern educational revival widened the gap between the schooling of whites and blacks at the same time that it extended opportunity for both groups. The same phenomenon occurred in the cities of the North, where separate schools for black children abounded as a result of legal or neighborhood segregation or of the gerrymandering of school districts. Also, while the comprehensive high school built upon the common elementary school became the standard pattern of American secondary education, the vocational high school was a common phenomenon in the larger cities and the presence of such schools resulted in differentiation along social class lines, as did the vocational tracks within comprehensive high schools. Moreover, within the vocational schools and tracks, there was growing differentiation along gender lines, even in so-called coeducational institutions, the most obvious example being the home economics courses that were seen during the first quarter of the century as preparing young women for their proper vocation, namely, homemaking. Intellectual and political divisions did arise over the wisdom of such differentiated arrangements. There were differences of opinion within the National Society for the Promotion of Industrial Education, for example, over whether young women should be prepared for employment in industry or taught to care for their homes and their children; and there was spirited debate within the National Association for the Advancement of Colored People over whether young blacks would do better with industrial education or general education. But these testified to dissonance within the movement and in the end had little effect on the direction of reform.

Second, the increasing structural differentiation in American schooling was paralleled by increasing curricular differentiation. One result of the progressive argument that the attractiveness, or "holding power," of the schools would be increased only as studies were seen by the pupils and their families as more useful and that studies would be seen as more useful as they were more vocational, was that different curricula would have to be designed for different groups of children, depending upon their various occupational preferences and destinations. Obviously, such differentiation would be one way of tailoring education to the needs and abilities of different children and classes of children, as those needs and abilities might be determined by standardized tests (another way, of course, would have been to teach a common curriculum in a variety of ways). Such a view was at the heart of the 1918 report of the National Education Association's Commission on the Reorganization of Secondary Education, entitled *Cardinal Principles of Secondary Education.* Twenty-five years earlier, the NEA's Commission on Secondary School Studies—the so-called Committee of Ten under the leadership of President Charles W. Eliot of Harvard—had argued for broadening the secondary-school curriculum to take account of the new classes of children entering the high schools in the 1890's; the four alternative curricula the Committee of Ten had proposed included a substantial core of academic subjects for all students, those bound for work as well as those bound for college—a common core that far outweighed the differing foreign-language and science requirements that marked the four curricula. The Commission on the Reorganization of Secondary Education, by contrast, proposed a common core that would be far less academically substantial—the recommendation was that the core be radically revised around the five objectives of health, command of fundamental

processes, worthy home membership, citizenship, and ethical character (the other two objectives featured in the report, namely, vocation
and worthy use of leisure, were obviously at the heart of specialized
or individualized studies)—and urged a much expanded differentiation of curricula, along lines that would be made possible by an
enlarged choice among subjects, a radical adaptation of content and
teaching methods, an increased flexibility in academic requirements,
and an extensive program of guidance and counseling heavily dependent upon testing. *Cardinal Principles* was in many ways an exemplary
progressive document, and it foreshadowed much that was to come.
But, as had often been the case with educational policy documents,
its recommendations regarding the curriculum signified less the setting of guidelines for the future than the ratification of innovations
well under way in many urban systems. Differentiation was already a
salient fact of American public school life by 1918, and with it came
a growing importance of the sorting function of the school with respect to vocation and life style.[9]

The issue of sorting was inextricably tied to the development of
intelligence and achievement tests and other instruments of educational measurement as part of the effort to build a rigorous and
dependable science of education. Beginning in the years between
1905 and 1908, when the French psychologists Alfred Binet and
Théodore Simon conceived the idea of an intelligence scale (a series
of problems of graded difficulty, each one corresponding to the norm
of a different mental level), educators on both sides of the Atlantic,
but notably in the United States, began to recognize that the scale
concept could be applied to intelligence, aptitude, and achievement,
and immediately thereafter testmakers undertook to develop instruments for appraising virtually every aspect of educational practice.
Edward L. Thorndike and his colleagues at Columbia's Teachers College developed scales for measuring achievement in arithmetic, hand-
writing, spelling, drawing, reading, and language ability. Charles
Hubbard Judd and his colleagues at the University of Chicago undertook similar efforts, particularly in connection with the monumental
1915 survey of the Cleveland schools. And Lewis M. Terman and his
colleagues at Stanford University undertook a revision of the Binet
scale and popularized the concept of the Intelligence Quotient as a
number expressing the relationship between an individual's mental

9. *Report of the Committee on Secondary School Studies* (Washington, D.C.: Government
Printing Office, 1893); and *Cardinal Principles of Secondary Education* (U.S., Bureau of Education, Bulletin, 1918, No. 35; Washington, D.C.: Government Printing Office, 1918).

age and his or her chronological age. By 1918, when the National Society for the Study of Education published its yearbook on *The Measurement of Educational Products,* Walter S. Monroe could describe more than a hundred standardized tests for measuring achievement in the principal elementary- and secondary-school subjects, and Thorndike could explain in a passage that would be widely quoted for a generation:

Whatever exists at all exists in some amount. To know it thoroughly involves knowing its quantity as well as its quality. Education is concerned with changes in human beings; a change is a difference between two conditions; each of these conditions is known to us only by the products produced by it—things made, words spoken, acts performed, and the like. To measure any of these products means to define its amount in some way so that competent persons will know how large it is, with some precision, and that this knowledge may be recorded and used. This is the general *Credo* of those who, in the last decade, have been busy trying to extend and improve measurements of educational products.

Clearly, Thorndike, Judd, and Terman saw themselves as experts seeking to place schooling on a sound scientific foundation—in that respect they were quintessentially progressive in orientation. Yet the freight of assumptions that entered into the formulation of that sound scientific foundation too often ended up supporting differentiation and sorting in American schools, and, with differentiation and sorting, a host of inequalities. The goal was commonly stated as one of individualizing instruction—the tests would help determine what any given student might best be offered at any given time; and one must acknowledge that as a result many young people were afforded opportunities they would have been denied on the basis of contemporary "common sense"—testing, for example, often opened up opportunities for immigrants and blacks to attend college. That said, however, it was but a brief leap from using tests as instruments of diagnosis to using them as determinants of placement. Did an IQ of ninety-five mean that Johnny needed special assistance in learning algebra, or that he should not be asked to learn algebra, or that he was incapable of learning algebra? Did it mean that Johnny should continue to study fractions and not go on to algebra, or that he should discontinue mathematics entirely and substitute woodworking? Did it mean that Johnny should be grouped with other children having similar IQ levels or with other children having very different IQ levels? One might put the questions and the answers variously; the fact is that, especially after the widespread use of the Army Alpha and Beta tests in classifying recruits during World War I, testing was increasingly used as a device for classifying schoolchildren, for grouping them within classrooms, and for streaming them into one school program or another. And there is no more vivid indication of the extent to which disagreement over the use and misuse of tests divided progressive educators than the sharp exchanges over the issue during the 1920's in the columns of the *New Republic.* [10]

The use of tests was but one example of a variety of political and intellectual differences within the progressive movement that exploded from time to time into conflicts quite as bitter as those between progressives and conservatives. There were, for instance, the running battles between labor unions and businessmen's associations over the structure of vocational education in the schools. On the national level, organized labor and organized business were both represented in the coalition brought together under the umbrella of the National Society for the Promotion of Industrial Education, however haltingly the American Federation of Labor under the leadership of Samuel Gompers took its place in the coalition, and both groups collaborated in supporting the Smith-Hughes legislation of 1917. But on the local level unions and businessmen's associations often clashed over whether there should be separate schools for those seeking trade and industrial training or whether they should be able to obtain such training in comprehensive high schools—the classic instance was the struggle in Illinois between 1913 and 1917 over the so-called Cooley bill that would have set up a dual system of general and continuing (vocational) schooling in Chicago, with the Chicago Commercial Club leading the forces favoring the measure and the Chicago Federation of Labor and the Illinois State Federation of Labor leading the forces that successfully opposed it. Both groups, of course, were working in the perceived self-interest of their constituencies. What is significant, however, is that both groups conceived of themselves as progressive forces, the business leaders of the Commercial Club and the former Chicago superintendent of schools who served as their educational adviser, Edwin G. Cooley, seeing themselves as proponents of economic development and social efficiency, the trade unions and their

10. Edward L. Thorndike, "The Nature, Purposes, and General Methods of Measurements of Educational Products," in National Society for the Study of Education, *Seventeenth Yearbook* (Bloomington, Ill.: Public School Publishing Company, 1918), Part II, p. 16.

civic-minded allies in the Chicago City Club and most of the local women's clubs seeing themselves as proponents of a common public school system free of social class segregation.

Similarly, there were the protracted battles between native-born reformers and immigrant groups over programs that would transform the school into a social center to serve the entire community. All might agree on the need for an enlarged curriculum, an expanded range of services to meet the requirements of broadened constituencies, and a lengthened school day to permit working adolescents and adults as well as children to take advantage of the school program. That said, when it came to the details there was often conflict. The struggles over the Gary Plan provide another classic case in point. Developed by a young progressive school administrator named William Wirt in the years following 1907 in the newly created steeltown of Gary, Indiana, the plan was intended to make the public school the hub of the social and intellectual life of its neighborhood by integrating classroom work with the activities of playgrounds, parks, libraries, gymnasiums, laboratories, machine shops, and assembly halls. Its goal was to unify general and vocational education and intellectual and moral education, and in the process to create a powerful new sense of community that would play a critical role in Americanizing immigrants. Given that large numbers of pupils at any time would be in the playgrounds or gymnasiums or assembly halls, a Gary school could accommodate twice as many students as a traditional school, with fewer classroom teachers. After the gifted young journalist Randolph S. Bourne visited Gary in 1915 to study the arrangement, he was moved to observe, "Those who follow Professor Dewey's philosophy find in the Gary schools—as Professor Dewey does himself—the most complete and admirable application yet attempted, a synthesis of the best aspects of the progressive 'schools of to-morrow.' " But, when John Purroy Mitchel, the Fusion mayor of New York City, became enamored of the plan after a visit in 1914 and set about introducing it into the New York City public schools, there was a political explosion, compounded of opposition from labor unions, immigrant groups, notably Jewish parents who saw the Gary Plan as offering a cheapened public education to their children, and teacher associations. By 1917 there was rioting at Gary schools in Manhattan, Brooklyn, and the Bronx; and in the mayoral election of that year the Tammany candidate, John F. Hyland, the Republican candidate, William Bennett, and the Socialist candidate, Morris Hillquit, all made opposition to the Gary Plan a central theme of their campaigns, with

Hyland and Hillquit sharply attacking Mitchel's increasingly strident claims that support of the Gary Plan represented one hundred percent Americanism. In the end, Hyland swept Mitchel out of office in the worst defeat of a Fusion candidate since 1898, and New York City soon abandoned the Gary reforms. However cynical some of the politicians may have been in seizing upon the issue for political advantage, the fact once again was that people and organizations that saw themselves as progressive were ranged on both sides of the controversy.[11]

The school's role in Americanization was yet another issue that led to sharp divisions among progressives, especially during World War I and the years immediately following. Schools had performed an Americanizing function throughout the latter decades of the nineteenth century, mostly by teaching youngsters the English language and the rudiments of American history and civics. Nevertheless, the same upsurge of nativism that led Congress in 1907 to create the Dillingham Commission to investigate the problems of the "new" immigration (the Commission's forty-one volume report, published in 1911, purported to document the "inferiority" of the "new" immigration) and that later led Congress drastically to curtail immigration through the Immigration Acts of 1921 and 1924, also set in motion the vast educational campaign known as the "Americanization movement." Under the prodding of the progressive reformer Frances Kellor and her Committee for Immigrants in America, the United States Bureau of Education established a Division of Immigrant Education (financed by funds Kellor raised from her wealthy friends) in 1914, the United States Chamber of Commerce formed an Immigration Committee during the winter of 1915–16, and the National Education Association created a Department of Immigrant Education in 1921; and school systems across the country organized comprehensive Americanization programs for immigrant children (and often for their parents as well). Such programs ordinarily involved a complex process of socialization that went far beyond instruction in English and civics to include training in personal cleanliness, middle-class values, and factorylike discipline, and, in many cases, the inculcation of disdain for the immigrant heritage. Whereas few voices outside the immigrant community itself had previously been heard questioning the assumption that immigrants needed to abandon their language, culture, and traditions in order to become Americans, a growing number

11. Randolph S. Bourne, *The Gary Schools* (Boston: Houghton Mifflin Company, 1916), p. 144.

of native-born as well as immigrant intellectuals now rejected that assumption in favor of more pluralistic and multicultural definitions of Americanism. John Dewey and Horace Kallen, for example, wrote of the need to redefine Americanism so that it would come to mean, not the abandonment of one identity in favor of another, but rather the combining or orchestrating of diverse identities. And the young writer Randolph Bourne, in a 1916 essay entitled "Trans-national America," sharply attacked both the melting-pot definition of Americanism and the Americanization movement that was propagating it, and called instead for a more cosmopolitan definition of Americanism that would embrace and preserve immigrant traditions. The issue died of its own accord during the late 1920's and 1930's, owing to the decline in immigration, at the same time that pluralistic definitions of Americanism became more fashionable.[12]

Yet another indication of dissonance among progressive school reformers was the split in the teaching profession symbolized by the separation between the National Education Association and the American Federation of Teachers. Since its founding as the National Teachers' Association in 1857, the NEA had claimed to represent the aspirations of a single unified education profession that brought together college and university leaders interested in school affairs, public school administrators, and classroom teachers. By the late 1890's, however, it had become a segmented organization, with such subunits as the Department of Superintendence (1870) and the National Council of Education (1884) comprising the powerful male leaders of the profession, and a subunit like the Department of Kindergarten and Primary Education comprising the less powerful women teachers. The organization remained small—its membership stood at 2,332 in 1900 and 6,909 in 1910; and, while a good deal of its work went on through its various departments, the leaders of the organization as a whole took as a given that the task of building a profession representing the expertise required for the proper conduct of the nation's schools took precedence over matters of teacher salaries, academic freedom, and working conditions in the schools—the assumption was that those matters would inevitably be taken care of as teachers acquired professional status. Beginning in 1897, however, with the de-

---

12. John Dewey, "Nationalizing Education," in National Education Association, *Addresses and Proceedings*, 1916, pp. 183–189; Horace Kallen, *Culture and Democracy in the United States: Studies in the Group Psychology of the American Peoples* (New York: Boni & Liveright, 1924); and Randolph Bourne, "Trans-national America" [1916], in *The History of a Literary Radical & Other Papers*, with an Introduction by Van Wyck Brooks (reprint ed.; New York: S. A. Russell, 1956), pp. 260–284.

velopment of the Chicago Teachers' Federation under the leadership, first, of Catherine Coggin, and then, of Margaret Haley, classroom teachers in a number of cities, notably Chicago, New York, Los Angeles, San Antonio, Gary, Oklahoma City, Washington, D.C., and Scranton, began to organize on a quite different basis. Predominantly women, they saw themselves as exploited by predominantly male administrators and boards of education, with no job security, no rights to academic freedom, and salary scales at approximately half of those for men of equivalent rank, training, and experience; and they made salaries, working conditions, and job security their primary concerns, believing that once salaries, working conditions, and job security improved, professional status would inevitably follow. Many of these teacher organizations affiliated in one way or another with the AFL—the San Antonio union in September, 1902, for example, and the Chicago Federation of Teachers, in November, 1902. And in 1916 the Chicago Federation of Teachers joined with two other Chicago teachers' unions and the one in Gary to form the American Federation of Teachers, which then made locals of the unions in New York City, Oklahoma City, Scranton, and Washington, D.C. By the 1920's, both the NEA and the AFT were seeking to represent American teachers. Both saw themselves as concerned with raising the quality of American schooling through the proper application of expertise—the NEA seeing itself as the bulwark of "professionalism," the AFT seeing itself as the bulwark of "democracy." And both, yet again, saw themselves as progressive.

What, then, were the outcomes of progressive school reform? As frequently occurs with reform movements, the language of education probably changed more rapidly than the practice of education, and small, specific, concrete changes in practice tended to be adopted more rapidly than larger, more general ones. Certainly those conclusions are suggested by Larry Cuban's findings in *How Teachers Taught: Constancy and Change in American Classrooms, 1890–1980* (1984). By 1940, he reported, progressive teaching methods—for example, increased levels of student participation through small group work, project activities, and field trips—were clearly in use by a significant minority of teachers and obviously considered respectable by professional norms, but most instruction remained traditional and teacher centered. More important, perhaps, he found that in instances where particular progressive techniques and reforms had been widely taken up, they were frequently adopted apart from the more subtle context in which they were intended to operate. Thus, industrial education, which was initially designed to give all youngsters an appreciation of the techniques at the heart of an industrial society, rapidly became vocational education, which conveyed to some youngsters the skills they would need for entry-level blue- or white-collar jobs. Activities, which were initially intended to concretize academic subject matter, soon became substitutes for academic subject matter. The project method, which Dewey's disciple William Heard Kilpatrick proposed as a progressive pedagogical device in 1918, soon eclipsed the more subtle relationship between the experience of the child and the content of the subjects that Dewey had set forth in *The Child and the Curriculum* (1902)—a development that Dewey himself subtly lamented in *Experience and Education* (1938). It is not merely that good theory was not always effected in practice, it is also that good theory was frequently pre-empted by bad theory. And, beyond that, there were inevitably the unintended consequences of reform. Thus, administrative changes that might have been intended to "take the schools out of politics" often simply subjected the schools to a new politics, which then frequently presented new problems for solution.[13]

Beyond a great variety of changes in public schooling, the progressive school movement, particularly between 1910 and 1930, became an important stimulus to the founding of independent schools. Some, like the Walden School in New York City or the Chevy Chase School in Maryland, were established by individual teachers seeking to apply particular pedagogical theories. Others, like the Park School in Baltimore, were established by groups of parents dissatisfied with the public schools. Still others, like the Oak Lane Country Day School in Philadelphia, were established by community groups attempting to make available a particular form of education. Given the enthusiasm that suffused the progressive movement and the widespread resistance to progressive ideas, it was only natural that certain individuals and groups would opt for the private school route. Although a few of these ventures catered initially to working-class children—one thinks of the Manumit School in Pawling, New York, or Caroline Pratt's original Play School in New York City's Greenwich Village—the costliness of private schools and the normal pedagogical conservatism of working-class parents tended to make independent progressive

13. Larry Cuban, *How Teachers Taught: Constancy and Change in American Classrooms, 1890–1980* (New York: Longman, 1984); John Dewey, *The Child and the Curriculum* [1902], in *John Dewey, The Middle Works, 1899–1924,* edited by Jo Ann Boydston (15 vols.; Carbondale: Southern Illinois University Press, 1976–1983), II, 273–291, and *Experience and Education* (New York: The Macmillan Company, 1938).

schools middle- or upper-class institutions. George S. Counts pointed to that inescapable fact at the 1932 convention of the Progressive Education Association in Baltimore, when he gave his address entitled "Dare Progressive Education Be Progressive?"[14]

Finally, it should be noted that the progressive movement exerted influence far beyond the borders of the United States. The works of Dewey were known in translation throughout Europe and the British Commonwealth and in some parts of Asia and Latin America. The works of the lesser progressives, for example, Kilpatrick, were also known in English and in translation. And the New Education Fellowship, with chapters throughout the world, provided a clearinghouse for American progressive ideas in a number of countries. In addition, in the extent to which progressive ideas made headway in American schools, they were exported as American models of schooling were exported. The export of black education on the Hampton and Tuskegee models to Africa during the 1920's has already been discussed. There was also considerable interest in American models of elementary education in Europe after World War I and in Europe and Asia after World War II, and in particular in Germany and Japan, where American occupation authorities imposed American versions of the progressive school as part of the effort to "democratize" both countries. In general, though, the exported versions of progressive schooling tended to be partial versions—the child-centered school in England, or social studies curricula in West Germany—and these in turn were inevitably further adapted by the countries that adopted them, according to the intentions of the borrowers and the circumstances in which the partial versions took root.

As has been noted, John Dewey liked to forecast during the later 1930's and 1940's that the time might soon be at hand when progressive education would be so widely accepted as good education that the adjective "progressive" might be dropped by reform-minded schoolpeople. For all intents and purposes that time arrived during the era following World War II. By the late 1940's and 1950's, progressive education had become the conventional wisdom in the United States, espoused by laypeople as well as professionals and embodied in the very language used to debate educational policy and practice. There were from time to time periods of conservative resurgence in the discussion of educational affairs. One such resurgence occurred during the mid-1950's, typified by the writings of Arthur E. Bestor, Jr.,

14. George S. Counts, "Dare Progressive Education Be Progressive?" *Progressive Education*, IX (1932), 257–263.

and Admiral Hyman G. Rickover; but the widely read reports of James B. Conant, former president of Harvard University, during the late 1950's and early 1960's tended to confirm rather than to revoke many elements of the progressive tradition. There were also, of course, periods of progressive resurgence like the one during the mid-1960's marked by the so-called Great Society reforms of the Johnson administration, with their emphasis on the advancement of equity through education. But through it all the secular trends continued much the same, namely, the extension of schooling at all levels, the expansion and differentiation of curricula, the individualization of school programs, and the socializing of school purposes, that is, the use of schools as instruments for solving various social and political problems of the larger society, for example, for advancing racial, ethnic, class, and gender equality, or for Americanizing new immigrants, or for reducing teenage pregnancy, or for resuscitating a lagging economy. The results of such efforts were not always measurable, and when measurable they were not always successful; but the effects on the schools themselves were significant and lasting. Progressivism may not have created the intentionally reformist society Dewey envisioned in *Democracy and Education* (1916), but it did bring into being the consciously politicized school on which Americans of all persuasions during the latter half of the twentieth century increasingly pinned their millennialist hopes and aspirations.[15]

III

Progressivism also influenced the colleges and universities during the last years of the nineteenth century and first years of the twentieth, though the reforms it engendered assumed even more varied forms than they did in the lower schools. The vocational theme was ubiquitous and central, as institutions sought to prepare young men and women for careers in an extraordinary range of occupations and at every conceivable level. Chancellor Francis Snow of the University of Kansas sounded the theme in a typical statement of the nineties intended to win taxpayer support for the university. "Let it be everywhere made known," Snow proclaimed, "that at the University of the State, every son and daughter of the state may receive the special training which makes chemists, naturalists, entomologists, electri-

15. John Dewey, *Experience and Education* (New York: The Macmillan Company, 1938), pp. 115–116, and "Introduction" in Agnes de Lima, *The Little Red School House* (New York: The Macmillan Company, 1942), p. ix.

cians, engineers, lawyers, musicians, pharmacists and artists, or the broader and more symmetrical culture which prepares those who receive it for that general, well-rounded efficiency which makes the educated man a success in any line of intellectual activity, ten years earlier in life than the uneducated man." In effect, all higher education was vocational insofar as it prepared students for adult occupational roles. And the University of Kansas was not alone in promising its students success in these roles.[16]

The scientific theme was ubiquitous and central too, though less with respect to the pedagogy than the substance and methods of the higher learning. The natural and social sciences expanded and proliferated; physics, chemistry, biology, geology, and astronomy; economics, politics, sociology, anthropology, and psychology—all developed rapidly, not only in schools of letters and science, but also in professional schools of agriculture, business, education, engineering, medicine, pharmacy, and social work. In addition, both the more traditional humanistic studies and the various professional fields were profoundly affected by new scientific approaches to their substance—thus, for example, the rise of scientific philology, scientific history, scientific medicine, and scientific law. And, most generally, there was the growing portrayal of the university as the creator of the disciplined scientific intelligence that would dispassionately attack and solve the problems of the emerging industrial society—in short, science would produce the experts who would serve the common good.

The social theme, which conceived of the school as a social center, cast the university in the role of a service center to the society at large. And indeed, the same movements in England that had given rise to the institutional church and social settlement movements, which had been so influential in the definition of the school as a social center, also gave rise to the university extension movement, which proved equally influential in the definition of the university as a service center. As the reform spirit swept through Oxford and Cambridge during the 1850's and 1860's, critics like William Morris at Oxford and Frederick Denison Maurice at Cambridge sharply attacked the aloofness of the two historic institutions and their remove from the life of the surrounding society. One response among several, including the institutional church, the social settlement, and the workingmen's college, was university extension. It began with the work of James Stuart, a fellow at Trinity College, Cambridge, who in 1867 started to offer

16. Francis H. Snow, "Inaugural Address," *University Review*, XII (1890), 6.

courses to local groups of workingpeople, lawyers, ministers, and teachers and in the process developed a paraphernalia of lectures, syllabi, homework assignments, discussions, and examinations that persuaded the university authorities to sponsor the work and assign university credit to those who completed it satisfactorily. By 1875 Cambridge enrolled some 7,300 students in extension courses. The idea soon spread to Oxford, which developed its own programs and which by 1887 enrolled some 13,000 students in similar courses. It was not long before the movement crossed the Atlantic and appeared in several American versions—in Philadelphia, as the work of the American Society for the Extension of University Teaching, which coordinated the efforts of various local colleges, universities, schools, and institutes in providing lectures to the public; in New York, as the work of the University of the State of New York (in effect, the state education department) in coordinating similar efforts by the state's institutions of higher learning; and in Indiana, as the effort of the Association of College Alumnae (later, the American Association of University Women) in much the same direction.[17]

More generally, the idea appeared in the programs of numerous individual colleges and universities. The University of Chicago under the leadership of William Rainey Harper provides an excellent case in point. Harper had had a brilliant career as an adult educator on the Sunday school and Chautauqua circuits long before he and John D. Rockefeller had begun to lay plans for a great university in the West. Harper deeply believed that the university, as the "keeper," "sage," "prophet," and "high priest" of democracy, owed it to a democratic society to disseminate its truths to the widest possible constituency. And, given that he was fully knowledgeable about contemporary English experiments, it should not be surprising that he built an aggressive and autonomous extension division, designed on the English model, into his initial plans for the university. Extension was to be organized into six departments, each with a secretary responsible to a director of extension. One of the secretaries would oversee lecture study, another, class work, and another, correspondence study; one would provide books and publications, another would conduct examinations, and another would train extension teachers. The division would have its own faculty, which would include individuals from other divisions of the university as well as men and women whose prime business would be extension teaching. Regular degree credit

17. R. D. Roberts, *Eighteen Years of University Extension* (Cambridge: Cambridge University Press, 1891), Appendices I, III.

could be obtained for extension work, but only on the basis of examinations held at the university. Harper's plans were never fully realized, but they did project the university into extension work on a broad scale throughout Chicago and its environs and, via correspondence courses, throughout the Midwest.[18]

Other institutions organized similar programs on a greater or lesser scale, notably the University of Wisconsin and the University of Kansas, both of which built on a fairly firm base of farmer interest in agricultural education. The movement waned during the late 1890's, however, and it was not until a number of institutions reorganized their programs after 1900 to move away from a fairly rigid adherence to the English model and take account of local needs and conditions that American university extension really flowered. On the eve of World War I, university extension was seen as "an organized effort to give to the people not in college some of the advantages enjoyed by the one-half of 1 per cent who are able to attend campus classes." Scores of institutions were involved, with programs that included correspondence courses, lecture courses, short courses, club study, training institutes, community forums, library service packages, and stereopticon slide demonstrations. Columbia University enrolled some 2,000 students in regular lectures and recitations leading to academic credit; Pennsylvania State College had 4,800 students in correspondence courses leading to the A.B. degree; the University of Michigan counted some 70,000 men and women in attendance at over 300 lectures; and the University of Kansas circulated almost 5,000 package libraries in connection with its high school debating league.[19]

Not surprisingly, the growing commitment of the universities, particularly the public universities, to service via extension programs led them to try to overcome their isolation from politics in favor of a greater sensibility to local political needs, in contrast to the effort of the lower schools to distance themselves from politics in order to preserve their integrity. But the seeming difference was more rhetorical than real. The same university that sought to be more responsive to local political needs nonetheless resisted local political interference in its professional appointments, while the same school system that tried to distance itself from local political chicanery sought to tie its

18. William Rainey Harper, "The University and Democracy," in *The Trend in Higher Education* (Chicago: University of Chicago Press, 1905), pp. 13, 16–20, 23–28, 28–32.

19. W. S. Bittner, *The University Extension Movement* (U.S., Bureau of Education, Bulletin, 1919, No. 84; Washington, D.C.: Government Printing Office, 1920), pp. 11, 12; and Louis E. Reber, *University Extension in the United States* (U.S., Bureau of Education, Bulletin, 1914, No. 19; Washington, D.C.: Government Printing Office, 1914), pp. 20, 32, 38, 39.

secondary school programs more closely to the requirements of local businesses. In the end, progressivism in both lower and higher education tried to bring the schools and universities closer to progressive politics, with its emphasis on administration by experts who would be responsive to the needs of the citizenry at large as those needs were defined by articulate, educated, white, native-born, and usually male representatives.

The great model of progressive higher education during the Progressive era was the University of Wisconsin during the presidency of Charles R. Van Hise (1903–1918). Many of the programs associated with the model had been inaugurated during the presidencies of Van Hise's predecessors, Thomas C. Chamberlin (1887–1892) and Charles Kendall Adams (1892–1902); but it was Van Hise who orchestrated them and brought them to a kind of apogee and, during the La Follette era in Wisconsin politics, publicized them throughout the country as the educational side of progressive politics. For Van Hise, who as a professor of geology had exemplified the cause of expert service to the state by his detailed studies of the mineral-bearing areas of the Lake Superior region, the obligation of the university was to undertake leadership in the application of science to the improvement of the life of the citizenry in every domain. This would be accomplished in three ways: first, by the extension of knowledge in every scientific field and the exploration of the uses of that knowledge through the systematic research of the faculty; second, through the contribution of the scientific expert to the improvement of agriculture, the development of industry, and the solution of social and economic problems, in part through the collaboration of university professors with government officials; and third, through a university extension program that carried the university's instruction to all members of the public at large. "I shall never be content," Van Hise declared, "until the beneficent influence of the University reaches every family in the state. This is my ideal of the state university." To these ends, Van Hise strengthened the research programs of the university as well as the university's commitment to academic freedom; he improved the training of experts, not only in agriculture, engineering, medicine, and law, but also in politics, economics, and history; he vastly expanded the programs of the extension division under the imaginative leadership of Louis E. Reber, who built the most comprehensive series of popularizing activities in the nation and in the process became the outstanding American leader of the extension field; and he presided aggressively over an increasingly heavy intellectual and professional traffic between the university and the agencies of state and local government, as scores of professors served on regulatory and investigatory commissions, helped draft legislation, and counseled various administrative authorities on the performance of their tasks. So much did the University of Wisconsin become for a time the quintessential American university that the liberal clergyman Lyman Abbott observed in 1906 that, while the pre-eminent goal of the English university was culture and the pre-eminent goal of the German university, scholarship, the pre-eminent goal of the American university was service.[20]

As publicized relentlessly by Van Hise and as celebrated in laudatory articles in *Collier's*, the *Survey*, the *Outlook*, and the *Review of Reviews* and in books like Charles McCarthy's *The Wisconsin Idea*, which appeared in 1912 with an Introduction by Theodore Roosevelt (and which Van Hise insisted that he never really liked), the Wisconsin model proved immensely influential. Delegations from the University of Georgia, the University of Kansas, and the University of Pennsylvania came to Madison to learn what they could for the benefit of their own institutions, and a steady stream of visitors from abroad came to consult, observe, and praise—one English educator insisted that more could be learned from the University of Wisconsin than from any other American educational agency. Van Hise, in turn, became the adviser to his fellow presidents, of private as well as public institutions, in matters ranging from curriculum development to legislative relations. Lincoln Steffens asserted to a Madison audience in 1913 that Van Hise was truly "in a class by himself among college presidents."[21]

Whatever the significance and influence of the University of Wisconsin model, it is important to note how much of the new enrollment in higher education during the Progressive era was absorbed, not by the state universities or indeed by the universities at all, but rather by a host of relatively new institutions of postsecondary education, to wit, the normal school, the nursing school, the private business or trade or technical school, and the private junior college. Charles McCarthy recognized this in *The Wisconsin Idea* (1912) when he included the Wisconsin system of normal schools in his chapter on education. Generally one- or two-year institutions under public aus-

20. Charles Van Hise, "Address before the Wisconsin Press Association" (Division of Archives, University of Wisconsin), p. 5; and Lyman Abbott, "William Rainey Harper," *Outlook*, LXXXII (1906), 110–111.
21. "Steffens Praises University," *Daily Cardinal*, November 14, 1913, p. 11.

pices, with associated networks of teacher institutes and other extension activities, normal schools across the country were as prototypical of the progressive service orientation in higher education as were the leading state universities: they presumed to prepare scientifically trained experts; they extended their learning to all comers; and they prided themselves on their sensitivity to popular need. In similar fashion, though somewhat more subject to market conditions, the private nursing, business, and trade schools articulated the same commitments and indeed frequently proved more accessible to the new clienteles seeking higher education, who for one reason or another found the universities—even the state universities—more forbidding, or expensive, or psychologically or geographically distant.

There was a surge in college and university enrollments after World War I, set in motion partly by young men who came for the Students' Army Training Corps in 1918 and then stayed after the Armistice. The number of students in higher education rose from 597,880 in 1919–20 to 1,100,737 in 1929–30 to 1,494,203 in 1939–40. Most of those students were seeking technical, preprofessional, or professional training, with the largest numbers in education, business, and engineering; and much of the increase was absorbed by the teacher education institutions and junior colleges. The University of Wisconsin and other state universities continued their programs of training, extension, and service much as they had earlier, and so did private institutions like the University of Chicago. State normal schools became teachers colleges; hospital training schools for nurses affiliated with colleges and universities and became two-year or four-year degree granting institutions; and the number of junior colleges rose from 207 in 1921–22 to 493 in 1931–32 to 624 in 1941–42.[22]

Yet progressive interest in the 1920's and 1930's, as evidenced by articles and editorials in the *Nation,* the *New Republic,* and the *Century,* underwent something of a shift away from the more popular public colleges and universities and their programs of training, extension, and service to the more elite colleges and universities and their programs of reformed liberal education—to A. Lawrence Lowell's experiments with tutorials at Harvard, to experiments with humanities and

22. The statistics of enrollment are given in U.S., Department of Education, National Center for Education Statistics, *Digest of Education Statistics, 1983–84* (Washington, D.C.: Government Printing Office, 1983), p. 8; the statistics of number of institutions are given in Leonard V. Koos, *The Junior College* (2 vols.; Minneapolis: University of Minnesota Press, 1924), I, 2; and Ralph R. Fields, *The Community College Movement* (New York: McGraw-Hill Book Company, 1962), p. 37. Fields includes the estimates of the United States Office of Education and the American Association of Junior Colleges; I have used the latter estimates.

contemporary civilization courses at Columbia, to Frank Aydelotte's experiment with honors programs at Swarthmore, to Alexander Meiklejohn's experiments with unified curricula, first at Amherst and then at the University of Wisconsin, and to Robert M. Hutchins's experiments with two-year baccalaureate programs at the University of Chicago. And throughout the liberal coverage of such experiments ran the subtle (and sometimes not so subtle) implication that too many young people were going to college in any case and that most of the "new students" were there for the wrong reasons and should really be discouraged, probably by the new technology of testing that had developed so rapidly in the period following the war.

Actually, the most auspicious progressive experiment in higher education of the interwar era was not Sarah Lawrence or Bennington or Black Mountain or Bard, however much they were universally viewed as progressive colleges; it was rather the General College at the University of Minnesota. The College was the creation of three men: President Lotus D. Coffman, who deeply believed that the state university ought to extend education to all people, that it ought to educate for "intelligent followership" as well as "intelligent leadership"; Dean John B. Johnston of the College of Science, Literature, and the Arts, who just as deeply believed that education had a responsibility to sort people on the basis of intelligence and aptitude and that only the upper strata of the population had the capacity for higher learning; and Malcolm S. MacLean, first director of the College and a tireless promoter of its values and programs. In contrast to those institutions that tried to discourage "new students" from coming at all, Minnesota welcomed them but, with the founding of the General College in 1932, assigned them involuntarily on the basis of tests and records to what was essentially a segregated institution with a separate curriculum leading to a two-year degree. The curriculum comprised a series of interdisciplinary survey courses in ten "areas of human living"—human biology; economics; home and family life; the arts; history and government; literature, speech, and writing; physical science; psychology; social problems; and contemporary affairs. The College began with 461 students in the autumn of 1932 and rapidly expanded to more than a thousand. The students were relentlessly studied and tested; and, on the basis of the studies and the tests, the curriculum became increasingly student-centered, in the fashion of the more child-centered progressive school programs of the 1920's and 1930's. Not surprisingly, there was sharp opposition on the part of some professors and some students, including some of the involuntarily assigned students, to what was too often referred to as a "dumbbell college" with a "watered down curriculum." Yet there was great interest outside, on the part of foundations such as the General Education Board and the Carnegie Foundation for the Advancement of Teaching, and on the part of other universities, notably the Universities of Oregon, Georgia, and Washington. In the end, the General College not only survived but prospered, and by the 1940's was performing much of what Burton R. Clark would call the "cooling-out function" that the community colleges of the post–World War II era would perform by segregating many of the "new students" seeking higher education, providing them with "life adjustment" and "personal development" courses, and enabling them to develop more "realistic" ideas of their own capabilities and aspirations. In the particular instance, "service" to the "new student" became a kind of insulating device for the traditional student and the traditional curriculum.[23]

World War II transformed American higher education and in particular the idea of service. On the one hand, it marked the beginning of the vast research enterprises commissioned by the federal government that would lead in the postwar era to what Clark Kerr called the "federal grant university." On the other hand, it provided the occasion for the Servicemen's Readjustment Act of 1944—the so-called G.I. Bill of Rights—that initiated the great postwar popularization of higher education, especially for men. Neither development derived primarily from educational concerns. The research enterprises were dictated by the needs of the war, while the readjustment legislation was designed primarily to placate organized veteran interests and to mitigate the effects of rapid demobilization on the economy and the society. Yet both had effects that reached far beyond any initial intentions.[24]

Given the experience of the SATC programs of 1918, it was anticipated that the G.I. Bill of Rights would create a temporary enrollment bulge in higher education and that the colleges and universities would soon return to their "normal" state. It was, after all, a federal legislative program directed overwhelmingly to men and, beyond

    23. Lotus Delta Coffman, *The State University, Its Work and Problems: A Selection from Addresses Delivered between 1921 and 1923* (Minneapolis: University of Minnesota Press, 1934), p. 51; and Burton R. Clark, "The 'Cooling-Out' Function in Higher Education," *American Journal of Sociology*, LXV (1959–60), 569–576.
    24. Clark Kerr, *The Uses of the University* (Cambridge, Mass.: Harvard University Press, 1963), chap. ii.

that, to veterans, a group generally older, more mature, and more preoccupied with family responsibilities than the traditional college student. No one anticipated the popularization of higher education that would result in its wake. To understand the longer-range effect, one must realize, not only that the veterans performed better at their studies than anyone had expected and that the expansive postwar economy was able to absorb them when they graduated, but also that President Harry S. Truman established a Commission on Higher Education in 1946 and that the Commission's report, *Higher Education for American Democracy* (1948), marked a turning point in American conceptions of the higher learning.

What the Truman Commission argued was that American colleges and universities could no longer consider themselves merely the instruments for producing an intellectual elite; rather, they would have to become "the means by which every citizen, youth, and adult is enabled and encouraged to carry his education, formal and informal, as far as his native capacities permit." The Commission asserted that at least 49 percent of the American population had the mental ability to complete at least 14 years of schooling and that at least 32 percent had the mental ability to complete an advanced liberal or specialized professional education. Moreover, in light of this, the Commission pointed to a historic gap between the educational potential of the American population and actual enrollments in the colleges and universities and urged an immediate doubling of higher education enrollments from the 2.3 million of 1947 to 4.6 million by 1960. To make this possible, the Commission recommended, first, that each state create mechanisms for statewide planning of new institutions of higher education; second, that an immediate expansion of community junior colleges be undertaken; third, that the federal government establish a program of undergraduate and graduate scholarships, based on need; and fourth, that historic patterns of discrimination in higher education, based on race, color, gender, and income, be attacked by federal legislation. The immediate response to the Commission's report in Congress was nil. No hearings were held; no legislation was enacted; no appropriations were made. But the long-range response by way of an acceleration of developments already in the making was considerable. States did create planning mechanisms; community colleges did multiply; the federal government eventually did create massive scholarship and loan programs; and historic patterns of discrimination did begin to decline, though they did not disappear. In effect, the Commission caught the spirit of the times and gave it voice and direction, as enrollments rose from 2.7 million in 1949–50 to 3.2 million in 1959 to 8.6 million in 1970 to 12.1 million in 1980.[25]

In much the fashion of the secondary schools, as higher education was popularized it was transformed, with the progressive idea of service holding the key to the transformation. The list of vocations for which higher education prepared grew by leaps and bounds: junior colleges prepared mechanics, hairdressers, office workers, and X-ray technicians; senior colleges prepared computer programmers, television writers, film makers, and systems analysts; and specialized professional schools prepared police officers, hotel managers, dental hygienists, and foreign service officers. Conversely, all these fields and a thousand others were seen as indefinitely perfectable by the application of scientific research performed in the institutions carrying out the training. And, by extension, the institutions carrying out the training stood ready to serve the public at all points with expert advice in the management of an ever more complex society. In effect, the higher education system was being called upon to produce and transmit knowledge at an unprecedented rate, in an unprecedented number of fields, and with a view to civic, national, and even international benefits.

That said, there were certain ironies with respect to service that raised fundamental political and social issues. For one thing, the very readiness of the federal-grant universities to serve the national interest via the great federally financed research laboratories, for example, the Argonne National Laboratory at the University of Chicago, the Lawrence Radiation Laboratory at the University of California at Berkeley, the Lincoln Laboratory at the Massachusetts Institute of Technology, and the Jet Propulsion Laboratory at the California Institute of Technology, to name but a few of the best-known laboratories of the 1960's, brought political tension to the universities as some students and faculty members attacked the idea of service to particular federal departments, especially the Department of Defense, as others attacked the idea of service to any federal department, and as still others attacked the idea of service itself. The severity of the tension was indicated by the attacks on President Clark Kerr of the University of California for merely describing the dilemmas of the federal-grant

25. *Higher Education for American Democracy: A Report of the President's Commission on Higher Education* (5 vols.; New York: Harper & Brothers, 1948), I, 101; and Thomas D. Snyder, *Digest of Education Statistics, 1987* (Washington, D.C.: Government Printing Office, 1987), p. 8.

university in *The Uses of the University* (1963)—opposition to the book became something of a rallying symbol for student and faculty activists during the later 1960's. And, while opposition to the federal-grant university was scarcely the sole issue in the widespread campus unrest of the late 1960's and early 1970's, which occurred, after all, in a context of fundamental cultural change coupled with vehement political opposition to the Vietnam War, it was surely a leading factor in that unrest. If the progressive goal of service was to remain the pre-eminent goal of the American university, as Lyman Abbott had suggested in 1906, the dilemmas Kerr referred to would have to be constructively contended with, if not resolved.

In addition, there was the question of whether the popularization of higher education was in the end a wholly democratizing movement. More men and women over a greater age range and representing a larger number of social, economic, racial, ethnic, and religious groups attended the colleges and universities than ever before. And they had available to them an ever greater range of curricular options. Yet, just as progressivism had fostered a differentiation of curricula in the high schools, along the lines suggested by the Commission on the Reorganization of Secondary Education in 1918, so did it foster the kind of structural differentiation at the college level that was augured by the General College at the University of Minnesota during the 1930's. The two great progressive models of universal higher education during the 1960's and 1970's were the three-tier system of the state of California and the open enrollment university of the City of New York. The former, developed under master plans prepared in 1948 and 1955, involved a lowest tier of some seventy junior colleges, a middle tier of some twenty state colleges, and a top tier comprising the nine campuses of the University of California. The three tiers were to be distinguished, on the one hand, by the differences in their academic missions—the junior colleges would take special responsibility for technical curricula leading to the Associate in Arts degree; the state colleges, for liberal arts and occupational curricula leading to the bachelor's and master's degrees; and the University of California, for undergraduate liberal and preprofessional and graduate and professional curricula—and, on the other hand, by the differences in their clienteles—the junior colleges were to be open to any graduate of an accredited California high school; the state colleges, to students in the upper third of the ability group; and the University of California, to students in the upper 12.5 percent of the ability group. However much these intended distinctions became blurred during the

1970's, the structural differentiation in the system created significant distinctions in the character, quality, and promise of the education the same student might receive at San Mateo Junior College, at San Francisco State College (later, University), and at the University of California at Berkeley. And it was significant that, when Clark Kerr moved from the presidency of the University of California to the chairmanship of the Carnegie Commission on Higher Education and then of the Carnegie Council on Policy Studies in Higher Education, the commitment to the sort of structural differentiation typified by the California system became embedded in the largest and most important body of policy literature on higher education to appear during the 1960's and 1970's.

Open enrollment, or the admission by right to the City University of New York of any graduate of an accredited high school in New York City, had been planned for during the late 1960's, with an anticipated target date somewhere in the 1970's; but it was adopted as a policy rather suddenly after a series of student sit-ins during the spring of 1970. Its novelty as instituted in September, 1970, inhered in two features: first, its sudden shift from a two-tier arrangement under which the two-year community colleges of the City University of New York were open-enrollment institutions and the four-year senior colleges selective institutions, to one in which both two- and four-year colleges became open-enrollment institutions (with places in the four-year colleges also guaranteed to all graduates of the two-year colleges); and second, the determination of the university, through curricular reform, supportive counseling, remediation programs, and a host of other special services, to provide equality of educational opportunity encompassing not only access but also outcome. Although controversial, the program flourished for five years, with results much like those of the midwestern state universities, which had long been open-enrollment institutions with revolving doors for the unsuccessful at the end of the first semester or the first year; but it foundered during the great New York City budget crisis of 1975, and the older two-tier system was reinstituted in the autumn of 1976. In the end, as with the high schools, a *de facto* structural differentiation deriving from differences in the social composition of the several borough populations in the city persisted even between 1970 and 1975, as the City College, with a predominantly black and Hispanic clientele, became a very different institution from Queens College, with a predominantly white clientele of Jewish and Italian descent.

Whether of the California or the New York variety, such structural divisions segregated not only people but functions, and in units that in the very nature of institutional life were increasingly competitive for personnel and resources. And in so doing they highlighted a historic tension within the progressive education movement, namely, the tension between the commitment to the creation of knowledge and the commitment to its popularization. On the one hand, progressives believed in the promise of science, not only in solving human problems but in preparing the experts on whom an urban, industrial society depended; on the other hand, progressives believed in the popularization of learning as the only sure foundation of democratic government. It was not merely that the segmentation of the higher education system separated the training, in Lotus Delta Coffman's words, of "intelligent leadership" from "intelligent followership"— and Coffman was fond of pointing out that no one led or followed in all things; it was that the necessary transformations of expert knowledge that were vital for its popularization—what James Harvey Robinson called "the humanizing of knowledge"—increasingly became the responsibility of people other than those who created it, with the result that the transformations were often inferior or simply not undertaken at all. It was a segmentation that might have seemed convenient and even efficient in the short run; but it was ultimately costly, not only in the missed associations of "leaders" and "followers," but also in the missed opportunities for that humanizing of knowledge that the more thoughtful of the progressives deemed so crucial to the conduct of informed public discussion.[26]

IV

The strong condemnation of discrimination by President Truman's Commission on Higher Education, and particularly of racial discrimination, was characteristic of the hopes and aspirations of progressives in the aftermath of World War II. The Commission's argument was that the nation's domestic economy could no longer countenance long-standing policies denying large numbers of Americans access to educational opportunity on the basis of race, class, gender, and national origin, and, further, that the nation's reputation abroad could ill afford the stigmata conferred by such policies. The dissenting opinion of four of the twenty-eight distinguished commissioners, however, was equally characteristic of progressive thought. "We recognize,"

26. Coffman, *The State University*, p. 51; and James Harvey Robinson, *The Humanizing of Knowledge* (New York: George H. Doran Company, 1923).

they wrote in the Commission's report, "that many conditions affect adversely the lives of our Negro citizens, and that gross inequality of opportunity, economic and educational, is a fact. We are concerned that as rapidly as possible conditions should be improved, inequalities removed, and greater opportunity provided for all people. But we believe that efforts toward these ends must, in the South, be made within the established patterns of social relationships, which require separate educational institutions for whites and Negroes." From the 1890's to the 1940's, progressives had been ambivalent on the issue of race, and for all the rhetoric of freedom during World War II, that ambivalence was very much alive.[27]

Five months after Truman appointed his Commission on Higher Education, he appointed a Committee on Civil Rights and asked the Committee "to inquire into and to determine whether and in what respect current law-enforcement measures and the authority and means possessed by Federal, State, and local governments may be strengthened and improved to safeguard the civil rights of the people." The Committee's report, entitled *To Secure These Rights* (1947), was in no way ambivalent about the problem of race: it combined an unqualified assertion that the matter of civil rights had become a national problem that affected every American with a ringing call for federal policies to guarantee the rights of all persons, wherever they lived and whatever their racial, religious, or national origins. The report traced the long-standing patterns of discrimination against Jews and Roman Catholics, against blacks and Native Americans, and against persons of Hispanic, Filipino, and Asian descent. It detailed the manifold ways in which discrimination was legally and illegally practiced. It pointed to the inextricable ties between discrimination in employment, housing, education, and health. It exposed the subterfuges by which blacks and immigrants were disfranchised. And it rejected out of hand the assumption that separate facilities for the races could ever be equal. "We believe that not even the most mathematically precise equality of segregated institutions can properly be considered equality under the law," the Committee maintained. "No argument or rationalization can alter this fact: a law which forbids a group of American citizens to associate with other citizens in the ordinary course of daily living creates inequality by imposing a caste system on the minority group." Finally, the Committee advanced a variety of recommendations, including the enactment by Congress of

27. *Higher Education for American Democracy*, II, 29.

a Fair Employment Practices Act, the enactment by the state legislatures of "fair educational practice laws for public and private educational institutions, prohibiting discrimination in the admission and treatment of students based on race, color, creed, or national origin," the creation of a permanent Commission on Civil Rights in the Executive Office of the President, and, in general, "the elimination of segregation, based on race, color, creed, or national origin, from American life."[28]

The situation in the schools and colleges more than justified the firm stand of the two commissions. In 1946–47, seventeen states (Alabama, Arkansas, Delaware, Florida, Georgia, Kentucky, Louisiana, Maryland, Mississippi, Missouri, North Carolina, Oklahoma, South Carolina, Tennessee, Texas, Virginia, and West Virginia) and the District of Columbia still required separate schools for blacks and whites by law; twelve states (Colorado, Connecticut, Idaho, Illinois, Massachusetts, Michigan, Minnesota, New Jersey, New York, Pennsylvania, Rhode Island, and Washington) specifically forbade the segregation of students on the basis of race or color, though in some of those states—Illinois, New Jersey, and Pennsylvania, for example—segregated schools for blacks were maintained in certain localities contrary to law; fourteen states (California, Iowa, Maine, Montana, Nebraska, Nevada, New Hampshire, North Dakota, Ohio, Oregon, South Dakota, Utah, Vermont, and Wisconsin) were silent on the matter of school segregation; and five states (Arizona, Indiana, Kansas, New Mexico, and Wyoming) maintained mixed or permissive arrangements by law—Arizona, for example, required segregation in its elementary schools and permitted it in its high schools; New Mexico prohibited segregated schools but permitted segregated classrooms within schools; Indiana, Kansas, and Wyoming generally permitted segregated schools.[29]

Basing his data on statistics drawn from the 1940 Census, the eminent black educator Charles H. Thompson detailed in stark fashion the inequalities in the educational opportunities and educational achievements of whites and blacks in the segregated systems. In the seventeen states and the District of Columbia where segregation was mandated by law, among persons twenty-five years of age and older,

28. *To Secure These Rights: The Report of the President's Committee on Civil Rights* (Washington, D.C.: Government Printing Office, 1947), pp. viii, 82, 168, 166.

29. George M. Johnson and Jane Marshall Lucas, "The Present Legal Status of the Negro Separate School," *Journal of Negro Education*, XVI (1947), 280–289; and Reid E. Jackson, "The Development and Character of Permissive and Partly Segregated Schools," *ibid.*, 301–310.

2.8 percent of the native whites and 11.7 percent of the blacks had not had a single year of schooling, and 11.6 percent of the native whites and 37.0 percent of the blacks were functionally illiterate; the median years of schooling for whites was 8.4, for blacks, 5.1; 13.2 percent of the whites had completed four years of high school, but only 2.9 percent of the blacks; 4.7 percent of the whites had had four years of college or more, but only 1.1 percent of the blacks. In the professions, there was one white physician to every 843 white individuals, but only one black physician to every 4,409 black individuals; one white pharmacist to every 1,714 white individuals, but only one black pharmacist to every 22,815 black individuals; one white lawyer to every 702 white individuals, but only one black lawyer to every 24,997 black individuals; and one white engineer to every 664 white individuals, but only one black engineer to every 130,700 black individuals. And at the same time the Committee on Civil Rights was conducting its inquiry, blacks in those seventeen states and the District of Columbia were at a marked disadvantage on every contemporary measure of school quality—the holding power of the schools, the length of the school year, pupil-teacher ratios, teacher salaries, the quality of school accommodations and equipment, the availability of special services, including transportation, current expenditures per student, and the availability of advanced graduate and professional education, public and private. Moreover, while nationwide and statewide data broken down by race and national origin were less plentiful, the 1940 Census indicated that the gap in educational attainment of whites and blacks was as significant—if not quite as great—in the North and West as it was in the South, though the national figures tended to reflect the fact that almost four-fifths of the nation's blacks lived in the seventeen states and the District of Columbia where school segregation was required by law.[30]

President Truman paid more than usual attention to the reports of his two commissions and incorporated many of their recommendations into his legislative program. In January, 1948, he included the securing of "essential human rights" as one of the five great goals he outlined in his State of the Union Message; and in February, he sent a civil rights message to Congress arguing that the federal government had a clear duty to ensure that the constitutional guarantees of individual liberty and of equal protection under the laws were not denied or abridged anywhere in the country and calling for legislation

30. Charles H. Thompson, "The Availability of Education in the Negro Separate School," *ibid.*, 263–265.

prohibiting lynching, outlawing the poll tax, and establishing a Fair Employment Practices Commission and a Commission on Civil Rights. Congress, however, was of no mind to enact such proposals. But Truman moved ahead under his executive powers in a number of domains, including education. In 1950, four years before the *Brown* decision, his Department of Justice argued for the overturn of the separate-but-equal principle; and in 1952 it submitted a brief generally supportive of the plaintiffs in the litigation that led to *Brown*. [31]

It was the Supreme Court, however, that most effectively placed the federal government on the side of desegregation, with the unanimous *Brown* decisions of 1954 and 1955. Not surprisingly, those rulings were greeted by a storm of opposition in the South. Less than two months after *Brown I* was handed down in May, 1954, the first white Citizens' Council was organized in Indianola, Mississippi, for the express purpose of resisting desegregation in the interest of preventing the "mongrelization" of the Caucasian race; and over the next months a citizens' council movement spread across the South dedicated not only to maintaining segregation but also to purging schools of "liberal" teachers and "liberal" books and, more generally, purging the South of the NAACP. Southern governors and legislators, led by Senators Harry Byrd of Virginia and James Eastland of Mississippi, revived John C. Calhoun's pre–Civil War doctrine of interposition, which held that the states had the right and the obligation to nullify unjust federal laws by interposing themselves between the federal government and the people, and, in the name of interposition, simply defied the Supreme Court's rulings. In addition, they enacted scores of laws intended to ensure the continuance of segregation—laws abolishing compulsory schooling, laws denying state funds to biracial schools, laws providing tuition grants to students who chose to attend segregated private schools in place of desegregated public schools, laws permitting districts to establish elaborate mechanisms for classifying, assigning, and transferring pupils. In 1955 a Federation for Constitutional Government was established to coordinate the fight against the Court and its desegregation mandates; and in March, 1956, 101 southern congressmen and senators issued a "Declaration of Constitutional Principles" denying the validity of the *Brown* ruling and declaring their intention to resist enforced integration by any lawful means. In the wake of this "massive resistance," as Byrd and his allies called it, violence and intimidation against blacks and moves

31. *Public Papers of the Presidents of the United States: Harry S. Truman, 1948* (Washington, D.C.: Government Printing Office, 1964), p. 3.

to disfranchise them intensified. The border states proved more amenable to the Court's rulings, not least because they had smaller percentages of blacks in their population and encountered less virulent white fears of black domination. Baltimore, Wilmington, San Antonio, Washington, St. Louis, and Louisville moved promptly to eliminate their dual school systems, in part by redistricting and assigning children to the schools nearest their homes, in part by permitting students to transfer to schools of their choice. Other communities followed more or less swiftly, depending both on the racial composition of their population and on the attitudes, the firmness, and the quality of leadership of state and local school and government officials.[32]

President Dwight D. Eisenhower endorsed the *Brown* decision several days after it was handed down; but he was a gradualist by nature and believed not only that the process of desegregation would take time but that it would only be hampered by extremists on both sides. His hand was forced, however, by events in Little Rock, Arkansas, in 1957. There, the doctrine of interposition was invoked in a pivotal test of the nature of American federalism. The Little Rock school board, under federal district court order, had adopted a plan to desegregate the schools gradually, beginning in September with the admission of nine black students to Central High School. Governor Orville Faubus, claiming he was acting in the interest of public order, called out the Arkansas National Guard to prevent the entry of the black students. The school board, joined by the mayor of Little Rock, maintained that it was the governor who was creating the problem, while the federal court ordered the governor to cease interfering with its order. The governor withdrew the guardsmen, but the confrontation had attracted a mob of white supremacist demonstrators; and, when the school actually opened and the black youngsters entered, the superintendent of schools became fearful for the youngsters' safety and sent them home in police cars. President Eisenhower, insisting that mobs would not be allowed to flout federal court orders, federalized the Arkansas National Guard and sent units of the 101st Airborne Division to Little Rock to enforce the court's decrees. The mob was quickly dispersed and the youngsters returned to school. Several months later, however, the school board petitioned for a delay in the implementation of its desegregation plan, claiming that the disrup-

---

32. *Brown v. Board of Education,* 347 U.S. 483 (1954); *Brown v. Board of Education,* 349 U.S. 294 (1955); John Bartlow Martin, *The Deep South Says "Never"* (New York: Ballantine Books, 1957), pp. 1–4; *Congressional Record,* 84th Congress, 2d sess., 1956, C11, 3948, 4004; and Robbins L. Gates, *The Making of Massive Resistance: Virginia's Politics of Public School Desegregation, 1954–1956* (Chapel Hill: University of North Carolina Press, 1964), pp. 117–118.

tions had seriously affected the educational program. The Supreme Court took the opportunity, in the resulting case of *Cooper v. Aaron* (1958), to rule that the right not to be discriminated against could not be abridged or nullified by the direct or indirect interposition of any state authorities, and further, that disruptions were not a basis for depriving black children of their constitutional rights. When Governor Faubus responded by closing the Little Rock high schools for 1958–59, a federal court ruled in the case of *Aaron v. McKinley* (1959) that Arkansas's school closing laws were unconstitutional. The high schools reopened in September, 1959, and remained open as desegregated institutions. Governor Faubus was rewarded by the Arkansas electorate with continuing re-election to the governorship until 1967.

Little Rock served notice that interposition as a legal doctrine was without merit and that there were limitations to the effectiveness of disruption as a tool of resistance to desegregation. Over the next six years, despite riots at the University of Georgia, bloodshed at the University of Mississippi, and Governor Wallace's personal blocking of the entrance at the University of Alabama, desegregation proceeded slowly but relentlessly in the colleges and universities of the South. There was also substantial movement in the lower schools of Oklahoma, Missouri, Kentucky, West Virginia, Maryland, and Delaware, where some 25 to 60 percent of black students attended biracial schools by 1962. But there was "token" desegregation at best in the lower schools of Texas, Georgia, Virginia, North Carolina, Arkansas, Tennessee, and Florida, and no desegregation whatever in the lower schools of Mississippi, Alabama, and South Carolina. And then, between 1963 and 1965, a series of Supreme Court decisions and congressional enactments changed the situation markedly. In *Goss v. Board of Education* (1963), the Court struck down a "minority to majority" transfer plan in Knoxville, Tennessee, whereby pupils could transfer out of schools where their race was in a minority into schools where their race was in a majority. In *Griffin v. County School Board* (1964), the Court flatly rejected an arrangement in Prince Edward County, Virginia, whereby the state had permitted the local board to close its schools rather than desegregate them and then provided for tuition grants and tax credits in support of private schools for whites only. And in *Bradley v. Richmond School Board* (1965), the Court ruled that the desegregation plans of local school districts were required to address the question of desegregation with respect to teachers as well as pupils. For all intents and purposes, the three rulings swept away the paraphernalia of "massive resistance."

The congressional legislation came in the context of a radically changed political situation. During the second Eisenhower administration, there had been sufficient bipartisan support for new civil rights legislation in Congress to permit passage of a moderate measure—the first enacted since Reconstruction—that established a Commission on Civil Rights within the executive branch (though without enforcement powers) and that provided for jury trials in contempt cases arising out of violations of the act; however, a section that would have given the attorney general the power to file suits to protect the right to vote and to seek desegregated school facilities was eliminated during the Senate's deliberations. Yet, in the meantime the civil rights movement that had begun with the Montgomery bus boycotts of 1955 was gaining momentum. In 1957 the Reverend Martin Luther King, Jr., founded the Southern Christian Leadership Conference to mobilize blacks in their effort to gain equal political, economic, and social rights; and in 1960 the sit-ins that would be such an important tactic of the more militant student-led effort began with the determination of four black students to desegregate a lunch counter in Greensboro, North Carolina. A second civil rights bill, extending the life of the Commission on Civil Rights, was passed in the spring of that year, but it gave little satisfaction to the black leaders. Recognizing the salience of the issue, John F. Kennedy sounded a strong civil rights theme in his 1960 presidential campaign, telling a Harlem audience in New York City, "If a Negro baby is born here and a white baby is born next door, that Negro baby's chance of finishing high school is about 60 percent of the white baby's. This baby's chance of getting through college is about a third of that baby's. His chance of being unemployed is four times that baby's." The "freedom riders" journeyed South in the summer of 1961 in the effort to desegregate bus terminals. Once elected, Kennedy was forced in 1962 to send troops to Oxford, Mississippi, to assure the admission of James Meredith to the University of Mississippi under a federal court order, and that only after two men had been killed in a riot at "Ole Miss." In April, 1963, Martin Luther King, Jr., led the blacks of Birmingham, Alabama, in demonstrations to end discrimination in restaurants and jobs, and the nation viewed on television the brutal use of dogs and fire hoses by Police Commissioner Eugene "Bull" Connor and his men against men, women, and children engaged in nonviolent protest. In June, Medgar Evers, the NAACP state secretary for Mississippi, was murdered. In August there was the great "March on Washington," in which almost a quarter-million people, black and white, gathered before the Lincoln Memorial to demonstrate in support of equal rights. And in September, after the schools of Birmingham had been desegregated under court order, a dynamite blast erupted at the Sixteenth Street Baptist Church directly after the conclusion of a Bible class, killing four black children. It was in the context provided by those awful events, so vividly conveyed via television to the nation's homes, that President Kennedy sent a spring civil rights bill to Congress, and it was in the context of those events that President Lyndon B. Johnson, following Kennedy's assassination in November, obtained passage of the bill.[33]

The Civil Rights Act of 1964 went significantly further than earlier measures in providing the protections necessary to guarantee the rights of blacks. Among other things, it empowered the attorney general to undertake legal action to achieve school desegregation and authorized federal assistance to districts desegregating their schools. It outlawed discrimination in any program receiving federal assistance and authorized the discontinuation of such assistance to programs where discrimination was found. It barred discrimination in most public accommodations, and it outlawed discrimination and segregation in most employment, establishing an Equal Employment Opportunity Commission to enforce compliance (but giving it little power to do so). As President Johnson remarked when he signed the bill, it was intended to "close the springs of racial poison."[34]

Re-elected in 1964 by a large majority, Johnson also moved to implement the Great Society program he had outlined in his campaign. Among the flurry of bills he sent to Congress were two that, once enacted, proved to be landmarks in the history of American education, the Elementary and Secondary Education Act of 1965 and the Higher Education Act of 1965. The first measure authorized federal assistance to school districts with large numbers of poor people (often, but not exclusively, people of minority background) as well as assistance for a variety of teaching materials and special services. The second authorized federal assistance for students attending two- and four-year colleges as well as assistance for the purchase of library materials and laboratory and teaching materials. Title I of the act also sought to attract the attention of the colleges and universities to solving the problems of housing, transportation, health, and employment in the cities, hoping thereby to create something of the same relationship between urban institutions of higher education and their

33. U.S., Congress, Senate, 87th Congress, 1st sess., Committee on Commerce, *Freedom of Communications,* Part I: The Speeches, Remarks, Press Conferences, and Statements of Senator John F. Kennedy, August 1 through November 7, 1960, pp. 582–583.

34. *Congress and the Nation, 1945–1964: A Review of Government and Politics in the Postwar Years* (Washington, D.C.: Congressional Quarterly Service, 1965), p. 1637.

communities as the Morrill Act of 1862 had created between the land grant colleges and their communities.

The passage of the Civil Rights Act of 1964 and the education acts of 1965, coupled with the growing impatience of the Supreme Court with resistance to its rulings in *Brown,* created a carrot-and-stick mechanism that dramatically hastened the pace of school desegregation. Federal expenditures for education rose rapidly, from $4.5 billion in 1966 to $8.8 billion in 1970 to $13.4 billion in 1974 to $19.5 billion in 1978—thus the carrot; and the Supreme Court continued to strike down devices for evading school desegregation—thus the stick. In *Green v. County School Board of New Kent County* (1968), the Court struck down a freedom-of-choice plan in New Kent County, Virginia, in which blacks could choose to transfer to a formerly all-white school and vice versa, maintaining, first, that *Brown* had charged school boards "with the affirmative duty to take whatever steps might be necessary to convert to a unitary system in which racial discrimination would be eliminated root and branch," and second, that no arrangement that left 85 percent of the black children in an all-black school could be judged satisfactory—boards were required to take measures "which promise realistically to convert promptly to a system without a 'white' school and a 'Negro' school, but just schools." In *Alexander v. Holmes County Board of Education* (1969), the Court rather sharply defined what "promptly" meant—the obligation of every school district was "to terminate dual school systems *at once* and to operate new and hereafter only unitary schools." And in *United States v. Montgomery County Board of Education* (1969), the Court established racial ratios for teacher assignments at the same time that it reaffirmed numerical goals for pupil assignment. With its rulings in *Green, Alexander,* and *Montgomery,* the Court's answer to the Deep South's "never" had become "now." Faced with federally initiated suits and cutoffs of increasingly substantial amounts of federal money, the South's "massive resistance" collapsed. By 1972, 91.3 percent of all southern black pupils attended biracial schools, as compared with 76.4 percent in the border states and 89.1 percent in the North and West. For all intents and purposes, the initial aims and aspirations of *Brown* had been achieved.[35]

35. U.S., Department of Education, National Center for Education Statistics, *The Condition of Education, 1980 Edition* (Washington, D.C.: Government Printing Office, 1980), p. 40; *Green v. County School Board of New Kent County,* 391 U.S. 437–438, 442 (1968); *Alexander v. Holmes County Board of Education,* 396 U.S. 20 (1969); and *Twenty Years after Brown: A Report of the United States Commission on Civil Rights* (Washington, D.C.: Government Printing Office, 1977), p. 50.

The mid-1960's, however, witnessed a transformation in those aims and aspirations that was fraught with significance. Two documents of the era were critical in initiating the transformation: the first was the so-called Coleman Report of 1966, the second was the Civil Rights Commission report of 1967 entitled *Racial Isolation in the Public Schools.* Title IV of the Civil Rights Act of 1964 had called for a survey "concerning the lack of availability of equal educational opportunity for individuals by reason of race, color, religion, or national origin in public educational institutions at all levels in the United States, its territories and possessions, and the District of Columbia." That survey was conducted in the fall of 1965 under the leadership of James S. Coleman of Johns Hopkins University and Ernest Q. Campbell of Vanderbilt University, using a sample of some four thousand schools. One key contribution of the survey was to go beyond the traditional measures of opportunity—such "inputs" as school facilities, teacher salaries, and expenditures per pupil—to include such "outcomes" as pupil achievement in reading and mathematics. On the basis of mass survey data using extant achievement tests, Coleman and his colleagues found that most American children attended schools where their own race was in the majority, that, despite the somewhat superior facilities of white schools, schools across the country were far more equal in measures of "input" than had been assumed; that the academic achievement of minority children was one or two years behind that of whites in the first grade and three to five years behind by the twelfth grade—in other words, the disparity not only went uncorrected by schools, it actually increased with schooling; and that, given those "outcomes," academic achievement seemed more related to family background than to school quality by any measure of "input" and that, beyond family background, the school factor that seemed to matter most with respect to academic achievement was the racial composition of the school.[36]

Racial Isolation in the Public Schools derived from the growing realization by the mid-1960's that, beyond legally enforced, or *de jure,* segregation in the schools, there were stubborn problems of *de facto* segregation, segregation resulting from housing patterns, social and economic stratification, and demographic factors, in school districts both North and South. Settling together in particular neighborhoods,

36. U.S., Congress, House of Representatives, 94th Congress, 1st sess., Committee on the Judiciary, *Civil Rights Acts of 1957, 1960, 1964, 1968,* p. 16; and James S. Coleman *et al., Equality of Educational Opportunity* (Washington, D.C.: Government Printing Office, 1966).

initially because of kinship and acquaintance and more generally because of such economic factors as rent levels and mortgage opportunities and such social factors as restrictive real estate covenants, discriminatory landlords, and outright prejudice backed by intimidation, blacks migrating from the South to the North and from the rural to the urban South had created far-flung ghettos in the central cities of the nation's metropolitan areas that no amount of school redistricting could correct. In the autumn of 1965, President Johnson asked the Civil Rights Commission to gather the data on *de facto* racial isolation in the schools, and the 1967 report was the result. Prepared under the leadership of William L. Taylor, David K. Cohen, and Thomas F. Pettigrew, and with an Advisory Committee that included, among fifteen distinguished educators and social scientists, Kenneth Clark and James Coleman, *Racial Isolation in the Public Schools* set forth findings documenting stark inequalities in the schooling of white and black children. Seventy-five percent of the black elementary-school pupils in the nation's cities were in virtually all-black schools, while 83 percent of the white pupils were in virtually all-white schools; moreover, the demographic trends, especially those associated with continued suburbanization, augured even further increases in this already high degree of racial isolation. Among the results of racial isolation were educational disparities. Black students typically did not achieve as well as white students, and the longer they remained in school the further behind they fell. Black students were less likely than whites to attend schools with well-stocked libraries, academically strong curricula, and competent, well-educated teachers; they were more likely to attend high schools that sent only a small proportion of their graduates to colleges and less likely to enroll in college. And finally, black students tended to perform better in desegregated schools than in racially isolated schools. As remedies, the report proposed programs of compensatory education (special services intended to correct the educational gaps between different groups of children) for racially isolated schools, city-wide plans that would make extensive use of magnet schools (schools with strong educational programs that would attract applicants from all over the city), educational parks that would combine schools for a variety of grade levels drawn from a wide attendance area with centers that would provide supplementary educational services, and arrangements for city-suburb collaboration. The Commission transmitted its report to the president with a number of recommendations for federal action, the most significant of which was the recommendation that Congress establish a uniform standard for the elimination of racial isolation in the schools, with the suggestion that schools whose enrollment of black pupils went much beyond 60 percent be judged unsatisfactory.[37]

The Coleman and the Civil Rights Commission reports marked a fundamental change in progressive aspirations for the schools, from equality of opportunity to equality of outcome, or, as the latter came to be called in the late 1960's, equity. The new aspiration threw emphasis on two concerns. First, insofar as some of the most intractable problems of race and education were no longer solvable by merely removing barriers through the desegregation of schools, there was a shift to a more affirmative policy of integrating schools. The Supreme Court explicitly adopted this position in *Green* and developed it further over the next few years in a series of cases that made school busing the central issue in school integration. Schoolchildren, of course, had long been transported to school by bus, mostly to achieve what were seen by their parents as the advantages of school consolidation but also for such diverse purposes as relieving overcrowding, gaining access to special services, and ensuring safety in travel. What was new, especially after *Green,* was the growing use of enforced as opposed to voluntary school busing as a means of achieving court-ordered school desegregation.

The Charlotte-Mecklenburg school system in North Carolina provided one such instance. A district serving more than 84,000 pupils in over 100 schools spread over some 550 square miles, its plan for desegregation involving rezoning and free transfer had been found inadequate by a federal district judge in light of *Green* because it had left some 14,000 of the 24,000 black children in the district in all-black or nearly all-black schools; as a remedy, the judge had ordered busing to achieve a further degree of integration. In *Swann v. Charlotte-Mecklenburg Board of Education* (1971), the Court unanimously directed school authorities to use every available device, including busing, to redistribute pupils for the purpose of achieving "the greatest possible degree of actual desegregation." Two years later, in *Keyes v. School District No. 1* (1973), the Court held that the Denver school board had pursued an intentional policy of segregation in a significant part of the district (a policy, incidentally, of segregating Mexican-American pupils, which made *Keyes* the first instance in which the *Brown* ruling was applied to an ethnic group); that the pursuit of such a policy in a significant part of the district created a strong presumption that

37. *Racial Isolation in the Public Schools: A Report of the U.S. Commission on Civil Rights* (Washington, D.C.: Government Printing Office, 1967).

segregated schooling had been similarly motivated in other parts of
the district; and that Denver was therefore bound by the injunction
in *Green* to desegregate the entire system "root and branch" and by
the injunction in *Swann* to use every available device, including sys-
temwide busing, to redistribute pupils in the interest of "the greatest
possible degree of actual desegregation." Then, in *Milliken v. Bradley*
(1974), the Court overturned a federal district court order creating a
new metropolitan school unit by joining the school district of Detroit
to fifty-three of the city's surrounding suburban school districts and
ordering a nine-member panel to draft a detailed plan to use busing
to create integrated schools throughout the metropolitan unit.
Doubtless reflecting the influence of President Richard M. Nixon's
four recent appointees, the Court thus set limits on how far it was
willing to go to achieve desegregation in metropolitan areas with
central-city ghettos. While the lower federal courts did on occasion
thereafter approve metropolitan busing plans, for example, in Wilmington and in Louisville, the combination of the Court's ruling in
Milliken, a declining interest on the part of President Nixon's departments of Justice and of Health, Education, and Welfare in instituting
school desegregation suits, and the sheer size and seeming intracta-
bility of the demographic situation, led to a decided slowing of the
pace of metropolitan efforts to achieve school integration. Interestingly, the Court returned to the Detroit situation three years later in
so-called *Milliken II,* holding that the lower courts did have the right
to order educational components such as reading programs, teacher
training programs, testing programs, and counseling programs as
remedies for the effects of *de jure* school segregation.[38]

There were two other domains of affirmative action toward equity
in education. One was language instruction. In *Lau v. Nichols* (1974),
the Court held against the San Francisco school system for failing to
provide instruction in the Chinese language for Chinese pupils who
did not speak English, maintaining that, whatever the identity of the
textbooks and curriculum, such students were "effectively foreclosed
from any meaningful education," and directing the schools to "rectify
the language deficiency" by establishing special language programs
for the non-English-speaking children. As one result of *Lau,* Congress
in 1974 passed the Bilingual Education Act, making special instruction in bilingual education available to all children of limited English-
speaking ability as a means of promoting educational equity.[39]

38. *Swann v. Charlotte-Mecklenburg Board of Education,* 402 U.S. 26 (1971).
39. *Lau v. Nichols,* 414 U.S. 566, 568 (1974).

The other domain of affirmative action toward the integration of schools and colleges was that of employment. Title VII of the Civil Rights Act of 1964 outlawed discrimination in employment based on race, color, religion, sex, or national origin and established the Equal Employment Opportunity Commission to enforce compliance. In addition, President Johnson in 1965 issued Executive Order 11246, requiring organizations holding government contracts in excess of $10,000 to take affirmative action in their practices with respect to race, creed, color, and national origin, in all aspects of their operation, and two years later Executive Order 11375, extending the requirement to include sex. In 1970, the requirements of Title VII and of Executive Order 11246 as amended were combined into a single requirement by the Equal Employment Opportunity Commission and in 1972 the EEOC was granted authorization to institute court suits in the process of enforcing compliance with the requirement. Vigorous enforcement by the Office for Civil Rights of the Department of Health, Education, and Welfare during the 1970's, requiring the collection and analysis of data by school systems and institutions of higher education and the development of plans with goals and timetables for the employment and assignment of personnel, led to a significant broadening of the social composition of school, college, and university faculties. But the program of affirmative action in employment was controversial from the beginning, with some contending that it was merely carrying out the mandate of the Civil Rights Act by actively removing historic discrimination in employment and with others maintaining that it violated the very meaning of the Civil Rights Act by making racial, religious, ethnic, and gender classifications central to employment. When the issue came to the Supreme Court in *University of California v. Bakke* (1978), the Court in a complex opinion attempted to give partial vindication to both views. It upheld the legality of affirmative action programs because of the diversity they lent to educational institutions and programs; but it struck down numerical quotas based upon race, religion, ethnicity, or gender. In effect, it left in place most of the apparatus established by HEW's Office for Civil Rights during the 1970's.

A second concern associated with the transformation of equality of opportunity into equity was a redirection of attention, from the "externals" of the educative process—facilities, teacher salaries, even the racial composition of the student body—to the "internals" of the educative process—cognition, locus of control (the student's sense of personal control over the social and physical environment), level of aspiration. Some policy makers contemplating the findings of *Racial Isolation in the Public Schools* recognized that there would be all-black or virtually all-black schools for years to come and concluded that the central objective of public policy should be to use what was known about the educative process to make those schools the best schools possible through the use of early developmental activities of the sort popularized by the Head Start experiments first undertaken under the Economic Opportunity Act of 1964, combining intensive, individualized instruction in the key skills of reading, writing, and arithmetic, special guidance and counseling activities, and supplementary educational services in such fields as the sciences, the arts, and physical education. (Some black nationalists made a virtue of necessity and claimed that all-black schools were superior to biracial schools in the opportunity they afforded for the nurture of black pride.) This shift of concern to the "internals" was strengthened by the findings of the various compensatory education studies undertaken by the National Institute of Education during the late 1970's, which held that such efforts contributed in significant ways to the academic achievement of all students, including minority students. Other policy makers, also contemplating the findings of *Racial Isolation in the Public Schools,* recognized that the problems of black education, black family structure, and black employment were inextricably intertwined, and that it was up to the black community to lead in attacking all those problems simultaneously if any was to be solved—the black family would not be strengthened in the absence of the education and training that were expected to lead to improved black employment; black schooling would not be as good as it could be unless black families were strengthened; and appropriate public policies to assist in these goals would not be forthcoming until blacks themselves considered the issues, proposed the policies, and led the efforts of implementation. When such a view was first proposed by Assistant Secretary of Labor Daniel Patrick Moynihan in 1964 and incorporated into a major address by President Johnson, both were pilloried as "racist" in many quarters; when similar views were incorporated into a Joint Center for Political Studies report entitled *A Policy Framework for Racial Justice,* issued in 1983 by a panel of leading black scholars, activists, and intellectuals, it marked the beginning of the development of a new black political and educational agenda for the later 1980's.

The *Brown* decision and the consequences that followed it have variously been referred to as a "second Declaration of Independence" and a "second Reconstruction." The first metaphor is perhaps too broad, hyperbole doubtless intended to mark the significance of the long-delayed promise of equality implicit in the *Brown* decision. The second is perhaps too narrow, though it does pose interesting questions. Both the first and the second "Reconstructions" initially focused on the South but in the end involved the entire nation. Both concerned historic issues of white-black relations and both raised profound questions of federal power vis-à-vis states' rights. Both involved the Supreme Court, the Congress, and the presidency in sometimes collaborative, sometimes conflicting roles. And both used schooling as a major instrument of political change as well as social redemption. But there were profound differences along with the similarities, especially in the central role of blacks in every phase of the more recent movement and in the sweep and durability of the results. In education, the post–Civil War Reconstruction laid the legal groundwork for public education in the South and the constitutional groundwork for *Brown* and the decisions that followed in its wake, insofar as they all derived from the Fourteenth Amendment. But the actual results in schooling for blacks were minimal, episodic, uncertain, and in the end long delayed.

The movement set in motion by *Brown* achieved far-reaching and durable results in practice. The results in the schools by 1972 have already been alluded to. Similarly, whereas at the time of *Brown* blacks had been admitted to only a handful of public and private colleges and universities in the southern states and the District of Columbia, by 1966 most southern institutions of higher education had signed agreements with HEW's Office for Civil Rights assuring their compliance with the nondiscrimination provisions of the Civil Rights Act of 1964, and by 1976 the percentages of blacks attending colleges and universities (9.1%) was very close to the percentage of blacks in the population. In addition, via the Civil Rights Act of 1964, the impact of *Brown* reached beyond blacks to other minority groups such as Mexican-Americans, Asian-Americans, Native Americans, and Americans of Puerto Rican background, as well as to women, to attack historic patterns of discrimination and segregation. There were limits to the reach of *Brown*, of course: poor blacks in the cities of the East and poor Mexican-Americans in the cities of the Southwest remained trapped in urban ghettos and ghetto schools made so by *de facto* degregation, and their situation was rendered even more intractable by the continuing process of suburbanization. And blacks and Hispanics in higher education were concentrated in undue proportions in public two- and four-year colleges, and, in the case of the blacks, in historically black institutions. To argue that the outcomes of *Brown* were significant and durable is not to argue that they conferred unmixed blessings of educational equity or that they went as far as they might have gone or should have gone; it is merely to contend that *Brown* set in motion a major thrust in the direction of greater racial and ethnic equality, in education as well as in many other domains of American society.

Chapter 6

CHILD SAVING AND SOCIAL
SERVICE AGENCIES

> Little by little we have been forced to recognize that neither the
> home nor the school, unaided, can properly guard the welfare of
> the child. We need the strength of the State to protect him from
> carelessness and selfishness, for the child is weak, and his natural
> protectors, individuals, are weak also.
>
> ELLA ARVILLA MERRITT

By the 1870's, common schools were ubiquitous in the United States,
however varied the forms they assumed from one community to another and the arrangements under which they carried on their work.
But common schools were merely one element in a much broader
configuration of education that had been widely developed during the
previous half century under the characteristic mixture of governmental and philanthropic sponsorship pioneered by the united evangelical
front, a configuration that included, not only common schools, but
also Sunday schools, academies, colleges, seminaries, publishing
houses, libraries, almshouses, orphan asylums, reformatories, and the
churches themselves. The common schools may have been distin-
guishable from the other institutions by virtue of their support by
taxation and their oversight by elected citizen boards; but the distinctions between the governmental and the philanthropic were less than
clear, and in the end the entire configuration was perceived by contemporaries as public in the more general sense in which that term
was used during the nineteenth century. Moreover, the ultimate mission of all the institutions was seen by the sponsors of the evangelical
movement as essentially the same: to nurture the good Christians who
would be the good citizens who would enable the Republic to fulfill
its destiny as a beacon of liberty to the world.

At the heart of the configuration was the family, which was deemed the primary and hence the most important of the educating institutions. As portrayed by a steady flow of literature from the evangelical publishing houses, the family was the most natural context for moral development and the most appropriate setting for early instruction—in effect, God's own nursery. And the key figure in familial education was the mother, the guardian of the home, who by virtue of God-given instinct had singular responsibility for producing the character and intellect required by citizens of a free society. "The formation of the moral and intellectual character of the young," argued Catharine Beecher, "is committed mainly to the female hand. The mother forms the character of the future man. . . . If this be so, as none will deny, then to American women, more than to any others on earth, is committed the exalted privilege of extending over the world those blessed influences, which are to renovate degraded men, and 'clothe all climes with beauty.'" Faith in the power of maternal education was unbounded, but not so complete as to prevent the evangelical movement from also erecting a vast apparatus that supplied parental advice in the form of magazines like the *Mother's Assistant* and handbooks like the Reverend Jacob Abbott's popular *Gentle Measures in the Management and Training of the Young* (1871), along with curriculum materials like the Rollo books, through which the same Jacob Abbott entertained a generation of children while instructing them in the rudiments of religion, ethics, history, geography, and science. Further, the evangelical movement complemented that publishing apparatus with a nationwide system of Sunday school literature that provided appropriate substantive fare for the entire household.[1]

Familial education, then, was at the heart of the educational system developed by the united evangelical front, and familial education was assumed to undergird all subsequent education. Most children, of course, grew up in families, though the leaders of the evangelical movement gave little indication that they understood the range and variation of familial forms and styles that prevailed throughout the nation. Yet they did understand that some children were not so fortunate as to have families and that some families simply failed (according to their lights) at the business of child rearing, so they developed, again, through a characteristic mix of governmental and philanthropic sponsorship, almshouses, orphan asylums, and reformatories. Such institutions were common by the 1870's, but they touched a

1. Catharine Beecher, *A Treatise on Domestic Economy for the Use of Young Ladies at Home and at School* (rev. ed.; Boston: Thomas H. Webb & Co., 1842), p. 37.

relatively small proportion of the population. Widowers with children most often remarried, providing the children with a newly constituted family. Widows with children frequently remarried or attempted to rear their children while earning a living, a situation in which the responsibilities of child rearing might well devolve upon older siblings. A common solution in such instances was for one or more of the children or for the widow and the children to join the household of a close relative—a brother or sister or the parent of the widow. The same disposition was commonly made of orphaned children, and indeed there were many cases in which members of the foster family were not kin. Obviously, therefore, although the nuclear family prevailed in nineteenth-century America, the extended family often assumed responsibility for dependent women and children, and most children who were not reared by their natural parents were reared by kin or by fictive kin within a foster family or an apprenticeship situation.

That said, there were families that did slip into dependency, there were orphaned children who were thrown upon the bounty of the community, and there were vagrant, incorrigible, and delinquent children whose families refused to rear them or who were judged incapable of rearing them; and it was for such individuals that almshouses, orphan asylums, and reformatories were created. All such institutions underwent a considerable evolution during the nineteenth century according to a rhetoric that abounded in family metaphors. The sponsors of such institutions increasingly pictured them as surrogate families that would provide the same beneficent and effective moral and intellectual education as the ordinary household; and, to that end, the sponsors sought to organize them according to routines that purported to incorporate the same "gentle but firm" rule that the didactic literature on familial education urged upon parents—indeed, a number of the orphan asylums and reformatories were actually organized as clusters of cottages, each overseen by a married couple referred to as "mother" and "father" by the inmates. The argument was that such routines would develop character in the dependent child and provide rehabilitation for the delinquent child. While the routines commonly ended up more firm than gentle, the rhetoric was sufficiently convincing for such institutions to have become increasingly common across the country during the middle third of the nineteenth century.

By the 1880's, however, there was a growing discomfort as to whether families, both natural and surrogate, were actually carrying out their responsibility for providing the solid foundation that the rhetoric of familial education assigned to them. Institutional church pastors like William S. Rainsford and Russell H. Conwell were finding the impoverished families of their extended parishes unable by dint of economic and social circumstances to rear their children in acceptable ways, with the result that the churches themselves, through day nurseries, kindergartens, mothers' clubs, and clinics, were having to create modes of assistance and support. Social settlement workers like Jane Addams and Lillian Wald were discovering as they reached out to their neighbors that children were locked in their homes for hours at a time or abandoned to the streets while their parents were at work and that assistance with child rearing was one of the most important services they could render. Moreover, they were finding that when immigrant slum families did devote themselves to child rearing, the folk wisdom they had brought with them from their native lands, particularly in matters of child health and nutrition, was insufficient to the task. Charles Loring Brace, the founder and for almost four decades the executive secretary of the Children's Aid Society in New York City, referred to the neglected children of the "outcast poor" as the most threatening members of the "dangerous classes" and conveyed the impression that unless immediate action was undertaken the more respectable classes would soon be overwhelmed. And Josiah Strong, predicting that such problems would only deepen as new waves of immigrants crowded into the burgeoning cities, perceived the making of a crisis that would ultimately test the nation's ability to fulfill its divine destiny.[2]

Concurrent with this growing sense of the breakdown of familial education, there arose a widespread skepticism about the institutions that were supposed to be serving as surrogate families for dependent youngsters. In almshouses where the young mixed freely with the old, children were found to be more often corrupted than properly educated. And in orphan asylums and reformatories, overcrowding, understaffing, and limited funding combined to defeat even the best-laid plans for quasi-familial governance and training. As early as the late 1850's, Brace had committed the Children's Aid Society to a program of placing vagrant children in rural foster homes rather than in institutions—"the best of all Asylums for the outcast child," he asserted in 1872, "is the *farmer's home.*" By the 1880's, a growing number of men and women concerned with the care of dependent children were inclined to agree with Brace's anti-institutional view. Asylums and

2. Charles Loring Brace, *The Dangerous Classes of New York and Twenty Years' Work Among Them* (New York: Wynkoop and Hallenbeck, 1872), p. 224.

reformatories might be necessities of last resort, but the natural family, however beset with problems and insufficiencies, was by far the superior agency of early education. Dollar for dollar, it was also more economical to shore up a child's family with moral, financial, and professional assistance than to institutionalize the child. "Constructive and preventive philanthropy," as the Boston philanthropist Joseph Lee put it, was better and cheaper than charity, on the one hand, or correction, on the other. And at the heart of constructive and preventive philanthropy was education.[3]

As with the progressive movement for school reform, such concerns multiplied during the 1880's, but remained scattered and sporadic. They coalesced into a genuine social movement called child saving during the 1890's. Jacob Riis's *The Children of the Poor* (1892) played much the same informing and galvanizing role for "child saving" as Joseph Mayer Rice's *The Public-School System of the United States* (1893) did for school reform. The National Conference of Charities and Correction and later the National Child Labor Committee served as vehicles for the development of the movement. And the establishment of the United States Children's Bureau in 1912 represented its triumph. However much the Children's Bureau would over the years fail to achieve the most cherished hopes of its founders, its great accomplishment would be in the domain of education. It would instruct generations of parents in the proper modes of child nurture, thereby providing the foundation of all subsequent education.

II

Church and settlement workers during the 1880's had begun to make systematic use of mothers' clubs as vehicles for imparting instruction in a wide range of familial pedagogy, from methods of infant feeding to methods of adolescent discipline. They perceived what they taught through the clubs to be the latest scientific techniques of physical and psychological nurturance, though as often as not their latest scientific techniques were little more than characteristic American common sense. However that may be, their use of clubs for that purpose was only one aspect of a much wider phenomenon of women joining in clubs for a variety of social, cultural, and political purposes. Female associations had emerged, of course, in connection with the evangelical crusade of the 1830's and 1840's, when women had participated

3. *Ibid.*, p. 225; and Joseph Lee, *Constructive and Preventive Philanthropy* (New York: The Macmillan Company, 1902).

in ever increasing numbers in the local, state, and national voluntary societies that were the driving force of the evangelical movement—religion and education, after all, were assumed to fall naturally within woman's "sphere"—with the result that a generation of women found in the evangelical movement an acceptable initial vehicle for interests and activities that went beyond the home. With the continuing decline in the birth rate during the post–Civil War era and with the development of a variety of labor-saving devices in the domain of household work, a growing number of middle- and upper-class women found themselves with more leisure and therefore the time to participate in a greater number and variety of associated activities. Important, too, the range of club concerns broadened as the argument was advanced that the domestic sphere was not merely confined within the four walls of the household but included the entire community—as the president of the Wisconsin Federation of Women's Clubs put it, women needed to "make the world itself a larger home." Hence, women's clubs interested themselves in the arts, literature, and community affairs as well as in the more traditional domains of religion and homemaking; and, in addition, they interested themselves in the plight of the less fortunate and on occasion, as did the churches and settlements, interested the less fortunate in doing something about their plight. By the 1890's, the clubs were multiplying geometrically—in Jane Addams's formulation, they served "subjective" as well as "objective" necessities for many women. And they also began, in the fashion of the time, to federate into national and international organizations.[4]

Not surprisingly, two domains in which women's clubs manifested special concerns were child study and education. Interest in child study arose during the later 1870's, with the vogue of Friedrich Froebel's writings that came in the wake of the kindergarten movement and the fascination those writings stimulated in the processes of "natural" development, particularly in connection with creative play. But child study came truly into its own during the 1890's under the enthusiastic leadership of G. Stanley Hall. A New Englander who had studied philosophy at Williams College, theology at Union Theological Seminary, and then psychology at Harvard, Leipzig, and Berlin, Hall had pioneered the experimental study of child development, using the questionnaire method of gathering data. As the founding presi-

4. Mrs. Arthur C. Neville, "President's Annual Address," in *Proceedings of the Fourth Annual Conference of the Wisconsin State Federation of Women's Clubs, 1900*, p. 7; and Rheta Childe Dorr, *What Eight Million Women Want* (Boston: Small, Maynard & Company, 1910), p. 327.

dent of Clark University, which opened in 1889, as the editor of the *Pedagogical Seminary,* which he established in 1891, and as the key intellectual figure in the international congress on experimental psychology and education at the Chicago Columbian Exposition of 1893, Hall made child study a national movement, with Clark University as its headquarters, the *Pedagogical Seminary* as its messenger, and a network of women's clubs as its driving force. In Hall's view, the promise of the movement was threefold: that the science of psychology had the potential of modernizing the practice of education; that a modernized child rearing and schooling had the potential for radically improving the prospects of humanity; and that the key to progress in these domains was to conduct child rearing and schooling in conformity with the principles of natural human development, as determined by science. Fundamental to the message of the movement was the application of the new theory of evolution. Ontogeny recapitulates phylogeny, Hall announced, following Ernst Haeckel—children in their development recapitulate the experience of the race. Moreover, they hold the key to goodness in the very process of their development. The task of family and school was therefore to adjust to that development and to foster it rather than to try to shape it or control it.

What Hall managed to accomplish in leading the movement was to enlist the women's clubs in gathering the data for the scientists at Clark to analyze and then in disseminating and putting into practice the scientists' findings—characteristically for the era, men did the theoretical work in the university and arranged for women to carry on the practical work in the field. Yet for the women there was the stimulating opportunity to participate in the development of the scientific truths that would transform education and to participate in the educational reform that would transform society. Thus, child study offered a secular version of the earlier evangelical crusade, and thousands of women across the country convened regularly to study and discuss every conceivable aspect of the moral, intellectual, and emotional development of children—the roots of loyalty and lying, the emergence of sex differences, the origins of the imagination, the manifestations and meaning of fear and anger, the rise and fall of interest in literature, history, geography, and arithmetic, and the periodicity of nascency and latency.

The inseparability of child study and education was clear from the beginning. The women who studied Froebel generally ended up being both enthusiasts about the mother's role in preserving the inborn goodness of the child and proponents of the kindergarten.

And, as for Hall, his conception of child study was pointedly linked to educational concerns from the outset. In fact, the whole purpose of working out a science of child development was to yield a science of education. As the new "laws" of natural development began to emerge at Clark, Hall energetically indicated their bearing on education. Young children were fundamentally different from adults; their fears and angers, their ideas of truth and falsehood, their inability sharply to distinguish between imagination and reality represented aspects of their natural development. For parents and teachers to meddle, constrain, prohibit, and punish was to defy the very nature of children and to threaten their health. A pound of health, growth, and heredity, Hall liked to tell his lecture audiences, "is worth a ton of instruction. The guardians of the young should strive first of all to keep out of nature's way, and to prevent harm, and should merit the proud title defenders of the happiness and rights of children. They should feel profoundly that childhood, as it comes fresh from the hand of God, is not corrupt, but illustrates the survival of the most consummate thing in the world; they should be convinced that there is nothing else so worthy of love, reverence, and service as the body and soul of the growing child." For parents this meant giving young children free rein rather than "invading" their leisure, indulgently treating them like the young animals they were (as they recapitulated the experience of the species) rather than forcing them to meet adult standards. For schoolteachers, it meant extending the informality of the kindergarten upward into the elementary grades and adjusting the curriculum to the rhythms of children's natural interests and needs— Hall spoke of the need for a *pedocentric* school, one that fitted the institution to the child, in place of the historic *scholiocentric* school, which fitted the child to the institution. It was nothing less than a Copernican revolution in pedagogy, and the mothers and school-teachers who responded to Hall's message became zealots, not only for kindergartens, but for a host of other progressive reforms ranging from the introduction of art, music, gardening, manual training, domestic science, and physical education into the school curriculum to the development of parks and playgrounds and the fostering of closer relationships among the institutions of child nurture.[5]

All these currents flowed into the work of the National Congress of Mothers, organized in 1897 by Alice McLellan Birney, an avid student of the ideas of Froebel and Hall, and Phoebe Apperson

5. G. Stanley Hall, "The Ideal School as Based on Child Study," *Forum*, XXXII (1901–2), 24–25.

Hearst, whom Birney interested in the possibility of a great national assembly of mothers in Washington and who in large measure underwrote its costs. The response to the "official call" to the National Congress was overwhelming; whereas a few hundred women had been expected, some two thousand actually participated. The presentations ranged from a lengthy keynote address on primitive motherhood by Frank Hamilton Cushing of the United States Bureau of American Ethnology to the concluding remarks on the need for women to organize by Ellen M. Henrotin, president of the General Federation of Women's Clubs. Lucy S. Bainbridge of New York City sketched a vivid picture of homes in "the submerged world" of poverty and the consequent need for day nurseries, while Maud Ballington Booth, founder of the Volunteers of America and the Volunteer Prison League, spoke of her work as a surrogate mother to scores of boys in prison. Margaret S. Sangster, the author who served as editor of *Harper's Bazaar* and who saw her writing as a mission to girlhood, sketched a reading curriculum for mothers wishing advice on child-rearing (she was full of admiration for Jacob Abbott's manuals of advice, along with his Rollo books), and Sallie Southall Cotten, a leader of the women's club movement in North Carolina, set forth a full-blown plan for a national training school for women, on the order of the Military Academy at West Point or the Naval Academy at Annapolis, that would create a truly scientific motherhood "which shall in time correct the errors of the past and redeem the future by penetrating the mysteries of heredity and controlling its possibilities." In the end, the congress passed resolutions endorsing the idea of a national training school for women, urging the states and territories to establish kindergartens and kindergarten training schools, and establishing the National Congress of Mothers on a permanent basis as an organization expressing "the earnest desire and determination of the women of our land and elsewhere to give the children committed to their care the advantages of pure thought and high endeavor."[6]

Aided by the enthusiasm of the delegates and the continued financial assistance of Phoebe Hearst, the National Congress prospered: it enrolled 60,000 members in 1915, 190,000 in 1920, 875,000 in 1925, and 1,500,000 in 1930 (it changed its name to the National Congress of Mothers and Parent-Teacher Associations in 1908 and to the National Congress of Parents and Teachers in 1924). It launched a monthly called the *National Congress of Mothers Magazine* in 1908 (it was

6. *First National Congress of Mothers, Washington, D.C., 1897*, pp. vii, 47, 211, 272.

renamed the *Child Welfare Magazine* in 1910), and it issued a continuing flow of leaflets and pamphlets as well as an eight-volume compendium of child care information entitled *Parents and Their Problems.* And it developed a series of techniques for the dissemination of its ideas. In general, the National Congress remained under the inspiration of Hall's psychology during its first quarter-century, however much that psychology may have declined in academic circles, with the result that adolescent problems came to the fore after the publication of Hall's two-volume work on *Adolescence* in 1904, matters of health and hygiene remained central, and, given Hall's hereditarian propensities, eugenics was a continuing preoccupation. In addition, school reform, especially the development of kindergartens; penal reform, including the establishment of juvenile courts; moral and religious training, along the lines suggested by George Albert Coe; and progressive womanhood, as incarnated in the new domestic science, were continuing themes.

The several strategies that the National Congress developed for disseminating its ideas were rooted in the evangelical movement and further refined by the institutional churches, the social settlements, and the Sunday school and Chautauqua movements during the 1880's and 1890's. They included group discussions, home visits to the poor, and participation in social reform. The group discussions were in the familiar mode of Sunday school and Chautauqua discussions: two or three of the articles on familial education and child care in each issue of the *National Congress of Mothers Magazine* would be specifically earmarked for discussion purposes; they were to be read in advance by club members and discussed under the supervision of designated discussion leaders; the result, of course, as with the similar techniques of the Sunday school and Chautauqua movements, was a national curriculum, in this instance, of parent education. A variant of the group discussion strategy emerged when lower-class women gathered in a church or settlement to receive middle-class ("scientific") tutelage on child rearing. There was discussion, to be sure, but the didactic character of the situation was even more crass. Home visits to the poor, of course, simply shifted the locale of the instruction from the church or the settlement to the impoverished household. Finally, participation in efforts toward social reform, especially school reform and penal reform, was seen as part of a more general effort to educate mothers with respect to their responsibilities to the "family" that was the community at large. In fact, it was this compelling sense of need for maternal action on behalf of the common good that most clearly distinguished the activities of the parent education movement in the pre–World War I era from its activities during the 1920's and 1930's.

The National Congress of Mothers and Parent-Teacher Associations did not spawn the Children's Bureau, but it might well have, for the commitments of the Congress were closely akin to what became the commitments of the Bureau. Indeed the Bureau might well have become one version of Sallie Southall Cotten's national training school for women. As it turned out, the Bureau was the creation of the network of women that grew up in connection with the social settlement movement, aided and abetted by the National Child Labor Committee, on the one hand, and the General Federation of Women's Clubs, on the other. The story has been told in detail by Nancy Pottishman Weiss in "Save the Children: A History of the Children's Bureau, 1903–1918." The idea of the Bureau originated with Lillian Wald, founder of the Henry Street Settlement in New York City, and Florence Kelley, general secretary of the National Consumers' League, who resided at Henry Street. Kelley had urged as early as 1900 the need for a federal commission that would collect information on children, much as the federal Department of Agriculture collected information on farming, and had published that suggestion in *Some Ethical Gains Through Legislation* (1905); Wald too had spoken from the first years of the century of a federal agency that would gather and disseminate information on the needs of children. At Kelley's suggestion, Wald got in touch with Edward Devine, who served with them on the National Child Labor Committee and who also edited *Charities,* with the request that he assist in advancing the idea. Devine responded by asking Wald to prepare a statement of the idea for publication in *Charities,* and promised to help. True to his word, he called the proposal to the attention of Theodore Roosevelt, who responded with characteristic enthusiasm, "Bully, come down and tell me about it" (Wald later recalled that, on the morning they were to call on Roosevelt, the secretary of agriculture was leaving for the South to investigate the threat posed by the boll weevil to the cotton crop; it occurred to her that no threat to children could have evoked comparable federal concern). A bill prepared by the National Child Labor Committee was introduced into the Congress in 1906, with strong support from Roosevelt, but it ran into stiff opposition, particularly from southern congressmen who perceived the Bureau as a radical scheme of "long-haired agitatists." The bill remained stalled for several years, while its proponents continued to claim, in the fashion of Wald, that the government was more interested in farm animals than in children. A White House Conference on Dependent Children in 1909, organized and led by Homer Folks, vice-chairman of the National Child Labor Committee, gave further publicity to the proposal, thereby enlarging the constituency behind it. Roosevelt renewed his support, arguing, "The National Government not only has the unquestioned right of research in such vital matters, but is the only agency which can effectively conduct such general inquiries as are needed for the benefit of all our citizens." Even so, it was not until 1912 that Congress finally passed the bill and President William Howard Taft signed it.[7]

As had been the case almost a half-century earlier with the federal Bureau of Education, the Children's Bureau was given the power to collect and diffuse information. Located organizationally within the Department of Commerce and Labor, it was authorized to "investigate and report to said department upon all matters pertaining to the welfare of children and child life among all classes of our people, and shall especially investigate the questions of infant mortality, the birth rate, orphanage, juvenile courts, desertion, dangerous occupations, accidents and diseases of children, employment, legislation affecting children in the several States and Territories." Provision was made for a chief to be appointed by the president, with the advice and consent of the Senate, for a small staff of fourteen, and for a total budget of just over $25,000; and, in response to critics who saw the long arm of the federal government about to invade the sacred precincts of the nation's homes, the specific injunction was included that "no official, or agent, or representative of said bureau shall, over the objection of the head of the family, enter any home used exclusively as a family residence."[8]

Once the bill had been signed, Jane Addams, Lillian Wald, and other members of the National Child Labor Committee worked for the appointment of Julia Lathrop as chief of the new Bureau, and Taft nominated her on April 17, 1912; upon confirmation by the Senate she became the first woman ever to head a statutory federal agency. She was an extraordinarily apt choice for the position. An alumna of Vassar College, Lathrop had joined the residents of Hull House in 1890. Becoming an invaluable associate of Addams and a close friend

7. Nancy Pottishman Weiss, "Save the Children: A History of the Children's Bureau, 1903–1918" (doctoral thesis, University of California at Los Angeles, 1974), pp. 55, 75; Lillian D. Wald, *The House on Henry Street* (New York: Henry Holt and Company, 1915), p. 165; and Robert H. Bremner *et al.*, eds., *Children and Youth in America: A Documentary History* (3 vols.; Cambridge, Mass.: Harvard University Press, 1970–1974), II, 762.

8. Bremner *et al.*, eds., *Children and Youth in America*, II, 774.

of Kelley (Kelley lived at Hull House before moving to Henry Street in 1899), she had participated in Hull House activities over the next twenty years. She had investigated county poorhouses and asylums, first as part of the Hull House neighborhood inquiries and later, after Governor John Peter Altgeld appointed her to the Illinois Board of Charities in 1893, as an official of the state; she had published the results of her investigations in *Suggestions for Visitors to County Poorhouses and to Other Public Charitable Institutions* (1905), along with strong recommendations that the indiscriminate mixing of young and old in state institutions be discontinued; and she had helped to obtain the legislation establishing the juvenile court in Chicago and had then assisted in raising the money to support the first of the court's probation officers. She had taught for a number of years at the Chicago School of Civics and Philanthropy, which was later incorporated into the University of Chicago; and, during a trip around the world with her sister in 1910–11, she had undertaken a study of the public school system of the Philippines. Once in office, she took aggressive advantage of the information-gathering powers of the Bureau, first to investigate infant mortality in a number of cities with a view to obtaining uniform birth registration procedures, and later, after her reappointment by President Woodrow Wilson, to study maternal deaths, juvenile delinquency, and illegitimacy. The quintessential progressive in her assumptions, she deeply believed that gathering the facts was the prelude to reform, since the very availability of the facts would compel reform. During the brief period between the time the first federal child labor law was enacted in 1916 and the time it was declared unconstitutional by the United States Supreme Court in 1918, she also led the Bureau in the vigorous enforcement of the law, enlisting Grace Abbott, another former resident of Hull House, as director of the newly created Child Labor Division within the Bureau. When Lathrop retired in 1921, Abbott succeeded her and served for thirteen years.

As the quintessential progressive, Lathrop also led the Bureau into education, where it exerted what was probably its most durable and far-reaching effect. Lathrop shared the conviction that Sallie Southall Cotten had articulated in her proposal for a national training school for women, namely, that the expertise was at hand to create a science of child rearing and that that expertise simply needed to be put into the hands of every mother. "Maternal affection is the most precious survival of instinctive life," Lathrop explained to a gathering of her fellow alumnae at Vassar College. "By its motive power millions of women daily perform miracles of patient toil but Nature has withdrawn from the human mother the instinctive wisdom which, as Febre has shown, she bestows so lavishly upon the hymenoptera [highly developed insects such as bees and wasps]. What may we not hope for the culture of the race when we put at the service of the human mother's intelligence the continually growing discoveries of research?" What Lathrop set out to do through the Bureau was to create national standards of child rearing based on those "continually growing discoveries of research" and to lay them before the nation's parents, especially mothers. As she once put the matter somewhat bluntly to an audience of schoolteachers, "Many parents need advice and are willing to take it, even from old-maid teachers."[9]

Lathrop's vehicles for furnishing the needed advice were three pamphlets prepared by Mary Mills West and "addressed to the average mother of this country": *Prenatal Care* (1914), *Infant Care* (1915), and *Child Care: The Preschool Age* (1918). West, a widow with five children of her own, was a University of Minnesota–trained researcher on the staff of the Bureau, though she was not a physician, a fact that later brought criticism of her selection to prepare the pamphlets. *Prenatal Care* was forty-one pages in length and ran the gamut from "signs of pregnancy" to "nursing the baby." West counseled engaging a doctor as early in the pregnancy as possible, consulting the doctor before engaging a nurse, bearing the child in a hospital, and, if confinement were planned for the home, securing the services of a visiting nurse. She stressed the utter necessity of "perfect cleanliness" during the confinement in the interest of avoiding "child-bed" fever. And she was uncompromising in her advice with respect to feeding: to nurse her baby was "the first duty of every mother," since "mother's milk is the perfect infant food." A lengthy glossary at the end translated the medical terms that were liberally sprinkled through the document into ordinary language. *Child Care: The Preschool Age* was eighty-eight pages in length and ranged from the living conditions of the child through such matters as food and clothing, exercise and play, discipline and education, and health and hygiene. West believed that a house with a yard was superior to an apartment for child rearing, that if children were regularly served wholesome and nutritious food "without comment or question" they would form proper dietary habits, that play was a "fundamental instinct" and that through play the child was laying "the foundation for a healthy adult life," that al-

9. Jane Addams, *My Friend, Julia Lathrop* (New York: The Macmillan Company, 1935), p. 40; and *Kindergarten-Primary Magazine*, XXXV (1913), 256.

though suppression and harsh punishment were to be avoided, the child was to "know no other way than to do what he is told," and that parents, in answering children's questions, had "boundless opportunity to lay the foundations of a broad and practical education." *Child Care* ended with detailed listings of sources for the further education of the interested parent.[10]

Prenatal Care and *Child Care* circulated briskly, but it was *Infant Care* that elicited the most widespread public interest. The pamphlet was eighty-seven pages in length and covered such topics as living conditions (West's preference for houses over apartments was again explicit), food, clothing, training, discipline, health, and hygiene. West again proclaimed the duty of mothers to nurse their babies; cleanliness was urged throughout; and the importance of establishing good habits through systematic training was strongly emphasized. Since good habits were the result of repeated actions, regularity in the infant's regimen was portrayed as vital: the infant was to be fed, bathed, and put to sleep at the same time each day; parents were not to succumb to the child's desire for play; and crying was not to be heeded. Toilet training was to begin in the third month; pacifiers and thumb-sucking were not to be tolerated (a pinned or sewed-down sleeve would quickly cure the latter); and the "injurious practice" of masturbation was to be eradicated as soon as discovered. As West summed it up, "Babies who are properly fed, who are kept clean, and have plenty of sleep and fresh air, and who have been trained in regular habits of life, have no cause for being 'bad' and are therefore 'good.' " Again, a listing of sources for the further education of interested parents concluded the document.[11]

The circulation of *Infant Care* astonished even those at the Bureau. Initially distributed at the request of individuals and organizations, it soon became a favorite gift of congressmen to their constituents. And, constrained as it was by limited publication budgets, the Bureau often found itself hard pressed to meet the demand. Beginning in 1921, the pamphlet was revised from time to time to keep up with new knowledge (and changing beliefs), but its distribution never flagged. By 1955, it had surpassed all other government publications, including the widely sought-after bulletins of the Department of Agriculture, with a total circulation of 35 million; by 1961 that figure had reached

10. Mrs. Max West, *Prenatal Care* (Washington, D.C.: Government Printing Office, 1913), pp. 6, 7, 32, 34, 26, 32, and *Child Care: The Preschool Age* (Washington, D.C.: Government Printing Office, 1918), pp. 28, 39, 47, 50.

11. Mrs. Max West, *Infant Care* (Washington, D.C.: Government Printing Office, 1914), pp. 62, 63.

45 million, and by 1972, 59 million. Also, initially printed in English alone, it was translated into Italian, German, Polish, Yiddish, Slovak, Hungarian, French, and Japanese by a number of the states as a service to their immigrant communities; and then, after World War II, it was translated into an even greater number of languages by the Department of State for circulation abroad. Whatever its ultimate readership and actual influence on child rearing—neither of which can ever be determined with precision—*Infant Care* has surely been one of the most significant educational documents of the modern era.

Several points, however, can be made about *Infant Care*. For one thing, it patently reflected the accepted medical advice of its era, and continued to do so through successive revisions. The chief manual of child care at the time West wrote the pamphlet was L. Emmett Holt's *The Care and Feeding of Children* (1894). Holt, one of the founders of pediatrics in the United States and for years professor of pediatrics at the College of Physicians and Surgeons and medical director of Babies' Hospital in New York City, was a pioneer in dispensing preventative medical advice as a primary technique of pediatric care. Recognizing that the chief causes of infant death at the turn of the century were digestive ailments, Holt saw sanitary reform, the improvement of the quality of city milk supplies, and infant hygiene as key weapons in the effort to reduce infant mortality. And in the domain of infant hygiene he saw three strategies as central: first, work with women's organizations in the development of a more scientific child rearing; second, the preparation of competent nursery attendants—to that end he established a Training School for Nursery Maids at Babies' Hospital; and third, the publication of suitable scientific material for home use. *The Care and Feeding of Children* was prepared in catechetical form as part of the third strategy; it quickly captured the field from the older evangelical manuals, and had gone through eight editions by the time West prepared *Infant Care*. As might be expected from a physician, the manual concentrated on matters of health, illness, and nutrition, but an emphasis on early training was also present. Nursing was essential, since there was no perfect substitute for mother's milk. In the absence of mother's milk, cow's milk was the best available substitute. Regularity in feeding was crucial—it must be established at the outset. Infants were not to be played with; crying was not to be indulged; thumb-sucking, which could lead to infection, was to be quickly eradicated; pacifiers were not to be permitted; and masturbation, the "most injurious of all these bad habits," was to be "broken up just as early as possible." West's debt in *Infant*

Care, not only to Holt but to the scores of more popular magazine articles that made Holt's preachments the commonplaces of the era, was unmistakable.[12]

During the 1920's, child-rearing ideas were profoundly influenced both by the behaviorism of John B. Watson and by the Freudianism of the mental hygiene movement. Watson's child-rearing manual, *Psychological Care of Infant and Child* (1928), dated from his period of "strict behaviorism," when he had carried his theories to the extreme and repudiated all "half-hearted" proponents of the behaviorist view. Although the book itself never enjoyed a large circulation—probably owing to the stridency of Watson's counsel, his disdain for what passed for child rearing in most households, his insistence on the radical inhibition of parental emotions, and his frank admission at the outset that he was addressing his manual to those mothers who had the "leisure to devote to the study of their children"—it did exert an important, if indirect, influence. In the end, the principal effect of the manual was to support and strengthen the behaviorist tendencies already present in Holt's *The Care and Feeding of Children* and the Bureau's *Infant Care.*[13]

The influence of the mental hygiene movement was quite different, thanks in large measure to Lawrence K. Frank's efforts through the Laura Spelman Rockefeller Memorial, a foundation created in 1918 by John D. Rockefeller in memory of his wife and endowed with $58 million. Frank had studied economics at Columbia and had then gone on to work, first, for the New York Telephone Company, and then, for the War Industries Board; there he had made the acquaintance of Wesley Clair Mitchell, the economist, and his wife, Lucy Sprague Mitchell, who had founded the Bureau of Educational Experiments in New York City in 1916 as an agency to develop a reformed schooling on the basis of the study of children. Under the influence of Lucy Sprague Mitchell and her associates, Frank became a mordant critic of contemporary schooling and a champion of the kind of progressive methods that would liberate youngsters from conformity to the traditional and the familiar and nurture in them a devotion to "science as the method of intelligence." When the economist Beardsley Ruml, who had recently assumed the leadership of the

12. L. Emmett Holt, *The Care and Feeding of Children: A Catechism for the Use of Mothers and Children's Nurses* (New York: C. Appleton and Company, 1894), p. 66.

13. John B. Watson, *Psychological Care of Infant and Child* (New York: W. W. Norton & Company, 1928), p. 7. For Watson's "strict behaviorism," see Lucille Terese Birnbaum, "Behaviorism: John Broadus Watson and American Social Thought, 1913–1933" (doctoral thesis, University of California at Berkeley, 1964).

Laura Spelman Rockefeller Memorial, invited Frank to prepare a proposal for a new program that the Memorial might undertake in the domain of education, he responded with a large-scale plan that involved, first, a series of child development research institutes at a number of the leading universities, second, a national network of parent organizations, coordinated by the Child Study Association of America and the National Council of Parent Education, that would involve parents in the systematic study of child development and child rearing, and, third, a series of instruments for popularizing the findings of the research institutes and the parent study groups, with a new periodical (it became *Parents' Magazine*) as the centerpiece. The effort was well financed during the later 1920's and enlisted the energies, not only of thousands of parents, but also of some of the nation's leading students of child development, including Adolf Meyer of the Johns Hopkins University, Arnold Gesell (G. Stanley Hall's former student) of Yale University, Helen Thompson Woolley of Teachers College, Columbia University, and the youthful Margaret Mead. During the later 1920's, the organizational apparatus the Laura Spelman Rockefeller Memorial erected conveyed a more or less eclectic version of the science of child development; after 1930 it served increasingly as a conduit for newer Freudian conceptions of child rearing that emphasized the centrality of the emotions in human development, the importance of personality adjustment, and the efficacy of more permissive processes of child rearing in fostering proper adjustment. And at the time of that shift a young pediatrician named Benjamin McLane Spock opened his practice in New York City, undertook postgraduate training at the New York Psychoanalytical Institute, and decided to accept an invitation from Donald Porter Geddes of Pocket Books, a pioneer in paperback publishing, to prepare a new child-rearing manual for parents.[14]

Spock had grown up in a well-to-do New Haven family, had attended Yale College and Yale Medical School, had interned at New York Nursery and Child's Hospital, which was affiliated with Cornell Medical School, and had then taken a residency in adult and child psychiatry at the Paine Whitney Clinic of New York Hospital—his training analysis was with Dr. Bertram Lewin, a disciple of Freud associated with the New York Psychoanalytical Institute. It was as a young pediatrician in New York City with training in psychoanalysis and with ties to organizations like the Psychoanalytical Institute and

14. Lawrence K. Frank, "Two Tasks of Education," *School and Society,* XV (1922), 659.

the Advisory Committee on Mental Hygiene of the Bureau of Child Hygiene, that Spock came to know Frank and Mead, and, most important for him, Carolyn Beaumont Zachry. Zachry had been educated at Teachers College, Columbia University, where she had completed a doctorate under William Heard Kilpatrick with a dissertation on the personality adjustment of schoolchildren and had then gone on to study with Carl Jung during the 1930's. An early fellow of the American Orthopsychiatric Association, she had directed an influential study of adolescent development for the Commission on Secondary School Curriculum of the Progressive Education Association and, as one outcome of that work, had become the founding director of a psychoanalytically oriented training center for child care professionals called the Institute for the Study of Personality Development. Having come to know Spock, she invited him to share in the work of the Institute and in the process became one of his most significant mentors. Years later, he credited her with having exerted the "broadest, deepest influence" on his ideas.[15]

In recognition of his growing reputation as an *avant-garde* pediatrician, Spock had been asked as early as 1938 to prepare a child-rearing manual for parents but had declined. When Geddes extended his invitation in 1943, Spock agreed, having concluded that there was no manual available that combined "sound pediatrics with sound psychology." He set to work on the project in the summer of 1943, but a tour of duty as a naval physician during World War II intervened, and the book was not published until 1946. One of the earliest volumes to appear concurrently in both hard-cover and paperback editions—the latter was entitled *Pocket Book of Baby and Child Care,* and later, simply *Baby and Child Care*—the book "took off," selling over a half-million copies during its first ten months and over 24 million by 1972.[16]

In outline, substance, and tone, Spock's manual was radically different from anything that had preceded it. In contrast to Holt, Spock gave a great deal of attention to parent concerns and to the "normal" course of child development—the research from Frank's child study institutes was formidable by the 1940's. In contrast to Watson, Spock began with a preface in which he urged his readers not to take his advice too seriously. "Books deal in generalities," he warned. "They

15. Hildegarde Dolson, "Who Is Dr. Spock?" *Ladies' Home Journal* LXXVII (March, 1960), 138.

16. Lynn Z. Bloom, *Doctor Spock: Biography of a Conservative Radical* (Indianapolis: The Bobbs-Merrill Company, 1972), pp. 101, 116.

can't go into all the possible variations." Hence, his book was to be considered "a source of helpful suggestions, not the final word." And, in contrast to both Holt and Watson, Spock urged parents to enjoy their babies, to be "natural" with them, to make their own decisions about breast feeding, not to worry too much about thumb-sucking and masturbation and certainly not to use restraints or punishments to eliminate them, to feel free to use pacifiers, and to discipline in ways that expressed the family's love for the child and that would foster the child's love in return. "Trust yourself" was Spock's message, though with frequent qualifiers about the need to consult with physicians.[17]

Spock's book was a watershed in American parent education, but it was a reservoir as well, for it brought together changes in knowledge and values that had been in the making for more than a decade, changes that were reflected in contemporary magazine articles on child rearing and in the 1942 and 1945 editions of the Children's Bureau's *Infant Care*. To argue thus is not to deny the freshness or originality of Spock's accomplishment; it is merely to contend that the book confirmed changes in child-rearing advice at the same time that it accelerated them. Put otherwise, Spock reached an audience that had been partially readied for what he had to say.

Who constituted the audience of the *Infant Care* manuals and of Holt's and Spock's best sellers? It is a commonplace to note that in conveying the best and latest medical advice, the authors inevitably assumed a middle-income situation and, often, middle-class values as well. The 1914 edition of *Infant Care* advised consulting a physician or nurse before confinement and the superiority of confinement in a hospital—the opposition to midwives, who were still prevalent in the urban, immigrant community, was patent in the failure to refer to them. The Bureau's contemporary studies of infant mortality, however, revealed instance after instance of home births where the family could afford to have neither nurse nor midwife in attendance but only experienced relatives. *Infant Care* counseled breast feeding at regular intervals throughout the day—it saw no decent substitute for mother's milk; by definition, mothers who had to work would fail in their responsibilities to their infants. *Infant Care* warned that babies without sunshine would "droop just as a plant does," and counseled that the room "in which the sun shines for the longest period of the day should be chosen for the nursery"; the family that lived in a dumbbell tenement was condemned to "drooping" children. One cannot quarrel

17. Benjamin Spock, *The Common Sense Book of Baby and Child Care* (New York: Duell, Sloan and Pearce, 1946), pp. 2, 21, 3.

with the effort to present sound medical advice to parents—if Holt and West saved infant lives by urging mother's milk in place of the contaminated cow's milk that was common in early-twentieth-century cities, they could scarcely be faulted, and nor could Spock when he consistently urged that children with high fevers be seen by a physician. The problem came when moral advice was proffered as medical advice and in the process collided with alternative ethnic or class values—this was as much a problem with the physicians' manuals as it had been with the ministers' manuals. Granted all that, there is ample evidence that the manuals, and especially *Infant Care,* were read by a broad cross-section of American parents and that the breadth of the cross-section increased as the literacy rate rose with compulsory schooling. The circulation rates alone would indicate that the audiences were not narrowly class-bound, though there is of course no telling what happened to the thousands of copies of *Infant Care* circulated by congressmen to their constituents. Beyond their circulation, however, there is the additional evidence of an unending flow of letters to the Children's Bureau and to Spock, commenting on the advice and asking for additional information, letters clearly written by a broad cross-section of the American population.[18]

In addition to the question of audience, there is the question of influence: Did the manuals actually affect the ways in which parents cared for and educated their children? Alice Hamilton, a physician who was a contemporary of Jane Addams and Julia Lathrop at Hull House and who later was a pioneer in the development of industrial medicine, liked to reminisce about the child-rearing instruction she regularly offered at the settlement. Speaking of the advice on feeding she proffered after having seen to it that the infants had been bathed, she noted, "Then I gave what I had been taught was the best advice about feeding babies—nothing but milk till their teeth came. When I see the varied diet modern mothers give their babies, anything apparently from bacon to bananas, I realize that those Italian women knew what a baby needed far better than my Ann Arbor professor did." She went on to remark about how ineffectual the advice had been in any case. "I remember a young mother who had brought her baby to me, showing me her fine specimen of a three-year-old son, and telling me of his difficulties when he was a baby. 'I gave him the breast and there was plenty of milk, but he cried all the time. Then one day I was frying eggs and just to make him stop I gave him one

18. West, *Infant Care,* p. 10.

and it went fine. The next day I was making cup cakes and as soon as they were cool I gave him one, and after that I gave him just whatever we had and he got fat and didn't cry any more.' " Hamilton's reminiscence suggests one answer to the question: Whatever influence the manuals may have exerted, it was never total and always filtered through a wide range of individual and group experience. That said, Urie Bronfenbrenner and others have presented a variety of data to the effect that child-rearing patterns in general did change during the 1940's and 1950's and very much in the direction of the shift discerned from Holt to Spock and in the several editions of *Infant Care*. But did the manuals occasion the change or merely reflect it, or did the change in both child-rearing advice and practice derive independently from other sources? The answer is, probably all three, in varying measures in varying circumstances. The sources of behavior are almost always multiple, though education is frequently one of them; and the sources of education are multiple too, so that it is rare that one can determine on any one-to-one basis the precise outcome of any particular educational effort or the precise educational source of any particular behavior.[19]

III

For all their talk about the primacy of the family, early-twentieth-century progressives were deeply ambivalent about familial education. On the one hand, they viewed the family as the pre-eminent nursery for the child's early mental, moral, and physical development, with the mother as the central agent in the process. On the other hand, they never really trusted the mother. Through ignorance, neglect, or adherence to outmoded—read "immigrant"—ways, mothers were seen as too often failing in their obligations and, in the end, miseducating. Hence, progressives pressed for parent education, so that children might be nurtured in accordance with the latest scientific knowledge. Yet, even when bolstered by parent education, families might err. Parents not only miseducated their children, they crassly exploited them, malnourishing them in order to save money, sending them prematurely to work in order to earn money, and in general failing to recognize them as the reformers did—as dependent beings in need of care and nurturance. Referring again to immigrants, progressives occasionally complained of the utter inability of parents

19. Alice Hamilton, *Exploring the Dangerous Trades: The Autobiography of Alice Hamilton, M.D.* (Boston: Little, Brown, and Co., 1943), pp. 69–70.

to educate in the first place. "If these children of illiterate immigrant parents cannot be placed in school soon after their arrival in this country," warned Sophonisba Breckinridge and Edith Abbott in *The Delinquent Child and the Home* (1912), "the way to delinquency through dependency is sure to be open to them."[20]

It was to the school that progressives turned as the institution that would at the least complement familial education and in many instances correct it and compensate for its shortcomings. The school would help rear the children of ordinary families, it would provide a refuge for the children of exploitative families, and it would acculturate the children of immigrant families. Moreover, the school would deliver whatever services children needed to develop into healthy, happy, and well-instructed citizens—it would provide meals for the poorly fed, medical treatment for the unhealthy, and guidance for the emotionally disturbed. It would send forth visiting teachers and visiting nurses for those unable physically to attend, and it would in turn refer to clinics, counseling centers, and social agencies those for whom its services were insufficient. Much as the church had stood at the hub of the configuration of education sponsored by the evangelical movement during the nineteenth century, the school stood at the hub of the configuration of education sponsored by the progressive movement in the twentieth. In effect, though progressives asserted the primacy of familial education, they advanced the pre-eminence of schooling.

There were those within the ranks who took note of the contradiction and objected. Joseph Lee, for example, the well-to-do president of the Massachusetts Civic League, as early as 1909 lamented the tendency of the school to accrete functions formerly carried out by the home. "A marked phenomenon of the time," Lee noted,

is the extent to which what used to be regarded as functions of the home are being taken over by other agencies. The home has ceased to be the industrial unit. With the coming of the apartment house it is ceasing to carry on even the domestic arts: sewing, cooking and housework. As a result of these recessions it has largely ceased to supply industrial and domestic training, and these duties have been taken over, as that of supplying general instruction had already been, by the school. In its cramped city surroundings, the home has ceased to be the playground even of the smaller children, and this gap also the school has largely filled. Even in the matter of physical care the school doctor and school nurse have, at first sight, apparently taken over what

20. Sophonisba Breckinridge and Edith Abbott, *The Delinquent Child and the Home* (New York: Charities Publication Committee, 1912), p. 65.

used to be functions of the home. Now comes the question of school feeding. At present the proposal is chiefly that of giving one meal a day; but a child without breakfast or supper is still underfed, and the question of giving all the meals is not far distant. Pure air is essential to life and vigor as is good food, and public provision of sleeping quarters must follow logically.[21]

Lee's point was not to quarrel with public provision for good schooling and for the child welfare services coming to be associated with good schooling. It was rather to ask how far provision for those services should be carried, and whether there was not somewhere "an invisible line beyond which we are no longer doing what we started out to do, but something else, or are undoing it." For Lee, the "invisible line" was the one beyond which the family was no longer able to carry out its obligation of physical and moral succor to the very young. Family relations were the oldest and most fundamental of all social relations; in their absence, people became subhuman. The family, Lee maintained, "is the mother of the affections, the first school and the best. It is the teacher of forbearance and of steady service. It is the first form of the state, the parent of all nations, and still the single cell of which all nations are composed." Were all the elements of familial education to be reallocated and well performed, but the family itself weakened, civilization would not survive.[22]

Lee was not a voice alone and indeed most of his fellow progressives would have nodded assent to his plea. But his arguments were in their very nature defensive. Where in the end should the line be drawn? It was all well and good, his progressive contemporaries agreed, to extol the virtues of the ideal family as a nursery of first-class education. But ideal families were few and far between in the nation's teeming cities; economic circumstances and conflicting values foreclosed that possibility. As Breckinridge and Abbott put it in *The Delinquent Child and the Home,* "The point of view of the parents with regard to much that is considered essential to the proper up bringing of the child often remains singularly un-American. For example, the immigrant child frequently suffers from the fact that the parents do not understand that the community has a right to say that children under a certain age must be kept in school. It seems, for example, unimportant to the Italian peasant, who as a gloriously paid street laborer begins to cherish a vision of prosperity, whether his little girls go to school or not. It is, on the contrary, of great importance that a sufficient dower be accumulated to get them good husbands; and to take

21. Joseph Lee, "The Integrity of the Family as a Vital Issue," *Survey,* XXIII (1909), 305.
22. *Ibid.,* 305, 313.

them from school and put them to work is, therefore, only an attempt to help them accomplish this desirable end." Even when the immigrant child was kept in school, Breckinridge and Abbott continued, the peasant became hostage to the child for "versions of what 'they all do in America' " and gradually parents found themselves "at a great disadvantage in trying to maintain parental control." Either way, the family was at a loss to fulfill the role Lee had set for it.[23]

This ambivalence of child welfare progressives about familial education led in part to the parent education movement; but it also led to the development of a considerable array of institutions to aid, assist, complement, and on occasion replace the family in the education of the young. The school was pre-eminent among such institutions, and the rapid spread of compulsory attendance laws attested to the progressive belief that, at least for the years between seven or eight and fourteen, fifteen, or sixteen, schooling should complement whatever education the family provided. Between 1890 and 1918, the twenty-three states that had not done so earlier enacted compulsory attendance laws—by 1918, all forty-eight states then in the union had such laws on their books. To be sure, they were not stringently enforced; what is more, as William M. Landes and Lewis C. Solmon have demonstrated, they more often confirmed high levels of school attendance than they caused them. Nevertheless, they served an important symbolic function during the years before World War I insofar as they testified to public acceptance both of extended child dependency—as Florence Kelley observed in 1903, "The best child-labor law is a compulsory education law covering forty weeks of the year and requiring the consecutive attendance of all the children to the age of fourteen years"—and of an expanded role for the state in the education of all children. Ella Arvilla Merritt, a staff member of the Children's Bureau, summed up one version of the progressive view in a talk she gave in 1919 on "What the Government Is Doing to Conserve Child Life." "We used to think that the care of our children was entirely an affair of the home," she noted. "It was a great step forward when, after much opposition, the idea that it is the duty of the State to furnish schools for its children and to see that they attend those schools, gradually found expression in our public school system and our compulsory education laws." But Merritt went further to make her most fundamental point: "Little by little we have been forced to recognize that neither the home nor the school, unaided, can properly

23. Breckinridge and Abbott, *Delinquent Child and the Home*, pp. 66, 67.

guard the welfare of the child. We need the strength of the State to protect him from carelessness and selfishness, for the child is weak, and his natural protectors, individually, are weak also. All the mother love and care in the world cannot avail against the dangers of a defective sewage system. We need also the knowledge of proper methods of care, which the government is better equipped than any other agency to obtain and to disseminate." Merritt was avowing the recognition of a need for greater state powers to protect the young, the weak, and the exploited that Florence Kelley in particular had fostered among the leaders, the staff members, and the far-flung supporters of the Children's Bureau, a recognition that provided an essential spur to their advocacy of compulsory school attendance laws.[24]

In addition to efforts to enhance the effectiveness of the school, child welfare progressives concerned themselves with the adequacy of nonfamilial care for children still too young to go to school. The initial age of entry into schooling had varied considerably during the nineteenth century, both from locality to locality and over time; on average it had tended to rise as the century progressed, to a point where it stood somewhere around the age of six or seven by the 1870's. Whereas it had not been uncommon for two- and three-year-olds to attend school in the eighteenth century, that practice had become rare in the nineteenth century, owing to the rise of the domesticity ethic with its assumptions and assertions about the superiority of familial education for very young children. It was clear, however, that single-parent families and families where both parents worked outside the home necessitated other arrangements. In some such situations, children stayed with kin or neighbors during working hours; in others, they stayed at home, often under the care of older siblings; in still others, they roamed the streets unattended; and, in still others, they worked alongside their parents. Out of such arrangements and in connection with them, formal and informal day nurseries developed—initially, households willing to board young children during working hours, and later, householdlike institutions of a similar sort. Like other quasi-familial institutions of the nineteenth century, they grew up under private, entrepreneurial, and philanthropic auspices,

24. William M. Landes and Lewis C. Solmon, "Compulsory Schooling Legislation: An Economic Analysis of Law and Social Change in the Nineteenth Century," *Journal of Economic History*, XXXII (1972), 54–91; Florence Kelley, "An Effective Child-Labor Law," *Annals of the American Academy of Political and Social Science*, XXI (1903), 443; and Ella Arvilla Merritt, "What the Government Is Doing to Conserve Child Life," *Kindergarten and First Grade*, IV (1919), 174.

and, like other such institutions, their quality varied considerably. With the rapid growth of cities, however, and the development of vast urban neighborhoods marked by poverty and family disruption, day nurseries became increasingly necessary. Once again, it was the institutional churches and social settlements of the 1880's and 1890's that became newly aware of the widespread need for such institutions among the poor. When Jacob Riis published *The Children of the Poor* in 1892, he was able to list twenty-eight formally organized nurseries in New York City, most of them associated with churches or charitable organizations. They were attempting to serve a population of a million and a half, of whom an estimated two hundred thousand were under five years of age. As Riis eloquently described, all too many of the two hundred thousand were left day after day to the streets and alleys of the slum.

We have a fairly good picture of these early day nurseries, not only in New York but across the country. Most of them were run by groups of philanthropically minded middle-class women to serve the families of the poor. Generally lodged in converted houses or brownstones or in annexes to churches or social settlements, they were open six days a week for twelve hours a day. Their principal concern was the physical care of the infants and children entrusted to them—feeding and bathing them and keeping them off the streets; but they prided themselves on teaching good habits of cleanliness, obedience, and industry as well—Riis liked to talk about the "soap cure," which he saw serving the purposes of physical and moral training simultaneously. Many of the nurseries operated in tandem with kindergartens, which also tended to be run by groups of philanthropically minded middle-class women to serve the families of the poor, and stressed the principles of learning through systematic play that were central to the Froebelian philosophy. The age demarcations between the two were neither sharp nor stringently enforced. As Riis observed, "There are lots of children who are kept at home because someone has to mind the baby while father and mother earn the bread for the little mouths. The kindergarten steps in and releases these little prisoners. If the baby is old enough to hop around with the rest, the kindergarten takes it. If it can only crawl and coo, there is the nursery annex." Further, as Riis also observed, some of the nursery-kindergartens also operated in tandem with playgrounds, which were developed as yet another expression of progressive concern.[25]

25. Jacob A. Riis, *The Children of the Poor* (New York: Charles Scribner's Sons, 1892), pp. 182, 181.

However well-meaning the ideals that spawned them, the day nurseries were often crowded and therefore run according to rather rigid versions of the already strict regimens common for the time. As one of the women long active at the Brightside Nursery on New York's Lower East Side recalled about its early years, "Regimentation was the rule rather than the exception. At the most, the older preschool group had a few hours of kindergarten, and the younger children had no education at all. The toys, frequently the discards of more fortunate boys and girls, were in the cupboards as much as in the children's hands. On the whole, the personnel was untrained and some were mentally dull." For all its shortcomings, however, its overcrowding did testify to the perception on the part of clients as well as sponsors that it was far superior to the streets.[26]

Many of the day nurseries also concerned themselves with the mothers, organizing classes in sewing, cooking, English, and child care as well as clubs that combined socializing with lectures on child rearing. Some even went so far as to organize training programs, via the nursery kitchen and laundry, so that the mothers might prepare themselves for service as domestics, and then maintained placement lists to help them find employment. Such activities, and indeed their central programs, involved the nurseries in the characteristic progressive ambivalence with regard to familial education. On the one hand, the nurseries were criticized for removing the children from their homes—a criticism they tended to meet by claiming that they were at best temporary, makeshift institutions that would surely disappear as soon as reform had conquered poverty. On the other hand, their sponsors did not hesitate to argue that whatever care they provided was superior to that of most slum homes. As the secretary of the New York Day Nursery Association put it in an address to the 1892 Conference of Day Nurseries, "Mothers who love their children, but are ignorant of every law of health, and compelled to live under the conditions of tenement house life, cannot do better than to place their little ones in a well-regulated nursery."[27]

It was in an effort to bolster familial education by enabling mothers to remain at home with their very young children that the mothers' pension movement was launched during the first years of the twentieth century. Its effective beginning came at the 1909 Conference on

26. Ethel Beer, *Working Mothers and the Day Nursery* (New York: Whitesude, Inc., and William Morrow Company, 1957), pp. 43–44
27. *Addresses Delivered at the Conference of Day Nurseries Held December 29th and 30th, 1892 in the Hall of the Young Women's Christian Association, New York City* (New York: n.p., 1893), pp. 67–68.

the Care of Dependent Children, which opened with remarks by President Roosevelt on the plight of widows and the need to help widowed mothers remain at home with their children, and which closed with a resolution stating: "Home life is the highest and finest product of civilization. It is the great molding force of mind and of character. Children should not be deprived of it except for urgent and compelling reasons. Children of parents of worthy character, suffering from temporary misfortune, and children of reasonably efficient and deserving mothers who are without the support of the normal breadwinner, should as a rule be kept with their parents, such aid being given as may be necessary to maintain suitable homes for the rearing of the children." In 1911, Missouri and Illinois enacted legislation providing for mothers' pensions; and, over the next seven years, thirty-seven of the forty-eight states followed suit. As a rule, the mother who received such assistance had to be "a proper person, physically, mentally and morally fit to bring up her children"; she had to provide proof of poverty and her dependent children had to be under a certain age, usually fourteen or sixteen. As a rule, too, appropriations were far short of what would have been necessary to assist all eligible claimants, with the result that, first, many who might have qualified did not receive such pensions, and second, those who did receive pensions— the recipients were prohibited from working—received too little. Finally, a number of localities required mothers to attend parent education classes as a condition of receiving their allowances. By 1931, every state except Georgia and South Carolina had arranged for such pensions, and in 1935, the aid-to-dependent-children provisions of the Social Security Act provided federal assistance to the state agencies carrying on the program.[28]

The rapid spread of provision for mothers' pensions inevitably affected the use of day nurseries after 1918; for all the inadequacies of the amounts of money available, the pensions patently increased the number and proportion of mothers who remained at home and cared for their very young children there. The tendency of public school systems to assume responsibility for kindergartens also doubtless affected day nurseries by reducing the number that functioned essentially as annexes to kindergartens. And a third major influence on day nurseries during and after the 1920's was the nursery school movement. Originating in England in the work of Rachel and Margaret McMillan, who in 1911 established an open-air school for six

28. Bremner *et al.*, eds., *Children and Youth in America*, II, 365.

young children in Deptford, a London slum, the movement began in the United States with the establishment of a cooperative nursery school by faculty parents at the University of Chicago in 1916 and of a laboratory nursery school under the auspices of the Bureau of Educational Experiments in New York City in 1919. The movement was aided during the 1920's by the widespread interest in child study set in motion by the Laura Spelman Rockefeller Memorial; and it was given extensive publicity among educated women in 1924 by a particular program of the Memorial that enabled the American Association of University Women, under the leadership of its education secretary, Helen Thompson Woolley, to oversee a national study of the nursery school that was for all intents and purposes conducted by its local chapters. The number of institutions actually called nursery schools did not increase rapidly—there were approximately three hundred by the early 1930's—but the influence of the nursery school on day nurseries in general was significant insofar as it broadened their concern from what was essentially custodianship, with proper physical care and a minimum of moral training, to a much wider range of social, educational, and developmental objectives. In addition to housing, caring for, and feeding children, day nurseries began to assume greater responsibilities for health maintenance, mental hygiene, constructive play, socialization, and preparatory experiences with storytelling, the exploration of nature, and the arts. Further, the new concern for the nursery as a site for child study intensified the interest in parent education activities. From a custodial institution operating for the convenience of mothers, the day nursery thus became much more an educational institution operating for the benefit of children.

That tendency was greatly strengthened by the decision of Harry Hopkins and his associates in the Federal Emergency Relief Administration in October, 1933, to include assistance to nursery schools for "young children of pre-school age in the homes of needy and unemployed parents" among the FERA's authorized programs—the goal being to provide jobs for unemployed teachers. Guidelines were quickly prepared with respect to building arrangements and equipment, personnel and personnel training, and programs—the last explicitly recommended observation in the nursery school by the child's parents, participation by parents in the school's activities, and parent study groups that would discuss with staff members such topics as "Ways of Helping Children Form Desirable Eating Habits" and "Desirable Ways of Guiding Children." When the Works Progress Administration was formally established in 1935, a Division of Education Projects assumed responsibility for the nursery school program and a parent education program. By 1937, the WPA was conducting 1,472 nursery schools across the country with an enrollment of 39,873 children. Some of the schools were operated as part of local public school systems, some as observation and training centers in universities, colleges, and normal schools, some as high school laboratories in connection with courses on child care (part of the home economics curriculum), and some as projects of local community agencies. What was especially significant, however, is that all were operated with public funds. In addition, the WPA that year sponsored 3,270 parent education classes with an enrollment of 51,093.[29]

With the shift of New Deal concerns to preparedness in 1940 and to mobilization and war in 1941, the WPA programs were gradually phased out in favor of defense-related activities. In June, 1941, Congress passed the Lanham Community Facilities Act, which authorized federal expenditures for the construction, provision, and operation of local facilities and services needed to further the preparedness effort in communities that were being particularly affected by the population shifts associated with defense activities. In 1942, the act was interpreted as permitting appropriations for day care services for children of working mothers, and in October of that year the first grants were made to operate day care centers, many of which had come into being under the WPA program. When the WPA program was discontinued on March 1, 1943, most of the WPA nurseries had ended up qualifying for Lanham Act assistance. By the end of the war in 1945, $45.8 million had been spent on child care facilities, $3 million for construction and $42.8 million for operating expenses; some 2,800 child care centers were operating with federal assistance; and one estimate put the number of children served at 1.5 million. In the shift from the WPA program to the Lanham Act program, however, two significant changes had occurred: the purpose of the effort had changed from the employment of teachers to the facilitation of working women, and the nature of the effort had changed from nursery schooling to child care. While these changes in no way precluded mixtures and overlappings of purposes and policies—most of the WPA nurseries did, after all, qualify as Lanham Act facilities—they

29. Doak S. Campbell, Frederick H. Bair, and Oswald L. Harvey, *Educational Activities of the Works Progress Administration* (Washington, D.C.: Government Printing Office, 1939), pp. 6–8, 110, 117; and U.S., The National Advisory Committee on Emergency Nursery Schools, *Bulletin of Information for Emergency Nursery Schools* (n.p., n.d.), p. 32.

were nonetheless important. They represented a cycling back to the earlier purposes and policies of the pre–World War I day nurseries; and indeed, for all the mixtures and overlappings of purposes that had occurred, when the Lanham Act funds were withdrawn in February, 1946, most of the 2,800 day care centers closed. A few states and cities continued public support for a few of the centers, but most did not. The expectation was that women, who had entered the labor force in large numbers during the war, would return to their homes in its aftermath and take their children with them. The expectation would prove incorrect. Between April, 1948 and March, 1966, the percentage of married women with children under six and husbands living at home who participated in the labor force would increase from 10.8 percent to 24.2 percent. But day care would go forward overwhelmingly under private auspices.[30]

IV

Florence Kelley's 1903 aphorism to the effect that the best child labor law was a well-drawn and stringently enforced compulsory schooling law had its obverse that was equally true, namely, that the best compulsory schooling law was a well-drawn and stringently enforced child labor law. Yet, for all her belief in regulatory legislation, Kelley was also a realist, who recognized that in the end the effectiveness of any child labor law or compulsory schooling law would depend, not only upon the compliance of the children, the parents, the employers, and the officials charged with enforcing the law, but also upon "the conscience of the community as a whole." And she recognized too that unless the schools were modified and "adapted to the needs of the recent immigrants in the North and of the poor whites in the South," unless the courses they offered were revised so as to appear worthwhile to the parents and interesting and attractive to the children, no amount of enforcement would suffice. Her analysis was characteristically incisive as well as typically progressive.[31]

By 1903, some two-thirds of the states had enacted some sort of compulsory school attendance law and some two-thirds had enacted some sort of child labor law setting age limits below which children were not permitted to work (though the same states did not always enact both sorts of laws). But the legislation itself was full of unclari-

30. U.S. Bureau of the Census, *Historical Statistics of the United States: Colonial Times to 1970* (2 vols.; Washington, D.C.: Government Printing Office, 1975), I, 134.

31. Kelley, "An Effective Child-Labor Law," 440, 443.

ties and confusions; in state after state, the age limits for attendance at school did not conform to the age limits in the child labor law; there were loopholes in both kinds of laws that permitted large numbers of exceptions; and the laws in any case were indifferently enforced. By way of testimony, the Census of 1900 reported 1.75 million, or 18.2 percent of the nation's 9.6 million children between the ages of ten and fifteen in gainful employment, and that figure was almost certainly low, since the enumerators excluded all children who worked less than half time. In Kelley's words, "the conscience of the community" had not been awakened.[32]

As progressive child savers viewed the situation, they concluded that a radical change was required, one that, as Julia Lathrop phrased it in testimony before a House committee, would put "child training in the place of child labor." And the achievement of the goal would require, first, a transformation in the public's perception of the young teenage child, and second, a transformation in the education that would be offered that child. The young "lad" or "lass," who had hitherto been considered sufficiently independent to work for wages in a textile factory or a department store, would have to be reconceived as a dependent child in need of instruction, formation, and care; and the education provided for that child would have to be transformed to render it useful, appealing, and realistic. Once again, the school would be the centerpiece, but a complex of clubs, playgrounds, camps, and other supervised facilities would assist in the task of forming the young teenager into an intelligent and productive citizen.[33]

No work contributed more fundamentally to altering the public perception of the young teenage child than G. Stanley Hall's massive study of *Adolescence: Its Psychology and Its Relations to Physiology, Anthropology, Sociology, Sex, Crime, Religion and Education,* published in 1904. Ten years in the making and well over a thousand pages in length, *Adolescence* presented a fascinating admixture of scientific data from around the world, authoritative opinion since the time of the ancient Greeks, and the highly individual reminiscences and interpretations of the author. Hall referred to it as his "first book"; it was also destined to be his *magnum opus.* An intensely personal document, it brought together everything he knew and believed about human development

32. U.S., Bureau of the Census, Special Reports, *Occupations at the Twelfth Census* (Washington, D.C.: Government Printing Office, 1904), p. lxvi.

33. U.S., Congress, House of Representatives, 64th Congress, 1st sess., *House Reports,* I, No. 46, p. 20.

and its bearing on education. Drawing upon his earlier studies of the "juvenile" stage of development, the period from about eight to about twelve years of age, Hall contrasted it sharply with the adolescent stage of development, the period from about twelve or thirteen through the early twenties. The first age was one of slowed physical growth and relative stability (Freud later called it the period of "latency"). Perception was "very acute," but reason, morality, religion, sympathy, love, and aesthetic enjoyment were "but very slightly developed." Never again, Hall counseled, "will there be such susceptibility to drill and discipline, such plasticity to habituation, or such ready adjustment to new conditions." By contrast, Hall continued, adolescence was unstable and unpredictable. Development quickened; the rate of growth in height, weight, and strength often doubled; the range of individual differences increased. The "cohesions between the elements of personality" loosened; perversions multiplied; sex worked its havoc "in the form of secret vice, debauch, disease, and enfeebled heredity"; new "repulsions" were felt toward home and school; and interest in adult life and vocations emerged.[34]

It was at precisely the crucial point of adolescence that Hall found American education most severely wanting. The adolescent required "a longer tether," but the schools continued to drill. The adolescent craved "large living wholes," but the schools dissected wholes into their elements. The adolescent was subject to spontaneous variation, but the schools purveyed ever more standardized curricula. The adolescent responded to "mental awakening" through "zest-provoking" pedagogies, but the schools served up information through lectures conveying bits and pieces. "Everywhere," Hall lamented, "the mechanical and formal triumph over content and substance, the letter over the spirit, the intellect over morals, lesson setting and hearing over real teaching, the technical over the essential, information over education, marks over edification, and method over matter." The United States was leading the world in the application of science, the development of industry, and the achievement of a "magnificent material civilization." It had become a pace setter in manners, morals, and religion; but it had forgotten that "for the complete apprenticeship to life, youth needs repose, leisure, art, legends, romance, idealization, and in a word humanism, if it is to enter the kingdom of man well equipped for man's highest work in the world."[35]

34. G. Stanley Hall, *Adolescence: Its Psychology and Its Relations to Physiology, Anthropology, Sociology, Sex, Crime, Religion, and Education* (2 vols.; New York: D. Appleton and Company, 1904), I, xix, ix, xii.
35. *Ibid.*, II, 453, 496, 530; I, xvii.

Repose, leisure, art, legend, romance, idealization—Hall's senti-mental portrayal of adolescence made it one with childhood and a world apart from adulthood; and that, coupled with his insistence upon the plasticity of adolescence, the vulnerability to perversion, and therefore the necessity for careful moral and intellectual nurturance, created a firm "scientific" base for the progressive cause. To send an adolescent to exploitative labor in the mills was, from the perspective of the individual, crassly to rob the youngster of the chance to mature into a decent human being, and, from the perspective of the society, utterly to ignore, in the words of the report of the 1909 Conference on the Care of Dependent Children, "the conservation of the produc-tive capacity of the people and the preservation of high standards of citizenship." Hall had written a powerful brief for Julia Lathrop's concern to put "child training in place of child labor."[36]

In the domain of youth training, as with other stages of develop-ment, progressives remained deeply committed to familial education, yet profoundly ambivalent about it. In the wake of Hall's *Adolescence,* a new "scientific" literature was developed to advise parents on the rearing of adolescents, along with a new scientifically based literature addressed to the adolescents themselves. One of the leading entre-preneurs in the production of such material was Professor Michael V. O'Shea of the University of Wisconsin. He served as editor-in-chief of *The World Book Encyclopedia,* a reference work specifically addressed to adolescents, and of *Junior Home Magazine,* a periodical similarly addressed to adolescents. He was also general editor of *The Childhood and Youth Series,* published by the Bobbs-Merrill Company, which was intended to give parents, teachers, and social workers "the best mod-ern knowledge about children in a manner easily understood and thoroughly interesting." Irving King of the University of Iowa con-tributed a general volume called *The High-School Age* (1914), which presented the "teen age" as a critical period during which the child's future is largely determined and counseled parents and teachers on how to cope constructively with the problems that would inevitably appear. There were several volumes on such particular problems as the inculcation of honesty and the nurture of careful habits of saving and spending. And, probably most interesting of all, there was a volume by Dorothy Canfield Fisher entitled *Self Reliance: A Practical and Informal Discussion of Methods of Teaching Self-Reliance, Initiative and Re-sponsibility to Modern Children* (1916). Arguing, much in the fashion of John Dewey in *The School and Society* (1899), that children in an earlier

36. Bremner *et al.,* eds., *Children and Youth in America,* II, 365.

era had learned self-reliance by participating in the family and neigh-borhood economy but were increasingly denied that opportunity by the conditions of urban, industrial life, Fisher advised parents on ways of creating situations in the home that would encourage children to learn self-reliance, much as Dewey had counseled teachers on ways of creating comparable situations in the school.[37]

Interestingly, the Children's Bureau had tended not to publish parent education materials on the rearing of adolescents during its early years, doubtless in part to avoid appearing to compete with the Bureau of Education, which had initially resisted its creation. During the 1930's, however, it did issue a bulletin called *Guiding the Adolescent* (1933), which took the general approach of Irving King's 1914 vol-ume, assuming the adolescent would experience "problems" in com-ing of age on which parents would need practical information and advice. Be that as it may, in the absence of inexpensive advice from the Children's Bureau, parent education materials dealing with the rearing of adolescents were, even more so than those dealing with younger children, middle-class oriented for middle-class consumers. They were neither read nor purchased by the parents of youngsters who were early sent to labor in the mills and mines, and the same was probably true of those well-to-do parents who sent their adolescent children to elite boarding schools like St. Paul's and Groton or Miss Porter's and Dana Hall.

The progressive commitment to familial education also played a role in the development of the juvenile court and the system of proba-tion associated with it. Dissatisfaction with the care children were receiving in asylums and reformatories, already widespread by the turn of the century, continued to mount, reaching something of an apogee in the report of the 1909 Conference on the Care of Depen-dent Children, which recommended that children be left in their own homes wherever possible; that, when for sufficient reason they needed to be removed from their own homes, they should be placed in foster homes wherever possible; that they should be placed in institutions only as a last resort; and that child care institutions should be con-ducted on the cottage plan, so that they would resemble homes as much as possible. The juvenile court, as developed in Chicago and Denver in 1899, seemed to satisfy those requirements admirably.

37. The quotation is from an unpaginated publisher's addendum to Dorothy Canfield Fisher, *Self-Reliance: A Practical and Informal Discussion of Methods of Teaching Self-Reliance, Initiative and Responsibility to Modern Children* (Indianapolis: The Bobbs-Merrill Company, 1916).

Juvenile offenders were detained in special facilities pending their hearings and were dealt with in a special court marked by an informal atmosphere and presided over by a special judge. The judge of the special court was assisted by probation officers, who were charged with making such investigations of the child's situation as the court might require, with representing the interests of the child when the case was heard, with taking such charge of the child before and after the trial as the court might direct, and with representing the court in the oversight of the child in instances where the child was found guilty of delinquency and returned to his or her home "on probation." In effect, the probation officer became a collaborator in the familial education of a delinquent. Although chronic insufficiencies of funds and heavy case loads never permitted the probation system even to approach the hopes of its sponsors, it did incarnate the progressive belief that even the poorest home was a better place for the rearing of children than the best institution.

Once again, then, this time in the case of adolescents, the progressives asserted their commitment to familial education. But in this instance, too, they ended up investing their energies in a reformed schooling that would try to take account of the phenomena Hall had described in *Adolescence*. Were adolescents newly interested in vocation? High schools would offer industrial and agricultural education for young men and domestic science for young women. Were adolescents interested in "large living wholes"? High schools would offer comprehensive courses in social studies in place of the separate disciplines of history and political science. Were adolescents preoccupied with sex? High schools would offer courses in family living and sex education. Did the range of individual differences increase among adolescents? High schools would offer differentiated curricula and varying versions of particular courses. Was adolescence a time of ebullient energy, of excess, of idealization? High schools would develop programs of athletic competition and social service. Was adolescence a time of plasticity, of unclarity, of susceptibility to perversion? High schools would establish guidance centers to ensure that youngsters entered upon the right path. In myriad ways, the developments in the secondary school curriculum associated with the progressive school reform movement, developments confirmed by the 1918 report of the Commission on the Reorganization of Secondary Education entitled *Cardinal Principles of Secondary Education*, accorded with the portrait of adolescence presented by Hall.

Beyond the school as well as in association with it, the progressives established ancillary institutions intended to strengthen the school's effort to shape adolescents in desirable social directions. Clubs, for example, were universally seen as powerful educative instruments for channeling youthful energy and idealism into worthy causes. The evangelical movement had used them fruitfully during the nineteenth century, not only through such organizations as the YMCA, the YWCA, and Christian Endeavor, but also as offshoots of larger adult movements, such as the Cadets of Temperance and the American Humane Education Society. The first decades of the twentieth century saw the rapid development of the Boys' Clubs of America (1906), the Boy Scouts of America (1910), the Camp Fire Girls (1912), and the Girl Scouts (1912). In the tradition of their nineteenth-century predecessors, these organizations prepared handbooks for local adult leaders on how to conduct chapters and issued periodicals such as *Boys' Life* and *The American Girl* for the youngsters themselves. Playgrounds, first established as philanthropic projects in New York, Boston, and Chicago during the latter years of the nineteenth century, also came to be seen as institutions that would seize upon the "play instincts" of the young (and the "gang instincts" of adolescents) to shape them, through supervised recreational activities, into socially responsible adults. Under the aegis of the Playground Association of America, founded in 1906 by Joseph Henry Lee, Luther Halsey Gulick, and Henry S. Curtis, public playgrounds became a nationwide objective of progressive youth workers, and in due course, a nationwide phenomenon. And summer camps, also begun during the latter years of the nineteenth century as projects in urban philanthropy, became more common during the first decades of the twentieth, not only as devices for providing slum children with summer vacations in the country, but also, under private auspices, as institutions for immersing youngsters in a "total educational environment" for a limited period of time. These institutions differed among themselves: playgrounds were much more commonly maintained under public auspices than summer camps, and the largest of the clubs were essentially private (though they did not hesitate, as in the case of the Boy Scouts of America, to put themselves forward as quasi-public). In addition, their clienteles, intended and actual, varied considerably: scouting was a middle-class activity conducted by middle-class adults for middle-class children; playgrounds, particularly during the first years of the century, were sponsored and conducted by middle-class adults for lower-class children; and different camps were operated by middle-class adults for both middle- and lower-class children. Whatever their differences, however, all these institutions claimed by the 1920's to be serving the cause of good citizenship. Moreover, each in its own way claimed to be collaborating with homes and schools in the proper nurture of adolescent children.

By the end of World War I, as child labor and compulsory attendance laws were beginning to be enforced more effectively, the so-called holding power of the schools tended to increase rapidly—secondary school enrollments rose from 1,115,000 in 1910, to 2,500,000 in 1920, to 4,812,000 in 1930. Yet when the Depression struck during the 1930's and President Franklin D. Roosevelt and his associates put together the congeries of programs that came to be known as the New Deal, it was not primarily to the schools that they turned in developing educational programs. They saw the "youth problem" as one of the critical issues facing the nation, but they conceived of it in terms of youth unemployment; and, suspicious of the people they associated with the "educational establishment," they were inclined to bypass the formal apparatus of schooling. Thus, the program of the Civilian Conservation Corps, established by executive order on April 5, 1933, set young men between the ages of eighteen and twenty-five to work on conservation projects; while the program of the National Youth Administration, established by executive order on June 26, 1935, provided funds for the part-time employment of needy students between the ages of sixteen and twenty-four to help them remain in school, as well as funds for the part-time employment of needy young people out of school who wished to gain work experience on projects of benefit to the communities in which they lived.[38]

Of the two programs, the CCC proved the more innovative and influential. Roosevelt had referred in his acceptance speech at the Democratic convention in July, 1932, to the need for a definite land policy to fight soil erosion and timber famine, and had gone on to suggest that as many as a million men could be employed in such a public work that would in the end be self-sustaining. In mid-March, 1933, he began to develop a plan for such a project in a memorandum to the secretaries of agriculture, war, labor, and the interior asking them to constitute themselves an informal committee of the cabinet to co-ordinate plans for the proposed Civilian Conservation Corps. Congress passed legislation authorizing the creation of such a corps toward the end of the month and Roosevelt signed the measure on March 31; his executive order creating the CCC was issued within the

38. U.S., Department of Education, National Center for Education Statistics, *Digest of Education Statistics, 1983–84* (Washington, D.C.: Government Printing Office, 1984), p. 8.

week. Uniting the goals of employment and conservation, the corps would enroll single young men between the ages of eighteen and twenty-five, drawn primarily but not exclusively from families on public relief, at salaries of $30 per month (of which a substantial portion would be allotted to their families), for "emergency conservation work." The Department of Labor would select the men; the War Department would enroll them and feed, clothe, and transport them to their camps; the Department of Agriculture and the Department of the Interior would select and supervise the work to be done and administer the camps (very soon, the War Department's role was expanded to embrace overall control of the CCC project, under the general supervision of the director). Robert Fechner, the widely respected vice-president of the International Association of Machinists, who had strongly supported Roosevelt in the election, was chosen to head the program. Enrollment began on April 6; the first men were accepted on April 7; and the first camp was established on April 27. The initial size of the corps was set at 250,000; that figure was raised to 360,000 in 1934 and to 520,000 in 1935. Also, the upper age limit for enrollment was shifted from time to time, and quotas of "local experienced men" (woodsmen who would bring special skills to the enterprise), veterans, and American Indians were added. Initial enlistments were set at six months with a one-year limit on the total time of service.

In a very real sense, life in the CCC was itself a form of education. To put several hundred young men from a variety of localities to work in a self-sustaining community where they could learn about everything from planting trees to getting along together, from eating certain foods to maintaining certain common standards of hygiene, was profoundly educative for many of the men. Beyond that, they were employed; they were earning money for themselves and their families; and they were performing socially useful work—to the sons of families on the relief rolls in the midst of a depression, those facts made a deep imprint on character. But almost from the beginning, there were pressures on Roosevelt and Fechner to take advantage of the possibilities for formal instruction (there was resistance as well—Colonel Duncan Major, who represented the War Department in the early stages of the project, lamented in a communication to Roosevelt's adviser Louis Howe, "We are going to be hounded to death by all sorts of educators. Instead of teaching the boys how to do an honest day's work we are going to be forced to accede to the wishes of the long-haired men and short-haired women and spend most of the time on some kind of an educational course"). In May, 1933, authorization was given to establish libraries in the camps and to offer instruction in forestry (by members of the Forest Service) and in vocational fields (by members of the Army) for CCC enrollees who desired it. As interest developed, the education program was assigned to the Office of Education, which appointed Clarence S. Marsh, dean of the evening session at the University of Buffalo, as educational director of the corps. Under his leadership (and after 1937 under the leadership of Howard Oxley, a former educational adviser to the Liberian government), a substantial program was devised that established many of the principles of modern adult education on a trial-and-error basis. By June, 1937, some 35,000 illiterates had been taught to read and write, more than a thousand of the enrollees had gained high-school diplomas, and thirty-nine had received college degrees. In addition, thousands of men had studied everything from carpentry, woodworking, boilermaking, and metalwork, to philosophy, economics, and social problems. Participation remained voluntary until 1937; thereafter it became compulsory and with compulsion came a greater degree of formalism. Nevertheless, the late 1930's also saw the introduction of an extensive guidance program that sought to assist the men in working out their own personal and vocational life goals during the period of their enlistment.[39]

With the preparedness effort of 1940 and 1941 and the entry of the United States into World War II at the end of 1941, the CCC came under a cloud. It sought to turn its energies to the war effort, performing useful work on military reservations and protecting vital forest regions; but, given its origins as a relief agency during the depth of the Depression, it was increasingly seen as an anachronism. Roosevelt remained committed to it and continued to fight for it in Congress, but public opinion, which had been highly positive during the 1930's, turned negative during the 1940's. In June, 1942, Congress voted to terminate the enterprise. Over the nine years of its operation, the corps had enrolled some 2,500,000 men. They had contributed massively to the conservation of the nation's resources by planting and protecting billions of trees, by halting the further erosion of millions of acres of soil, and by creating hundreds of parks and recreation areas. And in the process, they had contributed significantly to their own education. The corps had had its failures, to be sure: it had excluded women; despite a nondiscrimination clause in its authoriz-

39. The Major quotation is given in John A. Salmond, *The Civilian Conservation Corps, 1933–1942: A New Deal Case Study* (Durham: Duke University Press, 1967), pp. 48–49.

ing legislation, it had set quotas for blacks and had systematically discriminated against them (some 200,000 of the 2,500,000 enrollees had been black, though the economic plight of blacks during the Depression would have warranted a greater number); and in the bureaucratic infighting of the later New Deal it had consistently suffered from a limited vision of its possibilities. Such shortcomings notwithstanding, there can be no denying that the CCC represented one of the largest and most interesting educational experiments in the nation's history. The memory of that program would persist, along with the trees, the parks, and the recreation areas, as one of the more imaginative and durable contributions of the New Deal.

V

In his State of the Union message to Congress on January 8, 1964, President Lyndon B. Johnson declared an "unconditional war on poverty." It was to be a war, "not only to relieve the symptoms of poverty, but to cure it and, above all, to prevent it." It was a war in which child saving would play a central role, since one of the aims was to break the cycle of poverty by providing new opportunities to the coming generation.

The war Johnson announced had been in the making for at least a year. Toward the end of 1962, President John F. Kennedy had indicated to Walter Heller, chairman of the Council of Economic Advisers, his wish to go beyond the legislative accomplishments of the first half of his administration. "Give me facts and figures on the things we still have to do," he said. "For example, what about the poverty problem in the United States?" The "poverty problem" had not been high on Kennedy's agenda, nor had it been high on the nation's; but it had been high on Walter Heller's. Heller had been impressed by Michael Harrington's 1962 book, *The Other America: Poverty in the United States,* which sharply contradicted the widely held assumption that the United States had become an "affluent society," claiming that somewhere between forty and fifty million Americans lived in poverty and concluding with an impassioned plea for a comprehensive program to attack the conditions that led to and perpetuated poverty. Heller had also been persuaded by a series of memoranda prepared for the Council of Economic Advisers by Robert Lampman (whose work Harrington had cited), to the effect that the proportion of American families living in poverty (families with a total annual income of less than $3,000) had declined by about one percent a year from 1947 to 1956, but that the decline in percentage had slowed measurably since 1956, and that the number of people living in poverty had been increasing. In the face of such evidence, Kennedy had gradually become aware of the problem; but, as a political realist, he had also been aware that there was precious little political capital in antipoverty efforts—the impoverished as a political constituency were at best a powerless and inarticulate minority. Yet the civil rights movement had begun to alter that fact, as Kennedy and the public had become aware that a disproportionate number of blacks were to be found among the poor. As Kennedy put it in a 1963 message to Congress arguing that equal employment opportunity needed to be included among the civil rights of blacks, "There is little value in a Negro's obtaining the right to be admitted to hotels and restaurants if he has no cash in his pocket and no job."[40]

Heller began to work systematically on Kennedy's request in the spring of 1963; and, as the civil rights movement gained momentum during that summer, Kennedy became increasingly persuaded that he wanted to include legislation for an antipoverty program in his 1964 proposals to Congress. In September, Heller was asked to preside over a joint Council of Economic Advisers–Bureau of the Budget committee to develop such legislation, with a Thanksgiving deadline for the effort. Then Kennedy was assassinated on November 22; and, following a meeting with Heller two days after being sworn into office, Johnson made the antipoverty initiative his own. "That's my kind of program," he told Heller. "It will help people. I want you to move full speed ahead on it." The planning accelerated to meet Johnson's mandate, but it quickly became enmeshed in interagency rivalry. There was general agreement among the planners, however, that for the initiative to work and not end up simply one more effort in which the well-to-do ministered to their less fortunate countrymen, there would have to be comprehensive planning at the local level with maximum feasible participation of those who would be involved in the programs—the concept came to be known as community action. The log jam was broken only when, on February 1, 1964, Johnson announced the appointment of R. Sargent Shriver, the late President Kennedy's brother-in-law who had effectively established the Peace Corps in

40. Lyndon B. Johnson, "Annual Message to the Congress on the State of the Union, January 8, 1964," in *Public Papers of the Presidents of the United States: Lyndon B. Johnson, 1963–1964*, Book I (Washington, D.C.: Government Printing Office, 1965), p. 114; and John F. Kennedy, "Special Message to the Congress on Civil Rights and Job Opportunities, June 19, 1963," in *Public Papers of the Presidents of the United States: John F. Kennedy, January 1 to November 22, 1963* (Washington, D.C.: Government Printing Office, 1964), p. 488.

1961, as administrator of the war on poverty. In a frenetic few weeks of review and replanning, Shriver and his associates drafted the legislation that became the Economic Opportunity Act of 1964. Johnson sent the measure to Congress on March 16; the Senate passed the law on July 23 and the House, on August 8; and Johnson signed it on August 20.[41]

What were the Johnson administration's weapons in the war against poverty? To a remarkable degree, they were a congeries of progressive education programs that had been developing since the early years of the century. In effect, by the 1960's education had become the characteristic American mode of reform. This becomes even more apparent when it is recognized that the Elementary and Secondary Education Act and the Higher Education Act of 1965 were explicitly seen and presented as antipoverty measures that would complement the Economic Opportunity Act; indeed, it was doubtless the definition of the Elementary and Secondary Education Act as an antipoverty measure, with its all-important Title I authorizing what were by far the largest expenditures on behalf of disadvantaged children, that enabled the measure to overcome the historic resistance in Congress to general federal aid for the schools.

The Economic Opportunity Act itself provided for a wide range of programs for the poor, from legal assistance to health care to loans to needy farmers. Its centerpiece was the strategy embodied in the community action program, which explicitly encouraged local communities, with appropriate representation of residents and the poor, to develop their own plans for the attack on poverty. That the single most popular creation of community action programs across the country was Head Start, a program for the preschool children of poor families, was therefore profoundly significant. In addition, the act specifically provided for job training under a Neighborhood Youth Corps and a Job Corps, an adult basic education program (essentially but not exclusively an attack on adult illiteracy), and an Upward Bound Program to help promising low-income high school students prepare for entry into higher education.

The first Head Start programs were introduced in the summer of 1965. Several elements had figured in their creation. First, a number of educational psychologists, led by Benjamin Bloom of the University of Chicago, had come to the conclusion that the first few years of life

---

41. The Johnson quotation is given in Sar A. Levitan, *The Great Society's Poor Law: A New Approach to Poverty* (Baltimore: Johns Hopkins Press, 1969), p. 18.

were the "critical period" in human development during which the best chance existed for intervention that would enhance intellectual development (one might note the contrast with Hall's 1904 conclusion that adolescence was the "critical period"). Second, a number of experiments in "early learning" conducted during the early 1960's by investigators like Susan Gray and Martin Deutsch had demonstrated the effectiveness of certain strategies and activities in "enriching" the intellectual potential of young children—strategies and activities that were undertaken as a matter of course in middle-class homes but that were frequently lacking in lower-class homes (reading to children, for example, or conversing with them, or playing games with them, or undertaking collaborative tasks with them). And third, Shriver was eager to begin the community action programs with an enterprise that would be beneficial to the poor and at the same time relatively unthreatening to local political authorities.[42]

Head Start succeeded beyond Shriver's fondest hopes. A comprehensive program of child development directed primarily to four- and five-year-olds from low-income homes—frequently single-parent households in which no father was present—Head Start concerned itself with mental and physical health, child welfare and recreation, and remedial services, as well as with intellectual development. Moreover, parents were involved from the beginning, occasionally as planners, more often as paraprofessionals and volunteers. The response was overwhelming. A half-million children were enrolled during the first summer of 1965, and thereafter between 200,000 and 300,000 were enrolled annually in full-year programs, with large numbers of additional children in summer programs between 1966 and 1970. The parents were pleased and so were the professionals and paraprofessionals (who were given assistance in pursuing higher education after 1969) and the local political authorities. And the youngsters clearly profited. For a time, a 1969 evaluation by the Westinghouse Corporation cast doubt upon the enterprise with findings that the benefits of Head Start were ephemeral as the children proceeded into the elementary grades. But later studies during the 1970's and 1980's, particularly those carried out by David P. Weikart of the High/Scope

42. Benjamin S. Bloom, *Stability and Change in Human Characteristics* (New York: John Wiley & Sons, 1964); Susan W. Gray and Rupert A. Klaus, "An Experimental Pre-school Program for Culturally Deprived Children," *Child Development*, XXXVI (1965), 887–898; and Martin Deutsch, Elizabeth Taleporos, and Jack Victor, "A Brief Synopsis of an Early Enrichment Program in Early Childhood," in Sally Ryan, ed., *A Report on Longitudinal Evaluations of Preschool Programs* (Washington, D.C.: Office of Child Development, 1972), pp. 49–60.

Educational Research Foundation in Ypsilanti, Michigan, found significant and durable results, not only with respect to success in later schooling but also with respect to the ability to obtain and hold employment.[43]

The rapid success of Head Start led to the early introduction of supplementary and related programs through the Office of Economic Opportunity. Project Follow Through was inaugurated in 1967, as a program to extend Head Start services to Head Start children when they entered kindergarten and the elementary school. And a series of Parent and Child Centers (later Parent and Child Development Centers) was launched in 1967 as a demonstration program for families with children up to the age of three under which comprehensive health, education, and welfare services would be offered to the entire family in the home (whereas the center-based Head Start program for the four- and five-year-olds was seen as remedial, the Parent and Child Center program was seen as preventive). Neither of the two programs ever reached large numbers of children, but the establishment of the Parent and Child Centers did testify to the persistence of the progressive ambivalence concerning where children were best reared.

The job training programs of the Economic Opportunity Act attempted to bring together two somewhat different approaches to the problem of continuing high rates of unemployment among adolescents, especially adolescents from low-income families. In one view, the employment problems of adolescents were a consequence of their "inherent unemployability," that is, their inability to take and carry out the orders of supervisors, their inability to get along with other workers, their poor attendance and lack of punctuality, and in general their lack of motivation or sheer apathy. This "inherent unemployability" was assumed to stem from their lack of exposure to the world of work. The remedy, therefore, was a work experience program with a minimum training component. In the other view, the employment problems of adolescents were a consequence of a lack of "salable skills." In an increasingly technical and automated economy, the number of unskilled jobs was declining and would continue to do so; what

43. The statistics are given in Julius B. Richmond, Deborah J. Stipek, and Edward Zigler, "A Decade of Head Start," in Edward Zigler and Jeanette Valentine, eds., *Project Head Start: A Legacy of the War on Poverty* (New York: The Free Press, 1979), p. 142; D. P. Weikart *et al.*, "Longitudinal Results of the Ypsilanti Perry Preschool Project," *Monographs of the High/Scope Educational Research Foundation,* 1970, No. 1; and L. J. Schweinhart and D. P. Weikart, "Young Children Grow Up: The Effects of the Perry Preschool Program on Youths Through Age 15," *ibid.,* 1980, No. 7.

was needed for entry into the job market was a skill required by employers. The remedy, therefore, was an occupational training program.[44]

The National Youth Corps provided assistance for part-time work experience for low-income adolescents in the ninth to the twelfth grades of school so that they could finish their schooling, and work and training experience for unemployed and disadvantaged out-of-school adolescents between the ages of sixteen and nineteen, with employers in nonprofit institutions or public agencies (almost 50 percent of the young people ended up working in park maintenance or assisting in recreation and welfare activities—including Head Start programs). Between 1967 and 1972, almost a million young men and women were enrolled in the in-school NYC program, and almost a half-million in the out-of-school NYC program. The similarities to the National Youth Administration programs of the New Deal were patent.[45]

The Job Corps was designed for low-income adolescents between the ages of sixteen and twenty-one, but it differed from the National Youth Corps in that it removed enrollees from their homes to residential settings where they received lodging, clothing, meals, and health care, along with training in basic education and vocational skills. Some of the centers were located in rural areas and engaged in conservation work under the aegis of the Department of Agriculture. Others were located in urban areas and were operated by firms like International Business Machines or the Westinghouse Corporation, or by universities or other nonprofit organizations. The program was expensive, owing to its residential character and to the requirement that enrollees come from environments characterized by cultural deprivation or disrupted home life. Between 1966 and 1972, some 400,-000 young men and women participated. Once again, the resemblance to the CCC program of the New Deal era was patent.[46]

The Upward Bound and adult basic education programs reached smaller numbers of adolescents and adults than did the other job training programs of the Office of Economic Opportunity. Yet again,

44. Joseph D. Mooney, "Teenage Labor Problems and the Neighborhood Youth Corps," in Frederick H. Harbison and Joseph D. Mooney, eds., *Critical Issues in Employment Policies* (Princeton, N.J.: Industrial Relations Section, Princeton University, 1966), pp. 103–104.

45. The statistics are given in U.S., Office of Economic Opportunity, Office of Planning, Research and Evaluation, "Federal Youth Programs: A Discussion Paper," December, 1972, pp. 43, 45.

46. *Ibid.*, p. 42.

the precedents in the educational programs of the CCC during the 1930's and early 1940's were striking. The programs were not residential, as the CCC had been, but many of the counseling and educational methods they employed had been born and tested in the CCC and had entered the curricula of schools of education as time-honored principles of counseling and adult pedagogy.

The programs developed under the Economic Opportunity Act of 1964 did not account for the entire war on poverty. As has already been noted, the two education acts of 1965 were defined in part as antipoverty measures. In addition, there was extensive provision for child care under the amended Social Security Act and extensive provision for job training under the Manpower Development and Training Act of 1962 and the Vocational Education Act of 1963. Even so, the funds allocated to the war on poverty represented only a portion of the total federal welfare budget—by the late 1960's certainly under a third and probably more like a fourth. Whether the war would have been more successful with larger appropriations—and one must bear in mind that the war on poverty was surely lost as the war in Southeast Asia commanded increasing portions of the nation's resources—the education programs did seem to have made differences in the lives of their participants. There were exceptions, notably job training programs that prepared men and women for jobs that did not exist or went out of existence, owing to economic downturns or technological changes; but, at least for a time, the education programs embodied a national commitment to equity that clearly advanced the futures of many of the individuals involved.[47]

Beyond that, consensus had developed by the end of the 1970's about the value of a multifaceted federal education program that endured through the administrations of Presidents Richard M. Nixon, Gerald R. Ford, and Jimmy Carter. To be sure, the Office of Economic Opportunity was dismantled and its programs transferred to the departments of Labor and of Health, Education, and Welfare (later, the departments of Labor, of Education, and of Health and Human Services). And appropriations for many of the programs were severely curtailed and the relations between federal, state, and local authorities in the conduct and supervision of such programs drastically altered—that was surely the case when many of the job training programs were revised and regrouped under the provisions of the Comprehensive Employment and Training Act of 1973. Those facts

47. Levitan, *Great Society's Poor Law,* p. 10, and *Programs in Aid of the Poor for the 1970's* (Baltimore: Johns Hopkins Press, 1969), p. 13.

notwithstanding, the consensus endured. It was tested in 1971, when Congress passed the Comprehensive Child Development Act authorizing federal assistance for health, education, and welfare services for all children whose parents desired them and Nixon vetoed the act, and it was tested again in 1981, when President Ronald Reagan appointed Terrel H. Bell secretary of the Department of Education with instructions to arrange for the abolition of the department and the drastic reduction of the federal presence in education (neither had been accomplished by the end of Reagan's first term, when Bell departed), and in 1984, when Congress passed the American Conservation Corps Act, creating a latter-day version of the Civilian Conservation Corps, and Reagan pocket-vetoed it. The consensus was tested, but it did not dissolve. The issue of how, how far, and how aggressively education would be used as an instrument of federal policy persisted; the question of whether it would be so used seemed to have been settled.

Chapter 7

MEDIA OF POPULAR COMMUNICATION

> As a result of radio broadcasting, there will probably develop
> during the twentieth century either chaos or a world-order of
> civilization. Whether it will be the one or the other will depend
> largely on whether broadcasting be used as a tool of education or
> as an instrument of selfish greed.
>
> JOY ELMER MORGAN

On November 8, 1876, in the wake of the disputed Hayes-Tilden
election, the New York *Sun* had a circulation of 220,000; it claimed
that such a single-day sale had never before been "equaled or approached" by an American newspaper. On November 5, 1896, in the
wake of the bitterly fought McKinley-Bryan election, both the New
York *Journal* and the New York *World* printed almost a million and a
half copies. The difference testifies to a revolution that had occurred
in the intervening decades in the technology and the conception of
the American newspaper. And that revolution, most clearly manifested in the large cities, had profoundly altered the education that
American newspapers proffered to the American public.[1]

On the technological side, the Hoe "lightning press" of 1847, a
rotary press that had been able to print 8,000 sheets an hour (and in
improved versions, 20,000 sheets an hour), gave way to the Hoe
"double-supplement perfecting press" of the 1880's, which was able
to print, cut, fold, and deliver 24,000 twelve-page papers an hour (and
in improved versions, 48,000 twelve-page papers). In addition, processes for the large-scale production of paper from wood pulp rather
than rags were developed and refined during the 1860's and 1870's,
and improvements were also made in the size and speed of the Four-

1. The circulation statistics are given in *Sun,* September 3, 1883, p. 1; *World,* November
5, 1896, p. 1; and *Journal,* November 5, 1896, p. 1.

drinier papermaking machines with which the paper was manufactured. Finally, the Linotype machine was developed and perfected during the 1880's and 1890's; and during the same period the halftone photoengraving process was rapidly adopted, enabling newspapers to undertake much more in the domain of illustration.

Technology made it possible to meet the growing demand for newspapers; but the demand itself resulted from the interaction of demography with a radical alteration in the conception of what a newspaper was and what it was supposed to do. The essential demographic fact, of course, was urbanization and the concentration of literate audiences it made possible. The literacy rate for the nation at large rose from 80 percent in 1870 to 89.7 percent in 1900; and, while illiteracy ran higher in the cities owing to the presence of large numbers of immigrants who were either literate in a language other than English or entirely illiterate, the numbers of literate men and women that urbanization brought within easy distribution range of newspaper publishers by means other than the mails rose steadily. It was in an effort to attract an ever increasing share of that potential readership that the new conception of what a newspaper might be and do—a conception widely referred to as the "new journalism"—emerged.[2]

Joseph Pulitzer and William Randolph Hearst were the two individuals most closely associated with the new journalism of the 1880's and 1890's. Of the two, Pulitzer was surely the more original. Born in Hungary in 1847, he had left his homeland in 1864 in search of a military career and had ended up in the United States as a cavalryman in the Union Army. Mustered out in 1865, he had made his way to St. Louis, where he had been in turn a reporter for the *Westliche Post,* a German-language daily, a member of the Missouri legislature, an attorney, and the owner of the St. Louis *Post-Dispatch.* It was in the last capacity that he had begun to experiment with the newspaper crusades against municipal corruption that were to be a staple of the new journalism. But it was when he came to New York in 1883 and purchased the New York *World* from Jay Gould that he brought the new journalism into full flower.

Essentially, the new journalism was an effort to build circulation by transforming the content and character of the paper—by broadening its appeal both to readers of other papers and to those who had not hitherto been readers of newspapers. The effort was compounded

2. The statistics on literacy are given in U.S., Bureau of the Census, *Historical Statistics of the United States, Colonial Times to 1970* (2 vols.; Washington, D.C.: Government Printing Office, 1975), I, 382.

of six elements, some of which had been pioneered in one way or another by such early-nineteenth-century editors as James Gordon Bennett and Horace Greeley, but all of which, taken together, radically changed the nature of the news. First, Pulitzer sensationalized the content of the *World*, bringing to the forefront human interest material that ranged from lurid reports of crime and scandal to vivid accounts of the doings of the very rich. The stories were introduced by blaring two- and three-column headlines and written in a prose intended to shock and titillate. Second, Pulitzer greatly increased the paper's coverage of sports and recreation, dramatically reporting the great spectacles of the era, from boxing to baseball to bicycling, heightening reader interest with special attention to the leading rivalries among the contenders, the extraordinary compensation of the players, and the explosive hooliganism that occasionally broke out among the spectators. Third, Pulitzer complemented the news he reported with the news he created through stunts and crusades—news of reporter "Nellie Bly's" (Elizabeth Cochran's) impersonation of insanity in order to gain entry to the asylum on Blackwell's Island for an exposé of conditions there, or of the *World*'s campaign to raise funds for a pedestal for the Statue of Liberty. Fourth, Pulitzer enlivened the *World* with illustrations and cartoons—the drawings of Valerian Gribayédoff portraying famous personalities in the news, the diagrams of crime scenes with X marking the spot where the body was found, the political cartoons of Walt McDougall lambasting the candidates Pulitzer opposed, the comic strips of R. F. Outcault, introduced for children but read by adults as well. Fifth, Pulitzer specifically addressed parts of the paper to women and to young people as well as to men. The women's page included articles on the proper use of cosmetics, commentaries on the brewing of first-class coffee, hints on problems of interior decoration, and a regular column by "Edith" to her country cousin "Bessie" explaining the finer points of social etiquette in New York City, while a special section called "Youth's Department" carried puzzles, stories, and other juvenile reading matter. Finally, Pulitzer, like most of his contemporaries, printed all the advertising he could attract, but presented it in three- and four-column displays that, with the slogans, the drawings, and the other versions of human interest material, added to the vitality of the paper at the same time that it contributed to the exchequer.

Patently, the transformed *World* entertained as it informed; indeed, one way of describing the new journalism is to indicate that it shifted the traditional balance between information and entertainment in newspaper content decidedly toward entertainment. In one sense, the *World* fashioned the everyday life of the city into a continuing drama, a serial dime novel, a running vaudeville show, and an engrossing bazaar. For a couple of pennies a day, the reader had a bargain. But, beyond the entertainment, there was still the information. Pulitzer wanted the *World* to be both schoolmaster and tribune to its readers, to instruct them and from time to time to champion them. And, granted the sensationalism, the manufactured news, and the opinion that frequently masqueraded as news, the *World* did indeed educate its readers and did frequently take up their cause. As with any form of education, the readers came to the paper with their own interests, their own concerns, and the context of their own experience. But the *World* did engage them and in so doing informed them about slices of life in the city, the nation, and the world—about products for sale in the department stores, about fashions in clothing, about municipal, state, and national politics, about life in Egypt, Turkey, China, and Africa, about the wonders of science, and about the delights of sport. Its headlines helped immigrants learn English; its stories for young people helped boys and girls learn to read; its advice to women helped them rear their children; its features helped voters understand the political issues that faced them; and its drawings helped citizens recognize their elected officials. And, for all the cynicism of its stunts and crusades, the *World* did campaign for the eight-hour day, for Saturday half-holidays, and for weekly pay checks, issues important to workingpeople in the last years of the nineteenth century. Most important, perhaps, the *World,* like the New York *Herald* and the New York *Tribune* before it, proposed an agenda to its readers that it urged them to think about in common; and, while many of the items on that agenda were trivial and a few specious, many were of genuine moment to the local and national community.

If Pulitzer was the imaginative innovator of the new journalism, Hearst was its most dazzling practitioner. Born in San Francisco in 1863 to a well-to-do family, he attended St. Paul's School and Harvard College, though he failed to graduate from either. But he did, while at Harvard, become business manager of the *Lampoon* and in the course of that experience began a serious study of the newspaper business, taking Pulitzer as his model. And, when he was expelled from Harvard in 1885, he served for a time as a reporter on the *World.* In 1887, he persuaded his father to let him have the San Francisco *Examiner,* which the elder Hearst had bought in 1880 as a political organ and which he had operated at a loss for seven years. Following

Pulitzer's example, the young publisher went after circulation by bringing crime, sex, and sports to the forefront, by crusading fiercely against the Southern Pacific Railroad, by creating the Little Jim Fund to support the baby of a prostitute born in the city prison hospital, and by advertising himself and his paper in banner headlines. The elder Hearst died in 1891, leaving a fortune of $7.5 million to his widow. When the younger Hearst decided to enter the New York market in 1895 by purchasing the ailing New York *Morning Journal* (he renamed it the New York *Journal*), his mother advanced him the necessary capital. Within weeks, Hearst was locked in competition with his former idol. He ruthlessly lured away Pulitzer's ablest staff members and shamelessly mimicked his most innovative techniques, instituting them on an unprecedented scale with an unprecedented bravado. He set his price at a penny and claimed he would give his readers twice as much as the *World* for half the cost. With access to his mother's fortune, he was able to absorb his losses while building his circulation.

The great climax of the Hearst-Pulitzer competition came, of course, in connection with the Spanish-American War. The story is well-known. There had been insurrectionary movements in Cuba at least since the 1860's and 1870's, with the goal of independence from Spain. In addition, the United States had become increasingly involved in the island's economy, partly through a flow of American capital into the Cuban sugar industry and partly through the inevitable impact of American tariff policy. A rise in the tariff on sugar in 1894 had set off a depression on the island, which in turn had fanned the fires of the independence movement; and, when a group of Cuban insurrectionists called the Junta established themselves in New York and began to outfit filibustering expeditions and the Spanish navy moved to interdict them, American interests were soon involved. Stories of Spanish "atrocities" in the effort to suppress the insurrectionaries began to emanate from Cuba, as well as stories of Spanish "insults" to American ships in the effort to counter the filibustering, and newspapers across the country carried them under blaring headlines.

It was into this situation that Hearst moved with characteristic verve. As the story is told, Hearst in December, 1896, purchased a yacht and commissioned the writer Richard Harding Davis and the artist Frederick Remington to go to Havana and cover the escalating conflict between the Spanish authorities and the Cuban rebels. The two men were routinely barred from the "war zone" by the Spanish military authorities, with the result that there was little to report.

Remington wired Hearst: EVERYTHING IS QUIET. THERE IS NO TROUBLE HERE. THERE WILL BE NO WAR. WISH TO RETURN. Hearst is supposed to have replied: PLEASE REMAIN. YOU FURNISH THE PICTURES AND I'LL FURNISH THE WAR. Remington soon returned, but Davis remained in Cuba and wired a story of Spanish police boarding an American ship bound for Florida and searching three Cuban women passengers, claiming they were carrying information to Cuban insurrectionaries in New York. Hearst carried the story on the first page of the *Journal*, under a banner head, and added a half-page drawing on a second page of the search as envisioned by Remington, with the three women naked surrounded by Spanish policemen searching their clothing. Pulitzer responded by interviewing the three women when they arrived in Florida, discovering that they had been searched by matrons, not policemen, and carrying that story on the first page of the *World*, also under a banner head. Davis protested to the *World* that his story had been accurate but that Remington's drawing had created the misapprehension, and Pulitzer featured that too. And meanwhile, the circulation of both papers mounted.[3]

The competition continued for months; and, when the U.S.S. *Maine*, which had been ordered to Havana to protect American life and property, blew up in Havana harbor on February 15, 1898, both the *Journal* and the *World* exploited the disaster to the fullest, the *World* launching its own special investigation and the *Journal* claiming to have found a suppressed cable from the captain of the *Maine* claiming that the vessel had not been blown up by accident. There were ever shriller calls for war to avenge the nation's honor; and in due course, on April 11, 1898, President William McKinley asked Congress for the authority forcibly to intervene. The circulations of the *Journal* and the *World*—and of the interventionist press generally—had been rising steadily, and, with the war as the ultimate sensational story, circulation soared. Pulitzer stayed with the competition until the fighting ended and then withdrew, contending that the excesses to which the *World* had been driven by the *Journal* had subverted its quality.

The influence of the new journalism was widely felt, not only by newspapers like the Chicago *Daily Tribune* and the Boston *Herald*, which echoed Hearst's and Pulitzer's jingoism and mimicked their techniques, but also by newspapers like Adolph Ochs's *New York Times* and Whitelaw Reid's New York *Tribune*. But it was felt with a differ-

3. James Creelman, *On the Great Highway: The Wanderings and Adventures of a Special Correspondent* (Boston: Lothrop Publishing Company, 1901), pp. 177–178.

ence. Whereas the new journalism moved the balance of the news between information and entertainment decidedly in the direction of entertainment, its influence on papers like the *Times* and the *Tribune* was to brighten their format and enliven their substance at the same time that, in response to the sensationalism of Pulitzer and Hearst, they asserted the primacy of information, objectively presented and factually reported in a nonpartisan, almost clinical, fashion. To be sure, there were still judgments concerning what news was "fit to print," as Ochs's slogan for the *Times* put it, and the *Times* and the *Tribune,* content with smaller circulations, catered to a more select, more conservative, and better educated upper middle-class audience. They too educated, but with a different substance and a different pedagogy from those of the *World* and the *Journal,* thereby setting different agenda for different publics that brought different interests, concerns, and contexts to their encounter with the news.

The number of daily newspapers in the United States peaked around 1910, at some 2,600, of which the *World,* the *Journal,* the *Times,* and the *Tribune* were scarcely representative. Most of the dailies were small in size and circulation (the average circulation in 1910 was somewhat over 9,000 daily and somewhat over 25,000 Sundays), and catered to local audiences, reflecting the tastes of their editors, on the one side, and of their readers, on the other. Yet they were far from wholly local in character. For one thing, they came more or less under the influence of the new journalism, particularly as they sought commercial success through the increased advertising revenues that ordinarily flowed in the wake of increased circulation; for another, they felt the effects of new conventions of reporting the news, as journalism came to be seen as a profession to be practiced according to certain canons of quality. More important, perhaps, were three influences that made the education offered by the press increasingly cosmopolitan during the first years of the twentieth century.[4]

The first was advertising. The same urbanization that made possible the concentration of readership also transformed the market for consumer goods and for information about those goods. In contrast to their rural counterparts, people in cities increasingly ate commercially produced food, wore ready-made clothing, invested in household appliances as substitutes for household labor, and smoked cigarettes in place of smoking cigars or chewing tobacco, in deference to

4. *Historical Statistics of the United States,* II, 810.

the crowded conditions of urban life. As the size of potential markets expanded, manufacturers were able to distribute their products as well as information about them at declining unit costs. In the process, advertising grew exponentially, and the urban market gradually became national in character as well as increasingly metropolitan—that is, oriented to the tastes and styles of the larger cities, especially New York. The slogans and descriptions associated with Campbell's soups, Ivory soap, Kodak cameras, or Ingersoll watches could be used as effectively in Chicago as in San Francisco, or in a thousand smaller communities. The pioneer advertisers who wrote the descriptions and thought up the slogans even claimed that they were advancing the cause of education, by making their products known, and of democracy, by affording consumers a choice. However valid such boasts, what Daniel J. Boorstin has called consumption communities were among the first metropolitan communities of the modern era; and the press that served those communities gradually assumed a metropolitan character that did not long remain confined to the advertising columns.[5]

Second, the new journalism blunted the differences between newspapers and magazines. A paper like Hearst's Sunday *Journal* included as supplements the *American Women's Home Magazine,* the *American Magazine,* and the *American Humorist.* The first carried articles on fashion similar to those in the immensely popular *Delineator* and articles on child rearing similar to those in the best-selling *Ladies' Home Journal* (Kate Douglas Wiggin and Margaret Sangster wrote for both). The second carried the sort of miscellany one might find in *Collier's* or *The Saturday Evening Post.* And the third was the prototype of the modern comic book. Conversely, magazines like *Munsey's* or *McClure's* or *Cosmopolitan* (owned by Hearst after 1905), which boasted national circulations numbering in the hundreds of thousands, borrowed many of the techniques of the new journalism in both their fiction and their nonfiction. The magazines carried a huge volume of national advertising and joined with the newspapers in setting nationwide styles of journalism and hence a national agenda for public discussion. True, magazines tended to have a more socially restricted audience than newspapers like the *World* or the *Journal,* but they influenced those newspapers just as the papers influenced them. Beyond that, among the audiences they did serve, they created an interest in certain kinds

5. Daniel J. Boorstin, *The Americans: The Democratic Experience* (New York: Random House, 1973), pp. 137–148 and Part II.

of news that the newspapers found themselves providing when they boasted that they gave the public what it wanted. In effect, local audiences were not necessarily satisfied by local agenda.

Finally, in an age of organization, the press organized. The New York Associated Press, which had been formed in 1848, exploited the possibilities of the telegraph and the cable to the fullest. In addition, the United Press was organized in 1882, and quickly began to compete with the Associated Press. These two agencies, along with others like the Western Associated Press, furnished great quantities of news that local newspapers could never have afforded to gather on their own. Moreover, it was news that tended to be nonpartisan, at least in part because it was intended to be salable to papers of differing political persuasions; for the same reason, it tended to be cosmopolitan. Beyond the press associations, there were the newspaper chains, the most important of which were the Scripps chain, which began in 1878 when Edward W. Scripps purchased the Cleveland *Press* in association with his half-brothers and which numbered ten papers by 1910; the Hearst chain, which began with the San Francisco *Examiner* in 1887 and numbered six papers by 1910; and the Munsey chain, which began in 1901 when Frank Munsey purchased the Washington *Times* and the New York *Daily News* and which numbered five papers in 1910. The chains were developed differently and managed differently—Scripps tended to start new papers, while Hearst and Munsey tended to buy extant papers; but a combination of owner control and the demands of management efficiency inevitably made for certain common policies with respect to the style and content of the news.

Granted these influences countering localism, what in the end was the actual power of the press? Did an ever more national press at the turn of the century actually make for an increasingly national community? It probably helped, though the obverse is at least as true and in any case there is no way of knowing with certainty. Did the press in general and the *Journal* in particular bring on the Spanish-American War? It was often referred to by contemporaries as Hearst's war. The press surely helped, by exciting public opinion to the point where McKinley believed he needed to act. Again, there is no way of knowing with certainty. Did the press create the national market for cigarettes that developed with such extraordinary rapidity after 1890? It probably helped, though one ought not to deny the efficacy of a new mode of delivering the pleasures of nicotine. Chicago's leading advertising agency defined advertising in 1911 as "literature which compels action." Was it the cigarette advertising that compelled the action? Yet again, there is no way of knowing with certainty. The press surely educated in that it deliberately and systematically sought to transmit information, form attitudes, and shape behavior; but how much of a role it actually played in forming a national community or making a war or creating a taste must in the end remain moot.[6]

II

The year 1896, which witnessed new peaks in newspaper circulation deriving from the new journalism, also marked the beginning of the cinema revolution in the United States, as the nation's first projection of motion pictures on a screen before an audience that had paid to see them occurred in New York City. The *New York Times* took notice of the event on the day following the première, remarking the particular beauty of the umbrella dance done by "two precious blonde young persons of the variety stage," the extraordinary view of "angry surf breaking on a sandy beach near a stone pier," the excitement of a "burlesque boxing match between a tall, thin comedian and a short, fat one," and a "comic allegory called 'The Monroe Doctrine' "—all of it, according to the *Times* report, "wonderfully real and singularly exhilarating." The response to the innovation was electric, and it spread rapidly across the country. By 1910, hundreds of thousands of men, women, and children in cities of every size and kind were going regularly to storefront movie theaters as a favorite form of recreation and entertainment. A survey published that year in the *Review of Reviews* estimated that in New York alone there were approximately 450 such establishments with a seating capacity of 150,000 (the estimate was probably low). Chicago had 310, Philadelphia, 160, and St. Louis, 142, with a combined capacity of over 200,000. Many of the establishments were filled from morning through evening, with as many as a dozen seatings daily; and the audiences were as diverse as any to be found at the time, including women as well as men, young people as well as adults, the newly arrived as well as the native-born. Moreover, the enterprise was proving to be as profitable to its sponsors as it was entertaining to its clients. By 1913, a writer in the *American Magazine* was ready to call motion pictures the "new universal language," the great "art democratic." "For a mere nickel, the wasted man, whose life hitherto has been toil and sleep, is kindled with wonder; he sees alien people and begins to understand how like

6. *Altruism in Action—Concerning a Literature Which Compels Action* (Chicago: Lord & Thomas, 1911), p. 12.

they are to him; he sees courage and aspiration and agony and begins to understand himself. He begins to feel a brother in a race that is led by many dreams."[7]

As with newspapers, technology and urbanization combined to make possible the cinema revolution. The technology of the motion picture camera and projector had been slowly developed during the 1870's, 1880's, and 1890's, deriving from several sources in Europe and the United States. In England, the photographer Eadweard Muybridge, who had been working for some time on the problem of depicting accurately the movements of horses in motion, developed a battery of electrically operated cameras that would take photographs in rapid succession. In France, the scientist Étienne Jules Marey, who was working more generally on the problem of human and animal motion, developed a camera in the form of a rifle that was able to take a dozen photographs serially on a single plate of film in a second's time—a process that in subsequent models Marey transferred to a strip of film. In the United States, the inventor Thomas Alva Edison was seeking to develop a device that would combine with the phonograph to permit the portrayal of visual activity and audible speech in the presence of an audience. Edison met Muybridge in 1888 and Marey in 1889 and then set out, in collaboration with William K. L. Dickson, to develop a machine that would project the sort of strip Marey was using—actually, it was Edison who contributed the idea of perforating the strip so that it would move smoothly through the apparatus. In due course, Edison developed an apparatus called the Kinetoscope, which permitted viewers to watch an unenlarged 35-millimeter film strip pass behind a lens—the Kinetoscope was the basic machine in the so-called peep show films that were popular in city arcades between 1895 and 1905. Meanwhile, in 1895 and 1896, the brothers Louis and Auguste Lumière, working in France, Thomas Armat and C. Francis Jenkins, working in the United States, and Dickson, now working for a new American firm established in competition with Edison, came up individually with workable projection machines. Edison arranged to market the Armat-Jenkins machine under the name Vitascope, and indeed it was the Vitascope that projected the motion pictures shown in the New York première of 1896.

Urbanization, of course, contributed the same massive audience potential it did to the newspapers, but with two major differences.

First, literacy was not required to comprehend the new "art democratic"; hence, the potential audience was even larger. And second, it was an audience with increasing quantities of leisure time, as the workweek in commerce and industry gradually declined from fifty-five or sixty hours toward fifty, and hence increasingly in search of recreation. In response, recreational opportunities flourished, in forms ranging from saloons to burlesque theaters, from penny arcades to amusement parks. The storefront motion picture theaters reaped the harvest of that opportunity.

It was by no means foreordained that motion pictures would be used for popular entertainment. Muybridge and Marey, after all, were interested in studies of human and animal motion, while Edison was persuaded when he embarked upon his experiments that the phonograph and the motion picture projector would in the end be household playthings of the wealthy. Yet once the commercial possibilities of popular entertainment were recognized, a market rapidly developed, which groups in Europe and the United States organized to supply. Most of the early films ran for a minute or two and portrayed a single scene or incident—to recall the New York première, a dance, or a round of a comic prizefight, or a scene at a beach. The Lumière brothers, having perfected a relatively portable projector called the *cinématographe,* specialized in photographing actuality, beginning with slices of French life—foremen at work, children at a seaside, fishermen and their nets, a potato-sack race at a Lumière employees' picnic, and then, through a network of international agents, slices of life abroad—the arrival of the toreadors at a Spanish bullfight, the coronation of Nicholas II in Russia, the Melbourne races in Australia. By the end of 1897, the Lumière collection had grown to 750 films. Further, as the technology improved, the reels of film became larger, so that by the turn of the century a film could run as long as five to ten minutes. Proceeding somewhat differently, Edison constructed a substantial studio in connection with his laboratories at West Orange, New Jersey, and was therefore able to do much more with simulation. Among his early productions were *The Execution of Mary, Queen of Scots,* in which, at the crucial phase of the beheading, a dummy was substituted for the actress and the dummy was beheaded, and *Shooting Captive Insurgents, Spanish-American War,* in which the firing squad obviously shot blanks. The impact on audiences, however, was stunning. Once portable cameras became widely available, the only limits were set by the accessibility of the subject and the imagination of the photographer. Slices of everyday life continued to predominate; news items, both actual and simulated, grew in number; religious scenes made their entry (as early as 1897 a religious drama entitled *The Passion Play* was filmed at the unprecedented length of fifty-five minutes); and sex reared its head (in films like *The Typewriter,* which featured an employer kissing his secretary and being discovered by his wife, and *The Kiss,* which delivered precisely what its title promised and was considered sufficiently salacious to elicit demands for censorship).

The evolution of American films beyond these single-shot scenes was marked by the work of two central figures, Edwin S. Porter and David Wark Griffith. Porter joined the Edison company in 1896 as a mechanic and handy man but quickly moved to the making of the typical one-shot films of the turn of the century—*The Capture of the Biddle Brothers* was a two-minute shot of a simulated Western gun battle. He soon began to make films involving several shots in sequence—*New York City in a Blizzard* comprised four separate shots that shifted the camera and the scene—and in connection with that process he developed the idea, first, of using film to tell a story, and second, of drawing the substance of the story from the American popular idiom, for example, the activities of Western badmen. The result in 1903 was *The Great Train Robbery,* which combined twenty separate shots involving a variety of scenes and locations and which told a story of bandits taking possession of a train and robbing the passengers, of the recruitment of a posse, and of the killing of the bandits. The film was sensational, in much the same way that Pulitzer's and Hearst's human interest stories were sensational: it brought myth to life for audiences across the United States and in the process gave them a new way of encountering their history.

The Great Train Robbery was not the first of the narrative films, but it was the first classic of the genre. What David Wark Griffith did a dozen years later in *The Birth of a Nation* was to bring the techniques of the narrative film to a new level of artistry, while at the same time setting in motion a profound controversy over the film's particular interpretation of American history and its patent antiblack bias. Born in 1875 on what was left of a small plantation near Louisville, Kentucky, Griffith had grown up amid a combination of his mother's evangelical Methodism and his father's nostalgic reminiscences of service as a Confederate cavalry officer. The elder Griffith died when the boy was ten, leaving sufficiently large debts to force the family to give up the farm and move to Louisville, where Griffith worked, first, as a clerk and a factory laborer and, later, as an actor with a variety of theater companies. It was as an actor that he began his association with the motion picture industry—he played the lead role in *Rescued from the Eagle's Nest* early in 1908—and it was as an actor that he planned to continue; but in the informal arrangements of the industry in that era, he soon became involved in film making itself. Enjoying rapid success, he began to see in films a chance not only to make his mark commercially but also to reform the world—especially the sin-ridden urban world—and return it to the values he had learned from his parents. As one of the actresses who worked with him reminisced years later, "Griffith told us we were something new in the world, a great power that had been predicted in the Bible as the universal language. And it was going to end wars and bring about the millennium. Films were going to bring understanding among men—and bring peace to the world."[8]

The Birth of a Nation was born of that combination of entrepreneurial and evangelical zeal. Based on Thomas Dixon's novel *The Clansman* and supplemented by material from another Dixon book, *The Leopard's Spots,* and by Griffith's own reminiscences of his father's tales of the Civil War and Reconstruction, the film was divided into two parts. The first dealt with events leading up to the Civil War and with the war itself, including the surrender of Lee and the assassination of Lincoln. The second dealt with the exploitation of the newly emancipated Southern blacks by the carpetbaggers of the North and the scalawags of the South and featured the struggle of the Ku Klux Klan to liberate the South from the evils of northern domination and the folly of miscegenation. At the end of the second part, law and order were restored to the stricken land and Christ appeared to herald the beginning of the millennium in America. With a running time of three hours, the film was twice as long as the average contemporary feature; and, given the variety of substantive and filmic techniques Griffith introduced, audiences found it engrossing. The sentimentalism of the scenes of pre–Civil War plantation life, the grandeur of the monumental battle scenes, the viciousness attributed to the vengeful Northern victors, the terror of white women threatened with rape by blacks depicted as lecherous, the determination of the Klansmen as they rode to retrieve their way of life—all exerted awesome power over audiences who freely wept, shouted, and applauded as they viewed the film.

The film was extraordinary in other ways. Dixon, whose books

8. "Reel 1 Interviews . . . Lillian Gish," *Reel,* I (Winter, 1971), 11.

were blatantly ideological and whose goal in connection with *The Birth of a Nation* was nothing less than to convert the audiences that viewed it into thoroughgoing Democrats, wrote to President Woodrow Wilson, whom he had known at Johns Hopkins, and asked for an opportunity to show the film at the White House. Wilson acquiesced, and with members of his cabinet and staff actually viewed *The Birth of a Nation* on February 18, 1915. He is supposed to have said of the film, "It is like writing history with Lightning. And my only regret is that it is all so terribly true," though no written evidence of Wilson's endorsement has ever been found and he himself later disowned it. Other viewers, however, were outraged by the blatant historical and racial biases in the film. Jane Addams, Lillian Wald, and Jacob Schiff condemned the film outright, Addams calling it "a pernicious caricature of the Negro race." "You can use history to demonstrate anything when you take certain of its facts and emphasize them to the exclusion of the rest," she charged in an interview published in the New York *Post.* Oswald Garrison Villard, the editor of the *Post,* condemned it as "improper, immoral, and unjust" in its treatment of black American citizens. The NAACP fought the film in the courts, in the press, and before the National Board of Censorship, but was able to achieve at best only minor editorial changes. And, in the end, criticisms and protests were deluged by a flood of acclaim, best typified, perhaps, by a review in Hearst's *Journal* that declared: "Children must be sent to see this masterpiece. Any parent who neglects this advice is committing an educational offense. For no film has ever produced more educational points than Griffith's latest achievement."[9]

Obviously, the differences between Addams and Wilson, between the NAACP and the *Journal,* reflected different attitudes toward the problems of race; but they also revealed a profound ambivalence about the role of motion pictures in American life. Beyond the entertainment they provided, films patently educated. They conveyed information on current events, on matters of local and national interest, on the lives of world figures, and on the ways of foreign peoples. They revealed the activities, the styles, and the workings of the new metropolis to Americans across the country. And they provided new immigrants with a preliminary—if selective—view of American life and customs. A thoughtful commentator like Addams acknowledged this education; in fact, more than most of her contemporaries she recognized the potential power of films over the minds and hearts of metro-

9. New York *Evening Post,* March 13, 1915, p. 4; *New York Times,* March 31, 1915; New York *Evening Journal,* March 4, 1915, p. 15.

politan populations, especially the young. Yet she saw the evil too, and lamented the fact that immigrant parents exercised little control over the recreation their children indulged in, seeing the relentless pursuit of pleasure on the part of the young as the beginning of vice. Out of such ambivalence came demands, from progressives as well as conservatives, for didacticism in motion pictures, for tying them to the advancement of worthy values, and for regulation, ideally through self-censorship supported by the motion picture industry itself. The United States Supreme Court lent force to such demands when it ruled, in the case of *Mutual Film Corporation v. Industrial Commission of Ohio* (1915), that motion pictures were a business pure and simple and not organs of opinion protected by the free speech guarantees of the state and federal constitutions (that finding actually prevailed until 1952, when the Court held in the case of *Burstyn v. Wilson* that motion pictures were indeed a significant medium for the communication of ideas and hence subject to the protection of those free speech guarantees).

Motion pictures informed while they entertained; but they did more than inform. Like drama throughout history, they had immense power to affect the attitudes and beliefs of viewers, even—or especially—when they turned fact into fiction. And they accomplished this in part with a new grammar and rhetoric that Porter and Griffith had a prime role in developing—the grammar and rhetoric of montage, which related a story; of the flash back, which conveyed shifts in time; of the fade-in and fade-out, which conveyed shifts in place; of the close-up, which conveyed significance; and of lighting, which conveyed ambience and mood. In effect, whatever films taught by way of information and attitudes, they also taught a new language that viewers learned directly in the process of viewing. Whether or not it was a universal language, it quickly became a national language that in its very operation helped nurture a national community. It was the language through which Dixon hoped to make Democrats and with which Griffith hoped to Americanize the world.

III

World War I wrought profound changes in American education. As Wilson had moved, reluctantly, from a policy of neutrality to one favoring involvement on the side of the Allied Powers, he had been well aware that he presided over a deeply divided country. Business and labor had quarreled bitterly over wages, hours, and working conditions. Progressive reformers had fought vigorously to bring the enormous power of the trusts under some form of public regulation. Pacifist sentiment ran strong in many parts of the country; and millions of recent immigrants, including large numbers of first- and second-generation Americans of German, Austrian, and Hungarian descent, posed urgent problems of conflicting loyalty and commitment, which Wilson himself had repeatedly addressed during his first term in office. Moreover, Wilson had won his second term by the narrowest margin, after campaigning on the slogan "He kept us out of war," and after branding as disloyal opponents who charged him with pro-British sympathies. Then, within weeks after his election, he had gone before the Congress to ask for an increasingly stern series of measures that culminated on April 6, 1917, in a declaration of war, plunging the nation into a conflict unprecedented in its brutal tendency to engulf entire populations. As Wilson himself remarked, "It is not an army we must shape and train for war; it is a nation." In that task of training the nation Wilson enlisted the institutions of American education. And in the process of carrying out that task American education entered upon a new era.[10]

Wilson's instrument for training the nation for war was the Committee on Public Information. The idea for such a committee had been several months in the making. As early as February, 1917, as American involvement in the war had begun to seem likely, Walter Lippmann had written to Wilson from New York warning him of the difficulties that inevitably faced a democracy in attempting to recruit an army; and in subsequent letters and memoranda he raised the possibility of mobilizing public opinion around the idea of fighting a war to achieve a durable peace and recommended the establishment of a government clearinghouse that would provide a steady flow of information and at the same time counter rumors and lies. In March, a former student of Wilson's named David Lawrence, by then a reporter for the New York *Evening Post,* had also written the president, urging him to distinguish clearly in any declaration of war between the German government and the German people and to emphasize that the United States had no quarrel with the German people. In that same month, a journalist named Arthur Bullard had published a book entitled *Mobilising America* (1917), a copy of which had almost surely been read by Wilson's confidant Colonel Edward M. House, in which

10. United States Commission on Public Information, *National Service Handbook* (Red, White, and Blue Series, No. 2; Washington, D.C.: Government Printing Office, 1917), Title page.

Bullard pointed to the need for a spiritual mobilization of the entire people, using every organ of education and communication, if a modern war was to be fought and won. Also in March, members of Wilson's cabinet, especially Secretary of War Newton D. Baker and Secretary of the Navy Josephus Daniels, had met with representatives of the press to assure them that the administration had no intention of instituting the sort of rigorous censorship that several of the European countries had imposed but was interested rather in maximum publicity, subject only to the obvious limitations of secrecy concerning such matters as troop movements and battle plans.

As the censorship issue had begun to be discussed in the newspapers, a long-standing Wilson supporter named George Creel had written to his friend Daniels expressing interest in leading any censorship effort and urging that any such effort be based on publicity rather than suppression. Early in April, Creel had met with Daniels and Baker to develop plans for a department of information, while House had asked Lippmann to help formulate plans for a government "publicity bureau." Lippmann had responded with the outline of such a bureau on April 12; and, on that same day, Daniels and Baker, joined by Secretary of State Robert Lansing, had written Wilson recommending the creation of a Committee on Public Information that would combine the functions of censorship and publicity and "assure the publication of all the vital facts of national defense." America's great needs, the secretaries argued, were confidence, enthusiasm, and service, and those needs would not be fully met unless every citizen was "given the feeling of partnership that comes with full, frank statements concerning the conduct of the public business." The secretaries went on to urge that the chairman of the committee be a civilian, "preferably some writer of proved courage, ability, and vision, able to gain the understanding cooperation of the press and at the same time rally the authors of the country to a work of service," and that they themselves serve as the other members with the right to detail deputies to represent them. The following day Wilson created the Committee on Public Information by executive order, naming Creel as chairman and the three secretaries as the other members.[11]

The composition of the Committee was significant. Baker, a protégé of Tom Johnson, had been the progressive mayor of Cleveland when Wilson appointed him secretary of war—a seeming anomaly,

11. The letter from Lansing, Baker, and Daniels is given in full in James R. Mock and Cedric Larson, *Words That Won the War: The Story of the Committee on Public Information, 1917–1919* (Princeton: Princeton University Press, 1939), p. 50.

since he had been an avowed pacifist. Daniels had been the reformist editor of the Raleigh *News and Observer* and had overseen the Democratic publicity bureau in the campaign of 1912, when Wilson had appointed him secretary of the navy—another seeming anomaly, since he too had manifested clear pacifist propensities. Lansing was the conservative of the group, having practiced international law before Wilson appointed him to the State Department in 1914 and then to the secretaryship of state in 1915, after Bryan had resigned over Wilson's handling of the *Lusitania* affair—Daniels once said of him that in almost every policy "his mind ran along in harmony with that of J. Pierpont Morgan." But Lansing displayed little interest in the Committee, and Baker tended to defer to Daniels, which left Daniels and Creel in effective charge of the unit.[12]

Creel was the prototypical progressive. Born in 1876 in Lafayette County, Missouri, he had been educated in the Kansas City public schools, had worked for a time on the Kansas City *World* and the New York *Journal,* and had then returned to Kansas City to edit and publish a weekly called the *Independent,* which he had filled with reformist crusades against the local political machine. In 1909 he moved to Denver, where he wrote first for the Denver *Post* and then for the *Rocky Mountain News* and also developed a reputation as a free lance, preparing articles for *Everybody's, Pearson's,* and other magazines, coauthoring with Edwin Markham and Judge Ben Lindsey an attack on child labor entitled *Children in Bondage* (1914) and preparing *Wilson and the Issues* (1916) in connection with Wilson's campaign for re-election. And he espoused a wide range of progressive causes, from government regulation of utilities and transportation to universal military training, which he maintained would improve the quality of citizenship.

In addition to the lessons derived from this extended apprenticeship to progressive causes, Creel brought the zeal of a crusader to the CPI—Mark Sullivan once referred to him as the Billy Sunday of politics. Enlisting as associate chairmen Harvey O'Higgins, who had assisted Judge Ben Lindsey in the Denver Children's Court, Edgar Sisson, who had edited the reform-oriented *Cosmopolitan* magazine, and Carl Byoir, who had been circulation manager of *Cosmopolitan,* he set out energetically to vindicate his belief in expression rather than repression and in "the absolute justice of America's cause, the absolute selflessness of America's aims." He described his goal in the memoir he published in 1920:

12. Josephus Daniels, *The Wilson Era: Years of Peace—1910–1917* (Chapel Hill: University of North Carolina Press, 1944), p. 438.

While America's summons was answered without question by the citizenship as a whole, it is to be remembered that during the three and a half years of our neutrality the land had been torn by a thousand divisive prejudices, stunned by the voices of anger and confusion, and muddled by the pull and haul of opposed interests. These were conditions that could not be permitted to endure. What we had to have was no mere surface unity, but a passionate belief in the justice of America's cause that could weld the people of the United States into one white-hot mass instinct with fraternity, devotion, courage, and deathless determination.[13]

So far as Creel's belief in expression rather than repression was actually translated into policy, it was surely a carrot backed by a legal stick. Even before war was declared in April, Senator Lee S. Overman and Congressman Edwin Yates Webb, both Democrats from North Carolina, introduced a bill into Congress to define and punish espionage; but, while it passed in the Senate, it did not come to a vote in the House. Webb then reintroduced the bill on April 2, the day Wilson delivered his war message, and it was enacted in an amended version and signed by Wilson in June. While there was much self-congratulation by the press on the fact that an explicit censorship provision had been excised, the act did provide in Title I:

Whoever, when the United States is at war, shall willfully make or convey false reports or false statements with intent to interfere with the operation or success of the military or naval forces of the United States or to promote the success of its enemies and whoever, when the United States is at war, shall willfully cause or attempt to cause insubordination, disloyalty, mutiny, or refusal of duty, in the military or naval forces of the United States, or shall willfully obstruct the recruiting or enlistment service of the United States, to the injury of the service or of the United States, shall be punished by a fine of not more than $10,000 or imprisonment for not more than twenty years, or both.

In addition, Title XII made it illegal to send through the mails material that violated any provision of the act. Four months later, in October, Congress passed the Trading with the Enemy Act, which authorized the censorship of messages between the United States and foreign countries, which authorized the president to create a Censorship Board, and which banned from the mails any magazine or newspaper with a foreign-language article or editorial "respecting the government of the United States or of any nation engaged in the

13. Mark Sullivan, "Creel—Censor," *Collier's Weekly*, LX (November 10, 1917), p. 36; and George Creel, *How We Advertised America: The First Telling of the Amazing Story of the Committee on Public Information That Carried the Gospel of Americanism to Every Corner of the Globe* (New York: Harper & Brothers, 1920), p. 5.

present war" unless a sworn translation was filed with the postmaster, but authorizing the president to issue revocable permits excepting particular publications from the requirement so long as they carried no questionable material. And seven months after that, in May, 1918, Congress broadened the reach of the Espionage Act by making illegal any "disloyal, profane, scurrilous, or abusive language about the form of government of the United States, or the Constitution of the United States, or the military or naval forces of the United States, or the flag of the United States, or the uniform of the Army or Navy of the United States, or any language intended to bring the form of government of the United States, or the Constitution of the United States, or the military or naval forces of the United States, or the flag of the United States, or the uniform of the Army or Navy of the United States into contempt, scorn, contumely, or disrepute." Quite apart from the fact that Creel was appointed to the Censorship Board, he had behind his commitment to expression a continuing and severe threat of repression against those who refused to go along.[14]

Granted the legal stick behind his efforts, Creel zealously developed the media, the substance, and the forms of expression. He improvised organizations and units as he saw the need, and he recruited an extraordinary range of liberal, reform-minded journalists, intellectuals, artists, scholars, and men and women of affairs. In broad outline, the CPI included a Domestic Section, which began work immediately, and a Foreign Section, which swung into operation somewhat later, in October, 1917. The Domestic Section comprised at one time or another over a dozen divisions and bureaus. There was the all-important Division of News, which issued thousands of releases that appeared in some twenty thousand newspaper columns each week. There was the Division of Civil and Educational Cooperation which, under the leadership of the historian Guy Stanton Ford, produced over a hundred publications that sought to explain or justify American participation in the war, many of them written by scholars of the first rank. The division also issued a sixteen-page bulletin called the *National School Service,* which was distributed to schools across the country and which may have reached as many as twenty million homes. Ford actually conceived of the division as a new educational agency charged with instructing the public at large in the crucial issues facing the nation. There was a Division of Pictures and a Division of

14. Espionage Act of June 15, 1917, U.S., *Statutes at Large,* XL, Part I, 219; Trading with the Enemy Act of October 6, 1918, *ibid.,* 412; Amendment to the Espionage Act, May 16, 1918, *ibid.,* 553.

Films, responsible for obtaining pictorial material explaining and advancing the war effort—the film group arranged not only for the production of films like *Pershing's Crusaders* and *America's Answer* but also for the participation of stars like Mary Pickford and Douglas Fairbanks in the sale of Liberty Bonds. There was a Division of Four Minute Men, which sent some 75,000 speakers across the country into motion picture houses, concert halls, and other places of public congregation to deliver four-minute addresses on such topics as "The Danger to America," "Why We Are Fighting," and "What Our Enemy Really Is"—the speakers received the *Four Minute Men Bulletin* from Washington, setting forth the content of the various speeches, providing explanatory materials, and thereby ensuring that at any given time the talks being given would cover the same topics in essentially the same way. And there was a Speaking Division—occasionally referred to as the "Four Hour Men"—that, under the vigorous direction of Arthur E. Bestor, president of the Chautauqua Institution, enlisted the services of prominent individuals to lecture on topics as varied as the heroism of American soldiers and the need to conserve food (Bestor, incidentally, also had high hopes of converting Chautauqua into an instrument of patriotic propaganda).

There was a Division of Advertising, which arranged for millions of dollars' worth of donated advertising space for campaigns furthering the Red Cross, the YMCA and YWCA, draft registration, participation in Liberty Loans, the conservation of fuel, the extermination of rats, and the planting of war gardens; and there was an associated Division of Pictorial Publicity, which arranged for the memorable posters of Charles Dana Gibson, James Montgomery Flagg, Walter Whitehead, and Adolph Treidler—the depiction of women in the division's posters was especially interesting insofar as they were typecast, first, as the wives and mothers who stood behind their men in the American Expeditionary Force, second, as the victims of German brutality, and, third, as the symbols of American liberty and democracy. And there were bureaus of War Expositions, of State Fair Exhibits, and of Work with the Foreign Born, and a Division of Women's War Work—the last sent some fifty thousand letters of response to women across the country who had written to the government expressing concerns about conscription or some other aspect of war policy. In effect, Creel and his associates brought every available institution of education into organized support of the war, and used every major technique developed by the new journalism, the new advertising, and the new cinema.

The Foreign Section was less ambitious and less comprehensive. Creel himself initially led its work, conceiving its goal to be threefold; namely, to strengthen the people of the Allied Powers with "a message of encouragement," to preserve the neutrality of the neutral nations, while informing them of America's war aims, and to reach "the deluded soldiers and civilians of the Central Powers with the truths of the war" and, not least, with the stubborn fact of America's invincibility. The section comprised a Wireless-Cable News Service, which, with the assistance of the Navy, transmitted a daily news dispatch to a series of distribution points in Europe, Asia, and Latin America; a Foreign Press Bureau, which prepared and sent through the mails articles on American life, culture, and customs; and a Foreign Film Division, which exported several thousand reels of propaganda films, along with the equipment to project them, to Europe, Asia, and Latin America. These arrangements presupposed a network of agents who would receive and distribute the material, and Creel was assiduous in establishing that network in a score of countries, enlisting the aid, not only of American State Department and military intelligence personnel (and occasionally their Allied counterparts), but also of American private citizens abroad.[15]

In the end, probably the greatest contribution of the Foreign Section was to publicize Wilson and his war aims in advance of his participation in the peace conference—his popularity was unprecedented when he went to Versailles. As for the Domestic Section, its contribution was more powerful, more problematical, and less certain. For one thing, the CPI was only one among many organizations that were systematically disseminating domestic propaganda during the war— the Red Cross, the YMCA, the National Security League, and the League to Enforce Peace, among others, all mounted major programs. For another, the CPI, however much Creel was committed to expression rather than repression, did engage in censorship. As early as May 28, 1918, the Committee issued a "Preliminary Statement to the Press of the United States" that divided news into three categories, dangerous, questionable, and routine, and then attempted to define the differences. Later, the Committee became directly involved in evaluating material and clearing it as "authorized" or "passed." Beyond that, Creel was an active member of the Censorship Board and regularly took part in assessing films and periodicals as fit or unfit

15. Creel, *How We Advertised America*, p. 237.

for circulation in the United States or export abroad. Furthermore, there can be no denying that almost 2,200 men and women were prosecuted under the Espionage and Sedition Acts and that over a thousand of them were convicted, which could only have sent a chill through the nation's agencies of education and communication. Ultimately, however, the Committee did indeed mobilize public opinion across the country in favor of the war and in so doing represented an unprecedented government-sponsored educational effort that taught national values to a nationwide community. Indeed, it taught so well the slogans of a war "that would end all wars" and "make the world safe for democracy" that it almost certainly contributed to the disillusionment that followed in the wake of the Treaty of Versailles. And it taught so well, too, that men such as Walter Lippmann and Edward Bernays, who had participated in the effort, found themselves never again able to believe in the idea of democracy as a form of government in which rational men and women made up their minds on the basis of facts. Having dabbled in propaganda at high levels of government, they lost their faith in education, instead of assuming that since they had learned the difference between the two the average citizen could also learn and therefore continue to participate intelligently in the conduct of public affairs.

IV

November 2, 1920, marked the culmination of a bitterly contested presidential campaign. The Democratic candidate, Governor James M. Cox of Ohio, had called for the completion of the Wilson program for American participation in the League of Nations and for a vigorous American role in the shaping of the postwar world. The Republican candidate, Senator Warren G. Harding of Ohio, had called for a return to "normalcy." As Americans eagerly awaited the outcome, two men stood poised to demonstrate the remarkable capabilities of wireless transmission by broadcasting the results as they became available. In Detroit, under the auspices of the Detroit *News*, Elton M. Plant ran back and forth between the editorial room, where the returns came in over the telegraph wire, and a nearby conference room, where he shouted the returns into the "radiophone" transmitter of station 8MK. In Pittsburgh, under the auspices of the Westinghouse Electric and Manufacturing Corporation, Leo H. Rosenberg sat in a shack on the roof of one of the buildings of the Westinghouse works, received via telephone the returns that came to the Pittsburgh *Post* over the telegraph wire, and repeated those returns into the transmitter of station KDKA. Between bulletins, Rosenberg played music into the transmitter on a hand-wound phonograph. In both instances, the broadcasts were probably heard by several thousand people at most. But there was a crucial difference between the two. In Detroit, the *News* ran the broadcast as a stunt, assuming that those who received Plant's bulletins were radio buffs who would enjoy the prospect of knowing the outcome of the election before the candidates themselves. In Pittsburgh, Westinghouse ran the broadcast as part of a plan to create a market for home receivers it hoped to manufacture as a way of putting plant facilities idle since the war to good use—the plan was to provide regular broadcasts, advertised in advance, as a continuing service to those who bought the receivers. The *News* reported its stunt on November 3, and that was the end of it. Westinghouse created a sensation and in the process launched modern commercial broadcasting.

As with cinema, radio began with a technological revolution, the outcomes of which were only dimly perceived by those who set it in motion. As with cinema, too, the technological revolution was international in character. It began with James Clerk Maxwell's discovery at King's College, London, of the phenomenon of electromagnetic waves during the 1870's and Heinrich Hertz's confirmation of Maxwell's theory at the University of Bonn in 1889. The revolution was carried forward by the Italian inventor Guglielmo Marconi, who developed an apparatus that would transmit Morse code signals over distances without the necessity of wires. Marconi found no interest in the apparatus in the Italian Ministry of Post and Telegraph, so he took his invention to England, where its usefulness for ship-to-shore and ship-to-ship communication was immediately recognized. He then promptly patented his apparatus and founded the Wireless Telegraph and Signal Company, later Marconi's Wireless Telegraph Company, to manufacture and market it. Meanwhile, in the United States, Reginald Aubrey Fessenden, a native of Canada working under the aegis of the General Electric Corporation, developed a process in 1906 whereby the sounds of the human voice and of music could be continuously transmitted. And, also in 1906, a Yale-trained scientist named Lee De Forest developed a vacuum tube, called the Audion, that greatly facilitated transmission and reception over long distances. The following year he organized the De Forest Telephone Company to exploit the possibilities of the invention.

Given the widespread popular interest in scientific and technological tinkering in the United States, and the fact that both the transmitters and the receivers could be built relatively cheaply with readily available materials, an amateur movement of radio experimenters quickly burgeoned across the nation. Radio enthusiasts talked with one another, played phonograph records, transmitted weather reports and local news, and generally reveled in the possibilities of wireless telegraphy and telephony. At the same time, the United States government, through the departments of the Navy, of Commerce and Labor, and of the Post Office, became interested, with the Navy particularly concerned with the opportunities for ship-to-shore and ship-to-ship communication. Inevitably, given the limited number of wave lengths physically available for transmission, the amateurs, the commercial companies, and the government departments came into conflict, as amateurs drowned out vital naval communications and as the Navy pre-empted privileged commercial communications. In 1912, Congress addressed the conflict by legislation making it illegal to operate a radio station (transmitter) without a license from the secretary of commerce and labor, and also assigning certain bands for government—mainly naval—use and authorizing the president to commandeer or close down radio facilities in the event of war or other national emergency.

World War I dramatically hastened the development of radio technology, as the military uses of the new medium were aggressively exploited. Radio became important in military and diplomatic communication, intelligence work, and the dissemination of propaganda. Huge orders for equipment were placed by the Navy and the Signal Corps, and the companies that had become involved in the development of radio—General Electric, Westinghouse, the American Telephone and Telegraph Company, and the Marconi Wireless Company of America—prospered. More important in the long run, the war also brought both a heightened sense of the possibilities of radio and a sharpened competition between government departments and industrial concerns for control over its future. In 1919, under the aggressive leadership of Owen D. Young, a GE official who envisioned a quasi-public American monopoly exercising American domination over world communication, the Radio Corporation of America was formed. With Wilson's blessing, RCA promptly took over the Marconi land stations and ship installations that the government had seized during the war; and it also quickly reached agreements with GE and AT&T concerning exchanges of patents and domains of control. With the success of KDKA, Westinghouse also joined the RCA combine, under agreements whereby GE and Westinghouse would manufacture receivers and parts, AT&T would make and market transmitters, and RCA would market the receivers under its trademark. By 1921, American business was ready for the radio enthusiasm that gripped the country in the wake of KDKA's election night sensation.

The establishment of stations and the sale of receiving sets were nothing short of phenomenal. In 1921, the Department of Commerce issued twenty-eight licenses for new stations; during the first six months of 1922, it issued 354 more. The applicants ranged from newspapers to department stores to churches to universities, and the rhetoric of their hopes and plans would have led one to think that radio was the great panacea that democracy had been awaiting since its inception. The churches saw the word being proclaimed upon the housetops; the colleges saw a bonanza in home study; the newspapers saw new opportunities to convey information and in the process to build circulation; and purveyors of culture saw unprecedented opportunities to broaden their audiences. Obversely, the pressure for receivers was extraordinary. With several persons demanding every set available, 100,000 sets were produced in 1922, 500,000 in 1923, and 1,500,000 in 1924. By that year, 530 standard broadcast stations were regularly beaming programs to over a million homes, while thousands of radio buffs were intermittently beaming messages to one another. The interest of the public was unquenchable, but the cacophony that resulted from scores of transmitters of varying wattage, all transmitting at around 360 meters, was insufferable. In the absence of any regulatory body to bring order to the chaos, Herbert Hoover, whom Harding had appointed as secretary of commerce in 1921, moved into the vacuum.[16]

A Stanford-trained engineer who had won an international reputation as the "great humanitarian" through his efficient and effective operation of American relief efforts after the war, Hoover had accepted Harding's invitation to head the Department of Commerce only after Harding had promised him a more general voice in the economic policies of the administration. He had then set out to make the Department, which had traditionally lacked money, prestige, and influence, the source of a new progressivism that would flow, not from increasing government regulation, but rather from cooperative activities on the part of business stimulated and nurtured by an understand-

16. Hiram L. Jome, *Economics of the Radio Industry* (Chicago: A. W. Shaw Company, 1925), p. 70; and *Historical Statistics of the United States*, II, 796.

ing and sympathetic government. Hoover's preference for cooperation in lieu of regulation was not dissimilar, of course, from George Creel's preference for propaganda in lieu of censorship. Voluntarism was essential to both. Hoover's strategy for advancing cooperative activity was to organize promotional conferences that would bring the relevant groups together to undertake the necessary planning for cooperation and then arrange extensive publicity through the news media for the plans that emerged. His actions in connection with the radio enthusiasm of the early 1920's were exemplary. Aware of the developing chaos that was attending the rapid expansion of the industry and no doubt aware too that he was exceeding his powers under the Radio Act of 1912, Hoover called a Washington Radio Conference for February 27, 1922. Its purposes were to inquire into the "critical situation" that had arisen "through the astonishing development of the wireless telephone," to advise the Department of Commerce as to "the application of its present powers of regulation," and to formulate recommendations to Congress concerning legislation that might be needed. The conference duly convened, with representatives of RCA, AT&T, GE, and Westinghouse, as well as representatives of the government and of the so-called amateurs, and a few inventors and engineers. The discussions ranged from the possible role of advertising on radio to the use of radio as a tool of public education, though the principal theme was the need to bring order to the "mess" that characterized the air waves. In the end, the conferees resolved that the secretary of commerce should be given the legal authority to exert effective regulatory control over the industry. In the end, too, the conferees concluded that there was little promise in advertising—Hoover himself probably represented the prevailing opinion when he uttered his oft-quoted comment, "It is inconceivable that we should allow so great a possibility for service to be drowned in advertising chatter." Shortly after, Congressman Wallace H. White, Jr., of Maine, who had attended the conference, introduced a bill that would have given much stronger licensing power to the secretary of commerce; but there were those in Congress who already feared the power that Hoover might exercise if he gained control of American radio, so the bill failed. The radio boom continued, however, and with it the chaos in the air waves. Hoover called a second Radio Conference in 1923, and this time the conferees resolved that the secretary of commerce already had the authority to "regulate the hours" of programming and the "wave lengths of operation of the stations when such action is necessary to prevent interference detrimental to the public good"; and Hoover, with the industry behind him, proceeded with a sweeping reallocation of wave lengths that cleared up much of the problem.[17]

Meanwhile, the question of advertising was proving more thorny; for, once the novelty of broadcasting had worn off, there remained the persistent question of how to support it. In 1921 and 1922, most of the early stations were one- or two-person operations, with a series of unpaid speakers and performers providing the programs. There were those who thought that in the end broadcasting would be supported by tax funds or endowments, much in the fashion of public or private universities. Others—David Sarnoff of RCA was chief among them—believed that the industry itself, through a cartel like RCA, should maintain the stations and provide broadcasting as a service to those who owned the sets. AT&T, however, had another approach. Its telephones were open to any user who paid an appropriate toll. Its radiotelephone transmitters would be operated in the same manner—companies would buy the air time and sponsor programs, discreetly indicating by such titles as the *Eveready Hour* that they were thereby serving the public. Using station WEAF in New York City as its model, the company quickly demonstrated that sponsors were available, and, with them, revenues. Hoover sidestepped the issue in the Radio Conference of 1924, remarking acrimoniously that "If a speech by the President is used as the meat in a sandwich of two patent medicine advertisements, there will be no radio left." The Radio Conference of 1925, however, after lamenting the use of broadcasting for direct sales efforts, adopted a resolution, on the advice of Hoover, that ultimately settled the matter: "The problems of radio publicity should be solved by the industry itself, and not by Government compulsion and legislation." Thus freed to go its own way, the industry quickly cemented its relationship with—and reliance upon—the advertisers. In 1926, the leading companies renegotiated their respective roles in broadcasting. RCA, GE, and Westinghouse established the National Broadcasting Company, which would devote itself wholly to broadcasting and the use of AT&T's lines in the enterprise (when Arthur Judson of the Judson Radio Program Corporation found himself frozen out of NBC, he established United Independent Broadcasters, which later became the Columbia Broadcasting System); AT&T, in turn, sold station WEAF to RCA and moved out of broadcasting (NBC

---

17. Herbert Hoover, *The Memoirs of Herbert Hoover: The Cabinet and the Presidency, 1920–1922* (New York: The Macmillan Company, 1952), p. 140; and *New York Times*, March 25, 1923, I (Part 2), p. 5.

developed its "Red" network around WEAF and its "Blue" network around WJZ; in 1943, NBC-Blue was sold by order of the FCC and became the basis for the American Broadcasting Company). GE and Westinghouse continued to manufacture radio equipment, which RCA continued to market at the same time that it operated a number of its own radio stations. In effect, the advertiser had become the client, and the listener merely a consumer.[18]

A year later, based on recommendations from the Radio Conference of 1925, Congress passed the Radio Act of 1927. The legislation incorporated four principles: first, that the United States controlled the channels and merely licensed the stations to use them; second, that the standard for licensing would be "public convenience, interest, or necessity" (a phrase borrowed from public utility legislation); third, that nothing in the act was to be construed as giving any licensing authority the power of censorship over radio communication; and fourth, that licenses were to be given for stipulated periods of time and that no license was to be given to any company judged by a federal court guilty of seeking to monopolize radio broadcasting. The act established a Federal Radio Commission, with the authority to license stations, assign channels, and regulate broadcasting, though it also provided that the Commission would go out of existence after a year and its authority pass over to the secretary of commerce. Subsequent legislation renewed the life of the Commission, however, so that the body continued until it was made permanent by the Communications Act of 1934.[19]

With a pattern of commercial financing well established, with sufficient government regulation to bring reasonable order to transmission, and with improvements in the design of sets so that they became sufficiently compact and attractive to move from the family attic to the family living room (radio broadcasting thereby became "family entertainment"), the stage was set for the rapid development of the characteristic forms of radio programming. The variety show became a staple, in forms borrowed from vaudeville—Eddie Cantor and Rudy Vallee, as masters of ceremonies, became household names. The "Amos 'n' Andy" show, created by Freeman Fisher Gosden (Amos) and Charles J. Correll (Andy), brought the minstrel tradition to the air waves and combined it with the notion of serialization. The day-

18. *Radio Broadcast,* VI (December, 1924), 248; and U.S., Congress, Senate, 69th Congress, 1st sess., Committee on Interstate Commerce, *Radio Control: Hearings before the Committee on Interstate Commerce, January 8 and 9, 1926,* p. 67.

19. An Act for the Regulation of Radio Communication, U.S., *Statutes at Large,* XLIV, Part II, 1166.

time serial or "soap opera," directed mainly to housewives, made its appearance—"Clara Lu and Em" and "Betty and Bob" were among the earliest, and 1932 saw the beginning of "One Man's Family," about the Barbours of San Francisco, which was destined to become the longest-running uninterrupted serial in the history of American radio. Music remained a basic element in programming, though the earlier tendency to feature the classics slowly gave way to the more popular renderings of Kate Smith and Bing Crosby. News programs made their way slowly, in part because, with advertisers as sponsors, the disturbing, the unorthodox, and the controversial had to be avoided, and in part because the broadcasters wished to avoid conflicts with government. One form of news that was always welcome, of course, was sportscasting, where radio had a decided advantage over newspapers. Beyond all this, to recall Hoover's idea of the "inconceivable" in 1922, there was the constant "chatter" of advertising. By 1931, 33.8 percent of the NBC schedule and 21.9 percent of the CBS schedule were sponsored, and the sponsors had begun to develop their own characteristic forms of advertising, including the dramatized commercial, in which women praised the mildness of Lucky Strike cigarettes, men praised the taste and aroma of Chase and Sanborn coffee, and singers crooned "Che-e-ew Chiclets, and/Chee-ee-eer up!"[20]

With the onset of the Depression, the forms of radio programming that had become typical over the previous decade came under sharp attack, particularly from educators, churchmen, and farm and labor leaders. There was articulate concern about the "pollution of the air" by the advertisers and about the roseate view of American life (not to mention the bias) presented by networks whose explicit policies forbade programs that might disturb or undermine public faith and confidence. As Joy Elmer Morgan of the National Education Association charged in 1931, "There has not been in the entire history of the United States an example of mismanagement and lack of vision so colossal and far-reaching in its consequences as our turning over the radio channels almost exclusively into commercial hands." The election of Franklin D. Roosevelt in 1932 brought insistent demands for reform, including calls to scrap the entire system and put in its place a new arrangement that would reserve, as one measure submitted to Congress provided, a quarter of the available channels for assignment to educational, religious, agricultural, labor, cooperative, and other

20. Erik Barnouw, *A History of Broadcasting in the United States* (3 vols.; New York: Oxford University Press, 1966–1970), I, 245, 276.

nonprofit organizations. But the Communications Act of 1934 provided for no significant change beyond the establishment of a Federal Communications Commission on a permanent basis and the placing of telephone communication under its jurisdiction—the latter, incidentally, being the sole reform that Roosevelt himself had sought through the legislation. In the wake of the debate over the legislation, the networks did increase their public interest broadcasting, but the system itself and the substance of programming remained essentially the same. By 1940 there were 847 standard broadcast stations transmitting programs to more than 28 million households with radio sets across the country. Four out of five American households were receiving broadcasts.[21]

The 1930's were the so-called golden age of American radio, marked by Roosevelt's "fireside chats," which reached a nationwide audience of millions and which brought hundreds of thousands of letters to the White House; the concerts of the New York Philharmonic, the NBC Symphony, and the Metropolitan Opera; the entertainment of Jack Benny, Fred Allen, and Bob Hope; the dramatic presentations of the "Mercury Theater on the Air," including Orson Welles's *The War of the Worlds,* which caused panic across the country; the discussions of Lyman Bryson's "Invitation to Learning," which brought the classics to a weekly audience of over a million; the war reporting of Eric Sevareid, William L. Shirer, and Edward R. Murrow; and the news analysis of H. V. Kaltenborn and Elmer Davis. The 1930's were also the years of "Road of Life," "Backstage Wife," "Life Can Be Beautiful," "Little Orphan Annie," "Dick Tracy," "The Lone Ranger," Joe Penner, Walter Winchell, Father Charles Coughlin, "Professor Quiz," and "Kay Kyser's College of Musical Knowledge." According to a 1945 survey by the National Opinion Research Center, Americans generally thought better of radio than they did of their churches and schools; they preferred programs with advertising to programs without—many argued that they derived useful information from advertising; and they believed that radio programs added significantly to their general knowledge, their practical information, and their cultural enjoyment. Whatever judgments one might render of the cultural and intellectual standards of radio programming, and however much the advertisers had become the clients and the listeners the consumers, the listeners themselves saw radio as an important

21. Joy Elmer Morgan, "Education's Rights on the Air," in Levering Tyson, ed., *Radio and Education: Proceedings of the First Assembly of the National Advisory Council on Radio in Education, 1931* (Chicago: University of Chicago Press, 1931), p. 121.

medium of education as well as entertainment. Moreover, that education, beyond general knowledge, practical information, and cultural enjoyment, also offered formulas for solving personal problems, via the soap operas; needs and wants for consumer products, via the commercials; and, as with newspapers, an agenda of matters worth thinking about—politics, sports, the top tunes on the "Hit Parade," and the respective merits of various brands of coffee.[22]

On the eve of America's entry into World War II, Americans were being educated and miseducated by three quite different media purveying three quite different kinds of curricula under three quite different relationships with government. Radio was surely the most constant and the most pervasive. Under the gentle regulation of the Federal Communications Commission, which only rarely exercised its authority not to renew licenses, radio programming daily reached the vast majority of Americans in their living rooms with a varied, if bland, fare that taught everything from the meaning of Plato's *Republic* to the beauty of Mozart's symphonies, from the delights of one man's family to the advantages of irium, an ingredient in Pepsodent toothpaste that, apart from its mild detergent effect, had no advantages whatsoever. Cinema, enhanced by sound beginning in 1927, reached an audience of more than 80 million weekly, with films made bland by the industry-supported censorship of the Hays Office but nevertheless as varied as the mordant social criticism of Charles Chaplin's *Modern Times* (1936) and John Ford's *The Grapes of Wrath* (1940), the documentary portrayals of Pare Lorentz's *The Plow That Broke the Plains* (1936) and *The River* (1937), the artistry of Walt Disney's *Snow White and the Seven Dwarfs* (1938) and Frank Capra's *You Can't Take It with You* (1938), and the pabulum of a thousand grade-B Westerns, gangster episodes, and Cinderella stories. And newspapers, while they had declined in number by 1940 to 1,878 dailies, achieved a circulation of 41 million that year, the highest ever. The Scripps-Howard chain numbered nineteen dailies, and was considered the strongest of the national combines. The Hearst chain numbered seventeen, while the Munsey chain had fragmented after Frank Munsey's death in 1925. But it was not the chains that gave a common cast to newspapers across the country, but rather the wire services, the growing number of syndicated columnists and comic strips, network news broadcasts, which editors heard along with everyone else, and national advertising. Even stubbornly independent small-town newspapers like Wil-

22. Harry Field and Paul F. Lazarsfeld, *The People Look at Radio* (Chapel Hill: University of North Carolina Press, 1946), p. 6.

liam Allen White's celebrated Emporia *Gazette* manifested the similarity. Supported by a mix of advertising revenues and income from circulation, with the proportion of the first constantly rising, newspapers were partly free and partly beholden. Protected by the traditional guarantees of freedom of the press written into the federal and state constitutions, they were free of government or industry-sponsored regulation to a degree not true of radio or cinema, but their fare was often shaped or limited by their advertisers and by their incessant drive for circulation. Much the same was true of the great weekly and monthly mass circulation magazines of the era, from the *Saturday Evening Post* and *Collier's* to *Life* and *Look,* and including *Time,* founded in 1923 by Briton Hadden and Henry R. Luce, and *Newsweek,* founded in 1933 by a former *Time* foreign news editor, T. J. C. Martyn, both of which, as ventures in interpretive journalism, undertook quite consciously to instruct their readers in the larger meaning of current events.

With the entry of the United States into World War II in 1941, the question of propaganda again came to the fore. Roosevelt created the Office of War Information by executive order on June 13, 1942, with the journalist Elmer Davis at its head and with such people as Archibald MacLeish, the author and poet who had served as an editor of *Fortune* magazine, Robert E. Sherwood, the playwright, and Gardner Cowles, Jr., the editor and publisher of *Look,* as Davis's principal associates. The program of the OWI between 1942 and 1945 differed profoundly from that of George Creel's Committee on Public Information. For one thing, Roosevelt was less prepared than Wilson to concentrate great power in a single agency or a single group of men— the OWI's Voice of America may have demonstrated the most effective use of radio for conveying information overseas, but it was Frank Capra's *Why We Fight* films made by the Army Signal Corps that demonstrated the most effective use of film for conveying information at home. For another, the American people were less divided in their loyalties and their support for the war effort than had been the case in 1917. And, for yet another, Davis and his associates had not only a mature publishing industry to deal with but also mature film and radio industries—the necessity for collaboration was even more urgent. In the end, the OWI, like the CPI before it, engaged all the media for educating the public in the service of its cause, but it did so with a less shrill single-mindedness than the CPI and with a more sophisticated readiness to use information to counter propaganda. And, when the agency found itself committed to purveying a slogan like "unconditional surrender," it underwent sharp internal conflict over whether the slogan would facilitate or delay the successful conclusion of the war. Mostly the OWI conveyed in a variety of forms information on American life and ways, downplaying problems like discrimination against minorities and emphasizing American hopefulness, strength, and optimism. As a result, it left no bitter aftertaste of disappointment during the late 1940's, nor any lingering sense that democratic government was impossible because people were so easily manipulated, though it may well have contributed to the unfortunate sense of superiority that marked American participation in the affairs of the postwar world.

V

If the interbellum period was the great age of radio, the post–World War II period was the great age of television. Regular television broadcasting began in the United States on April 10, 1939, in connection with the New York World's Fair. Franklin D. Roosevelt and David Sarnoff both took part in the debut program, announcing the beginning of a new era, and were seen and heard on RCA television sets at the RCA exhibit at the Fair. Subsequent programs, transmitted daily either from NBC's recently built television studios in Radio City or from a two-bus mobile unit that roamed the streets of New York, included films, plays, musical selections, vaudeville acts, Dodger baseball games from Ebbets Field and Columbia football games from Baker Field, fashion shows, interviews, and occasional kitchen demonstrations. Within months, CBS and Dumont were also telecasting from New York, and within a year twenty-three stations were telecasting throughout the United States (unlike AM radio signals, television signals rarely reached beyond a hundred miles of the transmitter and frequently only thirty or forty, depending on the height of the transmitter antenna, the power of the signal, and the terrain between the transmitter and the receiver). Viewers by the thousands flocked to the RCA exhibit at the Fair to watch in awe, as did a select home audience—the first sets were costly—across the country.

For Sarnoff, the inauguration of regular telecasting was a personal triumph. Television technology had become available during the 1920's, largely through the experiments of Ernst F. W. Alexanderson at GE, Vladimir Zworykin at Westinghouse, and Philo T. Farnsworth, a brilliant young independent who sold the patent for his "dissector tube" to RCA; and Sarnoff had been among the earliest to recognize its potential. The onset of the Depression and the political battles surrounding the development of the FCC had delayed his plans, but by the mid-1930's he had committed large sums of RCA and NBC capital to the development of the new medium and its establishment on a firm commercial basis. The demonstration at the World's Fair launched his enterprise with impressive success, despite the fact that the FCC, which had jurisdiction over television broadcasting, had granted only limited licenses to the new stations (they could invite commercial sponsorship of experimental programs but they could not formally sell air time); and for a while it seemed as if the new industry might take off in a burst of television fever not unlike the radio mania of the 1920's. But it was not to be. The war intervened; the same assembly lines that had been set up to produce electronic equipment for television apparatus were capable of producing radar equipment for military apparatus, and for all intents and purposes television was put into mothballs.

With the conclusion of the war in 1945, Sarnoff's plans were finally realized. The FCC moved promptly to license television stations. The manufacturers of radar equipment quickly converted back to television sets, and the manufacturers of everything else seemed ready to advertise their wares. What is more, men and women who had lived for four years with restrictions, shortages, and sacrifices for high moral purpose lined up to buy television receivers. The spread of the new medium was no less extraordinary than the spread of radio after 1920. There were 30 commercial stations by the end of 1946 and 104 by 1950; 8,000 households had sets in 1946 and 5,000,000 by 1950. Ten years after that, almost 600 commercial and noncommercial stations were broadcasting programs to 45,750,000 households, representing over 80 percent of the households in the United States.[23]

Television programming combined the structure and substance of radio broadcasting with the language and techniques of cinema. From the beginning, the television set was in the living room and television entertainment was seen as "family entertainment." From the beginning, too, television programming was bounded by structures of scheduling, audience availability, commercial sponsorship, and government regulation similar to those of radio. The quarter-hour, half-hour, and hour format of programs, with a percentage of the time set aside for commercials; the awareness of a preponderantly female and preschool audience during weekday mornings and afternoons, of

23. *Historical Statistics of the United States*, II, 796.

a children's audience during late afternoons and early evenings and on Saturday mornings, and of a family audience during evenings and on Sundays; the inescapable facts of commercials and the inevitable relationships between audience size and advertising rates; and the basic requirements of "public interest, convenience, or necessity" as defined by the FCC at any given time—all were taken over from radio. And the very nature of television in uniting visual and auditory communications made it receptive, not only to the broadcasting of films initially made for exhibit in theaters, but also to the use of filmic techniques and filmic language in television productions. Granted this borrowing of structures, substance, and technique, the synthesis that resulted had characteristics unique to the medium—its immediacy, the sense it conveyed that the viewer was present at historic occasions and familiar with historic figures, its intensity, the result of the focus and caricature both necessitated and made possible by the small screen, and its compelling character, given the "realism" of its presentations and the fact that most of them were received in the home. In due course, the immediacy, the intensity, and the compelling character would combine to create audiences of a size unprecedented in history—the 65 million Americans who watched Mary Martin perform *Peter Pan* on television in 1955 or the 600 million individuals around the world who watched Neil A. Armstrong and Edwin Aldrin, Jr., step onto the surface of the moon in 1969—and those audiences would have undergone, at least in the objective sense, a common experience.[24]

Every genre of programming that had become familiar over radio early made its appearance on television; perhaps the most interesting difference lay in the fact that what proved to be durable staples on radio turned out to be far more ephemeral in the new medium. NBC early instituted the "Camel News Caravan," presided over by John Cameron Swayze, while CBS featured the Oldsmobile-sponsored "Television News with Douglas Edwards." Both were fifteen-minute programs that mixed films and commentary. Variety meant the "Texaco Star Theater," with Milton Berle, and the "Toast of the Town," with Ed Sullivan. Situation comedy meant "I Love Lucy," with Lucille Ball and Desi Arnaz. Drama meant the "Kraft Television Theater" and the "Goodyear Television Playhouse"—the latter presented

24. Erik Barnouw, *Tube of Plenty: The Evolution of American Television* (New York: Oxford University Press, 1975), p. 191; and Leo Bogart, *The Age of Television: A Study of Viewing Habits and the Impact of Television on American Life* (3d ed.; New York: Frederick Ungar Publishing Co., 1972), p. 355.

Paddy Chayefsky's *Marty*, one of the earliest archetypical television dramas, on May 24, 1953. Documentary meant "Victory at Sea," spliced together from World War II naval films. Children's programming meant Frances Horwich's "Ding Dong School." Comedy meant Jack Benny, who simply moved his entire troupe from radio to television. The same thing happened with popular music, as "Your Hit Parade" moved from radio to television. Classical music appeared in various forms, from the weekly broadcasts of the Chicago Symphony to "ABC's Concert," while the sorts of serious considerations of literature that had marked "Invitation to Learning" now appeared on "Now and Then," and, from time to time, on Alistair Cooke's "Omnibus." Daytime serials, starting slowly in the fifteen-minute format borrowed from radio, flourished in a thirty-minute format, and soon came to mean "Guiding Light," "Love of Life," and "Search for Tomorrow." And the commercials, among the most expensive elements in television programming, portrayed middle-class white Americans "moving up to Chrysler," "lighting up a Lucky," or quieting their nerves or their stomachs with Alka Seltzer. In every one of these domains, audience preferences seemed to shift rapidly and radically. The leading programs of the early 1950's were variety shows and drama anthologies; the leading programs of the later 1950's were quiz shows and Westerns; and the leading programs of the early 1960's were comedies. The principal durables of the era were "I Love Lucy" and "The Ed Sullivan Show." And, running underneath everything over the entire era, were such time-fillers as roller-skating derbies, wrestling matches, cartoons for children, and grade-B Hollywood movies on the so-called "Late Show."

However one might judge its overall quality—and Newton Minow when he was chairman of the FCC in 1961 watched television programming uninterruptedly for a time and pronounced it a "vast wasteland"—television proved capable of extraordinary feats in its coverage of the news, in its presentation of public affairs, and its capability of teaching while entertaining. One need only recall a few of the memorable programs of the 1950's and 1960's—the 1953 presentation by Edward R. Murrow and Fred W. Friendly of "The Case Against Milo Radulovich" on "See It Now" (Radulovich was an Air Force meteorologist who was asked to resign his commission as a lieutenant because of anonymous charges of radical inclinations against his father and his sister; he refused, was discharged, and was then reinstated after the program) and their 1954 report on Senator Joseph R. McCarthy; the 1954 coverage of the Army-McCarthy hearings; the so-called great debates of the Kennedy-Nixon presidential campaign of 1960; the live coverage of the civil rights movement during the early 1960's; the ABC documentary on Africa in 1967 and the CBS documentary entitled "Hunger in America" in 1968; the series of programs for preschool children genially presided over by Captain Kangaroo (Bob Keeshan). All of television programming educated (or miseducated): the news broadcasts conveyed information, the documentaries heightened awareness, the soaps conveyed formulas for resolving family conflicts, Captain Kangaroo taught about games and the world around us, and the commercials created wants and needs for consumer products—the pollster Louis Harris once went so far as to suggest that television commercials were among the many motivating forces of the civil rights movement, insofar as they showed poor black Americans an alluring view of how white Americans lived.[25]

Whatever the mix of the brilliant, the ordinary, and the worthless in the television programming of the 1950's and 1960's, there were the constant charges that, despite the requirements of the public interest, commercial broadcasting was failing to inform, educate, and entertain the public at the highest levels of quality and that, in fact, it was proffering an indefensible potpourri of violence, escapism, and pap that moved the young to aggressive behavior and their parents to intellectual and moral somnolence. Such charges, of course, had been heard since the commercialization of radio during the 1920's and had reached a peak during the early months of Franklin D. Roosevelt's first administration; but those who had leveled them had not achieved their goal of having a proportion of the available channels reserved for educational and noncommercial stations. That failure notwithstanding, a number of educational stations had come into being, mostly in association with the land grant universities of the Midwestern states; on the whole, however, the educational stations were poorly supported and limited in the scope and reach of their programming—a fact, incidentally, that made them ever vulnerable to criticism from commercial interests seeking to take over their licenses. When the FCC suspended television licensing for a time in 1948, claiming that the 108 stations already licensed were running into one another over the air waves, the issue rose again, but with a difference: this time the groups pressing for reserved channels had the assistance of the Ford Foundation's Fund for Adult Education and the ear of one

25. Newton D. Minow, *Equal Time: The Private Broadcaster and the Public Interest* (New York: Atheneum, 1964), pp. 48–64.

of the FCC commissioners, Frieda B. Hennock, a New York attorney whom President Harry S. Truman had recently appointed. After months of hearings, the FCC decided in 1952 to reserve 242 channels for noncommercial stations and the Fund for Adult Education made available matching grant funds to assist community organizations and educational institutions in activating such stations. The result was a rapid increase, first, in the number of such stations—from 10 in 1954 to 99 in 1964, and then, in the development of cooperative relationships among them; but they were not interconnected into a network and, despite the largesse of the Ford Foundation, they were relatively poorly financed, so that they continued to exercise local or regional rather than national influence. In response, a chorus of voices dismayed with the programming of commercial television and hopeful for a much greater contribution from noncommercial television—a chorus of voices backed by the Ford Foundation, the Carnegie Corporation of New York, and other philanthropic foundations—began during the 1960's to call for a substantial federal role in noncommercial television broadcasting. The television industry was vigorous in its resistance, claiming that it had faithfully served the public interest and convenience, that none of the alleged harmful consequences of the portrayal of violence had been proved, and that in effect the people were being given what they wanted—and at no cost.[26]

Within this context, the Carnegie Corporation of New York announced in November, 1965, the formation of the Carnegie Commission on Educational Television, with a grant of $500,000, to "conduct a broadly conceived study of noncommercial television" and to "recommend lines along which noncommercial television stations might most usefully develop during the years ahead." The announcement of the Commission followed a pattern of political activity that had become common by the 1960's. The National Association of Educational Broadcasters had resolved in 1964 to seek a presidential commission to study the financial needs of the educational television stations. The White House had responded with interest, but had suggested that the commission be privately established and financed. The Carnegie Corporation of New York, under the leadership of Alan Pifer, had been approached and had responded favorably. The membership of the Commission included, among others, James R. Killian, Jr., chairman of the Massachusetts Institute of Technology corporation, who had been President Dwight D. Eisenhower's science adviser,

26. Carnegie Commission on Educational Television, *Public Television: A Program for Action* (New York: Bantam Books, 1967), p. 20.

as chairman, James B. Conant, former president of Harvard, Lee A. DuBridge, president of the California Institute of Technology, Ralph Ellison, the writer, Oveta Culp Hobby, who had been President Eisenhower's secretary of HEW, Edwin H. Land, the president and chairman of Polaroid Corporation, Terry Sanford, the governor of North Carolina, Rudolf Serkin, the pianist, and Leonard Woodcock, vicepresident of the United Automobile Workers of America. Within the month, President Johnson wrote both Pifer and Killian, applauding the appointment of the Commission and expressing great interest in its recommendations. The Commission held hearings, visited ninetytwo educational television stations in thirty-five states (and several in foreign countries), and gathered data on historical, legal, and financial issues. The report was released in January, 1967, recommending that Congress establish a federally chartered, nonprofit, nongovernmental organization to be known as the Corporation for Public Television; that the Corporation be authorized to stimulate and support the production of television programs by public and private producers at the federal, state, and local levels, and to provide as quickly as possible for the interconnection of the nation's noncommercial television stations; and that Congress provide federal funds in support of the Corporation's activities to be raised through a manufacturer's excise tax on television sets.[27]

With the Commission's report in hand, Johnson in his education and health message to Congress on February 28, 1967, proposed the establishment of a Corporation for Public Broadcasting (representing the administration's intention to have educational radio as well as television within the purview of the Corporation), with financing at the level of $9 million for the initial year (the proposal for a tax on television sets was not incorporated). For all his rhetorical enthusiasm about the work of the Commission, Johnson himself did not assign a high priority to the measure—the Vietnam war was moving to the forefront of his concern. But the educational broadcasters marshaled impressive support for the measure; representatives of the FCC and the Department of Health, Education, and Welfare (the secretary of HEW was John Gardner, former president of the Carnegie Corporation) testified in favor of the bill; and representatives of the three networks not only did not oppose it but also gave it their assent— Frank Stanton went so far as to pledge that CBS would contribute $1 million to the work of the Corporation once it had been established.

27. *Ibid.*, p. vii.

Congress passed the bill and Johnson signed it on November 7, 1967, amid predictions that the Public Broadcasting Act of 1967 would prove as significant in the history of American education as the Morrill Act of 1862. The Corporation was duly established, with Frank Pace, former secretary of the army and former chief executive officer of General Dynamics Corporation, as chairman—it was an appointment that shocked the proponents of public television. The Corporation's appropriations rose steadily, from $5 million in 1969 to $152 million in 1980, but then declined for a time in the course of the budget reductions for domestic programs undertaken during the first Reagan administration.[28]

At its best, public television more than fulfilled the hopes of its proponents during the late 1960's and 1970's insofar as it offered a mix of public education and entertainment of generally higher quality than that of commercial television. The better continuing programs included the public affairs commentaries of the "MacNeil-Lehrer Report," "Bill Moyers' Journal," and "Black Perspectives on the News," the women's networking services of "Turnabout," the drama presentations of "NET Playhouse" and "Masterpiece Theater," the music, opera, and dance recitals of "Live from Lincoln Center," the science documentaries of "Nova," the children's activities of "Mr. Rogers' Neighborhood," and the culinary demonstrations of "The French Chef"; and there were such memorable specials as "An American Family" in 1973, "The Ascent of Man" in 1975, and "The Adams Chronicles" in 1976. It is likely that more people saw the 1977 broadcast of Mascagni's *Cavalleria Rusticana* than had seen the opera since its first performance, as was probably also the case with the 1979 broadcasts of Shakespeare's *Henry VIII* and *Romeo and Juliet.* And, in the domain of self-consciously didactic programs for children, probably the most extraordinary and influential programs of the era were the productions of the Children's Television Workshop. Conceived in 1968 by Joan Ganz Cooney, a public affairs broadcast journalist, and Lloyd N. Morrisett of the Carnegie Corporation of New York, the Workshop sought deliberately to marry the substance of the school curriculum to the techniques of television production. Financed initially by the Carnegie Corporation of New York, the Ford Foundation, and the federal government, "Sesame Street," first broadcast in 1969

28. Robert J. Blakely, *To Serve the Public Interest: Educational Broadcasting in the United States* (Syracuse: Syracuse University Press, 1979), p. 197; and U.S., Executive Office of the President, Office of Management and Budget, *Budget of the United States Government: Fiscal Year 1982* (Washington, D.C.: Government Printing Office, 1981), Appendix I, V19.

and addressed to preschool children—especially lower-class preschool children who often lacked both stable families and opportunities for formal preschool education—presented reading readiness exercises in the staccato rhythms of the television commercial. "The Electric Company," first broadcast in 1971 and addressed to slightly older children, did similarly with basic reading techniques, as did "Feeling Good," first broadcast in 1974 and addressed to teenagers, with the substance of health education. "Sesame Street" achieved approximately 90 percent "penetration" in the ghetto, and evaluation studies revealed that it clearly improved the reading readiness of ghetto children across the country. That it was also watched and profited from by middle- and upper-class children was surely ironic, given its objectives, though the phenomenon also testified to the program's extraordinary ability to draw audiences, to hold their attention, and, in fact, to instruct them, with measurable educational outcomes as well as considerable delight on the part of the children.

Granted these successes of public television, there were problems too. While contributions from governmental and private sources rose steadily, they failed to keep pace with the need, so that by the end of the 1970's the stations were running continuing fund-raising campaigns that were not too different from commercials. Beyond that, the Corporation for Public Broadcasting proved vulnerable to politicization, as President Nixon demonstrated when he used his appointment power to give the CPB board a more conservative cast. Most important, perhaps, the relentless advance of telecommunications technology during the 1970's rendered many of the assumptions that governed both commercial and noncommercial broadcasting increasingly out of date, as cable systems were established in the cities, as the reception of signals bounced off satellites became possible without network intervention, and as videodiscs, videocassettes, and videotext systems vastly broadened the substance that could be received on home television sets. A second Carnegie Commission on the Future of Public Broadcasting was created in 1977, under the chairmanship of William J. McGill, president of Columbia University, to explore these and other issues. Operating much in the fashion of the earlier Carnegie Commission, it issued its report, *A Public Trust*, in 1977, urging that the Corporation for Public Broadcasting be replaced by a Public Telecommunications Trust, with a "highly insulated, semiautonomous division" called the Program Services Endowment that would have "the sole objective of supporting creative excellence," that the federal contribution to public broadcasting rise to

$600 million annually by 1985, and that the number and interconnection of public radio stations be further increased at the earliest possible date. Probably the most interesting feature of the report, beyond its attempt to insulate public broadcasting from politicization, was its recognition that the new technologies made possible a more pluralistic programming for more diverse, if smaller, audiences on a financially feasible basis—a possibility referred to as narrowcasting. In any case, *A Public Trust* had little direct effect, either with President Jimmy Carter or with Congress; no legislation was proposed or enacted, and the goal of $600 million annually in federal support by 1985 proved ephemeral.[29]

One final point bears comment. During the early expansion of television broadcasting in the late 1940's and early 1950's, there were dire predictions that, in competition with the new medium, newspapers would go bankrupt, motion picture theaters would close down, and radio stations would become passé. As time passed, however, it became apparent that newspapers, cinema, and radio were profoundly affected by the rise of television, but in ways that changed rather than obliterated them. Americans read as much as ever in 1980, though what they read tended to be ever more specialized and job-related. Two out of three Americans read a newspaper every day, as contrasted with three out of four in the early 1970's, though newspaper circulation stood at approximately 62 million, very close to the 63 million of 1971. What was more significant, however, was that newspapers had been significantly modified; they could not "scoop" television on the announcement of news events, but they could give a fuller account of the meaning of news events than television, especially as television news became ever more dramatically presented in the relentless search for audience size. The result was that newspapers became more like general purpose magazines, with many more feature articles, while magazines tended to become ever more specialized in their content and audiences. Cinema changed radically, as the average weekly attendance fell from the highs of the late 1940's, which had reached around 90 million, to half that number in the 1960's and to 19 million by 1970. But, again, cinema proved adaptable and became more specialized in its address to specific age groups in motion picture theaters and to general audiences over television. As for radio, it was ubiquitous in the 1970's, with some 7,500 commercial stations (4,500 AM stations and 3,000 FM stations) and some 200 noncom-

29. Carnegie Commission on the Future of Public Broadcasting, *A Public Trust* (New York: Bantam Books, 1979), p. 14.

mercial stations broadcasting to an audience of close to 100 million people (only slightly lower than that of the television audience). But individual radio stations, like individual magazines, became more specialized in their audiences, and increasingly took account of the fact that, in addition to living rooms, they were now heard in kitchens, bedrooms, bathrooms, automobiles, and workplaces. In effect, the older communications media had not been displaced by the new one; rather, their functions, their substance, and their audiences had been dramatically rearranged and reallocated—along with their potential for education.[30]

VI

During the years following World War II, the United States quickly became the world's leading exporter of news, films, and television programs. It is interesting to note in this respect that, while the United States had dismantled its propaganda apparatus after World War I, it did not dismantle that apparatus after World War II. The Office of War Information was closed down in 1945, but the Department of State continued to carry on certain activities of the overseas branch through a unit initially named the Office of International Information and Cultural Affairs and then, later, the Office of International Information. Then, as part of the general governmental reorganization of 1953, the United States Information Agency was established, to function under the policy guidance of the State Department. As had the overseas branch of the OWI, USIA employed every medium of communication—newspaper columns, photographs, magazines, and books, radio programs (through the Voice of America), films, and television programs—to disseminate information about American life, American thought, and American domestic and foreign policies. The USIA was expressly prohibited from circulating its material in the United States—there was an articulate fear in Congress about any propagandizing of the American people by their own propaganda agency—but its material circulated widely throughout the world via a network of stations and libraries, usually associated with American embassies or consulates. There was an irony associated with the effort, however. As American newspapers, books, films, and television productions increasingly circulated abroad during the 1960's and

---

30. *New York Times,* September 8, 1983, pp. A1, B12; *Historical Statistics of the United States,* I, 400; Carnegie Commission on the Future of Public Broadcasting, *A Public Trust,* p. 329; and Bogart, *Age of Television,* pp. 413–414.

1970's, the pictures they conveyed of American life—from the violence portrayed on Westerns to the affluence portrayed on situation comedies to the scenes of childhood portrayed on "Sesame Street" (which appeared in translation in some seventy countries, either to teach the native language or to teach English)—became much more influential and pervasive in shaping overseas views of America than the materials circulated by USIA. Put otherwise, at the same time that American newspapers, films, and radio and television productions educated (and miseducated) the American people, they also educated (and miseducated) peoples around the world about the American people, and they did so much more powerfully than the carefully planned didactic efforts of the United States Information Agency.

To a considerable extent, the phenomenon was a result of the proliferation of nongovernmental agencies in marketing American communications materials abroad. The Associated Press and United Press International, which had become international news operations during the 1920's, served thousands of newspapers with dispatches gathered by hundreds of correspondents in scores of foreign bureaus and processed editorially through world desks in New York City. Along with Agence France-Press, Reuters, and Tass, they dominated the supply of news to the world at large, and particularly to the less developed countries. In addition, the New York Times News Service and the Washington Post–Los Angeles Times News Service served dozens of foreign as well as domestic subscribers, and special foreign language editions of *Time, Life, Newsweek,* and the *Reader's Digest* reached millions of individuals in Europe, Oceania, Asia, Africa, and Latin America—by the mid-1970's the international circulation of the *Digest* alone had reached 11.5 million.[31]

American film makers had begun early in the century to export their productions, and by the 1920's they were producing some 90 percent of the films shown abroad. This dominance persisted during the 1930's and was reinforced during the war years, when the raw materials, the production facilities, and the capital required for extensive film making were simply not available in most parts of the world. And in the immediate postwar years, Hollywood not only led the world in the production of new films but also exported hundreds of films made during the early 1940's and consigned to libraries after their initial runs. Then, after an initial period in which the film industry saw itself as in competition with the television industry—it was the

31. Samuel A. Schreiner, Jr., *The Condensed World of the Reader's Digest* (New York: Stein and Day, 1977), p. 181.

same period in which American films also began to be challenged in the export market by Italian, British, French, Indian, and Soviet films—Hollywood (and Chicago and New York) began to produce films for television, and especially the serial films, like "I Love Lucy," "Bonanza," "Ironside," and "Kojak," that became the staples of television during the 1960's. Finally, Hollywood realized the almost limitless market for reruns of its older productions that the voracious needs of television programming had created. The result by the 1960's and 1970's was a continuing American influence in the motion picture theaters of the world and a dominant American influence on world television. By 1974 American films accounted for some 50 percent of the world's screen time; upwards of 30 million people saw the average American film during its period of release for export; and American television programming accounted for the bulk of imported material in most of the non-Socialist countries and for some 15 to 20 percent of the total transmission time in the countries of Western Europe. In addition, there was the special situation of Canada, in which the bulk of the population lived within two hundred miles of the Canadian–United States border and was able to receive programming directly from U.S. television stations.[32]

The motivation behind this flow of news and entertainment was essentially though not wholly commercial. DeWitt Wallace reiterated time and again that the foreign editions of his *Reader's Digest* were instruments for exporting the American values of free enterprise, self-reliance, and democracy; and Henry Luce of *Time* and *Life* deeply believed that his magazines had an obligation to present the American way of life to the world at large—it was, in Luce's words, to be "the American century." Influential public officials like John Foster Dulles and William Benton, mindful of the power of the news to influence opinion abroad, also maintained that the free exchange of information was an integral element of American foreign policy—and indeed, the principle of "the free flow of information" became the bedrock of American policy during the early years of the United Nations and of its educational and cultural arm, UNESCO. Yet, that said, Wallace and Luce demonstrated again and again their readiness to discontinue international editions of their magazines when they did not turn a profit, and there can be no denying that the exporters of "I Love Lucy" and "Gunsmoke" were far more interested in profits than in propaganda.[33]

32. Thomas H. Guback, "Film as International Business," *Journal of Communication,* XXIV (Winter, 1974), 91; and Tapio Varis, "Global Traffic in Television, *ibid.,* 107.

33. Henry Luce, "The American Century," *Life,* X (February 17, 1941), 61.

For a time, the policy of the free flow of information seemed to serve the interests, not only of the United States and its allied industrial countries, but of the less developed countries as well, and especially of their educated elites, who were the principal consumers of American news, films, and television fare. In the theories of development that prevailed through much of the world during the 1950's and 1960's, the assumption was that modernization was a universal process that had begun in the West but that would soon be world-wide. As Daniel Lerner phrased the argument in his immensely influential book *The Passing of Traditional Society* (1958):

The Western model of modernization exhibits certain components and sequences whose relevance is global. Everywhere, for example, increasing urbanization has tended to raise literacy; rising literacy has tended to increase media exposure; increasing media exposure has "gone with" wider economic participation (per capita income) and political participation (voting). The model evolved in the West is an historical fact. That the same basic model reappears in virtually all modernizing societies on all continents of the world, regardless of variations in race, color, creed, will be shown. . . .

The argument, in effect, was that the West in general and the United States in particular, by sharing their news, their films, and their television programming, were hastening the process by which the less developed countries would become urban, industrial, wealthy, and democratic.[34]

From their first emergence, subscription to such ideas was scarcely unanimous. The Socialist countries saw little difference between what they perceived as the propaganda of the United States Information Agency and the propaganda of American newspapers, magazines, and films. Canadians had long been ambivalent about the torrent of print and audiovisual material that made its way north across the border, and during the 1960's that ambivalence turned increasingly to objection. And a wide range of European intellectuals, many though not all of them on the left, were scathing in their denunciation of the partisanship of American news and the low quality of American films and television programming. At least one response from the countries that found the dominance of American media products a matter of political and intellectual concern came in the form of individually set import quotas. And at least one American answer to such quotas was the coproduction of newspapers, films, and television programs, a procedure whereby information or entertainment materials were

34. Daniel Lerner, *The Passing of Traditional Society: Modernizing the Middle East* (Glencoe, Ill.: The Free Press, 1958), p. 46.

financed, produced, and marketed outside the United States by teams of foreign and American experts (and often wholly by nationals of the country where production was taking place, with financing and management in the control of absentee Americans). In some instances, as in a good deal of film making, coproduction turned out to be no more than a device for lowering production costs and avoiding import quotas, in the general fashion of multinational corporations. In others, as, for example, in the efforts of United Press International, there was a genuine effort to use foreign journalists to gather foreign news, though the decisions as to where to gather what news remained in New York. In still others, as, for example, in the efforts of the Children's Television Workshop to develop foreign-language versions of "Sesame Street," there was a transformation, not only of the language used, but also of the characters, the situations, and the events to make them culturally appropriate to "Sesamstrasse" (Germany), "Barrio Sesamo" (Spain), "Iftah ya Simsim" (Kuwait), and "Rechov Sumsum" (Israel); and indeed "Rechov Sumsum" was actually brought back to the United States as a device for teaching American children the language and culture of Israel (even so, ultimate control remained in New York).

A far more fundamental criticism of "the free flow of information" emerged during the 1970's. As sounded by President Urho Kekkonen of Finland at a symposium at the University of Tampere in 1974 organized around the findings of Dr. Tapio Varis to the effect that global traffic in television programming was a one-way flow from the industrial West to the rest of the world, the critique charged that the principle of the free flow of information had served as an instrument through which the industrial countries, particularly the United States, had exercised cultural and political hegemony over the rest of the world, particularly the less developed countries. What was needed, the critique continued, was a "balance of payments" in communication between nations (the use of the phrase from international economics was deliberate), an "equitable cultural exchange in place of the present disparity."[35]

Particularly in light of the growing availability and use of direct broadcast satellite communication during the 1970's, the issues Kekkonen raised became salient matters of international concern, especially in UNESCO, which was increasingly serving as the cultural forum and voice of the less developed countries. Charging that the

35. *Intermedia*, no. 3, 1973, p. 6.

free flow of information was really a form of media imperialism that went hand in hand with economic and political imperialism, representatives of the less developed countries argued that the information purveyed by the Western news services had a patent Western bias that rendered events of interest to the United States and the Western European countries overly important and events in the African, Asian, and Latin American countries either unimportant or of skewed importance—insofar as news set the agendas of public affairs, the agendas of the world were Western agendas. Moreover, they continued, the dominance of American films and television programming created the same problem with respect to American styles of life and thought as contrasted with Third World styles of life and thought—in short, American films and television programming were subversive of autochthonous ways of life. Put otherwise, the argument was that communications originating in the metropolitan centers of the industrial world were miseducating people in the localities of the Third World.

A series of resolutions and declarations presented and debated at the general conferences of UNESCO directed attention to the responsibility of national states for the regulation of the mass media of communication within their territories, to the need for a multidirectional flow of information around the world, to the obligation of the international community to lead in correcting the imbalance in information flow, and to the responsibility of journalists to assist in the effort. The debate quickly became politicized, with Western representatives resisting any attempt to limit the freedom of journalists to gather and report the news according to traditional Western standards of objectivity and with Third World representatives calling for the regulation of journalists in the interests of a more balanced flow of more accurate information. A Declaration adopted in Paris in 1978 included as Article VI the statement:

For the establishment of a new equilibrium and greater reciprocity in the flow of information, which will be conducive to the institution of a just and lasting peace and to the economic and political independence of the developing countries, it is necessary to correct the inequalities in the flow of information to and from developing countries and between those countries. To this end, it is essential that their mass media should have conditions and resources enabling them to gain strength and expand, and to co-operate both among themselves and with the mass media in developed countries.

Two years later, an International Commission for the Study of Communication Problems appointed by the director-general of UNESCO,

Amadou–Mahtar M'Bow, and presided over by the Irish diplomat Sean MacBride, issued a report under the title *Many Voices, One World.* It spoke of the "utmost importance" of "eliminating imbalances and disparities in communication and its structures, and particularly in information flows"; it argued for an international effort to break down concentration and monopolization in the media of communication to the end of a greater plurality of voices and views; and it recommended the "progressive implementation of national and international measures that will foster the setting up of a new world information and communication order." The appointment of the MacBride commission was intended to work out the differences among the various factions in UNESCO and to facilitate the development of a compromise position on the matter of an international communications policy. But the political differences between Western and Third World representatives over the issues only deepened in the wake of the Commission's report. In 1984, the United States formally withdrew from membership in UNESCO, charging that mismanagement and politicization had rendered the organization unable to carry out the mandates of its charter. The issues, of course, did not disappear. In fact, the rapid advance of communications technology during the 1980's only heightened their urgency, however much the participants in the debates continued to disagree on how those issues would be formulated and resolved. Meanwhile, American news, American films, and American television programming continued to exert a prodigious influence on peoples around the world.[36]

36. "Declaration on Fundamental Principles Concerning the Contribution of the Mass Media to Strengthening Peace and International Understanding, to the Promotion of Human Rights and to Countering Racialism, Apartheid and Incitement to War, 31 November 1978," in Kaarle Nordenstreng, ed., *The Mass Media Declaration of UNESCO* (Norwood, N.J.: Ablex Publishing Corporation, 1984), p. 274; and International Commission for the Study of Communication Problems, *Many Voices, One World: Towards a New, More Just, and More Efficient World Information and Communication Order* (Paris: UNESCO, 1980), pp. 253, 268.

PART III

THE INFORMED SOCIETY

The great social duty, therefore, is the universal diffusion of all the most important knowledge now extant in the world.

LESTER FRANK WARD

INTRODUCTION

The vision of a society made new by the widespread diffusion of knowledge became a commonplace of American political and intellectual discussion during the half-century following the Civil War. Yet what was remarkable about that commonplace was the passion with which it was articulated and the millennial expectations with which it continued to be invested. The poet-journalist Walt Whitman rhapsodized in *Democratic Vistas* (1871) about "a programme of culture, drawn out, not for a single class alone, or for the parlors or lecture-rooms, but with an eye to the practical life, and west, the working-man, the facts of farms and jackplanes and engineers, and of the broad range of the women also of the middle and working strata, and with reference to the perfect equality of women, and of a grand and powerful motherhood." From his earliest writings to his last, the sociologist Lester Frank Ward put forward "the distribution of knowledge" as the critical social reform that would ultimately underlie all other reforms. "Of all the panaceas that have been so freely offered for the perfectionment of the social state," he observed in 1897, "there is none that reaches back so far, or down so deep, or out so broad, as that of the increase and diffusion of knowledge among men. But the increase of knowledge—the discovery of wholly new truths—is attended with such a charm that it may be trusted to take care of itself. The great social duty, therefore, is the universal diffusion of all the most important knowledge now extant in the world." And the philosopher John Dewey referred again and again to the long-standing monopolies of learning that had been associated with traditional society and the revolution that had been set in motion with the coming of industrialism. "Printing was invented; it was made commercial," Dewey observed in *The School and Society* (1899).

375

Books, magazines, papers were multiplied and cheapened. As a result of the locomotive and telegraph, frequent, rapid, and cheap intercommunication by mails and electricity was called into being. Travel has been rendered easy; freedom of movement, with its accompanying exchange of ideas, indefinitely facilitated. The result has been an intellectual revolution. Learning has been put into circulation. While there still is, and probably always will be, a particular class having the special business of inquiry in hand, a distinctively learned class is henceforth out of the question. It is an anachronism. Knowledge is no longer an immobile solid; it has been liquefied. It is actively moving in all the currents of society itself.[1]

For all the commitment to diffusion, however, there remained a "politics of knowledge"—the phrase is Ellen Condliffe Lagemann's—that had to be contended with. Who would decide upon "the most important knowledge now extant" that needed to be distributed? Contemporary with the "liquefaction" of knowledge to which Dewey metaphorically referred, there arose a new complex of scientific and cultural elites, each claiming the special expertise to rule upon what knowledge might be of most worth in one domain or another. There were the scholars of the arts and sciences, of medicine and law, and of the other emerging professions in the universities; there were the scientists in the research institutes, the industrial laboratories, and the agricultural experiment stations; and there were the custodians of learning in the libraries and museums, who often allied themselves with the new families of wealth in the burgeoning cities, their hope being to humanize the urban environment and civilize the immigrant masses who inhabited it through the beneficent effects of culture. For such individuals and groups, the distribution of knowledge was a relatively simple matter of diffusing as widely as possible the truths and beauties that they judged timeless and universal.[2]

Others saw the process as more complex. The historian James Harvey Robinson took note of the new architecture of knowledge that was inextricably tied to the rise of modern science, an architecture comprising a host of disciplinary, subdisciplinary, and crossdisciplinary specializations, each with its coterie of experts, its scholarly organizations, and its learned journals, and argued the need for a continuous process of "humanizing" if knowledge was to be made truly accessible to ordinary men and women. "It has become apparent that we must fundamentally reorder and readjust our knowledge before we can hope to get into the current of our daily

1. Walt Whitman, *Prose Works 1892*, edited by Floyd Stovall (2 vols.; New York: New York University Press, 1963–1964), II, 396; Lester Frank Ward, *Dynamic Sociology* (2 vols.; New York: D. Appleton and Company, 1883), II, 598, and *Glimpses of the Cosmos* (6 vols.; New York: G. P. Putnam's Sons, 1913–1918), VI, 33; and John Dewey, *The School and Society* [1899], in *John Dewey: The Middle Works, 1899–1924*, edited by Jo Ann Boydston (15 vols.; Carbondale: Southern Illinois University Press, 1976–1983), I, 16–17.

2. Ellen Condliffe Lagemann, "The Politics of Knowledge: The Carnegie Corporation and the Formulation of Public Policy," *History of Education Quarterly*, XXVII (1987), 205–220.

thought and conduct," Robinson argued in *The Humanizing of Knowledge* (1923). "It must be re-synthesized and re-humanized. It must be made to seem vitally relevant to our lives and deeper interests." The task seemed to Robinson at the same time so important and so difficult that he proposed yet another coterie of experts, namely, writers whose task it would be "to bring home to the greatest possible number of readers as much knowledge as possible, in the most pleasing, effective, and least misleading manner."[3]

Still others thought the problem went far beyond merely making expert knowledge comprehensible and palatable to the public at large. They questioned whether the formal scientific knowledge of the experts was the sole knowledge worth having and worth distributing. John Dewey returned again and again in his writings to the relation between science and common sense and to the uselessness of scientific knowledge that did not in the end assist in the reconstruction of common sense. And, in *Art as Experience* (1934), he pointed to the arts as aspects of the diurnal experience of ordinary people rather than as symbols of quality abstracted from experience and stored in cultural institutions. In a related vein, Jane Addams queried the separation of theory from practice that she saw emerging in the new research universities; the librarian and museum director John Cotton Dana insisted that libraries and museums draw upon the resources of their surrounding communities for their collections; and the critic Gilbert Seldes argued that the popular arts as exemplified by Al Jolson's singing, Ring Lardner's writing, Charlie Chaplin's acting, and Irene Castle's dancing were more worthy, interesting, and expressive of the best in American life than much of what was featured in the libraries, museums, concert halls, and opera houses of America's leading cities. Dewey, Addams, Dana, and Seldes were calling attention to the importance of embracing the vernaculars that provided a genuine basis for American culture and education.[4]

In contemplating the needs for knowledge that were emerging in metropolitan America, Herbert Spencer's question, "What knowledge is of most worth?" could not be avoided. And the various ways in which various groups of Americans answered that question and pressed their answers in the affairs of schools, colleges, cultural agencies, workplaces, philanthropic foundations, and government institutions remained at the heart of the politics of education throughout the twentieth century.

3. James Harvey Robinson, *The Humanizing of Knowledge* (New York: George H. Doran Company, 1923), pp. 100, 104.

4. John Dewey, "Common Sense and Science: Their Respective Frames of Reference," *Journal of Philosophy*, XLV (1948), 197–208; Ellen Condliffe Lagemann, ed., *Jane Addams on Education* (New York: Teachers College Press, 1985), pp. 37–38 and *passim;* John Cotton Dana, *A Plan for a New Museum: The Kind It Will Profit a City to Maintain* (Woodstock, Vt.: Elm Tree Press, 1920); and Gilbert Seldes, *The Seven Lively Arts* (New York: Harper & Brothers, 1924), p. 309.

Chapter 8

THE NATURE AND USES OF KNOWLEDGE

> The knower is an actor, and co-efficient of the truth on one side,
> whilst on the other he registers the truth which he helps to create.
>
> WILLIAM JAMES

On a cloudy October afternoon in 1869 Charles W. Eliot, the recently appointed thirty-five-year-old president of Harvard College, delivered his inaugural address in the First Parish Church of Cambridge, Massachusetts. Confident, serious, and forceful in his delivery, Eliot set before his hearers a vision of what the American university needed to become if it would fulfill its responsibilities to the urban, industrial society that was coming into being. "The endless controversies whether language, philosophy, mathematics, or science supply the best mental training, whether general education should be chiefly literary or chiefly scientific, have no practical lesson for us today," he began, disposing in a sentence of a generation of academic controversy over the relative merits of different subjects. "This university recognizes no real antagonism between literature and science, and consents to no such narrow alternatives as mathematics or classics, science or metaphysics. We would have them all, and at their best."[1]

Eliot then proceeded to detail the measures he believed would project Harvard into the modern world. In every domain of learning, he argued, Harvard needed to search out the most effective methods of instruction: languages had to be taught more systematically, the sciences more inductively, mathematics and history more vividly, and philosophy less dogmatically. Written examinations for admission needed to be set, with students selected on the basis of intellectual

---

1. Charles William Eliot, "Inaugural Address as President of Harvard, 1869," in Richard Hofstadter and Wilson Smith, eds., *American Higher Education: A Documentary History* (2 vols.; Chicago: University of Chicago Press, 1961), II, 602.

promise and strength of character and then offered as wide a choice as possible among subjects. The professors were "the living sources of learning and enthusiasm," but they needed to be paid better and permitted a greater flexibility in their teaching if able individuals were to be attracted to academic work. The governing boards had the high responsibility of maintaining the freedom, the intellectual quality, and the financial stability of the institution. And the president had the crucial obligation to "watch and look before—watch, to seize opportunities to get money, to secure eminent teachers and scholars, and to influence public opinion towards the advancement of learning;—and look before, to anticipate the due effect on the university of the fluctuations of public opinion on educational problems; of the progress of the institutions which feed the university; of the changing condition of the professions which the university supplies; of the rise of new professions; of the gradual alteration of social and religious habits in the community." In sum, the university needed to accommodate itself to changes in the character of the society for which it existed. "The institutions of higher education in any nation are always a faithful mirror in which are sharply reflected the national history and character," Eliot observed. "In this mobile nation the action and reaction between the university and society at large are more sensitive and more rapid than in stiffer communities."[2]

Eliot's inaugural was quickly recognized for what it marked, namely, a turning point in American higher education. His cousin Theodore Lyman, a member of the Board of Overseers, noted in his diary, "I had looked for a very good, sound discourse, but this went far beyond all I had expected! It was in style clear, elegant, and terse; in matter comprehensive and critical. His views of what a university should be were beyond praise. Such a volley never was fired before in these old walls; and yet there was nothing 'radical' about it. They were one and all content with this address—most were even enthusiastic." And the young philosopher John Fiske, a member of the faction seeking university reform in Cambridge, wrote to his wife, "I never before heard a speech so grand and impressive. It lasted an hour and three quarters; and during all you might have heard a pin drop, save when the old arches rang with thunders of applause. We are going to have new times here at Harvard. No more old fogyism, I hope."[3]

2. *Ibid.*, 615, 621–622.
3. The quotations are given in Henry James, *Charles W. Eliot: Founder of Harvard University, 1869–1909* (2 vols.; Boston: Houghton Mifflin Company, 1930), I, 226–228.

The members of the Corporation who chose Eliot to succeed Thomas Hill in the presidency of Harvard knew well that they were appointing anything but a fogy. Born in 1834 to a well-to-do Boston family with close ties to Harvard—his father was treasurer of the college between 1842 and 1853 and two of his aunts were married to Harvard professors—Eliot had attended the Latin School and then Harvard, where he had demonstrated particular interest in chemistry and mathematics. Upon graduation from Harvard in 1853, he had become a tutor in mathematics and then an assistant professor of mathematics and chemistry, and had quickly made a name for himself as a would-be reformer interested in high academic standards, laboratory work, and the extension of the principle of elective studies. When the Corporation had passed him over for the Rumford Professorship in 1863, however, he had felt obliged to leave Harvard. Thereafter, he had traveled in Europe, where he had had the opportunity to study French and German higher education and to work for a time in the laboratory of the eminent chemist Hermann Kolbe; and he had then been appointed to a professorship of chemistry at the newly founded Massachusetts Institute of Technology in 1865. He was serving at MIT when Hill resigned from the Harvard presidency in 1868. Although he had been immediately perceived by some as a candidate, the situation had been complicated, on the one hand, by sharp divisions between reformers and conservatives on the faculty and among the alumni, and, on the other hand, by Eliot's own strong articulation of a reformist position in two articles he had published in the *Atlantic Monthly* in 1869. There he had combined a detailed review of recent American efforts to change the curriculum of the colleges with a caution against any attempt to organize American higher education on a borrowed European model. "The American university has not yet grown out of the soil . . . ," he noted. "When the American university appears, it will not be a copy of foreign institutions, or a hot-bed plant, but the slow and natural outgrowth of American social and political habits, and an expression of the average aims and ambitions of the better-educated classes. The American college is an institution without a parallel; the American university will be equally original." It was to building "the American university" that Eliot would subsequently devote his career.[4]

Samuel Eliot Morison once remarked that Eliot's mind was Roman rather than Greek or Hebraic—he was first and foremost an organizer

4. Charles W. Eliot, "The New Education: Its Organization," *Atlantic Monthly*, XXIII (1869), 204, 216.

rather than a theoretician or a lawgiver. That being the case, it is scarcely surprising that Eliot's vision of the American university was implicit in the reforms he introduced at Harvard and widely disseminated via the model he developed there. The institution whose presidency he accepted in 1869 was small in size, local in orientation, and provincial in character. The college was the heart of the enterprise, with some five hundred undergraduates and a faculty of twenty-three. The curriculum was mostly prescribed, emphasizing Latin, Greek, and mathematics, and including some work in philosophy, history, physics, chemistry, French, and German. A smattering of elective studies was available in the sciences and the modern languages. In addition to the college, there was a law school that granted the LL.B. degree to any student who remained in residence for eighteen months, a medical school from which students who had attended for two terms and who had served an apprenticeship with a practicing physician could receive the M.D. degree upon passing ten-minute oral examinations in five of nine principal subjects, a divinity school that for all intents and purposes did not grant degrees, and a scientific school that could boast an eminent faculty but that maintained pitifully low standards for entry and exit. Eliot moved promptly and aggressively to make Harvard larger in size, national and even international in orientation, and cosmopolitan in character. The undergraduate offering was dramatically broadened; the work of the scientific school was for all intents and purposes folded into that of the college; a Graduate Department (later, the Graduate School of Arts and Sciences) was established in 1872 with the privilege of granting earned master's and doctor's degrees; the three professional schools were placed on a graduate level, with sequential curricula capped by written examinations; and the scholarly quality of the faculties was improved by more careful national and international recruitment and by improved salaries for full-time service. By 1894, after twenty-five years in office, Eliot had created the foremost model of the new American university—foremost insofar as it became the most widely acclaimed and the most widely imitated.[5]

Beyond the model that permitted Eliot to teach by example, he published widely in journals that were read, in his words, by "the better-educated classes." Politically a Mugwump Democrat, he articulated a clear vision of the democracy that was to sustain the new American university and in turn be served by it. In Tocquevillian

5. Samuel Eliot Morison, *Three Centuries of Harvard, 1636–1936* (Cambridge, Mass.: Harvard University Press, 1936), p. 336.

fashion, he celebrated the national commitment to universal man-
hood suffrage, the widespread publicity given public affairs, the universal schooling that enabled all to partake of that publicity (he was
well aware that universal schooling was less than universal in his time,
but he never addressed the issue forthrightly), the general toleration
of religion and the unprecedented mixing of individuals of varying
religious, ethnic, and class backgrounds (Eliot wrote little about race
and was reluctant to acknowledge the value of women's higher education), the diffusion of material well-being among the people at large,
the opportunity for the competent to rise in the world, particularly
through education, and the general optimism of the people and their
openness to change and innovation. And he praised the readiness of
Americans to accept the leadership of the "best men," the preachers,
teachers, jurists, physicians, seers, and poets whom the transformed
Harvard would select, train, and imbue with a spirit of public service.
To his friend James Bryce's query as to why Americans did not elect
their best men to public office, Eliot responded that the real leaders
in the United States were not necessarily elected officials but rather
those preachers, teachers, jurists, physicians, seers, and poets. It is
reported that Ralph Waldo Emerson sat "right in front" at Eliot's
inauguration in the First Parish Church, "listening and smiling and
assenting"; one wonders what the aging sage of Concord would have
thought of his "American scholar" turned university-trained expert![6]

Eliot dealt frequently in his writings and addresses with the special
relationship between a democratic polity and its system of schooling;
and, more than many of his contemporaries, he attempted to view that
system whole, from the kindergarten through the university. What
principles did Eliot see guiding the development of a democratic
school system? In the first place, such a system needed to emphasize
a "progressive acquisition of an elementary knowledge of the external
world"—beginning with the study of nature and proceeding to the
formal material of geography, meteorology, botany, and zoology.
Second, it needed to stress a similar acquisition of "the human
part"—the story of the human race, including "the immense product
of the imagination in art and literature." Third, it needed to include

6. Eliot, "The New Education," *Atlantic Monthly*, XXIII (1869), 216; and James, *Charles W. Eliot*, I, 228. President M. Carey Thomas of Bryn Mawr College scolded Eliot for his views on women's education in an 1899 address, referring to them as a "dark spot of mediaevalism" in his "otherwise luminous intelligence"; see M. Carey Thomas, "The Bryn Mawr Woman," in Barbara M. Cross, ed., *The Educated Woman in America: Selected Writings of Catharine Beecher, Margaret Fuller, and M. Carey Thomas* (New York: Teachers College Press, 1965), p. 142.

the manual and moral training associated with preparation for an occupation—training that included not only accurate handwork but also the qualities of patience, forethought, and good judgment in productive labor. And fourth, it needed to teach by precept, by example, and by reading that the supreme attainment for any individual is vigor and loveliness of character. Finally, a democratic education needed to plant in every child's mind "certain great truths which lie at the foundation of the democratic social theory," among them, the interdependence of individuals, the unity of the democratic community (which implied the important need to Americanize the "rising tide" of immigrants), the satisfactions to be derived from service to one's fellow human beings, and, interestingly, respect for expertise in every field of human activity. "Confidence in experts, and willingness to employ them and abide by their decisions, are among the best signs of intelligence in an educated individual or an educated community," Eliot counseled; "and in any democracy which is to thrive, this respect and confidence must be felt strongly by a majority of the population." In a sense, one principal function of a democratic education would be to teach the community to appreciate the products of the new American university. And indeed the new university too would have special commitments. It should teach all the great languages and all the great literatures, all of human history, the development and functioning of all major human institutions, everything that has been learned about the domain of nature, and the expertise of all the learned and scientific professions. It should be a seeker after new truths and a storehouse of the truths that have been learned. And it should exert a broad, public, beneficent, unifying influence upon the community at large. The kinship to the ideas John Dewey was working out at the same time in treatises like *The School and Society* (1899) is unmistakable and reveals the currency of such ideas among the educational reformers of the era—one understands why in 1919 the organizers of the Progressive Education Association would ask Eliot to be their president. But there were also crucial differences between Eliot and Dewey that are worthy of note, particularly in the relationship they saw between the democratic community and its experts. What Eliot—and later Walter Lippmann—wanted the community to accept as a matter of faith, Dewey—and Jane Addams—wanted to be the basis of an ever widening shared understanding.[7]

Eliot was well aware that his views on education reflected an expli-

7. Charles William Eliot, *Educational Reform: Essays and Addresses* (New York: The Century Co., 1898), pp. 316–317, 403, 404, 405, 413, 412.

cit definition of "the cultivated man" (again, given his ideas on the education of women, the phrase was specific rather than generic). He recognized two differences between his own definition and those that had prevailed earlier in the century. First, the horizon of the human intellect had "widened wonderfully" during the century as a result of the scientific method of inquiry; and second, it had come to be accepted (following Emerson) that the kinds of bodily skill associated with handwork or drawing or piano playing as well as an intimate acquaintance with nature itself were essential elements of culture. "The idea of culture has always included a quick and wide sympathy with men," he noted; "it should hereafter include sympathy with nature, and particularly with its living forms, a sympathy based on some accurate observation of nature." Granted these fundamental shifts, Eliot's ideal of culture stressed the sorts of character that derived from participation in the world, the ability to express oneself with accuracy and elegance, acquaintance with "some part of the store of knowledge," since culture could no longer imply a knowledge of everything, and, important, some form of "constructive imagination" coupled with an appreciation of the great variety of forms of constructive imagination that were coming into being. "We must extend our training of the imagination beyond literature and the fine arts to history, philosophy, science, government, and sociology," he counseled. "We must recognize the prodigious variety of fruits of the imagination that the last century has given to our race."[8]

It is interesting to compare such remarks with the contents of Eliot's "Five-Foot Shelf"—the fifty-odd volumes he selected shortly after his retirement in 1909 as a working substitute for a good liberal education obtained in school during one's youth. The venture has often been seen as anomalous with the rest of Eliot's career, especially in view of the commercialism that surrounded it; but there is a sense in which, just as the transformed Harvard he brought into being best illustrates his ideal of higher education, the Five-Foot Shelf best illustrates his idea of cultivation. It included such standards as Homer, Plato, Plutarch, and Virgil, but it also included writings by Benjamin Franklin, Adam Smith, Charles Darwin, Michael Faraday, Louis Pasteur, and Edward Jenner. Collier, the publisher of the Five-Foot Shelf, claimed to have sold some 350,000 sets, including 17,500,000 volumes, and that does not account for all the numerous imitations

8. Charles W. Eliot, "The New Definition of the Cultivated Man," in William Allan Neilson, ed., *Charles W. Eliot: The Man and His Beliefs* (2 vols.; New York: Harper & Brothers, 1926), I, 191, 193, 202.

issued by competing publishers and advertised as "recommended by President Eliot."[9]

Almost from the time he was appointed to the Harvard presidency, Eliot became influential, first in the affairs of education and then more broadly in public affairs. He played an important role in counseling the trustees of the Johns Hopkins University and in directing their attention to the candidacy of Daniel Coit Gilman for the Hopkins presidency, and he remained in touch with Gilman's efforts thereafter—indeed, he often found himself prodded to action at Harvard by what Gilman had done at Hopkins. The pattern was repeated with other institutions, and in the end Eliot was in touch with every major university president of his time. He was the chairman and the chief figure in the NEA's Committee of Ten on Secondary School Studies, and wrote the Committee's report of 1893, which proved so influential in standardizing secondary school curricula, in achieving parity for the modern languages and the newer scientific subjects in those curricula, and in continuing, at least for a time, a system of secondary school instruction whereby terminal students studied the various subjects in precisely the same fashion as college-bound students. And later, he figured importantly in the work of such organizations as the College Entrance Examination Board, the General Education Board, the Carnegie Foundation for the Advancement of Teaching, and the Carnegie Endowment for International Peace. He advised Wilson on how to maintain American neutrality during the early years of World War I; he advised the United States Senate on the candidacy of Louis D. Brandeis for the Supreme Court; and he advised the Chinese government on how to obtain expert advice without falling under the control of Western governments. And, beyond his counsel to the "best men," the Five-Foot Shelf made him a familiar presence across America. However much his mind may have been Roman rather than Greek or Hebraic, his views were widely sought after and listened to.

Eliot was the foremost member of the generation of university organizers that built the American university. They were a varied lot, in some ways quite different from one another, and they created very different institutions. Daniel Coit Gilman's Johns Hopkins was far more receptive to pure research than Eliot's Harvard, while Andrew Dickson White's Cornell was far more receptive to practical research. Nicholas Murray Butler's Columbia developed a much broader range of professional studies, while James McCosh's Princeton remained

9. James, *Charles W. Eliot,* II, 196, 200.

content with a much narrower range of traditional liberal studies. And Charles Van Hise's University of Wisconsin developed a far richer conception of service, while Timothy Dwight's Yale manifested one that was at best constricted. Nevertheless, the development of an American university out of the American soil was a central concern to all of them, and one can grant the differences without minimizing the commonalities that inhered in all the models—in their forms of organization, in their joining of a liberal arts college to postgraduate academic and professional schools, and in their triune commitment to teaching, research, and service. Eliot articulated these commonalities, though in a sharply restricted form that was addressed to the "better-educated classes" and that conceived of those classes as comprising white men of Anglo-Saxon, Protestant background; and the transformed Harvard he created and led embodied those commonalities with enduring influence.

II

In 1910, Eliot prepared a preface for a new Everyman's Library edition of Herbert Spencer's *Education: Intellectual, Moral, and Physical,* which had first appeared in the United States in 1860. Eliot was warm in his praise of Spencer's ideas—they had, after all, profoundly influenced his own writings. They "have been floated on a prodigious tide of industrial and social change," Eliot observed, "which necessarily involved widespread and profound educational reform." As a matter of fact, Spencer had found a more spirited interest and a more ready market for his ideas in the United States than in his own country. Although the four essays that went to make up *Education: Intellectual, Moral, and Physical* had initially appeared in British periodicals, it was in the United States that they had first been published in book form. And, as Spencer himself observed in his *Autobiography,* in England his ideas had encountered a mixture of hostility and apathy, and indeed his *Social Statics* (1850) and his *Principles of Psychology* (1855) had actually been published at a loss. In the United States, his ideas had quickly become the vogue; by the 1870's, it was no longer possible to embark upon the serious study of philosophy or the natural or social sciences without contending with Spencer.[10]

One reason for the difference was the aggressive sponsorship of Edward Livingston Youmans. An autodidact who wrote textbooks on

10. Charles W. Eliot, Introduction to Herbert Spencer, *Essays on Education and Kindred Subjects* (New York: E. P. Dutton & Co., 1910), p. xvii.

chemistry and domestic science and who annually made the rounds of the lyceum circuit lecturing on the wonders of modern science, Youmans formed a friendship and a business association with the publisher William H. Appleton during the late 1840's that was to prove immensely fruitful to both men. Following Youmans's counsel, Appleton became the leading American publisher of the new science. Enjoying Appleton's support, Youmans published *The Culture Demanded by Modern Life,* an anthology of "addresses and arguments on the claims of scientific education," in 1867; he founded *Appleton's Journal,* dedicated to "the diffusion of valuable information on subjects of public importance," in 1869; he undertook editorial direction of the International Scientific Series of works by distinguished scientists, which eventually ran to over fifty volumes, in 1871; and he established the *Popular Science Monthly,* committed to the diffusion of scientific knowledge, in 1872. It was in the effort to obtain a contribution from Spencer to *The Culture Demanded by Modern Life* that Youmans first wrote the Englishman during the winter of 1859–60. Youmans had read *Social Statics* and *Principles of Psychology* as well as several of Spencer's articles and the prospectus of his projected ten-volume synthetic philosophy, and had become sufficiently converted to Spencer's ideas to arrange for American publication (through Appleton), first, of *Education: Intellectual, Moral, and Physical,* then of *Social Statics* and two books of essays, and then of the entire series that became the synthetic philosophy. In addition, he had featured Spencer's writings in *Popular Science Monthly* and persuaded him to prepare *The Study of Sociology* (1874) for the International Scientific Series. As Spencer's ideas gained favor in the United States, Youmans became one of his chief interpreters to the American public; and, when Spencer paid his much commented-upon visit to the United States in 1882, it was Youmans who served as host, traveling companion, chief of arrangements, and director of publicity.[11]

Beyond the sponsorship of Youmans, however, there was a more fundamental reason for the popularity of Spencer. During the years following the Civil War, the social dislocations associated with industrialization and urbanization were compounded by the intellectual dislocations associated with the challenge of Darwinism. As reports of Darwin's findings and theories appeared in magazines and newspapers, their challenge to the traditional doctrines of special creation and eternal forms became ever more clear and compelling, and

11. E. L. Youmans, *The Culture Demanded by Modern Life* (New York: D. Appleton and Company, 1869), Title page; and *Appleton's Journal,* I (1869), 22.

Americans were forced to wrestle with the question of whether there could ever be a reconciliation between scientific knowledge and Christian belief. Spencer offered them an all-encompassing philosophy that answered the question in the affirmative—nothing scientists could ever learn about the world would violate the special domain of religion, namely, worship of "the Unknowable." And, beyond that affirmative answer, he provided a philosophy that was accessible to and could be appreciated by an extraordinary range of individuals, from the learned scientist to the cracker-barrel intellectual. Oliver Wendell Holmes remarked that Spencer had "come nearer to the realization of Bacon's claim of all knowledge as his province than any other philosopher of his time"; and John Fiske said of his work that it had surpassed that of Aristotle and Newton, much as "the railway surpasses the sedan-chair, or as the telegraph surpasses the carrier-pigeon." For many, he seemed to incarnate the scientific spirit of the age. Moreover, that scientific spirit was joined, on the one hand, to a fierce individualism suspicious of government authority, and, on the other hand, to a firm belief in progress as the unalterable course of nature. It is little wonder, as Richard Hofstadter once observed, that the generation that took Grant as its hero took Spencer as its thinker.[12]

Spencer's *Education* was a mélange of argument, opinion, and theory sharply critical of existing practice in the schools and colleges, and, more generally, of the existing values of Anglo-American high culture. The four essays had been written as part of the spirited Victorian debate over the conflicting claims of an education rooted in classical languages and literature and an education rooted in the substance and methods of science, and as such they had a polemical quality about them—Eliot referred to their "aggressive" tone—that lent added force to their arguments. "To prepare us for complete living," Spencer declared, "is the function which education has to discharge; and the only rational mode of judging of any educational course is, to judge in what degree it discharges such function." And what was complete living? Spencer divided it into five categories: those activities ministering directly to self-preservation; those that secured the necessities of life; those concerned with the rearing and disciplining of children; those that maintained proper social and polit-

12. Herbert Spencer, *First Principles of a New System of Philosophy* (2d ed.; New York: D. Appleton and Company, 1864), Part I; [Edward Livingston Youmans, ed.], *Herbert Spencer on the Americans and the Americans on Herbert Spencer* (New York: D. Appleton and Company, 1883), pp. 84, 51; and Richard Hofstadter, *Social Darwinism in American Thought, 1860–1915* (Philadelphia: University of Pennsylvania Press, 1944), p. 21.

ical relations; and those devoted to the gratification of tastes and feelings. The ideal education was simply "complete preparation in all these divisions." Measured against these criteria, Spencer found conventional education sadly lacking. In four of the five domains, what the schools and colleges offered was seriously deficient; and in one, namely, the rearing and disciplining of children, there was no preparation whatever. What was Spencer's remedy for these deficiencies? In a word, "science." For the maintenance of health, for earning a living, for parenthood, for civic duty, for the perfect production and highest enjoyment of the arts, and for discipline in all its forms, intellectual, moral, and religious, science was the most effective, productive, and economical study of all.[13]

Spencer's *Education* made an important impact on American schools and colleges, mostly by accelerating utilitarian tendencies that had been central in American life since the days of Benjamin Franklin. It surely influenced Eliot's efforts on behalf of a "new education" rooted in the modern languages, the natural sciences, and mathematics, and it obviously played a role in Eliot's formulations on behalf of the NEA's Committee of Ten. Yet, however great the impact of *Education,* it was Spencer's more general philosophical writings that exercised the largest influence on American educational thought and practice. As the leading proponent of evolution to the American people, Spencer sounded throughout his work the principle that history was the progressive adaptation of constitution to conditions, or put otherwise, the adjustment of human character to the circumstances of living. Human beings, he argued, were infinitely more the creatures than the creators of history. And, because the development of mind followed evolutionary processes and because evolutionary processes worked themselves out over time, independent of immediate human acts, education could never be a significant factor in social progress. The only thing teachers could do was provide the knowledge that would enable people to adapt to their circumstances; any change in the circumstances themselves would have to follow the inexorable course of evolution.[14]

That there were reformist implications in this view is evident from Spencer's preachments in *Education.* The aim of education was preparation for life. Instruction would have to begin with objects rather than abstractions to take account of the development of mind. Moral-

---

13. Eliot, Introduction to Spencer, *Essays on Education,* p. vii; and F. A. Cavenagh, ed., *Herbert Spencer on Education* (Cambridge: Cambridge University Press, 1932), pp. 10, 14, 54.

14. *Report of the Committee on Secondary School Studies Appointed at the Meeting of the National Education Association, July 9, 1892* (Washington, D.C.: Government Printing Office, 1893).

ity was best taught by connecting acts with their consequences. The health of the body was inseparable from the health of the mind. These and other dicta, much in the reformist tradition of Bacon, Locke, and Pestalozzi (Spencer was familiar with their writings), followed in Spencer's view from the laws of nature. But they followed within the context of a larger system in which the ultimate goal of education was the adaptation of individuals to circumstance. "Reforming men's conduct without reforming their natures is impossible," Spencer wrote in *Social Statics;* "and to expect that their natures may be reformed, otherwise than by the forces which are slowly civilizing us, is visionary. Schemes of discipline or culture are of use only in proportion as they organically alter the national character, and the extent to which they do this is by no means great. It is not by humanly-devised agencies, good as these may be in their way, but it is by the never-ceasing action of circumstances upon men—by the constant pressure of their new conditions upon them—that the required change is mainly effected." If most efforts toward reform were visionary, state-sponsored efforts were most visionary of all; for, in Spencer's view, each institution of the social organism, like each part of the individual organism, was best fitted to perform one particular function, and the function of the state was to administer justice, not to reform the world and certainly not to try to reform the world through education.[15]

Widely known in general outline, Spencer's philosophy had a marked impact upon the entire generation of American thinkers, though it propelled them to conclusions that were often divergent and occasionally opposed. Nowhere was that diversity of thought more striking than in the theories of education and culture that came to the fore during the half-century following the Civil War. In 1872, for example, William Graham Sumner, who would soon take up his duties as Yale's Professor of Political and Social Science, read Spencer's *The Study of Sociology* as it appeared serially in the *Contemporary Review.* An 1863 graduate of Yale, Sumner had gone on to study at Geneva, Göttingen, and Oxford before returning to the United States in the autumn of 1866 to take up a tutorship at Yale and to study for orders in the Protestant Episcopal Church. It was in the course of preparing his sermons as rector of the Church of the Redeemer at Morristown, New Jersey, that Sumner turned to the Spencer essays for clarification of his views on political economy. They proved a revelation. Years later, he reminisced about their impact.

15. Herbert Spencer, *Social Statics; or, the Conditions Essential to Human Happiness, Specified, and the First of Them Developed* (New York: D. Appleton and Company, 1882), p. 384.

THE INFORMED SOCIETY

These essays immediately gave me the lead which I wanted, to bring into shape the crude notions which had been floating in my head for five or six years, especially since the Oxford days. The conception of society, of social forces, and of the science of society there offered, was just the one which I had been groping after but had not been able to reduce for myself. It solved the old difficulty about the relation of social science to history, rescued social science from the dominion of the cranks, and offered a definite and magnificent field for work, from which we might hope at last to derive definite results for the solution of social problems.

In effect, Sumner was converted to Spencer and to sociology at one and the same time.[16]

What did Sumner find in *The Study of Sociology* that stimulated the initial conversion, that led him to use the volume as a textbook in his Yale courses, and that led in 1879–80 to his celebrated clash with President Noah Porter over the suitability of the book for Yale students? Essentially, he found a vision of a true social science that located the moving forces of society, not in divine interposition or in the actions of individual men and women, but in the inexorable workings of the evolutionary process. "The implication throughout the argument," Spencer wrote in the conclusion, "has been that for every society, and for each stage in its evolution, there is an appropriate mode of feeling and thinking; and that no mode of feeling and thinking not adapted to its degree of evolution, and to its surroundings, can be permanently established." The bearing of this on public and private effort was in Spencer's view inescapable.

Though the process of social evolution is in its general character so far pre-determined, that its successive stages cannot be ante-dated, and that hence no teaching or policy can advance it beyond a certain normal rate, which is limited by the rate of organic modification in human beings; yet it is quite possible to perturb, to retard, or to disorder the process. . . . Though, by maintaining favorable conditions, there cannot be more good done than that of letting social progress go on unhindered; yet an immensity of mischief may be done in the way of disturbing and distorting and repressing, by policies carried out in pursuance of erroneous conceptions. And thus, notwithstanding first appearances to the contrary, there is a very important part to be played by a true theory of social phenomena.

In sum, the primary role of social science was preventative—the avoidance of harm.[17]

16. "Sketch of William Graham Sumner," *Popular Science Monthly*, XXXV (1889), 266.
17. Herbert Spencer, *The Study of Sociology* [1874] (reprint ed.; Ann Arbor: University of Michigan Press, 1961), pp. 356, 365–366.

Sumner spent the rest of his life explaining the bearing of Spencerian principles, first, on the central social questions facing contemporary American society, and then, on the development of a comprehensive science of society based on data concerning all human institutions from primitive times to the present. The effort yielded a spate of brilliantly polemical treatises with such titles as "What the Social Classes Owe to Each Other" (in which he argued the responsibility of individuals to look after their own welfare, leaving to the public the responsibilities of sympathy, the mutual redress of grievances, and the extension of opportunity for life chances) and "The Absurd Effect to Make the World Over" (a mordant criticism of proposals to reconstitute the industrial system on the principles of democracy for their failure to perceive the inextricable tie between capitalism and democracy). More important for education, it also yielded a masterwork called *The Science of Society,* which was unfinished at the time of Sumner's death in 1910, except for a lengthy prolegomenon on the role of custom in the development of human institutions entitled *Folkways: A Study of the Sociological Importance of Usages, Manners, Customs, Mores, and Morals* (1906). His argument there was that the "folkways" are not "creations of human purpose and wit" but rather "products of natural forces which men unconsciously set in operation"; that the folkways are "right" and "true" in their very nature, because they are traditional and exist in fact; that when the folkways are invested with doctrines of rightness and truth they become "mores"; that the most essential education of any individual is the business of learning the mores, a process that goes forward naturally beginning at birth and continues over a lifetime; that the main justification of popular schooling is not the instruction of the masses but the selection and training of "men of genius"; and, finally, that the job of statesmen is not to try purposefully to change the mores but rather to perceive changes in the mores that are already under way and seize upon the opportunities inherent in those changes to effect useful social policies.[18]

William Graham Sumner read Herbert Spencer and incorporated Spencer's conservatism full-blown into his own social philosophy. Lester Frank Ward also read Spencer but reacted sharply against Spencer's conservatism, transforming it into one of the most influential reformist philosophies of the Progressive era. Born in Joliet, Illi-

18. William Graham Sumner, *Folkways: A Study of the Sociological Importance of Usages, Manners, Customs, Mores, and Morals* [1906] (reprint ed.; Boston: Ginn and Company, 1940), pp. 4, 28, 29, 34, 628.

nois, in 1841, Ward was for all intents and purposes an autodidact. Although he earned three degrees and a medical diploma from George Washington University, then known as Columbian College, his real education came from voracious reading coupled with tireless observation of natural phenomena. He mastered seven languages and read easily in four others; he acquainted himself with virtually all of the leading scientific treatises of his day, and, as part of that effort, he made himself thoroughly familiar with Spencer's works as they appeared. Yet, as Ward observed the phenomenon of evolution, he concluded that there was more to it than the progressive adaptation of constitution to conditions. Spencer, he argued, had described merely physical, or animal, or genetic evolution, a process essentially planless in character. But Spencer had ignored the crucial fact that with the emergence of mind the very character of evolution changes. Mind is "telic," it has purposes, it can plan, Ward observed in describing a new dynamic phase of evolution. "The office of mind," he counseled, "is to direct society into unobstructed channels, to enable these forces to continue in free play, to prevent them from being neutralized by collision with obstacles in their path. In a word, mind has for its function in civilization to preserve the dynamic and prevent the statical condition of the social forces, to prevent the restoration of equilibrium between the social forces and the natural forces operating outside of them." With mind at work, evolution was no longer blind, but instead telic, purposeful, and capable of conscious direction toward worthy social ends.[19]

Developing this formulation in a work entitled *Dynamic Sociology* (1883), Ward, unlike Spencer and Sumner, brought education to the forefront of human activity; it was to be the single most important function of government, the "great panacea" for all social ills. Indeed, when Ward began work in the spring of 1869 on the manuscript that would become *Dynamic Sociology,* he conceived of it as "a book on the subject of education"; and, though the lengthy discussion of education ended up coming last in the finished work, it was one of the earliest sections he drafted. Logically, the section dominates the latter half of the work. Having reasoned that the entry of mind into the evolutionary process had inaugurated a new dynamic phase in the history of the world, Ward reasoned further (following Auguste Comte) that the state had also gone through an evolutionary process, from tyranny to aristocracy to the physiocratic (laissez-faire) democ-

19. Lester Frank Ward, *Dynamic Sociology* (2 vols.; New York: D. Appleton and Company, 1883), I, 698.

racy of the eighteenth century to the plutocratic democracy of the nineteenth. The problem of the age, Ward maintained, was to move from plutocratic democracy to a next phase, which, following Comte, he called sociocracy. This was the final stage in the evolution of the democratic state (and indeed the final stage of political history—a secular millennium). It would be marked by perfect equality, perfect comity, and the freely given loyalty of the citizenry, and it would be brought into being by education. Ward's reasoning was simple: progress rested on dynamic social action; dynamic social action derived from informed public opinion; informed public opinion derived from widely diffused accurate knowledge; and widely diffused accurate knowledge was the result of a proper education.[20]

What would be the characteristics of a proper education? Ward defined it as "a system for extending to all the members of society such of the extant knowledge of the world as may be deemed most important." In contrast to an education derived from experience, a proper education would planfully transmit knowledge; in contrast with an education based on discipline, it would assume that character and intellect flowed from the possession of knowledge rather than vice versa; in contrast to an education associated with traditional culture, it would be useful rather than ornamental; and in contrast to an education stressing research, it would concentrate exclusively on imparting information already discovered to those who did not yet have it. In general, the system would be marked by three "cardinal principles." First, it would ignore differences in the mental capacity of various minds and concentrate solely on increasing the content of all minds. Second, it would be "the exclusive work of society itself," that is, it would be public in all aspects. And third, it would be truly universal—as Ward put it, it would benefit society by preventing the encroachments of the ignorant upon the intelligent at the same time that it prevented the encroachments of the intelligent upon the ignorant. Ward never faced squarely the crucial question of who would decide what parts of "the extant knowledge of the world" were "most important" for the citizenry at large, though there is evidence that, again following Comte, he would have located the responsibility in presumably selfless groups of social scientists chosen to administer the affairs of the sociocratic state.[21]

At a time when Spencer's books were being devoured by a large and

20. Bernhard J. Stern, ed., *Young Ward's Diary* (New York: G. P. Putnam's Sons, 1935), p. 317.

21. Ward, *Dynamic Sociology*, II, 568, 571.

appreciative general audience and Sumner's essays were being pored over by an elite conservative cognoscenti, the first edition of *Dynamic Sociology* sold fewer than five hundred copies. But the work was rediscovered, so to speak, after 1890, when Albion W. Small, then president of Colby College, came upon it and proclaimed it the most vital diagnosis of cosmic and social problems to have appeared in two centuries. A second edition, issued in 1896, circulated more briskly and soon earned for Ward a reputation as the "father of American sociology." Ward, in turn, went on to publish a succession of major sociological works, including *The Psychic Factors of Civilization* (1893), *Pure Sociology* (1903), and *Applied Sociology* (1906). In 1906, he left his position in Washington as a paleontologist with the United States Geological Survey to accept a professorship of sociology at Brown University, where he remained until his death in 1913. His later works refined many of his concepts, but *Dynamic Sociology* remained his masterpiece, prefiguring all the principal themes of his later work. Its equalitarianism, which insisted, first, that there were no race, gender, or social-class differences in intellect, and second, that, given individual variations, the ordinary capacity for knowledge was far in excess of the knowledge possessed; its feminism, which propounded a theory of the social and intellectual equality of women (Ward later proclaimed their superiority to men); its practicalism, which emphasized dynamic action as the end product of accurate knowledge; its conception of the distribution of knowledge as the leading function of the state; and its vision of popular education as the great mainspring of rational social progress were revolutionary in character. They lent scientific expression to many of the reform themes of the Progressive era, and they provided alternatives to the formulations of Spencer and Sumner that would fuel American debates over education for years to come.

Ward was lionized as much after the appearance of the second edition of *Dynamic Sociology* as he had been ignored after the appearance of the first. His colleagues in the field of sociology were not reticent in their criticisms, but neither were they reticent in their regard. A generation of sociologists celebrated Ward's role in the establishment of the discipline in the United States; and, when the American Sociological Association was organized in 1905, Ward was elected the first president. The honor was more than symbolic; for, however much his younger colleagues had gone beyond him, he had in many ways set the problematics of their work. And in the process he had placed the theory and practice of education at the heart of the new scientific study of society.

Two younger academics were especially significant in carrying Ward's analyses forward and in the process exerted an important influence on social and educational thought in their own right. One was Albion Small of the University of Chicago, the other, Edward Alsworth Ross of the University of Wisconsin. An early graduate of the Johns Hopkins University, Small left the presidency of Colby College in 1892 to go to the University of Chicago, where he established the first graduate department of sociology in the country. There, he developed Ward's conception of education as a critical factor in the improvement of society. In an 1896 address to the National Educational Association entitled "The Demands of Sociology upon Pedagogy," Small argued that education needed to place the new generation in contact with the three great realities of modern life—interdependence (the recognition that in the urban, industrial world no one lived unto himself); cooperation (the correlate of interdependence); and progress (the realization that new individuals and new circumstances would forever necessitate new social arrangements). What is more, Small continued, contact with these new realities needed to be active and action-oriented. "If I am not mistaken, he maintained, "a consensus is rapidly forming, both in pedagogy and in sociology, to the effect that action in contact with reality, not artificial selection of abstracted phases of reality, is the normal condition of maximum rate and symmetrical form of personal development. Sociology consequently joins with pedagogy in the aim to bring persons, whether in school or out of school, into as direct contact as possible with the concrete conditions in which all the functions of personality must be applied and controlled. In these conditions alone is that balanced action possible which is the *desideratum* alike of pedagogical and social culture." Sociology, he concluded, "knows no means for the amelioration or reform of society more radical than those of which teachers hold the leverage." When Small's colleague John Dewey formulated his pedagogic creed for the *School Journal* the following year, the University of Chicago published Small's address and Dewey's creed in a single pamphlet.[22]

Edward Alsworth Ross too was an early graduate of Johns Hopkins who had gone on to teach at Indiana, Cornell, Stanford, and Nebraska before settling in Wisconsin in 1906. It was during his tenure at Stanford that he developed the treatise that was published in 1901 under the title *Social Control: A Survey of the Foundations of Order,* in

22. National Educational Association, *Proceedings and Addresses,* 1896, pp. 175, 184.

which he explicated the processes by which education contributes to social progress, on the one hand, and, via the transmission of values and habits by parents, clergymen, schoolteachers, political parties, and "ethical elites," to social stability, on the other. In the course of his analysis, he distinguished sharply and importantly between class control and social control. The former meant leadership by a self-styled elite and inevitably resulted in deep social cleavage; it was in its nature immoral, parasitical, and ineffectual. The latter made possible the essential stability within which individual liberty and egalitarian mobility might flourish, a stability that facilitated the "ennobling of new fortunes, the opening of careers to talent, the equalization of opportunities, the dissolving of hereditary classes." In the end, however, it was different instrumentalities that most clearly distinguished the two: the former used force, fraud, and superstition to achieve its purposes, the latter used persuasion and teaching. Ward praised the treatise to the skies as "at once brilliant and profound"; Small hailed it as "something approaching a relevation"; and Theodore Roosevelt and Oliver Wendell Holmes sent letters of appreciation. Ross's progressive credentials had been well established in 1900, when he had been dismissed from the Stanford faculty at Jane Stanford's behest for his views on railroad regulation and the free coinage of silver. Unlike Ward, he was not an egalitarian, he was not a feminist, and he did not believe in the equality of races. But he remained an articulate proponent of social and economic reform and a consistent supporter of workingpeople and farmers in their confrontations with big business. More important here, *Social Control* established him as a progressive in education, whose formulations would continue to influence pedagogical theory and practice right up to the beginning of World War II.[23]

Although not an academic, one other social theorist of the Progressive era merits attention as a disciple of Ward, namely, Charlotte Perkins Gilman. Gilman had grown up in the family of Frederick Beecher Perkins, where she had imbibed all the innovative independence and eccentricity of the Beecher tradition, particularly as reflected in the lives of Harriet Beecher Stowe, Catharine Beecher, and Isabella Beecher Hooker. Although she had had some schooling at the Rhode Island School of Design and had later lived for a few

23. Edward Alsworth Ross, *Social Control: A Survey of the Foundations of Order* (New York: The Macmillan Company, 1901), pp. 378–379; Bernhard J. Stern, ed., "The Ward-Ross Correspondence," *American Sociological Review*, XII (1947), 706, Note 7; and Albion Small, "Review of *Social Control*," *American Journal of Sociology*, IX (1904), 578.

months at Hull House, she was essentially self-educated, having read voraciously from adolescence and having sharpened her wit in incessant debate with her male as well as female kin and friends. A constraining first marriage left her first separated and then divorced with a daughter to support, and it was force of circumstance that led her to a career of lecturing and writing. Having developed strong feminist and suffragist convictions, she came upon Ward's writings as a revelation, and when she met him personally at the Woman's Suffrage Convention of 1896 she cast him immediately as one of her heroes. In a series of books that included *Women and Economics: A Study of the Economic Relations Between Men and Women as a Factor in Social Evolution* (1898), *Concerning Children* (1900), *The Home: Its Work and Influence* (1903), *The Man-Made World; or, Our Androcentric Culture* (1911)—dedicated to Ward "with reverent love and gratitude"—and *His Religion and Hers: A Study in the Faith of Our Fathers and the Work of Our Mothers* (1923), she developed a sociology that merged a radical feminism with a profound commitment to a radically reformed education that began with a radically altered child rearing, continued through a radically changed training in church and school, and culminated in a radically transformed conception of work and the workplace. She was surely the leading intellectual of the women's movement during her lifetime, and the power and relevance of her ideas remained remarkably vigorous during the revival of that movement after World War II.[24]

III

William James initially encountered Spencer's writings during the early 1860's when he read *First Principles* as it appeared chapter by chapter in the English periodical press. He reported that he was initially "carried away with enthusiasm by the intellectual perspectives which it seemed to open." He was soon jolted from that enthusiasm, however, by the mordant criticisms of his "maturer companion," Charles Sanders Peirce. "I felt spiritually wounded," he recalled, "as by the defacement of a sacred image or picture, though I could not verbally defend it against his criticisms." Whatever those spiritual wounds, James soon moved to his own vigorous rejection of Spencer's philosophy. "Apart from the great truth which it enforces, that everything has evolved somehow," he later observed, "and apart from the

24. Charlotte Perkins Gilman, *The Man-Made World, or, Our Androcentric Culture* (New York: Charlton Company, 1911), p. 3.

inevitable stimulating effect of any such universal picture, I regard its teachings as almost a museum of blundering reasoning."[25]

At the heart of James's objection was Spencer's insistence that what he called the general evolutionary law of life, namely, "the adjustment of inner to outer relations," applied as well to the process of mental development, leaving the principal office of mind that of mirroring the external environment and thereby enabling the organism to adjust to that environment. In James's view, that insistence denied the active character of mind in which, first, mind helps determine what actually constitutes the reality of the environment, and second, mind plays a role, not only in enabling the organism to adapt to its environment, but also in transforming the environment. James set forth these criticisms in his "Remarks on Spencer's Definition of Mind as Correspondence," which William T. Harris printed in the *Journal of Speculative Philosophy* in 1878. "I, for my part, cannot escape the consideration," he wrote there, "forced upon me at every turn, that the knower is not simply a mirror floating with no foot-hold anywhere, and passively reflecting an order that he comes upon and finds simply existing. The knower is an actor, and co-efficient of the truth on one side, whilst on the other he registers the truth which he helps to create."[26]

That same year, 1878, James signed a contract with the New York publisher Henry Holt to produce a textbook on psychology. It was published twelve years later as *The Principles of Psychology.* James began the work with Spencer and then spent some 1,400 pages concretizing the basis of his objections and setting right Spencer's "blundering reasoning." "At a certain stage in the development of every science," he noted in the opening pages, "a degree of vagueness is what best consists with fertility. On the whole, few recent formulae have done more real service of a rough sort in psychology than the Spencerian one that the essence of mental life and of bodily life are one, namely, 'the adjustment of inner to outer relations.' Such a formula is vagueness incarnate; but because it takes into account the fact that minds inhabit environments which act on them and on which they in turn react; because, in short, it takes mind in the midst of all its concrete relations, it is immensely more fertile than the old-fashioned 'rational psychology,' which treated the soul as a detached existent, sufficient

25. William James, "Herbert Spencer" [1904], in *Essays in Philosophy* (Cambridge, Mass.: Harvard University Press, 1978), p. 116.

26. William James, "Remarks on Spencer's Definition of Mind as Correspondence" [1878], *ibid.*, pp. 7, 21.

unto itself, and assumed to consider only its nature and proportion."
Vagueness incarnate—Spencer became the foil against which James
would fashion his philosophy of activism, empiricism, pluralism, and
free will.[27]

James was born in 1842 in New York City, the eldest child of an
extraordinary family that could live in comfort owing to inherited
wealth. His father, a writer on religious subjects, had made a lonely
spiritual odyssey from the stern Presbyterian orthodoxy of his youth
to a rather more benign, nonsectarian Swedenborgian Christianity;
his mother, the strong-willed "protective spirit" of the family, followed her husband in intellectual affairs while providing the moral
and physical sustenance that made his literary efforts possible. Together, they believed that the proper education of the children was
their own central responsibility, with the result that the family traveled
frequently for the edification of the youngsters and there was little
concern with uninterrupted periods of formal schooling. William
early displayed a scientific bent but also clearly had artistic talent. A
year of formal study in the studio of William Morris Hunt in 1860
persuaded him he would never be a first-class painter, and in 1861 he
entered the Lawrence Scientific School and for all intents and purposes remained at Harvard until his death in 1910. Upon graduation
from Lawrence in 1864 he entered the Harvard Medical School, inter-
rupting his work there, first, to go on an expedition headed by Louis
Agassiz to collect zoological specimens in the Amazon basin, and
then, to study in Europe, and obtained his M.D. in 1869. There
followed a period of intense depression during another sojourn in
Europe, marked by an overwhelming sense of powerlessness and an
anguished fear of madness, from which he is supposed to have recovered by adopting the French philosopher Charles Renouvier's views
on free will. In an oft-cited diary entry for April 30, 1870, James wrote,
"I think that yesterday was a crisis in my life. I finished the first part
of Renouvier's second 'Essais' and see no reason why his definition
of free will—'the sustaining of a thought *because I choose to* when I
might have other thoughts'—need be the definition of an illusion. At
any rate, I will assume for the present—until next year—that it is no
illusion. My first act of free will shall be to believe in free will." As
Howard M. Feinstein has observed, the diary entry itself was more
dramatic than any action that followed from it. The depression lin-
gered on, and it was probably only James's subsequent acceptance of

27. William James, *The Principles of Psychology* (2 vols.; New York: Henry Holt and Company, 1890), I, 6.

the psychiatric view that madness is not wholly hereditary (and hence, wholly determined) that relieved his anguish. However that may be, he was appointed instructor in physiology at Harvard in 1872, began to teach psychology in 1875 and philosophy in 1879, and became professor of philosophy in 1885. With the publication of *The Principles of Psychology* in 1890, he achieved national and indeed international renown.[28]

The Principles of Psychology was a remarkable work by any measure. Written in a style laced with illustrations from everyday life, it summed up a generation of physiological and psychological research in Europe and the United States and wove it into a coherent whole. The problematics of the work was not unlike that of Spencer's *Principles of Psychology,* but the orientation, the data, and the argument were a world apart. Man was presented as a biological creature within the scheme of evolution, whose behavior was founded upon certain instinctive tendencies to react. Upon these tendencies rested both habitual and voluntary action. As a result of the repetition of acts, habits emerged, testifying to the plasticity of the human nervous system. Once formed, they increasingly governed behavior until eventually they became the overwhelming determinants of social and personal character. There was a paradox about habit, however, for, the more the details of life were given over to it, the further the higher powers of mind were released to do their own proper work. Here, James's central concept was consciousness, or the "stream of thought." Insisting that life itself rather than any formal notions of mind or soul must be the starting point of psychology, James pictured consciousness as an intensely active phenomenon continually engaged in attending, emphasizing, ignoring, and interpreting the raw data of immediately felt experience. Mind was ever "a theatre of simultaneous possibilities," he observed, and it was the fate of each individual to be constantly choosing: what is perceived, what is known, and, ultimately, which of many possible selves one would become. Once again, the knower was the actor, whose very act of knowing transformed the world.[29]

With the completion of the *Principles,* James turned increasingly to the philosophical problems that had occupied him intermittently since 1878. The result was the emergence over the next twenty years

28. Leon Edel, *Henry James* (5 vols.; Philadelphia: J. B. Lippincott, 1953–1972), I, 47; Henry James, ed., *The Letters of William James* (2 vols.; Boston: Atlantic Monthly Press, 1920), I, 147, by permission of the Houghton Library, Harvard University, and Alexander R. James, literary executor; and Howard M. Feinstein, *Becoming William James* (Ithaca: Cornell University Press, 1984), pp. 309–315.

29. James, *Principles of Psychology,* I, 224, 288.

of a full-blown system that Ralph Barton Perry once called "the most perfect philosophical expression of American individualism." In 1897 a volume of essays called *The Will to Believe* gave forceful statement to James's deep-seated voluntarism, his faith in a society of moral individuals, each courageously living life according to hopes, possibilities, and aspirations deeply held. A series of articles written in 1904–5, and posthumously published as *Essays in Radical Empiricism* (1912), set forth a metaphysical notion of "pure experience" that rejected ancient dualisms between thought and object, knower and known, in favor of a unitary view in which "the parts of experience hold together from next to next by relations that are themselves parts of experience." And finally, the essays on *Pragmatism* in 1907 and on *The Meaning of Truth* in 1909 elaborated the now-famous thesis that "The truth of an idea is not a stagnant property inherent in it. Truth *happens* to an idea. It *becomes* true, is *made true* by events. Its verity *is* in fact an event, a process: the process namely of its verifying itself, its verification."[30]

In all of this, James conceived of thought as essentially purposive, having constant reference to action or to the possibility of action, and of knowledge as deriving from thought acted upon, from ideas tested in practice. Moreover, he saw the development of knowledge as a process in which all individuals participated, each in a unique way as part of a unique experience. "The process here is always the same," James explained.

The individual has a stock of old opinions already, but he meets a new experience that puts them to a strain. Somebody contradicts them; or in a reflective moment he discovers that they contradict each other; or he hears of facts with which they are incompatible; or desires arise in him which they cease to satisfy. The result is an inward trouble to which the mind till then has been a stranger, and from which he seeks to escape by modifying his previous mass of opinions. He saves as much of it as he can, for in this matter of belief we are all extreme conservatives. So he tries to change first this opinion, and then that (for they resist change very variously), until at last some new idea comes up which he can graft upon the ancient stock with a minimum disturbance of the latter, some idea that mediates between the stock and the new experience and runs them into one another most felicitously and expediently.

This new idea is then adopted as the true one. It preserves the older stock of truths with a minimum of modification, stretching them just enough to

30. William James, *Essays in Radical Empiricism* [1912] (Cambridge, Mass.: Harvard University Press, 1976), p. 4, *The Meaning of Truth* [1909] (Cambridge, Mass.: Harvard University Press, 1975), p. 7, and *Pragmatism* [1907] (Cambridge, Mass.: Harvard University Press, 1975), p. 97.

make them admit the novelty, but conceiving that in ways as familiar as the case makes possible. . . . New truth is always a go-between, a smoother-over of transitions. It marries old opinion to new fact so as ever to show a minimum of jolt, a maximum of continuity.

Thus did James at the same time explain the development of new knowledge in the world and the learning of that knowledge by the individual. It was a continuing process in which ordinary men and women participated in the creation and incorporation of what eventually came to be regarded as common sense in the daily living of the common life. And James marveled, on the one hand, at the richness, the diversity, and indeed the daily heroism involved in that common life, and, on the other hand, at the capacity of the ordinary individual, rarely used to the fullest, to contribute fruitfully to that common life. Like Lester Frank Ward, he understood the hereditary differences in temperament and intelligence among individuals, but he deeply believed that individuals as a rule "use only a small part of the powers which they actually possess and which they might use under appropriate conditions."[31]

James was among the most widely read of American philosophers. He had critics in abundance, who deplored what they saw as either the naive subjectivism or the narrow utilitarianism of his philosophy; but he was also taken to heart by innumerable progressives who found in his ideas a source of tremendous hope and inspiration for the future. As James's younger colleague George Santayana once remarked, "James felt the call of the future and the assurance that it could be made far better, totally other, than the past." Yet, however much James's philosophy ennobled the ordinary individual, it was not generally read by ordinary individuals. Rather, it was popular insofar as it was addressed to and read by a wide range of intellectuals and men and women of affairs. Whereas Ward influenced other sociologists who in turn influenced a broader public, James addressed that broader public directly. And his concern, as David A. Hollinger has pointed out, was to extend to all domains of knowledge, scientific as well as religious, "the culture of inquiry," the processes of testing, creating, and incorporating knowledge that he described in *Pragmatism.*[32]

John Dewey, of course, was one of the intellectuals who avidly read

31. James, *Pragmatism,* pp. 34–35, and "The Energies of Men" [1907] in *Essays on Faith and Morals* (New York: Longmans, Green and Co., 1949), p. 221.

32. George Santayana, *Character and Opinion in the United States, with Reminiscences of William James and Josiah Royce and Academic Life in America* (London: Constable and Company, 1920), p. 88; and David A. Hollinger, "William James and the Culture of Inquiry," *Michigan Quarterly Review,* XX (1981), 264–283.

James and was deeply influenced by him. In fact, his reading of *The Principles of Psychology* was a case study of James's generalizations about the incorporation of new knowledge by the individual. Coming in the midst of Dewey's intellectual odyssey from the Hegelianism he had imbibed at Johns Hopkins to his own characteristic instrumentalism, the work contributed much of "new direction and quality" to his thinking. He was especially taken with the idea of an objective psychological theory firmly rooted in evolutionary biology, an idea that, as he himself noted, worked its way slowly into every domain of his thought and profoundly transformed his beliefs. In 1904, James, doubtless seeing many of his own ideas reflected back from Dewey at the University of Chicago, wrote an admiring review of the collection Dewey and his colleagues had published under the title *Studies in Logical Theory* (1904), in which he roundly praised the "masterly pragmatic production" of the "flourishing school of radical empiricism" at Chicago. Six years after that, on the occasion of James's death, Dewey wrote of the "precious gift" James had contributed to American philosophical thought. "I love, indeed, to think," he commented, "that there is something profoundly American in his union of philosophy with life; in his honest acceptance of the facts of science joined to a hopeful outlook upon the future; in his courageous faith in our ability to shape the unknown future. When our country comes to itself in consciousness, when it transmutes into articulate ideas what are still obscure and blind strivings, two men, Emerson and William James, will, I think, stand out as the prophetic forerunners of the attained creed of values."[33]

The instrumentalism that would be fundamental to Dewey's own conception of knowledge and culture fit squarely, of course, within the American tradition that honored common sense and everyday experience—a tradition that included Emerson and James, among others. It was already explicit in the essays Dewey contributed to *Studies in Logical Theory*, and he developed it in considerable detail in *How We Think* (1910), where he argued that the origin of thinking is always "some perplexity, confusion or doubt"; that thinking generally moved through a series of steps in which a problem is defined, suggestions (ideas, hypotheses) for solving the problem are developed, the implications of the several suggestions are conjectured (reasoning),

33. John Dewey, "From Absolutism to Experimentalism," in George P. Adams and Wm. Pepperell Montague, eds., *Contemporary American Philosophy: Personal Statements* (2 vols.; New York: The Macmillan Company, 1930), II, 24; James, "The Chicago School," in *Essays in Philosophy*, p. 103; John Dewey, "William James," in *Characters and Events: Popular Essays in Social and Political Philosophy* (2 vols.; New York: Henry Holt and Company, 1929), I, 109, 117.

and at least one of the suggestions for solving the problem is tested in practice and evaluated; and that the most effective way of training people to think effectively is to begin with typical problems from their experience to be solved by "personal reflection and experimentation" and thereby assist them in acquiring "definite bodies of knowledge leading later to more specialized scientific knowledge." And he refined his instrumentalism in more technical terms in his *Essays in Experimental Logic* (1916), where he reprinted his contributions to *Studies in Logical Theory* and added a number of essays on the nature of knowledge and of judgments of practice, and in *Logic: The Theory of Inquiry* (1938), where he related his instrumentalism to "interpretation of the forms and formal relations that constitute the standard material of logical tradition." One of the most important undertakings of the *Logic* was its connecting of scientific inquiry with ordinary common sense, a connection that, in the first place, removed the distinction in kind between formal research and ordinary reflective inquiry, and that, in the second place, socialized inquiry by indicating its origins in common sense and its rooting in the "social relations" of its time. "Scientific subject-matter and procedures," he maintained, "grow out of the direct problems and methods of common sense, of practical uses and enjoyments, and . . . react into the latter in a way that enormously refines, expands, and liberates the contents and agencies at the disposal of common sense."[34]

Implicit in this conception of thinking was a revised conception of knowledge that was far more inclusive and dynamic than traditional views. Dewey developed it most fully in an article he prepared for Paul Monroe's *Cyclopedia of Education* (1911–1913), which became an important vehicle for his less technical writings on philosophy, education, and culture (he wrote over a hundred pieces for the *Cyclopedia*, some of them quite lengthy). The term "knowledge" in Dewey's view included at least four distinct meanings: first, knowledge in the sense of intelligently acquired skill—the knowledge of how to walk, talk, skate, or get along with one's neighbors; second, knowledge in the sense of acquaintance or familiarity with persons, places, and situations—the knowledge of one's neighborhood or workplace; third, knowledge attained indirectly through learning from others—information; and fourth, rational, or scientific, knowledge. In the first three

34. John Dewey, *How We Think* [1910], *John Dewey: The Middle Works, 1899–1924*, edited by Jo Ann Boydston (15 vols.; Carbondale: Southern Illinois University Press, 1976–1983), VI, 188, 312 [italics removed], and *Logic: The Theory of Inquiry* (New York: Henry Holt and Company, 1938), pp. iii, 66.

types of knowledge, Dewey explained, "intelligence or reflective thought is used, but only secondarily. It is employed as a means of gaining control of things; in enlarging acquaintance with them; in apprehending and understanding things reported by others. It is not, however, used in any sense as a source of knowledge for its own sake." As information is amassed and systematized, Dewey continued, some individuals become interested, not merely in familiarity, but in rational demonstration and the discovery of new knowledge; and thus a fourth kind of knowledge comes into existence, namely, rational knowledge, or science. Like information, Dewey pointed out, such knowledge is also indirect, but it is indirect in a new sense of dependence upon logical data and premises. "From this point of view, knowledge is identical with *science,* and we have no logical right to denominate intelligent skill, matters of acquaintance, of information, *knowledge,* unless they are reduced to general principles and are connected with one another in systematic ways. Otherwise they represent beliefs, opinions, rather than knowledge."[35]

Closely related to Dewey's conception of knowledge was his reformulation of the meaning of culture. Like his onetime colleague at the University of Chicago Thorstein Veblen, Dewey sharply attacked traditional definitions of culture, rooted as they were in the civilization and literature of the ancient world and the Renaissance and revitalized by the nineteenth-century European reaction against eighteenth-century naturalism. Such definitions advanced a class-bound ideal, he maintained, that divided the world into people of leisure, who needed the refinement of culture, and people who worked with their hands, who did not; beyond that, the ideal implicit in traditional views of culture was anachronistic, born of a premodern world. The rise of industrialism, of social and economic interdependence, and of political democracy necessitated a radically different view of culture. "Culture," he concluded, "is the social insight and spirit to which useful skill, knowledge of fact, and trained mental power must all be made to contribute. Where they are isolated from active participation in culture, utility becomes mechanical routine, or else skill in purely egoistic pursuits; information becomes an accumulation and memorizing of a mass of miscellaneous facts that have no bearing upon conduct, and discipline becomes a formal gymnastic of specialized mental habits or 'faculties.' On the other hand, culture when isolated tends to become a purely external polish and refinement, a mark of

35. John Dewey, "Knowledge" [1912], *John Dewey: The Middle Works,* VII, 266–267.

an invidious class distinction." Following this formulation, he argued in *Democracy and Education* (1916) that there were no bodies of knowledge intrinsically endowed with liberating or cultural powers per se, that any subject could be cultural in the degree to which it was pursued and apprehended in its widest possible range of meanings. There was perhaps no better definition of culture, he maintained, "than that it is the capacity for constantly expanding the range and accuracy of one's perception of meanings." Finally, in *Art as Experience,* Dewey democratized the domain of the aesthetic by making it a quality of the "doing" and "undergoing" involved in experience, including ordinary experience, connected, on the one hand, with intelligent behavior and, on the other hand, with the living of life in a particular society.[36]

Dewey propounded his ideas on the need for a radical reconceptualizing of the phenomena of thought, knowledge, and culture at many levels to many audiences—in technical papers in the *Journal of Philosophy,* in books as recondite as *Logic* and as accessible as *Reconstruction in Philosophy* (1920), in more popular articles in the *Nation* and the *New Republic,* in addresses before labor unions and political gatherings, in the manifestoes of educational and cultural organizations. If James sought to explain the culture of inquiry to a relatively broad audience of intellectuals and people of affairs, Dewey sought to explain his socialized version of the culture of inquiry to an even broader cross-section of his fellow Americans. He was in many ways—to borrow from Carlyle and Emerson—the representative American of his time, insofar as he incarnated the finest aspirations of his countrymen at the same time that he articulated those aspirations and brought them to common consciousness.

The very success of James and Dewey in articulating certain aspirations of their fellow Americans did leave them vulnerable to critics who questioned or condemned those aspirations. Santayana was writing not a little ironically when he observed that James felt the call of the future and the assurance that it could be made far better and totally other than the past. He was in truth criticizing what he saw as the superficiality of James's religious views, in the course of a work that commented mordantly on the moral emptiness, the naive millennialism, and the crass materialism of American culture. Not surprisingly, the work in which he undertook that critique, *Character and Opinion in the United States* (1921), quickly made him a hero of a genera-

36. John Dewey, "Culture" [1911], *ibid.,* VI, 407, *Democracy and Education* [1916], *ibid.,* IX, 130, and *Art as Experience* (New York: Minton, Balch & Company, 1934), chap. iii.

tion of young independent literary-social critics that had begun to form during the period of World War I. The intellectual leader of that younger generation was Van Wyck Brooks, whose essays published as *America's Coming of Age* (1915) and *Letters and Leadership* (1918) posed the problem of a fundamental split in American life between the "Highbrow" idealism of American philosophy and letters and the "Lowbrow" opportunism of everyday affairs, and called upon American writers to create a usable past that would serve as the basis of a noble and vital American culture. Pragmatism, Brooks asserted, had failed dismally to achieve that task. The patron saint of the younger generation was Randolph Bourne, whose essays in the *Seven Arts* magazine condemning the moral insufficiency of the philosophy that had enabled his mentor, John Dewey, to support American participation in the war, had become a clarion call to youthful critics throughout the country, and whose untimely death in the influenza epidemic of 1918 had given Brooks the opportunity to canonize him in his introduction to the posthumous anthology of Bourne's writings entitled *History of a Literary Radical and Other Essays* (1920). And the *enfant terrible* of the younger generation was H. L. Mencken, who pilloried James and Dewey in the *Smart Set* as the "Great Thinkers" who had propounded the "serpent's metaphysic" of pragmatism on behalf of all "right-thinking and forward-looking men."[37]

Of all the youthful critics who answered Brooks's call, none remained more steadfastly devoted to the enterprise than Lewis Mumford. Born in New York City in 1895 to a lower middle-class family that reared him in an aura of genteel poverty, Mumford attended the Stuyvesant High School with the thought of becoming an engineer but subsequently turned to journalism and enrolled in night classes at the College of the City of New York, intending to major in philosophy. There he encountered the work of the Scottish sociologist and city planner Sir Patrick Geddes, who would profoundly shape his writing in the years to come. Mumford never completed the work for the bachelor's degree at CCNY. He served in the Navy for a time, spent a brief sojourn in London after his discharge, and then returned to New York to heed Brooks's call for writers who would reclaim the best of America's cultural heritage. Brooks himself considered Mumford the best of the younger generation, the one to whom he felt "most sympathetic and closely allied." As he observed in his autobi-

37. Van Wyck Brooks, *Three Essays on America* (New York: E. P. Dutton & Co., 1934), pp. 17, 19, 171; and H. L. Mencken, "Professor Veblen and the Cow," *Smart Set*, LIX (May, 1919), 138, 139.

ography, "I had a fraternal feeling for him that steadily grew with the years, and I connected this with a remark of William James in a letter to his friend Josiah Royce: 'In converse with you I have always felt that my life was being lived importantly.' "[38]

Mumford began his quest for a usable American past in three works of the 1920's, *The Story of Utopias* (1922), *Sticks and Stones: A Study of American Architecture and Civilization* (1924), and *The Golden Day: A Study of American Literature and Culture* (1926). In the first, he propounded the thesis that human beings lived in two worlds, the ideal world within (Mumford called this the "idolum") and the real world without. The world within could serve as a refuge from the world without or as a tool for reconstructing it, he observed. His purpose in reviewing the utopias of the West was to encourage his contemporaries to develop their own visions of a better community on earth.[39]

In *Sticks and Stones,* Mumford sounded the themes that would echo through his work for the next half-century. Life in the medieval village had been an organic whole, he maintained; architecture, institutions, and people had been integrally related and governed by a coherent religious ideal. But modernity had destroyed that integrity: the centrifugal forces of Protestantism, capitalism, science, and democracy had torn it asunder. By the time the New World had been settled, these forces had been in the ascendancy. Even so, the first New England settlements had been in their own way integral wholes—"In the villages of the New World there flickered up the last dying embers of the medieval order." But the "diaspora" of the pioneers out from these seaboard settlements had destroyed their coherence and opened the way for the forces of Protestantism, capitalism, science, and democracy to triumph; and, with the rise of the machine age, vision had failed and leadership had fallen into the hands of the "busy people" with the "mechanical ingenuity" and the "imbecile power." What was needed was a transformation of values that would replace the depredations of the machine with a concern for the quality of community life. "The pioneer inheritance of the miner," Mumford argued, "coupled with the imperial inheritance of the hunter-warrior, out for loot, lie at the bottom of our present-day social structure; and it is useless to expect any vital changes in the milieu of architecture until the miner and the hunter are subordinated to relatively more

38. Van Wyck Brooks, *An Autobiography* (New York: E. P. Dutton & Co., 1965), pp. 405–406.
39. Lewis Mumford, *The Story of Utopias* (New York: Boni and Liveright, 1922), p. 13.

civilized types, concerned with the culture of life, rather than with its exploitations and destruction."[40]

In *The Golden Day,* Mumford reviewed the literature that in his view had gone hand in hand with the developments chronicled in *Sticks and Stones.* There had been a "golden day" in American letters, presided over by Emerson, that had reflected the coherence of the New England town. That had been followed, alas, by the age of the "pragmatic acquiescence"—acquiescence in the exploitativeness of the machine civilization, marked by the narrowness and superficiality of James's philosophy ("One searches James's pages in vain for a *Weltanschauung:* but one gets an excellent view of America. . . . Beside the richness of Emerson's thought, which played over the whole field of existence, James was singularly jejune") and the inelegant blandness of Dewey's ("No one has plumbed the bottom of Mr. Dewey's philosophy who does not feel in back of it the shapelessness, the faith in the current go of things, and the general utilitarian idealism of Chicago"). Pragmatism had articulated what was characteristic in American life, its utilitarianism, its mechanism, its love of technique, while ignoring the imaginative, the artistic, and the poetic ("The deficiencies of Mr. Dewey's philosophy are the deficiencies of the American scene itself"). What was needed, once again, was a compelling vision of what it might mean "to live a whole human life," in effect, a new "idolum."[41]

Mumford's lifelong effort to formulate the new idolum was carried out in two phases. The first was "The Renewal of Life" series, comprising *Technics and Civilization* (1934), *The Culture of Cities* (1938), *The Condition of Man* (1944), and *The Conduct of Life* (1951); the second was a two-volume study entitled *The Myth of the Machine,* comprising *Technics and Human Development* (1967), and *The Pentagon of Power* (1970). Both works incorporated sweeping—indeed bravura—examinations of cultural history, the first going back to "the dawn-age of our modern technics" between 1000 and 1750, the second going back even further to the "invisible machine" that anticipated the machine itself in ancient Sumer and Egypt. Both involved a didactic interpretation of cultural history. Both sought a "re-harmonizing" of educative institutions, not only of schools and universities, but also of museums and

40. Lewis Mumford, *Sticks and Stones: A Study of American Architecture and Civilization* (New York: Boni and Liveright, 1924), pp. 14, 73, 237, 227.
41. Lewis Mumford, *The Golden Day: A Study of American Literature and Culture* (New York: Horace Liveright, 1926), pp. 183–184, 256, 261, 279.

theaters, libraries and reading rooms, even factories and laboratories, that would thrust the arts to the forefront of diurnal life and facilitate people in developing and sharing their own artistic conceptions of a revitalized, organic society. And both concluded with prophetic visions of whole men and women living humane lives in a transformed, integral culture.[42]

For all the rich detail and incisive commentary of Mumford's analysis, however, the outlines of the truly integrated culture he so zealously sought remained unclear, still to be developed. As one critic remarked of "The Renewal of Life" series, the four books "cannot be gospels for our time, they are at best only vast and learned sketches of the modern gospels that still remain to be written." Mumford saw the formulating of those gospels as a continuing, universal human task and, in the end, the most important task of modern society. Interestingly, having begun by rejecting the philosophy of James and Dewey, Mumford came full circle to the enterprise of James and Dewey and to a mode of analysis that was far from alien to the one they taught. Where Mumford differed profoundly from them was in his oppositional stance toward modern American culture. In effect, "The Renewal of Life" series and *The Myth of the Machine* were the most sweeping and learned indictment ever mounted of the institutions of modern America. Yet, when the dust of the attack had settled, Mumford's vision of a new and better world was strangely lacking.[43]

IV

In the autumn of 1921, as the disenchantment deriving from the war deepened among American intellectuals and as the return to "normalcy" promised by President Warren G. Harding proceeded apace, a writer named Harold E. Stearns persuaded Van Wyck Brooks to join him in gathering together a group of younger critics to undertake a wide-ranging assessment of American culture in all its aspects. The symposium that resulted, published in 1922 under the title *Civilization in the United States: An Inquiry by Thirty Americans,* reviewed the American achievement in science, philosophy, poetry, art, theater, politics,

42. Lewis Mumford, *Technics and Civilization* (New York: Harcourt, Brace and Company, 1934), p. 111, *The Myth of the Machine: Technics and Human Development* (New York: Harcourt, Brace & World, 1967), pp. 188–194, and *The Culture of Cities* (New York: Harcourt, Brace and Company, 1938), p. 477.

43. Peter Firchow, "Lewis Mumford," in A. Walton Litz, ed., *American Writers: A Collection of Literary Biographies,* Supplement II, Part I (New York: Charles Scribner's Sons, 1981), p. 499.

medicine, law, education, and much else, and expressed a near-unanimous judgment. To the question, What is authentic and durably excellent in American culture, the response was, Very little! Like Mumford, who prepared the article on "The City" for the symposium, most of the contributors were of a younger generation that was avidly reading *The Education of Henry Adams* and resonating to its *fin-de-siècle* arguments that education had failed because the culture it was intended to sustain had dissolved into chaos. "Something must be radically wrong with a culture and a civilization when its youth begins to desert it," Stearns lamented; and, along with large numbers of his contemporaries, he left for Paris in search of the truly authentic and excellent—and, not incidentally, of himself. In the end, he never really found either. Others, however, both in the United States and abroad, conducted that search more fruitfully, among them, a young journalist named Gilbert Seldes.[44]

Seldes had grown up in a utopian community in Alliance, New Jersey, that had been organized on principles laid down by Count Tolstoy and Prince Kropotkin. He had had his formal education at Harvard and had then served as a reporter, a music critic, an associate editor of *Collier's*, and the managing editor of the *Dial* before going off to Paris—for a "holiday," as he put it—to write a book about popular culture in America. Published in 1924 as *The Seven Lively Arts*, it maintained not only that there was much of great worth in American culture but that it was to be found, not in bogus imitations of European styles in the traditional elite arts, but rather in original creations in the new popular arts. After commenting at length on the cinema, jazz music, newspaper satire, the revue (including musical comedy and ballroom dancing), vaudeville, the circus, and the comic strip, Seldes summed up his argument in nine arresting statements patently intended to shock: that Al Jolson was more interesting to the intelligent mind than John Barrymore; that Ring Lardner and Mr. Dooley at their best were more entertaining and more important than James Branch Cabell and Joseph Hergesheimer; that George Herriman's daily comic strip, "Krazy Kat," was "easily the most amusing and fantastic and satisfactory work of art produced in America to-day"; that Florenz Ziegfeld was a better producer than David Belasco; that one film by Mack Sennett or Charlie Chaplin was worth the entire oeuvre of Cecil B. DeMille; that "Alexander's Ragtime Band" was

---

44. Harold E. Stearns, ed., *Civilization in the United States: An Inquiry by Thirty Americans* (New York: Harcourt, Brace and Company, 1922); and Harold Stearns, *America and the Young Intellectual* (New York: George R. Doran Company, 1921), p. 159.

musically sounder than "The Rosary"; that the circus was often more artistic than the Metropolitan Opera; that Irene Castle was "worth all the pseudo-classic dancing ever seen on the American stage"; and that the civic masque (a form of Elizabethan drama) was not perceptibly superior to the Elks' Parade in Atlantic City.[45]

Clearly, beyond the shock value of the statements themselves, Seldes was advancing a series of propositions about popular culture, namely, that there was no opposition between the elite and the popular arts—indeed, that the only opposition was between both at their best and the "middle or bogus arts"; that the lively arts in America were more interesting to the adult cultivated intelligence than most of what passed for art in cultured society; and that a "genteel tradition" about the arts had prevented a proper appreciation of the popular arts and in the process had encouraged abuse rather than the thoughtful criticism that was merited—criticism intended to develop appropriate standards for the popular arts and thereby hold them to the highest possible levels of performance. In effect, Seldes was arguing to the authors of *Civilization in the United States* that they had looked in the wrong places for the authentic and the excellent, that a popular (democratic) culture produced new forms of authenticity and excellence for which appropriate standards needed to be developed, and indeed, that those new forms of authenticity and excellence were worthy, not only of criticism, but also of wide communication, dissemination, and appreciation.[46]

Seldes's arguments set in motion a debate that would continue energetically over the next half-century. His reviewers divided sharply in their response to his work. Edmund Wilson, writing in the *Dial*, praised the book as "a genuine contribution to America's new orientation in the arts which was inaugurated by *America's Coming of Age.*" Thomas Craven, on the other hand, writing in the *Nation*, found the book innocent at best and utterly misguided at worst. "Criticism today is permeated with the ambition to level objective values," he maintained. "Mr. Seldes is only one of many who, under the pressure of a new attitude toward creativeness, have lost their bearings. . . . Art is produced only when the suggestive quality remains subordinate to the object; when the content is so wedded to the form that no separation is possible. In the 'lively arts' all is suggestion, and the form is

45. Gilbert Seldes, *The Seven Lively Arts* (New York: Harper & Brothers, 1924), pp. xi, 309.
46. *Ibid.*, p. 349.

completely overridden by the comic idea. These expressions cannot be considered as objectively valuable—their significance is purely sociological. The surest test of aesthetic validity is permanence of appeal."[47]

Seldes himself returned to the issue in three subsequent books. In *The Movies Come from America* (1937), he reviewed the development of cinema from its earliest days, attempting to apply the new standards of judgment he had called for in 1924. In general, he remained an *aficionado* of the movies, but expressed concern over the continuing sacrifice of quality to profits by the large studios and urged patrons to make their preferences known to the producers. In *The Great Audience* (1950), the distress he expressed about the movies was extended to all the popular arts, particularly in the forms conveyed by cinema, radio, and television—Seldes had been director of television programming for CBS from 1938 to 1945. The producers, he charged, had catered to the lowest common denominator of the audience they served; they had conveyed a "flat and limited picture of life" and had actually encouraged people to limit the range of their emotions and interests—in effect, they had made teenagers of everyone. Finally, in *The Public Arts* (1956), he united the optimism and appreciation of *The Seven Lively Arts* with the foreboding and concern of *The Movies Come from America* and *The Great Audience* in a treatise that conceived of the public arts as embracing both popular entertainment and broadcast communications and characterized them as of near-universal accessibility and appeal, popularized content, and in varying degree governed by public law. "They belong to the people," Seldes argued, "and consequently the people have certain rights and duties in respect to them." Borrowing from the work of the Canadian economist Harold A. Innis, Seldes maintained that the communications industry in the United States was undergoing revolutionary changes in the shift from print to electronic transmission and that whenever such changes in the means of communication occur social changes of equal consequence are sure to follow. "I suggest," Seldes concluded, "that, as the fundamental values of our lives and those of our children will be affected by the revolutionary change in entertainment and communications which I have described in this book, we have an obligation to control the speed and direction of this change." It was that obligation of the public to the public arts that Seldes hoped to establish. Given

47. Edmund Wilson, "The Seven Low-Brow Arts," *Dial*, LXXVII (1924), 250; and Thomas Craven, "Art and Jazz," *Nation*, CXIX (1924), 290. By permission of the *Nation*.

the influence of those arts in shaping the national taste and culture, the responsible carrying out of that obligation meant nothing less than the public controlling its own education.[48]

Seldes's optimism that the public could and should control its own education through the popular arts surely represented the most hopeful formulation of the problem among his contemporaries. From one quarter, T. S. Eliot maintained that true culture was inseparable from religion and could flourish only in an organic social structure that fostered its hereditary production and transmission by an elite class. Absent the return of such an organic social structure in the United States, true culture was doomed. From another quarter, Clement Greenberg argued that true culture could emanate only from an *avant-garde* with a superior comprehension of historic and objective values, and that the only culture that could emanate from Hollywood movies, Tin Pan Alley, or the comic strips was *Kitsch,* a mechanical quasi-art, produced for profit according to formula, that was the epitome of all that was spurious in contemporary life. True culture was possible, but it had little chance of being popularized. And from yet another quarter, Dwight Macdonald charged that the culture produced for popular consumption—the novels of Edna Ferber, Fannie Hurst, and James Michener, the art of Norman Rockwell, and the philosophy of Norman Vincent Peale—was popular neither in the sense that it disseminated high culture nor in the sense that it represented folk art. In fact, it was not popular at all, it was a new phenomenon in history that Macdonald referred to as mass culture, or "masscult," neither popular nor culture. It was a product of the masses who had come into being with the industrial revolution. "Up to then," Macdonald explained, "there was only High Culture and Folk Art. To some extent, Masscult is a continuation of Folk Art, but the differences are more striking than the similarities. Folk Art grew mainly from below, an autochthonous product shaped by the people to fit their own needs, even though it often took its cue from High Culture. Masscult comes from above. It is fabricated by technicians hired by businessmen." Macdonald saw the principal cultural movement of the post–World War II era as the emergence of what he called "midcult," a vulgarization of high culture intended to please the masses, exemplified by such works as Thornton Wilder's *Our Town* and Archibald MacLeish's *J. B.* For Macdonald, midcult was about all America could aspire to culturally. He brushed aside Seldes's hope that the people

48. Gilbert Seldes, *The Great Audience* (New York: The Viking Press, 1950), pp. 250, 263, 291, and *The Public Arts* (New York: Simon and Schuster, 1956), pp. 301, 302.

could control the public arts and force the producers to issue work of high quality. The only solution he could propose was to disaggregate Seldes's "great audience" into its component taste publics and then try to create a new public for high culture—a solution the Columbia sociologist Herbert Gans incorporated into the more general solution he proposed in 1975 under the title *Popular Culture and High Culture: An Analysis and Evaluation of Taste.* [49]

One might note, too, that, while many critics were less optimistic than Seldes concerning the possibility of public participation in the setting of high but democratic standards for culture, at least one critic, the Canadian Marshall McLuhan, actually developed a caricature of Seldes's optimism. A professor of English at the University of Toronto, McLuhan had been educated at the University of Manitoba and at Cambridge, where he had been deeply influenced by the New Criticism of I. A. Richards and F. R. Leavis, and had spent the first twenty years of his career producing a steady flow of academic essays on Tennyson, Keats, Poe, Eliot, and Pound—with an occasional venture into the aesthetics of advertising and the cultural significance of baseball. Then, during the early 1950s, he had come upon the work of his colleague at Toronto, the economist Harold A. Innis, just as Seldes had done, and had accepted as revelation Innis's sweeping assertion that changes in the predominant media of communication held the key to history insofar as they changed social meanings, altered the character of knowledge, and created and destroyed monopolies of knowledge and with those monopolies, constellations of power. *The Mechanical Bride: A Folklore of Industrial Man,* published in 1951, represented McLuhan's attempt to apply Innis's theory to the contemporary cultural situation. He argued in that work that modern culture, and particularly advertising, had thrown men and women into a "collective dream" from which they could escape only by a prodigious exercise of critical intelligence. Moreover, given the unprecedented power of the modern media of communication, the traditional classroom could contribute little toward this critical intelligence—it could never "compete with the glitter and the billion-dollar success and prestige of this commercial education. Least of all with a commercial education program which is disguised as entertainment and which by-passes the intelligence while operating directly on the will and the

49. T. S. Eliot, *Notes Toward the Definition of Culture* (New York: Harcourt, Brace and Company, 1949); Clement Greenberg, "Avant-Garde and Kitsch," *Partisan Review,* VI (Fall, 1939), 40; and Dwight Macdonald, *Against the American Grain* (New York: Random House, 1962), pp. 13–14, 38, 71.

desires." Critical intelligence would have to be exercised through the very media that had created the collective trance in the first place.[50]

Subsequently, in *The Gutenberg Galaxy: The Making of Typographic Man* (1962) and *Understanding Media: The Extensions of Man* (1964), McLuhan developed his own sweeping interpretation of history, according to which the preprint, preliterate, oral/aural, scribal culture of medieval Europe had been replaced by the typographic, visual, linear culture of modern Europe, with its print-initiated splits between head and heart and technique and meaning and its glorification of mechanization and respectability. The typographic, visual, linear culture of modern Europe had in turn been replaced by the electronic, oral/aural culture of the "global village" that was the modern interdependent world, with its new opportunities to grasp processes whole and instantaneously and thereby to do away once and for all with historic splits between head and heart and technique and meaning. In the new electronic culture, McLuhan explained,

the medium is the message. This is merely to say that the personal and social consequences of any medium—that is, of any extension of ourselves—result from the new scale that is introduced into our affairs by each extension of ourselves, or by any new technology. . . . The instance of the electric light may prove illuminating in this connection. The electric light is pure information. It is a medium without a message, as it were, unless it is used to spell out some verbal ad or name. This fact, characteristic of all media, means that the "content" of any medium is always another medium. The content of writing is speech, just as the written word is the content of print, and print is the content of the telegraph. If it is asked, "What is the content of speech?," it is necessary to say, "It is an actual process of thought, which is itself nonverbal." An abstract painting represents direct manifestation of creative thought processes as they might appear in computer designs. What we are considering here, however, are the psychic or social consequences of the designs or patterns as they amplify or accelerate existing processes. For the "message" of any medium or technology is the change of scale or pace or pattern that it introduces into human affairs.

In the new electronic culture as McLuhan depicted it, education became not so much a matter of transmitting information or knowledge as a training of the sensibilities to discern large patterns and processes, to seek and find wholes. Beyond that, since the principal business of the electronic world consisted in the movement and process-

50. Herbert Marshall McLuhan, *The Mechanical Bride: A Folklore of Industrial Man* (New York: The Vanguard Press, 1951), pp. v, 72.

ing of information, the classroom shrank immeasurably in power and significance as the entire global village became the primary teacher.[51]

Just as William James's conception of active mind had set James apart from Herbert Spencer, so did Gilbert Seldes's faith in an intelligent community set him apart from Marshall McLuhan. That said, however, there were also striking resemblances between McLuhan's cosmology and Lewis Mumford's. For both men, the organic unity of the medieval world had been shattered by the centrifugal force of the modern world, and with it the integrity of the individual psyche; and, for both men, the great need of contemporary life was the re-creation of wholeness. In Mumford's writing, the artistic vision held the key to that wholeness; in McLuhan's, the electronic revolution necessitated it and the choice was left to individual societies as to whether they would acquiesce in the drift into totalitarianism or work assiduously toward a human world order (one always wondered in reading McLuhan whether the bleakness of George Orwell's *1984* was predetermined in any case). In both instances, the knowledge of most worth was artistic knowledge and it would make the creation and appreciation of that knowledge the leading business of everyday life.

McLuhan and Mumford were both widely read during the 1960's and early 1970's, particularly by those disillusioned with what they saw as the technocratic character of American culture, though Mumford enjoyed nothing approaching the vogue of McLuhan. Indeed, for a time McLuhan rose to a popularity rarely enjoyed by an academic critic; he became a hero of the popular culture and the foremost expounder—and defender—of its techniques and values. His celebration of the "new electronic technology that extends our senses and nerves in a global embrace" made him a prophet of the television industry and especially its advertisers—TV favored paperbacks, Zen, and small cars, he told them. And his aphorisms about TV being "the Bauhaus program of design and living, or the Montessori educational strategy, given total technological extension and commercial sponsorship," became conversation pieces on the cocktail party circuit. They also brought him an unending stream of lecture invitations, and the kind of controversy that inevitably enhances popularity. It was a popularity that proved ephemeral, however; by the early 1980's McLuhan was far less widely read and well regarded. But there re-

51. Marshall McLuhan, *The Gutenberg Galaxy: The Making of Typographic Man* (Toronto: University of Toronto Press, 1962), p. 31, and *Understanding Media: The Extensions of Man* (New York: McGraw-Hill Book Company, 1964), pp. 7–8.

mained a core of truth and incisiveness in his analysis that continued to illuminate discussions of educational affairs, especially as these pertained to the sweeping social and intellectual effects of the electronic media of communication.[52]

V

That late-twentieth-century commentators as different as Gilbert Seldes and Marshall McLuhan should have found insight in the writings of Harold A. Innis is worthy of note. In an earlier time, a cultural critic like Charles W. Eliot could discuss the nature and value of knowledge without specifying the scholarly theories and standards of measurement upon which his views were based; by the 1950's, that was becoming less and less possible, as scholars like Innis were beginning to develop special branches of the social sciences devoted to analyzing the nature, character, production, distribution, and social impact of knowledge. Interestingly, Innis had begun his career as an economist concerned with questions of industrial organization. Indeed, it was in connection with a projected history of the Canadian paper and pulp industry in the 1940's that he had redirected his reading and research toward the history of printing and journalism, and, more generally, communications. His *Empire and Communications*, which advanced his theory about changes in communications media altering the character of knowledge and the structure of power in societies over time, appeared in 1950, and *The Bias of Communication*, a series of papers further developing the theme, in 1951. Given that he had taken his doctorate at the University of Chicago at a time when the tradition of inquiry associated with Thorstein Veblen was still strong, Innis's intellectual odyssey was not surprising; but the fact is that he came at best obliquely to the study of how the character and distribution of knowledge shift over time and in the process transform society.

Much the same might be said of the economist Fritz Machlup. Born in Austria in 1902, Machlup had taken his doctorate at the University of Vienna in 1923 and had become a successful business-man in the Austrian paper industry when the rise of Hitler led him to migrate to the United States, where he launched an academic career, first at Harvard, and then, successively, at the University of Buffalo, Johns Hopkins University, Princeton University, and New York Uni-

52. McLuhan, *Understanding Media*, pp. 80, 325, 326, 322.

versity. His specialties were capital formation, international trade and finance, and the economics of monopoly and competition, subjects on which, between 1925 and 1962, he published a score of books in German, French, Italian, Spanish, and English. It was in connection with his studies of monopoly and competition that he had become interested in the economics of the patent system; it was in connection with the economics of the patent system that he had become interested in industrial research and development; and it was in the process of studying the economics of industrial research and development that his interests had broadened to embrace the entire system by which a society creates and distributes knowledge. The result was the publication in 1962 of a magisterial work entitled *The Production and Distribution of Knowledge in the United States.* A commitment to the elaboration and updating of the ideas and data associated with that study was destined to consume Machlup's interests and efforts until his death in 1983.

The Production and Distribution of Knowledge in the United States was one of the seminal studies of the 1960's, whose often unacknowledged influence continued to reverberate, not only through the study of economics, but through every domain of public and private policy making for education. Machlup was more than usually latitudinarian in the definitions he developed for his analysis. He defined the production of knowledge as not only the creation of "socially new knowledge" but also the conveying of old knowledge to formerly ignorant individuals, so that the production of knowledge included not only discovering, inventing, designing, and planning but also disseminating and communicating. After reviewing contemporary distinctions between knowledge and information (most of them kindred to Dewey's definition of information as knowledge learned from others), he decided to define knowledge as inclusive of the ordinary meanings of information. He distinguished among five classes of knowledge, depending on the relation of knowledge to the knower: practical knowledge, "useful in his work, his decisions, and actions," including professional knowledge, business knowledge, workman's knowledge, political knowledge, household knowledge, and other practical knowledge; intellectual knowledge, "satisfying his intellectual curiosity, regarded as part of a liberal education, humanistic and scientific learning, general culture"; small-talk and pastime knowledge, ranging from gossip to jokes to light entertainment; spiritual knowledge, "related to his religious knowledge of God and of the ways to the salvation of the soul"; and unwanted knowledge, usually accidentally acquired and aimlessly retained—Machlup argued that the last category was of interest to the economist because of the resources committed to conveying such knowledge throughout the society. Machlup then defined a broad range of knowledge producing industries and occupations, including education (in the home; on the job; in the church; in the armed forces; in schools, colleges, and universities; and in public libraries), research and development units and agencies, the media of communication (printing and publishing; photography and phonography; stage, podium, and screen; radio and television; advertising; telephone, telegraph, and postal service; and conventions); information machines (printing trades machinery; musical instruments; motion picture apparatus and equipment; telephone and telegraph equipment; signaling devices; measuring and controlling devices; typewriters; electronic computers; other office machines and parts); and information services (professional services; financial and business services; and governmental services). The sweep of the undertaking was breath-taking, and it conveyed more dramatically than any other analysis the extraordinary range of a modern society's apparatus for producing and distributing knowledge. More important here, Machlup's definition of education was broader than most; but when one recognized that didactic books, periodicals, films, and radio and television programs could educate, that physicians educated when they counseled their patients on prophylactic and therapeutic regimens, that conventions systematically arranged opportunities for instructive interchange—in effect, that education was inseparable from much that Machlup defined as the production and distribution of knowledge—the bearing of his undertaking on educational thought was inescapable.[53]

In the end, Machlup concluded that the United States in 1958 spent approximately $136 billion on the production and distribution of knowledge, with roughly 28 percent contributed by government, 31 percent by business, and 41 percent by consumers. He estimated further that the total constituted approximately 29 percent of the gross national product for the year; and he judged that the share of knowledge production and distribution in GNP had been increasing for some years and would continue to increase. Finally, and extremely important, he estimated that, of the final product, the "investment" part, that which would raise future productivity, was greater than the "consumption" part—in other words, that the burden, not merely of

53. Fritz Machlup, *The Production and Distribution of Knowledge in the United States* (Princeton: Princeton University Press, 1962), pp. 7, 8, 21, 22.

TABLE I

U.S. Expenditures on the Production and Distribution of Knowledge, 1958

Education	$ 60,194 million	(44.1%)
Research and development	10,990 "	(8.1%)
Media of communication	38,369 "	(28.1%)
Information machines	8,922 "	(6.5%)
Information services (incomplete)	17,961 "	(13.2%)
	$136,436 million	(100.0%)
The expenditures were made by		
Government	$ 37,968 million	(27.8%)
Business	42,198 "	(30.9%)
Consumers	56,270 "	(41.3%)
	$136,436 million	(100.0%)
The total is divided between		
Final product (investment or consumption)	$109,204 million	(80.0%)
Intermediate product (current cost)	27,232 "	(20.0%)
	$136,436 million	(100.0%)

what was defined as education and research and development, but of the entire enterprise of the production and distribution of knowledge was an investment that would contribute to continued economic growth.[54]

Machlup's treatise was published at the beginning of what proved to be an explosion of interest in the relation between education and economic development during and after the late 1950's. At the University of Chicago, Theodore W. Schultz and his colleagues, notably Gary S. Becker, produced a spate of articles and monographs on the idea of education as a capital investment in human beings and of the role of that investment in economic growth. At Princeton University, Machlup's colleagues W. Arthur Lewis and Frederick H. Harbison issued a steady flow of research on the role of education in human resource development. And, as the economics of education moved rapidly to the heart of the problematics of economics, individual scholars at a score of universities as well as at the National Bureau of Economic Research and in federal and state government agencies worked on particular aspects of the problem: Jacob Mincer at Columbia estimated the contribution of on-the-job training to the American economy; Edward F. Denison of the United States Bureau of Economic Analysis calculated the contribution of the advance of knowledge to economic growth; and Robert M. Solow of the Massa-

54. *Ibid.*, pp. 361–362. Reprinted by permission of Princeton University Press.

chusetts Institute of Technology calculated the contribution of technical progress to economic growth. Much of the work of the 1960's concentrated on the contributions of schooling and college and university attendance to economic development; later, during the 1970's, Becker, Mincer, and others began to focus on education in the family. And in 1979, Lewis and Schultz shared the Nobel Prize in Economics, in part for their work on the importance of investment in human beings as a major factor in economic growth and development.

Most of this work was highly technical and abstruse and therefore accessible at best to a small, if influential, scholarly audience. On occasion, a brief treatise like W. Arthur Lewis's *Education and Economic Development* (1964) or Frederick H. Harbison's *Human Resources as the Wealth of Nations* (1973) would synthesize the work for more general audiences; but even then the audiences were much like those William James reached with his more popular lectures—they comprised intellectuals in other fields and men and women of affairs. Nevertheless, the influence of the work was far-reaching, as the conception of the production and distribution of knowledge as a substantial factor in human resource development and, through human resource development, in economic growth, made its way into the policy documents of public and private agencies and eventually into legislation, appropriations measures, and public and private welfare, manpower, and education programs. Edward F. Denison's *The Sources of Economic Growth in the United States and the Alternatives Before Us* (1962) was prepared for and disseminated by the Committee for Economic Development, and Theodore W. Schultz's *The Economic Value of Education* (1963) was commissioned as a policy document by the Ford Foundation's Program in Economic Development and Administration. And the fact that the efforts of the Carnegie Commission on Higher Education and the Carnegie Council on Higher Education were presided over by a labor economist, Clark Kerr, left an unmistakable imprint on the documents the Commission and the Council produced and the policies they advocated. Domestically, Machlup's paradigm and its extensions undergirded federal aid programs in education during the 1960's and 1970's; and in foreign affairs, they encouraged a shift in aid programs from an earlier emphasis on industrialization and capital accumulation to a later emphasis on the education and training of the work force and an indigenous leadership, including teachers in every domain of what Machlup called the knowledge industries. In a sense, Machlup's paradigm and its extensions also lent new scientific validity and specificity to Lester Frank Ward's primordial faith in the efficacy of knowledge widely distributed, to John Dewey's deep-seated conviction that the content and character of culture itself needed to be democratized in a democratic society and connected with the world of everyday affairs, and to Marshall McLuhan's imaginative formulations concerning the role of information transfer and processing in the "global village." In addition, by establishing beyond a doubt the centrality of an unprecedented range of accessible knowledge in providing the quality of life to which the human beings of that world aspired, they profoundly illuminated the unprecedented responsibility of education in its manifold forms. As early as 1776, Adam Smith had stressed in *The Wealth of Nations* the role of "the acquired and useful abilities of all the inhabitants or members of the society" as one element of fixed capital. "The acquisition of such talents," Smith explained, "by the maintenance of the acquirer during his education, study, or apprenticeship, always costs a real expense, which is a capital fixed and realized, as it were, in his person. Those talents, as they make a part of his fortune, so do they likewise of that of the society to which he belongs." It remained for American economists of the twentieth century to develop that view and explore its profound significance for the world in which they lived.[55]

55. Adam Smith, *An Inquiry into the Nature and Causes of the Wealth of Nations* [1776], edited by Edward Cannan (New York: Random House, 1937), pp. 265–266.

Chapter 9

PLACES OF CULTURE

A museum is an educational institution, set up and kept in motion that it may help the members of its community to become happier, wiser and more effective. It can help them only if they use it. They can use it only if they know of it. And only when they know much about it can they get from it much help.

JOHN COTTON DANA

The autodidact remained a familiar figure on the American scene during the last decades of the nineteenth century and first decades of the twentieth—the man or woman with a common school education who read systematically over a lifetime. The better-known of the autodidacts are well remembered through their autobiographies—the inventor Thomas A. Edison, who was withdrawn from school after a few months and who, having been taught to read at home by his mother, read omnivorously all the rest of his life; the journalist Edward Bok, who learned English at a public school after coming to the United States at the age of six and who used his first earnings as an office boy at Western Union to buy a set of *Appleton's Cyclopedia of Biography*, thereby to embark upon a systematic program of lifetime reading; the writer Charlotte Perkins Gilman, who developed her feminist theories in part from her systematic study of the writings of Edward Bellamy and Lester Frank Ward; the novelist and lecturer Hamlin Garland, who began a program of self-instruction during the early 1880's, using John Richard Green's *A Short History of the English People* and the *Chambers's Cyclopaedia of English Literature*. True, one must bear in mind the fact that one of the enduring influences of Benjamin Franklin's *Autobiography* has been its encouragement to Americans to style their autobiographies as successful ventures in self-education. That said, however, the better-known autodidacts were representative of a significant group of Americans who actually

426

did obtain their education largely through purposive reading and reflection. Not all Americans were literate, of course, and not all Americans who were literate read books—some read nothing, some read newspapers and other periodicals, which were far more readily available and accessible than books, and those who did read books read them for a variety of purposes, from entertainment and diversion to study and self-improvement, and they read them in a variety of ways. People read alone and in family groups, in libraries, churches, schools, and colleges, and in YMCAs, women's clubs, and Chautauqua circles. Jane Addams read George Eliot's *Romola* to the first visitors to Hull House; the members of Nationalist Clubs read Edward Bellamy's *Looking Backward* together; the members of synagogues proceeded annually through the Pentateuch; and young men and women read the poetry of love to one another. Most of those who educated themselves read systematically in one way or another, but not all who read systematically educated themselves.

In one sense, since virtually any book can be used for instructional purposes, all authors, for better or for worse, are potentially educators. But publishers, in deciding what to print, in which style, and for what markets, play a central role in determining which authors shall actually have the opportunity to teach. Obviously, therefore, it was of considerable educational significance that, with the expansion of the population and the secular rise in literacy rates after the Civil War, both the number of publishers and the volume of publishing rapidly increased. The industry became increasingly concentrated in New York—by the early 1880's more than a score of the larger houses were located within walking distance of one another near Astor Place and dozens of others within a mile's radius—though significant clusters of publishing houses remained in Boston, Philadelphia, and Chicago. Roughly two thousand books were published in 1880, with the largest numbers of titles in the domains of fiction, juveniles, religion, biography, and education and language. The total rose fairly steadily to a peak of approximately thirteen thousand in 1910, then declined to a nadir of under six thousand in 1919, then rose during the 1920's, declined during the Depression, and rose rapidly after World War II. The leading categories shifted from time to time, with law tending to replace biography during the later 1880's and 1890's, and with philosophy, literature, science, and social science edging out fiction and juveniles during the first decades of the twentieth century.[1]

Publishers circulated their books through booksellers in the cities

1. John Tebbel, *A History of Book Publishing in the United States* (4 vols.; New York: R. R. Bowker, 1972–1981), II, 676.

and towns. In 1876 *Publishers Weekly* sponsored a contest open to subscribers and employees of subscribers—essentially publishers, booksellers, and their clerks—concerning what works should form the nucleus of a well-stocked bookstore, the prize going to the entry listing the greatest number of books agreed upon by the other contestants. The leading titles in the biography category were John Foster, *The Life of Charles Dickens;* Washington Irving, *The Life of George Washington;* James Boswell, *The Life of Samuel Johnson;* Plutarch, *Lives;* and Frederic W. Farrar, *The Life of Christ.* The leading titles in the fiction category, excluding works by Bulwer, Dickens, George Eliot, Scott, and Thackeray, which were assumed to belong on every list, were Charlotte Brontë, *Jane Eyre;* Dinah Maria Muloch, *John Halifax, Gentleman;* Mrs. Alexander (Annie F. Hector), *The Wooing O'T;* Augusta J. Evans, *St. Elmo;* and Blanche Willis Howard, *One Summer.* The leading works of reference, other than the Bible, were Webster's unabridged dictionary, Cruden's *Concordance of the Bible,* Lippincott's *Pronouncing Gazetteer,* and *Chambers's Encyclopaedia.* The contest did not go on to belles-lettres, though if it had the works of Emerson and Longfellow would surely have been among the leaders. Interestingly, not a single woman appeared among the contestants—bookselling was apparently a male occupation—but the five most mentioned works of fiction had all been written by women. Granted that the titles listed were eminently salable at the time, at least in the eyes of the booksellers who read *Publishers Weekly,* what is striking about the list as a whole is the overwhelmingly didactic character of the works. The biographies were meant to instruct through exemplary lives; the fiction was meant to instruct through plots that ended in the triumph of middle-class values (John Halifax, the orphan, made his way in the world through the sheer excellence of his character; Edna, the heroine of *St. Elmo,* not only married Sir Roger, the worldly sophisticate, but reformed him as well); and the reference works were meant to convey useful information. Clearly, then, not only textbooks and reference books, but most books remained didactic.

In part, of course, the Victorian conventions that bound authors, publishers, booksellers, and book buyers in a common sense of what was appropriate substance for books dictated this style—even books designed to divert and entertain were expected to have some redeeming moral value. But it was more than a matter of convention. Through much of the nineteenth century, and especially during its latter decades, outright censorship and suppression prevailed. Nathaniel Hawthorne's *The Scarlet Letter* was condemned in some communities and Walt Whitman's *Leaves of Grass* was condemned in others. Congress enacted legislation in 1842 prohibiting the importation of obscene goods into the United States, and in 1865 and 1872 prohibiting the circulation of obscene books and pamphlets through the mails; and New York State enacted legislation in 1868 outlawing obscene literature. Thereafter, the tempo of suppression increased, owing largely to the efforts of the evangelical Protestant crusader Anthony Comstock of New York City. Working with a YMCA group that became the Society for the Suppression of Vice, Comstock succeeded, first, in enforcing the New York law, and later, on March 7, 1873, in obtaining congressional passage of a strengthened version of the 1865 and 1872 legislation and in having himself appointed as the Post Office Department's special agent for the enforcement of the new law. Since obscenity was rarely clearly defined and since most of the leading publishing houses were controlled by men similar to those who controlled the Society for the Suppression of Vice—white, native-born Protestants—Comstockery, as George Bernard Shaw once labeled it, joined with convention to narrow the boundaries of what was considered publishable. Comstockery began to wane during the 1930's, with the landmark decision of Judge John M. Woolsey in the Federal District Court (S.D.) of New York on December 5, 1933, holding that James Joyce's *Ulysses* could not be declared obscene under the federal laws, and with the subsequent American publication of *Ulysses* by Random House. Even though censorship and suppression by no means vanished, the courts increasingly curtailed the role of government as censor, publishers became more and more venturesome, and community tastes broadened. As a result, the range and variety of legitimate publications expanded significantly. In due course, the market replaced the government as arbiter of what was appropriate in the literary domain.

The predominance of market factors led to continuing diversification in what was published and in the standards for judging the quality of what was published—the controversy between Gilbert Seldes and his opponents echoed through twentieth-century criticism. The Bible remained the all-time and continuing best seller, followed by cookbooks (*Better Homes and Gardens Cook Book*), detective and mystery books (Mickey Spillane and Erle Stanley Gardner), religious books (Charles Monroe Sheldon, *In His Steps;* Fulton Oursler, *The Greatest Story Ever Told*), juveniles (*Boy Scouts Handbook, Girl Scouts Handbook,* Little Golden Books), child-rearing books (Mrs. West, *Infant Care;* Benjamin Spock, *The Common Sense Book of Baby and Child Care*), and reference books (dictionaries; J. K. Lasser, *Your Income Tax*). The didactic theme remained strong, the vogue of Spillane notwithstanding, and publishers remained among the foremost distributors of educational materials. Moreover, market factors commonly combined with organizational technology to make the publishers' dissemination efforts more systematic and at the same time more profitable.

One of the earliest devices of the publishers developed in response to the challenge of the market was books about how to educate oneself through reading. Such counsel had been a staple of the handbooks on how to live directed to young men and women during the pre–Civil War era—William A. Alcott's *The Young Man's Guide* (1838) and *Letters to a Sister; or, Woman's Mission* (1849) were representative and continued to circulate well into the 1870's and 1880's. What emerged in the post–Civil War era, however, was the manual addressed wholly to the needs of the reader engaged in self-education. Two works of the 1880's are illustrative. In *Books and How to Use Them: Some Hints to Readers and Students* (1883), John C. Van Dyke, at the time assistant librarian of the Gardner A. Sage Library of the New Brunswick Theological Seminary and later a well-known art critic and president of the National Institute of Letters, began with the advice, "There is no easy method of obtaining knowledge. You can not distill it from your own individual and unaided thought; nor can it be obtained by observation, or gathered by experience alone. There is but one true way, and that is a hard, wearisome one; for it is only by comparison of your thought, observation, and experience, with the thoughts, observations, and experiences of many men, through the medium of books, that you are enabled to gain true wisdom." For those who were ready to embark upon the "hard, wearisome" journey, Van Dyke went on to provide counsel on how to read, when to read, where to read, and what to read. A final section counseled the advantages of cultivating the "good graces" of librarians. *Hints for Home Reading: A Series of Chapters on Books and Their Use* (1883) was a collection of essays that had appeared in the *Christian Union,* edited by Lyman Abbott. It too provided advice on how, when, where, and what to read; but it went beyond the Van Dyke manual in including several lists of suggestions for home libraries put together by the publishers' father, George Palmer Putnam, as well as advertisements on the endpapers of "Putnam's Handy-Book Series of Books for the Household," which included handbooks on everything from *How to Educate Yourself* to *How to Make a Living.* G. P. Putnam's Sons had provided not only a teacher for the autodidact (*Hints for Home Reading*) but a curriculum (the

Putnam lists) and curriculum materials (Putnam's Handy-Book Series) as well.[2]

George Palmer Putnam's lists, manifesting the cultural altruism of the nineteenth century, included works from a variety of publishers. It would take no great leap of marketing imagination for publishers of the twentieth century to conform their lists of recommended books to their lists of published books. However that may be, the genre of the *vade mecum* for the reader bent on self-education became a staple of American publishing. In fact, Mortimer J. Adler's *How to Read a Book* (1940) rose to the top of the best-seller list shortly after it appeared and remained there for more than a year (it was subsequently translated into French, Spanish, Swedish, German, and Italian). "Education is still open to all of us—whether we have had a schooling or in spite of it," Adler proclaimed in the Preface. "But only if we know how to read." Adler billed his book as an outline of "the steps one must take in learning how to read." Far more sophisticated than its predecessors, his treatise concentrated less on when and where to read than on what to read and how to read properly. For Adler, proper reading involved three stages: a first, in which the reader grasped the work as a whole; a second, in which the reader grasped the progress of the author's argument; and a third, in which the reader evaluated the argument and decided whether or not he or she was in agreement with it. Once a person had learned how to read properly, the only works worth reading were the classics, those that had stood the test of time. Adler concluded his treatise with two lists of books worth reading, one of the "great" books of the Western world, none of which had initially appeared after the nineteenth century, and the other of "good" books of the contemporary era. In due course, Adler joined with others in having a revised list of great books published in a uniform edition and in working out arrangements for groups of men and women to study the great books in local public libraries. Once again, there was a teacher, a curriculum, and a body of curriculum materials; and, in this instance, there was in addition an institutional setting and an organizational arrangement for self-education and mutual education via those materials—in effect, a system of education.[3]

The variety of such systems developed by American publishers during the late nineteenth and twentieth centuries was remarkable.

2. J. C. Van Dyke, *Books and How to Use Them: Some Hints to Readers and Students* (New York: Fords, Howard, and Hulbert, 1883), pp. 8, 133; and *Hints on Home Reading: A Series of Chapters on Books and Their Use* (New York: G. P. Putnam's Sons, 1883), Endpapers.

3. Mortimer J. Adler, *How to Read a Book: The Art of Getting a Liberal Education* (New York: Simon and Schuster, 1940), pp. viii (italics removed), 375.

The efforts of the Sunday school movement to create its own curriculum materials have already been described. The production of such material was a leading concern, not only of the American Sunday School Union, but also of such houses as the Methodist Book Concern in New York, the Presbyterian Board of Publications in Philadelphia, the Colored Methodist Episcopal Church publishing unit in Jackson, Tennessee, and the Deseret Sunday School Union in Salt Lake City, as well as some of the more general publishers like the Fleming H. Revell Company, which started in religious publishing but broadened, and Harper & Brothers, which started as a general publisher but carried on a substantial business in religious materials. The Sunday school movement also made wide use of the device of having the chapters of prospective books published initially as articles in periodicals and then in book form, as well as the technique of subscription publishing and bulk sales, frequently arranged by colporteurs, in which single or multiple copies of publications went automatically to subscribers through the mails. The Chautauqua movement employed similar techniques. Indeed, when the Chautauqua Literary and Scientific Circle was organized in 1878 as a "company of pledged readers," a "school at home, a school after school, a 'college' for one's own house" and the sponsors early encountered difficulty in supplying members with the required readings, John Heyl Vincent and his associates established the Chautauqua Press for the express purpose of ensuring that those works would be available in good time, in sufficient quantity, and at reasonable cost. Once again, subscriptions and bulk sales were commonly employed. In yet another domain, the United States Department of Agriculture collaborated with the United States Government Printing Office in developing similar techniques for the circulation of government publications on agriculture, horticulture, animal husbandry, and farm management to the nation's farm families. And, in yet another domain, the Grolier Society used similar arrangements, enhanced by advertising and canvassers, to finance the production and sale of reference works, especially *The Book of Knowledge,* which it marketed to families in parts as a well-illustrated children's encyclopedia. Such arrangements were further developed during the twentieth century by the publishers of magazines, who combined secondary uses of their substantive matter with secondary uses of their subscription lists to create and market popular teaching materials for the family—the several Time-Life nature, science, and history series of the 1970's were notable examples.[4]

4. John H. Vincent, *The Chautauqua Movement* (Boston: Chautauqua Press, 1886), pp. 73, 75.

One variant of the subscription plan was the book club, an arrangement that had precedents in some of the marketing arrangements of the American Tract Society during the nineteenth century as well as in the book guilds of the Weimar Republic that attempted to supply cheap editions of the classics to a war-weary and inflation-impoverished German population. The modern model was the Book-of-the-Month Club, organized by Harry Scherman, Robert K. Haas, and others in 1926 as a subscription sales operation that would have a board of literary experts and celebrities select one title each month from the lists of recently published or about-to-be-published works and send that book to the subscribers at a special price made possible by bulk printing and purchasing. The first selection, sent to 4,750 initial members, was Sylvia Townsend Warner's *Lolly Willowes;* the second, sent to 12,500 members, was T. S. Stribling's *Teeftallow;* the third, sent to 13,500 members, was Esther Forbes's *O Genteel Lady.* Later, book "dividends" and "alternative selections" were made available. The principles, however, were early clear: selection by experts; easy purchase by members; and the advantages of bulk acquisition and repeat sales for the organizers. Once again, albeit without a curriculum and with a less strident didacticism in evidence, there were teachers in the form of literary experts who did the choosing, and there were curriculum materials. The idea spread like wildfire. The Literary Guild was launched in 1927, along many of the same lines. And soon after there came the Religious Book Club, the Catholic Book Club, the Children's Book Club, the Free Thought Book of the Month Club, the Crime Club, the Detective Story Club, the Book League of America, the Business Book Club, the Scientific Book Club, and the Early Years Book Club. Like subscription selling in general, the club arrangement continued with a variety of twists and refinements into the 1970's and 1980's, in the process coming to include new educational media, like long-playing records and cassette tapes, as they appeared.

The years following World War II were a boom period for American publishing. The industry grew rapidly but underwent marked transformation. On the one hand, firms that had long been independent and family owned went public, and, having gone public, frequently ended up in mergers with other publishing firms and, beyond that, as components of diversified corporate conglomerates in which the "bottom line" or profitability became ever more important. On the other hand, publishing remained a relatively accessible industry; anyone who wanted to publish a book could do so via the so-called vanity presses with a relatively small capital investment, and hundreds of individuals and groups did so. "The essence of publishing is pure entrepreneurship," observed Dan Lacy, the managing director of the American Book Publishers' Council in 1963. Publishing proceeded on many levels and with many purposes in mind, but there could be no denying the essential role of profits in the enterprise. And, while the open market of American publishing made it possible for the autodidact to choose from among an astonishing variety of "curriculum materials," that variety was not endless. The market too exerted its constraints, kindred in some respects to convention and Comstockery, but different in others. The *avant-garde* book that had not yet found its prospective audience, the traditional book that was "out of style," the arcane book that appealed to a narrow public—these and others like them had difficulty getting published in the 1970's and 1980's. And, as the price of books rose steadily, book ownership became more and more a luxury. Comstockery had weakened considerably, though it was by no means dead; and taste had broadened immeasurably; but the reader bent on self-education still found limitations, however free the market of ideas had become.[5]

II

The tradition of self-education combined with the tradition of voluntary association to produce an infinite variety of groups within which men and women pursued knowledge in post–Civil War America. People not only read books and attended lectures together in libraries and churches, YMCAs and women's clubs, Chautauqua circles and social settlements, scientific academies and learned societies, they also discussed those books and lectures and in the process of sharing knowledge often contributed to its advancement. The records of the Chautauqua Literary and Scientific Circle are replete with instances. John Heyl Vincent created the CLSC in 1878 as a systematic program of home reading organized and overseen by the leadership of the central Chautauqua. The program as Vincent described it was designed "to promote habits of reading and study in nature, art, science, and in secular and sacred literature, in connection with the routine of daily life (especially among those whose educational advantages have been limited), so as to secure to them the college student's general outlook upon the world and life, and to develop the habit of close, connected, persistent thinking." It was intended to encourage study

5. Dan Lacy, "The Economics of Publishing, or Adam Smith and Literature," *Daedalus*, XCII (1963), 44.

"by text-books which shall be indicated; by local circles for mutual help and encouragement in such studies; by summer courses of lectures and 'students' sessions' at Chautauqua; and by written reports and examinations." It was designed to proceed over four years, according to a specified reading list that during the 1880's included such standard popular works as John Richard Green's *A Short History of the English People,* Charles Merivale's *A General History of Rome,* Henry White Warren's *Recreations in Astronomy, with Directions for Practical Experiments and Telescopic Work,* and J. Dorman Steele's *Fourteen Weeks in Human Physiology,* and during a later period added such works as Richard T. Ely's *An Introduction to Political Economy* and *The Strength and Weakness of Socialism,* Jane Addams's *Twenty Years at Hull-House,* and *The Autobiography of Lincoln Steffens.* In addition, the list stipulated specially prepared CLSC textbooks published by the Chautauqua Press that ranged in character from a collection of lengthy excerpts from James Bryce's *The American Commonwealth* issued under a new title, *Social Institutions of the United States,* to a tract called *Good Manners: A Few Hints about Behavior.* The chief innovations in Vincent's plan, which he patently drew from his experience in the Sunday school movement, were the local circles for mutual help and encouragement and a monthly publication called the *Chautauquan,* which was designed to assist both solitary readers and the study circles with texts of some of the required readings, various sorts of background material, hints toward more effective study, questions for contemplation and discussion, and news of readers and circles around the country. Those who completed the four-year course received a diploma at a special "Recognition Day" ceremony held in connection with the annual summer Chautauqua assembly in upstate New York.[6]

Over 8,000 men and women enrolled in the Circle during the first year, and 1,718 of them received diplomas four years later, with over 800 actually attending the Recognition Day ceremonies. The enrollment rose to almost 200,000 during the early 1890's and to over 300,000 by 1918, after which it declined in the face of competition from the new popular media of communication. John F. Noffsinger estimated in 1926 that during the first two decades of the venture some 10,000 local circles sprang up, a quarter in villages of less than 500 in population and a half in communities between 500 and 3,500 in population.[7]

6. Vincent, *Chautauqua Movement,* p. 75.
7. *Ibid.,* p. 112; Arthur Eugene Bestor, Jr., *Chautauqua Publications: An Historical and Bibliographical Guide* (Chautauqua, N.Y.: Chautauqua Press, 1934), p. 12; and John S. Noff-

The circles included an extraordinary range of individuals—college graduates and those with only a year or two of schooling; physicians, lawyers, ministers, teachers, bookkeepers, tradespeople, housewives, and servants; individuals professing every religious creed and none; teen-agers and octogenarians. There was a Chickasaw Circle in the Indian Territory during the 1880's and a Look Forward Circle in the Nebraska Penitentiary during the 1890's. Since most of the circles were in smaller communities, they often constituted the only adult group beyond the church specifically dedicated to cultural purposes. And, as the participants shared their knowledge, interests, and interpretations of the books they read, in living rooms, churches, and later in libraries, a remarkable variety of educational outcomes ensued. A circle in Lewiston, Maine, purchased a telescope and studied the craters of the moon; a circle in Burlington, Iowa, studied chemistry under the tutelage of a local physician; a circle in Garrison, Iowa, sponsored classical evenings with readings and dramatic presentations; and a circle in Cincinnati not only proceeded in German since a number of the members could not read English, but also arranged cultural programs at which members presented their own papers, poems, and readings. Many a circle began with reading and soon became the nucleus of a local women's club or civic organization. And there was no knowing the number of individual cases in which the CLSC activities contributed to careers in writing, teaching, or journalism.[8]

Somewhat more spontaneous and less formal exchanges of knowledge occurred in the work of the social settlement. There, the goal of the residents was not only, in Jane Addams's words, "to share the race life, and to bring as much as possible of social energy and the accumulation of civilization to those portions of the race which have little," but also to deepen the knowledge of the already well educated, first, by enriching it with the contributions of people from other ethnic, social, and religious traditions, and second, by testing it in a concerted effort to improve the living conditions of the poor. Addams and Starr may have begun in 1889 by reading George Eliot *to* the first visitors from the neighborhood, but they and their associates soon went beyond that to study Dante *with* their neighbors and eventually moved on to develop the sort of reciprocal interpretation that was

singer, *Correspondence Schools, Lyceums, Chautauquas* (New York: The Macmillan Company, 1926), p. 109.

8. Bestor, Jr., *Chautauqua Publications*, p. 12; and Noffsinger, *Correspondence Schools, Lyceums, Chautauquas*, p. 109.

essential to the purpose of the Hull House Labor Museum. The extension of knowledge derived from such exchange was more than a matter of cumulation; it involved a transformation in the very nature of knowledge and in the idea of what constituted worthwhile knowledge.[9]

Other instances of the mutual sharing of knowledge occurred in the development of social and political movements. The local lodges of the Farmers' Alliances during the 1880's and 1890's, for example, ordinarily named one among their members to the office of "lecturer" and charged him with the responsibility of suggesting subjects for systematic discussion and obtaining materials to serve as the bases for that discussion. Many of the lodges collected small circulating libraries that included such works as Edward Bellamy's *Looking Backward,* Ignatius Donnelly's *Caesar's Column,* Terrence V. Powderly's *Thirty Years of Labor,* William A. Peffer's *The Farmer's Side,* and James B. Weaver's *A Call to Action.* Alliance papers like Jay Burrows's *Alliance* (later the *Farmers' Alliance*) carried discussion questions addressed to these and similar books, and indeed the editors saw themselves and were seen by others as leaders of broad public education, "not only in matters relating to agriculture, but also in subjects of political and economic science." Similar educational components marked the development of the union movement and the Socialist movement. Eugene Victor Debs helped organize a lodge of the Brotherhood of Locomotive Firemen in Terre Haute, Indiana, during the 1870's and then served as national secretary and treasurer of the Brotherhood and editor of the *Firemen's Magazine* from 1880 to 1892, playing much the same educational role as Burrows in the Alliance. And Morris Hillquit undertook his first systematic study of the Socialist literature as a clerk in the office of the Socialist Labor Party where, amid continuing debates on that literature, he also assisted in publishing the *People,* the official organ of the party—thereby continuing his own education at the same time that he began to educate others. In all of this, knowledge was not only transmitted, it was also transformed, as Americans worked out their own distinctive versions of populism, socialism, and unionism.[10]

At a more sophisticated, less popular level, the St. Louis Philosophical Society played a similar role in the education of its partici-

9. Jane Addams, "The Subjective Necessity for Social Settlements" [1892], in Christopher Lasch, ed., *The Social Thought of Jane Addams* (Indianapolis: The Bobbs-Merrill Company, 1965), p. 29.

10. C. S. Walker, "The Farmers' Movement," *Annals of the American Academy of Political and Social Science,* IV (1894), 793–794.

pants. Not only did the members systematically read, study, translate, and discuss the writings of Hegel and Kant—recall that they started the *Journal for Speculative Philosophy* and with it made the Philosophical Society a center for the international exchange of philosophical ideas; they also developed a characteristically American Hegelianism that was an important philosophical school in its own right and exercised a profound influence on American education. In addition to the Philosophical Society, St. Louis also boasted an Academy of Science, established in 1856. Members of the Academy reported on new species of natural history objects found in the environs; they heard lectures by the state geologists of Missouri, Kansas, and Illinois on the rock formations of the region; they exchanged notes and opinions on recent publications; they collected books for the Academy's library and specimens for the Academy's museum; and they published a series of *Transactions* that appeared continuously for more than a century. Like its counterparts in Cincinnati, Cleveland, Louisville, Milwaukee, and Chicago, the St. Louis Academy reflected the boosterism that led many a Midwestern city to aspire to become the Athens of America, but it also contributed significantly to a basic understanding of the geology and natural history of the Midwest.

Such local associations, along with the colleges and universities of the time, were the "habitats of knowledge"—the phrase is Daniel J. Boorstin's—of late-nineteenth-century America, and they were legion. They tended in their membership and activities to blur the lines between amateurs and professionals, teachers and learners, theoreticians and practitioners, disseminators of existing knowledge and producers of new knowledge—these lines would harden toward the end of the century as inquiry in the sciences became more specialized and taste in the arts and humanities more rigidly defined. And, whatever the range of their activities, they tended also to be centers for the preservation and dissemination of knowledge insofar as they almost always incorporated libraries and occasionally museums as well. At the very least they were critically important vehicles for the education of their members and they often reached beyond their membership to a larger public through their programs of lectures and discussions and their collections of books and specimens—it was partly a quest for financial support and partly an expression of a widely felt social responsibility to diffuse knowledge and uplift taste. In the process, the associations served as important vehicles of public education.[11]

11. Daniel J. Boorstin, "Universities in the Republic of Letters," *Perspectives in American History*, I (1967), 377.

As cities burgeoned during the later nineteenth century, cultural institutions multiplied in number and expanded in size at the same time that they manifested the same more general tendencies toward consolidation, on the one hand, and specialization, on the other, that marked other domains of the emerging urban, industrial society. One could see the process in St. Louis, where during the 1870's there was a conspicuous overlap between the leadership of the Academy of Science and the leadership of the Medical Society of Missouri, the St. Louis Philosophical Society, the St. Louis Library Association, the Mechanics Institute, the Franklin Society (a lyceum with a literary bent), the public schools, the O'Fallon Polytechnic Institute, the Manual Training School, and Washington University. The Reverend William Greenleaf Eliot, who for all intents and purposes was the founder of Washington University, spoke for many when, soon after migrating west from New England, he observed that it was the responsibility of those who valued literature and religion and sensed the importance of education and morality to come forward and establish institutions by which public opinion might be elevated and public taste purified. Interestingly, too, though Washington University scientists published frequently in the *Transactions* of the Academy of Science during the 1860's and 1870's, they began to send their work to the more specialized national journals during the 1880's and 1890's, leaving their places in the *Transactions* to be taken increasingly by amateurs, secondary-school teachers, and graduate students—it was a process manifest in all of the other major cities as academies were either taken over and transformed by professional scholars or deserted by the professionals and left to amateurs and aspiring professionals.

In Chicago, as Helen Lefkowitz Horowitz has noted, a range of institutions quite similar to those of its archrival, St. Louis, had appeared by the 1870's. The Chicago Public Library was established after the Great Fire of 1871, to receive the books that had been sent from England and a number of other European nations. The Chicago Academy of Sciences had been founded the same year as the one in St. Louis by the same sorts of individuals, interested in the same kinds of programs. Although it was distinguished from its St. Louis counterpart by the presence of a paid professional scientist as secretary and curator, it also published a continuing series of *Transactions;* it also held regular meetings at which members and visitors discussed the flora, fauna, and geological phenomena of the region, with a bit more emphasis on fish, given Chicago's location on Lake Michigan; and it also maintained a museum, which was destroyed in the Great Fire but resuscitated on a small scale in 1894, as an institution of popular science education. The Athenaeum had been established in 1871 as a vehicle to bring lectures and courses to workingpeople. In addition, a host of clubs, associations, and societies of various sorts organized the artistic, musical, and cultural life of the city along ethnic (the Orpheus Gesangverein), religious (the YMCA), class (the Chicago Biennial Musical Festival Association), and professional (the Chicago Academy of Design) lines.[12]

Then, beginning in 1879, in what Horowitz has called a burst of "cultural philanthropy," grand metropolitan institutions were established to promote an implicitly elite-defined structure for the community. Under the leadership of Charles L. Hutchinson, a leading banker and businessman, a generation of wealthy Chicagoans transformed the Chicago Academy of Design, which had originally been organized by artists, into, first, the Chicago Academy of Fine Arts, and then, the Art Institute of Chicago, a great downtown museum dedicated to the highest standards of European painting and sculpture. In addition, using bequests from Walter Newberry and John Crerar, groups from essentially the same socioeconomic background created the Newberry Library and the Crerar Library as great downtown libraries dedicated to the highest standards of literature and book collecting. Further, with the munificent gifts of John D. Rockefeller, a board of trustees again representative of the same group created the University of Chicago. And finally, following upon the World Columbian Exposition of 1893, a similar board created the Field Columbian Museum to house the natural history exhibits that had been displayed at the Exposition. As Horowitz has persuasively argued, the elites that established and developed these institutions—elites joining well-to-do philanthropists with an emerging class of professional humanistic and scientific scholars—had a clear educational program in mind, one that envisioned the museums and libraries as great civilizing institutions that would place Chicago on a par with Renaissance Florence and contemporary London while also in the process taming the turbulent Chicago population during a period of ethnic, religious, class, and racial strife. In Matthew Arnold's formulation, they saw themselves as protagonists of "culture" who, by making available the best that had been thought and said in the world, would stave off the anarchy they perceived as just over the horizon. In culture at its best and highest,

12. Helen Lefkowitz Horowitz, *Culture & the City: Cultural Philanthropy in Chicago from the 1880s to 1917* (Lexington: University Press of Kentucky, 1976).

they saw the means of spanning the chasm that had grown up between the various segments of the population and of ultimately re-establishing community.[13]

In New York, too, a similar configuration of institutions was created by a similar elite for similar purposes. Their great efforts centered in the development of Central Park, reflecting Frederick Law Olmsted's vision of a beautiful, ordered environment in which the various segments of the city's population might mingle in harmonious relationship (Olmsted also designed Riverside Park and Morningside Park in New York, South Park in Chicago, and the Washington University campus in St. Louis); in the establishment of the American Museum of Natural History in 1869, the Metropolitan Museum of Art in 1870, and the New York Public Library in 1895 (as a consolidation of the extant Astor and Lenox Libraries and the contemplated library mandated by the will of the late Samuel G. Tilden); and in the transformation of Columbia College into a university. And they very much shared the Arnoldian vision of culture as a disciplining education for the turbulent urban populace.

In Washington, D.C., the presence of numerous scientists working in such government agencies as the Smithsonian Institution, the Library of Congress, the Bureau of American Ethnology, the Geological Survey, the Weather Bureau, the Naval Observatory, the National Zoological Park, the National Arboretum, and the various bureaus of the Department of Agriculture combined with Washington's special role as a capital city to make possible an extraordinarily lively scientific elite that centered in the American Association for the Advancement of Science, the Philosophical Society of Washington, the Anthropological Society of Washington, the National Academy of Sciences, the Washington Academy of Sciences, and the Cosmos Club.

One can discern similar phenomena with interesting variations in Boston, Philadelphia, and other cities. A number of circumstances made for the differences, including the fact that elites differed in character—Boston's Puritan upper class, as E. Digby Baltzell has argued, proved more uniform and more socially responsible during the later decades of the nineteenth century than Philadelphia's Quaker upper class; and Boston, with a long history and the oldest institution of higher learning in the United States, had a larger and more specialized intellectual community than Chicago during the 1880's and

13. *Ibid.*; and Matthew Arnold, *Culture and Anarchy* [1869], edited by J. Dover Wilson (Cambridge: Cambridge University Press, 1932), p. 6 and *passim*.

1890's. Cities also differed in the size and diversity of their populations—Washington and St. Louis had smaller and less varied minority communities than Chicago, and the vigor and quality of local institutions of higher learning varied—the University of Chicago was newer and smaller in the 1890's than Harvard, and the University of Pennsylvania was older and more fully developed in the 1890's than Columbian University—later the George Washington University. And what might loosely be described as different local histories also played a part, for example, the fact that Philadelphia hosted an international exposition in 1876, Chicago, in 1893, and St. Louis, in 1904, with Washington and Boston not having hosted one.[14]

The philosophy of culture that these various urban elites acted upon during the last third of the nineteenth century has been described as late American Victorian. It was essentially British-American in character, marking a "climactic era of modernization" for the English-speaking peoples, and essentially Protestant and middle-class. It was highly self-conscious, rooted in the culture of evangelicism but receptive to the new sciences, and much committed to individual and social improvement. It tended to be cosmopolitan rather than parochial, national rather than regional or local, and interdenominationally moralistic rather than narrowly sectarian. It celebrated culture over materialism, discipline over liberty, rationality over the emotions, excellence over equality, and nonpartisan reform over partisan politics. It preached the virtue of art but made certain that art would serve the cause of virtue. And it was relentlessly didactic, drawing upon every technique of persuasion—in effect, every available means of education—to convey its outlook upon the world and thereby enforce its standards and patterns of behavior. It was a culture that dominated many institutions of late-nineteenth-century American education—schools, colleges, and universities, most certainly, and with them many of the publishing houses, social settlements, women's clubs, libraries and museums, and associations for the advancement of the arts and sciences.[15]

A number of points must be made about this late Victorian culture and its influence upon American education writ large. For one thing, it was a remarkably coherent culture but there were strains and con-

14. E. Digby Baltzell, *Puritan Boston and Quaker Philadelphia: Two Protestant Ethics and the Spirit of Class Authority and Leadership* (New York: The Free Press, 1979).

15. Daniel Walker Howe, "American Victorianism as a Culture," *American Quarterly*, XXVII (1975), 512.

flicts within it. Jane Addams learned about the role of art in narrowing
the gap between social classes from reading the Victorian novelist
Walter Besant and the Victorian critic John Ruskin and from observing the work of the Victorian cleric Samuel A. Barnett at Toynbee
Hall, but her efforts at Hull House placed her a world apart from her
friend Charles Hutchinson on the matter of how art should be displayed, enjoyed, criticized, and experienced. Hutchinson located the
Art Institute downtown and followed the cosmopolitan standards of
Renaissance painting and sculpture in attempting to civilize and uplift
the community; Addams located the Hull House Labor Museum in an
immigrant neighborhood and sought to follow the indigenous standards of immigrant craftspeople in attempting to civilize and uplift the
community. Hutchinson and Addams were both Victorians, but their
Victorianism led them in profoundly different educational directions.

Beyond the matter of internal conflicts, it is important to bear in
mind that, even though late Victorian culture was the dominant culture of its time, it was not the sole culture. St. Louis included a large
German community, whose cultural life revolved around organizations like the *Bestrebung,* a *Turnverein* that sponsored not only physical
culture activities but also lecture courses and dramatic presentations,
the *Philodramatische Gesellschaft,* an amateur theatrical group, the *Lese-
verein,* a library and reading room, and newspapers like the *Anzeiger des
Westens* and the *Westliche Post.* Chicago included large ethnoreligious
subcommunities whose configurations of culture and education have
already been discussed, and Washington also included a substantial
black community whose cultural life revolved around the black
churches as well as more elite associations like the Medico-Chirurgical
Society and the Bethel Literary and Historical Society, newspapers
like the *Bee* and the *Colored American,* and, particularly for teachers,
Howard University. More than other ethnic groups, the Germans
contributed significantly to late American Victorianism—the work of
the St. Louis Philosophical Society is a leading example; and certainly
as much as any group the black middle class created its own version
of late American Victorianism—the culture of Washington's black
intelligentsia is a leading example. Such cross-fertilization notwithstanding, the fact remains that many ethnic, religious, and racial
groups in late-nineteenth-century America maintained their own distinctive cultures centered in their own distinctive configurations of
educative institutions.

Finally, late Victorian culture reinforced the metropolitanizing trend inherent in the geographic, demographic, and technological facts of turn-of-the-century American life. The cultural philanthropists of Chicago and other cities hoped to recreate in the United States institutions on a par with the British Museum, the Louvre, and the Uffizi Gallery; and, in an extraordinarily short period of time, their wealth and determination enabled them to do so. One outcome was that the great metropolitan centers of culture they established in the United States were more oriented toward so-called world-class standards in art, music, and literature than toward indigenous standards, with the result that these centers failed to encourage the vernaculars of American cultural life. Beyond that, in accepting and promoting that which was world-class, these institutions encouraged a standardization of culture that had not been evident earlier, when cultural institutions were rooted essentially in localities. One could debate the merits of this trend toward more uniform standards, set in fewer and fewer centers of culture and increasingly in New York City; but there could be no mistaking the trend itself or its continuing significance for American education.

The values and ideals of late American Victorianism persisted well into the twentieth century, indeed, in some quarters right down to the 1980's; but they also came under increasing criticism after the 1890's, first, from social scientists and social philosophers who attacked their ethnic, religious, and racial ethnocentrism; then, from the artists and writers who answered the calls for innovation from such critics as Harriet Monroe, Robert Henri, Van Wyck Brooks, and Alfred Stieglitz; and later, from a growing segment of the generation that came of age during and after World War I. By the 1920's, the assault on Victorianism was direct, concerted, and widespread; as demystified by novelists like Sinclair Lewis and Theodore Dreiser and social scientists like Robert S. and Helen M. Lynd and Margaret Mead, Victorianism came increasingly to be seen as materialist, repressive, conformist, and fearful—genteel and inhibited at its best, hypocritical at its worst. Yet, much like the pre–Civil War evangelical movement, late American Victorianism left in its wake a congeries of characteristic cultural institutions, notably libraries and museums, that continued to carry on their educative functions well after the values that had been instrumental in their creation had begun to wane. Over time, and particularly after World War I, those institutions became subject to many of the same popularizing tendencies that marked the contemporary schools and colleges.

III

There were some four thousand libraries with holdings of a thousand volumes or more in the United States by the mid-1890's, including the public community libraries of the twenty-nine states and the District of Columbia that had enacted enabling legislation by 1896 (they numbered roughly a thousand), the great endowed private libraries like the Newberry and the Crerar in Chicago, the Enoch Pratt in Baltimore, and the New York Public, the specialized business, professional, and scientific libraries that had grown up under the auspices of particular associations, mostly in the cities, and indeed the Library of Congress. They were marked by a wide range of institutional missions. Some saw themselves as "people's colleges" committed to the widest possible diffusion of knowledge; others, as "workshops" committed to placing their collections at the disposal of scholars and legislators; and still others, as "storehouses" committed to the preservation of the world's knowledge. For example, both the Chicago Public Library and the Newberry Library spoke of themselves as serving the public, but the Chicago Public Library did so by seeking to cater to the tastes of a wide variety of user groups, including immigrants who read only in foreign languages, and to facilitate access to its collections through hours that would enable every social class to use them, while the Newberry, though prepared to sponsor lecture series for the edification of the public, opened only during regular business hours and remained closed during evenings and Sundays, making it difficult for those who worked at jobs other than scholarship to avail themselves of its resources.[16]

The single most significant influence on library development during the period from 1898 to 1909 was Andrew Carnegie's benefaction of over $39 million to 1,408 communities for library buildings. Carnegie chose libraries as a philanthropic domain for several reasons, partly because he himself had profited from a local mechanics' library as a working boy in Pittsburgh, partly because the gift of a library building was one that could call for continued community commitment and participation through the maintenance of the library, but

16. Alexander Summers and Henderson Presnell, "Statistics of Libraries and Library Legislation in the United States," in U.S., Bureau of Education, *Report of the Commissioner of Education for the Year 1895–96* (2 vols.; Washington, D.C.: Government Printing Office, 1897), I, chaps. viii–ix; and John Y. Cole, "Storehouses and Workshops: American Libraries and the Uses of Knowledge," in Alexandra Oleson and John Voss, eds., *The Organization of Knowledge in Modern America, 1860–1920* (Baltimore: Johns Hopkins University Press, 1979), pp. 364–385.

probably mostly because libraries were institutions that could assist those who were already prepared to help themselves. Carnegie began in 1886 by giving close to $2 million for library buildings concentrated principally in cities and towns where the Carnegie industries were located. Then, encouraged by the results of those ventures, he opened the opportunity to the rest of the country. Until 1911, when the Carnegie Corporation of New York was created to carry on the Carnegie philanthropies, he managed the gifts himself, in collaboration with his secretary, James Bertram; after 1911, the Corporation, with Carnegie as president, Bertram as secretary, and a former Carnegie financial secretary named Robert Franks as treasurer, managed the gifts. Carnegie insisted that the libraries established with his gifts be community libraries, the property of all, open to all, and maintained by taxes. "I do not think," he wrote to a group of applicants in 1904, "that the community which is not willing to maintain a library had better possess it. It is only the feeling that the Library belongs to every citizen richest and poorest alike, that gives it a soul, as it were. The Library Buildings which I am giving are the property of all the members of the community which maintains them." Many of the communities receiving gifts used them to erect buildings for libraries already in existence and took the opportunity to place those libraries on a continuing basis of public support. Others, particularly in the South, used them to create libraries where none had existed. And indeed, coming as they did at a time when many states were enacting legislation establishing state public library programs overseen by state library boards, the Carnegie gifts also served more generally as a stimulus to library development.[17]

During the early 1920's, the acting president of the Carnegie Corporation, Henry S. Pritchett, commissioned a study by William S. Learned, a colleague of Pritchett's on the staff of the Carnegie Foundation for the Advancement of Teaching, on the role of the public library that was published in 1924 as *The American Public Library and the Diffusion of Knowledge*. In a terse, brilliantly argued monograph, Learned reviewed the history of "the diffusion of knowledge in the United States," pointing on the one hand to the new demands created by the rise of near-universal literacy and on the other hand to the rapid rise in the number of knowledge-generating agencies and institutes, reviewing the services in knowledge diffusion carried on by the

17. The quotation from Andrew Carnegie is given in George S. Bobinski, *Carnegie Libraries: Their History and Impact on American Library Development* (Chicago: American Library Association, 1968), p. 43.

print media, by films, by lectures, and by museums, setting forth the vision of a "community intelligence service" in each city and town across the country where a trained "intelligence personnel" would reorganize knowledge and make it available to the citizenry, and arguing, with examples from Newark, Cleveland, Indianapolis, and a dozen other cities, that the public library had the best chance of any extant institution for meeting this pressing educational need (one might note both the similarities and differences in Learned's intelligence services in localities and Walter Lippmann's roughly contemporary intelligence services in the federal government). Learned also pointed to the rapid growth of a library profession since the organization of the American Library Association in 1876 and the development of the first schools of library science and service at Columbia and Syracuse Universities in New York, the Drexel Institute in Philadelphia, and Simmons College in Boston, and indicated the requirement for large numbers of professionally trained, specialized librarians implicit in his proposals. The Corporation never proceeded on Learned's overall set of recommendations, though it did, characteristically, put large amounts of money into the development of professional schools of library service, particularly the one at the University of Chicago. And Learned's vision, of the public library as a "community intelligence service," came to dominate the rhetoric of library professionals during the next half-century, making them the single most articulate group pressing for the popularization of library services in both public and private libraries.[18]

It proved difficult to make libraries truly accessible, however, and even more difficult to attract a genuine cross-section of the public to avail themselves of library services once they had become accessible. In these two problems lay the difficulty of realizing Learned's vision. A major survey of library accessibility and use during the 1930's carried out by Louis R. Wilson, dean of the University of Chicago Library School, found that there were grave inequalities in the accessibility of libraries across the United States, from region to region (high in New England, New York, and California, low in the southeastern and southcentral states), between city and country (exceedingly low for urban and rural blacks), and grave inequalities in use even where libraries were accessible (registrants ranged from 2 percent in Mississippi to nearly a third of the inhabitants of California). Beyond the obvious sources of these inequalities in geography, economics, social status, and schooling among different segments of the population, Wilson commented mordantly on the attitudes of American librarians that kept the services of libraries from being fully used ("The attitude that 'book learning' is of little value to the Negro has given way but slowly").[19]

A decade later, another survey of library usage carried out by a team of social scientists under the leadership of Robert D. Leigh, dean of the Columbia University School of Library Service, came up with much the same result. Commenting on the "typical" public library in the "typical" American community, Bernard Berelson concluded in *The Library's Public* (1949), "Although most adults in the community like the public library, most of them do not use it. Like many other civic facilities in the town, the public library is used by only a minority of the population. In many respects they constitute a separate group within the town." Berelson went on to detail the extent to which libraries were used principally by children and young people in connection with their school work and by a small number of adults who tended to have more formal education than most. Once again, the reality was a far cry from Learned's vision.[20]

During the post–World War II era, with increased amounts of federal and state money available to them, librarians "reached out" to their clienteles in an effort to achieve a broader pattern of use. Collections were diversified on the basis of reader polls; adults were offered vocational counseling and job information; children were assisted with their homework; and special exhibits were arranged for Labor Day, Open School Week, Black History Month, and the International Year of the Child. There were storytelling circles for youngsters, great books discussion groups, adult education courses, and individual reading programs devised on the basis of individual interests and needs by librarians called learning consultants. But the patterns of differential access and usage persisted into the 1970's and 1980's. The libraries were popularized but they did not become truly popular. The nation of readers read, but they looked elsewhere for their "intelligence services"—to the popular media of communication and to a host of adult education courses provided by schools and colleges and increasingly by employers in workplaces.

19. Louis R. Wilson, *The Geography of Reading: A Study of the Distribution and Status of Libraries in the United States* (Chicago: University of Chicago Press, 1938), pp. 116, 423, 442.

20. Bernard Berelson, *The Library's Public* (New York: Columbia University Press, 1949), p. 124.

There were several hundred museums in the United States by the mid-1890's, the exact number depending on how one defined a museum and what minima one set with respect to size and support. There were the great museums of art, like the Philadelphia Museum of Art, the Metropolitan Museum of Art in New York, the Boston Museum of Fine Arts, and the Art Institute in Chicago, and there were the lesser art museums like the Rhode Island School of Design Museum of Art and the Wadsworth Atheneum in Hartford. There were the great museums of science, like the Academy of Natural Sciences in Philadelphia, the American Museum of Natural History in New York, the Field Columbian Museum in Chicago, and the National Museum of the Smithsonian Institution in Washington, and the lesser science museums like the Boston Society of Natural History Museum and the Medical Museum of the Armed Forces Institute of Pathology in Washington. There were also the museums of art and science associated with colleges and universities, like the Trumbull Gallery at Yale and the art galleries at Amherst, Princeton, Smith, and Wellesley and the Peabody Museum of Archeology and Ethnology and the Gray Museum of Comparative Zoology at Harvard. There were the museums of history, including large numbers of local institutions like the Essex Institute in Salem, Massachusetts, and the New York Historical Society and in addition many county and state institutions. And there were the "cabinets of curiosities" in local libraries, lyceums, and colleges, the historic houses like Washington's Headquarters at Newburgh, New York, and the more popular "museums" of the sort pioneered by P. T. Barnum in New York—too informal to be counted, and yet very much museums in the public mind.

Museums had been seen as educational institutions since the efforts of Pierre Eugène Du Simitière and Charles Willson Peale during the early national period. And many museums of the 1890's were founded and conducted with explicit educational purposes in mind— the Boston Society of Natural History Museum and the American Museum of Natural History were leading examples, as were the local and state historical societies and, of course, the museums associated with colleges and universities. But even more than libraries, the great museums of the period, however much they voiced the rhetoric of education, conceived of themselves as agencies of preservation, custodianship, research, and display rather than of diffusion, interpretation, and popularization. They were storehouses first, workshops second, and people's colleges a poor third if at all.

One can see this in the Boston Museum of Fine Arts, founded in 1870 and opened in 1876, which saw itself as an educational institution from the first. The act of the Massachusetts legislature creating the museum spoke of a corporation "for the purpose of erecting a museum for the preservation and exhibition of works of art, of making, maintaining, and exhibiting collections of such works, and of affording instruction in the fine arts." There was a more particular notion of education implicit in the efforts of the first trustees as well, voiced by one of the founders, Charles Callahan Perkins, in a report he prepared for the American Social Science Association in 1870. Perkins argued there that museums had a didactic as well as an aesthetic function, namely, to elevate the public taste in such ways as to improve morals, on the one hand, and the design of industrial products, on the other—the combination, incidentally, was quintessentially late American Victorian. Hence, although the museum actually operated a School of Drawing and Painting from its earliest years, it is clear that the trustees saw their educational responsibilities as extending far beyond the instruction of novices in the arts to the enlightenment of the public at large—a function they discharged, as did the trustees of the Newberry Library, simply by granting the public at large free admission two days a week. Another great museum of the period, the Metropolitan Museum in New York, institutionalized similar aspirations. The first director of the Metropolitan, Luigi Palma di Cesnola, likened the museum to an "object-library and lecture room" that would provide "silent but sure" instruction to the casual visitor at the same time that it furnished the serious student with "the most perfect means for reaching perfection in his special branch of study or art, and for attaining that end by the shortest and most unerring path." Once again, the museum was seen as having a didactic as well as an aesthetic function; it would educate simply by collecting, preserving, and displaying.[21]

However paradigmatic the purposes of the Museum of Fine Arts and the Metropolitan may have been, as the number of museums increased after 1895, so did the diversity of museum interests and emphases. There were approximately 600 in 1910 and some 2,500 when Laurence Vail Coleman published the first great survey of American museums in 1939 under the title *The Museum in America* (the

21. Massachusetts, *Acts and Resolves Passed by the General Court of Massachusetts,* 1870, p. 4; Charles C. Perkins, *Art Education in America* (Cambridge, Mass.: Printed for the American Social Science Association at the Riverside Press, 1870); and Luigi Palma di Cesnola, *An Address on the Practical Value of the American Museum* (Troy, N.Y.: Stowell Printing House, 1887), pp. 11–12.

study, like the great library surveys mentioned above, was supported by the Carnegie Corporation of New York). Most of the 2,500 museums had been established after World War I, and represented an astonishing range of specialties. There were children's museums like the Junior Recreation Museum of San Francisco, which included both science and art exhibits; trailside museums like the Todd Wild Life Sanctuary at Hog Island, Maine; company museums like the Studebaker Museum of Transportation at South Bend, Indiana; school-system museums like the Nature Exhibit of the Los Angeles Public Schools; planetariums like the Buhl Planetarium and Institute of Popular Science at Pittsburgh; anthropology museums like the Gila Pueblo at Globe, Arizona; and applied science museums like the New York Museum of Science and Industry. Individual gifts remained the prime source of support for a majority of the museums—both large benefactions and recurrent membership dues, though 722 of the 2,500 institutions Coleman surveyed were public and many of the others received public support on a partial or intermittent basis. An American Association of Museums was established in 1906—Coleman was the director when he did the Carnegie survey—for the purpose of representing museum workers and their interests. By the 1930's it had a membership of some 200 institutions and roughly a thousand museum professionals, trustees, and patrons. But, given the diverse world of museums, it was nowhere near as coherent or as unified in the philosophy it articulated, and nowhere near as powerful, as its supporters would have liked.

Coleman argued in his report that the great opportunity for American museums during the years ahead was to move toward a larger place in education. "Heretofore," he noted, "teaching has been largely the business of a few conventional agencies—the school and the college, in particular—but observers see that some of the less practical agencies, including museums, are now adjusting their methods and finding means of working in broader ways. Museums, like libraries, stand right in line for this responsibility because they are so much better grounded than most of the social, business, and governmental agencies now swinging into educational work, and also because they have collections that must inevitably be drawn upon for interpreting nature to man and man to himself."[22]

Coleman was able to offer this argument in 1939 because of a gradual but pronounced change of attitude toward the museum as an

22. Laurence Vail Coleman, *The Museum in America: A Critical Study* (3 vols.; Washington, D.C.: The American Association of Museums, 1939), III, 318–319.

educative institution, both within and without the museum world. Many, of course, continued to hew to more traditional positions concerning the nature of museum education. Benjamin Ives Gilman of the Boston Museum of Fine Arts had gone so far as to argue that an institution dedicated to the preservation and exhibition of works of fine arts was not an educational institution, either in essence or in its claims to consideration. "By no liberality in the definition of the word education," he had written shortly after the turn of the century, "can we reduce these two purposes, the artistic and the didactic, to one. They are mutually exclusive in scope, as they are distinct in value." But others, like John Cotton Dana of the Newark Museum, had begun to argue otherwise. Dana had come to the Newark Museum from a career in librarianship in which he had vigorously preached the development of genuine community libraries. "A collection of books gathered at public expense does not justify itself by the simple fact that it is," he had argued. "If a library be not a live educational institution it were better never established." Dana conceived of the museum, too, as a community institution, ideally rooted in the life of the community and dedicated to the people who lived there. "A museum is an educational institution," he observed in 1917, taking clear issue with Gilman, "set up and kept in motion that it may help the members of its community to become happier, wiser and more effective. It can help them only if they use it. They can use it only if they know of it. And only when they know much about it can they get from it much help." Further, Dana reasoned, people would neither know nor care about a museum unless its collections had a clear and direct connection with their lives. "What Newark men and women and children would welcome," he observed concerning the principles on which he had developed the museum collections there, "and would use to add to the interests of their lives and to the improvement and general efficiency of their business and work-a-day lives,—this we thought should be slowly and carefully discovered by study, observation and trial,—and so the museum would grow." In other words, to make a museum a center for popular education, it would have to be made interesting via the nature and organization of its contents.[23]

Dana was a pioneer but in many ways a maverick. When Francis Henry Taylor moved from the directorship of the Worcester Museum

23. Benjamin Ives Gilman, "On the Distinctive Purpose of Museums of Art," *Museums Journal,* III (1903–4), 216; John Cotton Dana, *Libraries: Addresses and Essays* (White Plains, N.Y.: H. W. Wilson Company, 1916), p. 8, *Museum,* I (May, 1917), 2, and *The New Museum* (Woodstock, Vt.: Elm Tree Press, 1917), p. 12.

of Art, where he had made the museum a community center for the entire Worcester region, to the directorship of the Metropolitan Museum of Art in 1939, the call for museums to become institutions of popular education gained a more attentive hearing. Taylor put the case directly in an address to the American Association of Museums shortly before going to the Metropolitan, in terms so striking that his remarks were reprinted in the *Atlantic Monthly:*

We have reached a critical period in American museums, as anyone confronted with a budget can tell too plainly. It is impossible for us to continue as we have done in the past. The public is no longer impressed with the museums and is frankly bored with their inability to serve it. The people have had their bellyful of prestige and spending of vast sums of tax-levied or tax-exempted funds for the interest and pleasure of the initiated few. We must stop imitating the Louvre and the Kaiser Friedrich and solve this purely American problem in a purely American way.[24]

Taylor understood the forces that were bringing Dana's and his own position to the forefront—budgets; and he understood, too, that the "purely American way" of attacking the problem was popularization. Museums increasingly needed public funds, in the form of tax money or membership dues from ever larger audiences. They were in the market for scarce resources, and it was only by bringing the diffusion of knowledge to parity with preservation and custodianship and by reaching out to persuade expanding audiences of their worth that they could prosper. For these reasons, Taylor quite literally transformed the Metropolitan Museum, and his successors, James Rorimer and Thomas Hoving, confirmed the transformation. The transformation was partial, however. The older standards of the collections were preserved, while the collections were aggressively publicized. Hence, it was in other museums across the country, particularly the local historical museums, that the transformation Dana had urged for community institutions was more fully achieved, particularly as federal assistance became available during the 1960's and 1970's from the United States Office of Education, the Institute of Museum Services, the National Endowment for the Arts, and the National Endowment for the Humanities. Two reports of the 1970's and 1980's, *Museums USA* (1974) and *Museums for a New Century* (1984), confirmed the shift in the museum world at large. "No longer elite preserves," wrote Hamish Maxwell, the chief executive officer of Philip Morris Incorpo-

24. Francis Henry Taylor, "Museums in a Changing World," *Atlantic Monthly*, CLXIV (1939), 790.

rated, a major sponsor of the latter report, "museums are now part of a popular movement in which more Americans attend cultural events than professional sports. But museums can do more, and this report shows how. . . . The report makes a persuasive case that museums can supplement universities as centers of research and teaching." The body of the report went on to provide dozens of instances of the triumph of the community museum as an institution of community education.[25]

Two brief postscripts are necessary to this account of triumphant popularization. The first is signaled by Maxwell's suggestion that museums could *supplement* the work of universities as centers of teaching and research. In fact, the universities had won an earlier triumph of their own in the allocation of educational functions at the turn of the century that is worthy of note. The configuration of education that emerged in Chicago may be taken as an example. The University of Chicago had joined with the Art Institute and the Field Columbian Museum in the effort to organize the cultural life of the city. What the museums soon found, however, was that to collaborate with the burgeoning university was to be all but subsumed by it—in fact, William Rainey Harper actually tried to incorporate the Art Institute and the Field Museum as departments of the university. The collaboration continued, but it was unequal from the outset, for the university had the certificatory power of the degree and, with it, the power to create and develop professions. It did not have to happen that way; the Art Institute and the Field Museum might well have expanded their formal teaching, petitioned the legislature for the right to grant degrees, and prevailed. But they did not, and their boards of trustees, overlapping as they did with the board of the university, informally acquiesced in the allocation of educational functions, as Harper and his successors built their own monopolies of certifying power in the domains of intellect and culture. Years later, those monopolies would be broken, not by cultural institutions like museums, but rather by workplace-related institutions like the General Motors Institute in Michigan, the Rand Graduate Institute of Policy Studies in California, and the Wang Institute of Graduate Studies in Massachusetts.

The second postscript concerns the educational role of international expositions in American life. In essence, they were temporary museums, though their displays often found permanent homes in institutions like the Field Museum and the New York Museum of

25. *Museums for a New Century: A Report of the Commission on Museums for a New Century* (Washington, D.C.: American Association of Museums, 1984), p. 9.

Science and Industry. And, as temporary museums, they sought to teach, not only certain specifics through their exhibits, their ceremonies, and their international congresses, but also certain larger cultural ideals. Daniel H. Burnham's design for the World Columbian Exposition in 1893, the so-called White City, presented an ideal Chicago to Chicagoans, Americans, and the world that was not different from the ideal Chicago embodied in Charles L. Hutchinson's Art Institute, and indeed the several foreign pavilions, conveying ideal national images, were not different in concept from the Hull House Labor Museum, except that they were designed by governments rather than workingpeople and they were seeking to create a world community rather than a neighborhood community. Later, the commissioners for the New York World's Fair of 1939 presented an ideal New York—they called it the World of Tomorrow—to New Yorkers, Americans, and the world that was not different from the ideal New York embodied in Henry Robinson Towne's Museum of Science and Industry, and again, the foreign exhibits conveyed the vision of a world community of nations—ironically, on the very eve of World War II. And several decades after that, the American pavilion at the Brussels World's Fair of 1958, where Vice President Richard M. Nixon and Premier Nikita S. Khrushchev of the USSR carried on their famous "kitchen debate," presented an ideal America to Americans and the people of the world that was not different from the ideal America embodied in the National Museum of the Smithsonian Institution as well as in a hundred local history and industry museums across the United States. International expositions were in their very nature metropolitan phenomena—their economics, their politics, and their ultimate reason for being made them prime vehicles for local and national boosterism; and, as metropolitan phenomena, they gathered and offered a common experience to audiences far more variegated and cosmopolitan than any permanent museum. The influence of the successful ones was immediate and powerful, not only on technology and architecture, but also on the social sentiments of those who attended. The stark realities of urban life always lay ominously behind the utopian displays of exposition, as in Depression Chicago of 1893 and in Depression New York of 1939, and the contrasts were unavoidable; and the Berlin and Cuba confrontations of the early 1960's lay just over the horizon from the Brussels Fair. But for moments, at least, visitors to the expositions could share a special sense of community, however evanescent it might have been.

IV

John Cotton Dana was not only an original thinker, he was also a man of commitment, who worked zealously to realize his vision of libraries and museums as educational centers with roots sunk deep into the communities they served. As a librarian at Denver (1889–1897) and at Springfield, Massachusetts (1898–1901), he lengthened library hours to make the collections truly accessible to the entire community. He removed the railings and the locked glass doors and placed both the circulating and the reference collections on open shelves. He culled the collections of rarely used materials, consigning them to annexes where they would remain on call, and filled their places with materials in greater demand. He diversified the collections, stocking foreign-language materials for immigrants, children's materials for the young, and specialized materials relating to the leading local trades and industries. And he involved the library in the work of the public and private schools, the churches and Sunday schools, the women's clubs, the literary, historical, and scientific societies, and the business and professional associations. Further, as a museum director and librarian at Newark (1901–1929), he collected flora, fauna, minerals, paintings, bookplates, prints, craftwork, schoolwork, and manufactured products drawn from the surrounding region—in effect, visual representations of the life and culture of the community. He lent collections of artifacts to other community institutions; he imported, created, and exported special exhibitions of every kind; he welcomed community clubs and societies that wished to use the museum's facilities and organized the museum's own clubs and societies to advance its educational programs; he organized an on-the-job training program for college graduates who wanted to go into museum work; and he advertised the programs at the museum tirelessly, so that the public would know what was available.

Dana's ideas were radically new when he first enunciated them, and even at the time of his death in 1929 the Newark Library and Museum were widely known as interesting but unusual institutions. The idea of reaching out to all classes of the community as a clientele for libraries and museums was slowly gaining recognition, but the idea of filling libraries and museums with materials reflecting and relating to the life of the surrounding community was still utter heresy—culture remained something removed, historic, and abstruse. Yet, with a rapidity Dana could not have anticipated in his lifetime, ideas such as his came into their own, as American intellectuals, shaken by the Depression, undertook a new search for a usable past marked much more by a critical appreciation of the American heritage than by a disdainful rejection of it. "We need to know what kind of firm ground other men, belonging to generations before us, have found to stand on," the young writer John Dos Passos observed. The literary expatriates who had gone to Europe to find themselves as well as true cosmopolitan values found instead, as had generations of young travelers before them, that they rediscovered America. By 1927, Louis Bromfield could write enthusiastically from Paris, "I feel more American than I have ever felt before." And as Malcolm Cowley would write of the whole generation in *Exile's Return,* "In Paris or Pamplona, writing, drinking, watching bull-fights or making love, they continued to desire a Kentucky hill cabin, a farmhouse in Iowa or Wisconsin, the Michigan woods, the blue Juniata, a country they had 'lost, ah lost,' as Thomas Wolfe kept saying; a home to which they couldn't go back." In an extraordinarily short time, a sea change occurred in the dominant values and sensibilities of the intellectual community, as the debunking of the 1920's gave way to the affirmations of the 1930's and as artists and writers began to find richness and worth in the common life they had earlier ridiculed. Nowhere was the shift better symbolized than in the work of Van Wyck Brooks, who in the 1920's had answered his own call for a usable past with studies of how the narrowness and superficiality of American culture had thwarted the full maturing of Mark Twain and Henry James and who in the 1930's produced a series of panegyrics to the abundance and quality of American culture, notably, *The Flowering of New England* (1936) and *New England Indian Summer* (1940).[26]

It was during this period of renewed cultural nationalism, of the rediscovery of America, so to speak, that the New Deal arts projects launched the federal government upon a large-scale venture in popular education that had profound and lasting effects on American life and thought. As has often been the case with federal education activities, those responsible for the program launched it on other grounds, in this instance, as a venture in public employment; but there is every evidence that they were well aware of the educational aspects of what they were undertaking and wholly conscious of the cultural choices they were making. The effort began with the Public Works of Art

26. John Dos Passos, *The Ground We Stand On: Some Examples from the History of a Political Creed* (New York: Harcourt, Brace and Company, 1941), p. 3; Louis Bromfield, "Expatriate—Vintage 1927," *Saturday Review of Literature,* III (March, 1927), 1; and Malcolm Cowley, *Exile's Return: A Literary Odyssey of the 1920's* (New York: The Viking Press, 1951), p. 9.

Project (PWAP) of the Treasury Department in 1933. George Biddle—who had gone to Groton and Harvard with Franklin Delano Roosevelt, who had abandoned the legal career for which he had prepared in favor of a career as an artist, and who had studied, among others, with Diego Rivera, a leader of the Mexican muralists who had covered the public buildings of Mexico City with depictions of the aspirations of the Mexican revolution—wrote to Roosevelt suggesting that American muralists be invited to decorate a public building under government auspices in order to exemplify the possibilities of a socially oriented public art. Roosevelt was taken with the idea and referred Biddle to Assistant Secretary of the Treasury Lawrence W. Robert, who was curator of public buildings. Robert informed Biddle that the new Department of Justice Building in Washington's federal triangle would be a possibility. Biddle lobbied for his proposal with Eleanor Roosevelt, Secretary of Labor Frances Perkins, Secretary of the Interior Harold L. Ickes, and Assistant Secretary of Agriculture Rexford G. Tugwell; he sought tentative commitments to work on such murals from Thomas Hart Benton, Reginald Marsh, Boardman Robinson, and others; and he made contact with another Treasury Department official, Edward Bruce, an expert on international monetary policy who had had for a time a quite successful career as a painter. Out of the effort, with funds allocated from Harry Hopkins's Civil Works Administration, came the Public Works of Art Project, through which over three thousand artists across the country produced some four hundred murals, thousands of oils, watercolors, and prints, hundreds of sculptures and drawings, and scores of craft objects ranging from batiks to pottery—all of them intended, in the words of PWAP directives, to provide a permanent record of the aspirations and achievements of the American people. Of all these renderings, it was the murals—in post offices, courthouses, and community centers—that quickly came to symbolize government art in the public mind. Many of them were actually painted cooperatively, with a leading artist planning the work and his collaborators assisting him in producing it—Grant Wood worked that way as an assistant professor of art at the University of Iowa and his colleagues received academic credit for their work, and in fact the group became so cohesive that when cuts came in the funds for the program they pooled their resources to stay together.

The Public Works of Art Project ended in April, 1934, when the funds from the Civil Works Administration ran out, and was succeeded by a Section of Painting and Sculpture in the Treasury Department (it was renamed the Section of Fine Arts in 1938 and then transferred to the Federal Works Agency in the 1939 reorganization of the executive branch). Under Bruce's direction, the Section continued to decorate public buildings, mostly post offices, with murals and occasionally with sculptures depicting the American scene. In a thousand communities, most of them without museums, art dealing with American life was thus brought to people whose only previous experience with art had often been limited to advertisements in newspapers and magazines and the stereotypical reproductions traditionally available as gifts. Beyond that, the PWAP, as one of the initial efforts of the Civil Works Administration, demonstrated the feasibility of the much broader program of government participation in the arts that was mounted through the Federal Emergency Relief Administration and the Works Progress Administration. Hopkins, who had been Roosevelt's state relief director when Roosevelt was governor of New York and whom Roosevelt appointed to head, first, the FERA (and CWA) and, then, the WPA, believed that work relief was superior to direct relief and that artists and writers were as much entitled to work relief as any other segment of the unemployed—indeed, he had put artists to work painting murals in settlement houses as part of New York's relief effort. Given the task of administering the New Deal's emergency relief effort during the winter of 1933–34, Hopkins not only responded to Biddle's request for the funds to launch the PWAP, he also put writers to work surveying local archives in Minnesota and interviewing ex-slaves in the Ohio Valley, and he put musicians and actors to work in New York and California presenting concerts and shows in schools, libraries, and hospitals. Finally, in the aftermath of Roosevelt's sweeping victories in the off-year elections of 1934, he helped persuade Roosevelt to organize and finance the Works Progress Administration to carry on useful work projects designed to provide maximum employment in localities across the country.

One small division of the WPA was the Federal Art Project, generally known as Federal Project No. 1, or Federal One, as the first of six projects within the WPA to aid educational, professional, and clerical workers. It comprised four units: the Federal Art Project, headed by Holger Cahill; the Federal Music Project, headed by Nicolai Sokoloff; the Federal Theatre Project, headed by Hallie Flanagan; and the Federal Writers' Project, headed by Henry G. Alsberg. Cahill was a self-educated Minnesotan who had worked at a series of menial jobs until he had moved to New York on the eve of World War I and settled into a career as a writer. He had attended Thorstein Veblen's lectures at the New School and John Dewey's lectures at Columbia; and in 1919 he had begun to study art seriously, working subsequently with John Cotton Dana at the Newark Museum and with Alfred H. Barr, Jr., at the Museum of Modern Art. Sokoloff, who had been born in Kiev, had attended the Yale School of Music, had concertized as a violinist in Europe and the United States, and had been the first conductor of the Cleveland Symphony Orchestra.

Flanagan had attended Grinnell College—she and Harry Hopkins had grown up in Grinnell and had gone to school and college a year apart—and, after the sudden death of her husband in 1919, she had persuaded the head of the English Department at Grinnell to permit her to offer a course in drama. Under the influence of George Pierce Baker of Harvard, with whom she had worked in 1923, she had developed the course into the Grinnell Experimental Theatre; and, after moving to Vassar College in 1925, she had been able to travel to Europe on a Guggenheim Fellowship and in particular to see how the Russian theater, under the leadership of Constantine Stanislavsky and his student Vsevelod Meierhold, had become an instrument of popular education in the aspirations of the Russian revolution. She was well aware of the distinction between education and propaganda, and later she would deplore the Stalinist policies that sent Stanislavsky and Meierhold into exile. But she gleaned from her experience in the USSR the commitment to a vital national American theater that would involve its audiences spiritually and physically and would touch on the substance of their lives, and she used the Vassar Experimental Theatre as the vehicle to develop her ideas. And Alsberg was a New Yorker who had attended Columbia College and the Columbia Law School and, like Biddle and Bruce, had abandoned the law, in his case for a career as a writer. As a foreign correspondent after World War I, he had come to know Prince Kropotkin, Alexander Berkman, and Emma Goldman and had collaborated with them on a number of projects; and, as a philosophical anarchist living in Greenwich Village, he had moved easily among the writers and artists who congregated there in search of aesthetic fulfillment. Hopkins's assistant Jacob Baker thought that Alsberg's acquaintance with a wide variety of creative individuals would be helpful in publicizing the work of the Civil Works Administration and he called Alsberg to Washington to work with the relief program for writers. Since he was already on the scene, it was an easy step to put him in charge of the Writers' Project.

Hopkins brought the four heads together for the first time in the spring of 1934, at Alsberg's home. President Roosevelt had spoken enthusiastically of cultural enrichment as part of the New Deal's broader commitment to social justice. Access to the arts was part and parcel of the decent life to which every American was entitled, he had claimed, and he was particularly interested in having good art made available to the smaller communities of the nation. Hopkins shared that enthusiasm and went beyond to envision the arts as instruments of social reform that would heighten public consciousness concerning the demands of social justice. The directors talked animatedly about the opportunity that lay open to them. Alsberg spoke of producing a series of authentic guidebooks, one for each state, that would accurately portray the variegated natural and cultural riches of the United States. Cahill spoke of a nationwide network of community art centers where unemployed artists could gather and document the local folk art—the decorative doorknobs and weather vanes, the functional quilts and glassware—for a great index of American design. Sokoloff spoke of traveling symphony orchestras and chamber groups that would bring first-class music to people who had never been able to hear a live performance. And Flanagan spoke of a theater that would dramatize the great issues of the day in living newspapers and in plays specially commissioned by American playwrights—as she later recalled, it was a time when everything seemed possible. After the usual frenetic bureaucratic maneuvering during the spring and summer, the funds for Federal One became available and the four directors proceeded with the work of "art for the millions."[27]

The four programs developed with considerable individuality, given the differences in the temperaments and aspirations of the directors as well as in the domains over which they presided. What was remarkable, though, was the features that soon came to mark the effort as a whole. For one thing, Federal One was first and foremost a public employment program, and over the years in which the program flourished writers and artists were afforded the opportunity to practice their professions while earning a modest living. In all, the four programs employed some 45,000 men and women during the spring of 1936, some 37,000 during the spring of 1937, and some 28,000 during the spring of 1938 (the Music Project was consistently the largest, the Writers' Project, the smallest). Not only were the arts in a variety of forms made available to Americans who had not experienced them, but a generation of artists and writers was enabled

27. Francis V. O'Connor, ed., *Art for the Millions: Essays from the 1930's by the Artists and Administrators of the WPA Federal Art Project* (Greenwich, Conn.: New York Graphic Society, 1973).

to preserve and develop its talents. In addition, coming as they did during a period of cultural nationalism and rediscovery, a period, too, when the popular front in politics brought radicals of diverse persuasions together in cultural as well as political organizations, the several projects were able to generate what was in retrospect clearly an American school of indigenous art that drew its substance and inspiration from everyday American life. Much of that art was at best ordinary; some of it was contrived, propagandistic, and patently substandard; some of it—the paintings of Jack Levine and Jacob Lawrence, the sculpture of Louise Nevelson, the *Index of American Design*, the *New York City Guide*—was truly remarkable and in the end quite durable. New forms were pioneered. Given the mix of the highly competent and the barely competent that the relief rolls produced, the collaborative venture proved a useful and innovative device. The collaborative mural, the collaborative guidebook, the living newspaper, with its serial recitation, the civic orchestra—all were vehicles for making the most of a variety of talent and ability. In addition, given the wish, at least in the art, theater, and music programs, to involve audiences, muralists like Lucienne Block devised techniques for consulting with the clients of the institutions for which they were producing the murals while the work was in progress; the Audience Research Department of the Theatre Project surveyed the men, women, and children of the project's audiences to determine their response to what had been shown and the kinds of works they would prefer to see in the future; and the Composers' Forum—Laboratories of the Music Project made it possible for audiences to discuss with composers works that had just been performed. Finally, while Shakespeare plays and Beethoven symphonies were brought to more diverse audiences than ever before, a great variety of American work was brought as well—Marc Blitzstein's *The Cradle Will Rock*, Sinclair Lewis's *It Can't Happen Here*, Eugene O'-Neill's *The Fountain, Anna Christie*, and *Marco Millions*, the remarkable jazz version of Gilbert and Sullivan's *Mikado* that one of the Theatre Project's black companies performed across the country under the title *Swing Mikado*, and the countless renderings of American compositions of Sokoloff's bands and orchestras. Whatever else it achieved, this indigenous art educated: it interpreted American culture to Americans; it documented the ethnic and regional variety in that culture; and it introduced millions of Americans who had never before visited a museum or attended a concert or a play to an indigenous art that surely heightened their sensibility with respect to their own lives and times. Equally important, beyond the educational potential inherent in the art itself, the artists and writers of Federal One systematically taught men, women, and children, in community art centers, in social settlements, in libraries, in hospitals, and in schools, as classes in writing, painting, music and drama were conducted across the country.[28]

Interestingly, the WPA had a formally constituted library program, but none for the museums, the difference probably testifying, first, to the public perception of libraries as public institutions whereas museums were still seen as essentially private, and second, to the large number of unemployed men and women who saw themselves as librarians in contrast to the relatively smaller number who saw themselves as museum workers. During 1936 and 1937, approximately fifteen thousand individuals were supported in library work, performing tasks that included cataloguing and recataloguing projects, bookbinding and book repair projects, and collecting and duplicating projects. Most important, perhaps, WPA workers extended library services to some two million Americans, mostly in the South, who had not previously had access to libraries, through some 2,500 new libraries and some 2,000 traveling libraries. Laurence V. Coleman lamented in his 1939 survey that most of the funds that had come to museums during the New Deal had gone for capital outlays, with little for personnel and collection development. Yet he chose not to mention the hundred-odd community art centers in cities and towns across the country, where artists and craftspeople gathered to share their experience, where local art and craft work was collected, documented, and exhibited, and where classes were conducted for adults and children. Those centers were surely museums in the definition of John Cotton Dana. Beyond that, Coleman could not have known how profoundly the art being produced during the 1930's would shift the character of formal museum collections during the 1950's and 1960's in the directions Dana had envisioned.[29]

Finally, there was the inescapable question of censorship. Hopkins had assured his directors of a free, adult, and uncensored opportunity, but public convention and Washington politics were to belie that assurance in both the short and the long runs. The Music Project and the Writers' Project were relatively free of problems, owing to the uncontroversial character of guidebooks and Sokoloff's preference

28. William F. McDonald, *Federal Relief Administration and the Arts* (Columbus: Ohio State University Press, 1973), chap. xiii.

29. Carleton B. Joeckel, *Library Service* (Washington, D.C.: Government Printing Office, 1938), pp. 54, 58; and Coleman, *Museum in America*, I, 190.

for the European masters. But the Art Project encountered criticism of various sorts, from Des Moines Public Library officials to the effect that Harry D. Jones's mural in the children's reading room was grotesque and frightening, from a Roman Catholic judge in the New York County Courthouse to the effect that Attilo Pusterla's mural portraying the history of justice included a portrait of Martin Luther, and from the Chicago *Tribune* to the effect that the murals of Mitchell Siporin and Edgar Britton were "un-American" and obviously done under Communist influence. And the Theatre Project was under constant attack for the contents of its living newspapers and for its socially conscious plays like *Injunction Granted* (a prolabor account of the union movement), *Power* (an attack on the electric industry), and *The Revolt of the Beavers* (a play depicting a successful workers' revolution in Beaverland, which Brooks Atkinson referred to as "Mother Goose Marx" in the *New York Times*). And in fact, after a highly publicized Congressional investigation in the spring of 1939, Congress abolished the Theatre Project in the Relief Bill for 1939–40, leaving the other three projects of Federal One to linger on until 1943 with ever more stringent personnel requirements, drastic reductions in federal appropriations, and new requirements of local sponsorship. Eventually, like the CCC, Federal One fell victim to the war.

V

There was a "culture explosion" in the United States after World War II that closely paralleled the upward extension of popular schooling and that doubtless in part derived from it, though the combination of economic growth and increased leisure made possible by the technological advances achieved during and following the war was also an important factor. By every quantitative measure, more Americans participated more intensively in the arts than ever before. They painted, sculpted, printed, wove, played music, wrote fiction and nonfiction, and joined in the work of amateur theater companies; they visited museums, attended concerts, plays, and poetry readings, and enjoyed music and drama of every sort and variety in their homes via phonograph, radio, and television; and they supported the cultural activities of their fellow Americans with their taxes, their ticket purchases, and their philanthropic contributions. Exuberant optimists like the author Alvin Toffler proclaimed the arrival of a new renaissance, of culture popularized and democratized; despairing pessimists like the music critic Harold C. Schonberg responded that more was invariably worse, that culture spread wide was inevitably spread thin; and thoughtful critics like David Riesman and Jacques Barzun granted the reality of the quantitative increase and pondered its inevitable effects on intellectual and cultural standards.[30]

It was within the context of that culture explosion that the federal government became, as one historian put it, a "reluctant patron" of the arts, in the process coming to contend with many of the dilemmas that had marked federal cultural policy during the New Deal era. One such dilemma concerned what sorts of art the government ought to sponsor—in the highly politicized atmosphere of the early 1950's, this dilemma was heightened by continuing charges and countercharges involving the loyalty of artists and the appropriateness of their creations. A typical controversy revolved around a mural in the Rincon Annex of the San Francisco Post Office that had been painted by the artist Anton Refregier; it portrayed the history of San Francisco in a series of twenty-nine panels that included, not only the gold rush, the great earthquake of 1906, and the signing of the United Nations Charter in 1945, but also the riots against the Chinese, the trial of Tom Mooney, and the labor strife that had continually plagued the waterfront. Patriotic groups objected to the content of the mural and to Refregier's stylized realism, and California Representative Hubert B. Scudder actually introduced a resolution into the House of Representatives that would have directed the administrator of the General Services Administration to remove the mural on the grounds that it reflected unfavorably on the character of the California pioneers. A well-organized defense by the Bay Citizens' Committee to Protect the Rincon Annex Murals eventually quashed Scudder's resolution and the mural was saved, but the controversy was characteristic of the era.[31]

Roughly contemporary with the hearings on the Rincon Annex mural was the conflict over what books would appear in the approximately two hundred libraries and information centers that the United States International Information Administration maintained overseas. During the winter of 1952–53, after Senator Joseph R. McCarthy had charged the State Department with being "soft on Communism,"

30. Alvin Toffler, *The Culture Consumers: A Study of Art and Affluence in America* (New York: St. Martin's Press, 1964); Harold C. Schonberg, "Lowered Values: The Second-Rate Is Taking Precedence Over the Better Things in Music," *New York Times*, May 28, 1961, II, p. 9; David Riesman, *Individualism Reconsidered, and Other Essays* (Glencoe, Ill.: The Free Press, 1954), p. 184 and *passim;* and Jacques Barzun, *Music in American Life* (Bloomington: Indiana University Press, 1963).

31. Gary O. Larson, *The Reluctant Patron: The United States Government and the Arts, 1943–1965* (Philadelphia: University of Pennsylvania Press, 1983).

the IIA had begun to remove from its overseas libraries the novels of Howard Fast and Walter Duranty, the poetry of Langston Hughes, the political commentary of Vera Micheles Dean, and the sociological analysis of Robert and Helen Lynd. When the removals became public, they were widely denounced in the press as government censorship and "book-burning," charges that brought not only a series of denials and "clarifications" from the IIA but also a series of resignations by its leaders. As was often the case with such matters, the outcome was inconclusive, even after McCarthy had been censured by the Senate and his influence had begun to wane.[32]

There were kindred conflicts during the 1950's over what sorts of paintings and drawings would be included in the traveling exhibitions that the IIA sent abroad from time to time. In that domain, the chief congressional critic was Representative George Dondero of Michigan, who was unremitting in his denunciations of what he perceived as the subversive social, intellectual, and cultural influences of cubism, dadaism, expressionism, surrealism, and abstractionism, and who consequently saw the inclusion in government-sponsored exhibits of works by such artists as Ben Shahn, William Zorach, Robert Motherwell, Jack Levine, and Jackson Pollock as "un-American" and unrepresentative of the American people. As Jane De Hart Mathews has demonstrated, Dondero's animus was more than a simple matter of political opportunism; it was an exercise in cultural politics as well, as he had the consistent support in his crusade of traditionalist artists who were ever ready to serve up damaging information about their modernist colleagues and in the process to reinforce Dondero's tendency to identify modernism with subversion.[33]

It was precisely this sort of controversy over what kinds of art the federal government ought to support that led many Americans of all political persuasions to resist government subsidies to the arts—as the painter Larry Rivers once remarked, "The government taking a role in art is like a gorilla threading a needle. It is at first cute, then clumsy, and most of all impossible." And yet there was growing pressure during the 1960's from both the humanities and the arts communities for government subsidies comparable to those that flowed to the natural sciences, the argument being that matters of social and aesthetic value were quite as important to the national life and welfare

32. "Book Burning," *New Republic*, CXXVIII (June 29, 1953), 7–11; and Martin Merson, "My Education in Government," *Reporter*, XI (October 7, 1954), 15–27.

33. Jane De Hart Mathews, "Art and Politics in Cold War America," *American Historical Review*, LXXXI (1976), 762–785.

as matters of scientific knowledge and hence quite as worthy of public support. There were tentative efforts to obtain federal aid to the arts and humanities during the Kennedy administration, but the break-through came during the extraordinary period in 1965 when Lyndon B. Johnson exploited his sweeping election victory over Barry Gold-water to push a number of path-breaking measures through the 89th Congress, including the "National Foundation on the Arts and Humanities Act of 1965," which Johnson signed on September 29. The legislation stated that "a high civilization must not limit its efforts to science and technology alone but must give full value and support to the other great branches of man's scholarly and cultural activity." It defined the humanities as including languages, linguistics, litera-ture, history, jurisprudence, philosophy, and archaeology, and the arts as including music, dance, drama, folk art, creative writing, archi-tecture, painting, sculpture, photography, graphic and craft arts, in-dustrial design, costume and fashion design, motion pictures, televi-sion, radio, and tape and sound recording. The National Foundation itself comprised three institutions: the National Endowment for the Arts, the National Endowment for the Humanities, and the Federal Council on the Arts, the last named to consist of twelve agency ad-ministrators, including the chairmen of the NEA and NEH, charged with coordinating the Foundation's activities with those of other fed-eral programs.[34]

The activities of the two endowments can be gleaned from their annual reports, which convey in detail their general policies and their specific grants. Suffice it here to make several points concerning the bearing of their efforts on education in the large. For one thing, the appropriations of the two endowments rose steadily between 1966 and 1980, from some $2.5 million each to approximately $100 million each, with the most rapid increases coming during the 1970's. Sec-ond, from the beginning there were substantial provisions for match-ing funds from private individuals and institutions. Third, both En-dowments—the Arts Endowment from the beginning—subsidized arts councils and humanities councils at the state level and arranged for them to have funds for their own programs that were supposed to take account of particular local and regional opportunities. Fourth, given the support for arts and humanities efforts from other branches

34. The Rivers quotation is given in David Halberstam, "Art Leaders Give Their Plat-forms," *New York Times*, April 28, 1961, p. 33. U.S., Congress, 89th Congress, 1st sess., 1965, *United States Code: Congressional and Administrative News* (St. Paul: West Publishing Company, 1965), I, 809, 810.

of the federal government (the Corporation for Public Broadcasting, for example, or the Smithsonian Institution, or the Department of Education), the NEA and the NEH by no means accounted for the total federal contribution to arts and humanities programs; and, given continuing support from the private sector in the form of ticket purchases and admissions fees by patrons and benefactions of various sorts from private individuals and institutions, the NEA and NEH by no means accounted for even the bulk of financial support for the arts and humanities.

Most important, perhaps, in terms of the traditional tensions within American education, both Endowments, the Arts Endowment decisively under Livingston Biddle and the Humanities Endowment decisively under Joseph Duffey, moved in the direction of a radical pluralism in the projects and institutions they assisted and advanced. The Arts Foundation supported, not only the work of elite arts agencies like the Metropolitan Opera and the Los Angeles Symphony, but also studies of the art of tattooing, documentaries on the cuetro (a traditional Puerto Rican musical instrument), and the actual business of basket weaving by the Mohawk Indians and quilt making by Afro-American Mississippians. In like fashion, the Humanities Endowment supported, not only translations of the fragments of Theophrastus and conferences on the relation of John Locke's thought to political philosophy in the 1680's, but also studies of Native American religions as they related to tribal identity, oral histories of the Cuban refugees in Florida and the Indochinese refugees in Ohio, and cultural assessments of the sixty to seventy-five ethnic groups in the environs of Fresno, California. As a result, the culture explosion of the postwar era, which itself involved an extraordinary range of tastes, styles, and standards, was afforded additional scope and force. In effect, the 1960's and 1970's saw the development and flourishing of many musics, many arts, and many literatures in the United States directed to many audiences displaying many tastes and preferences. Baroque music, abstract impressionist art, and haiku, initially reflecting the arcane tastes of artistic elites, became popularized, not least via the enterprising efforts of the record, the advertising, and the publishing industries. And jazz, belly dancing, and the primitive paintings of Grandma Moses, initially reflecting more popular tastes, were taken up by newly formed artistic elites, who, in the fashion described by Gilbert Seldes, proceeded to develop standards for judging them as genres. Moreover, as this congeries of artistic and literary products was exported abroad, it constituted a remarkably cosmopolitan influence extending out from the metropolis of the United States to other parts of the world. In a sense, Herbert Gans's taste cultures came into being on a world-wide basis, as youngsters from Paris to Tokyo danced to American rock and roll and as wealthy collectors from Paris to Tokyo bought abstract expressionist paintings.

The culture explosion had profound educational significance for the American people, as ever larger segments of the population participated in and partook of the arts and humanities—it is indicative that when Ronald Berman became head of the Humanities Endowment in 1971, he arranged for NEH assistance to Fritz Machlup's elaboration and updating of his 1962 study of *The Production and Distribution of Knowledge in the United States* and indeed reprinted Machlup's essay "Learning More about Knowledge" in the Seventh Annual Report of the Endowment. Equally important, large portions of NEA and NEH funds went, not only to schools, colleges, and universities, but also to libraries, museums, and other cultural agencies for the development of explicitly educational projects. By the end of the 1970's, the nation's thirty thousand libraries and five thousand museums were more decisively and self-consciously in the business of education than ever before, and what was striking about their educational programs was their extraordinary diversity. American culture had been popularized in substance as well as audience, with prodigious significance for American education writ large.[35]

35. U.S., National Endowment for the Humanities, *Seventh Annual Report, 1971–72,* pp. 18–19. The statistic for the number of libraries does not include elementary- and secondary-school libraries.

Chapter 10

PLACES OF WORK

The New York Central lines have established what is called by those responsible for it "a rational apprentice system." . . . They take an old steam pump, run it by compressed air in the school room, and let the apprentices see the way it works, take it apart and examine into the valve motion, make drawings of the various parts, calculate the cubical contents of the cylinders, study the various mechanism [*sic*], and then go out into the shop and grind the valves. In other words, starting with the pump, they work down through the various subjects of arithmetic, geometry, mechanical drawing, mechanics, etc., as applied to the action of the pump.

CARROLL D. WRIGHT

The processes of industrialization during the decades following the Civil War brought painful problems to the nation's farmers. Whereas 51.6 percent of gainfully occupied or employed Americans worked in agriculture in 1870, that number declined to 48.8 percent in 1880, to 42.5 percent in 1890, and to 37.7 percent in 1900. Moreover, those who remained in agriculture experienced severe financial difficulties. Farm prices fell markedly—the price of wheat declined by three-quarters between 1866 and 1896, and the price of corn, by two-thirds—at the same time that the price of land rose. And, with mechanization moving relentlessly forward and agriculture becoming increasingly commercialized, farmers found themselves undercapitalized and facing ever rising transportation costs from railroads, storage costs from elevator operators, processing costs from machinery owners, and interest costs from the banks—all at the same time that they were barraged by advertisements for ready-made clothing, canned foods, cookstoves, kerosene lamps, and pianos. Little wonder that speakers at Grange and Alliance meetings talked darkly of exploitation by vast trusts conspiring with a bribed government, and little wonder, too, that the young flocked to the cities in search of a better life.[1]

For all their emphasis on agitation and organization, however, and on the political activism that culminated in the Bryan campaign of 1896, the Grange and the Farmers' Alliances were also part of a nationwide effort to improve the quality and productivity of American agriculture during the last decades of the nineteenth century—an effort, ironically, that in its success was partly responsible for the problems of oversupply that were one factor in the decline of prices. The heyday of the Grange, of course, came during the mid-seventies, when membership soared to three-quarters of a million; thereafter membership declined, though the organization continued strong and articulate in its own right and as an important component in the Farmers' Alliance movement. And, from the beginning, the Grange was deeply committed to the application of science to agriculture and to the diffusion of scientific knowledge among farmers. The Alliances flourished during the 1880's and 1890's with a much more sharply focused emphasis on politics; yet the Alliances too maintained a vigorous program of education for the improvement of farming—indeed, contemporaries were fond of referring to the Agricultural Wheel (which later became a component of the Southern Alliance) and the Alliance itself as "schools" and "universities" of the rural population. In localities across the country, members of Grange and Alliance lodges and locals gathered to hear lectures and to conduct discussions about crop diversification, the improvement of livestock lines, the propagation of fruit trees, the renewal of worn-out soils, and the comparative advantages of deep versus shallow plowing (while their wives dealt similarly with cooking, canning, and gardening, in the traditional gender allocation of agricultural tasks). In addition, they arranged visits to one another's farms for the purpose of mutual instruction and assistance and they collaborated in the organization of district and county fairs, where they saw exhibitions of agricultural products and demonstrations of new machinery, and of farmers' institutes, where they had the chance to hear professors from the state

1. U.S., Bureau of the Census, *Historical Statistics of the United States, Colonial Times to 1970* (2 vols.; Washington, D.C.: Government Printing Office, 1975), I, 138; and Simon Kuznets, *National Income: A Summary of Findings* (New York: National Bureau of Economic Research, 1946), p. 41.

agricultural colleges give "plain talks on plain subjects" (whatever the aspirations to "plainness," the announcement of a professorial lecturer all too often had the effect of emptying the hall).[2]

As the effects of education became evident in improved yields, the Grange and the Alliances also became important lobbying groups, first, for state-supported agricultural institute programs, through which well-planned short courses of a day's or two days' duration would be brought to the localities—the model referred to was often the teachers' institute; then, for the agricultural colleges themselves, as farmers began to see those institutions as *their* institutions; and, later, for agricultural experiment stations. These had begun to develop during the 1870's and were then made available nationwide by the Hatch Act of 1887, which provided annual federal appropriations of $15,000 for the establishment, under the aegis of the United States Department of Agriculture, of an agricultural experiment station within each of the Morrill Act colleges that would acquire "useful and practical information" and "promote scientific investigation and experiment respecting the principles and applications of agricultural science."[3]

Finally, and perhaps most important, the educational programs of the Grange and the Alliance, insofar as they dealt with the politics and economics of agriculture, transformed the farmers' views of themselves and their work. Jeffersonian images of God's chosen people living in the righteous ways of self-sufficiency began to be replaced by images more appropriate to an increasingly metropolitan nation—images, on the one hand, of exploited producers who needed to organize in order to wrest the full rewards of their labor from grasping bankers and politicians, and, on the other hand, of small businessmen competing in the markets of an interdependent commercial-industrial economy. It was as exploited producers that farmers, radicalized by the educational efforts of Alliance lecturers, took a leading role in helping to organize the People's Party and to manage its campaigns during the 1890's. It was as small businessmen seeking the financial returns of improved quality and productivity that farmers, more oriented toward the emphasis on education inherent in Progressive reform, began actively to reach for the knowledge being

2. C. S. Walker, "The Farmers' Movement," *Annals of the American Academy of Political and Social Science*, IV (1894), 793; Colorado, *Annual Report of the Secretary of the State Board of Agriculture, 1891*, p. 74; and A. E. Paine, *The Granger Movement in Illinois* (Urbana: University Press, 1904).

3. An Act to Establish Agricultural Experiment Stations, in U.S., *Statutes of the United States of America, Passed at the Second Session of the Forty-Ninth Congress, 1886–1887*, p. 440.

developed and purveyed by the agricultural colleges, the experiment stations, and the research bureaus of the state and federal departments of agriculture.

Leaflets, magazines, clubs, institutes, fairs, lecturers, and short courses (not only in local communities but also at the agricultural colleges themselves) all represented a remarkably complementary configuration of education addressed to farmers who were increasingly disposed to take advantage of what it had to offer. And yet it is probable that only a minority of American farmers actually availed themselves of formal and informal agricultural education during the first years of the twentieth century—a minority composed of those more schooled, more conscious of the potential value of scientific knowledge, and more ready to change habitual ways of doing things in light of scientific knowledge. As with libraries, an educational opportunity offered to all tended to be used most by those who already enjoyed many of the advantages the educational opportunity was intended to confer.

One of those most acutely aware of the problem was Seaman A. Knapp. A New Yorker who had been educated at Union College and who had taught for a time in the private academies of upstate New York, Knapp had moved to Iowa in 1866, where he had combined a career in farming, first, with a Methodist pastorship, subsequently, with the superintendency of the state school for the blind and the editorship of the *Western Stock Journal and Farmer,* and then, with a professorship and the presidency at the Iowa Agricultural College at Ames. He had early become interested in scientific stock breeding, had been one of the organizers and the first president of the Iowa Improved Stock Breeders' Association, and had become sufficiently convinced of the potential of scientific agriculture to have drafted in 1882 the so-called Carpenter Bill (providing for federal appropriations to agricultural experiment stations), which was much like the measure that became the Hatch Act in 1887. At the same time, however, particularly during his years at Ames, he had become suspicious and on occasion disdainful of the professors who were his colleagues—as supervisor of the college farm he was doubtless skeptical of what many of the students brought from their academic coursework, and as president of the college he was increasingly impatient with academic politics. However that may be, when a large land syndicate that wished to develop a flourishing rice industry in southwestern Louisiana invited Knapp to join the venture as its chief agricultural expert at a salary substantially higher than the one he enjoyed at

Ames, he accepted and moved to Lake Charles, Louisiana, in 1885. There, Knapp created a series of demonstration farms, each run by a family recruited especially for the task, that exemplified the possibilities of colonizing the land and at the same time introducing crops that would prove profitable. Knapp the farmer maintained that it was simply good, common-sense agricultural techniques that had made for the success of the demonstrations; but Knapp the educator had in fact created a new technique. "We then learned the philosophy and the power of agricultural demonstrations," he later recalled.[4]

From that time forward, Knapp became the enthusiast of the demonstration farm as the answer to the nation's agricultural problems. In 1898, Knapp's old friend from Iowa days, James Wilson, whom President William McKinley had appointed secretary of agriculture, asked Knapp to join the Department as a special agent to coordinate the Department's effort to find and test superior varieties of rice. Four years later, when the Department set out to rejuvenate southern agriculture, Wilson asked Knapp to lead that effort, and it was in connection with his work as Special Agent to Promote Agriculture in the South that Knapp found the opportunity to propagate his demonstration method. Interestingly, the first support came, not from the farmers themselves, but from businessmen like E. H. R. Green, president and general manager of the Texas Midland Railroad, who was eager to develop the economy of the region served by the road. Green, on behalf of the local businessmen and farmers of Terrell, Texas, where the headquarters of the railroad was located, asked Knapp to visit the community and advise the farmers on the problems they faced. Knapp went to Terrell in 1903 and proposed that the community leaders create a farm demonstration project in which a local farmer of their choice would agree to follow the instructions given him for improving the productivity of his farm and a sufficient sum of money would be raised to guarantee the farmer against loss in the venture. The committee of businessmen and farmers selected Walter C. Porter's farm for the experiment, with a 70-acre plot of Porter's 800-acre property actually committed to the work. The land had been planted with cotton or corn for twenty-eight years, without fertilizers, and was on its way to exhaustion. Knapp selected particular varieties of corn and cotton seeds, but beyond that proposed only basic improvements— better planting, more careful cultivation, and the application of fertilizer in large quantities. Porter claimed that in the end he had cleared

4. Seaman A. Knapp, "An Agricultural Revolution," *World's Work*, XII (1906), 7734.

$700 more than he would have cleared using his traditional methods. It was easy enough for Porter's neighbors in an earlier day to reject the advice of experts who claimed to have gotten superior yields at the model farm of the agricultural college; it was more difficult once they had seen Porter employing techniques that they themselves were perfectly capable of imitating, on land that was not fundamentally different from their own. The example of a well-known neighbor turned out to be a teaching innovation of incalculable value.

Knapp's demonstration in Terrell might have had local impact at best had Texas not been caught in a boll weevil plague in 1903 that had all but panicked the state's farmers and businessmen. Given demands that the Department of Agriculture take dramatic action, given that Porter had achieved his results despite an attack by boll weevils on his cotton crop, and given that the Bureau of Entomology of the Department of Agriculture had discovered that the boll weevil did not begin to multiply each year until late July, so that early plantings of early maturing varieties of cotton might avoid the worst of their depredations, Knapp was invited to apply his demonstration methods on a broader scale. With additional money from Congress and with the cooperation of the railroads serving Texas, he was able to appoint a score of special agents. In addition, he was able to obtain a ripple effect from his primary demonstration projects by enlisting some fifteen to twenty farmers in each county to serve as cooperators—men who would also follow the instructions given them, usually by mail, and report on their results. Moreover, persuaded that the South's need was not merely to overcome the boll weevil epidemic but, more generally, to upgrade its agriculture, Knapp seized the opportunity to have the projects teach methods of improved farming and farm management. And, in so doing, he continued to stress common-sense principles rather than radically innovative techniques. "The work is in no sense experimental," Knapp wrote in 1908; "no experiments are tried; the instructions are not new nor doubtful; everything recommended has been fully tested by practical farmers." The goal was innovation, to be sure, but the primary pedagogical concern was to ensure the kind of broad-scale participation that would prove that the average farmer could farm more effectively.[5]

The success of the demonstration work as it expanded soon made Knapp something of a legend in Texas—though less so in Washington, where bureaucratic competition within the Department of Agri-

5. Seaman A. Knapp, "The Farmers' Co-operative Demonstration Work," *Southern Planter*, LXIX (1908), 226.

culture led to criticism of his charisma. In 1905, President David F. Houston of Texas A & M College chanced to remark in a conversation with Wallace Buttrick of the General Education Board, "There are two universities in Texas. One is at Austin and the other is Dr. Seaman Knapp." Given that Buttrick was searching at the time for promising ways to use the Board's resources in the cause of Southern regeneration, the remark proved providential for Knapp's efforts. Once Buttrick had met Knapp, he was convinced he had found his answer; and, after the usual round of negotiations, an agreement was reached whereby the Board would become a silent partner of the Department of Agriculture in sponsoring Knapp's work. Beginning with a grant of $7,000 for 1906, the Board increased its contribution each year until 1914, when passage of the Smith-Lever Act rendered private assistance no longer necessary.[6]

GEB involvement in the dissemination of Knapp's technique was especially significant for at least three reasons. First, although Knapp claimed to be much interested in reaching black as well as white farmers, he was reluctant to employ black agents, maintaining that they would create problems with southern white clients. Prodded by the Board, however, he developed cooperative relationships with Tuskegee Institute in Alabama and Hampton Institute in Virginia and, with Board funds, began to employ black agents. Second, although Knapp's program was aimed primarily at adult farmers, he was well aware of the value of using the demonstration ideas with young people, and Board funds enabled him to employ agents explicitly charged with reaching southern youngsters through boys' corn clubs and girls' tomato clubs. Finally, given his understanding that the problem of economic regeneration was not merely one of greater productivity but also one of better farm management, Knapp developed a home demonstration program for women that dealt with the improvement of everything from sewing to canning to gardening, and Board funds made it possible for him to employ the first home demonstration agents to carry on this work.

The coalitions that Knapp developed in support of his efforts were characteristically progressive; they included reform-minded businessmen, farmers, church workers, journalists, and educators—all roles Knapp himself had played in his long and varied career. When President Theodore Roosevelt created a Commission on Country Life in 1908 and charged it with gathering information and formulating

6. The Houston quotation is given in Raymond B. Fosdick, *Adventure in Giving: The Story of the General Education Board* (New York: Harper & Row, 1962), p. 41.

recommendations for relieving rural distress, the membership comprised the same sorts of individuals—Liberty Hyde Bailey, the dean of the New York State College of Agriculture at Cornell University and an internationally known horticulturalist, who had become the great champion of country life in his popular books and articles; Henry Wallace, editor of the influential *Wallace's Farmer;* Walter Hines Page, who at the time was editing the *World's Work;* Kenyon Butterfield, president of the Massachusetts Agricultural College and a powerful figure in the Association of American Agricultural Colleges and Experiment Stations; Gifford Pinchot, Roosevelt's friend who was chief of the forestry bureau of the Department of Agriculture; Charles S. Barrett, president of the Farmers' Educational and Cooperative Union, which had been founded in Texas in 1902; and William A. Beard, editor of *Great West Magazine* in California and chairman of the Sacramento Valley Improvement Association and of the National Irrigation Society. The Commission surveyed a half-million rural Americans (not all of them farmers) with a twelve-item questionnaire concerning farm life in their neighborhoods (over a hundred thousand were returned); it conducted a vigorous correspondence with informed leaders throughout the nation; it held hearings in twenty-four states and the District of Columbia; and it invited rural communities to hold meetings in local schoolbuildings and to transmit the results of the meetings to the Commission.

The Commission delivered its report to Roosevelt in January, 1909, charging that agriculture was nowhere near as commercially profitable as it ought to be and that social conditions in the rural regions of the country fell short of their possibilities as a result. The Commission held that the chief causes of these conditions lay in ignorance, poor communication, the lack of decent schooling, and the absence of effective leadership. And the Commission proposed that the most promising remedies lay in scientific surveys of rural conditions, a coordinated program of education for country life involving churches, schools, libraries, agricultural societies, YMCAs, and the extension activities of the land grant colleges, and the improvement of communication through economical highway systems and a parcel post. In effect, a panel of progressives had recommended to a progressive president a characteristically progressive program centering in reform through an education that would diffuse socially relevant, expert knowledge. Roosevelt was delighted with the report and sent it on to Congress for consideration and action. Congress was uninterested and not only refused Roosevelt's request for an appropriation to print and publicize the findings but ordered the Commission to cease its work. President William Howard Taft, who took office in March, was also uninterested, with the result that the Commission's work for all intents and purposes died aborning.[7]

Yet, granted its failure on the legislative side, the Commission was immensely successful in mobilizing and articulating public opinion, especially on the needs of rural education. The Association of American Agricultural Colleges and Experiment Stations, which had been working for several years under Butterfield's leadership to formulate a federal program of assistance to extension work, took the opportunity of the report to redouble its efforts and succeeded in having Representative James C. McLaughlin of Michigan introduce a bill into Congress in December, 1909. McLaughlin's measure soon encountered two complexes of problems that would stall the effort for five years. First, there were competing measures for a more comprehensive program of federal aid to vocational education that would include trade and agricultural schools as well as extension activities; and second, there was sharp competition between the agricultural colleges, whose extension programs revolved around publications, institutes, and short courses, and the Department of Agriculture, whose extension programs revolved around Knapp's demonstration system. Finally, bills sponsored by Congressman Ashbury F. Lever of South Carolina and Senator Hoke Smith of Georgia were passed in the House and Senate early in 1914 and a conference version was enacted and signed by President Woodrow Wilson in May.

The Smith-Lever Act provided that "in order to aid in diffusing among the people of the United States useful and practical information on subjects relating to agriculture and home economics, and to encourage the application of the same," there might be inaugurated, in connection with the college or colleges in each state receiving the benefits of the Morrill Act of 1862 and the so-called Second Morrill Act of 1890, "agricultural extension work which shall be carried on in cooperation with the United States Department of Agriculture." And it stipulated affirmatively that "cooperative agricultural extension work shall consist of the giving of instruction and practical demonstrations in agriculture and home economics to persons not attending or resident in said colleges in the several communities, and imparting to such persons information on said subjects through field demonstrations, publications, and otherwise; and this work shall be

7. *Report of the Commission on Country Life, with an Introduction by Theodore Roosevelt* [1911] (Chapel Hill: University of North Carolina Press, 1944).

carried on in such manner as may be mutually agreed upon by the Secretary of Agriculture and the state agricultural college or colleges receiving the benefits of this act." In addition, it stipulated negatively that "no portion of said money shall be applied, directly or indirectly, to the purchase, erection, preservation, or repair of any building or buildings, or the purchase or rental of land, or in college-course teaching, lectures in colleges, promoting agricultural trains [traveling displays of agricultural products and implements commonly sponsored by the railroads to stimulate economic development], or any other purpose not specified in this act, and not more than 5 per centum of each annual appropriation shall be applied to the printing and distribution of publications." Obviously, the program as enacted was a clear victory for the Department of Agriculture.[8]

The Smith-Lever Act created under federal auspices a configuration of education that proved extraordinarily effective in the continuing modernization of American agriculture. Scientific knowledge developed in the agricultural colleges and particularly in the experiment stations would not only be transmitted through courses at the colleges but also conveyed through demonstrations and publications to practicing farmers and their families. And the arrangement would be subject to continuing negotiation between the Department of Agriculture and the agricultural colleges and their experiment stations. It was a configuration the ingenuity and significance of which has been justly celebrated, but it was a configuration fraught with tensions—the tension between those who wished the experiment stations to produce quick solutions to practical problems and those who wished them to pursue scientific inquiries that might in the end prove fruitful in practice, the tension between those who wished to extend systematic teaching from the colleges of agriculture and those who wished to extend transferable agricultural and home economics demonstrations, the tension between those who wanted an emphasis on local solutions to local problems and those who wanted a national network of cosmopolitan-oriented institutions. The tensions proved healthy in the long run, and indeed the solutions changed over time, particularly as farmers and their families enjoyed increasing opportunity for general and vocational education in schools and colleges and became ever more entrepreneurial in the process. But the tensions persisted as irritants, too, and needed to be constantly renegotiated, even as a community of background and outlook developed among the kinds of

8. An Act to Provide for Cooperative Agricultural Extension Work, in U.S., *Statutes at Large*, XXXVI, Part I, 372–374.

individuals who staffed the colleges, the experiment stations, the bureaus of the Department of Agriculture, and the extension system itself.

Finally, and ironically, as Grant McConnell has pointed out, the extension system created by the Smith-Lever Act provided a new basis of political power for the nation's farmers, symbolized by the American Farm Bureau Federation. The arrangements for financing the work of the county agents who were at the heart of the system provided for federal, state, and local contributions, and for continuing advice from county organizations of farmers and other leaders that would be nonpolitical, nonsectarian, and nonsecret and generally representative of the farm population at large. These organizations, which came to be called farm bureaus, were first created by the county agents to assist them in their work and, once created, ended up working with the county agents in a symbiotic relationship. And, after the local organizations created the American Farm Bureau Federation in 1920, a powerful national voice of the American farm community was in place, with a network of local officials paid and sponsored in large measure by public agencies. The Smith-Lever Act had thus created the kind of rooted national organization that the Populists had dreamed about but failed to achieve. The organization came into its own during the New Deal and continued as a major voice of American agricultural interests, though the small farmer that the Farm Bureau claimed to represent increasingly disappeared in favor of an agribusiness comprising huge firms not different from the vast businesses that had haunted the Populists in their nightmares of the 1890's. The farmer had achieved through organization what he had not been able to achieve as an individual, but the individual farmer on the family farm had become a rarity on the American scene by the 1980's.[9]

II

Both the number and the percentage of Americans involved in nonagricultural pursuits expanded rapidly during the half-century following the Civil War, with some of the most dramatic increases occurring in the domains of transportation, manufacturing, and trade and distribution. The development of the railroad and telegraph systems during the middle third of the century led to significant improvements in the speed, the volume, and the regularity of shipments and communi-

9. Grant McConnell, *The Decline of Agrarian Democracy* (Berkeley: University of California Press, 1953).

cations, making possible in turn a fundamental transformation in the production and distribution of goods. In agriculture, the transformation was marked by the emergence of the grain elevators, the cotton presses, the warehouses, and the commodity exchanges that seemed to so many of the nation's farmers the visible signs of a vast conspiracy against them. In manufacturing, the transformation was marked by the emergence of a "new factory system" in which plants became larger, more complex, and more systematically organized and managed. And in distribution, the transformation was marked by the emergence of the jobber, the wholesaler, and the mass retailer. These changes radically altered the nature of work during the half-century between 1870 and 1920. To be sure, there were still small shops, where skilled craftsmen manufactured products ranging from newspapers to cabinets to plumbing fixtures. There were the sweatshops in city tenements, where groups of men and women in household settings manufactured clothing or cigars on a piecework basis. And there were factories in fields such as metalwork where individual contractors and subcontractors presided over what were essentially handicraft proprietorships that coexisted within a single building. But, as the number of wage earners in manufacturing rose from 2.7 million in 1880 to 4.5 million in 1900 to 8.4 million in 1920, the number of huge plants like the Baldwin Locomotive works in Philadelphia or the McCormick Reaper works in Chicago burgeoned, as did the size of the average plant (the Baldwin works had 600 employees in 1855, 3,000 in 1875, and 8,000 in 1900; the McCormick works had 150 employees in 1850, 4,000 in 1900, and 15,000 in 1916). By 1920, at least in the northeastern quadrant of the United States, where most of the nation's manufacturing wage earners were concentrated, three-quarters of those wage earners worked in factories with over 100 employees and 30 percent worked in factories with over 1,000 employees.[10]

Within this context of rapid industrialization, changes that had been occurring in the apprenticeship system since the 1840's and 1850's went forward at an accelerated pace. In some of the traditional trades that had been only moderately affected by the new technology—printing, for example, or plumbing, or bricklaying, or carpentry—apprenticeship, backed by strong craft unions, remained the leading entree into the work. But the apprenticeships tended to be

10. *Historical Statistics of the United States*, I, 138; and Daniel Nelson, *Managers and Workers: Origins of the New Factory System in the United States, 1880–1920* (Madison: University of Wisconsin Press, 1975), pp. 6–9.

informal—only a small percentage involved formal indentures, with the result that the statistics of apprenticeship almost always under-reported the phenomenon, and only a fraction of the teaching was systematic. In other domains, for example, in the textile industry, where there had been no formal apprenticeships since the 1840's and 1850's because operatives in the mills could learn the few simple skills they needed to operate and tend the machines on the job in a matter of days, apprenticeship was merely the entry rung on the employment ladder, no longer serving educational purposes. And in still other domains, for example, the shoemaking industry, apprenticeship had all but disappeared during the 1840's and 1850's, as a former craft had become mechanized and rationalized and as operatives in the factories no longer needed the complex skills associated with shoe-making but rather the simpler skills associated with machine tending.

The last pattern came increasingly to prevail during the half-century following 1870, as, first in textiles and shoemaking, and then in distilling, cigarette making, watchmaking, glassmaking, flour milling, and automobile manufacture, a combination of coal and electric power, technological innovation, and the rationalization of production and management rendered traditional craft skills outmoded and substituted for those craft skills the ability respectively to perform highly discrete and particular tasks with the assistance of machines. The result by the turn of the century was a widespread perception that apprenticeship as traditionally conceived and practiced was mori-bund. The perception reflected the fact that the number of appren-ticeships had climbed only modestly in comparison with the rapid increase in the overall number of persons involved in manufacturing. Also, it was widely assumed that the growing specialization of labor had sharply reduced the proportion of factory operatives who needed to have overall knowledge of the productive process and that appren-ticeship was increasingly viewed as unprofitable by the employers who paid for it, the workers who did the teaching, the parents of the youngsters who served as apprentices, and the youngsters them-selves. And, adding to all this, there was the constant argument of proponents of vocational schools that apprenticeship had become irreversibly inefficient and exploitative and that it was no longer possi-ble to carry on decent vocational education in the workplace.[11]

Particularly after the organization of the National Society for the Promotion of Industrial Education in 1906, the vocational school

11. Paul H. Douglas, *American Apprenticeship and Industrial Education* (New York: privately published, 1921), p. 74; and *Historical Statistics of the United States*, I, 138, 143.

gained increasing support in the education community as the ideal agency to prepare young people for work. But there were those who continued to point to the strengths of properly conducted apprenticeships. Carroll D. Wright, the president of Clark College at Worcester, was one such individual. Wright readily conceded the inadequacies of what he called "the old apprenticeship system": it was exploitative, in that it held young people at substandard wages long after they had learned what they needed to know to do a journeyman's job; and it was inefficient, in that it trained young people for specific skills but conveyed none of the theory underlying those skills and hence left them unprepared to find meaning in their work or to cope with technological change. But Wright was equally ready to argue the ineffectiveness of the vocational school: it conveyed some of the theory needed by young workers and it made a respectable beginning at teaching some of the required skills; but under no circumstances could it prepare full-fledged workers prepared to take up a trade. What was needed, Wright maintained, was "an enlightened, coordinated system that shall secure all that can be gained from the apprenticeship system and all that can be gained from modern schools for trades and industrial education generally."[12]

In 1908 Wright carried out a survey for the United States Bureau of Education of what he called "the modern apprenticeship system." Essentially, the examples he offered involved various combinations of classwork and shopwork, not unlike the combinations offered by the manual training schools and the trade and industrial schools that had grown up in the wake of the Philadelphia Centennial Exposition of 1876. The General Electric Company at Lynn, Massachusetts, for example, had arrangements for a four-year apprenticeship in which the company carried on both academic and shop instruction during working hours. The academic instruction, which came during the first two years, comprised work in arithmetic, elementary algebra and trigonometry, mensuration, elements of machines, power transmission, strength of materials, mechanics, elementary electricity, mechanical drawing, machine designing, and jig and fixture designing. The shopwork, under the supervision of a foreman, ordinarily started with errand running and unskilled labor, then moved on to simple work at the bench, such as chiseling and plain filing, the cleaning of small castings, or assisting the stockkeeper in the handling of small tools

12. Carroll D. Wright, "The Apprenticeship System as a Means of Promoting Industrial Efficiency," in National Society for the Promotion of Industrial Education, *Bulletin No. 5* (New York: National Society for the Promotion of Industrial Education, 1908), p. 31.

and stock materials, and finally progressed to tool- or diemaking or machine work. The company required sufficient numbers of machinists so that apprentices headed for machine work had their shop training in a special room under the supervision of a mechanic specifically chosen for his skill as a teacher. The smaller number of apprentices headed for pattern making or foundry work pursued all their skill training in the shops themselves. Interestingly, the New York Central Railroad had arrangements paralleling those of the General Electric Company, but in reverse order. Instead of proceeding from theory to practice, from academic work to shopwork, the railroad's apprentices proceeded from practice to theory. "They take an old steam pump," Wright explained, "run it by compressed air in the school room, and let the apprentices see the way it works, take it apart and examine into the valve motion, make drawings of the various parts, calculate the cubical contents of the cylinders, study the various mechanism [sic], and then go out into the shop and grind the valves. In other words, starting with the pump, they work down through the various subjects of arithmetic, geometry, mechanical drawing, mechanics, etc., as applied to the action of the pump." Given their concern for the practical, Wright continued, the railroad's managers had found trade school courses inadequate as preparation for their workers. Again, not surprisingly, Wright found their experience in setting up their education programs of great importance in "illustrating the most advanced type of apprentice systems."[13]

A quite different pattern was maintained by R. Hoe and Company, a manufacturer of printing presses. In 1872, Hoe had established a special night school of its own for apprentices who worked for the company during the day. The course of instruction, comprising work in English, mathematics, geometry, and freehand and mechanical drawing, was specifically designed to extend over the four-year period of apprenticeship and roughly to conform to the shop instruction going forward during the day; the course ran from September through May each year, three nights a week. A variant of the Hoe arrangement was conducted by the Brown-Ketcham Iron Works in Indianapolis, where the night school for apprentices was carried on by the local YMCA, at a cost of $6 a year to the students. Clearly, the common element in all these arrangements was the provision for actual experience in the workplace. For Wright, such experience was crucial to the preparation of competent workers.

13. Carroll D. Wright, *The Apprenticeship System in Its Relation to Industrial Education* (U.S., Bureau of Education, Bulletin, 1908, No. 6; Washington, D.C.: Government Printing Office, 1908), pp. 14, 34, 35.

Given that the so-called new apprentice system took form during the Progressive era, one might expect a revival of state efforts to regulate apprenticeship "in the best interests of the child." Characteristically, Wisconsin in 1911 enacted what came to be seen as a model state apprenticeship law. The measure was part of a more general legislative effort to provide for a state-wide system of industrial education that included a compulsory school law requiring all employed workers between the ages of fourteen and sixteen to attend school for four hours a week and all apprentices to attend school for five hours a week. Specifically, the apprenticeship law set the conditions of indentures, stipulated that "the whole trade, as carried on by the employer" be taught, and that the five hours a week of schooling include English, civics, business practices, physiology, hygiene, and the use of safety devices, and required that a certified copy of the indenture be filed by the employer with the state commissioner of labor. The apprentice law was amended in 1915 to place the supervision and direction of the system under the state industrial commission and to give the commission extensive powers to classify trades and industries, to construct and supervise apprentice contracts, and to mediate differences between apprentices and employers. Acting under the amended law, the commission created a state apprenticeship board, composed of representatives of the employers, the unions, and the state continuation schools, and served by a full-time paid secretary, who also acted as supervisor of apprentices.[14]

In another pioneering effort, during the 1920's, the American Construction Council, composed of representatives of all elements in the construction industry, from the architects and engineers to the contractors and manufacturers to the chambers of commerce and construction unions, created a General Apprenticeship Committee and charged it with developing industry-wide standards for the training of apprentices. Franklin D. Roosevelt, who was president of the Council, spoke of the need to place skilled manual labor on a par with the clerical and nonmanual occupations in public esteem and to create a greater public appreciation of craftsmanship. Later, during Roosevelt's presidency, a Federal Committee on Apprentice Training was established under the National Recovery Administration in 1934, and the Fitzgerald Act was passed by a unanimous Congress in 1937, directing the secretary of labor "to formulate and promote the furtherance of labor standards necessary to safeguard the welfare of apprentices, to extend the application of such standards by encourag-

14. Wisconsin, *Session Laws, 1911,* p. 381.

ing the inclusion thereof in contracts of apprenticeship, to bring together employers and labor for the formulation of programs of apprenticeship, to cooperate with state agencies engaged in the formulation and promotion of standards of apprenticeship, and to cooperate with the National Youth Administration and with the Office of Education of the Department of the Interior." The Federal Committee on Apprentice Training was made a permanent body within the Department of Labor and a Bureau of Apprenticeship was created within the Department to conduct activities under the Act. One of the first efforts of the Bureau under the Fitzgerald Act was to draft a model voluntary state apprenticeship statute and persuade states to adopt it, with the result that a strong federal-state partnership, acting collaboratively with industry-wide councils like the American Construction Council, became the regulatory mode in the domain of apprenticeship. It was a pattern that has prevailed to the present.[15]

Apprenticeship, at least as defined in state and federal law during the twentieth century, usually involved a minor sixteen years of age or older in a contractual relationship with an employer, whereby the minor received instruction in a trade, craft, or business. In addition, as there had always been, there were informal apprenticeship systems within business and industry whereby workers learned to carry out a job that was new to them through the assistance of other workers or of supervisors. The learner was usually a novice in an entry level job or a person recently promoted to a new job with new responsibilities. And the means of learning ranged all the way from the "pick-up method," in which the worker gained the requisite knowledge and skills to perform the job on a hit-or-miss basis through trial and error and informal questioning; to the understudy or helper method, in which the worker was assigned to a fellow worker who knew the job and gained the requisite knowledge and skills through a combination of imitation, questioning, and teaching; to the training method, in which the worker was taught by the supervisor who oversaw his or her work, either individually or as part of a group; to the "vestibule school" method, in which the worker was systematically instructed in the department in which the work was to be done before actually taking up the work as a helper, understudy, or trainee; to the "training department" method, in which the worker was systematically instructed in a special department of the company with explicit responsibility for training and education.

15. U.S., *Statutes at Large*, L, Part I, 664.

The growth and systematization of such learning and teaching systems within business and industry were among the most significant educational developments of twentieth-century America. There is obviously no way to mark the beginning of any or all of them. The establishment of the Hoe Company school in 1872 is often taken as a benchmark event, as is the organization of the National Association of Corporation Schools in 1913. But those events involved schooling, while corporation programs of education from the beginning embraced a much broader variety of educational arrangements and techniques. In fact, the development of education programs within business and industry is much more fruitfully viewed in its relation to several of the larger social and intellectual movements that marked the rise of American industry during the twentieth century. The first such connection came early in the century, when the notion of scientific management associated with Frederick W. Taylor, Frank B. Gilbreth, and Sanford E. Thompson swept the business community. As part of that movement, education came to be seen as one important means of promoting efficiency—in fact, in its statement of objectives the National Association of Corporation Schools maintained: "Corporations are realizing more and more the importance of education in the efficient management of their business. The Company school has been sufficiently tried out as a method of increasing efficiency to warrant its continuance as an industrial factor."[16]

It was during the early years of the century that many of the firms that constituted the initial membership of the NACS first created their schools. Typical of the era was the program that the department store magnate John Wanamaker organized in 1897 as the John Wanamaker Commercial Institute. Wanamaker himself claimed that the Institute, organized as part of the Philadelphia store, was nothing less than a school of practice in business methods, "giving daily opportunities to obtain a working education in the arts and sciences of commerce and trade." The curriculum of the school included reading, writing, arithmetic, English, spelling, stenography, commercial geography, commercial law, and business methods; the faculty consisted of twenty-four teachers, some drawn from the store, others from the Philadelphia schools. New employees spent two sessions a week at the school in the morning; more advanced employees spent two sessions a week in the evening, after having supper in the store's cafeteria. In addition, boys and girls alike were organized into drill companies—

16. National Association of Corporation Schools, *Bulletin No. 2* (New York: National Association of Corporation Schools, 1914), front matter.

separated along gender lines—designed to teach the lessons of "discipline, organization, precision and obedience" and to provide the "health lessons of muscular training that give bodily strength without which successful mental work is impossible." So far as Wanamaker was concerned, the educational program more than paid for itself. "Unintelligent and wasteful labor has lessened," he observed. "The wisdom of co-operation and mutual helpfulness has been recognized. Knowledge of merchandise, its production, distribution and uses has been increased. Principles of control and government and organization have developed."[17]

The second connection between education programs in the workplace and more general social and intellectual movements developed during and after World War I, when the gospel of "welfarism"—the provision of services to employees in the hope that they would come to feel positively toward their companies and thereby resist the blandishments of union organizers—swept American industry. Education was one of the leading services provided, the goal being not only the development of technical skills but also the advancement of Americanization, more stable family life, and more rewarding recreation. Companies made substantial contributions to local public schools so that the children of their employees might have a better general education, and they sponsored homemaking classes, sewing schools, and instruction in English and civics for their employees and their families. Beyond that, they established libraries and published house organs filled with company chitchat, inspirational messages, and soft-selling editorials intended to unify the so-called company family. The company-wide education program that the International Harvester Company launched in 1908 and rapidly expanded during the succeeding decade was prototypical. It started with a school for apprentices but soon came to include courses in everything from mechanical drawing to shopwork—in fact, Harvester offered to teach any course that five or more employees might apply for. It also involved a large-scale Americanization program conducted by the YMCA, using methods developed by Peter Roberts, head of the Association's industrial department, a series of libraries and clubhouses, and a publication called *Harvester World* that regularly brought the company's messages to employees. The Americanization work waxed and waned with the nationwide Americanization effort between 1914 and 1924, but the more general program continued over the years, despite the fact that,

17. John Wanamaker, "The John Wanamaker Commercial Institute—A Store School," *Annals of the American Academy of Political and Social Science*, XXXIII (1909), 151, 153–154.

like most ventures in "welfarism," it did not succeed in weaning the workers from union organizers.

A third general spur to the growth of workplace education developed during the first years of the century with the organization of the General Electric Research Laboratory in 1900, the Westinghouse Research Laboratory in 1903, and the research and experimental division of the American Telephone and Telegraph Company in 1907, though it came to fruition during the 1920's when several hundred industrial laboratories were established for the purpose of applying the findings of scientific research to the creation of new products, the improvement of old products, and more generally, the achievement of greater productivity. Until World War II, the education associated with industrial laboratories tended to be an elite enterprise involving highly trained scientific and technical workers within the laboratories themselves, within the upper reaches of management, product development, and production design and operation, and within associated departments of science, engineering, and business in the universities. During and after World War II, however, the fruits of industrial research began to be utilized more generally in the curricula and pedagogy of company education programs, and it became increasingly the case that the most advanced educational arrangements were to be found in those industries with the greatest investment in organized research and development.

The educational efforts of the Bell Telephone Company furnish an excellent example. The company was early involved in the business of education because of the need to train telephone installers and operators, and from the first years of the century it had sponsored operators' schools and installers' schools—really "vestibule schools"—that offered courses extending over one or more weeks that combined training in the technology of the telephone with telephone company policy concerning service and customer relations. From the first years of the century, too, the Bell Company and its principal subsidiary, Western Electric, had maintained industrial research laboratories. In 1907 three heretofore independent laboratories were combined to form the research and experimental division and in 1912 the division was charged with developing a practicable long-distance telephone system. Later, in 1925, Bell Laboratories was formally established as a separate unit within the company. For some forty years thereafter, the educational operation (except at the upper reaches) and the research operation ran in parallel lines, the educational effort extending into virtually every phase of the company's operation and the laboratories producing an extraordinary flow of scientific and technological advance, from John Bertrand Johnson's contributions to the clearing away of circuit noise during the 1920's to Harald T. Friis's pioneering work on microwave technology during the 1930's to Claude E. Shannon's fundamental work on information theory during the 1940's. During the 1950's, however, under the leadership of Mervin J. Kelly, the third president of Bell Laboratories, the laboratories undertook, first, a major effort toward the continuing education of their own scientific and technical staff, and second, a more systematic, scientific approach to the design and delivery of training and education for the entire Bell system. In effect, the laboratories, working with the system-wide Human Resource Department, created a complex educational network that involved facilities ranging from spare rooms in local telephone offices to the university-style campus at Lisle, Illinois, curricula ranging from self-instruction for foremen to carefully designed programs of classroom instruction for managers, and a budget of a billion dollars a year. There were administrative and organizational changes with the court-ordered division of the Bell system in 1982, but the concept of a close relationship between research and education continued.

Five additional observations bear comment. First, it is obvious that the demands of efficiency, welfarism, and science frequently coincided. John Wanamaker doubtless believed he was building company loyalty with his drill teams, along with "discipline, organization, precision and obedience"; International Harvester was doubtless trying to enhance efficiency with its welfare program; and the Bell system was doubtless seeking to advance efficiency and loyalty at the same time that it attempted to build the fruits of applied scientific research into the substance and pedagogy of its training and education programs. In short, the educational outcomes of the scientific management movement, the welfare capitalism movement, and the industrial research movement were by no means mutually exclusive.

Second, it should be borne in mind that the effort to tie research to education in industry was essentially different from the effort to tie research to education in agriculture, insofar as the independent farmer, as an entrepreneur, had a greater stake in adopting new methods than did the wage-earning worker (in contrast to the stock-owning manager). As agriculture became increasingly industrialized during the twentieth century and as the number of employee-owned firms increased after World War II the difference may have narrowed, but it remained one of the persistent problems of education within industry to enlist the genuine interest of the workers. Third, much like the companies themselves, the various trade associations that grew up during the twentieth century in connection with the various segments of American industry also carried on educational activities, through individual courses arranged with colleges and universities, through specially designed programs that they themselves conducted, and through periodic conventions at which the displays, the talks, and the more systematic public relations activities all instructed. And fourth, beginning in 1945, when the General Motors Institute in Flint, Michigan, a wholly owned subsidiary of the General Motors Corporation, was empowered to grant engineering degrees, a select number of association and corporation programs won state authorization for the granting of undergraduate and graduate degrees—in a 1985 survey she undertook for the Carnegie Foundation for the Advancement of Teaching, Nell P. Eurich found over a dozen such programs, granting everything from the bachelor's degree to the doctorate, with others in the making.[18]

Finally, and important, workingpeople developed their own programs of education, often in collective opposition to the programs of businessmen. As labor educators were wont to point out, the very act of organizing and maintaining a union—the recruitment of members, the gaining of recognition, the negotiation and administration of an agreement, the handling of grievances—proved a continuing education for the workers who were involved. And the conduct of a strike often intensified that education, as the consciousness of issues was heightened, and the sense of group cohesiveness deepened. Thus, to take but one notable example, when American businessmen at the end of World War I developed and publicized the so-called American Plan, preaching the virtues of antiunionism and the open shop, American workers responded with some 3,600 strikes in 1919 alone, involving over four million workers. The result was an educational experience that led many workers beyond such traditional issues as higher wages and shorter hours to demands for nationalization of the railroads and coal mines and worker control of industry.

Not surprisingly, workingpeople also established a number of more formal educational programs and institutions, often in collaboration with socialist intellectuals. The socialist movement itself employed every conceivable educational device, including leaflets, pamphlets, books, and periodicals, lectures, lyceums, study circles,

18. Nell P. Eurich, *Corporate Classrooms: The Learning Business* (Princeton, N.J.: The Carnegie Foundation for the Advancement of Teaching, 1985), pp. 89–95.

discussion meetings, and formal classes, to popularize its critique of capitalist institutions and its characteristic battery of social and economic remedies. And in 1906, the Rand School of Social Science was organized in New York City under the aegis of the Socialist Party systematically to develop and expound socialist theory. Most often, however, particular unions undertook their own programs of training and education, usually stressing the techniques of organization and collective bargaining. Thus, the International Ladies' Garment Workers' Union established its own Educational Department in 1916, with Juliet Stuart Poyntz as director and Fannia M. Cohn as secretary; and the Amalgamated Clothing Workers of America followed suit in 1919, with J. B. S. Hardman as director. In addition, labor colleges were organized, modeled after such English prototypes as the Workingmen's College in London and Ruskin College at Oxford, to offer courses directed to those preparing for service in the labor movement. The best-known were Brookwood Labor College (1921–1937) at Katonah, New York, which was organized under the leadership of the Socialist leaders James Maurer and A. J. Muste and which offered theoretical work in social history and philosophy as well as practical work in union organizing and the analysis of strike situations, along with opportunities for the writing and performing of labor drama; and the Bryn Mawr Workers' Summer School (1921–1938), which was organized by M. Carey Thomas and Hilda "Jane" Worthington Smith along the lines of Ruskin College at Oxford to exemplify the commitment to educating workingwomen for life rather than livelihood, which meant courses in literature, history, hygiene, science, and modern industrial society rather than in union organizing and strike management. Finally, there were such collaborative activities as the Workers' Education Bureau of America, organized in 1921 as a clearinghouse for labor education throughout the United States, and the AFL-CIO National Labor Studies Center (later, the George Meany Center for Labor Studies) at Silver Spring, Maryland, organized in 1970 as an institute for the practical training of potential leaders of the labor movement in the diurnal affairs of unionism.

III

The professions flourished in the more complex and specialized society that came into being during the decades following the Civil War. The traditional professions of medicine, law, and divinity expanded rapidly, as did fields aspiring to professional status such as dentistry,

PLACES OF WORK 493

engineering, teaching, nursing, and librarianship. One result was that the total number of Americans involved in professional service rose from 372,000 in 1870, to 944,000 in 1890, to 1,758,000 in 1910. Moreover, the shift from apprenticeship to schooling as the preferred mode of entry into both the old, established and the newer, aspiring professions, already manifest during the second third of the nineteenth century, accelerated. In consequence, the number of medical schools rose from 78 in 1876 to 135 in 1910, of law schools, from 42 in 1876 to 114 in 1910, and of theological schools, from 124 in 1876 to 184 in 1910; the number of graduate schools for the training of college and university teachers increased; and special training schools for the occupations aspiring to professional status made their appearance and multiplied. In effect, as Burton Bledstein has observed, the Gilded Age was also a guilded age, in which one of the important boundaries that was developed to regulate the social experience of individuals and groups was the boundary marked by professional status.[19]

In medicine and law, the era between 1870 and 1910 witnessed the emergence of distinctive new models of graduate professional training that would dominate those fields through most of the twentieth century—in medicine, the model was the one William Henry Welch and his colleagues worked out at the Johns Hopkins Medical School; in law, it was the one Christopher Columbus Langdell and his colleagues worked out at the Harvard Law School. Both models were developed during periods of professional expansion that were also marked by widespread dissatisfaction with contemporary professional training and practice; and both imposed drastically altered standards upon their respective fields. Yet they could not have been more different in the solutions they embodied to the problems of professional education.

Medical education at the time of Welch's appointment as professor of pathology at the Johns Hopkins University in 1884 was a combination of apprenticeship, the study of textbooks such as Caspar Wistar's anatomy, Robley Dunglison's physiology, and George Wood's medicine, and formal lectures. Most aspiring physicians entered the pro-

19. *Historical Statistics of the United States*, I, 140–141; U.S., Bureau of the Census, *Special Census Report on the Occupations of the Population of the United States at the Eleventh Census: 1890* (Washington, D.C.: Government Printing Office, 1896), p. 11; U.S., Bureau of Education, *Report of the Commissioner of Education for 1900–01*, II, 1732–1733, *Report of the Commissioner of Education for the Year Ended 1910*, II, Statistical Tables 75–78; *Biennial Survey of Education, 1920–22*, II, Table 7; and Burton J. Bledstein, *The Culture of Professionalism: The Middle Class and the Development of Higher Education in America* (New York: W. W. Norton & Company, 1976), p. 56.

fession via one or another of the proprietary medical schools that had grown up by the score during the nineteenth century. Generally organized and staffed by local practitioners and often closely allied with local medical societies, these schools offered what were essentially didactic lectures on the principal medical subjects, that is, anatomy, physiology, chemistry, surgery, medicine, therapeutics, pharmacology, and obstetrics. The total course ordinarily ran from one to three years in length and the degree generally carried with it the legal right to practice.

The heart of Welch's new medical curriculum lay in three major reforms. First, the preclinical subjects of anatomy, physiology, pharmacology, and pathology were taught via laboratory inquiry—following the teaching of the great European investigators who had revolutionized the study of physiology and medicine, notably Pierre Louis and later Louis Pasteur at Paris, Carl Ludwig at Leipzig, and Robert Koch at Breslau, Welch displayed an inveterate preference for facts over theories and for inquiry over didactics. Second, Welch made his own subject, pathology, the keystone of medical science as defined within the medical school. In consequence, the essence of medicine came to be conceived as the diagnosis and cure of disease. Third, building on the plans developed by John Shaw Billings during the 1870's, Welch made the hospital central to the life of the medical school and the medical school central to the life of the hospital. He arranged for the clinical subjects of medicine, surgery, and obstetrics to be rooted in the ongoing life of the associated teaching hospital—a new institution in its own right insofar as hospitals had not previously had their own laboratories—so that students learned through a combination of inquiry and practice conducted under expert supervision. As Billings once put it, "the sooner he [the student] can begin to profitably receive instruction by the bedside of the sick, or rather to instruct himself there, the better. Nothing can take the place of this; if it be not obtained before graduation, when errors can be prevented by the teacher, it must be obtained afterward at the expense of the first patients who present themselves." In addition, Welch insisted that the teaching hospital be linked to the medical school via an appointment system whereby professors in the medical school also served as heads of their respective departments in the hospital, an arrangement that not only made them responsible for the delivery of medical services and the organization of medical instruction but also permitted them to integrate advanced medical students into the life of the hospital in such a way that they could serve with maximum effectiveness while

they learned with maximum efficiency. The result was a profound
change in medical education as well as in the hospital as a site for the
professional practice of medicine. Professional preparation for medicine became a combination of scientific inquiry in the laboratory, via
the preclinical subjects of anatomy, pharmacology, physiology, and
pathology, and supervised practice, via training in the clinical subjects
of surgery, medicine, and obstetrics; while hospitals became places
where research and instruction were central rather than peripheral to
the work routine of the professional staff.[20]

Legal education at the time of Langdell's appointment as dean of
the Harvard Law School in 1870 was in its own way much like medical
education, a combination of apprenticeship in a law office, study of
textbooks on the law by commentators such as St. George Tucker,
James Kent, and Joseph Story, and formal lectures. If there was a
difference, it lay in the fact that most aspirants to the law entered the
profession via apprenticeship and self-study, assisted from time to
time by lectures purchased on a course-by-course basis. The primary
claim of the law schools was not that they could substitute for law
office training but rather that their lectures represented a more efficient way of teaching the general principles of law than the haphazard
instruction given by busy practicing attorneys.

The heart of Langdell's law curriculum lay in the case method of
instruction, the doctrinal analysis of appellate court opinions. Rather
than studying the commentaries of Tucker, Kent, or Story, students
were presented with the cases themselves and asked to derive their
own commentaries in the form of general principles. And, rather than
listening to lectures on the general principles of law, students were
confronted with a Socratic dialogue in which the professor sought at
the same time to elicit "true" rules and to inculcate proper modes of
legal reasoning. At bottom, the case method rested on three assumptions—that lawyers would be better trained in law schools than in law
offices, that law schools would be better established within universities than independent of them, and that for law to be worthy of a place
in the universities it would have to become a science—Langdell once
observed that the case book became for the law school what the
laboratory was for the physics department. After students had
grasped the science of law, everything of significance for the practice
of law would follow. In sum, preparation for the law became the study,

20. John S. Billings, "Suggestions on Medical Education" [December 6, 1877], in Alan
M. Chesny, ed., "Two Papers by John Shaw Billings on Medical Education," *Bulletin of the
Johns Hopkins Hospital,* LXII (1938), 326.

via the case method, of a baker's dozen of core subjects—property, common law pleading, contracts, torts, and criminal law during the first year; and equity, evidence, corporations, sales, agency, persons, bills and notes, and constitutional law later on.[21]

One would look in vain for a similarly determinative model in the field of theology. Given the essential fact of denominationalism, theological education during the 1880's and 1890's was even more varied and fragmented than legal or medical education, ranging from Bible college work, really at the secondary-school level, extending over several months and requiring no particular standards for admission, a pattern common among a number of the fundamentalist sects; to some of the more formally organized programs of the Lutherans, Baptists, Disciples of Christ, and Roman Catholics that combined academic and theological training in a four-year undergraduate curriculum; to the graduate, professional seminary programs that required a bachelor's degree for admission and featured a three-year curriculum that commonly combined studies in Hebrew and Greek exegesis, church history, systematic theology, pastoral theology, and homiletics, with more or less of an opportunity to engage informally in the practical work of churches, missions, YMCAs and YWCAs, and social settlements. A great deal of attention was given in the literature of theological education to an essay Charles W. Eliot published in 1883 under the title "On the Education of Ministers," in which he called for a thorough undergraduate preparation in the Greek, Latin, Hebrew, and German languages, in spoken and written English as well as English literature, and in psychology, political economy, history, and the natural sciences, followed by a three-year professional curriculum that would include Semitic studies, New Testament criticism and exegesis, ecclesiastical history, comparative religion, psychology, ethics, and philosophy of religion, systematic theology, homiletics, and practical work in "charitable and reformatory methods, and the contest of Christian society with licentiousness, intemperance, pauperism, and crime." By the 1890's, the work of the Harvard Divinity School embodied much of the substance and spirit of what Eliot had urged. It was explicitly "unsectarian," in that scholarship rather than subscription to any particular creed defined the general outlook of the school; it aspired to "objectivity," with the result that the historical approach was favored throughout the curriculum— indeed, the historical approach became the hallmark of the school;

21. Christopher Columbus Langdell, "Harvard Celebration Speeches," *Law Quarterly Review* (London), III (1887), 124.

and it sought breadth of training, via reliance upon the elective system, not only within the curriculum of the school, but also more generally within the university and especially the faculty of arts and sciences. Granted Eliot's influence on the Harvard Divinity School, however, neither Eliot nor the Harvard Divinity School was particularly influential on any other divinity school. The institution that most closely resembled the Harvard Divinity School was the Union Theological Seminary in New York, which owed no debt to Eliot or to Harvard; and neither Harvard nor Union exercised any determinative influence on theological education at large. In contrast to legal and medical education during the twentieth century, the central fact of theological education remained the fact of pluralism.[22]

Professionalization, of course, required more than a particular kind of education; it inevitably involved some form of professional association, some kind of licensing by the state, and some sort of code of ethics that would be enforced by a recognized authority through widely understood procedures, to which members of the profession were expected to subscribe. Medicine and law could boast all of these by 1900; clergymen, of course, were certified, not by the state, but rather by the several religious communities, each acting according to its own discipline. Yet, granted the multiplicity of factors involved in professionalization, occupations seeking professional status were invariably caught up in the effort to define an appropriate education for entry into the work, and what is striking is the immense variation in the forms of education that emerged. Dentistry, not surprisingly, sought to develop paradigms that closely followed medicine; in fact, there were many efforts during the nineteenth century to make dentistry a subspecialty of medicine, and Harvard actually moved in that direction with the establishment of the D.M.D. program in the Harvard Medical School. Engineering developed paradigms that combined general education in the humanities, a solid grounding in mathematics and the sciences, and specialized work in drawing, mechanics, the applications of science, and shopwork, all of it on the undergraduate level and the shopwork taking a considerable range of forms, from simple observation of technicians at work to actual labor in an ongoing industrial establishment, though rarely constituting more than a small fraction of the curriculum.

College and university teaching developed a paradigm in which three years of graduate instruction in an academic discipline concen-

22. Charles W. Eliot, "On the Education of Ministers," in *Educational Reform: Essays and Addresses* (New York: The Century Company, 1898), p. 82.

trated wholly on training for scholarship, to the exclusion of systematic preparation for teaching; while elementary- and secondary-school teaching developed an alternative paradigm that enlisted most teachers through normal schools at the secondary level and a very few through teachers colleges, with the programs concentrating on subject matters and methods of teaching, to the exclusion of training for scholarship. Preparation for business and management followed the pattern of law, insofar as few school programs provided for internships or practical experience, but it diverged from the legal pattern insofar as most programs were carried on at the undergraduate level; much the same was true of preparation for librarianship, accounting, and pharmacy. Preparation for nursing combined theoretical work with supervised experience, but mostly at the secondary level, not unlike the work of the normal schools.

The differences among the several professions reflected much more than the accidents of history. As one can observe with special clarity in the relationships between associated "male" and "female" professions, they derived as much from fundamental differences in the size, structure, prestige, and social composition of the occupational groups seeking professional status. Medicine and nursing provide a case in point. Both had undergone tremendous change by 1920, the most vital development in each having been the acceptance of a more scientific, hospital-based preparatory training. That similarity notwithstanding, the differences between the two were patent. Although there were essentially the same numbers of formally trained nurses and physicians in 1920, the overwhelming number of nurses were women in the employ of private, eleemosynary, and public hospitals, while the overwhelming number of physicians were male and self-employed. Beyond that, most of the nurses had been prepared in hospital training schools at the secondary level, while most of the physicians had been prepared in medical school programs that had followed upon some sort of postsecondary schooling. Most important, perhaps, doctors prescribed for their patients, while nurses, however vital their services, merely carried out the doctors' orders. Nursing did change during the decades following 1920, but gender relationships between physicians and nurses, which mirrored gender relationships in general, tended to make a mockery of enthusiastic talk by nursing leaders of a nursing profession.

That said, one must note, too, that as the quest for professional status went relentlessly forward—in a classic article the sociologist Harold L. Wilensky called the phenomenon "the professionalization of everyone"—the concept of profession itself broadened; and the broadening raised profoundly significant problems of educational policy. Emerging as a major force in the shaping of policy at the turn of the century, philanthropic foundations early recognized these problems, and some, notably the Carnegie Foundation for the Advancement of Teaching, addressed them with far-reaching consequences. As Ellen Condliffe Lagemann has pointed out in her history of the Carnegie Foundation, Henry Smith Pritchett, the astronomer who served as the Foundation's first president, was profoundly distressed by the social and intellectual turbulence that marked the emergence of urban, industrial society during the last quarter of the nineteenth century and deeply committed to having the Carnegie Foundation serve as a "great agency" to reform American education so that it could more effectively prepare the scientifically trained experts that Pritchett believed were needed for social, political, and intellectual leadership. Among these experts, he ranked physicians high within the professional hierarchy he hoped to help create, and schoolteachers low. And, in keeping with this belief, the Carnegie Foundation's study of medical education, the famous Flexner Report, advocated a high-standard paradigm of professional training that was intended to limit access to the profession, whereas the Foundation's later study of teacher education by William S. Learned and William C. Bagley recommended a pattern that was essentially trade education rather than professional education. Subsequently, as "the professionalization of everyone" proceeded, the very same Foundation would become a major advocate of higher standards for teacher education and greater professional status for teachers.[23]

The constant press for more education as more occupations sought and achieved professional status did not in the end reduce differences among the professions. Thus, education for medicine and law became wholly graduate education, along the lines of the Welch and Langdell models; education for dentistry and optometry sought eagerly to follow the medical model but tended to lag in achieving it. Education for business, engineering, journalism, accounting, librarianship, teaching, nursing, and social work moved slowly to the postsecondary level and then to various mixes of undergraduate and graduate training. And education for new fields aspiring to professional

23. Harold L. Wilensky, "The Professionalization of Everyone," *American Journal of Sociology*, LXX (1964–65), 137–138; Ellen Condliffe Lagemann, *Private Power for the Public Good: A History of the Carnegie Foundation for the Advancement of Teaching* (Middletown: Wesleyan University Press, 1983), chap. iii and *passim;* and Ernest L. Boyer, *High School: A Report on Secondary Education in America* (New York: Harper & Row, 1983), pp. 174–185.

status, such as corrections, hotel management, and undertaking, tended to begin at the junior college level and then to move gradually toward bachelor's and master's degree programs. Yet, significantly, even after teacher education and nursing education had been dramatically upgraded in the 1960's, teachers and nurses, still articulating the rhetoric of professionalism, joined the union movement in large numbers and related to school and hospital administrators through collective bargaining rather than professional colleagueship. And even as corrections officers designed programs of corrections education that they hoped would win them professional status, they too unionized, as did their supervisors, and dealt with their elected and appointed commissioners through collective bargaining. Amitai Etzioni coined the term "semi-professions" to deal with the irony during the late 1960's, but in the end the term clouded as well as clarified distinctions.[24]

Four additional points bear comment. First, most professional education between 1870 and 1910 was classroom education in the didactic mode—Welch's model was the exception rather than the rule, even after it came to dominate medical education—and indeed most professional education in 1970 was classroom education in the didactic mode. Yet all the professions and subprofessions without exception experimented with a wide variety of arrangements for training in practice, from the model school to the management internship, from the cooperating industrial or architectural firm to the cooperating library or pharmacy, from the simulated newsroom of the journalism schools to the war games of the military academies. And that experimentation created important educational ventures in the workplace, often less formal than the apprentice training programs and vestibule schools of industry and more collegial in character, but no less significant. What is more, particularly in the period after World War II, when continuing education for the professions began to develop on a large scale, first on a voluntary basis and later on the basis of state mandates for continued licensing, those educational ventures expanded rapidly, often in cooperation with professional schools or professional associations but often managed by educational leaders within the workplace—the technical, scientific, and management training of the Bell telephone system, described earlier, was one among many possible examples—or by independent consultants who began to specialize in the continuing education of professionals. The resultant enterprise was sufficiently large so that by the 1970's it was a matter of competition as well as collaboration within the professions as to who would conduct continuing education, on what basis and where, as well as who would pay for it and who would reap the financial rewards.

Second, with the professionalization of the various health services—not only nursing but nutrition, rehabilitation, pharmacy, clinical psychology, public health work, hospital social work, and hospital administration—the teaching hospital became the educational center for a wide range of professions, conveying formal instruction in the arts and skills associated with the various specialties at the same time that it proffered informal instruction in the relationship of each specialty and its practitioners to all the others. Put otherwise, John Shaw Billings's vision of the hospital as an institution for research and instruction as well as for the delivery of medical services was vastly expanded to embrace the full range of proliferating health and health-related professions. None achieved the close integration of academic and clinical instruction that ideally characterized medical education, but all reached some measure of integration; and in the process the modern hospital became a leading center for the preparatory and continuing education of professionals.

Third, the model schools that had been associated with normal schools from the early decades of the nineteenth century became, like teaching hospitals, important centers of education, not only for the youngsters who attended them but also for the teachers who worked in them. Increasingly called laboratory schools after the institution developed by the Deweys at Chicago, these schools often consciously modeled themselves after the teaching hospital, conducting systematic research into pedagogical problems, maintaining joint appointments with the schools or departments of education with which they were affiliated, and paying careful attention to the instruction of aspiring teachers and supervisors. Beyond that, in the classic examples at the University of Chicago, Teachers College, Columbia University, the University of Wisconsin, the University of Illinois, and the University of California at Los Angeles during the first third of the century, the social organization of the laboratory school was as radically transformed as the social organization of the teaching hospital. When the affiliated laboratory schools fell out of favor during the second third of the century, partly because they had become favored institutions for the education of faculty children and partly because they were expensive institutions to run, the effort was made to create similar arrangements with public school systems; but the effort achieved less certain success, owing, on the one hand, to the legal restrictions involved and, on the other hand, to the lack of clearly defined lines of authority between the school systems and the teacher-education institutions with which they collaborated. Nevertheless, as the number and variety of professionals engaged in school functions increased during the 1950's and 1960's—one thinks of guidance counselors, school nutritionists, school nurses, attendance officers, and curriculum specialists, to name but a few—the university-affiliated school system, like the teaching hospital, became a leading center for the preparatory and continuing education of professionals.

Finally, with the rise of knowledge-generating organizations during the twentieth century, particularly research universities, research institutes, research laboratories, and research libraries, a new kind of workplace was created in which certain kinds of education, notably independent study and collegial instruction, came to the fore. University faculty members taught students, of course, but they also pursued independent study and taught one another, and the same was true of the specialized scholars in organizations like the Smithsonian Institution in Washington, the National Institutes of Health in Bethesda, the National Bureau of Economic Research in Cambridge, the Battelle Memorial Institute in Columbus, the Rand Corporation in Santa Monica, and the Huntington Library, Art Collections, and Botanical Gardens in San Marino. When all was said and done, it was the research university, with its congeries of departments, schools, centers, institutes, laboratories, museums, observatories, and affiliated hospitals and school systems, that became the greatest of all the centers for the preparatory and continuing education of professionals, including the professionals who constituted its core faculties.

IV

Education within the military establishment represented a fascinating combination of informal apprenticeship, indoctrination, vestibule schools, and technical and professional training, geared during the century following the Civil War to cycles in which the armed services, kept small in accordance with traditional American suspicions regarding standing military forces, were rapidly expanded from time to time to meet the needs of military exigency. They were increased by enlistments to some 236,000 men during the Spanish-American War and then reduced in 1901 to 112,000, then increased by enlistments and conscription to just under 3,000,000 men (along with some 34,000 women volunteers) during America's participation in World War I and again reduced to under 270,000 in 1922, and then increased by enlistments and conscription again to some 12,000,000 men (and, by the end of the war, just under 300,000 women volunteers) during World War II and then reduced less drastically after that war as the concept of the "force in being" replaced the concept of a small standing military and as conscription continued during a troubled era of peace interrupted by the Korean and Vietnam wars. In 1973, the force in being changed significantly with the ending of conscription and the establishment of an all-volunteer military.[25]

During the first two-thirds of the nineteenth century, the military had sponsored professional education for officers and on-the-job training for enlisted men. The United States Military Academy had been established at West Point in 1802 and, during the superintendency of Sylvanus Thayer between 1817 and 1833, had developed the distinctive curriculum that would mark its work for more than a century. Thayer, taking into account requirements that had been set by Congress in 1812, had organized the curriculum of the academy around a characteristic system of discipline, a characteristic pedagogy, and a characteristic content. The system of discipline had been strictly hierarchical, involving a commandant of cadets, with responsibility under the superintendent for discipline and training, who was assisted by a group of subordinate military officers, who were in turn responsible for a corps of cadets with its own cadet officers, mostly first- and second-classmen. The pedagogy had involved small classes that met regularly, with each cadet reciting daily and being graded for his recitation. And the curriculum had been wholly prescribed, extending over four years, with the emphasis in classroom work on engineering subjects including drawing, mathematics, French (an absolutely utilitarian requirement, since many of the engineering and mathematics textbooks were available only in French), chemistry, natural philosophy, geography, history, and moral philosophy, and with the emphasis during summer encampments on military exercises. When the Naval Academy was established in 1845, it had adopted much of the so-called Thayer system. Thus, by the time of the Civil War, elite officers in the regular Army and Navy—there had always been other roads to commissions than the academies—were receiving a distinctive formal training, most of it on the undergraduate level, explicitly designed to

25. *Historical Statistics of the United States*, II, 1141.

produce professional military leaders. Enlisted men learned what they needed to know from their peers and from the noncommissioned officers of their units and ships. The skills of a rifleman or cavalryman or seaman or naval gunner were readily learned on the job by the time-honored methods of imitation, trial-and-error, correction, and repetition. The one other element in the system came through the provisions of the Morrill Act of 1862, where Congress mandated that the land grant colleges include military science and tactics in their curricula. Morrill's arguments for the provision were that the need for officers in the rapidly expanding Union armies could be better met by a military reserve prepared through civilian educational institutions than by a build-up of professional officers prepared at an enlarged West Point. The legislation had little chance to affect the Union armies in any significant way, but it did profoundly affect the United States Army in the years that followed.

During the period between the Civil War and World War I, professional education for the officer class expanded and proliferated, while general education for enlisted men under military auspices was begun on a small scale. The military and naval academies proceeded along the lines set by the Thayer system, with continued emphasis on engineering, mathematics, and technical subjects. In 1866, 1888, and 1891, Congress made provision for the detailing of Army officers who would serve as professors of military science and tactics to the land grant colleges, and many of the states made enrollment in military science and tactics courses mandatory for students attending land grant institutions. More significant, however, was the creation of graduate military education in the form of the specialized infantry, ordnance, quartermaster, engineer, and artillery schools, of a Naval War College and an Army War College, of an Army General Service and Staff School—later, the Command and General Staff School—and of a postgraduate division at the Naval Academy that offered courses in ordnance, mechanical engineering, radio, shop management, naval architecture, and civil engineering. Instruction for enlisted men "in the common English branches of education, and especially in the history of the United States" was mandated by Congress in 1866 and made compulsory by Army regulations in 1889, frequently but not always under the supervision of Army chaplains; but neither officers nor enlisted men were reputed to be much interested in formal academics and in general what they wanted and needed to know continued to be learned informally from peers and noncommissioned officers. In effect, both the Army and the Navy on the eve of World

War I were somewhat isolated American subcommunities, tightly organized, rigidly disciplined, and in many respects monastic.[26]

World War I marked a great divide. For one thing, as the size of the military increased from 180,000 on the eve of American entry into the war to almost 3,000,000 some nineteen months later, largely through conscription (from which one could not escape by hiring a substitute), the armed forces became much more representative of the American population at large. For another, given the fact that conscription brought large numbers of recent immigrants into the Army, whose loyalty, rightly or wrongly, became a matter of concern (actually, aliens never constituted more than ten percent of the armed forces), the troops came to be viewed as a special target audience for the kinds of propaganda the Committee on Public Information was directing to the domestic population at large. And, for another, given the expectation of large casualty rates owing to the murderous character of machine-gun and trench warfare, and given as well the stark fact that French troops had already mutinied by the time the United States entered the war, there was a particular concern for the morale of the ground forces, where the largest numbers of immigrants were concentrated.

During the initial phase of the war, the Army was reluctant to deal with the matter of morale, preferring to leave the question to such private welfare agencies as the YMCA, the National Catholic Welfare Board, the Jewish Welfare Board, and the Salvation Army. By the spring of 1918, however, owing largely to the efforts of General Edward L. Munson, a Medical Corps officer who believed that "the efficiency of an army as a fighting force obviously depends on the willingness of its component individuals to contend and if necessary to die for ideas and ideals," the General Staff decided to have the Army itself undertake the task of systematically maintaining morale. The mission was assigned, first, to the Training and Instruction Branch, which disagreed with the need for such training, and then to the Intelligence Branch, which viewed the task as part of the more general need to protect troops from influences tending to impair military efficiency that derived from other than armed forces. Not surprisingly, little happened. Finally, in October, the General Staff created a separate Morale Branch under General Munson's leadership, and a morale officer was designated for each regiment and training camp with responsibility for mounting an aggressive "Will to

26. U.S., *Statutes at Large*, XIV, 336.

Win" campaign, using many of the materials and techniques of the Committee on Public Information. The Morale Branch survived beyond the Armistice in November by taking on many of the welfare activities earlier carried by the YMCA and other social service organizations, but when the Army was reorganized in 1921 the branch was dissolved.[27]

Beyond the general orientation and indoctrination that were intended to maintain high morale, the Army soon found itself also involved in literacy, technical, and leadership training. Literacy training derived from the fact that, on the basis of the Army Alpha and Army Beta tests, roughly a quarter of the enlisted men were labeled illiterate (the figure, incidentally, included those literate in languages other than English as well as those who had not had more than three years of schooling). Men labeled illiterate were assigned, along with men designated physically or mentally handicapped, to "development battalions," where they were given training for a time in the hope of equipping them to perform useful if menial tasks. Literacy training was ordinarily part of the curriculum, and many of the men learned to read simple messages and to write letters home during their service in development battalions.

In February, 1918, the War Department created the Committee on Education and Special Training and charged it with developing programs that would supply the enlisted and commissioned technicians that were needed by the rapidly expanding Army. The Committee quickly organized a series of intensive eight-week courses designed to produce specialists in a wide range of technical skills, and established a host of sites in vocational schools, colleges, and training camps, where the courses could be offered, mostly by civilian instructors. The Committee also organized the Students' Army Training Corps, through which potential officers might remain in colleges until called to active service and enroll for the general and technical courses that would prepare them for their duties. The hope was that the program would benefit the colleges by preserving their enrollments at the same time that it benefited the Army (later, when the draft age was lowered from twenty-one to eighteen, those enrolled in the SATC were actually inducted). The program was launched with much fanfare on October 1, 1918, but was rapidly dismantled after the Armistice in November. As was the case with a number of World War I programs, it was officially judged a success, though it was never really given an effective test.

One additional program was created by General John J. Pershing for the American Expeditionary Forces during the months after the Armistice. Amid a hue and cry for rapid demobilization, Pershing was faced with the problem of maintaining a large army with little to do; and, in general orders issued early in 1919, he established post schools that would provide elementary and secondary education for all soldiers who wished it, educational centers associated with the several corps and divisions that would offer more advanced general and technical education, and an AEF college staffed by officers and enlisted men with the appropriate academic training and experience. The University of the American Expeditionary Forces in France actually began instruction on March 19, 1919, at Beaune, with six thousand students enrolled in over two hundred courses and with opportunity for would-be teachers to undertake student teaching in the post schools. There were also arrangements under which those with the necessary qualifications might pursue advanced work at French and English universities—some six thousand men actually attended French institutions, mostly the Sorbonne and Toulouse, and some two thousand English institutions, mostly Oxford and Cambridge. For a few months, all of these programs flourished and there was a heady sense both in Europe and in the United States that formal education and training had become a permanent feature of Army life. With the drastic cuts in troop strength and financial support mandated by Congress in 1920 and 1921, however, education was once again de-emphasized and the more traditional aspects of garrison life came again to the fore.

World War II marked another great divide in the history of education in the armed forces, owing principally to the rapid mechanization of war. During American participation in World War I, it had been estimated that some fifty out of every one hundred men had required special qualifications or training as technicians. By mid-1942, General Brehon Somervell of the Army Service Forces estimated that some sixty-three out of every one hundred men were being assigned to duties requiring specialized training; and by mid-1943 that figure had risen to some ninety out of every one hundred men. To mount the educational effort implied by these statistics meant that the armed forces had to provide or contract for programs that would make illiterates literate in a matter of weeks, that would furnish huge numbers of automobile and aircraft mechanics, bookkeepers, carpenters, dental hygienists, medical corpsmen and pharmacist's mates, quartermasters, signalmen, and torpedomen in a matter of months, and sufficient numbers of engineers, meteorologists, navigators, fluent speakers of Japanese, and able practitioners of surgery in a matter of years. Beyond that, given the development of the arts of propaganda during the 1930's, it was taken as a given among the civilian and military leaders that all troops would require the kind of information and education that would enable them to understand why they were fighting the war and to what ends, and it was also taken as a given that many of the men would have comfortable leisure time available to them and that the pursuit of education was a worthy use of that leisure time.[28]

The result was an educational program of unprecedented size and complexity. It included arrangements for literacy courses at reception centers across the country, using specially prepared materials like the *Soldier's Reader* and the *Army Reader* and technical schools of every sort and variety, staffed and operated by the armed forces themselves to train enlisted men in the skills needed to pursue the war. It involved contractual arrangements with civilian educational institutions—vocational schools, colleges, and universities—to provide specialized training in foreign languages, psychological testing, engineering, medicine, dentistry, military government, and other needed professional skills, as well as a vast information and education program conducted under the auspices of the Information and Education Division, led by General Frederick H. Osborn—one far more subtle and sophisticated than the one conducted by the Morale Division in World War I. In addition, a program of correspondence courses conducted by the United States Armed Forces Institute that at its peak enrolled over 600,000 men, and innumerable programs of classroom instruction in general and liberal subjects were organized and offered at the post, ship, and theater of operations levels. What is more, as had been the case after World War I, there were substantial programs of formal education in the posthostilities era, and these were generally better planned and organized than their earlier counterparts, partly because the occupations of Germany and Japan required larger numbers of troops over longer periods of time and partly because of the knowledge gleaned from the educational experiments of the post-Armistice period in 1919 and the precedents set by them.

With the technological revolutions of the electronics and nuclear

28. Brehon Somervell, "Education and the Armed Forces," *Journal of the National Education Association*, XXXII (October, 1943), 185–186.

eras, there could be no turning back from the need for and commitment to education on the part of the military during the post–World War II era. Indeed, the armed forces actually featured the opportunities for education and training they made available as part of their recruiting campaigns. The Air Force established its own air academy for the training of officers in 1954—one also modeled on a modified Thayer system but with greater opportunity for general education and for elective courses. ROTC and NROTC programs in colleges and universities across the country continued to be the main sources of the reserve officers for the expanded forces that fought in Korea and in Vietnam. And new specialist postgraduate schools were created to teach the sciences and arts associated with such developing fields as nuclear submarine warfare and missile and antimissile warfare. Finally, given the heated ideological context within which the Korean War was fought, troop information and education programs during the 1950's not only sought to "motivate and inform" military personnel with the "facts" that would enable them to discharge their duties "with understanding," they also began systematically to try to "offset the effects of enemy propaganda." Particularly after political charges from the far right that American soldiers had not fought well in Korea—charges subsequently disproved in scholarly studies and Senate hearings held during the early 1960's—the programs became increasingly militant in character, contrasting sharply in their emphasis on systematic indoctrination with the more moderate emphasis on information and orientation during World War II. One outcome was that the armed forces drew back from dealing with morale during the later 1960's, with the result that the troops who fought in Vietnam often had little sense of why they were there. In one study by the sociologist Charles C. Moskos, Jr., in 1967, twenty-seven of thirty-four soldiers queried in the field about their involvement in the Vietnam War answered in terms of personal misfortune—"My tough luck in getting drafted!"[29]

One of the most far-reaching changes of the post–World War II era was set in motion by President Harry S. Truman's executive order of July 28, 1948, abolishing racial segregation in the armed forces. On the eve of World War II, blacks had constituted some 5.9 percent of the Army, and there had been only five black Army officers, three of

29. Stephen D. Westbrook, "Historical Notes," in Morris Janowitz and Stephen D. Westbrook, eds., *The Political Education of Soldiers* (Beverly Hills, Cal.: Sage Publications, 1983), pp. 265, 270; and C. C. Moskos, Jr., *The American Enlisted Man* (New York: Russell Sage Foundation, 1970), pp. 148–149.

them chaplains. The Navy had permitted blacks to join as enlisted men but only to serve as stewards in the messman's branch. And the Marine Corps had simply barred blacks from enlisting. All of the services had accepted blacks for duty during the war itself but, with a few notable exceptions like the 99th and 553d Fighter Squadrons and the 332d Fighter Group, had generally segregated them in all-black units and assigned them to quartermaster, engineer, and transportation work, much of which was simply heavy-duty labor. With astonishing rapidity during the years following 1948, the armed forces were integrated, blacks were given the opportunity to enter the entire range of military occupation specialties and to compete for promotion to noncommissioned and commissioned ranks, and as a result the number and percentage of blacks in all the services increased. By the mid-1950's, well before the effects of *Brown v. Board of Education* had begun to be felt in civilian life, the armed forces had become a major avenue of educational opportunity and social mobility for blacks. Moreover, with the improvement in the public schooling available to blacks that came in the 1960's and 1970's, ever larger numbers of blacks who wished to do so were able to meet the entrance requirements of the several services. Even taking account of the period of the Vietnam war, when a disproportional number of blacks were drafted and actually saw combat, the armed services in the long run became one of the important providers of technical education for blacks, including lower-class blacks, as well as of job opportunities in which that technical education could be put to direct and immediate use in career advancement.

Many of the same phenomena were set in motion by the Women's Armed Services Act of 1948, which established a permanent place for women in the Army, the Navy, the Marine Corps, and the Air Force. Much as blacks had been confined to all-black units and assigned to menial duties in support services during World War II, women had been organized in all-female units and assigned jobs traditionally associated with women's work—nursing, quartermaster and transportation services, clerical duties, and the like. In addition, they had been set apart in special organizations like the WAC, the WAVES, and the WAFS. Hence, the Act of 1948 was intended to introduce a more effective integration into the services. Stereotypes died hard, however, and indeed there was even more ambivalence about the integration of women than there was about the integration of blacks. It was not until the 1970's that the barriers really began to topple and the number of women in the armed forces rose significantly. Women continued to be barred from certain combat roles; but, as they gained access to a growing range of military occupation specialties as well as to the three service academies and most of the postgraduate military schools, the armed services became for them, too, an important provider, not only of technical and professional education, but also of job opportunities.

Conscription ended in 1973, and for the first time since World War II the United States maintained a force in being made up wholly of volunteers. The men and women of that force had greater opportunity for general, technical, and professional education than any in recent military history—during the late 1970's as many as one in four or one in five of the enlisted men and women were in classrooms on any given day. Yet, interestingly, the men and women of that force also had less systematic opportunity for information, education, and orientation leading to an understanding of its mission than any in recent military history. The situation was at the least ironic, and to some, alarming. There was spirited public discussion during the late 1970's and early 1980's about how well such a force would perform in the heat of battle, given that military service was increasingly seen as a job or a career rather than a responsibility of citizenship. And there was discussion too of the obverse set of problems that the sociologist Morris Janowitz raised in a 1983 treatise entitled *The Reconstruction of Patriotism: Education for Civic Consciousness.* Military service, Janowitz argued, had always been more than merely a test of civic obligation; it had been an incomparable form of civic education that in its very nature had taught large numbers of Americans the responsibilities that must inevitably accompany civic rights. Americans were abandoning that form of education, Janowitz continued, at precisely the time the schools were abandoning systematic instruction in patriotism and civic commitment. The result in his opinion was a crisis that could be resolved only by a new conception of national service that would proceed on a voluntary basis, involve both governmental and private organizations, and include both military and civilian options. Janowitz was well aware that, beyond the matter of cost, one of the formidable barriers to the acceptance of such a program lay in the negative attitudes of the very young people for whom the program would be designed. Yet he deeply believed that there was no alternative to national service if a true civic consciousness was to be nurtured—schools and colleges were simply incapable of teaching the nature of political obligation. Janowitz recognized the dilemma, but refused to turn away from it. "The vitality of democratic citizenship," he concluded, "cannot be maintained by the existing range of political forms, such as voting and political participation. Historically, citizenship and patriotism have included various forms of local self-help currently associated with the idea of community or national service. Participation in these activities gives the idea of obligation concrete meaning. The need to make use of this tradition has grown, ironically, with the growth of the welfare state. The first step to make is voluntary national service available to all young men and women."[30]

V

Americans had been exporting technical expertise through education in the workplace for several generations by the time of World War II. James Bolton Davis had introduced American methods of cotton cultivation into Turkey during the 1840's, under the personal aegis of Secretary of State James Buchanan; John Adams Church had introduced American mining techniques into China during the 1860's, on the invitation of Viceroy Li Hung-chang; Charles J. Murphy had taught the cultivation of Indian corn throughout Europe during the 1880's, under the auspices of the Department of Agriculture; and Gerow Brill had established a full-fledged agricultural center for the training of agricultural leaders in China during the 1890's, under the joint auspices of Cornell University's Agricultural Experiment Station and the Department of Agriculture. And, during the first years of the twentieth century, agricultural missions under the auspices of the Department of Agriculture, or of foreign governments interested in improving production, had become fairly common in Asia, Africa, and Latin America. In addition, beyond the efforts of governments, particularly after World War I, there had been the numerous technical missions sponsored by religious organizations, philanthropic foundations, and business concerns that had established and maintained a host of institutions offering education, from schools and colleges to scientific laboratories, public health stations, agricultural demonstration projects, and industrial training enterprises. Not all of these missions had been successful, and few of those that had succeeded had displayed any genuine insight into some of the larger social and cultural consequences of their efforts—the disruptions occasioned by missionary activity in China during the 1920's were but one among many examples. Yet the fact was that, while Americans continued to

30. Morris Janowitz, *The Reconstruction of Patriotism: Education for Civic Consciousness* (Chicago: University of Chicago Press, 1983), p. 203.

import technical expertise throughout the twentieth century—from methods of German scientific research during the early years of the century to methods of Japanese business management during the later years—Americans increasingly exported technical expertise as well, and with it, a vast variety of American educational institutions for conveying and communicating that expertise.

The post–World War II era marked a watershed in such efforts, as the American government embarked upon a large, systematic, and sustained effort to share American technical expertise with the non-Communist world, and especially with the so-called underdeveloped nations. As much as any single event, President Harry S. Truman's Inaugural Address signaled the change. In a lengthy section on international relations, Truman assured the world of continuing American support for the United Nations, of continuing American contributions to world recovery, and of continuing American efforts to strengthen "freedom-loving nations against the dangers of aggression." He then added a fourth point: "We must embark," he said, "on a bold new program for making the benefits of our scientific advances and industrial progress available for the improvement and growth of underdeveloped areas."[31]

On June 24, 1949, Truman sent a special message to Congress recommending legislation authorizing the so-called Point Four programs. Essentially, he envisioned two categories of assistance, both vital and both closely interrelated. The first category embraced "the technical, scientific and managerial American knowledge necessary to economic development," including "not only medical and educational knowledge, and assistance and advice in such basic fields as sanitation, communications, road building and governmental services, but also, and perhaps most important, assistance in the survey of resources and in planning for long-range economic development." The second category embraced capital investment—the production machinery and equipment and the financial aid that would enable the underdeveloped nations to build the transportation and communication facilities, the irrigation and drainage projects, and the public utilities that were crucial to the extractive, processing, and manufacturing industries. "Technical assistance is necessary to lay the groundwork for productive investment," Truman observed. "Investment, in turn, brings with it technical assistance. In general, however, technical surveys of resources and of the possibilities of economic

31. *Public Papers of the Presidents of the United States: Harry S. Truman, 1949* (Washington, D.C.: Government Printing Office, 1964), p. 114.

development must precede substantial capital investment. Further-more, in many of the areas concerned, technical assistance in improv-ing sanitation, communications or education is required to create conditions in which capital investment can be fruitful."[32]

The legislation that had made possible the so-called Marshall Plan—the Economic Cooperation Act of 1948—had been directed primarily to Europe, though it had encompassed aid to countries in other parts of the world, notably East and Southeast Asia. As such, it had involved mostly the financial aid necessary for economic recon-struction and recovery. What was new about the Point Four program, as embodied in the Foreign Economic Assistance Act that Truman signed on June 5, 1950, was the substantial provision for government programs of technical assistance in the form of what one State Depart-ment publication called "know-how" and "show-how." Experience had indicated, the publication maintained, that the United States and other countries with advanced technical and scientific resources could make them available to underdeveloped areas in a variety of ways. These included assisting with basic surveys of economic problems; furnishing expert advisers or missions to proffer advice; helping to establish and operate research centers and laboratories; developing demonstration projects; providing on-the-job training; translating and publishing specialized reports; facilitating exchanges of students and teachers in technical fields; bringing workers, supervisors, engi-neers, and executives to the more advanced countries to observe or train in their industrial and other establishments; and establishing and operating technical libraries and film services. In effect, from the giving of advice to the development of demonstrations, the legislation put the federal government squarely in the business of exporting American education—not only schools and colleges but all the institu-tions, arrangements, and techniques that had been developed over more than a century for educating adults in their workplaces.[33]

Drawing as they did on available experience, Point Four programs sent overseas every conceivable device of American agricultural and industrial education. Demonstration farms were created in the vil-lages of India and through them new lines of seeds and methods of cultivation were introduced that doubled and tripled wheat and po-tato yields. Bulldozers were brought to Jordan in a giant water devel-

32. *Ibid.*, p. 330.
33. U.S., Department of State, *Point Four: Cooperative Program for Aid in the Development of Economically Underdeveloped Areas* (Department of State Publication 3719, Economic Cooper-ation Series 24, January, 1950; Washington, D.C.: Government Printing Office, 1950), pp. 3–4.

opment project and Jordanians were taught to operate and service the bulldozers through on-the-job training programs that combined vestibule-type instruction with methods of understudy. A literacy program in El Salvador was carried out through a Radio School of the Air that, combined with single-channel receiving sets in the villages, made impressive inroads into rural illiteracy. And a country-wide education campaign in Paraguay used traveling public health units to convey simple demonstrations of the virtues of adequate sanitation and boiled drinking water. Beyond these large government programs, there were also the numerous smaller efforts mounted by private firms in which training programs were developed in connection with particular processes and machinery—the programs of American petroleum companies in Venezuela and Saudi Arabia were among the leading examples.

Educational enterprises such as these burgeoned under the Mutual Security Agency after 1951, the Foreign Operations Administration after 1953, the International Cooperation Administration after 1955, and the Agency for International Development after 1961—the names were more than cosmetic, conveying as they did the shifting concerns that underlay American programs for the export of technical expertise. Given that most of the underdeveloped world was rural, the farm demonstration methods of the Department of Agriculture were everywhere in demand. By the late 1950's, under the auspices of the International Cooperation Administration, demonstrations had been central in introducing the moldboard plow into Iran, the cultivation of fertilized rice into Liberia, the row planting of corn into Europe, the use of hybrid corn seed into Egypt, the use of artificial insemination for the improvement of the quality of herds into Iran, and the use of commercial fertilizer into India. Along with agricultural demonstrations, public health instruction in village centers had contributed dramatically to the reduction of malaria in Taiwan, of smallpox in the Middle East, and of yaws in Latin America; while industrial training programs had helped introduce modern tire recapping into Indonesia, a grape bottling industry into Japan, wallboard production into Turkey, can lid gasket manufacture into Iran, and a ceramics industry into the Philippines.

One aspect of this government activity that was especially significant as an example of the use made of education as a means of cultural transfer was the Peace Corps, created by President John F. Kennedy in 1961. The idea of a program through which young Americans might engage in public service overseas had been discussed in Washington since early 1960, and Kennedy himself had formally proposed it during his campaign for the presidency in the autumn of that year. He created it by executive order on March 1, 1961, with his brother-in-law, R. Sargent Shriver, as director (it was later formally established by the Peace Corps Act, which Kennedy signed on September 22, 1961). The purpose of the program, as stated in the Act, was to "make available to interested countries and areas men and women of the United States qualified for service abroad and willing to serve, under conditions of hardship if necessary, to help the peoples of such countries and areas in meeting their needs for trained manpower, and to help promote a better understanding of the American people on the part of the peoples served and a better understanding of other peoples on the part of the American people." Volunteers were sent only to countries that requested them, to work on projects mutually agreed upon by those countries and Peace Corps officials. And, while no age limits were set by the legislation, it was anticipated, and indeed the anticipation was correct, that most of the volunteers would be recent college graduates in their twenties. The program grew rapidly, to slightly over four thousand by the end of 1962, to some seven thousand in 1963, to almost twelve thousand in 1965, and to a peak of some fifteen thousand in 1967. Volunteers were serving in thirty-seven countries in 1962, in forty-six in 1963, in fifty in 1967, and in sixty-nine in 1974. Most of the volunteers worked as schoolteachers, and many of them taught English to speakers of other languages. But they also served in agricultural demonstration work, vocational training, rural community development, youth club organization, and public health instruction. As with more general technical assistance programs, much of the work, whatever it was called, involved teaching.[34]

Finally, quite apart from government sponsorship or assistance, there was the burgeoning program of educational enterprise carried on by American corporations as they increased their overseas activities during the 1960's and 1970's. A 1967 survey of forty-five American multinational firms doing business in Latin America revealed something of the range and variety of educational efforts mounted within the private sector—on-the-job instruction in fields like sales and marketing, financial operations, personnel management, and general administration; classroom instruction in accounting, engineering, and languages; industrial training in a host of skills, from

34. Peace Corps Act, U.S., *Statutes at Large*, LXXV, 612; and Brent Ashbranner, *A Moment in History: The First Ten Years of the Peace Corps* (Garden City, N.Y.: Doubleday & Company, 1971), pp. 113–114, 136–137.

soldering to data processing; and course offerings in public speaking and personal development—and all these apart from whatever training firms offered in their own particular styles and customs of operation. While government programs may have waxed and waned according to the special outlooks of successive administrations, private programs grew steadily with the expansion of American capital investment overseas.[35]

For a time there was a heady optimism about such programs and a confident sense that the less developed nations would proceed through the same "stages of economic growth" toward "modernization" as had the more developed nations of the West. And then, during the 1970's, that optimism and that confidence began to wane. For one thing, even in instances where technical expertise had been shared altruistically, there remained the stubborn facts of social, political, and cultural differences: the food supplies did indeed increase in many regions, but the birth rate increased more rapidly; manufacturing did indeed take root in many regions, but government authorities were unable to provide the stable political conditions under which the fruits of industrial development could be widely reaped; the income of some of the less developed nations did indeed grow, but it was distributed even more inequitably than before; and the wealth of some of the less developed nations did indeed increase, but instead of becoming more autonomous they remained even more dependent upon the political and economic power of the more developed nations. It was not merely that capital and expertise would not transform nations apart from supportive structures of political and social institutions; it was that investments of capital and technical assistance too often were more costly than the fruits they yielded. The sadness of the expectations of the 1960's when confronted with the realities of the 1980's was poignantly captured by a lecture the eminent African educator W. Senteza Kajubi delivered at Teachers College, Columbia University, in 1982, in which he reviewed the educational development of the newly emergent African nations during the 1960's and 1970's:

In the last two decades a great deal of investment has been made in education with a view to promoting economic and social development in Africa. National governments devote very high proportions of their recurrent and development budgets to education. Organs of the United Nations, friendly governments, and philanthropic organizations have also directed large sums

35. Leon Weintraub, *International Manpower Development: A Role for Private Enterprise in Foreign Assistance* (New York: Frederick A. Praeger, 1969), pp. 62–80.

of money and technical assistance toward education with the hope of lessening the economic and social development gap between Africa and the rest of the world.

The green revolutions that were expected from education, however, have not yet occurred. On the contrary, the scenario that Africa presents after two decades of independence is still one of acute and worsening poverty and social and political turmoil. . . . Although Africa has vast virgin arable lands and enormous economic potential awaiting fuller development, abject poverty, malnutrition, kwashiorkor, and starvation are endemic and widespread throughout the continent. In other words, despite the heavy investment in education, Africa remains a problem continent and a disaster area in perpetual crisis.

In few of the less developed regions of the world would Kajubi's lament have failed to apply.[36]

36. W. Senteza Kajubi, "Higher Education and the Dilemma of Nation-Building in Africa: A Retrospective and Prospective View," in Andrew Taylor, ed., *Insights into African Education: The Karl W. Bigelow Memorial Lectures* (New York: Teachers College Press, 1984), pp. 43–44.

PART IV

A METROPOLITAN EDUCATION

———————————

Till the Great Society is converted into a Great Community, the Public will remain in eclipse. Communication can alone create a great community. Our Babel is not one of tongues but of the signs and symbols without which shared experience is impossible.

JOHN DEWEY

INTRODUCTION

The United States became a metropolitan society in the century following 1876. The loosely knit "island communities" of the nineteenth century were gradually transformed into the closely integrated metropolitan communities of the twentieth—communities in which individuals came to be defined more by the facts of race, class, ethnicity, religion, and occupation than by the place where they happened to live, and to be regulated more by the rules and policies of governments, professions, and formal institutions than by the unspoken conventions of localities. Metropolitan society was marked by highly interdependent economic, political, and social systems made possible by the technologies of mass production, rapid transportation and communication, large-scale organization, comprehensive planning, and bureaucratic management. And it relied for its effective operation on an ever more complex apparatus of education that included child care facilities and social service agencies of every sort and variety, schools and colleges offering an increasingly standardized curricular fare to an ever broadening age group of the population, cultural institutions dedicated to the advancement and diffusion of every conceivable domain of the arts and sciences, and a vastly enlarged network of popular communications that helped purvey the goods and services made available by a consumer economy at the same time that it informed, instructed, and entertained.[1]

Metropolitan society was a new phenomenon in human history, unprecedented in its size, scope, and character. Not surprisingly, its emergence evoked an infinitely varied response from contemporary scholars and commentators, ranging from the heady optimism of the entrepreneurs, who saw in the metropolis an ever expanding market for their

1. Robert H. Wiebe, *The Search for Order, 1877–1920* (New York: Hill and Wang, 1967), p. xiii.

products and as a result the possibility of a new golden age for the average individual, to the mordant pessimism of Freudian and Marxian critics, who saw in the metropolis the source of a lost individuality that was nothing less than a retreat into barbarism. The German sociologist Georg Simmel, in a classic essay entitled "The Metropolis and Mental Life" (1903) that came to be widely known among American social scientists, commented ambivalently on the intensity of stimulation in metropolitan experience, the punctuality, calculability, and exactness required for transactions, the reserve demanded to make close contact with strangers even minimally tolerable, and the impersonality and anonymity that marked most human relationships. "On the one hand," he observed, "life is made infinitely easy for the personality in that stimulations, interests, uses of time and consciousness are offered to it from all sides. They carry the person as if in a stream, and one needs hardly to swim for oneself. On the other hand, however, life is composed more and more of these impersonal contents and offerings which tend to displace the genuine personal colorations and incompatibilities. This results in the individual's summoning the utmost in uniqueness and particularization, in order to preserve his most personal core. He has to exaggerate this personal element in order to remain audible even to himself." As a consequence, Simmel continued, both forms of individuality, each a way of defining the individual's role in metropolitan society, struggled for dominance. "It is the function of the metropolis," he concluded, "to provide the arena for this struggle and its reconciliation." A half-century later, in *The Secular City* (1965), Harvey Cox left ambivalence behind to celebrate the fullness of liberty in the metropolis and to invite all who would participate to help define its disciplines.[2]

Simmel's English contemporary Graham Wallas was equally convinced that metropolitanization had brought into being a new world that was profoundly altering human nature and that demanded the most fundamental inquiry and action if the public happiness was to be preserved. "We must let our minds play freely over all the conditions of life," he counseled in *The Great Society* (1914), "till we can either justify our civilization or change it." Wallas's student Walter Lippmann, to whom *The Great Society* was dedicated, took up the challenge in his early writings; and, the more he contemplated the new metropolitan world that was coming into being, the more he abandoned the hopeful socialism with which he began in favor of a pessimistic elitism that held out little hope for a society governed by average men and women. John Dewey, who wrote *Democracy and Education* (1916) and *The Public and Its Problems* (1927) also in light of Wallas's *The Great Society,* rebutted Lippmann's pessimism, maintaining that the diversity and variegation of metropolitan society left

2. Georg Simmel, "The Metropolis and Mental Life," in *The Sociology of Georg Simmel,* edited by Kurt H. Wolff (Glencoe, Ill.: The Free Press, 1950), p. 422.

the way open for the fullest development of human personality and that the real problem was ultimately one of transforming the great society into the great community. A half-century later, the historian Daniel J. Boorstin mordantly pictured the development of that great society into what he called "everywhere communities," communities that "floated over time and space" and that comprised men and women "held together less by their hopes than by their wants, by what they made and what they bought, and by how they learned about everything."[3]

What was striking about many of these commentaries was the extent to which they depicted education as an all-powerful force that worked some sort of uniform influence upon millions of minds and personalities—Lippmann's metaphor in *Public Opinion* of the stereotypical "pictures in our heads," put there by an all-powerful press, was perhaps the prototypical example. Yet, when one stopped theorizing about how human beings in some kind of imagined, faceless "mass" might respond to an increasingly standardized education and started to inquire into how individual human beings actually did respond to that education, the reality was quite otherwise. Individuals in the metropolis came to the education proffered them with their own temperaments, histories, and purposes, and different individuals interacted with given configurations of education in various ways and with various outcomes. A score of children in the same classroom taught the same curriculum took away various versions of what had occurred, some similar and some quite different; the same was true of a score of adults visiting the same museum and a score of families in the same city or in different cities (or different countries) viewing a televised soap opera like "Dallas."[4]

Metropolitan education remained a complex phenomenon, fraught with accident, irony, and contradiction. What was taught was not always what was learned, and vice versa. And when what was taught was actually learned, it was always learned in context and hence learned individually. And what was learned frequently had nothing to do with anything that was taught but rather with what a particular individual set out to study for his or her own purposes. To be aware of such complexity is to recognize that metropolitan education may have proffered common messages and provided common experiences to populations of a size unprecedented in history; but those populations interpreted those messages and experiences variously, doubtless extending the domain of the common, but also expanding the range of the unique. To paraphrase Simmel, the metropolis was the arena of both processes, as well as of their continuing tension and reconciliation.

3. Graham Wallas, *The Great Society: A Psychological Analysis* [1914] (reprint ed.; Lincoln: University of Nebraska Press, 1967), p. 15; and Daniel J. Boorstin, *The Americans: The Democratic Experience* (New York: Random House, 1973), p. 1.

4. Walter Lippmann, *Public Opinion* (New York: Harcourt, Brace and Company, 1922), chap. i.

Chapter 11

INSTITUTIONS

> This instrument can teach, it can illuminate; yes, and it can even inspire. But it can do so only to the extent that humans are determined to use it to those ends. Otherwise it is merely wires and lights in a box. There is a great and perhaps decisive battle to be fought against ignorance, intolerance and indifference. This weapon of television could be useful.
>
> EDWARD R. MURROW

The American household changed significantly during the century following 1876, as families became smaller and more diversified, as women in ever larger numbers entered paid employment outside the home, as schooling and a variety of social services became widely available, and as the instruments of popular communication made their decisive entry into American living rooms. The consequences for education, not only as it proceeded within the household, but also as it was provided by other agencies, were profound.

The size of the average American household declined, from 4.9 persons in 1890, to 4.3 in 1920, to 3.4 in 1950, to 2.8 in 1980. There were still very large and very small households, and households generally remained embedded in networks of kin; but the average American household included fewer children and fewer adults, that is, fewer siblings, aunts, uncles, grandparents, and boarders. Further, both the absolute number of divorces and the rate of divorce rose, with the result that, even with a relatively high rate of remarriage, there were more single-parent households. In addition, there was a growing participation of married women, and, among them, mothers of school-age children, in the work force, particularly during and after World War II. Thus, whereas 26 percent of married women with children between the ages of six and seventeen were engaged in or seeking work in 1948, 51 percent were doing so in 1974. Inevitably, familial education changed as a result, in character, content, and intensity, as well as in who taught what to whom.[1]

American families also became increasingly diverse, as successive waves of immigrants arrived from countries throughout the world—mostly from Europe during the years before World War I, from Europe and Latin America during the 1930's, 1940's, and 1950's, and from Latin America, the Middle East, and east and southeast Asia during the 1960's and 1970's. What is more, as the process of Americanization went forward, there was the further variegation introduced by the co-presence of first-, second-, and third-generation families from each of the several ethnoreligious traditions, proving more or less "unmeltable" in their ethnic and religious affiliations and marrying more or less easily across ethnic and religious boundaries. The Isei of California insisted that their children learn Japanese, the Mexicans of Texas insisted that their children learn Spanish, the Lutherans of Missouri insisted that their children learn German, and the Jews of New York insisted that their children learn Hebrew; but family traditions were inevitably and inexorably modified by participation in the larger community, however much families tried to insulate and isolate their young. Finally, of course, there were also the distinctive family forms of intentional communities, ranging from Shaker colonies where adults were celibate and no children were born, to cooperative communes where all the men were considered to be wedded to all the women in one large extended family, which in turn accepted responsibility for rearing the children born of shifting sexual liaisons within the family.

Granted this extraordinary diversity, there were numerous efforts to portray the "typical American family" during the early decades of the twentieth century. Robert S. Lynd and Helen Merrell Lynd discovered at least one version of that family in their studies of Muncie, Indiana, during the 1920's and 1930's. What the Lynds set out to investigate were the ways in which the processes of industrialization had affected the values and personalities of Americans. As the source of their data, they sought a "typical" American community, essentially

1. U.S., Bureau of the Census, *Historical Statistics of the United States, Colonial Times to 1970* (2 vols.; Washington, D.C.: Government Printing Office, 1975), I, 41, 64, and *Statistical Abstract of the United States: 1985* (Washington, D.C.: Government Printing Office, 1984), p. 41; Paul Glick and Andrew J. Norton, "Perspectives on the Recent Upturn in Divorce and Remarriage," *Demography*, X (1974), 301–314; and U.S., Bureau of the Census, *Household and Family Characteristics: March 1984* (Current Population Reports, Series P-20, No. 238; Washington, D.C.: Government Printing Office, 1985), p. 4.

self-contained (not a satellite city), somewhere between 25,000 and 50,000 in population, including a small proportion of blacks and immigrants, located if possible in "that common-denominator of America, the Midwest," and experiencing a sufficiently rapid rate of growth "to insure the presence of a plentiful assortment of the growing pains accompanying contemporary social change." The city they chose, Muncie, was an expanding factory town with a population of roughly 38,000 that were overwhelmingly white and of old stock and drawn from the surrounding countryside. Portraying late-nineteenth-century Muncie as a quiet county seat where people "lived relatively close to the land and its products" *(Gemeinschaft)*, the Lynds set out to chronicle the transformation wrought by industrialization *(Gesellschaft)*. Acting with their research associates as participant observers and describing the diurnal life of Muncie much as anthropologists might describe the life of a preliterate tribe, they grouped their findings under six headings: getting a living; making a home; training the young; using leisure; engaging in religious practices; and engaging in community activities. The result was an aura of scientific detachment and objectivity that lent particular strength to the description.[2]

Given the Lynds' decision to exclude all data on Muncie's blacks, and given that the overwhelming proportion of the whites in Muncie were native-born, the family the Lynds portrayed as typically American was the white, native-born family of middle America during the 1920's; in consequence, the Lynds' ethnography confirmed and detailed the notion of typicality that had been conveyed by a good deal of contemporary fiction. The families of Muncie tended to live in one-family houses, each on its own separate patch of ground; working-class families had less inside space and smaller yards, business-class families had more inside space and larger yards, despite the fact that working-class families tended to be larger than business-class families. Child rearing was generally conceived in Muncie chiefly in terms of "making children conform to the approved ways of the group." A "good" home would secure the maximum of conformity, a "bad" home, a bare minimum. But there was widespread lament by the 1920's to the effect that the rise in opportunities for associations outside the home was making it more difficult to secure adherence to traditional ways. Most important, perhaps, parents found themselves increasingly sharing the traditional tasks of familial education with schools. Following well-established gender distinctions, mothers took

2. Robert S. Lynd and Helen Merrell Lynd, *Middletown: A Study in American Culture* (New York: Harcourt, Brace and Company, 1929), pp. 7–8.

responsibility for teaching the traditional tasks of homemaking— cooking, sewing, housework—to their daughters, and fathers took responsibility for teaching the skills associated with earning a living to their sons. But, with the changes in the nature of work associated with industrialization, fathers could no longer pass on the skills of craft and trade via formal or informal apprenticeships, and mothers, more and more of whom were employed outside the home, could no longer devote so much time to teaching homemaking to their daughters, who were often uninterested in any case in learning "old-fashioned" practices. Increasingly, therefore, it was the schools more than the family that prepared young men and women for vocations—one might even venture that guidance counselors who advised the young on vocations had pre-empted traditional parental responsibilities. Moreover, in addition to these formal programs, there were the innumerable school-based and church-based clubs that took youngsters out of the home and, through carefully arranged group activities, taught skills and values formerly conveyed within the household.[3]

These problems of role strain and shared responsibility peaked in the high school, where the phenomenon of adolescence manifested itself in increasingly intense peer relationships revolving around the substance of radio programs and motion picture films, popular magazines, clubs, dates, and a social life that more and more involved the automobile. A survey of some eight hundred high school sophomores, juniors, and seniors in Muncie revealed that 55 percent of the boys and 44 percent of the girls had been at home fewer than four evenings out of seven during the previous week. The contrast between that experience and the experience that the parents had undergone as teenagers was at the least striking; and, not surprisingly, there was articulate concern on the part of many parents that the values and standards being taught within the household were being seriously eroded by the early sophistication deriving from peer associations outside the household. Some parents sought to solve the problem by reassertions of adult authority; others, seeking the kinds of "adjustment" preached by the new parent-education literature of the 1920's, made efforts to develop more "democratic" relationships with their adolescent children, marked by more frank and symmetrical exchanges of ideas and opinions.[4]

Withal, Muncie's households remained the sites of considerable formal and informal education across the entire life-span. As the Lynds summed up the experience of childhood:

3. *Ibid.*, p. 132.
4. *Ibid.*, pp. 135, 143–144.

From birth until the age of five or six a child is reared almost entirely in the individual home by his parents, under whatever conditions or according to whatever plan or lack of plan their habits and inclinations may favor. He may live in a home where getting a living is the dominant concern of both parents or where the mother, at least, devotes much of her time to her children; in a home of affection or of consistent bickering; of any variety of religious or political affiliation or use of leisure; he may be "made to mind" by spanking or bribing, or he may rule the house; he may be encouraged to learn or told "not to ask so many questions"; he may be taught to tell the truth or laughed at as "cute" when he concocts little evasions—unless he is "cruelly treated" no one interferes. From five or six to twelve or thirteen the home still remains the dominant formal agency responsible for the child, but supplemented by compulsory schooling and by optional religious training and the increasing influence of playfellows. After the age of twelve or thirteen the place of the home tends to recede before a combination of other formative influences, until in the late teens the child is regarded as a kind of junior adult, increasingly independent of parental authority.

Moreover, despite the movement of growing numbers of women into paid employment outside the home, the Lynds found that almost half of both business-class and working-class mothers were spending sixteen hours a week or more with their children; and, at least among the business-class fathers, there was a heightened sense of the importance of parental responsibilities and a heightened concern for the performance of those responsibilities. Beyond the education of children by adults, there were the countless activities in which adults educated one another, as knowledge gained in women's club or men's club meetings was brought home for further discussion, as radio programs or motion pictures or magazines provided a common fare for conversation, or as shared experiences were recalled and reflected upon. And indeed, there were the inevitable instances in which the young taught the old, as when a daughter taught a mother what she had learned in her home economics class or when a grandson taught a grandfather how to start an automobile or strum a tenor banjo. Finally, as children and grandchildren married and established their own households, the processes of familial education continued across household boundaries, with the telephone now facilitating communication, not only from one Muncie neighborhood to another, but from Muncie to other cities.[5]

Two follow-up studies were done on Muncie, one by the Lynds during the 1930's and one by Theodore Caplow and his associates during the 1970's. The Lynds sought to assess the impact of the

5. *Ibid.*, p. 132.

Depression on the culture of Muncie; Caplow and his associates sought to assess the tension between continuity and change in the culture of Muncie over a half-century. And, while the focus of both investigations was on change, the message of both was the profound force of continuity. With respect to Muncie's families, the Lynds' study of the 1930's dramatized the growing gap between social classes and especially between the extremes of the social class system—between the despairing members of lower-class families standing in long lines waiting for food doles and the self-conscious members of the emergent upper-class in their newly built mansions on Muncie's "West End." Across classes, however, the study discovered the stubborn persistence of family ways, including familial education. Yet the content of familial education, especially in the domain of values, was increasingly conflicting and confused. As the Lynds put it, despite a rigorous adherence to traditional ways, "the range of sanctioned choices confronting Middletown youth is wider, the definition of the one 'right way' less clear." And, more generally, for all the optimism and boostering at the heart of what the Lynds called "the Middletown spirit," a spirit widely shared across social class lines, there was also fear and uncertainty, especially among the working-class families that had suffered the effects of the Depression most traumatically. Put in educational terms, the modes and processes of familial education remained much the same, as did the tensions involved in sharing the education of the young with other institutions; but the curriculum of familial education was even less assured than it had been a decade earlier.[6]

Caplow and his associates also reported striking continuities in family life, indeed, more extensive continuities than were perhaps justified by the objective data. In the matter of divorce, they argued that no great increase in divorce rates had occurred between the 1920's and the 1970's. Muncie had seemed to the Lynds to have had an unusually high divorce rate during the 1920's, as compared with the federal Census statistics; and subsequent studies by Samuel H. Preston and John McDonald had established that Indiana during the 1920's had had the highest crude divorce rate of any state east of the Mississippi. Nevertheless, Caplow and his associates questioned whether the federal Census statistics had been accurate and whether indeed there had been as great a rise in divorce rates during the 1960's and 1970's as the Census statistics had indicated. In the matter

6. Robert S. Lynd and Helen Merrell Lynd, *Middletown in Transition: A Study in Cultural Conflicts* (New York: Harcourt, Brace and Company, 1937), ɔ. 175.

of what had seemed to be a growing gap between adolescents and their parents, Caplow and his associates also found less change than they had expected—indeed, the similarity in parent-child relationships from 1925 to 1975 led Caplow and his associates to conclude that the changes the Lynds had reported in their original study between families in the 1880's and families in the 1920's had been far more profound than the changes after the 1920's. "The decisive transition from a traditional to a modern family configuration," they reported, "from child labor to prolonged education, from the hand-powered to the machine-powered home, and from an enclosed to an open community had been accomplished by 1925. . . . Today, Middletown has become, for the first time in its history, a place where the experience of the present generation resembles the experience of the past generation and prefigures the probable experience of the next generation." In fact, the greatest change in Muncie's family life reported by Caplow and his associates had been the intrusion of the popular media of communication into the life of the household. Ninety-eight percent of Muncie's households owned at least one television set, and nearly half had more than one set—many, three or four; and the amount of time Muncie's residents devoted to viewing television was remarkable. According to one estimate, the median for the entire population was 28 hours per week, with elderly women (35 hours), elderly men and middle-aged women (32 hours), and pre-school children (29 hours) having the highest rates, and adolescents (21 hours), the lowest rates. What puzzled Caplow and his associates was where all that time had come from. What were the activities that had been replaced? Not newspaper reading. Not radio listening. Not film viewing. Not book reading. And not attendance at sports. In the end, the Caplow report left the question unanswered.[7]

One can make too much of the Middletown studies. Muncie's population had doubled by the 1970's, to around 70,000, but the community remained scarcely representative of metropolitan America. It had diversified, too, but only moderately as compared with cities like Los Angeles or Pittsburgh or Atlanta. Suburbanization was a major demographic phenomenon of the post–World War II era, bringing significant changes in the character of familial education; and the concurrent deterioration of central cities was no less signifi-

7. Theodore Caplow et al., *Middletown Families: Fifty Years of Change and Continuity* (Minneapolis: University of Minnesota Press, 1982), pp. 21, 23–25; and Samuel H. Preston and John McDonald, "The Incidence of Divorce Within Cohorts of American Marriages Contracted Since the Civil War," *Demography*, XVI (1979), 1–25.

cant. But one could learn little of such phenomena from the Middle-town studies. More important, perhaps, the very fact of the Lynds' search for typicality led the Middletown studies to downplay the plu-ralism and variegation of American familial education.

Consider, for example, the special qualities of Italian-American familial education, particularly as it extended over several genera-tions. The families that migrated from Italy to American cities like Buffalo or Rochester or Omaha or Cleveland (frequently a period of three or four years elapsed between the time the male breadwinner arrived and the time he was able to bring his wife and children to join him) brought powerful traditions of in-group solidarity, familism, sharply defined gender differentiation that stressed the high status of males and the reflective status of females, strong adult prerogative in decisions concerning marriage and the choice of occupation, and patterns of self-help among kin and *compari*. Such families tended to settle in homogeneous ethnic subcommunities—really colonies—within which networks of kin and *compari* were supportive of these old-country traditions, thereby providing external reinforcement of the education conveyed within the household. Over time, as second- and third-generation Italian-American families shared the education of their children with public as well as parochial schools, community agencies, and the popular media of communication, the youngsters became aware of alternative ways and values and found some of them attractive. What is more, despite the strong familism of the traditional Italian-American community, some of the young married exoga-mously across ethnic and religious lines. Obviously, ethnoreligious differences notwithstanding, there was a common secular trend to-ward a diminution of the influence of familial education—in that respect, at least, Muncie families were indeed typical. Obviously, too, however, even as Italian-American families were "Americanized," they preserved vestiges of the older values and traditions; and, as the third and fourth generations began to search for their "roots"—a common phenomenon in the 1970's and 1980's—many of those val-ues and traditions were self-consciously reclaimed through self-edu-cation and mutual education deliberately pursued by the newly emerging elders.

A somewhat different complex of phenomena marked Mexican-American familial education in the cities and towns of the Southwest. Like Italian-American families, Mexican-American families brought powerful traditions of in-group solidarity and familism, and sharply defined gender differentiation that stressed the high status of males and the derivative status and domestic role of females, forceful adult involvement in career and marital decisions, and patterns of self-help within a kinship system that included fictive as well as biological kin, especially godparents. Again, like Italian-American families, Mexican-American families tended to settle in homogeneous subcommunities—*barrios*—within which networks of kin and kith supported the maintenance of the Mexican ways taught within the family. Mexican-American families readily accepted American material goods, but they carefully sustained Mexican traditions through the maintenance of the Spanish language, the preservation of tales *(cuentos)*, ballads *(corridos)*, and proverbs *(dichos)*, the celebration of saints' days, and the support of old-fashioned healers *(curanderos)*. That notwithstanding, Mexican-American young women did increasingly become wage earners during the early years of the twentieth century; Mexican-American children did adopt American customs and demand greater freedom from parental control; and the Americanization programs conducted by churches, schools, and community agencies during the second and third decades of the century did inevitably influence the character of Mexican-American familial education. In these ways, the common secular trend toward less powerful familial education was evident; and yet the geographical proximity of Mexico and the constant flow of new migrants across the border, coupled with continuing ethnoreligious discrimination on the part of native-born Americans (including the maintenance of ethnically segregated public schools), led to a different mode of assimilation to American society. In contrast to the Italian-American community, the Mexican-American community was marked by lower rates of naturalization and intermarriage (the great change came after World War II), a slower entry into public life (again, there was a pronounced shift after World War II), and the eventual emergence in the Southwest of a border culture that was neither wholly American nor wholly Mexican.

With respect to immigrant families, Josef J. Barton has explored the fascinating question of whether household education combined with school education in such ways as to assist or hinder social mobility in the second and third generations by comparing the experience of Italians, Slovaks, and Romanians in Cleveland during the period from 1890 to 1950. Most immigrants from all three groups entered Cleveland as blue-collar workers and most remained so, though a small percentage of manual workers did climb into white-collar jobs— as clerks or proprietors of small shops, saloons, or other commercial establishments. Among men in the first generation, the Romanians had enjoyed a modest advantage in such mobility. Among the men of the second generation, the Romanians maintained a decided advantage in such mobility, owing in part to the fact that Romanians of the first generation had fewer children and were therefore able to bestow greater advantages upon each child, particularly in launching them into middle-class occupations, and in part to the effective use they made of opportunities for schooling. But the effects of schooling were not independent of other factors, particularly the economic status of the family and the educational correlates of that status, to wit, members of the first generation who had moved into middle-class occupations tended to value education more, especially as it assisted the next generation in preserving and improving upon that middle-class status. As Barton summed it up:

Ethnicity . . . was a differentiating factor in the process of career mobility. The role of ethnic group membership appears even more striking in patterns of cumulative mobility. Second-generation Rumanians moved quickly into white-collar jobs, only one-fourth of the Italians, and fewer than one-fifth of the Slovaks, enjoyed comparable status. Rumanian sons of middle-class fathers achieved a remarkable level of continuity with their origins, for 93 percent ended their careers in professional or managerial occupations. Only about 40 percent of second-generation Italians and Slovaks, however, managed to remain in white-collar positions.[8]

Finally, there was the special set of phenomena that affected black familial education in the cities of the North during the same era. The so-called Great Migration of rural southern blacks to the cities of the Midwest and Northeast began in earnest during the 1890's, continued into the first decade of the twentieth century, then doubled in the second decade and virtually doubled again in the third decade. The shock the migrants encountered in adjusting to new regions as well as to urban ways was not unlike the shock migrants from Italy encountered—with the added burden of race difference. There were small numbers of middle-class blacks in most northern cities during the early decades of the twentieth century, but they tended to see their hard-earned status imperiled by the newcomers and perceived little by way of common cause with them. Whereas the Italian-American subcommunity practiced mutual assistance in recruitment to employment and concentrated in certain domains of the economy, the black subcommunity entered the urban job market more individually, less

8. Josef J. Barton, *Peasants and Strangers: Italians, Rumanians, and Slovaks in an American City, 1890–1950* (Cambridge, Mass.: Harvard University Press, 1975), p. 141.

assisted by kin and kith, and at the bottom of a wide range of unskilled occupations. Black families were large; their children had unequal access to schooling owing to racial discrimination; and, even when their children were able to obtain schooling, their families and the networks of which their families were part were less able than white immigrant families to assist them in obtaining the kinds of employment that would be associated with upward social mobility, owing to discrimination in employment. A small proportion of blacks defied the predictions, obtained additional schooling, and went on to careers as white-collar workers, professionals, and entrepreneurs, most often serving black clienteles. A much larger proportion found themselves locked into dead-end jobs or chronic unemployment. Among this latter group, after New Deal welfare policies began to make public assistance available to female-headed families, the men began to defer or eschew marriage, leading to the rise in female-headed, impoverished black families after World War II. Some of these families, often assisted by networks of kin, provided the familial education that, coupled with adequate schooling and decent opportunities for employment, enabled their children to go on to productive and satisfying lives and to form two-parent Afro-American families that were as typical in their own right as the families of Muncie. But most were unable to do so and their children ended up illiterate, alienated, and unable to function productively except in the "hidden economy" of hustling, drugs, and outright criminal activity, or in another generation of female-headed impoverished families supported by public welfare funds. By the early 1980's, more than half of black American families with children had only one parent present; most such families were female-headed; and most were poor. They too had become typical in their own right, and the education they proffered was profoundly different from that of middle-class, two-parent Afro-American families, or of third-generation Italian-American families, or of the families that Caplow and his associates described in Muncie.[9]

II

Churches and synagogues seemed to manifest an ever greater presence in American life during the years after 1876. Church membership statistics are notoriously inaccurate, but there was clear indication of growing affiliation on the part of the American people, with

9. U.S., Bureau of the Census, *Household and Family Characteristics: March 1984,* p. 4.

TABLE II

Percentage of the National Population with Religious Affiliation, 1890–1980

	1890	1916	1936	1960	1980
Population	63,056,000	101,961,000	128,181,000	180,671,000	226,546,000
Church Members	21,699,000	41,927,000	55,807,000	114,449,000	134,817,000
Percentage	34	41	44	63	60

the proportion of the population reporting church/synagogue membership rising from 40 percent in 1890 to 63 percent in 1960, probably peaking some time during the 1960's, and then falling off to 60 percent in 1980. When the Bureau of the Census in 1957 asked a national sample of people fourteen years of age and older, "What is your religion?" over 96 percent indicated some religious preference, with over 78 million listing that preference as Protestant, over 30 million as Roman Catholic, almost 4 million as Jewish, and over a million as "other," and with almost 4 percent, or over 4 million people, indicating no religious preference or no religion at all. The number of separate religious groups and denominations remained large: there were at least 143 in 1890 and 142,000 churches and synagogues, 256 in 1936 and 180,000 churches and synagogues, and 222 in 1980 and 333,000 churches and synagogues; and those statistics did not include a plethora of small groups representing new churches coming into being, churches that had splintered off from the larger denominations in disputes over doctrine or governance, and miscellaneous groups outside the Judeo-Christian or Buddhist traditions. Yet, for all this pluralism, the Roman Catholics, the Baptists, and the Methodists were consistently the largest denominations during the twentieth century; and, when the Lutherans, the Presbyterians, and the Episcopalians were added to those, most church members were accounted for.[10]

These gross statistics should not obscure the continuing dynamism of American religion during the late nineteenth and twentieth centuries. The great revivals of the 1890's and the 1960's occasioned

10. *Historical Statistics of the United States,* I, 8; U.S., Bureau of the Census, *Religious Bodies: 1916* (2 vols.; Washington, D.C.: Government Printing Office, 1919), I, 29, *Religious Bodies: 1936* (2 vols.; Washington, D.C.: Government Printing Office, 1941), I, 86, *Statistical Abstract of the United States: 1985* (Washington, D.C.: Government Printing Office, 1984), p. 51, "Religion Reported by the Civilian Population of the United States: March 1957," *Current Population Reports,* Series P-20, No. 79, February 2, 1958, p. 6; *Historical Statistics of the United States,* I, 391; and Constant H. Jacquet, Jr., ed., *Yearbook of American and Canadian Churches, 1980* (Nashville, Tenn.: Abingdon Press, 1980), p. 242.

surges of membership in the traditional churches as well as resurgences of piety among those already affiliated. Yet, contemporary with these forces of renewal was the continuing process whereby ethnoreligious institutions of every sort and variety were established by the immigrants who came from Europe, Asia, Central and South America, Africa, and the Middle East—Ukrainian Catholic and Eastern Orthodox churches and Russian Jewish synagogues during the 1890's, and Dominican Pentecostal and Vietnamese Catholic churches and Arabic Mohammedan mosques during the 1960's. In addition, older lower-class churches like the Baptist and the Methodist became more "respectably" middle class, and their places were taken by newer lower-class churches like the Assemblies of God and the Fruit of Islam. Also, the secularization that had begun in the eighteenth century with the legal disestablishment of religion, which had been fairly well concluded in the nineteenth, gradually removed the churches as churches from direct participation in politics. Yet, the churches were in the vanguard of the early-twentieth-century crusade that culminated in the ratification of the Eighteenth Amendment; they were the seedbeds of the civil rights movement of the post–World War II era; and they provided the leadership for the antiabortion campaigns of the 1970's and 1980's.

As in the national period, the churches and synagogues continued to serve as centers of a wide range of formal and informal education. The Christian service, as it had been for centuries, was itself a system of instruction, whether in the more liturgical version of the Roman Catholics and Episcopalians, or in the more prophetic version of the Unitarians and Universalists, or in the freer mix adopted by the Pentecostalists. And the Jewish service continued in the age-old pattern of the systematic reading of the Torah over the course of a year of Sabbaths. Priests, ministers, and rabbis continued to instruct their congregations in correct doctrine and ceremonial as well as in the meaning of correct doctrine and ceremonial for the affairs of everyday life, not only in Sabbath services and mid-week lectures and prayer meetings, but in an extraordinary array of special gatherings—mothers' and fathers' clubs, young people's classes and senior citizens' organizations, ladies' aid societies and men's sodalities. In addition, the clergy also borrowed every conceivable instrument of education and entertainment from the secular world in their effort, on the one hand, to enhance their effectiveness, and, on the other hand, to meet the competition of alternative ways of spending the Sabbath—not only oratorical devices, but also pedagogical aids like films, plays, and musical presentations. Sermons increasingly dealt with the diurnal problems of parishioners; participation was gradually broadened beyond traditional responsive reading and hymn singing; and in Reform temples during the 1920's and in Catholic churches during the 1960's the services were conducted in English. New editions of the Bible appeared during the 1960's and 1970's, not only to incorporate the findings of new scholarship, but also to render its contents more popular, more readable, and more comprehensible to the untutored; and indeed the substance of Scripture was also increasingly conveyed in novel forms, from comic books to films to presentations by folk guitarists. Moreover, the so-called electronic church—comprising the hundreds of evangelical broadcasting stations that burgeoned during the 1960's and 1970's—served largely to complement and strengthen the work of the churches themselves (it tended to be listened to and watched by churchgoers and served to confirm rather than to detract from churchgoing). Further, for all the pluralism of American religious life, this complex of formal and informal education proved sufficiently effective at the very least to nurture a widespread piety—or acknowledgment of piety—on the part of the American people. In Gallup polls conducted during the 1940's, the 1960's, and the 1970's, the vast majority of Americans, over 90 percent in every instance, acknowledged belief in God—in contrast, incidentally, with significantly lower percentages in several of the countries of Western Europe; and in similar polls inquiring into church attendance, between a third and a half of the Americans queried reported weekly, and well over half, monthly or more often. Granted continuing differences in doctrine and discipline from one church to another, what was also noteworthy about the findings of such polls was the widespread acceptance of a common, Judeo-Christian creed, diffuse in its message, hopeful in its outlook, and concerned with individual moral self-improvement within the context of family, church, and local community.[11]

In addition to continuing their historic instruction in the fundamentals of doctrine and the liturgy, churches and synagogues broadened the domain of their concern—broadened their curricula, so to speak; they extended the range and variety of the ancillary institutions they designed and adopted to assist them in carrying out their educational mission; and they reached out ever more aggressively to the unaffiliated and the unbelieving. In the fashion of the pioneering

11. Jackson W. Carroll *et al.*, *Religion in America: 1950 to the Present* (San Francisco: Harper & Row, 1970), chap. iv.

institutional churches of the late nineteenth century, they involved themselves in child care, vocational training, general education, occupational placement, recreation, athletics, family counseling, the teaching of English to immigrants, citizenship education, alcohol and drug rehabilitation, the discussion of political and social issues, and the mobilization of political and social publics; and in fact studies carried out during the 1950's and 1960's found that for single men and women who lived alone and for others who did not live in familial households, churches and synagogues increasingly functioned as family surrogates. And, in the fashion of the evangelical movement, churches and synagogues spawned clubs, classes, societies, day care centers, Sabbath and weekday religious schools, Christian and Jewish academies, libraries, lyceums, forums, research and study units, summer camps, retreat centers, mission houses, fairs, publishing houses, broadcasting stations, film production units, professional and learned societies, trade unions, and sororal and fraternal associations. If in the 1860's and 1870's a large proportion of the libraries of the United States were church and Sunday school libraries, in the 1960's and 1970's a large proportion of the day care centers of the United States were sponsored by the churches and synagogues. Also in the fashion of the evangelical movement, they carried their efforts well beyond the walls of even this panoply of institutions, in the form of home ministries that gathered congregations in family living rooms, coffee house ministries that sought the unchurched in their places of recreation and relaxation, hospital ministries that sought to instruct the sick while comforting them, prison ministries that sought to instruct wrongdoers while rehabilitating them, and street ministries that sought to instruct the unfortunate while assisting them. And cutting across all such efforts and in a sense enveloping all of them were the great interdenominational efforts of revivalists such as Billy Graham and authors such as Joshua Loth Liebman.[12]

Granted their limitations, the Muncie studies, already discussed, shed considerable light on the multiplicity of ways in which the educational efforts of churches and synagogues interacted with the educational efforts of families in American localities. In 1890, the base year of the Lynds' first study, Muncie had a population of 11,345 and Delaware County, in which it was located, had a population of 30,131.

12. Charles Y. Glock, Benjamin B. Ringer, and Earl R. Babbie, *To Comfort and to Challenge: A Dilemma of the Contemporary Church* (Berkeley: University of California Press, 1967), chap. iii; and Eileen W. Linder, Mary C. Mattis, and June R. Rogers, *When Churches Mind the Children: A Study of Day Care in Local Parishes* (Ypsilanti, Mich.: The High/Scope Press, 1983).

There were fourteen churches in Muncie itself and fifty-three in the county as a whole. The 1890 Census identified 6,722 church members in the county, of whom 2,761 were Methodists, 1,161 were United Brethren in Christ, and 979 were Disciples of Christ. Muncie had no United Brethren of Christ church and one Disciples of Christ church. It also had an African Methodist Episcopal church, a Presbyterian church, a Universalist church, a Roman Catholic church, and a Protestant Episcopal church, as well as Baptist, Methodist, Lutheran, Christian, and Congregationalist churches, a Church of God, a Friends meeting house, and a Jewish congregation that met in the homes of its members. The Lynds estimated on the basis of interviews with residents during the 1920's concerning their parents' church attendance around 1890 that approximately half the population of Muncie attended religious services regularly during the 1890's, a percentage that would seem high in relation to the Census figure of church members but not impossible, given the flurry of revivals toward the end of the century. In any case, the next three decades brought rapid growth and considerable diversification to Muncie's religious life, including the organization of a number of fundamentalist and Pentecostal congregations. Meanwhile, the older churches prospered and consolidated their position in the city, building imposing stone edifices in the heart of the downtown section.[13]

What the Lynds found during the 1920's was a pervasive belief in Muncie in the truth of Christianity (the exception, of course, being the Jews), in the sacredness of the Bible, and in the appropriateness of church membership and attendance. In addition, they found that the home continued to serve as an important site of religious observance and instruction, though less important than in earlier times—a group of six ministers the Lynds interviewed judged that only a small percentage of their congregations still had daily family prayers and that anywhere from 10 percent to 30 percent regularly read the Bible at home. The same ministers testified to the continued significance of Sunday schools, though they noted that there had been little change in Sunday school work since the 1890's and that more and more often the students were arriving in class with their lessons unprepared. In addition to Sunday schools, the YMCA and YWCA were heavily involved in Bible teaching, not only during the school year, but also during summer vacations. Finally, the churches had vastly expanded their efforts to incorporate some of the secular interests of their

13. Theodore Caplow et al., All Faithful People: Change and Continuity in Middletown's Religion (Minneapolis: University of Minnesota Press, 1983), chap. ii.

members, through a plethora of social clubs of every sort and variety. The Lynds noted little mixing of blacks and whites in church or YMCA and YWCA activities; indeed, in the main they saw the churches as essentially confirming the property-centered values and social structure of the city and putting their imprimatur on the social system that industrialism had wrought. Beyond that, for all the religious subscription and activity they had chronicled, they saw religion as a kind of premodern survival slowly giving way before the advance of secularism—a judgment especially interesting since Robert Lynd was a graduate of the Union Theological Seminary in New York who had intended to be a Presbyterian minister before entering the field of social research and the Muncie study was originally sponsored by the Institute of Social and Religious Research.[14]

When the Lynds returned to Muncie in the 1930's, they found that the churches had grown apace with the population—there were 65 congregations in 1935, representing 22 denominations; and they found support for their earlier observation that religious beliefs and practices were among the most slowly changing of human activities. Moreover, they also found support for their earlier sense that, for all their "Rock of Ages" permanence, the churches were becoming increasingly irrelevant to the real needs and problems of Muncie's industrial society. The Lynds had little further to report about religion, condensing their entire discussion into a single, brief chapter. On the other hand, the study done by Caplow and his associates in the 1970's contradicted the Lynds at virtually every point. They found religion in Muncie not only alive and well but flourishing. A 1976 directory listed 145 churches, representing an even greater heterogeneity than in the 1920's, and indeed representing a genuine growth—whereas there had been 810 persons per church in 1890 and 798 per church in 1925, there were 550 per church in 1976. Attendance remained strong on the Sabbath and on other days when church activities were scheduled; and it remained strong, too, at such church-sponsored external activities as home prayer and Scripture study groups, Gospel-music concerts, and religious club activities. Along with continuing high rates of religious observance and participation, Caplow and his associates found continuing widespread subscription to a common creed that professed belief in God, in the sacredness of the Bible, and in the efficacy of prayer. What was novel, perhaps, was that an earlier censoriousness on the part of the churches had given way to a perva-

14. Lynd and Lynd, *Middletown*, pp. 357–358 and *passim*.

sive tolerance; people were attached to their faiths but reluctant to impose them on others—as Caplow and his associates put it, "Religious fervor no longer goes hand in hand with missionary zeal." Beyond all else, though, Caplow and his associates found no evidence of a retreat of religion in the face of an aggressive, all-powerful secularism. The only retreat they noted was from the sphere of public politics; in the private domain, religion played as vital and significant a role as ever.[15]

As in the case of familial education, the Muncie studies convey little of the ethnoreligious variegation of American church and synagogue education. One need only look at the role of the Roman Catholic Church in its various ethnic versions to gain a sense of that variegation. As in Europe, Italian-Americans were ambivalent toward the church: on the one hand, it shared the language, the traditions, the values, the icons, and the ideologies of their close-knit, homogeneous communities; on the other hand, they brought with them to the United States historically uncongenial attitudes toward the church as an institution. Those attitudes may have limited the church's influence as an agency of social and moral education; nevertheless, the church did play a powerful role, not only in transmitting a characteristically Italian version of Roman Catholic doctrine and liturgy, but also in supporting and sustaining such characteristically Italian values as familism, male dominance, and female subordination. Much the same can be said with respect to the role of the Roman Catholic Church in the Mexican-American communities of the Southwest. The Slovak Catholic Church played a quite different role in the life of Slovak-American subcommunities, owing to its particular history in Europe. There, the Magyar leaders of Hungary had turned the Slovak schools into state schools and had used those schools to carry forward a deliberate policy of Magyarization. By way of response, the Slovak clergy had been forced to turn their own educational efforts largely to preserving the social and moral character of the Slovak community. The result in the United States was an immediate and persistent suspicion of public schools, however great the advantages they might have conferred with respect to social betterment (M. Mark Stolarik has advanced such an analysis to explain the different rates of social mobility of Slovaks and Romanians Josef J. Barton found in Cleveland; given their ethnoreligious history in Europe, Slovaks were taught and learned a different conception of success, namely, commu-

15. Lynd and Lynd, *Middletown in Transition*, chap. viii; and Caplow *et al.*, *All Faithful People*, p. 69, chap. ii, p. 98.

nity cohesion and stability rather than individual striving and mobility). Similarly, the black Pentecostal churches that appealed to the poor, southern, rural blacks who flocked to the cities of the Midwest and Northeast during the years between 1900 and 1940 stood at the heart of black networks of family and kin, conveying a rich emotional experience of private hope for salvation in a situation where the diurnal affairs of economic, social, and political life were dominated by the harsh realities of racial prejudice and discrimination.[16]

The number of priests, ministers, and rabbis increased during the twentieth century, but it declined steadily in proportion to the American population and in proportion to church and synagogue membership. The proportion remained consistently higher among blacks than among whites, the ministry being one of the few professions early open to blacks. Members of the clergy continued to constitute an immensely diverse group, ranging from the inspired but unschooled ministers of some sects and denominations, who served on a part-time basis and depended upon other jobs for their livings, to the highly professional, well-schooled ministers of other sects and denominations, who served on a full-time basis and were accorded full salaries and perquisites by their congregations. C. Luther Fry's analysis of unpublished data collected in connection with the 1926 Census of Religious Bodies revealed that five out of every eight ministers of white denominations and one out of every four ministers of black denominations claimed to be graduates of a college or seminary, with the Roman Catholic Church having the highest percentage of college-trained men. Among Protestant bodies, 80 percent of the white ministers of towns and cities claimed to be graduates, while fewer than 50 percent of those in rural areas claimed to be graduates. These differences persisted over the next half-century, though the gaps between Catholics, Protestants, and Jews, between whites and blacks, and between those who served in urban and rural areas narrowed. The number and proportion of women who served as members of the clergy was minuscule at the beginning of the century and remained so until the 1970's, when it began to rise slowly but significantly. By the early 1980's, the proportion of women theological students enrolled in Protestant theological seminaries was approaching 25 percent; and, while not all of those women would end up as members of the clergy, their presence did augur continued change in the gender

16. M. Mark Stolarik, "Immigration, Education, and the Social Mobility of Slovaks, 1870–1930," in Randall M. Miller and Thomas D. Marzik, eds., *Immigrants and Religion in Urban America* (Philadelphia: Temple University Press, 1977), pp. 103–116.

composition of the profession. In the early 1980's, too, a small number of women were serving as Reform Jewish rabbis (it was not until 1985 that the Jewish Theological Seminary of America ordained the first Conservative woman rabbi). Women continued to be barred from serving as Roman Catholic priests, though the larger problem of that church was the crisis during the 1960's and 1970's created by the decline of vocations, not only for the priesthood, but also for its orders of teaching nuns and brothers.[17]

III

Schooling had become prevalent in the United States by the 1870's— the majority of American children attended common schools for a few years between the ages of six or seven and twelve and became literate in the process, though a great deal of training in literacy continued to go forward in households and churches. The century following the 1870's witnessed a remarkable development of schooling, as Americans attended school in ever greater numbers over ever longer periods of the year during ever more extensive periods of their lives. School enrollments rose steadily, in their own right, in proportion to the overall number of young people, and in proportion to the population as a whole. By 1940, the average American twenty-five years of age or older had completed 8.6 years of schooling; by 1980, that figure had risen to 12.5 years of schooling. Moreover, given that the average length, at least of the public-school year, had risen over time, from some 144 days in 1900 to some 178 days by 1950 (it tended to remain at around 178 days over the next thirty years), the increase represented by that increment of 3.9 years was all the greater.[18]

During the decades following 1876, city school systems tended to lead in the development of school innovation and systematization, and it was in the cities that the eight-year elementary school assumed its classic form. A survey of eighty-two cities undertaken by the United States Bureau of Education in 1888–89 revealed that the average number of hours students spent in actual study and in recitations of

17. C. Luther Fry, *The U.S. Looks at Its Churches* (New York: Institute of Social and Religious Research, 1930), pp. 62–66; and Jacquet, ed., *Yearbook of American and Canadian Churches, 1985*, p. 271.

18. Thomas D. Snyder, *Digest of Education Statistics, 1987* (Washington, D.C.: Government Printing Office, 1987), pp. 8, 35. Compare the table with the classic Department of Education historical table on enrollment in educational institutions by level of instruction and by type of school in W. Vance Grant and Thomas D. Snyder, *Digest of Education Statistics: 1983–84* (Washington, D.C.: Government Printing Office, 1983), p. 8. See also *Historical Statistics of the United States*, I, 381; and *Statistical Abstract of the United States: 1985*, p. 134.

TABLE III

Enrollment in Educational Institutions, by Level and Control of Institution: United States, 1879–80 to Fall 1980—(In thousands)

Year	Total, all levels	Total, elementary and secondary	Public schools			Private schools[1]			Higher education[2]		
			Total	K–8	Grades 9–12	Total	K–8	Grades 9–12	Total	Public	Private
1	2	3	4	5	6	7	8	9	10	11	12
1879–80	—	—	9,868	9,757	110	—	—	—	116	—	—
1889–90	14,491	14,334	12,723	12,520	203	1,611	1,516	95	157	—	—
1899–1900	17,092	16,855	15,503	14,984	519	1,352	1,241	111	238	—	—
1909–10	19,728	19,372	17,814	16,899	915	1,558	1,441	117	355	—	—
1919–20	23,876	23,278	21,578	19,378	2,200	1,699	1,486	214	598	—	—
1929–30	29,430	28,329	25,678	21,279	4,399	2,651	2,310	341	1,101	—	—
1939–40	29,539	28,045	25,434	18,832	6,601	2,611	2,153	458	1,494	797	698
1949–50	31,151	28,492	25,111	19,387	5,725	3,380	2,708	672	2,659	1,355	1,304
Fall 1959	44,072	40,857	35,182	26,911	8,271	5,675	4,640	1,035	3,216	1,832	1,384
Fall 1969	59,124	51,119	45,619	32,597	13,022	[3]5,500	[3]4,200	[3]1,300	8,005	5,897	2,108
Fall 1970	59,853	51,272	45,909	32,577	13,332	5,363	4,052	1,311	8,581	6,428	2,153
Fall 1979	58,215	46,645	41,645	27,931	13,714	[3]5,000	[3]3,700	[3]1,300	11,570	9,037	2,533
Fall 1980	58,414	46,318	40,987	27,674	13,313	5,331	3,992	1,339	12,097	9,457	2,640

1. Beginning in fall 1980, data include estimates for an expanded universe of private schools. Therefore, these totals may differ from figures shown in other tables, and direct comparisons with earlier years should be avoided.

2. Data for 1879–80 through 1949–50 include resident degree-credit students enrolled at any time during the academic year. Data for 1959 include resident degree-credit students enrolled during the fall term of academic year 1959–60. Data for the years 1969 through 1980 include all resident and extension students enrolled at the beginning of the fall term.

3. Estimated.

—Data not available.

Note.—Elementary and secondary enrollment includes pupils in local public school systems and in most private schools (religiously affiliated and nonsectarian), but generally excludes pupils in subcollegiate departments of institutions of higher education, residential schools for exceptional children, and Federal schools. Elementary enrollment includes a relatively small number of prekindergarten pupils. Higher education enrollment includes students in colleges, universities, professional schools, teachers colleges, and 2-year colleges. Because of rounding, details may not add to totals.

SOURCE: U.S. Department of Education, National Center for Education Statistics. *Statistics of State School Systems; Statistics of Public Elementary and Secondary School Systems; Statistics of Nonpublic Elementary and Secondary Schools;* academic year and fall reports on enrollment in institutions of higher education; and Center for Education Statistics, "Common Core of Data" and "Fall Enrollment in Colleges and Universities" surveys; and unpublished projections. (This table was prepared January 1987.)

class exercises over the eight years of elementary schooling totaled 7,000, of which 1,188 hours were devoted to reading, 1,190 to arithmetic, 616 to spelling, 559 to writing, 500 to geography, 300 to grammar, 150 to history, and the remainder to such subjects as science, singing, drawing, physical training, manual training (for boys), and sewing and cooking (for girls). Rural elementary schools were less likely to be fully graded and systematized. Many of them remained one-room affairs, with a single teacher overseeing children ranging in age from six through twelve, thirteen, or fourteen. Many such schools could, however, boast a rough tripartite organization into primary, intermediate, and advanced work, with reading, writing, spelling, and arithmetic stressed in the primary phase, geography and nature study added in the intermediate phase, and history and grammar added in the advanced phase, and with drawing, singing, and moral instruction included at appropriate levels throughout.[19]

The high school came into its own during the decades after 1876, and soon became the dominant mode of secondary education—enrollment in public high schools began to exceed enrollments in private secondary schools (mostly academies) during the late 1880's. From 1890 to 1930, public high school enrollments virtually doubled every decade. And, as the numbers and percentages of so-called terminal students—students who were not preparing for college—increased, the high school curriculum gradually broadened. During the years from 1890 to 1910, largely influenced by the formulations of the Committee of Ten on Secondary School Studies, the curriculum featured Latin, German, French, English literature, history, algebra, geometry, physics, and chemistry. During the years from 1910 to 1930, the numbers and percentages of young people studying Latin, German, algebra, geometry, physics, and chemistry declined; the numbers and percentages studying French, English literature, and history held steady or rose; and the numbers and percentages studying such newer subjects as general science, manual training, home economics, bookkeeping, and typewriting increased rapidly. As has been remarked, when the Committee on the Reorganization of Secondary Education recommended in 1918 a transformation of the substance of the traditional subjects to take account of the interests and needs of a more diverse student body as well as a greater differentiation of

19. U.S., Bureau of Education, *Report of the Commissioner of Education for the Year 1888–89* (2 vols.; Washington, D.C.: Government Printing Office, 1891), I, 373–410; and William T. Harris, "Elementary Education," in Nicholas Murray Butler, ed., *Education in the United States* (2 vols.; Albany, N.Y.: J. B. Lyon Company, 1900), I, No. 3, 33–35.

curricula, it merely confirmed a series of changes that was already well under way.

Two new organizational units also gained a permanent place in the American school system: the kindergarten and the junior high school. The kindergarten had first appeared during the 1850's under private auspices, introduced by the disciples of the German pedagogue Friedrich Froebel. The first public school kindergarten was established in 1873 as part of the St. Louis school system during the superintendency of William T. Harris, when Susan E. Blow, a native of St. Louis who had taken a kindergarten training course with Maria Boelte, a student of Froebel's widow, offered to oversee a kindergarten class and instruct a teacher in kindergarten methods gratis if the school system would provide the teacher, the room, and the equipment. The experiment was a success; other kindergartens were organized; and Blow was soon able to devote herself entirely to training kindergarten teachers. The innovation spread rapidly during the 1880's and 1890's, so that by the turn of the century there were 225,394 kindergartners in the United States, some 58 percent of them in public school facilities. Rooted in a combination of Froebelian idealism and "scientific" studies of child development, kindergartens employed set routines of play through organized stories, songs, and games, and through the manipulation of so-called gifts and occupations—colored forms and shapes through which children might gain a progressive series of sense impressions at the same time that they began to realize what the Froebelians saw as such elemental human truths as the principles of unity and of the mediation of opposites. From the beginning, there was criticism of orthodox Froebelian methods as overly formal and rigid; and, as might be expected, variant versions of the kindergarten developed. But it remained a form of education that placed children and their presumed needs as children at the heart of the educative process rather than the substance of a curriculum and the presumed need to convey it to all children. During the 1920's and 1930's, as increasing percentages of women entered the labor market, nursery schools also came into their own, extending many of the methods of the kindergarten downward to three-and four-year-olds. By 1980, 36.7 percent of three- and four-year-olds were enrolled in schools and 93.2 percent of five-year-olds.[20]

The junior high school emerged out of criticism of the eight-year elementary school and the four-year high school as inefficient and

20. Grant and Snyder, *Digest of Education Statistics: 1983–84*, pp. 8, 43.

ineffective. As early as the 1880's, Charles W. Eliot began to call the elementary school to task for wasting time in the seventh and eighth grades, where endless review and repetition seemed to dominate. Eliot believed that in place of such review and repetition a useful beginning could be made on several of the secondary school subjects, notably algebra, geometry, natural science, and foreign languages, especially on the part of students who would not be going on to college. Later, the Committee of Ten, of which Eliot was chairman, included such a recommendation in its report. During the first years of the twentieth century, even though the 8-4 organization of elementary and secondary schooling was increasingly the standard, there was a wide degree of variation, with many localities having 7-4 and 9-4 organizations, with others having 8-3 or 8-5 organizations, and with still others having even more significant departures from the norm. In addition, there was a good deal of experimentation with one or another such variation by particular localities. Further, a number of localities began to try 6-6 organizations and to break those organizations down further to 6-2-4 or 6-3-3 organizations. In 1909, the cities of Columbus, Ohio, and Berkeley, California, formed three-year units that combined the seventh and eighth grades of the elementary school with the first year of the high school, and each subsequently claimed to have established the first junior high school. But the fact is that intermediate units between the elementary school and the high school were springing up across the country at that time, and any claim to priority would be at best moot.

As the new unit began to emerge in a fairly standard three-year form, its protagonists formulated rationalizations for its existence. Child development scholars pointed to the need for a special school concerned with the *Sturm und Drang* of puberty. Efficiency experts pointed to the need, in educational terms, for a more productive use of the seventh and eighth grades and, in financial terms, for a less wasteful use of resources in increasing the holding power of the school system. And academic theorists pointed to the need for young people to have a chance to explore differing vocational possibilities and hence differing academic emphases, during their early adolescence. On balance, it was probably a combination of the academic drive toward differentiated curricula and the financial need in many districts to take the enrollment pressures off both the elementary school and the high school by erecting a single junior high school building that accounted for the rapid growth in the number of junior high schools during the years following World War I. In the end, the junior high school never quite realized the hopes of its proponents, one of the prime reasons being that the Smith-Hughes Act of 1917 made federal funds available for vocational education addressed to persons over fourteen years of age. And, during the 1950's and 1960's, a new variant 4-4-4 organization, with the intermediate school called the middle school, came into style, supported by arguments that the ninth year ought really to be returned to the high school and that the better grouping was one that joined young people in late childhood and early adolescence. The argument was at the least supported by the steadily declining age of puberty in the United States and the increasing sophistication of preadolescent children owing to the contents of television programming.

The most obvious shifts in curricula during the twentieth century among the several school levels involved the admission of new subjects at all levels, the transformation and reorganization of the substance of traditional subjects, the movement of some subjects from one level to another, and the addition of so-called extracurricular activities at all levels. The admission of new subjects at the elementary level involved much more instructional attention to art, music, drama, dance, and physical training, though it should be borne in mind that together these subjects rarely accounted for much more than 20 percent of the instructional time at the elementary level. And the admission of new subjects at the junior and senior high school level involved much more instructional attention to the arts, physical training, vocational education, and so-called personal development subjects, including driver education. The transformation and reorganization of the substance of traditional subjects is best illustrated by the conversion of history, geography, and civics into the social studies. At the elementary level, this involved the discussion of self in relation to family and community, of other cultures (e.g., the Eskimos), and of such problems as health and the environment; at the junior high school level, it involved United States history and geography, world history and geography, and the history and geography of the state in which the school was located; and, at the senior high school level, it involved American history and government and a range of possible electives from economics and psychology to human relations and current events. In ways similar to the social studies, reading, writing, speaking, and literature became the language arts, while biology, physics, geology, and chemistry became general science. The movement of subjects from one level to another was constant: to take but a few examples from the curriculum reform movement of the 1950's, set theory moved from the college to the elementary school in many of the so-called new mathematics programs; anthropology moved from the college to the junior high school in "Man: A Course of Study"; and calculus moved from the college to the twelfth grade in many of the nation's more academically oriented high schools. The development of the extracurriculum involved clubs of every sort and variety at all levels of the school, more or less meaningful attempts at student government, and a plethora of athletic teams, orchestral, choral, and dramatic groups, debating societies, and trips to faraway places, be they farms, cities, or the nation's capital.

The residual category that Henry Barnard in the nineteenth century called "supplementary schools"—schools for the deaf, the blind, the mentally handicapped, or the delinquent or unmanageable—persisted into the twentieth. Often starting under philanthropic or religious auspices, such institutions increasingly became parts of state public school systems during the 1870's and 1880's. Then, as better methods of diagnosis and treatment became available, as the assumption spread that handicapped and difficult children not only were educable but had a right to an education, and as state financing of education became more generous and more reliable, they expanded in number. Many of the schools were residential and hence costly; many were not supported at the level that would have been required to offer a first-class education; some were hellish places, where children were ignored or abused by untrained personnel. Such problems notwithstanding, the number of special schools climbed steadily until the 1960's and 1970's, when there was a dramatic shift in opinion among educators of so-called exceptional children. Reflecting the more general movement of the era toward "deinstitutionalization" of the deviant and the handicapped, those educators began to hold that the policy of isolating handicapped and delinquent children in special classes and special facilities, even when putatively done for their own good, was morally wrong and educationally undesirable and that such children would do better if they were placed more in the mainstream of education and then given additional special services. The shift of opinion was written into federal legislation in the Education for All Handicapped Children Act of 1975, which extended and expanded a series of federal programs for improving the education of handicapped children at the same time that it asserted their right to an education in the least restrictive environment appropriate to their needs. Congress never really appropriated the amounts of money that would have been required to realize the ideals embodied in the act, but the effect of the legislation, when joined to state court rulings confirming the policy of least restrictive environments, was to slow the development of new special schools for educating the handicapped and to hasten the closing of some of the existing ones.[21]

Approximately 90 percent of the children in American elementary and secondary schools during the twentieth century were enrolled in public schools—the percentage in 1899–1900 was 92; in 1919–20, 93; in 1939–40, 91; in 1959, 86; and in 1980, 89. These schools varied widely in size and character, depending upon the structure of the state school system of which they were part (some states contributed a good deal of tax money to local school systems; others, comparatively little), the taxable wealth of the localities in which they were located, and the ethnic, religious, racial, and social class composition of the population they served. Schools tended on the average to become larger over time, as local districts consolidated voluntarily or under county, city, or state mandate—there were 117,000 local school districts in 1939–40, 41,000 in 1959–60, and 16,000 in 1980—and schools tended to become more similar, as mass textbook publishing, state and national testing programs, and national reports sponsored by philanthropic foundations, professional associations, and the federal government exerted ever more powerful effect.[22]

The public schools prided themselves on being "common" schools, that is, schools that enrolled children of all races, classes, religions, and ethnic backgrounds and that in the process continually honored and renewed the American commitment to democracy. And indeed there was some basis in fact for the claim, insofar as the structural segmentation of students according to social and religious background that had traditionally prevailed in Europe was less marked and less rigid in the United States. Moreover, in many of the relatively homogeneous hamlets and small towns of mid-America during the early decades of the twentieth century, virtually all children did in fact attend common elementary schools and those who proceeded further did in fact attend a comprehensive high school. But the "commonness" of the public school was severely limited by a wide range of structural divisions both among and within schools—by the *de jure* segregation of black children in the South and of Native American children in the West, by the *de facto* segregation of black and Puerto Rican children in the North, of Chicano children in the South-

---

21. *Journal of the Rhode Island Institute of Instruction,* I (1845–46), 60; and U.S., *Statutes at Large,* LXXXIX (1975), 773.
22. Snyder, *Digest of Education Statistics: 1987,* pp. 8, 70.

west, and of Asian children in the Far West, by the segregation and tracking of inner-city children according to criteria that frequently stressed social class background (for example, vocational aspiration), and, granted the fundamental difference owing to the element of choice, by the voluntary withdrawal of any number of social, religious, and ethnic groups into private and parochial schools (Irish Catholics in Boston, German Lutherans in Milwaukee, the Amish in Lancaster, Pennsylvania, the Hasidic Jews in Brooklyn, and the well-to-do at the Groton School in Groton, Massachusetts, or the Foxcroft School in Middleburg, Virginia). Beyond that, during the 1970's and 1980's the idea of the common public school itself came under sharp challenge, not only from religious subcommunities seeking public support for their own private schools, but also from proponents of voucher plans and parental choice plans who envisioned public schools that in their very nature would not be common schools.

The private schools also varied widely in size and character, depending upon the purposes for which they were organized, the policies set by their controlling bodies, the wealth they had behind them, and, again, the ethnic, religious, racial, and social class composition of the clienteles they served. The overwhelming majority of private schools were conducted under religious auspices, and the overwhelming majority of those were conducted by the Roman Catholic Church. The right of such schools to exist and to satisfy the requirements of state compulsory schooling laws was challenged during the 1920's by nativist and other groups wishing to compel all children to attend public schools; and in 1922 a coalition of such groups in Oregon, using the initiative and referendum, obtained legislation requiring that all children between the ages of eight and sixteen attend public schools, beginning in 1926. But in 1925 the United States Supreme Court struck down the law as unconstitutional, holding that its enforcement would effectively have deprived private and religious schools of their property without due process of law. The number and percentage of children enrolled in religious schools grew after 1925, until the 1960's and 1970's, when a combination of financial stringency and a declining number of vocations reduced the capacity of Roman Catholic schools to accept all the children whose parents wanted them to attend. There was a concurrent growth of so-called Protestant academies during those decades, private, religiously oriented schools organized principally by white Protestant fundamentalist congregations in an effort to escape what they perceived to be the religious and moral latitudinarianism of the public schools or mandates concerning racial desegregation; but, although that growth was rapid, it did not match the decline in the numbers of Roman Catholic schools.[23]

Finally, there were throughout the twentieth century significant numbers of private nonsectarian schools—independent schools, both eleemosynary and entrepreneurial—that catered to particular kinds and classes of students with curricula featuring one or another emphasis not to be found, or at least perceived as not to be found, in the public schools—traditional academic emphases, progressive emphases, character-development emphases, military emphases, athletic emphases, or artistic emphases. Some of those institutions, like the Phillips Academy at Andover, Massachusetts, or St. Paul's School at Concord, New Hampshire, or Abbot Academy at Andover, or the Stuart Hall School at Staunton, Virginia, started out as private academies during the nineteenth century, and, when forced to find a special role in the face of competition from public high schools during the 1880's and 1890's, turned themselves into elite boarding schools. Others, like Miss Porter's School in Farmington, Connecticut, or Miss Hall's School in Pittsfield, Massachusetts, were started by ambitious educators with some special notion of what schooling ought to be, and carried on as individual proprietorships for a generation or two. Still others were begun with a special need in mind—of children who were handicapped, or chronically ill, or consistently troublesome—and lived from hand to mouth when clienteles proved difficult to attract or unable to pay tuition fees at levels sufficient to keep the enterprises solvent.

The gross categories of "public" and "private" were doubtless useful for purposes of administration and governance; but it was more subtle distinctions based on tradition, on the social background of staff and clientele, and on social context that ultimately affected the kind and quality of education a school provided. A Roman Catholic school conducted by the Religious of the Sacred Heart of Jesus and Mary and enrolling the daughters of upper-class families was more like a nearby public school in a well-to-do suburb than it was like a Roman Catholic inner-city parish school. A rural Protestant academy in southern Illinois was more like a nearby rural public school than either was like a public or private school in Chicago. And an inner-city

23. *Pierce v. Society of Sisters,* 265 U.S. 510.

public high school stressing science and mathematics in the Northeast was more like a diocesan high school down the street than it was like a comprehensive public high school in the same city. For all the standardization of curricula and pedagogy that had come to mark American schools by the 1970's and 1980's, significant differences in the character and quality of individual schools persisted.

The size of the teaching force in kindergartens, elementary schools, and secondary schools grew at a pace faster than school enrollments, from 399,047 in 1890, to 719,188 in 1920, to 1,045,125 in 1950, to 2,465,340 in 1976, with the result that the average class size declined and there were many more subject-matter specialists as time passed. The percentage of women teachers increased from 66 percent in 1890 to 86 percent in 1920, which represented something of a peak, and then declined to 79 percent in 1950 and 67 percent in 1976. A study of the social composition of the teaching profession published in 1911 revealed that the "typical" American teacher was female, the native-born daughter of native-born parents, and twenty-four years of age. She had begun teaching at the age of nineteen, after four years of training beyond the elementary school. Her salary after five years in service was $485 a year. As time passed, the "typical" American teacher was older, and as teaching became more and more of a career, in contrast to a temporary job, she was better educated—by 1960, 62 percent of all teachers held bachelor's degrees and 24 percent held master's or doctor's degrees; by 1976, 62 percent held bachelor's degrees and 38 percent held master's or doctor's degrees—and better paid—by 1960, the average public school teacher earned $5,174 per year, and by 1976, $13,895, in current dollars. As time passed, too, earlier differences in the education, salary, outlook, and gender of elementary-school and secondary-school teachers became ever narrower; and, as the school system became more and more rationalized and bureaucratized, a growing number of supervisors and administrators, most of them male, came to fill managerial positions that placed them in hierarchical relationships with still mostly female classroom teachers—the similarities to gender segmentation in other fields, notably health care, were patent. Finally, though teachers had long been organized into professional associations of various sorts, beginning in the 1960's they became ever more effectively and articulately organized, as the American Federation of Teachers grew rapidly in size and influence, and as the National Education Association behaved increasingly like an alternative union to the AFT, and indeed as state and local teacher associations lobbied effectively in legislative halls and bargained effectively with state and local boards of education.[24]

IV

New colleges and universities were established in large numbers after the Civil War—the 1880's were something of a boom period for college founding—and college and university enrollments climbed steadily, though it was not until after 1910 that they began to climb rapidly. Resident, degree-credit enrollments in higher education constituted 1.6 percent of the age group between eighteen and twenty-four in 1880 and 2.9 percent in 1910; that figure then rose to 4.7 percent in 1920, to 7.2 percent in 1930, and to 9.0 percent in 1940. Moreover, if one were to include nonresident, non–degree-credit enrollments, not only in colleges and universities, but also in post-secondary commercial and correspondence institutions, the percentages would be significantly larger. After World War II, higher education began to be truly popularized, fueled initially by the scholarships made possible (overwhelmingly to men) under the G.I. Bill of Rights and then by the loans and grants made available under the National Defense Education Act of 1958, the Higher Education Act of 1965, and the Higher Education Amendments of 1972. By 1980, enrollments of all levels in some three thousand institutions of higher learning totaled 12,097,000.[25]

As had been the case before the Civil War, new institutions were founded for a great variety of purposes—to accommodate special clienteles like women or blacks or Hispanics or Native Americans; to feature special curricular emphases like engineering or business or teaching or nursing or agriculture or the military arts and sciences or the "great books" or "interdisciplinary studies"; to represent special

24. U.S., Office of Education, *Biennial Survey of Education: 1928–1930* (2 vols.; Washington, D.C.: Government Printing Office, 1932), II, 8; W. Vance Grant and Leo J. Eiden, *Digest of Education Statistics: 1980* (Washington, D.C.: Government Printing Office, 1980), pp. 11, 56; Lotus Delta Coffman, *The Social Composition of the Teaching Population* (New York: Teachers College, Columbia University, 1911), p. 80; and U.S., Department of Health, Education, and Welfare, National Center for Education Statistics, *The Condition of Education: 1979 Edition* (Washington, D.C.: Government Printing Office, 1979), pp. 82, 158.

25. Seymour E. Harris, *A Statistical Portrait of Higher Education* (New York: McGraw-Hill Book Company, 1972), pp. 412–413; Snyder, *Digest of Education Statistics, 1987*, p. 8; and Colin B. Burke, "The Expansion of American Higher Education," in Konrad H. Jarausch, ed., *The Transformation of Higher Learning 1860–1930: Expansion, Diversification, Social Opening, and Professionalization in England, Germany, Russia, and the United States* (Chicago: University of Chicago Press, 1983), pp. 108–130.

religious values or outlooks; or to serve particular localities or regions. And, as also had been the case before the Civil War, not all the institutions that were founded survived—as late as the 1970's, for example, 76 new private colleges were founded, but 141 closed and 44 were forced to give up their independence through mergers with other institutions. Finally, as had been the case before the Civil War, many colleges and universities came into being through a continuing process of institutional upgrading—business schools and academies became junior colleges, junior colleges became senior colleges, normal schools became teachers colleges, teachers colleges became state colleges, and state colleges became state universities.[26]

With the increase in numbers came a corresponding diversification of the college and university population, though the rates of diversification were neither steady nor proportional to the population at large. The number and proportion of women in the colleges increased from 1880 to 1920, but the proportion then declined until the later 1950's, when it began to increase again and eventually rose to over 50 percent during the late 1970's. There was some diversification by social class between 1880 and 1920, but one study of a representative sample of undergraduate liberal arts institutions during the mid-twenties revealed that 98 percent of the undergraduates were native-born and that 88 percent of their fathers and 90 percent of their mothers were also native-born, and indeed that 91 percent of both their fathers and their mothers were descendants of the "older" immigrations from northern and western Europe. Beyond that, there were high concentrations of segments of the undergraduate population in particular institutions: the vast majority of blacks were in all-black institutions; and a large percentage of young men and women from farming and working-class families were in teacher training institutions and schools of nursing. And, most interesting, it was not the state universities or the Morrill Act colleges that attracted the largest increases in student enrollment during the years between 1880 and 1910 but rather the medical and nursing schools, the education schools, and the small private coeducational colleges, frequently aided by denominations, that served particular localities or regions. Later, after World War II, it was indeed the state institutions, along with the local junior colleges, that absorbed the largest increases.[27]

26. *Chronicle of Higher Education*, June 30, 1980, pp. 7–8.
27. Patricia Albjerg Graham, "Expansion and Exclusion: A History of Women in American Higher Education," *Signs*, III (1977–78), 766; and O. Edgar Reynolds, *The Social and Economic Status of College Students* (New York: Bureau of Publications, Teachers College, Columbia University, 1927).

The leading reform in higher education during the half-century following the Civil War was the development of the American university as an institution offering postgraduate instruction in the arts, the sciences, and the professions with an emphasis on scientific inquiry leading to new knowledge and public service. There had been attempts earlier in the nineteenth century to develop genuine university studies—one thinks of Henry Philip Tappan's efforts at the University of Michigan and Leonidas Polk's in connection with the University of the South. But Tappan's hopes had foundered on the shoals of university politics, and Polk's on the shoals of the Civil War. It was not until the resources became available through private philanthropy and government largesse during the 1870's and leaders with the vision of a university uppermost in mind came into a position to command those resources that genuine universities came into being in the United States. And they came into being in a variety of forms in a variety of places.

The vision of the university was brought in part from Europe. There, particularly in Germany, the universities, and especially their faculties of philosophy, had come alive under the ideal of *Wissenschaft*—pure, ordered scientific knowledge, produced as the fruit of disinterested scientific inquiry. Substantial numbers of Americans had gone to Germany to study at the universities—some two hundred during the first half of the nineteenth century and some nine thousand during the second, with as many as two thousand going during the 1880's alone—and had tasted of the excitement of the systematic search for truth, guided by the associated principles of *Lehrfreiheit* (freedom of teaching) and *Lernfreiheit* (freedom of learning). Albeit with somewhat roseate memories, they had returned to the United States disdainful of the parochial colleges that had trained them and determined to create American universities on the German model. And, whereas the resources had not been available in the pre–Civil War era, they had become available by the 1880's and 1890's, through the Morrill land grants and the tax revenues of the federal and state governments, and through the fortunes of men like Ezra Cornell, Johns Hopkins, Jonas Clark, and John D. Rockefeller, men who were coming to feel not only the obligation of stewardship with respect to their fortunes but also the sense that the rise of the United States to its appropriate place among the nations of the world was dependent upon the development of great American universities. Cornell joined with Andrew Dickson White; Clark, with G. Stanley Hall; and Rockefeller, with William Rainey Harper; and Daniel Coit Gilman built on the legacy left by Johns Hopkins to create four early models of the American university. Charles W. Eliot, partly with the German model in mind and partly with the competition from Gilman's Hopkins, found among the Boston Brahmins the wealth he needed to transform Harvard, and Nicholas Murray Butler did likewise in New York with Columbia; Charles Van Hise formed an alliance with the Wisconsin legislature, as did James Burrill Angell with the Michigan legislature. Thus did American universities take form.

The Johns Hopkins University under Gilman served the ideal of pure research and only as an afterthought established an undergraduate college. Cornell University under Andrew Dickson White sought to honor Ezra Cornell's aspiration to "found an institution where any person can find instruction in any study" and, though Cornell University never embodied the aspiration literally, it embodied it sufficiently to become a very different university from Johns Hopkins. Wisconsin and Michigan, recognizing that their revenues came from the people of their states, celebrated the ideal of service, though they did so in different ways, Wisconsin featuring its services to farmers, Michigan seeking to develop a cosmopolitan scholarship that transcended state boundaries. John D. Rockefeller remarked that his contributions to the University of Chicago were "the best investment I ever made in my life." Jonas Clark, by contrast, became disenchanted with G. Stanley Hall's aspirations to build a great university and in the end withdrew his affection and his support from the university that bore his name. Harvard and Columbia invested their rapidly expanding endowments well during the first years of the twentieth century and flourished in their new-found wealth; Johns Hopkins insisted that the trustees of the university keep the Baltimore and Ohio Railroad stock that constituted the larger part of his fortune, and when the stock plummeted in value, the university suffered a significant setback. Suffice it to say that out of the mix of vision, resources, leadership, and luck, the American university developed in a variety of forms.[28]

With the emergence of the research university came a number of associated phenomena that increasingly marked American higher education during the twentieth century. For one thing, the commitment to *Wissenschaft* during a period of rapid expansion in the amounts and kinds of knowledge led to a proliferation of scholarly fields and subfields and a corresponding specialization on the part of academic

28. *Autobiography of Andrew Dickson White* (2 vols.; New York: The Century Co., 1905), I, 300; Thomas Wakefield Goodspeed, *A History of the University of Chicago: The First Quarter-Century* (Chicago: University of Chicago Press, 1916), p. 398.

INSTITUTIONS 559

scholars. The individual who might have professed history in 1880 professed European or American history in 1910 and ancient or medieval or modern European history or colonial or nineteenth-century American history in 1940. Departments came into being representing these scholarly fields and subfields, and, with departments, the competition for personnel and funds that inevitably marks organizational units. As universities expanded in size and complexity and in the process became collections of schools, departments, and institutes, administrators were needed to mediate the tensions and the competition that resulted. Presidents, who had formerly managed, taught, raised funds externally, and disciplined students internally, became Thorstein Veblen's "captains of erudition," academic counterparts of the "captains of industry" who were leading the new colossal businesses like Standard Oil and United States Steel. And, under the presidents, an assortment of vice-presidents, deans, directors, department chairmen, and heads of administrative offices emerged. Whatever the particular ideal a university sought to serve, as a large, complex organization it ended up a bureaucracy, concerned with efficiency and fairness. And, inevitably, bureaucracy affected the academic enterprise.[29]

Beyond their role as managers, the leaders of the new universities were organizers and consolidators, who gathered together under the umbrella of the university formerly discrete and independent operations. William Rainey Harper, to take but one of the leading examples, arranged affiliations between the University of Chicago and four liberal arts institutions (Des Moines College, Kalamazoo College, John B. Stetson University, and Butler College), a polytechnic institute (Bradley Institute), and a medical school (Rush Medical College). He also incorporated Colonel Francis W. Parker's Chicago Institute (a teacher training institution with an attached elementary school), the Chicago Manual Training School, and a preparatory school known as the South Side Academy into the university and joined them to the University Elementary School that the Deweys had founded in 1896 to form a new School of Education. And, through the efforts of Professor Wallace W. Atwood, he established close relations with the Chicago Academy of Sciences. When Jane Addams refused Harper's offer to affiliate Hull House with the university, he created the University of Chicago Settlement and made it a site for the research of the social

29. Thorstein Veblen, *The Higher Learning in America: A Memorandum on the Conduct of Universities by Business Men* [1918] (reprint ed.; Stanford, Calif.: Academic Reprints, 1954), chap. iii.

service faculty and its students. And, after the commercial failure of an independent University of Chicago Press that Harper had brought into being under a special arrangement with the Boston publisher D. C. Heath, he assumed control of the press and made it the vehicle for a vast program of scholarly outreach, including the publication of more learned journals than any other university at the turn of the century. In addition, Harper encouraged individual departments and faculty members to participate actively in the political affairs of the city, particularly those bearing on the school system, social welfare activities, and municipal reform. It is little wonder that the university came to be known as "Harper's Bazaar" during his reign, or indeed, that many of these grandiose beginnings were not able to be carried forward after Harper's death of cancer in 1906 at the age of forty-nine.

Finally, as part of their effort at organization and consolidation, the leaders of the new universities played a central role in the movement to have their institutions standardize academic and professional curricula and credential the teachers of those curricula. Unlike the German universities that served as their models, the new American universities were never as effective in having the holders of their doctorates assume leading posts in American public affairs as they were in boosting them to leadership in American academic and professional affairs. College graduates and law school graduates came increasingly to dominate state legislatures and governments, and in that respect the leading private universities in the Northeast and the leading state universities in the South, the Midwest, and the West achieved considerable influence; but holders of research doctorates did not achieve similar public prominence. That said, because holders of doctorates did come to dominate the faculties of universities, colleges, and professional schools, as well as the leadership positions of professional associations and public school systems, they exerted a firm hold on the business of credentialing. And, through their services in the presidencies and on the boards of the new philanthropic foundations, the leaders of the new universities exercised profound influence.. This was particularly true of the Carnegie Foundation for the Advancement of Teaching, founded as a pension fund in 1906 but operated by its first president, Henry S. Pritchett, and its first board, which included, among others, Eliot of Harvard, Butler of Columbia, David Starr Jordan of Stanford, Jacob Gould Schurman of Cornell, Woodrow Wilson of Princeton, and Arthur Twining Hadley of Yale, as a standardizing agency, initially for the American professions, and later, for American education at large.

After World War II, with the infusion of large amounts of federal money into the great research universities, all these tendencies were magnified a hundredfold. Bureaucracy became more pronounced than ever, as government accounting and personnel regulations were superimposed upon the already well-developed machinery of university administration. Schools, departments, and institutes, particularly those in the natural sciences and medicine that were able to attract large government and foundation grants, became exceedingly powerful and virtually independent—the federally supported research-oriented medical school, represented in the central university administration by the ubiquitous vice-president for medical affairs, was the foremost example; and, particularly during the great expansion of the 1950's and 1960's, the president was less and less a "captain of erudition" and more and more what Clark Kerr called a "captain of the bureaucracy" who was often little more than a "galley slave on his own ship." Consolidation went forward relentlessly, as universities incorporated not only the schools of newly professionalizing occupations—of police administration and hotel management—but huge applied research facilities that inquired into everything from atomic weaponry to genetic engineering. And in the process the university moved ever more to the heart of the economy and the polity, advising officials, credentialing and canonizing experts, and standardizing vast domains of intellectual life, from professional curricula to scientific classifications to information systems.[30]

If the leading reform in American higher education was the rise of the research university, it should be noted immediately that many institutions made the conscious choice not to try to become research universities. Some of the older colleges felt the tension during the 1880's and 1890's between intellect and piety and between the specialization—and fragmentation—that marked the university and the more traditional commitment to educating "the whole man," and, notwithstanding some curricular modification, opted for tradition. President Julius H. Seelye of Amherst College proclaimed in his inaugural address in 1877 that "the corner stone and the top stone and the informing law" of the "whole educational fabric" of the college would be Christian faith and Christian freedom, and he reiterated

30. Clark Kerr, *The Uses of the University* (Cambridge, Mass.: Harvard University Press, 1963), p. 33.

from time to time thereafter that Amherst's work was not professional but rather the work of discipline and culture. "Education is the creation and training of character," he observed in an 1893 charge to the new pastor of the Amherst College Church. "What men are, not what they know, tests the work of the college."[31]

Just as Amherst decided not to be a university but rather to continue in a more traditional mode, so did Olivet College in Michigan and Beloit College in Wisconsin. Other institutions—Bowdoin College in Maine and Wesleyan College in Connecticut—made half-hearted attempts to turn themselves into universities and failed; having failed, they decided to make a virtue of necessity and reconciled themselves to traditional collegiate education. Still others, like Occidental College in California and Hood College in Maryland, were founded for the explicit purpose of offering a traditional liberal education. In addition, it should be borne in mind that traditional liberal education came in variant versions—during the 1880's and 1890's Wesleyan encouraged electives while Amherst discouraged them; fifty years later, Amherst encouraged electives while St. John's College in Maryland, committed to a curriculum featuring the great books of the Western world, discouraged them. Beyond that, there were the ever present colleges featuring technical, preprofessional, and professional education in agriculture, art, Bible studies, business, divinity, engineering, law, medicine, music, nursing, pharmacy, and teaching. And, with the multiplication of junior colleges after World War II, the variation extended still further to include aeronautics, ceramics, computer science, court reporting, fashion design, film studies, funeral service, museum studies, and secretarial studies—to name but a few.

Whether or not an institution opted for collegiate or university status or for liberal or technical education, its curriculum was likely to broaden; only in the rare instance of a college like St. John's in Maryland was there a single focus of study for all students throughout the four years, with little opportunity for election. The number of liberal arts departments in the universities burgeoned, as did the number of courses; and the same phenomenon could be observed in the colleges, despite regroupings from time to time in the interest of integration. To cite but one example, Amherst College offered 83 trimester courses in the mid-1870's and 203 by the turn of the cen-

---

31. *Addresses at the Inauguration of Rev. Julius H. Seelye, to the Presidency of Amherst College, June 27, 1877* (Springfield, Mass.: Clark W. Bryan & Company, 1877), p. 31; and Julius H. Seelye, "Charge to the Pastor of Amherst College Church" [November 17, 1893] (unpublished ms., Julius Hawley Seelye Papers, Amherst College Archives, Amherst College). By permission of Amherst College Library.

tury, then 112 full-year courses by the mid-1920's, after a decade of
effort by President Alexander Meiklejohn and Dean (later President)
George Daniel Olds to achieve greater synthesis in the curriculum,
and then 353 semester courses by the mid-1950's. Clearly, the idea
of some core of studies constituting a liberal education being required
of all students was a thing of the past, however frequently that idea
was propounded in the inaugural and graduation oratory of college
presidents; in its place arose combinations of requirements and electives, newly constituted "general education" courses on "the Western
tradition" or "the natural sciences," and newly devised "integrating
seminars" in the senior year. In the end, it was a combination of
utilitarianism on the part of the students, political compromise on the
part of the faculty, and the availability of financial resources that drove
the curriculum. One of the early studies of the Carnegie Commission
on Higher Education during the 1970's, by the distinguished British
scientist and educator Sir Eric Ashby, was aptly titled *Any Person, Any
Study* (1971); and the final pronouncement of the Carnegie Council
on Higher Education a decade later was no less aptly titled *Three
Thousand Futures* (1980).[32]

The latter title was more than a commentary on the individual
balancing of revenues and opportunities that each of the American
colleges and universities would have to undertake in order to vouch-
safe its future during the demographic downturn in potential students
predicted for the 1980's and 1990's. It was also a commentary on the
almost infinite diversity of the nation's three thousand institutions of
higher education. Quite apart from the differing ideals they served—
technical training or Christian culture or personal growth or service
to the community or the disinterested search for truth—the colleges
and universities developed profoundly different "cultures" within
which their students were immersed while pursuing their formal studies. The culture of Rockford Seminary when Jane Addams and Ellen
Gates Starr were students there celebrated the values of Christian
service and missionary work, and those values were learned by the
students along with the formal substance they were taught in their
courses. Rockford College continued to celebrate those values during
the 1890's and the first years of the twentieth century and, in so doing,
created a very different atmosphere for higher education from that of
Bryn Mawr College in Pennsylvania, where the emphasis was on rigorous scholarship and systematic research in the best fashion of the

32. The statistics of Amherst College courses are based on the Amherst College cata-
logues for 1874–75, 1900–1901, 1925–26, and 1954–55.

men's liberal arts colleges. And both of those cultures differed profoundly from the culture of Hunter College in New York City, a tuition-free commuter institution that prepared large numbers of young women for positions as teachers in the public and parochial schools of the City. Beyond the ideals espoused by trustees, presidents, and faculties, college and university cultures were profoundly influenced by the social backgrounds of the students who attended, so that, whatever values the Hunter College faculty chose to celebrate, the exigencies of life for Hunter's lower- and middle-class students were inescapably influential on their education.

Finally, quite apart from the college culture, there was the critical role that the students themselves played in their own education, whether through debating societies and political associations, of the sort that proved so influential in the life of the young Walter Lippmann, or the protests against the restrictive paternalism of Fisk University and Howard University that provided one crucible for the emergence of the "New Negro" that the black philosopher Alain Locke portrayed so vividly in 1925, or the various organizations of the student political left during the 1920's and 1930's that provided the basic education for a generation of social theorists as varied as James Wechsler, Daniel Bell, and Irving Howe, or the various student organizations associated with the civil rights movement and the protests against the Vietnam war in the 1960's, which were so effective, not only in changing the governance structures of American colleges and universities—however temporarily, but also in helping to achieve some of the goals of the civil rights movement and in turning American public opinion against the war. David Riesman once described American higher education as a "snake-like procession," with Harvard in the lead and all other institutions seeking to emulate Harvard, even as Harvard itself changed. However suggestive, the metaphor was surely an exaggeration, given the tremendous differences, not only from one institution to the next, but in the ideals different institutions sought to serve and in the models they sought to imitate.[33]

Whatever the power and influence of trustees, presidents, and students in shaping the character of American higher education during the twentieth century, the faculty played an increasingly critical role in determining what would be taught and how. The academic career changed tremendously during the years after the Civil War,

33. Alain Locke, ed., *The New Negro* (New York: Albert & Charles Boni, 1925); and David Riesman, *Constraint and Variety in American Education* (Lincoln: University of Nebraska Press, 1956), p. 25.

particularly with the rise of the university, as members of the academic profession were increasingly drawn from secular sources rather than the ministry, increasingly educated in a specialty rather than in a broad field or in several broad fields, increasingly certified by a doctorate from a university rather than by ordination, and increasingly oriented toward research rather than teaching, whatever the actual balance of their duties in reality. Membership in the profession was increasingly heterogeneous, too, though for much of the twentieth century college and university teaching was mostly the preserve of white, native-born, Christian males. Moreover, even as diversification increased it did so at different speeds in different domains—education departments opened up to women professors earlier than physics departments; sociology departments opened up to Jewish professors earlier than English departments; social work schools opened up to black professors earlier than medical schools. In 1870, 12 percent of American faculty members were women and in 1880 that proportion had risen to 36 percent, owing largely to the opportunities created by the expansion of women's colleges, teachers colleges, and schools of nursing. Thereafter, the proportion fell to 20 percent by 1890, rose slowly to another peak of 28 percent by 1950, and then fell to roughly 25 percent by the mid-seventies. The proportion of women on the faculties of the leading graduate schools of arts and sciences remained well under 5 percent for most of that period. The percentages of blacks, Hispanics, and Asians, outside the special situation of black professors at black colleges, were minuscule. Yet, granted its unrepresentative character, the academic profession came into its own during the twentieth century, exerting a powerful influence over the internal affairs of colleges and universities and, as colleges and universities moved from the periphery to the center of public life, exerting a powerful influence on public affairs as well.[34]

V

Colleges and universities were transformed from elite into popular institutions during the twentieth century, as ever higher proportions of the population attended them. And, beyond attendance at colleges and universities, participation in formal and informal adult education activities—through proprietary and correspondence schools, job training programs, and courses offered under the auspices of churches, synagogues, libraries, and museums—also grew rapidly, to

34. Graham, "Expansion and Exclusion," 766–768.

a point where by the early 1980's it was estimated that some 21 million Americans were enrolled in adult education courses of one sort or another, a figure representing almost 13 percent of the adult population. Yet, whatever the prevalence of school and college going and whatever the popularity of courses taken in settings other than schools and colleges, no institutions were as pervasive in their reach and effect as the media of popular communication. For all intents and purposes, at least in the form of television, they reached the entire American population, over the entire life span, and for a significant part of each day. As a result their educative impact was ubiquitous and powerful, and their educational potential profound.[35]

Newspapers by the 1870's had evolved into what was clearly a characteristic American form. They were privately owned and entrepreneurial—provincial and state governments had been out of the business of censoring newspapers since the later eighteenth century and the First Amendment to the federal Constitution had precluded federal regulation, however much that interdict may have been ignored in some of the indictments handed down under the Sedition Law of 1798. They tended to be local, since, despite a substantial development of transportation and traditionally favorable postal rates, the size of the United States and the costs and difficulties of transportation continued to militate against a national press. They appeared frequently—by 1870, there were 574 dailies, with a combined circulation of 2.6 million, and 4,295 weeklies, with a combined circulation of 10.6 million. And, at least in their most general, popular form (there continued to be specialized newspapers bringing specialized fare to specialized clienteles), they regularly combined five elements: advertisements for goods and services, along with several other kinds of commercial announcements; information about public affairs—reports of important policy statements, legislative debates, court decisions, diplomatic and military ventures, and other matters of local and national interest; opinion about public affairs, ideally demarcated from the information though not always demarcated in practice; feature stories intended to entertain while they informed, on topics ranging from murder trials to athletic competitions; and cultural materials—literature, poetry, and advice and instruction on topics of various kinds, from how to cook to how to get ahead in the world. What the "new journalism" of Pulitzer and Hearst did was to liven up the style of the popular dailies to make them more attractive to larger

35. U.S., Department of Education, National Center for Education Statistics, *The Condition of Education: 1983 Edition* (Washington, D.C.: Government Printing Office, 1983), pp. 157–171.

TABLE IV

Year	Number of Groups	Number of Dailies	Percent of Total Dailies Group-Owned	Percent of Daily Circulation of Group-Owned Dailies
1910	13	62	—	—
1930	55	311	16.0	43.4
1960	109	552	31.3	46.1
1978	167	1,095	62.5	72.2

and more heterogeneous audiences and in the process to readjust the balance of the several substantive elements—more entertainment and less information on public affairs. But the "new journalism" did not in the end alter the characteristic American mix of advertising, information, opinion, entertainment, and culture. And indeed, it was that same substantive mix that dominated the content of broadcasting from the late 1920's on.[36]

That said, several points might be made concerning the characteristic mix and the institutions that purveyed it. First, newspapers became big businesses during the age of Pulitzer and Hearst and commercial radio and television stations were big businesses almost from the beginning. With bigness, not surprisingly, came concentration of ownership, the separation of ownership and management, bureaucratic organization, and the effort to maximize profits. Newspaper ownership in the United States never reached the degree of concentration of ownership that prevailed in Canada and in Europe. Nevertheless, there was a steady increase in concentration during the twentieth century, marked by a growing number of newspaper groups (chains) owning growing numbers of dailies.

By 1978, too, the ten largest newspaper groups controlled 17 percent of the nation's daily newspapers and 39 percent of the nation's daily circulation. The effects of such concentration on the quality of newspapers was from the beginning moot. For proponents of combination, group ownership brought improvement through greater efficiency and higher standards; for opponents, group ownership reduced the range and variety of editorial content and opinion. Of course, concentration of ownership prevailed in broadcasting from the earliest days of the Columbia Broadcasting System, the National Broadcasting Company, and the American Broadcasting Company; though, again, the effects of concentration on the substance and quality of broadcasting were the subject of vehement debate. And, particularly during the years after World War II, there arose the phenome-

36. *Historical Statistics of the United States,* II, 810.

TABLE V

Year	Number of Cities With Daily Papers	Number of Cities With Two or More Dailies	Percent of Cities With Two or More Dailies
1923	1,297	502	38.7
1943	1,416	137	9.7
1963	1,476	51	3.5
1978	1,536	35	2.3

non of cross-ownership of radio and television stations by newspaper groups and of newspapers and radio and television stations by conglomerate organizations, though tendencies toward concentration in those directions were reversed during the later 1970's when the Justice Department and the Federal Communications Commission resolved to limit the number of cross-ownerships as a means of promoting the public interest in diversified communications media. Whatever the debate over the effectiveness of combination, the fact is that the editor-entrepreneur of the late nineteenth century soon became an anachronism. One could celebrate the independence of a J. W. Gitt of the *York Gazette and Daily* or of a Henry Beetle Hough of the *Vineyard Gazette* as late as the 1970's, but the Gitts and the Houghs were the exception rather than the rule. The most obvious result of concentration over the years was a steady decline in the number of cities with two or more daily newspapers. A similar trend in broadcasting was precluded by FCC action during the 1960's limiting the number of stations any group could own in the same market.[37]

Beyond the effects of concentration, there were the continuing and ubiquitous effects of the effort to maximize profits on the balance and quality of newspaper and broadcast content—effects that ranged from the outright suppression from time to time of reportage offensive to large advertisers to the sacrifice of *pro bono* reporting on public affairs in the interests of profitable presentations of popular entertainment. True, there were newspapers like the *New York Times* and the *Washington Post* that managed to be profitable at the same time that they maintained editorial independence and excellence; and there were occasions on which the networks presented courageous reporting of the most controversial public affairs. But again, such newspapers and such broadcast coverage were exceptions rather than the rule. "This instrument can teach, it can illuminate; yes, it can even inspire,"

37. Benjamin M. Compaine, ed., *Who Owns the Media? Concentration of Ownership in the Mass Communications Industry* (White Plains, N.Y.: Knowledge Industry Publications, 1979), pp. 21, 23, 18. By permission of G. K. Hall & Co., Publishers.

Edward R. Murrow said of television in a celebrated 1958 address excoriating the networks for ignoring public affairs in their relentless search for profits. "But it can do so only to the extent that humans are determined to use it to those ends. Otherwise it is merely wires and lights in a box. There is a great and perhaps decisive battle to be fought against ignorance, intolerance and indifference. This weapon of television could be useful."[38]

Second, as newspapers became pervasive through much of the society (and it is well to recall that illiteracy persisted during the twentieth century), newspaper advertising, along with magazine advertising, mail-order advertising, and later roadside and billboard advertising, connected with a market economy to enhance a culture of consumption by teaching the values and attitudes of consumption. Several late-nineteenth-century developments played a role in this. Standardized goods in standardized formats in standardized packages at standardized prices became increasingly available through American industry—processed foods; ready-made clothing; household implements, furniture, and equipment; patent medicines; and the like. And retail stores were designed and redesigned to accommodate, display, and sell such goods—the great urban department stores of the era were the premier examples of such establishments. In such a situation brand names became significant; in transactions that were no longer based on face-to-face acquaintance and knowledge they conveyed not only a sense of the reliability and authenticity of a product—in a word, its predictability—but also a sense of identifiable status and fashion to be achieved by the purchase of the product. One could live a certain style of life by owning and using a certain kind of toothpaste or camera or suit of clothes or automobile. What newspaper advertising conveyed was, first, information—information about the characteristics of the product, about the quality of the product in relation to rival products, about the price of the product, and about where and how the product might be obtained; second, the stimulus to obtain the product, usually by attempting to establish some connection between the product and the aspirations or well-being of the potential purchaser; and third, and more generally, a confirmation of the values of consumption in the market, of the desirability of purchasing, having, and using the products made available by manufacturers. Whatever one might make of those values, the fact is that advertising educated: it conveyed information; it taught values and attitudes; and indeed it nurtured sensibilities. At one level, it confirmed the styles and designs

38. *In Search of Light: The Broadcasts of Edward R. Murrow, 1938–1961,* edited by Edward Bliss, Jr. (New York: Alfred A. Knopf, 1967), p. 364.

of the products it proffered—Michael Schudson has described this
sort of teaching by calling advertising "capitalist realism," in contrast
to the sort of art that came during the 1920's and 1930's to pass for
"socialist realism." At another level, advertising style itself became
influential in other domains, in the presentations of goods in department stores, of art in museums, and of displays in fairs. It would be
simplistic to argue that advertising in and of itself created the culture
of consumption; it was at best one of many factors. But advertising did
nurture, transmit, and enhance the culture of consumption and in so
doing lent it continuous stimulus and vitality.[39]

Commercial broadcasting via radio and television adopted all the
assumptions and values of newspaper advertising—advertising agencies were a well-developed business by the 1920's and were influential
in the transfer—and adapted them, first, to auditory style, and later, to
audiovisual style. By 1935, the total expenditure for advertising in all
media for the entire nation was $1.7 billion, of which $762 million was
spent on newspaper advertising and $113 million on radio advertising.
By 1970, the total expenditure had risen to $19.6 billion, of which $5.7
billion was spent on newspaper advertising, $1.3 billion on radio
advertising, and $3.7 billion on television advertising. Clearly there
had been, not only a significant rise in the overall amount of advertising, but also a significant shift in where the advertising dollars went and
how they were spent. In addition, the FCC regulated the proportion of
time on the air that broadcasters might devote to advertising as well as
the content of advertising in general and of advertising addressed to
special groups, for example, children. Be that as it may, advertising
continued to sustain, transmit, and elaborate the culture of consumption and to lend it stimulus and vitality. And, particularly through radio
and television, its slogans and tunes became the common fare of a
national community. Recall Daniel J. Boorstin's suggestion that advertising contributed to the creation of "consumption communities," that
is, communities that came into being by sharing one or another product. One might question the nature of the community that ownership
and use of a product might create; but there was no doubt but that
some advertising created such communities through the sharing—
however superficial and momentary—of certain language, music, and
symbols, and the values that attached to them.[40]

39. Michael Schudson, *Advertising, the Uneasy Persuasion: Its Dubious Impact on American Society* (New York: Basic Books, 1984), chap. vii.

40. *Historical Statistics of the United States*, II, 855–856; and Daniel J. Boorstin, *The Americans: The Democratic Experience* (New York: Random House, 1973), pp. 145–147.

Advertising was the staple fare of the media of popular communication and in a sense the most consistent fare across the several media. Beyond the advertising, of course, there was the remaining content of information, opinion, entertainment, and culture that constituted the "news" of the newspapers and the "programming" of the broadcasting stations. With respect to the newspapers, a variety of studies of their content during the 1920's revealed a decided shift away from the political reporting, editorial opinion, and cultural material that had dominated newspaper columns since Horace Greeley's era and toward a variety of features like sports reporting, police and crime news, and stories about fashion, clothing, and the home, all of which might be grouped under the category of entertainment. Studies of the content of radio broadcasting in the 1930's revealed a similar emphasis on entertainment, with the dominant categories being music and drama (mostly soap operas).

And studies of the content of television broadcasting in the 1950's revealed much the same emphasis on entertainment, with drama, music, comedy-variety, and quiz shows being the staples of the daily program diet. As has been argued in Chapter 7, all of this material could educate, insofar as it conveyed information, taught values, and nurtured sensibilities; and it could do so increasingly for a nationwide audience—the millions who partook of "Amos 'n' Andy" on the radio or of "Dear Abby" in the newspapers, or the tens of millions who partook of "Dynasty" over television. Further, with the concentration of ownership by the several newspaper groups, with the rise of the wire service and the syndicated feature, and with the control of programming by the broadcast networks, there was less and less variation in what Americans in different localities and regions saw and heard. Especially after World War II, the content of newspapers and of radio

TABLE VI

Percentages of Radio Program Content				
	NBC		CBS	
	1933	1939	1933	1939
Music:				
Classical and semiclassical	26.9	14.1	8.8	6.2
Dance and light	40.4	43.1	45.4	30.8
Drama	11.2	20.1	18.1	26.6
Other	21.5	22.7	27.7	36.4

and television programming became ever more national in character.[41]

Finally, both the reporting of public affairs and the expression of editorial opinion about public affairs changed markedly during the years following 1932. For one thing, while it may have been Woodrow Wilson who invented the presidential press conference, it was Franklin D. Roosevelt who mastered it as a device for managing the news; and, not surprisingly, it was Roosevelt, too, who was the first to make full use of radio as an instrument for informing the public directly about his policies (in the process winning public support for them). Moreover, the ability of radio to report events instantaneously and directly from the places where they occurred began the process whereby newspapers would have to change the character of their reporting to take account of the fact that their readers would increasingly be encountering the news for a second time. Radio, and later television, exploited this advantage of the instantaneous to the fullest, requiring newspapers increasingly to transform their reporting into feature writing. And, in so doing, radio and television, even more than newspapers, threw the weight of the news to the dramatic event or the controversial person rather than the important trend. More and more, what would entertain or titillate as it informed was preferred over what would merely inform; and indeed, as television news became big business and big entertainment in and of itself during the 1960's and 1970's, whatever would not only entertain but also meet the business needs of rapid filming and cheap transmission increasingly became the news of the day.

Beyond the matter of news selection and emphasis, there were important differences in the conventions of newspaper news and television news that Paul Weaver first directed attention to in the 1970's. The two genres were similar enough in some respects: both were current accounts of current events, and both sought to cover current events by means of reportage. But there were differences in style and approach that led in the end to differences in content and meaning. For one thing, the newspaper had more space for more stories of greater average length; the television program had less time for fewer stories of briefer length. For another, newspaper news stories early adopted an intensely impersonal, "objective" voice—the reporter tended to remain apart from the story; television news was audiovisual, with the

41. Llewellyn White, *The American Radio: A Report on the Broadcasting Industry in the United States from the Commission on Freedom of the Press* (Chicago: University of Chicago Press, 1947), p. 66. By permission of the University of Chicago Press.

reporter either present or reporting via voice-over—the reporter was part of the story. Third, newspaper news, even with photographs, rarely relied on the spectacular to hold the attention of the audience to the extent that television news did—one task of television news was to hold the viewer to the channel for the programs following the news. And fourth, newspaper news early developed the stylistic convention of leaving the interpretation or meaning of the news open, for the reader to discern or develop independently; television news early developed a stylistic convention of "wrapping up" the meaning of the news event and providing closure for the viewer. These differences in convention almost surely led to differences in the way the news informed and shaped opinion—put otherwise, educated—though the precise nature of these differences and their bearing on public affairs remained moot and unclear during the early 1980's.[42]

Lastly, there was the shift in the function of editorial opinion, as the untrammeled right of the newspaper editor to urge what he would upon his readers, a right increasingly limited, of course, by the concentration of ownership, contrasted with the obligation of the broadcaster to serve the public interest by devoting a reasonable proportion of broadcast time to matters of public concern and to provide a rostrum for the presentation of differing viewpoints concerning those matters—the obligation, established by the Communications Act of 1934 and subsequent congressional legislation as well as by rulings of the FCC and the federal courts, was embodied in the so-called Fairness Doctrine. The obligation came under increasing attack from the broadcasters, who claimed it was onerous and unmanageable. But they were unable to prevail in Congress, before the Commission, or in the courts, so they discharged the obligation through a variety of stratagems such as the panel discussion, the debate, and the formal editorial with opportunity for responses and rejoinders. In the end, however, the conventions of television news may have been more powerful in their educational effects than the stratagems for presenting diverse views—once again, the precise nature of these effects and their bearing on public affairs was at best inconclusive during the early 1980's.

The craft of journalism was increasingly professionalized during the twentieth century, though it was always possible to become a

42. Paul H. Weaver, "Newspaper News and Television News," in Douglass Cater, ed., *Television as a Social Force: New Approaches to TV Criticism* (New York: Praeger Publishers, 1975), pp. 81–94, and "Is Television News Biased?" *Public Interest*, No. 26 (Winter, 1972), 57–74.

journalist without specific training for the field. During the 1880's and 1890's, the image of the journalist as one who put out a local weekly and served simultaneously as publisher, editor, reporter, and printer began to give way to an image of the journalist as newspaper reporter. Moreover, as newspapers expanded their coverage to include sports, recreation, entertainment, the comings and goings of society, and cultural affairs, reporters began to specialize in particular domains, though many newspapers made it a practice to move reporters from one domain to another. Later, the idea of the journalist came also to include individuals who worked in radio and television broadcasting, wire services, news magazines, and press associations, as well as in the business and commercial activities associated with journalism. The Bureau of the Census estimated that there were 32,000 reporters and editors in 1900, 61,000 in 1930, and 103,000 in 1960. And, as the numbers rose and the requirements of the work increased, there were efforts to introduce vocational and professional training for the work. By 1910, there were ten four-year collegiate programs in the United States specifically designed to train journalists, along with any number of individual courses at particular institutions; by 1980, there were 300 such programs, 216 of which enrolled 91,000 students. Yet many journalists continued to enter the field without any college work at all or with college work in programs other than journalism. Finally, the social composition of the profession broadened, from one almost exclusively white, Protestant, and male in 1900, with a handful of women and blacks, to one that included 30 percent women and 4 percent blacks by the 1980's. Beyond that, there was a vast increase in the range of compensation. While a good city reporter could earn as much as $5,000 annually during the 1880's, most reporters earned between $800 and $1,200 annually. A century later, the average male journalist earned $21,000 annually and the average female journalist, $15,000; but anchor newspeople on television could earn over $100,-000 annually and the stars of television journalism, over $2,000,000. What is more, a leading television newsman like Walter Cronkite of CBS could achieve a measure of recognition and trust on the part of the American people that quite literally rivaled that of the president of the United States.[43]

43. *Historical Statistics of the United States,* I, 140; Frank Luther Mott, *American Journalism: A History, 1690–1960* (3d ed.; New York: The Macmillan Company, 1962), p. 499; David H. Weaver and C. Cleveland Wilhoit, *The American Journalist: A Portrait of U.S. News People and Their Work* (Bloomington: Indiana University Press, 1986), pp. 19, 43; and *Columbia Journalism Review,* XXV (November/December, 1986), 47.

Chapter 12

CONFIGURATIONS

According to present indications, New York is approaching this conception of metropolitan excellence; it is unquestionably becoming the most highly organized and the most distinguished collective expression of American social life.

HERBERT CROLY

Jean Gottmann argued in *Megalopolis: The Urbanized Northeastern Seaboard of the United States* (1961) that the forces that had created an interrelated metropolitan region extending from southern New Hampshire to northern Virginia were sufficiently prevalent in the nation at large—and indeed throughout the world—for the region to serve as a laboratory in which one might "study the new evolution reshaping both the meaning of our traditional vocabulary and the whole material structure of our way of life." With Gottmann's argument in mind, one might study the development of education in metropolitan New York during the years following 1876, not as a representative metropolis with representative configurations of education, but rather as an archetypical metropolis with archetypical configurations of education, illustrative, to paraphrase Gottmann, though in larger and more intense versions, of what other American metropolises had been and would be experiencing during the twentieth century.[1]

---

1. Jean Gottmann, *Megalopolis: The Urbanized Northeastern Seaboard of the United States* (New York: The Twentieth Century Fund, 1961), p. 9. For the argument concerning New York as an archetypical metropolis, see Ira Katznelson, "New York City: Notes on the Formation of a Research Planning Committee," in the Social Science Research Council's newsletter *Items*, XL (December, 1986), 57–61.

II

New York City had begun an explosive population growth during the later eighteenth century that did not taper off until the 1940's and 1950's. The population stood at 3.4 million in 1900, two years after the consolidation of Kings, Richmond, and parts of Queens into Greater New York; and that figure rose to 5.6 million in 1920 and to 7.9 million in 1950, where it remained for a couple of decades (with the extensive migration to the suburbs roughly balanced by a sizable influx of migrants from the South, from Puerto Rico, and from abroad) and then declined to 7.1 million in 1980. In 1900, 84 percent of the white heads of families in the city were either themselves foreign-born or the children of immigrants; in 1940, that figure was still as high as 65 percent. The origins of the foreign-born population were exceedingly varied, with the principal concentrations having come from Italy, Russia, Ireland, Germany, Poland, Austria, and Great Britain. In addition, there was a large black population, primarily but not exclusively native-born, which increased from 92,000 in 1910 to 458,000 in 1940, to 1,784,000 in 1980, and a substantial population of Puerto Rican birth, which increased from 61,000 in 1940 to 430,000 in 1960 and which stood at approximately 400,000 in 1980 (of a total of 861,000 of Puerto Rican birth or descent). Predictably, household education was extraordinarily diverse in New York City, with respect to everything from language and values to relationships with neighbors and kin. Predictably, too, religious institutions were also diverse. A fairly reliable 1952 survey indicated that New Yorkers reported themselves as 47.6 percent Catholic, 26.4 percent Jewish, and 22.8 percent Protestant; but these figures would have to be further refined within the several categories to indicate Irish Catholics, Italian Catholics, Hispanic Catholics, and Ukrainian Catholics; Reform Jews, Conservative Jews, Orthodox Jews, and various sorts of ultra-Orthodox Jews; and a host of Protestants ranging from high Episcopalians to Pentecostal sectarians. Further, there were small groups of Japanese Buddhists, Turkish Moslems, and Chinese Confucians. In New York, as elsewhere, many churches, synagogues, temples, and mosques brought together clusters of ethnoreligious families joined together for the preservation of a particular way of life, forming in the process the beginnings of particular configurations of education that later added schools, clubs, libraries, workplaces, and summer camps dedicated to similar goals. Those configurations became the teaching arms of the several immigrant communities, seeking to preserve particular traditions at the same time that they mediated the influence of the dominant American culture. They also served as the central social institutions of a variegated pattern of ethnoreligious neighborhoods—of Chinatown in lower Manhattan, of the Greek quarter in Astoria, of the Polish community in Greenpoint, and of the Italian community in the Bronx.[2]

Given its demographic base and institutional specialization, nineteenth-century New York had already developed a complex configuration of educative institutions that included not only households, churches, schools, colleges, newspapers, and workplaces, but also rehabilitative, recreational, and cultural agencies of every sort and variety. During the twentieth century, all the components of that configuration became larger, more intricate, and more specialized. Enrollment in the public school system rose from 553,000 in 1900, to 1,064,000 in 1930, and then declined to 987,000 in 1960 and to 944,000 in 1980; but it is important to recognize that the gross enrollment figures covered a wide range of schools—not only elementary schools, junior high schools, and comprehensive, academic, and technical senior high schools, but also specialized academic and vocational schools of music, the performing arts, food trades, needle trades, printing trades, and the like, special schools for difficult children, delinquent children, deaf children, visually impaired children, and mentally handicapped children, and a variety of evening schools and part-time continuation schools. In addition, the school system provided a wide range of specialized health and welfare services, from dental care to school lunches.[3]

Several points might be made about this system, the largest of its kind in the United States. First, under the leadership of Superintendent William H. Maxwell, a nationally known educator who served from 1898 to 1918, the system, like urban school systems across the country, became increasingly centralized, with a single board of edu-

2. Ira Rosenwaike, *Population History of New York City* (Syracuse: Syracuse University Press, 1972), pp. 90, 102, 141, 151–152, 161; U.S., Bureau of the Census, *1970 Census of Population,* I (Characteristics of the Population), Part 34 (New York), Section 1, Table 7, *1980 Census of Population,* I (Characteristics of the Population), Chapter A (Number of Inhabitants), Part 34 (New York), Table 6, and *1980 Census of Population and Housing,* III (Summary Characteristics of Governmental Units and Standard Metropolitan Statistical Areas), Part 34 (New York), Table 1; and Evelyn S. Mann and Joseph J. Salvo, *Characteristics of New Hispanic Immigrants to New York City: A Comparison of Puerto Rican and Non-Puerto Rican Hispanics* (New York: New York City Department of City Planning, 1984), p. 25.

3. New York (City), Department of Education, *Third Annual Report of the City Superintendent of Schools, 1901,* pp. 19–20, Board of Education, *Thirty-Third Annual Report of the Superintendent of Schools,* 1931, p. 550, Board of Education, *Sixty-Third Annual Report of the Superintendent of Schools, 1960–1961,* p. 64, and Board of Education, *School Profiles, 1980–1981.*

cation and a single superintendent of schools exercising immense powers over administration, curriculum, personnel, and the purchase and dispensation of equipment and services. Yet that fact notwithstanding, individual schools within the system differed widely from one another in intellectual and social ambience, depending upon such factors as the neighborhood in which they were located, the social-class and ethnoreligious character of their clienteles, and the experience, capabilities, and outlooks of their teachers and administrators. Second, New York City's schools, again, like schools across the country, were deeply influenced by the progressive education movement, not only in their move toward centralization—the assumption was that a highly visible board and an expert professional superintendent would be accountable, responsible, economical, and competent—but in the widespread use of testing to determine children's individual needs and achievements (testing was introduced on a large scale under Maxwell's successor, William L. Ettinger), in the broadening of the school program during the 1920's (Ettinger's successor, William J. O'Shea, liked to refer to the school as the "mother of the city's children"), in the introduction of more child-centered approaches under the so-called experiment with the activity program in the elementary schools during the 1930's, and in the continuing focus on vocational preparation in the secondary schools during the decades after World War I. Third, as the schools assumed an ever broader range of social responsibilities, they frequently served, much as the churches did, to gather groups of families into what became, with clubs, libraries, and other educative institutions, configurations of education, some, in relatively homogeneous neighborhoods, with particular ethnoreligious flavors, others, in more heterogeneous neighborhoods, with more cosmopolitan, secular flavors. Fourth, given their roots, on the one hand, in the variegated neighborhoods of the city, and, on the other hand, in the borough and city-wide politics of the city, and given, too, the number of jobs involved in the school system, the schools became one continuing focus of ethnoreligious politics in the city. Native-born Protestants, Italian and Irish Catholics, East European and German Jews, and more recently arrived black migrants from the South and Hispanic migrants from the Caribbean competed vigorously with one another through alternative political strategies, alternative programs, and alternative candidates for public office—two typical instances of such competition were the fight over the Gary Plan that dominated the mayoral election of 1917 and the fight over local community control that dominated the city's school affairs during the 1960's. Finally, given the extraordinary diversity of New York City's population, different individuals and groups used the schools for varying purposes and the schools performed a range of functions for different individuals and groups, serving as social elevators for some, as assimilators and Americanizers for others, as trainers in vocational skills for others, and as domains of failure and oppressive compulsion for still others.[4]

Alongside the public school system were several substantial religious school systems, a large number of independent schools, and a mind-boggling range of special entrepreneurial schools that taught everything from diamond cutting to radio and television repair. The largest of the religious school systems was the Roman Catholic, which enrolled 79,000 children in 1900, 186,000 in 1930, 332,000 in 1960, and 212,000 in 1980. Like the public school system, it underwent considerable centralization and bureaucratization during the twentieth century; though, like the public school system, too, it comprised individual schools that differed markedly from one another, depending upon their location, the ethnic and social-class backgrounds of their clienteles, and the particular orders of sisters or brothers who conducted them. Catholic schools tended to be somewhat more conservative than the public schools with respect to educational philosophy and curricular and pedagogical innovation, though like the public schools they performed different functions for particular groups, serving Irish and Italian constituencies during the 1920's and 1930's as confident transmitters of traditional ethnoreligious culture and serving white, Hispanic, and black middle-class families during the 1950's and 1960's as racially integrated but somewhat socially select alternatives to the public schools. A number of other religious schools and school systems served other ethnoreligious communities throughout the city.[5]

The independent schools played an important role in the education of special clienteles. Some, like the Collegiate School or the Trinity School, had begun as charity schools attached to some of the city's oldest churches and were converted into college preparatory schools during the 1880's and 1890's; others, like the Browning School and the City and Country School, were begun by forceful

4. The O'Shea quotation is given in New York (City), *Fiftieth Annual Report of the Superintendent of Schools, 1948*, p. 92.

5. *Catholic Directory, 1901*, pp. 109–111, 115, 192–206; *Catholic Directory, 1931*, 148, 133–139, 253–260, 264–265; and *Catholic Directory, 1961*, pp. 167–174, 330–333. The 1980 statistics were provided by the Office of the Superintendent of Schools, Archdiocese of New York, and the Office of Catholic Education, Diocese of Brooklyn.

educator-proprietors with philosophies of education they wanted to put into practice. Many catered to a particular social class or to families that wished a particular kind of education for their children; others were simply businesses that accepted everyone who applied and promised an "individualized" education to all who attended. Single-sex schools were frequently paired—Trinity and St. Agatha's, for example, or St. Hilda's and St. Hugh's—and clusters of schools with socially similar clienteles were joined to clubs, churches, summer camps, and the colleges their alumni most often attended, to form configurations of education identifiable along class, ethnic, or religious lines.

The entrepreneurial schools taught everything from acting to yoga. The Delehanty Institute in the later 1920's prepared thousands of young men and women for the examinations through which they might gain access to the city's civil service positions. The New York Schools of Music in the 1930's gave five thousand lessons a week on the piano, violin, tenor banjo, guitar, saxophone, trumpet, and trombone. The Arthur Murray School of Dancing in the 1940's taught thousands of men and women to do the rhumba and the samba. The Berlitz Schools of Language in the 1950's taught thousands to speak in foreign tongues using the oral methods that had been developed for the armed services during World War II. The Katharine Gibbs School in the 1960's prepared hundreds of young women and a few young men in the arts of secretarial and business services. The Stanley H. Kaplan Education Centers in the 1970's prepared thousands of young men and women in the arts of test taking. And the Ultissima Beauty Schools in the 1980's prepared thousands of young men and women for careers as hairstylists and cosmetologists. And to these more formal entrepreneurial schools must be added infinite numbers of formal and informal apprenticeships conducted by the city's firms in the worlds of manufacturing, merchandising, fashion, design, information processing, the arts, and entertainment.

The same range and diversity marked the academic institutions of higher learning in the city. The College of the City of New York had been founded in 1847 (initially as the Free Academy) to provide free higher education to deserving young men, and Hunter College had been founded in 1870 (initially as a normal school) to perform a similar function for deserving young women. Brooklyn College was added in 1930 and Queens College in 1937—making four public institutions offering tuition-free undergraduate education to residents of the city (in addition, City College conducted the Townsend

Harris High School and Hunter College conducted the Hunter College Model School and the Hunter College High School, all three institutions being designed for academically talented children from the five boroughs). Later, after World War II, the four colleges were joined together to form the core of the City University of New York, which would eventually comprise a graduate school, ten four-year undergraduate institutions, and seven two-year community colleges, along with a medical school and a law school; and that university would become the largest city-sponsored institution of higher learning in the world.

In addition, there were by the 1930's the two older independent universities, Columbia University and New York University, and the more recently founded Long Island University, as well as several church-related institutions such as Fordham University (Roman Catholic), Wagner College (Lutheran), and Yeshiva University (Jewish). There were also a host of specialized institutions such as Finch College, Pratt Institute, Pace Institute, Parsons School of Design, New York Law School, New York Medical College, the New York School of Interior Design, the American Academy of Dramatic Arts, the Juilliard School of Music, the Brooklyn Polytechnic Institute, and the Rockefeller Institute. All of these institutions prospered after World War II, and some of the more specialized, like Pace, transformed themselves into large, multipurpose universities.

The development of Columbia under Presidents Frederick A. P. Barnard (1864–1889), Seth Low (1889–1901), and Nicholas Murray Butler (1902–1945) beautifully illustrates the various phenomena of consolidation that went into the making of the great research universities during the last decades of the nineteenth century and first decades of the twentieth. It was under their leadership that Barnard College, Teachers College, the New York College of Pharmacy, and the College of Physicians and Surgeons (along with the Presbyterian Hospital) were brought solidly within the Columbia orbit. They also worked out collaborative teaching and research arrangements with the Union Theological Seminary, the American Museum of Natural History, the New York Botanical Garden, and a number of other academic and cultural institutions. They assisted various schools and departments in inaugurating some scholarly journals and in bringing others to Morningside Heights—by 1904 thirty-five learned periodicals under the control of the university or its officers issued from Columbia. They organized a university press, which assumed many of the functions of scholarly publishing formerly borne by commercial publishers. They arranged extension courses to disseminate the university's knowledge to a wider public. And, beyond extension courses, they set out to move the university from the periphery to the center of New York City affairs. When Low in 1896 pushed a resolution through the trustees designating the institution "Columbia University in the City of New York," he was reaching for much more than a clarification of the difference between the faculty of arts and the university in all its parts; he was indicating an effort to involve the university and its professors more directly in the public life of the city. Moreover, given the national and international ambitions of Low's successor, Butler, both for himself and for Columbia, it was but an easy extension of Low's initiative to involve Columbia in the public affairs of the nation and the world.

Several of the same phenomena can be noted in the development of New York University during the chancellorships of Henry Mitchell MacCracken (1891–1910) and Elmer Ellsworth Brown (1911–1933)— indeed, MacCracken anticipated many of the innovations he and Brown would seek in an 1892 address to the Nineteenth Century Club entitled "A Metropolitan University." The Metropolis Law School, which maintained high admission standards, required three rather than two years of study for the degree, and followed the case methods pioneered by Langdell at Harvard, was brought within the orbit of the university and merged with the extant university law school. The Bellevue Hospital Medical School was also incorporated and merged with the university medical school, bringing the hospital too, an institution supported by the city, into relationship with the university. The New York–American Veterinary College was similarly incorporated and actually served for several years as the State University Veterinary College for the eastern part of the state, until the university closed it down in 1922 because of the uncertain financial support of the legislature. And the New York College of Dentistry was incorporated in 1925. In addition, the university started a School of Commerce in collaboration with the New York State Society of Certified Public Accountants, a School of Retailing in collaboration with a group of the city's department stores, and a College of Fine Arts in collaboration with the National Academy of Design. The university also spread its work over two campuses, one in Washington Square and one in the Bronx, believing, in the words of MacCracken, that it should try to extend its presence as well as its influence throughout the city. It made its Washington Square undergraduate college and its law school coeducational, believing that women deserved greater, and more equal, opportunities for liberal and professional education. It created a university press in 1916. And it established a series of short courses in advertising in collaboration with the Advertising Club of New York, and an Institute of International Finance in collaboration with the Investment Bankers' Association of America.[6]

In effect, both Columbia and New York University saw themselves as research universities especially adapted to the metropolitan environment, and their capacity to assume coordinating roles vis-à-vis a variety of other knowledge developing and disseminating institutions testified to their success in the effort. However, they developed somewhat differing models of the research university. Columbia, in creating the first of its so-called nonprofessional graduate schools in 1880, described the School of Political Science as "designed to prepare young men for the duties of public life"; but it proposed to carry out that aim through the development of what were seen as the branches of the political sciences, namely, political economy, political and constitutional history, and constitutional, international, and administrative law. And indeed it was in the development of those political sciences that Columbia made one of its greatest marks. New York University's model was more utilitarian. "The notion of a university as a place to give men knowledge without reference to anything in particular and without their earning their livelihood," MacCracken observed, "is a nonsensical notion. The first work of the university is to train men for the dozen different professions which may be properly so called." And, while the university did develop a graduate school and while it did contribute its share to the development of the several academic disciplines, its emphasis was clearly on preparing young men and women for positions of responsibility in the community at large. The models were kindred, but the differences were crucial, and each served as a compelling example of the emerging metropolitan university.[7]

Beyond Columbia, NYU, and the fledgling Long Island University, Fordham University, along with the College of Mount Saint Vincent, Manhattan College, St. John's College, and, after 1936, Marymount College, was part of the configuration of education that served New

6. Henry Mitchell MacCracken, *A Metropolitan University* (New York: The Christian at Work, 1892).
7. Columbia College, *Report of the Committee on the Statutes and Course of Instruction as to a Scheme of Instruction for Graduates; a Provision of Electives in the Undergraduate Course; and the Institution of a School of Political Science, Presented to the Trustees, May 3, 1880*, p. 12; Columbia College, Minutes of the Trustees, May 3, 1880 and June 7, 1880 (Columbiana Collection, Columbia University); and MacCracken, *Metropolitan University*, p. 28.

York's Roman Catholic community (though it must be borne in mind that the several Catholic institutions were very different in character and served very different clienteles); Wagner College was part of the configuration of education that served New York's Lutheran community; and Yeshiva College, along with the Jewish Theological Seminary, the Hebrew Union College, and a dozen small rabbinical seminaries, was part of the configuration of education that served New York's Jewish community. Similarly, the several more specialized institutions tended to form educational alliances with the business and professional institutions and groups they sought to serve—Pratt Institute collaborated with architectural firms in organizing apprenticeship opportunities; Pace Institute, with accounting firms; Parsons School of Design, with advertising and fashion firms; and the American Academy of Dramatic Arts, with the city's theaters.

In addition to the schools, colleges, and universities, there were by the 1930's more than a dozen art museums, a score of historical museums, five science museums, and a half-dozen botanical gardens and zoological institutes. There was a collection of libraries that included the New York Public Library, with its main reference department and its three-score local circulation branches and subbranches, and a fascinating sprinkling of independent libraries, ranging from the Grolier Club Library to the library of the American Numismatic Society. And then there was the congeries of concert halls, theaters, and art galleries, where artists, patrons, and critics joined to perform, display, discuss, and anoint, and, in the process, to set standards and styles. In manifold ways, these institutions also formed networks of learning with one another, with the universities of the city, and with practitioners of the arts and sciences. Columbia under Seth Low succeeded in developing a network that joined the American Museum of Natural History, the New York Botanical Garden, and the New York Academy of Sciences with the School of Mines and the Graduate Faculty of Pure Science of the university; but Columbia failed in the attempt to develop a comparable network that would have involved the Metropolitan Museum of Art, the National Academy of Design, the Society of American Artists, and an informal group of practicing artists that clustered around such painters and critics as John LaFarge and Kenyon Cox. Later, New York University under Elmer Ellsworth Brown was more successful in developing such a network, owing to the fact that the university had maintained a chair of fine arts from its earliest days (Samuel F. B. Morse had been appointed professor of fine arts in 1832), as well as to its historic relationships with the artists of Greenwich Village (some of whom, like Winslow Homer and Aaron

Draper Shattuck, had been its tenants in the university building on Washington Square before it was demolished in 1894) and to arrangements worked out with the National Academy of Design. And, quite apart from the universities, the artists worked out their own networks of learning, around organizations like the National Academy of Design and the Society of American Artists as well as around associations like the Lotos Club, the Salmagundi Club, and the National Arts Club, which in their own right became "habitats of knowledge" and, at least for some, centers of education. And there were similar networks of authors and publishers, revolving around organizations like the Salmagundi Club, the Grolier Society, and the P.E.N., and of actors, revolving around organizations like the Players. All of these associations were elite in character, confining their membership almost exclusively to white, Protestant, middle- and upper-class men of Anglo-Saxon background, a fact that inevitably limited the scope and richness of the knowledge and learning they could offer; but all of them did educate and all were thought to be and thought of themselves as cosmopolitan.[8]

New York City's rehabilitative and custodial system included, in addition to the domestic relations court and its affiliated probation officers and social service workers, a potpourri of public, quasi-public, independent, and church-related institutions—jails and reformatories, orphan asylums and settlement houses, child guidance clinics and municipal shelters, custodial facilities euphemistically known as training schools and almshouses euphemistically known as hospitals. In 1939 the city's *Directory of Social Agencies* listed some eight hundred institutions and organizations operating in the fields of health, family service, recreation, vocational guidance, and custodial and correctional supervision, of which roughly a hundred were departments of government; and they oversaw everything from the care of foundlings to the care of the aged. Later, after World War II, federal, state, and local expenditures for such services would increase exponentially; but New York would maintain its pattern of public and private religious and independent organizations in the delivery of such services, preferring to subsidize the full range of alternatives rather than to funnel public moneys solely through public institutions, as was almost entirely the case with the schools.[9]

In the realm of popular communications, New York by the 1930's

8. Daniel J. Boorstin, "Universities in the Republic of Letters," *Perspectives in American History*, I (1967), 377.
9. [New York City] Welfare Council, *Directory of Social Agencies, 1939–40* (New York: Columbia University Press, 1939).

could boast eight daily mass-circulation newspapers, thirty-five foreign language dailies, and three Negro weeklies. The city also housed fourteen radio stations, all of which could be heard within the metropolitan area and many of which could be heard elsewhere. A half-century later, the city would have only five locally produced daily, general mass-circulation newspapers (the *Times,* the *News,* the *Post,* the *Wall Street Journal,* and *Newsday*), along with *USA Today,* produced largely in Washington, D.C.; it could also boast eleven Chinese-language dailies, two Spanish-language dailies, two Greek-language dailies, an Italian daily, a black daily, and several dozen weeklies and biweeklies issued in Arabic, Armenian, Estonian, French, Finnish, German, Hebrew, Hungarian, Latvian, Lithuanian, Norwegian, Russian, Swedish, and Yiddish. In addition, the city was headquarters for twenty-nine radio stations that could be heard through much of the metropolitan area (including stations broadcasting in Spanish, French, Italian, Greek, Chinese, Arabic, and Russian), seven broadcast television channels, and a half-dozen public access cable channels from which regular and occasional programs emanated in a wide range of foreign languages. Further, beyond the channels themselves, the city was the site for the production of a vast array of television programs, both by the broadcasters themselves (including not only CBS, NBC, and ABC, but also Channel Thirteen/WNET, a public broadcasting channel, which had its broadcast facilities in Newark but its production facilities in New York) and by independent producers such as Home Box Office, the Warner/Amex Satellite Entertainment Company, and the Children's Television Workshop. As the country's leading center of publishing, the city also sent forth annually a profusion of books, magazines, and other printed matter for mass and specialized consumption. And finally, one must add to these a vast range of social and cultural clubs, associations, and organizations, an infinite variety of crafts, businesses, services, and industries, and the countless comings and goings of individuals and groups from every corner of the nation and the world for purposes of commerce, convention, and tourism, to gain a sense of the complexity of the city as an originator, mediator, and transmitter of ideas—in sum, as a center of education.[10]

At least one additional point should be made. The remarkable growth of the city during the early decades of the century created a metropolis too vast for any single individual to grasp, conceive, or

10. *Ibid.; Working Press of the Nation* (1986), I, 6/2–6/11, and III, 2/223–2/224; and *New York Times,* September 15, 1985, A-42.

comprehend as a whole. By the 1930's, there were more Italians in New York City than in Rome, more Irish than in Dublin, more blacks than in any African city, and more Jews than in any other city of the world. For all intents and purposes, a person experienced New York City through one or another of its neighborhoods or its distinctive communities: the Lower East Side, or Astoria, or Borough Park, or Yorkville, or Harlem, or Riverdale. As the writer Alfred Kazin reminisced about his boyhood in Brownsville during the 1920's, "We were of the city, but somehow not in it. Whenever I went off on my favorite walk to Highland Park in the 'American' district to the north, on the border of Queens, and climbed the hill to the reservoir from which I could look straight across to the skyscrapers of Manhattan, I saw New York as a foreign city." And, as the social worker Lillian W. Betts wrote of the Italian community on the Lower East Side, "After a little while it occasioned no surprise to meet grandparents whose own children were born in New York who had never crossed to the East Side of the Bowery, never seen Broadway, nor had been North of Houston Street." Such localism had profound implications for the configurations of education in New York City. Even in eighteenth-century Dedham, one could live one's early years within a cluster of families dominated by a revivalist pastor and only later enter into significant association with other sorts of children and adults in a district school. Similarly, in nineteenth-century Macoupin County, Illinois, one could live to adulthood largely within the confines of a world bounded by Lutheran households, a Lutheran church, and a Lutheran school. And neither eighteenth-century Dedham nor nineteenth-century Macoupin was isolated or insulated; they were both in continuing communication with external cultural and religious institutions committed to education. In twentieth-century New York City, however, the power of particular configurations of education, on the one hand, and of external influences, on the other, had increased. One could grow up in Brownsville within a network of institutions that served the Jewish community there and have little to do with the outside world until going to the Brooklyn Public Library, or taking a job, or being drafted into the army; and if one avoided going to the library and worked in an all-Jewish establishment and was not called for military service, one could live one's entire life within the confines of the Jewish community, only dimly aware of external influences. Similarly, one could grow up in Harlem after it had become predominantly black in the 1930's and 1940's, within a network of black familial, religious, and public institutions and have little to do with the outside world, once again, until voluntarily venturing forth or going to work or joining the military. And indeed, in a society that practiced racial segregation, venturing forth to the "wrong" place in the "wrong" way was discouraged by a variety of means that ranged from subtle warnings to violent exclusion—a black woman, for example, could venture to Beekman Place to work as a domestic, but her adolescent son and his friends could be viewed with suspicion if they strolled through the same neighborhood. As a result, the Brownsville Jew and the Harlem black could come of age in an immense, cosmopolitan city within fairly confined configurations of household, synagogue or church, school, and peer group, never visiting a museum or a botanical garden or an institution of higher learning or a midtown department store. In other words, people could receive a profoundly limited education amid abundant opportunities.[11]

Several additional observations might be made concerning the dynamics of education in New York City, particularly as they changed over time. For one thing, the various aspects of the education undergone by any particular individual or group at any given time might be consonant or dissonant, depending upon a variety of circumstances, both planned and accidental. The public schools, for example, were consciously committed to a program of Americanization that for many teachers meant systematically divesting immigrant children of their native language and culture. "Americanization is a spiritual thing difficult of determination in mere language," Superintendent Ettinger explained in a 1918 interview with the *Evening Post.* "Broadly speaking, we mean by it an appreciation of the institutions of this country, absolute forgetfulness of all obligations or connections with other countries because of descent or birth." Such an interpretation obviously cast the schools in opposition to the efforts of those families, churches, and synagogues that wished to preserve particular ethnoreligious traditions and pass them on to the younger generation. In fact, the matter went even further, since some reformist educators saw the child taught American ways in the public school as a prime instrument for educating the parent to those American ways. Moreover, the process was seen to involve not only a new language but new standards of behavior, dress, morality, and hygiene. In such situations, collisions between opposing programs of education were inevitable, and indeed, such collisions became the stuff of a genre of ethnic fiction that ranged from Mario Puzo's *The Fortunate Pilgrim* (1964),

11. Alfred Kazin, *A Walker in the City* (New York: Harcourt, Brace and Company, 1951), p. 11; and Lillian W. Betts, "The Italian in New York," *University Settlement Studies,* I, No. 3 (1905), 90–91.

about the Italian experience, to Chaim Potok's *The Chosen* (1967), about the Jewish. In other circumstances, it was less a program than a chance encounter—with a friend in the neighborhood, a social worker in a nearby settlement house, a book in a nearby library—that set in motion a discordance between what a family was seeking to convey and what a youngster was attempting to learn.[12]

Second, particular social groups related variously to particular educative agencies at any given time, and those relationships also changed over time. For example, Italians who arrived in the city at the turn of the century found the Roman Catholic Church at best a strange institution, vastly different from the Church they had known in Italy. It stressed regular church attendance and doctrinal orthodoxy, it engaged in ceaseless fund raising, and it insisted that parishioners send their children to parochial schools. The Italians were lax about church attendance, they were resistant to fund raising, and they were nowhere near as ready as the Irish to send their children to parochial schools. The resulting estrangement made the Church far less influential in the education of recently arrived Italian-Americans than it was in the education of Irish-Americans. Interestingly, the second generation of Italian-Americans adjusted more fully to the Church's norms and expectations and participated much more fully in its activities; and the Church, in turn, created many more Italian parishes and staffed them with priests of Italian background. The rapprochement that resulted made the Church much more influential in the education of second-generation Italian-Americans. In the matter of schooling, recently arrived Russian Jews at the turn of the century were more eager to send their children to the public schools and to keep them there as long as possible than recently arrived Italian Catholics. And yet, by the end of the Depression, the schooling patterns of both groups had begun to converge. Further, one notes in the earlier era the clash within both groups between familial efforts to transmit an ethnoreligious heritage and public school Americanizing efforts. By the 1930's and 1940's, however, both groups had sufficiently mastered the politics of public schooling in the city to have forced an accommodation on the part of the school system to many of their special demands.

The same sorts of dynamics marked the experience of the Puerto Ricans, who came to New York City in such large numbers during the years after World War II. They too found the American Catholic Church vastly different from the Church they had known in Puerto

12. [New York] *Evening Post,* August 9, 1918, p. 7.

Rico, especially in light of Francis Cardinal Spellman's decision in 1939 to follow a policy of integrated parishes in the city. Also, like the Italians, they brought strong traditions of patriarchalism, marked gender differentiation, and family solidarity, all of which were sharply challenged as the young learned American customs in the schools and from their American-born peers. And, like the Italians, too, they were less committed to lengthy schooling for their children and less willing to submit meekly to school-based programs of Americanization featuring English as the sole language of instruction. But there were profound differences as well, associated with the geographical proximity of Puerto Rico (the Puerto Rican influx was often referred to, not as a migration, but rather as a process of commuting), with the racial discrimination to which Puerto Ricans of darker complexion were subjected upon arrival in New York, and with the availability of more extensive welfare services in the city during the 1950's and 1960's.

It should be noted that such changes in the relationship of particular groups to particular educative institutions were by no means always an accommodation to some universal norm. The history of New York's black community during the twentieth century is illustrative. Herbert Gutman included a detailed comparison of the structure of black, Jewish, and Italian families during the early years of the century in *The Black Family in Slavery and Freedom, 1750–1925*. His data, taken from a 1905 census, indicate that, granted differences in the age distribution and sex ratios of the three communities (the black community was generally older, included greater numbers of single women living as lodgers or with relatives or alone, and had larger ratios of marriageable women to men than the Italian and Jewish communities), nuclear, extended (nuclear families residing with additional kin), and augmented (nuclear families residing with additional unrelated boarders) families predominated in all three communities, though the black community included a somewhat larger percentage of subfamilies headed by women. Twenty years later, after the Great Migration of blacks from the South, the percentage of black nuclear families had declined and the percentages of black extended, augmented, and subfamilies had increased. But the changes were incremental, and not unlike those experienced by the Italian and Jewish communities. A series of changes in the black family structure did take place, however, after the post–World War II migration of blacks from the South that introduced more fundamental differences, among them, a dramatic rise in the percentage of female-headed subfamilies coupled with a dramatic rise in the number and percentage of children born to teen-age mothers. Such families, commonly matrifocal in structure and embedded in kin, were often transient, dependent, and impoverished, and, as a consequence, were poorly able to relate to the local public schools. The result was, on the one hand, high rates of failure, retardation, absenteeism, and eventual dropping out on the part of the children, and, on the other hand, a lack of accommodation on the part of the public schools to the special needs of this group. The outcomes in chronic dependency, continuing poverty, poor health, and social pathology were endemic in New York City and indeed in every metropolis in the country with a major inner-city population of poor blacks. What is more, such developments were by no means confined to the black community during the 1970's and 1980's; they characterized other impoverished communities as well, particularly the Hispanic community. However that may be, the point is that there were profound differences from the Italian and Jewish communities of New York in patterns of institutional accommodation and, as a result, in patterns of education.[13]

Among the many sources of these widening social and educational disparities were historic differences in the economic opportunities available to blacks, Italians, and Jews. As Suzanne Windholz Model has demonstrated in a detailed study of employment in New York City during the twentieth century, blacks, Italians, and Jews all carried to New York during the early years of the century certain characteristic skills related to the social positions they had occupied in the places from which they had come. The blacks had "served and carried" for southern whites and they began by serving and carrying for northern whites; the Italians had been builders since ancient times and they entered construction work in New York in large numbers; the Jews had been in trade and commerce in Eastern Europe and they continued in trade and commerce in New York. In addition, Jewish workers were the most likely of the three groups to find themselves working for Jewish employers; Italian workers frequently but less often found themselves under the supervision of Italian gatekeepers (padroni); and blacks were relatively unlikely to find themselves working for black employers or under the supervision of black gatekeepers. One result was that Jews and Italians were more likely to enter employment through kinship ties than blacks, and hence more likely to be aided by familial education, since most of what needed to be known to obtain and hold an entry level job could be learned in the household and the rest learned readily in the workplace itself. Later, when

13. Herbert G. Gutman, *The Black Family in Slavery and Freedom, 1750–1925* (New York: Pantheon Books, 1976), pp. 521–530.

the political accommodations of the 1950's and the affirmative action programs of the 1960's and 1970's assisted blacks in gaining access to public and civil service (and later private) employment, kinship ties and familial education could help only in limited measure—there were requirements of formal education and formal certification. One result was an economic bifurcation of the black community. Some blacks were assisted in rising to middle- and upper middle-class status, partly through the formal education system; but when they moved out of the ghetto they left behind a disastrously isolated underclass. Kinship ties, and with those ties the advantages of familial education, could not help blacks seeking civil service positions in the same way they had helped Jews in the garment business or Italians in the construction industry. Put otherwise, however much caste, class, and color surely played their roles in the cycle of deprivation that plagued segments of the black community, so did historic social and cultural factors perpetuated through particular relationships with educative institutions.[14]

Finally, there were the changing relationships of various social groups with the city's institutions of higher education, especially the public colleges and universities. At the beginning of the century, college-going was an elite activity involving small numbers of young people, overwhelmingly males of middle- and upper-class background. The undergraduate colleges of Columbia University and New York University enrolled mostly white, native-born young men of Protestant background, along with small numbers of others, including a few of German-Jewish background (the social backgrounds of the young women at Barnard College were not dissimilar). The student bodies at CCNY and Hunter College were somewhat more heterogeneous, but reflected essentially the same pattern. By the end of World War I, however, over three-quarters of the undergraduates at CCNY and over a third of the undergraduates at Hunter were of Jewish background. While the overall numbers of undergraduates at the two public institutions remained small during the 1920's, the changed social composition of the two student bodies was significant—CCNY prepared large numbers of Jews and Hunter prepared large numbers of Jews and Roman Catholics for positions in the city's public school system. Thus, during the Depression, secondary school enrollments rose rapidly in New York as elsewhere and there were few jobs for

14. Suzanne Windholz Model, "Ethnic Bonds in the Work Place: Blacks, Italians, and Jews in New York City" (doctoral thesis, University of Michigan, 1985). Model's analysis refers essentially to native-born American blacks, and does not include latter-day black migrants from the Caribbean or from Africa.

graduates of secondary schools, with the result that there were growing numbers of applicants for the limited number of places at CCNY and Hunter (and at the newly established Brooklyn College and Queens College) and the entrance requirements soared.

In the immediate post–World War II era, the student bodies of all four city colleges were composed of varying proportions of young men and women of Jewish, Italian, and Irish background as well as small numbers of blacks. Columbia and New York University broadened their admissions policies to take in large numbers of non-Protestant whites along with small numbers of blacks, and other institutions like Fordham, Long Island University, and Pace Institute expanded rapidly and heterogeneously. It was at the private institutions, therefore, that many of the blacks who made their way into the civil service system during the 1960's and 1970's obtained their formal education. The great change that came with the inauguration of open admissions at the City University in 1970 was that many more undergraduates of Irish, Italian, Hispanic, and Asian backgrounds as well as many more blacks were able to gain access to the public system, a goodly percentage by transferring from the private colleges but a significant number by entering anew. The curtailing of open admissions after 1975 coupled with the introduction of tuition fees at the undergraduate colleges of the City University significantly restricted enrollment; but by every measure the broadening of access effected by open admissions during the early 1970's, together with the related broadening of curricula, equipped large numbers of working-class and lower-middle-class blacks and Hispanics to enter technical, semiprofessional, and professional occupations in the public sector that would have been closed to them in an earlier era.

III

The consolidation of counties and cities that created Greater New York in 1898 was simply a stage in the process of metropolitanization, the development of a multiplicity of social, economic, and cultural relationships between a central core area where jobs, transportation and communication agencies, business headquarters, manufacturing plants, wholesaling, retailing, and entertainment districts, and educational and cultural agencies were concentrated, and a surrounding peripheral area, where many of the people who worked at the jobs in the core area or who produced the products needed to feed and service the core area or who patronized the shops, restaurants, and educational and cultural agencies of the core area, lived. New York,

TABLE VII

Population of Greater New York, Metropolitan New York, and Megalopolis

Year	Greater New York	New York Metropolitan District	New York SMSA	New York SCSA	New York Metropolitan Region	Megalopolis
		(Retrojected from 1980)				
1900	3,437,202	4,607,804				
1920	5,620,048	7,910,415				
1940	7,454,995	11,690,520				
1956					15,375,000	
1960	7,781,984		9,539,655	15,404,756		37,000,000
1980	7,071,639		9,120,346	16,121,297		

Yonkers, New Rochelle, Jersey City, Newark, Rockville Centre, Mineola, Greenwich, and Stamford were clearly delineated political entities located in three different states; yet, they were inextricably tied to one another by the easy movement of people, goods, money, and ideas across their political boundaries. The United States Census Bureau tried to take account of the phenomenon, first, with the concept of the Metropolitan District, then, with the concept of the Standard Metropolitan Statistical Area, and then with the concept of the Standard Consolidated Statistical Area. The Regional Plan Association tried to take account of the phenomenon by developing the concept of the New York Metropolitan Region, comprising twenty-two counties in the states of New York, New Jersey, and Connecticut. And Jean Gottmann tried to take account of the phenomenon by developing the concept of the Megalopolis to cover the single inter-related urbanized region extending from the southeastern parts of New Hampshire to the northeastern parts of Virginia. New York City itself comprised 365.4 square miles; the New York Metropolitan District (1940), 2,560.9 square miles; the New York Standard Metropolitan Statistical Area (1980), 1,382 square miles; the New York-Northeastern New Jersey Consolidated Statistical Area (1980), 4,824 square miles; the New York Metropolitan Region (1956), 6,914 square miles; and Megalopolis (1960), 53,575 square miles.[15]

15. Warren S. Thompson, *The Growth of Metropolitan Districts in the United States: 1900–1940* (Washington, D.C.: Government Printing Office, 1947), pp. 30, 40; U.S., Bureau of the Census, *1970 Census of Population*, I, Part 34, Section 1, Table 7, *1980 Census of Population*, I, Chapter A, Part 34, Tables 6, 29, 30; Edgar M. Hoover and Raymond Vernon, *Anatomy of a Metropolis: The Changing Distribution of People and Jobs Within the New York Metropolitan Region* (Cambridge, Mass.: Harvard University Press, 1958), p. 4; and Gottmann, *Megalopolis*, pp. 26–27.

The metropolitan area and region of which New York was the center was marked by a number of characteristics, none of them unique except in aggregate size and combination. In the first place, there was not only a high degree of concentration and crowding of people, things, and functions (concentration and crowding, along with social and economic integration, were the central criteria for the Census Bureau designations of Standard Metropolitan Statistical Areas and Standard Consolidated Statistical Areas), but also a high degree of variation in people, things, and functions. What is more, that concentration and variation also extended to communities and subcommunities within the metropolitan area or region, so that, as settlement expanded simultaneously out from the central core and out from the peripheral cities and towns, the several clusters of population became at the same time competitive and complementary. Put otherwise, the metropolitan region came to be marked by the concentration of variety, by what Jean Gottmann called "manifold concentration" and "polynuclear structures." Concurrently, the entire region, rural portions as well as urban portions, was transformed by new relationships, as formerly general farms became truck gardens and dairy farms and as formerly general industrial areas became the locales of specialized production.[16]

One could observe the phenomena within the confines of New York City proper, in the different ethnic, religious, residential, economic, and social characteristics of various neighborhoods—of Harlem, Riverdale, Wall Street, the garment district, and the farms of Richmond Valley in the southern portion of Staten Island. The same variation extended to politically independent communities, in the differences between Scarsdale, a carefully planned and carefully zoned upper-middle-class bedroom community with no industry, in Westchester County, north of New York; Hoboken, an industrial city with heavy concentrations of Irish-American and German-American workingpeople in its residential sections, in Hudson County, west of New York; and New Brunswick, a college town with a mix of agriculture and agricultural services in nearby Dayton and Deans, industry (the Johnson & Johnson pharmaceutical plant), and services (Rutgers University), in Middlesex County, south of New York. Moreover, communities changed seasonally and over time: the shore towns of New Jersey had small, relatively homogeneous permanent populations during the winter and large, relatively heterogeneous transient popu-

16. Gottmann, *Megalopolis*, p. 25.

lations during the summer; and, in the period between 1945 and 1985, Dayton and Deans were transformed from agricultural communities into bedroom communities with substantial developments of single-family suburban houses and shopping centers. And new communities came into being: before 1947 there was no Levittown in Nassau County, to the east of New York; it was built *ex nihilo* by the firm of Levitt and Sons as a suburb of one-family houses for middleclass families seeking to escape from the central city; and, by the 1970's, it could boast a population of 65,000, even though it remained unincorporated as a political entity.

One of the chief elements in the process of metropolitanization was the ability of people, things, money, and ideas to achieve relatively easy, cheap, and rapid movement through the metropolitan region. Such movement was facilitated from the nineteenth century on, first, by the development of the port of New York—the city was situated on the greatest natural harbor in the Western hemisphere—through dock, ferry, and shipping services, and, by way of extension, through the development of the Erie Canal and subsequently, the New York State Barge Canal System; then by the development of steam-powered railroad systems, including elevated systems within the city, with bridges and tunnels crossing the Harlem, East, and Hudson Rivers; then by the development of the electric-powered subway system; then by the development of roads, bridges, and tunnels to facilitate automobile, truck, and bus traffic; and finally, through the development of the city's airports, notably, Newark Airport, La Guardia Airport, and Kennedy Airport, which made New York a center of regional, national, and international air traffic. In addition, owing largely to the crucial importance of its financial services, the city early became a hub of telegraph, telephone, and international cable services, services that became the basis for the electronic services associated, first, with broadcasting, and later, with the more general collecting, processing, and storage of information that made New York in the 1980's what the Port of New York and New Jersey Authority called the prime "teleport" in the world.[17]

In 1940, the population of New York City was 7.5 million, while the population of the metropolitan area was 11.7 million; in 1980, the population of the city was 7.1 million, while the population of the consolidated area was 16.1 million. Given the combination of concentration and variation and the facilitation of access that metropolitani-

17. Desmond Smith, "Into City," *New York,* XIV (February 9, 1981), 27.

zation had made possible (though not always achievable, owing to differences in wealth, motivation, know-how, and the capacity to appreciate), what was provided educationally and culturally was an unprecedented density of potential clientele for an unprecedented range of potential opportunities. The concentration of clientele had several implications at least. For one thing, it meant a concentration of potential donors who might contribute financial and other resources—for Columbia University, a specialized library, perhaps; for the Metropolitan Museum of Art, a collection of paintings; for the *New York Times,* an infusion of capital. For another, it meant a concentration of individuals of skill, taste, and discrimination, in effect, a concentration of connoisseurship and expertise—for Columbia, this might meant an organization of "friends of the library"; for the Metropolitan, a discriminating audience for collections of Chinese ceramics or medieval sculpture; for the *Times,* avid followers of its crossword puzzles, its recipes, or its coverage of the world of computing; and for all educational and cultural institutions, a steady supply of experts. And for yet another, it meant a concentration of audiences of individuals interested in what educational institutions might have to offer—for Columbia, students for its adult education courses; for the Metropolitan, visitors to its "blockbuster" exhibitions such as "Treasures of the Vatican" or "Van Gogh at Arles"; and for the *Times,* the steady readership that made it throughout the twentieth century the city's pre-eminent newspaper of record. The density of clientele also made possible the unparalleled range of opportunity inherent in specialization, and, within specialization, minority, dissenting, and arcane tastes. For Columbia, this meant an extraordinary range of linguistic studies; for the Metropolitan, an incomparable Assyrian collection; for the *Times,* bureaus in a score of foreign capitals and resident authorities on architecture, cookery, education, health, language, religion, stamps, philanthropy, and style.

The benefits of concentration and variation were patently available within the city proper; they were vastly extended by the specialization, the complementarity, the reinforcement, and the competition that came with metropolitanization. Columbia University, for example, had an even larger potential clientele of donors, connoisseurs, experts, and students for its programs; and it could share the world of higher education with such complementary institutions as Rutgers University, with its School of Agriculture, and the Merchant Marine Academy at Kings Point. It also had to face, not only the traditional competition of New York University, but also the increasingly spirited competition of Hofstra University on Long Island. So it was also with the Metropolitan Museum, which could share the world of art with the Newark Museum, with its excellent collections of American folk art. And so it was also with the *New York Times,* which enjoyed a wide readership throughout the metropolitan area, and which, in response to that readership, sought to cover Long Island and Newark but in the end could not cover them as well as *Newsday,* which started as a local Long Island newspaper but by the 1970's and 1980's was challenging the *Times* for a metropolitan readership, or as the Newark *Star-Ledger,* which had no national pretensions but which covered Newark far better than the *Times.* Moreover, one could quickly recognize the further extension that came with Megalopolis. The potential clienteles became even larger, and the specialization, complementarity, reinforcement, and competition even more intense. For Columbia, there was the competition and complementarity of Harvard, Yale, Princeton, Johns Hopkins, and, in special fields, a dozen other institutions; for the Metropolitan Museum, there were the collections of the Smithsonian, the National Gallery, and the Boston Museum of Fine Arts; and for the *Times,* there was the complementarity and competition of the Washington *Post, USA Today,* the Baltimore *Sun,* the Philadelphia *Inquirer,* and the Boston *Globe.* And in all these institutions, there were the concentrations of what Gottmann referred to as the "quarternary occupations," those "supplying services that require research, analysis, judgment," in short, the sorts of information services at the heart of an advanced industrial and service economy.[18]

IV

The Bureau of the Census defined a metropolis on the basis of the size and density of a city's population and the extent of that city's social and economic integration with its environs; and surely those were necessary criteria for a metropolis. But were they sufficient? The young editor of the *Architectural Record,* Herbert Croly, raised the question in a 1903 article he wrote for that journal under the title "New York as the American Metropolis." For at least a half-century, Croly observed, New Yorkers had made incessant and noisy claims that the city was the metropolis of the United States; but they had rarely understood that the quality of being metropolitan was not merely a matter of population size. To be truly metropolitan, Croly

18. Gottmann, *Megalopolis,* p. 580.

continued, a city needed to "reflect large national tendencies" and in the process to "sum them up and transform them." It must not only mirror typical American ways of thought and action, it must anticipate, define, and realize ideal national modes of thought and action. It must be both a concentrated and a selected expression of the national life. "According to present indications," Croly concluded, "New York is approaching the conception of metropolitan excellence; it is unquestionably becoming the most highly organized and the most distinguished collective expression of American social life."[19]

Croly, of course, was a native New Yorker and could be forgiven some local boosterism. Yet the discussion of New York's unique role in the nation's affairs was something of a commonplace by the turn of the century, and in any case there could be no denying some of the data Croly cited in support of his case. By the time he wrote, New York had been the largest American city for several generations and it had achieved a decisive pre-eminence in the nation's commercial, financial, and industrial affairs. It not only boasted the greatest concentration of commerce, wealth, and corporate leadership. it also exerted a large measure of hegemony in the nation's commercial, financial, and industrial affairs. When the Populists waged their campaigns against the remote Eastern interests they saw burdening their lives from afar, they meant most often interests that were centered in New York.

Pre-eminence in cultural, intellectual, and educational affairs was another matter, however, and in those domains New York in 1903 stood at best on an uncertain threshold. One result of the accumulation of wealth in the city during the post–Civil War era was the pouring of fresh resources into such older institutions as Columbia University during the era of Low and Butler and New York University during the era of MacCracken and Brown and the establishment of such newer institutions as the American Museum of Natural History, the Metropolitan Museum of Art, and the New York Public Library. Still, probably the most important element in the rise of New York to metropolitan status in the cultural domain was the increasing concentration of the publishing industry in the city during the post–Civil War era and the shift in the intellectual center of publishing from Boston to New York around the turn of the century. Alfred Harcourt described the shift in a 1937 reminiscence entitled *Publishing Since 1900*, in which he contrasted the traditional Victorianism of such Boston houses as Houghton Mifflin and Little, Brown with the more *avant-garde* cosmopolitanism of such New York publishers as B. W. Huebsch and Alfred A. Knopf. What is more, the cosmopolitanism Harcourt described was advanced by the establishment in New York of branches of such influential English houses as Macmillan, Longman's, Green, and the Oxford University Press. In addition, New York was also by 1900 the premier center of magazine publishing; it served as headquarters for such mass circulation monthlies as *McClure's* and *Munsey's* and a host of more specialized journals iike *Scribner's,* the *Forum,* the *World's Work, McCall's,* and the *Review of Reviews.* Publishing brought concentrations of authors, editors, artists, and critics, in short, of intellectuals; and these intellectuals formed acquaintances, friendships, and networks, then clubs and associations, and then neighborhood communities.[20]

The best known of the neighborhood communities was probably Greenwich Village. Intellectuals began to gather there during the first years of the century, drawn by the remove of the area from the frenetic diurnal life of the city—the narrow, winding streets of the Village with their row houses set the neighborhood off from the main arteries of business traffic, at least until the Seventh Avenue subway was built in 1917—and by the combination of low rents and old-fashioned taverns, shops, and restaurants. Those who gathered there have been portrayed as young, poor, in flight from stifling midwestern towns, and in rebellion against their parents; but, as Kenneth S. Lynn has pointed out, their average age in 1912 was around thirty, they were as often rich or comfortable as they were poor, they came as often from Chicago, St. Louis, New England, or even other parts of New York City as they did from Gopher Prairie, and they as frequently confirmed their parents' teachings as they rejected them. However that may be, they gathered from all parts of the United States and from Europe as well, and they made the Village a crossroads of *avant-garde* ideas and a mecca of creative writing, painting, sculpture, and theater. Their ideas were not immediately accepted. Publishing may have become more cosmopolitan but it was still markedly conservative, and it was some time before the older houses and the older magazines rose to the opportunity of publishing Floyd Dell, Waldo Frank, Theodore Dreiser, Willa Cather, Sinclair Lewis, Edmund Wilson, Edna St. Vincent Millay, and William Rose Benét. Yet, as Alfred Harcourt remarked, new publishers like Huebsch and Knopf and new

20. Alfred Harcourt, *Publishing Since 1900* (New York: New York Public Library, 1937).

magazines like *Bruno's Weekly, Rogue, Pagan, Quill,* and the *Masses* did open up opportunity to *avant-garde* authors, and in due time the older publishers followed suit. And, if the traditional theaters and the traditional galleries and museums were as wary of the new as the traditional publishers, the artists themselves created the Provincetown Playhouse and the Photo Secession Gallery. In time, especially during the years after World War I, the styles of the Village became the styles of middle America, in literature and the arts and, more generally, in design and fashion. The metropolis, which had, in Croly's words, drawn energy and talent from every part of the country, had also created a concentrated and selected expression of the national life and then disseminated it. In Dreiser's novels, Eugene O'Neill's plays, Millay's poems, Alfred Stieglitz's photographs, and Robert Henri's paintings, national tendencies had been transformed into national ideals—or anti-ideals—and those ideals had been presented to the nation as its own.[21]

The Village may have been the best known of the neighborhood communities of intellectuals during the first decades of the century, but it was not the only one. Harlem also became during the years before World War I a crossroads of *avant-garde* ideas and a mecca of creative activity on the part of blacks. W. E. B. Du Bois moved there in 1910 as editor of the *Crisis,* the monthly publication of the NAACP. James Weldon Johnson moved there in 1914 and remained for the next seventeen years as an editorial writer for the *New York Age* and, after 1916, as field secretary and then executive director of the NAACP. Marcus Garvey moved there in 1916 and a year later founded a New York branch of the Universal Negro Improvement Association, through which he hoped to teach his fellow blacks that they were a noble people with a great history and a great destiny, namely, to return Africa to the Africans. Langston Hughes, Claude McKay, Nella Larsen, Jessie Fauset, and Countee Cullen wrote novels and poems attempting to define the identity of blacks and their place in American life—were they essentially white people with black skins or were they made different from whites by a unique Afro-American history? Richmond Barthé, Palmer Hayden, Charles Alston, and Aaron Douglas made the same attempt in sculpture and painting; and James Weldon Johnson edited a collection of black spirituals in collaboration with J. Rosamond Johnson, while Arthur Fauset recorded folk tales associated with black history. Interestingly, the quest was for a high

21. Kenneth S. Lynn, "The Rebels of Greenwich Village," *Perspectives in American History,* VIII (1974), 333–337.

culture, so that virtually no attention was devoted to the possibilities of jazz, which was so much a part of the black artistic experience in New Orleans and Chicago. Be that as it may, Harlem became a magnet for black intellectuals. Langston Hughes, who was living in Mexico during the early 1920's, reminisced years later that his father, a wealthy rancher and miner, wanted him to go to Switzerland to be trained as an engineer but he himself wanted to go to Harlem. "More than Paris, or the Shakespeare country, or Berlin, or the Alps, I wanted to see Harlem, the greatest Negro city in the world." And, like the Village too, Harlem's styles spread across the country.[22]

There were lamentations that Greenwich Village and Harlem were no longer centers of creative vitality by the 1930's, that the pall cast by the return to "normalcy" and later by the Depression had drained both communities of their genuine intellectuals and left in their place pseudo-intellectuals playing at creativity. The lamentations were unjustified, since both the Village and Harlem continued to attract writers, artists, and intellectuals in unusually large numbers until well after World War II. In addition, other neighborhood communities of writers and artists grew up in the city—the community on the Upper West Side of Manhattan, for example, that came to house so many of the refugee intellectuals who fled Hitlerism during the 1930's, or the community on the Lower East Side of Manhattan, called the East Village or Soho, that came to house so many of the artists associated with the so-called New York School during the 1950's and 1960's. And all these communities continued to attract talented and ambitious men and women from across the country—and increasingly the world—and all were the crucibles for the development of new ideas and new styles—Croly's "national ideals"—and the sources of their dissemination back across the country and increasingly throughout the world. In 1970, when the sociologist Charles Kadushin asked a national sample of American authors and editors to name the country's most influential journals of opinion and the most prestigious intellectuals who wrote for them, 70 percent of the editorial offices of the twenty-five leading journals mentioned were located within ten miles of the Empire State Building, and over half of the seventy leading intellectuals mentioned were located within fifty miles of the Empire State Building.[23]

The publishers provided the initial media for the dissemination of

22. Langston Hughes, *The Big Sea* (New York: Hill and Wang, 1963), p. 62.
23. Charles Kadushin, *The American Intellectual Elite* (Boston: Little, Brown and Company, 1974), pp. 22, 30, 41.

New York ideas and styles. Trade books and "little magazines" of limited, elite circulation were the first instructors. Later, textbooks for every level of schooling, from the primary grades through the university, and mass circulation magazines reached broader audiences. During the 1930's, for example, Harold Rugg, a professor at Teachers College, Columbia University, who had imbibed the heady brew of Village intellectual life during the previous decade, wrote a series of social studies textbooks that were widely adopted by school systems across the country, textbooks embodying interpretations of American life that had become prevalent among Village intellectuals. The books were subsequently ousted from the schools after charges by the American Legion that they were "subversive," but their influence in disseminating the views of New York intellectuals was nevertheless substantial. Similarly, magazines like *Time, Newsweek, Life, Look,* and the *New Yorker* gave currency during the 1930's and 1940's to ideas that had been *avant-garde* in New York during the 1920's. Clearly it was a sign of the times when Gardner Cowles decided, in launching *Look* on behalf of Cowles Communications, to edit it from New York and not from Des Moines, Iowa, the center of the Cowles interests. Also, during the 1930's, the concentration of advertising firms on Madison Avenue and of corporate headquarters on Manhattan island combined with the location in the city of the Columbia Broadcasting System, the National Broadcasting System, and the American Broadcasting System to make New York the pre-eminent originator, mediator, and disseminator of radio and television advertising, news, opinion, entertainment, and culture. Thereafter, the city became the national gathering place of ideas, intelligence, and styles, which were refracted back to the nation at large through network broadcasting.

In all of this, national boundaries meant less and less, especially after World War I. Bergsonian, Freudian, and Marxian ideas were current in the Village during the 1920's and 1930's, as were styles of European painting, sculpture, and theater; and indeed European intellectuals were present in significant numbers for shorter or longer sojourns. Obversely, the Village's writers and artists were known in person and by their works in London, Paris, and other European capitals, especially during the period of fashionable expatriation during the 1920's. Later, *Time, Newsweek, Life, Look,* and the overwhelmingly popular *Reader's Digest,* which was edited in suburban Pleasantville in Westchester County, north of the city, and which, though scarcely *avant-garde,* did disseminate many a Village idea in attenuated form, circulated abroad in significant numbers and in special foreign editions. And, after World War II, American television programming, from the products of the Children's Television Workshop to the soaps and serials filmed on the city's streets, became the standard fare of international television. In addition, New York styles of architecture (for example, the glass skyscraper typified by Lever House), engineering (for example, the steel suspension bridge typified by the George Washington Bridge), painting (for example, the abstract expressionist paintings of Jackson Pollock, Willem de Kooning, Hans Hofmann, and Mark Rothko), and fashion (for example, the blue jeans designs of Gloria Vanderbilt or Calvin Klein, designs drawn on Seventh Avenue in New York's garment district but increasingly, in the 1970's and 1980's, manufactured in Hong Kong or Korea) were exported through the mechanism of the market, the necessary tastes having been developed through the age-old techniques of modeling and imitation. More and more during the post–World War II era, the city fulfilled Croly's criteria of a metropolis on a world-wide rather than merely a national basis—it drew energy and talent from throughout the world and not only reflected but transformed large national and international tendencies, refracting and then broadcasting American ideals and American versions of cosmopolitan ideals back upon the world from which it drew.

New York was scarcely the sole American metropolis of the twentieth century. Chicago, Los Angeles, and other cities performed many of the same functions as New York, with different emphases and different specializations. Moreover, the development of jet transportation and electronic technology during the latter decades of the century made it likely that there would be more rather than fewer metropolitan regions. But New York was the pre-eminent American metropolis of the twentieth century. Further, at least during the 1970's and early 1980's, it was the pre-eminent world metropolis. Whether and how long it would remain so was in the end of less moment than the recognition that its educational functions were among the most powerful forces of teaching and learning to manifest themselves in the history of humankind.

Chapter 13

LIVES

The metropolis of the United States is made up mainly of people different from the country whose culture it modified. Nowhere, either in the present world or in history, was another case of a city exercising the influence of a metropolis on a country without being made up of people of that country.

MARK SULLIVAN

To foreign and American observers alike, New York was a city of cities. It was not merely that Manhattan's Lower East Side was as different from the Bushwick section of Brooklyn as Chicago was from Milwaukee, it was that one could grow up on the Lower East Side in a Russian city, an Italian city, a Romanian city, or an Irish city—the Jewish writer Abraham Cahan once referred to the Lower East Side as "the metropolis of the ghettos of the world." It was often remarked that, even though America, paralleling its metropolis, was less a country than a country of countries, there remained something paradoxical about the archetypical American metropolis being populated overwhelmingly by foreigners. "What, indeed, is a New Yorker?" asked the English journalist Charles Whibley in 1907. "Is he Jew or Irish? Is he English or German? Is he Russian or Polish? He may be something of all these, and yet he is wholly none of them. Something has been added to him which he had not before. He is endowed with a briskness and an invention often alien to his blood. He is quicker in his movement, less trammeled in his judgment. Though he may lose wisdom in sharpening his wit, the change he undergoes is unmistakable. New York, indeed, resembles a magic cauldron. Those who are cast into it are born again." And a quarter-century later, the American journalist Mark Sullivan, commenting on the relationship between New York and the nation at large on the eve of World War I, remarked, "The metropolis of the United States is made up mainly of people different from the country whose culture it modified. Nowhere, either in the present world or in history, was another case of a city exercising the influence of a metropolis on a country without being made up of people of that country."[1]

The paradox posed by Whibley and Sullivan was ultimately resolved in their minds by the development of an emergent cosmopolitanism. The archetypical New Yorker became the archetypical American by being "born again," to use Whibley's phrase. And that rebirth was most often associated with processes that involved education. Whether one cast the business of becoming an American in the metaphor of a melting pot (Whibley's "cauldron") or a blending (Sullivan's "hybrid") or a mosaic or an orchestration of diversity, one tended to see in the American a metropolitan character—Whibley noted the qualities of briskness, inventiveness, quickness of movement, and untrammeled judgment (elsewhere, he remarked the sharp, cruel distinctions between riches and poverty, intelligence and boorishness, beauty and ugliness); Sullivan, somewhat disdainfully, noted a too-easy penchant for the new. Both observed the emergent quality of cosmopolitanism: the metropolitan American was coming into being, not yet fully formed, not wholly discernible.[2]

That said, the metropolitan American was also infinitely variegated, the result of the diverse modes of education that marked a metropolis like New York. And, to the end of understanding that variegation and diversity, it is worth considering the education of a number of New Yorkers who came of age during the late nineteenth and twentieth centuries. Like the metropolis itself, they are presented, not as representative, but as archetypical, as indicating, perhaps in starker and more intense forms, the dynamics of the education other Americans had been and would be experiencing during the twentieth century.

II

Alfred E. Smith, Jr., was born on the Lower East Side in 1873 to Alfred E. Smith, Sr., and his second wife, Catherine Mulvehill Smith. The elder Smith was of Italian and German descent and had served in the "Bowery Boys" regiment during the Civil War; his wife was the

---

1. A. Cahan, *Yekl: A Tale of the New York Ghetto* (New York: D. Appleton and Company, 1896), p. 28; Charles Whibley, *American Sketches* (Edinburgh: William Blackwood & Sons, 1908), pp. 25–26; and Mark Sullivan, *Our Times: The United States, 1900–1925* (6 vols.; New York: Charles Scribner's Sons, 1926–35), IV, 200.

2. Whibley, *American Sketches*, p. 26; Sullivan, *Our Times*, IV, 208.

daughter of recent Irish immigrants. Alfred grew up in a world closely circumscribed by his family, the St. James Roman Catholic church, and the parish school, which was run by the Christian Brothers. Alfred E. Smith, Sr., owned and operated a small trucking company, which consumed his energies six days a week, leaving Sundays for family, church, and the occasional ceremonies of the local volunteer fire company with which he was associated. Catherine Mulvehill Smith reared Alfred and his sister in the traditions of religious piety, strict morality, and familial loyalty—his devotion to her was such that even as an adult he would kneel to receive her blessing. But she also allowed him the independence to roam the neighborhood, climb upon the riggings of the ships that docked in the harbor, volunteer at the local fire house, and listen to the incessant political conversation there and everywhere else in the neighborhood where groups of men gathered to talk. The family was far from well off; indeed, when the elder Smith died in 1886 on the eve of Alfred's thirteenth birthday, the family was virtually without resources. But the Lower East Side had not yet become the teeming slum it would be in the 1890's and after; and young Alfred enjoyed early years of calm stability in a working-class neighborhood where people were familiar to one another and bound by the ties of common tradition and similar circumstances.

St. James, with some sixteen thousand communicants during the 1870's, was the largest Roman Catholic parish in the city, comprising for the most part Irish and Italian working-class families. Under the energetic leadership of Monsignor John Kean, who came to St. James in 1879, the church reached out to parishioners of all ages through a plethora of clubs, societies, and associations. Alfred belonged to the parish youth group, served as an altar boy, and later took part in the St. James Dramatic Society—he recalled Father Kean as "a powerful and magnetic personality," who had exercised "a strong influence on the young people of the parish." Alfred also attended the parish school from 1880 to 1888; his academic record was undistinguished, but he displayed a sufficient talent for elocution at the age of eleven to win second prize in a city-wide contest. Alfred's active involvement in the life of the parish not only strengthened and complemented his mother's teaching at home; it also enabled him to meet the leading politicians of the neighborhood and afforded him the opportunity to develop his skills as a speaker, initially in the elocution classes at school and later in the presentations of the dramatic society.[3]

3. Alfred E. Smith, *Up to Now: An Autobiography* (New York: The Viking Press, 1929), p. 40.

After Alfred's father died, his mother took a job at the nearby umbrella factory where she had worked before her marriage, and young Alfred began to sell newspapers after school. In a matter of months, however, his mother's strength gave out and she subsequently rented a basement room from her landlady and established a store, where Alfred and his sister worked after school and on Saturdays. The income proved insufficient to maintain the family, and in 1888 Alfred dropped out of school and obtained a job as a truck chaser, relaying pick-up and delivery notices to the drivers as they made their way back and forth across lower Manhattan. The job was the first of several that projected him increasingly into the commercial life of the city. He subsequently held positions as a shipping clerk for an oil company, as a bookkeeper and general fill-in at the Fulton Fish Market, and as a shipping clerk for the Davison Steam Pump Works in Brooklyn. The rather remarkable ability to get along with many different kinds of people that his various jobs required him to develop would serve him well when he later entered the world of politics (he once remarked in the state legislature during an exchange in which various members were referred to as Yale men and Harvard men that he was "an FFM man," meaning the Fulton Fish Market, otherwise known as the school of hard knocks; granted the characteristic humor and hyperbole, it was also testimony to the primary educational importance for him of work-related personal acquaintances).[4]

During Smith's early years as a wage earner, politics became a focal point for his unusual energy and ambition. "The neighborhood political club was always the center of all activity," he later recalled; it sponsored picnics in the summertime, it assumed responsibility for charitable relief to local families in need, it arranged Christmas parties, and it provided "advice and information on any subject." Election Day was one of the most important holidays of the year, and the respect accorded those in the neighborhood who had been appointed to political positions—in pre–civil service days these included policemen, firemen, and district court clerks—did not escape the notice of the eager lad. Young Smith had listened throughout his youth to the local political orators, notably Congressman W. Bourke Cockran and State Senator Thomas F. Grady—he admired Grady in particular for his "faculty in making himself understood" and for his insistence upon always giving his listeners "something to remember and something to think about." In 1894, drawing upon the skills he had shar-

4. *Ibid.*, pp. 111–112.

pened in the school elocution classes and the church dramatic society, Smith began giving his own political speeches in favor of the anti-Tammany candidate for governor, Timothy J. Campbell, who won the election. It marked the beginning of his political career.[5]

Over the years, Smith had several mentors who recognized his talent for public speaking, his ability to deal with a wide variety of people, and his basic decency. One was Henry Campbell, a local grocer who exhibited "a rather fatherly interest" in the young man. Campbell had watched Alfred play as a child, serve at the church, and later go to work after the death of his father. Seeing a good deal of potential in Smith, he obtained a job for him in 1895 as a process server in the office of the commissioner of jurors. The job offered, beyond an increase in salary, an opportunity to explore all of Manhattan and the Bronx and in doing so to become acquainted with "all kinds of people, from the small storekeeper in Fordham to the broker and banker on Wall Street." Smith enjoyed the nonmenial labor and the new associations and soon rose to the position of investigator, checking exemptions from jury duty. The salary also enabled him to marry Catherine Dunn, who became his lifelong helpmate, his constant supporter, and the mother of their five children.[6]

Another mentor was Thomas Foley, a local saloonkeeper who was widely known among the children of the neighborhood for his great generosity. Young Smith early formed a friendship with Foley; and, when Foley fought with Patrick Divver in 1901 over the leadership of the Tammany Hall district in which Smith lived, Smith joined forces with Foley and ended up on the winning team. Later, when Foley became dissatisfied with the state assemblyman from the Fourth Ward and his first choice as a replacement refused to run, Foley, at Campbell's suggestion, chose Smith for the nomination (Smith had deliberately been patronizing Foley's saloon in order to be available if opportunities should arise). Smith won the election; and it is testimony to his growing powers of political persuasion that he had the support of both the Foley and the Divver factions. Henry Campbell, eager for Smith to present himself properly, took the young novice to Brooks Brothers and bought him the wardrobe he would need for the legislative sessions and formal occasions he would be required to attend in Albany.

Smith approached his legislative career in 1904 with characteristic verve and with the eager desire to learn that had guided him in every

5. *Ibid.*, pp. 28, 51–52.
6. *Ibid.*, pp. 55, 56.

job he had ever held. Once embarked upon his duties, however, he felt for the first time at a disadvantage because of his lack of formal schooling. He found that he did not "really know what was going on" and had great difficulty understanding pending bills, even after studying them at night after each session. Still, he was re-elected and in the 1905 legislature was assigned to the Committees on Banks and on Public Lands and Forestry, despite the fact, as he later observed, that he had never been in a bank except to serve a jury notice and had never seen a forest. He thought for a time about relinquishing his seat, but his determination to master the business of the legislature came to the attention of Speaker James J. Wadsworth, who took a personal interest in Smith and gave him committee assignments that would help him better understand what was going on. By the end of 1906, Smith felt that, with his nighttime study and the encouragement of Wadsworth, he had "made so much headway" that he could actually look forward with pleasure to the next election. Meanwhile, under the tutelage of Foley, he refrained from speaking in the chamber until he had "something to say" and avoided making promises until he was sure he could "deliver." Further, he listened attentively to his constituents in the Fourth Ward and began to shape his activities to their needs. His first speech in the Assembly called for more equitable representation for the city in the legislature, and among the earliest measures he introduced were bills to control utility rates, insurance premiums, and banking practices. He soon became known as a champion of the people against the interests, but his approach was far more pragmatic than programmatic; he was merely seeking to meet the needs of his constituency as he understood them, as often as not with the Tammany machine as the go-between.[7]

The fire at the Triangle Waist Company on March 25, 1911, in which 146 employees, most of them young women, lost their lives because they had been locked into their work area, set in motion the next phase of Smith's political education. In the wake of the tragedy, a Committee on Safety was formed to make certain nothing of the sort would ever happen again. One result of the Committee's agitation was the creation of a legislative commission to look into the need for more effective laws pertaining to fire safety and, more generally, to investigate the whole domain of labor relations. Smith helped establish the commission and then became a member, along with his friend Robert F. Wagner from the senate, and several private citizens, including

7. *Ibid.*, pp. 71, 76.

Simon Brentano, the publisher, Mary Dreier, the labor advocate, and Samuel Gompers, the president of the American Federation of Labor. The proceedings proved a revelation to the maturing assemblyman. He traveled widely through the state, looking into factory conditions and hearing testimony from businessmen and labor leaders. And, even more important, he entered into continuing association with a group of reformers whose work had brought them into intimate relationship with the problems of the poor—Henry Moscowitz, head of the Madison Street settlement, Belle Israels (later to be the wife of Henry Moscowitz) of the Educational Alliance, Frances Perkins, head of the Committee on Safety, and Joseph M. Proskauer, a leader of the Citizens' Union. The experience joined a firsthand view of New York's industry to the insights of a group of activists arguing the need for legislation requiring improved working conditions and healthier living conditions for workingpeople. As a result of the commission's investigations, Smith and Wagner were able to introduce a series of bills that began to assign to government the positive role of protecting those unable to protect themselves. Beyond that, the Moscowitzes, Perkins, and Proskauer became Smith's advisers for the remainder of his political career.

Smith later served as governor of New York and as the Democratic candidate for president of the United States in the unsuccessful campaign of 1928. His education certainly did not cease, but it would never again be as intense as it had been in the New York legislature. As he himself remarked in 1925, after taking the oath of office as governor for the third time in the Assembly chamber, "This is the sixteenth time that I have taken the oath of allegiance to the state in this room. I have a deep and abiding affection for the Assembly chamber. It has been my high school and my college; in fact, the very foundation of everything that I have attained was laid here."

The education Smith had gained in the Assembly served him in good stead through 1928; thereafter, it seemed to serve him less well. Having accepted the American dream of an open society, he was shaken by the bigotry he encountered in the presidential campaign; having been schooled in the politics of loyalty, he could not understand Franklin D. Roosevelt's continuing indifference to his views; and having risen in the world through his own efforts, he could not come to terms with the New Deal. The same education that had, along with great effort and some incomparable good luck, carried him to national eminence, in the end rendered him unable to contend with the emerging problems of a transformed America. He died in 1944 a disappointed man, not so much angry or alienated—he was, after all, something of a fatalist—as resigned and uncomprehending.[8]

III

Elizabeth Dodge Huntington Clarke was born to Cleveland Hoadley Dodge and Grace Parish Dodge at the family's summer mansion (called Greyston) in Riverdale, on August 10, 1884. She grew up in Manhattan, but spent weekends and summers in Riverdale by the shore of the Hudson River. The Dodges belonged to a prominent and wealthy New York family that had first arrived in the city in 1806, when Elizabeth's great-great-grandfather, a successful merchant and devout evangelical Protestant named David Low Dodge, had moved there from Connecticut. Elizabeth's great-grandfather, William Earl Dodge, Sr., proved to be an even more successful businessman than his father. His marriage to Melissa Phelps in 1828 united two families of wealth and led eventually to the formation of Phelps, Dodge & Company. As William Earl Dodge, Sr.'s, fortune increased, so did his dedication to Christianity. He helped found the Young Men's Bible Society of New York and the New York City Mission and Tract Society and was a leader in the development of the National Temperance Society. William Earl Dodge, Jr., never took the vow of temperance, but he continued in his father's philanthropic and evangelical tradition, contributing during the course of his lifetime to the work of such organizations as the Young Men's Christian Association, the American Museum of Natural History, the Metropolitan Museum of Art, the Bronx Zoo and Botanical Garden, and Robert College in Istanbul. His son Cleveland Hoadley Dodge also united an interest in philanthropy with a dedication to Christian service; and, while playing an active role in the continuing development of Phelps, Dodge & Company also took an interest in national politics by supporting first Theodore Roosevelt and then Woodrow Wilson.

In her memoirs, Clarke described her father as "the leader of our expeditions." He led Elizabeth, her younger sister, Julia, and her younger twin brothers, Cleveland and Bayard, on many long walks around Greyston and along the Hudson. In a more spiritual vein, he also led them to become committed Christians, dedicated to the service of others. His readings from the family Bible inspired Elizabeth with a love of the Scriptures and with an urgent wish to live her

8. *Ibid.*, p. 296.

Christianity. Grace Parish Dodge played the role of sustaining help-mate and mother, administering a large and complex household at the same time that she readily made herself available to her children, comforting, teaching, and encouraging them and possibly even creating spaces in which they might gain autonomy, given the fairly strict constraints set by their powerful father. Both Dodges were also active in the work of the Riverdale Presbyterian Church, where Cleveland H. Dodge served as superintendent of the Sunday school. Elizabeth and her siblings attended the classes taught by Kate Dodd, the pastor's daughter, and helped organize their own local Christian Endeavor Society. At the age of fourteen, Elizabeth joined the church, and later recalled of that moving occasion, "I felt I then gave my life to Jesus as Lord, a commitment which has been strengthened by life's many experiences in times of stress."[9]

Family and church provided the principal elements in Elizabeth's early education. She was tutored at home for a time and then attended the Brearley School in Manhattan from 1898 to 1903; but she maintained that she learned less at school than she did at home and at church. Her teachers at the Brearley encouraged her to continue on to college and she herself wanted very much to go to Bryn Mawr with many of her classmates; but her father insisted that college was unnecessary for women unless they were headed for a specific career such as teaching or nursing. The elder Dodge also systematically instructed Elizabeth in the multifarious ways in which one did the work of the church and charities.

As she grew older, Elizabeth became increasingly interested in Christian service. Yet, for all her father's assiduous instruction, it was clear that many of his activities, particularly those associated with business and politics, were not open to women, and indeed that even some of his philanthropic activities either excluded women or relegated them to marginal roles. In the end, therefore, it was her paternal aunt, Grace Hoadley Dodge, rather than her father or indeed her more domestically inclined mother, who became the leading role model for Elizabeth. Of all the relatives Clarke described in her memoirs, none was accorded as much respect or seemed to have exercised as much influence on her as Grace Hoadley Dodge. Barred from business or political activities because of her sex, Grace Dodge had devoted her considerable executive abilities to organizing and promoting educational and charitable groups for women. Although she

9. *The Joy of Service: Memoirs of Elizabeth Dodge Huntington Clarke* (New York: National Board of the Young Women's Christian Association, 1979), pp. 216, 26.

successfully preserved and tried to teach the virtues of domesticity, she also led an active life outside the home as a philanthropist. She sponsored working girls' clubs and served on the New York City Board of Education; she started the Kitchen Garden Association that eventually led to the founding of the New York College for the Training of Teachers, later, Teachers College, Columbia University; she helped organize the Greenhouse Library, which later became the Riverdale Library and Neighborhood House; and she served as president of the board of trustees of the American College for Girls in Turkey.

Given Elizabeth's aspirations, Grace Dodge provided a perfect model. Both were the eldest children in their families, and both were more outgoing than their sisters. Elizabeth scorned the idea of being a debutante, just as her aunt had scorned it a quarter-century earlier. Both preferred hard work at Christian service to the goings-on of society, and Elizabeth especially admired Aunt Grace's ability to inspire religious fellowship and devotion. Beyond providing a model, Grace Dodge enlisted Elizabeth's participation in her work. She urged Elizabeth to attend the 1905–6 YWCA meetings at her Manhattan home, where she successfully reconciled members of the International Board with members of the American Committee. During her presidency of the YWCA, she appointed Elizabeth treasurer of the Territorial Committee for New York and New Jersey. Elizabeth soon rose to the chairmanship of the Territorial Committee. As the territory expanded, she eventually became chairman of the New England field committee and served on the National Board. As her responsibilities within the organization expanded, so did her organizational skills—always under the watchful eye of Aunt Grace. She crisscrossed her territory, speaking at colleges and to women's groups about the YWCA. She also started two summer camps for women. By 1915 she had traveled from Portland, Maine, to Los Angeles, attending national conferences and delivering speeches on the work of the "Y."

The opportunities Elizabeth was offered through service expanded her purview beyond the world of family, church, and neighborhood; and travel served a similar function, especially the trip she took with her father to the Near East and Europe in 1910. For the first time, she visited Robert College, where her father was president of the board of trustees. She also met her future husband, the Reverend George Huntington, who was a professor there. And she subsequently joined Grace Dodge in Berlin for the world YWCA conference, where Dodge was the American delegate. It was only then that

she began fully to comprehend the international scope and significance of the YWCA.

Elizabeth had cherished the hope of some day serving as a missionary. That hope was realized in 1916 when she married George Huntington and joined him in Turkey. A graduate of Williams College and
of the Hartford Theological Seminary, Huntington shared his wife's
enthusiasm for mission work. They deeply believed their services
would be especially useful in preaching Christ's word in a Moslem
country, and their marriage reinforced and deepened their evangelical commitments.

World War I provided numerous opportunities for Christian service on the part of the Americans in German-occupied Istanbul. When
the food shortage became severe, Robert College was forced to send
home its boarding students. The head of the engineering school
devised a grain mill so that faculty members could prepare their own
flour for bread. The hunger and suffering occasioned by the war
intensified the Huntingtons' efforts to help the people of the city.
Dismayed by the plight of the Armenians, Elizabeth Huntington did
what she could to create jobs for the widows and find homes for the
orphans. She scrounged up old rags and commissioned women to
embroider the material so that soldiers might purchase the products
as gifts to send home. She also prodded her father to raise money for
Near East relief. Later, after the war, she became secretary of the
Relief Committee headed by Caleb Gates, the president of Robert
College, which received funds from the United States for Armenian
and Syrian relief and sent them on to missionaries. She also dedicated
herself to the "moral and spiritual upbuilding" of women recently
emancipated from purdah and strove through various organizations
to unite Greek, Armenian, Catholic, Protestant, Jewish, and Moslem
women "into one sisterhood with the principles of Christ to guide
them."[10]

As was frequently the case with missionaries, Elizabeth Huntington's commitment to educating foreign women revealed a considerable ethnocentrism. She deeply believed that fresh air would
strengthen the Moslem girls and develop their commitment to Christianity, just as the YWCA camps she had started in New England had
in her view strengthened American girls and developed their commitment to Christianity. Hence, in 1921 she opened a camp for Turkish
girls on the Bosporus Sea. At first, parents forbade their daughters to

10. Mrs. George Huntington, "In Constantinople during the War," *Women's International
Quarterly*, IX (1919), 12.

spend nights away from home, but eventually the idea became fairly popular. Another program she inaugurated was a business class in which young women would learn secretarial skills. Many businessmen came to postwar Istanbul, and the demand rose for qualified secretaries. Elizabeth Huntington, realizing that few Turkish women possessed the skills of typing and dictation, helped the service center in Istanbul offer training courses for aspiring secretaries. Once again, the American YWCA set the pattern. Beyond these educational activities, Huntington also served as a trustee of the American Hospital in the city.

In all these efforts, Huntington continued to draw on the example of Grace Dodge, in the process deepening her own faith in one of her aunt's favorite preachments—"In quietness and confidence will be your strength." That influence notwithstanding, Huntington's work also bore the marks of the twentieth century. Except for her service as president of the board of the American College for Girls, Dodge's activities had been primarily limited to New York. Huntington's service carried much more of an international flavor. By 1914, she had been to Europe four times and to the Near East, twice. Those travels provided, not only pleasure, but opportunities for continuing education, through the people she met and through the understanding she gained of different customs and cultures. She found her visits to Jerusalem particularly satisfying insofar as they heightened her appreciation of Christianity. In 1914 she traveled with her brother Cleveland to Palestine and later recalled, "It was a great thrill for me to see those Holy Places. . . . This trip helped me understand the history of the Jews and the life of Jesus in a very real way." In 1922 she took her first plane ride from Paris to London, and in 1951 she flew across the Atlantic for the first time. From that year on she flew to Turkey nearly every year to attend board meetings at Robert College.[11]

When George Huntington's paralysis, caused by a 1933 attack of poliomyelitis, forced the couple to return to the United States, Elizabeth Huntington continued to pursue her work with the YWCA. George died in 1953, and three years later Elizabeth married Dumont Clarke, a minister who was involved in the effort to reinvigorate rural parishes by having farmers set aside an acre, "the Lord's acre," the produce of which would go to the church. Their union further strengthened her dedication to Christian service, both of her marriages thus reinforcing the beliefs, values, and aspirations she had

11. *Joy of Service,* pp. 46, 90.

learned as a child and young woman. Dumont Clarke died in 1960; Elizabeth Clarke carried on in her YWCA activities until her death in 1976. At the time of her death, she lived on the same estate in Riverdale where she had been born ninety-two years before. The continuities, not only of outlook, but of place and daily routine, that one could observe in her life were remarkable. That as an old woman Clarke could walk the same hills her father had walked with her as a child bespoke the stability amid change and the localism amid cosmopolitanism that could continue to mark an individual's experience with education even during a metropolitan era.

IV

Morris Raphael Cohen was born in Minsk, in Russian Poland, the fifth or sixth child of Abraham Mordecai Cohen and Bessie Farfel Cohen, on July 25, 1880. His father was unable to make an adequate living as a carpenter and businessman, so in the winter of 1883–84 he went to the United States in search of better opportunities, apprenticing Morris's elder brothers, Tom and Sam, to a shoemaker and a tailor, respectively, and leaving Morris and his younger sister, Florence, with their mother, who eked out a living as a peddler of bakery products and produce. The result was a lonely childhood for Morris, who came to adore his mother as nurturer and provider and to view his father as a largely unknown figure ("My relations with my father were not on the whole happy," he would later recall). Abraham Cohen returned from the United States in the spring of 1887 but went back a few weeks later, taking Tom and Sam with him. Morris was then sent to live with his maternal grandparents in the village of Neshwies, where he came under the watchful eye and stern discipline of his grandfather, Hirsch Farfel ("Life in Neshwies was a vast improvement over my previous existence," he observed, "and the companionship of my grandfather was the central feature of it"). At Neshwies he continued the schooling he had begun in Minsk, developing his facility with Hebrew, systematically studying the Torah, and learning to translate the Torah into the vernacular, namely, Yiddish. The studies of the heder were closely linked with his grandfather's systematic teaching of religion at home; and both, needless to say, were in turn linked with the systematic teaching of the synagogue. Deciding under his grandfather's influence that he would like to begin Talmudic studies, and there being no qualified teacher of Talmud in Neshwies, Morris returned in 1890 to his mother's home in Minsk, where he continued his work on Torah and began his instruction in Talmud. But he also discovered outside the heder that his command of Yiddish gave him access to a much broader literature of history, belles-lettres, and social commentary. He began avidly to read everything from serious novels to "penny dreadfuls." In the process, the pious Talmudist soon began to be transformed into the enlightened secularist; and it was the enlightened secularist that Abraham Cohen brought to New York City in 1892 with the rest of the family.[12]

The Cohens settled on the Lower East Side, where Abraham worked as a presser in a sweatshop and the family participated in the program of the Neshwieser Verein, one of the scores of ethnoreligious benevolent organizations that performed social and religious services while maintaining a familiar aura of the "old country." In September, 1892, Morris and his sister began their public schooling. Having no English, they were placed in the "ABC class" with the youngest children. Thereafter, Morris was rapidly skipped and promoted, winning prizes for his work in arithmetic and composition, and completing the grammar school course in 1895, with a gold medal for the highest grades in his class on the entrance examinations to City College. Among the many outcomes of his schooling between 1892 and 1895 was a lifelong love of English literature. Along with the writings of Scott, Byron, Macaulay, and Carlyle, he also discovered the *Autobiography* of Benjamin Franklin, which he claimed "exercised the most practical influence" on him at the time; and, like many another teen-ager so influenced, he dutifully started a diary that, at least for the period of his adolescence, became an important vehicle of self-scrutiny and, hence, of self-education. He also began early to make use of the Aguilar Free Library of the Educational Alliance, which was his major source of books in English, and regularly read the *Arbeiter Zeitung,* from which he imbibed a heady brew of Yiddish literature and Socialist commentary.[13]

Cohen entered CCNY in 1895 and was graduated in 1900—the extra year was a so-called subfreshman year at Townsend Harris Hall, the preparatory school that was associated with City College. He completed a solid program of liberal studies, winning the Ward Medal in Logic and the Belden Medal in Mathematics; and, owing to the absence of a decent library at the college, began to frequent the

12. *A Dreamer's Journey: The Autobiography of Morris Raphael Cohen* (Boston: The Beacon Press, 1949), pp. 42, 49, 47.

13. *Ibid.,* p. 85; and Leonora Cohen Rosenfield, *Portrait of a Philosopher: Morris R. Cohen in Life and Letters* (New York: Harcourt, Brace & World, 1962), pp. 5–24.

Columbia University Library. Yet, if Cohen seemed to flourish at CCNY, it was not solely a result of his formal college studies. Like many young immigrants and children of immigrants in that era, he plunged zestfully into the intellectual life of the Lower East Side. Even as a grammar school student, he had participated in the Sunday night meetings of the Bryant Literary Society; and, when that had dissolved in the summer of 1896, he involved himself in the work of a group of CCNY students who called themselves the Young Men's Literary Society, serving as editor of their journal. He also became active in the Socialist Labor Party and helped organize a Marx Circle that met from time to time at the Henry Street Settlement and various other places to read and argue over Marx's *Capital* and other socialist classics. In 1898, under the guidance of the labor leader and social reformer Edward King at the Educational Alliance, he was drawn into the Comte Synthetic Circle, where, in addition to the classics of social theory, he came to know the woman who would later become his wife, Mary Ryshpan, and a number of her friends, including Leonora O'Reilly, one of the founders of the Women's Trade Union League of New York.

It was also at the Alliance that Cohen met the man who was probably, next to his grandfather, his most important teacher, Thomas Davidson. With King a fierce defender of the intellectual and aesthetic life, much in the fashion of Matthew Arnold, Davidson organized a course on "Social and Historic Culture" at the Alliance that met on Saturday evenings during the first months of 1899. Cohen and Ryshpan and several of their friends attended regularly and found the experience exhilarating as Davidson lectured on everything from the new higher criticism of the Bible to the latest writings of William James. When Davidson approached Cohen at one of their meetings and remarked, "You have a fine mind. You ought to cultivate it," and later invited him, first to his room on Stuyvesant Square, and later, to his house at Glenmore in the Adirondacks, offering him maintenance in return for services at the summer school he conducted there, Cohen's exhilaration turned into enchantment. Davidson became the revered master and Cohen the reverent disciple. The following year, 1899–1900, in collaboration with Davidson and David Blaustein, the superintendent of the Educational Alliance, Cohen helped launch the evening classes at the Alliance that subsequently became the Breadwinners' College, Cohen himself teaching "the history of civilization." Then, in September, 1900, Davidson died. Cohen and others of his disciples organized a Thomas Davidson Society, dedicated to the ideals of the late philosopher, with the Breadwinners' College and a series of evening preparatory classes as its centerpiece. Cohen persisted in the effort until it dissolved in 1917; but he continued to be inspired by Davidson's example long after. He would make an annual pilgrimage to Glenmore for forty years; and, for the rest of his life, he would refer to Davidson as his "beloved teacher."[14]

Armed with his bachelor's degree, Cohen taught the common school subjects for a year at a private school conducted by Rabbi David Davidson (no relation to Thomas Davidson) and then for another year in a public school on 70th Street and Second Avenue. Then, in 1902, he obtained an appointment at City College to teach mathematics in the preparatory department at Townsend Harris Hall, and was thereby rescued from "the dreary task of teaching public school children who did not want to learn that in which I had no particular interest." His principal energies, of course, went into the work of the Thomas Davidson Society and its Breadwinners' College; and, in addition, he enrolled for graduate study at Columbia University, with Frederick J. E. Woodbridge in philosophy, Felix Adler in ethics, and Franklin Giddings in sociology, among others. Cohen had come to know Adler as a neighbor of Thomas Davidson's at Glenmore and as a familiar figure at the Educational Alliance and in other organizations on the Lower East Side, and Adler had doubtless had word of Cohen's intellectual promise from Davidson. When Cohen handed Adler an outstanding paper on Aristotle's theory of the state in the Columbia course, Adler was moved, first, to create a part-time position for Cohen as his assistant at the Ethical Culture Society and, subsequently, to arrange for a fellowship from the Society under which Cohen could study for the doctorate at Harvard. As a result, Cohen was able to spend the years between 1904 and 1906 in Cambridge, studying philosophy with William James, Josiah Royce, Ralph Barton Perry, Hugo Münsterberg, and George Herbert Palmer (it has properly been characterized as the golden age of Harvard philosophy), collaborating with Frank Parsons of the Bureau of Economic Research to organize a Breadwinners' College in Boston, leading the Cambridge Ethical Culture Society, sharing quarters for a time with a third-year law student named Felix Frankfurter, and serving for a year as assistant to Professors James and Münsterberg. In addition, he carried on a remarkable correspondence with Mary Ryshpan, to whom he had become informally engaged in 1903, that served, some-

14. *Dreamer's Journey*, pp. 104, 110; Morris Raphael Cohen to Thomas Davidson, June 9, 1900, June 17, 1900, in Rosenfield, *Portrait of a Philosopher*, pp. 62, 63.

what in the fashion of the earlier diary, as another vehicle of reflection and self-scrutiny. He completed a thesis on "Kant's Doctrine as to the Relation Between Beauty and Happiness" in the spring of 1906; he married Mary on June 13 (Solomon Ryshpan approved the match, because Cohen, as a scholar, though scarcely orthodox, was appropriately learned—not unlike a rabbi); and he was awarded the doctorate at the Harvard commencement a fortnight later. He returned to City College with what President John H. Finley characterized as the finest set of recommendations he had ever read.[15]

There followed a discouraging period of six years in which Cohen was unable to arrange a transfer from the Townsend Harris mathematics department to the City College philosophy department (with the notable exception of Adler at Columbia, Jews were not welcome in philosophy departments during the early twentieth century); then, another such period in which, having arranged such a transfer under the beneficent aegis of Professor Harry Allen Overstreet, Cohen seemed locked into an assistant professorship that provided inadequate support for his wife and three children; and finally, with his promotion to a full professorship in 1921, a period of growing influence, initially within the world of City College, and increasingly in the world outside the college.

Philosophers, in the classic fashion of Socrates, have traditionally educated themselves through dialogue (conversation and correspondence), reading, and reflection. Cohen used all three creatively as he clarified and refined his ideas. He wrote principally in the fields of philosophy of science, philosophy of law, philosophy of history, and logic, publishing a collection of Charles S. Peirce's essays with a lengthy introduction in 1923, *Reason and Nature* in 1931, *Law and the Social Order* (a collection of his papers) in 1933, *An Introduction to Logic and Scientific Method* (with his former student Ernest Nagel) in 1934, *The Meaning of Human History,* which he believed to be his magnum opus, in 1947, and *A Dreamer's Journey,* the unfinished autobiography that he saw as "the vehicle by which almost all that my life has meant can be expressed—even all that my philosophic reading and reflection have meant to me," in 1949. Cohen suffered a stroke in 1942, and *The Meaning of Human History* and *A Dreamer's Journey,* along with a number of other books by Cohen published in the 1940's and 1950's, had to be completed under the editorship of his son Felix Cohen. Several of the posthumous works (Cohen died on January 25, 1947),

15. *Dreamer's Journey,* pp. 128, 135.

especially *King Saul's Daughter* (1952) and *American Thought* (1954), were fragmentary at best. But in the end, it was an imposing body of scholarship that did much to pave the way for the criticism of pragmatism that found increasing favor during the 1940's and 1950's. Beyond that, Cohen's was a critical philosophy that revealed one special domain of the learning to be derived from dialogue and reflection, namely, the education inherent in intellectual controversy. In a career of contention against the metaphysics of William James and the logic of John Dewey, the legal realism of Hessell Yntema and Karl Llewellyn, and the historical relativism of Charles A. Beard and Carl L. Becker, Cohen steadily sharpened his own ideas and in so doing sharpened the ideas of others and thereby heightened the quality of philosophic discussion. In the continuing process of clarification lay the key to the phenomenon—again, one going back to ancient times— by which Cohen's own continuing education became one aspect of the larger education of the public.[16]

V

Mary Ryshpan Cohen has always appeared as an obscure, if beloved, wife and helpmate in the autobiographical and biographical material on Morris Raphael Cohen. Yet she deserves closer scrutiny as a fascinating individual in her own right; and indeed her educational career exemplifies both the opportunities and the dilemmas that faced gifted women during the late nineteenth and early twentieth centuries. She was born in 1880 on the Lower East Side, the second youngest of Solomon and Sheba Ryshpan's eight or nine children and the first born in the United States. The Ryshpans had migrated from Russian Poland shortly before Mary's birth and had taken up residence on East Broadway, within a block of the Henry Street Settlement. Solomon Ryshpan, who may have worked for a time in the jewelry business and who later managed to acquire some real estate in Brooklyn, was a devoutly orthodox Jew who considered any institution other than the orthodox home and the synagogue itself as at best alien and at worst corrupting. Of his children, only one was a son and therefore in his mind suited for extensive schooling; daughters, he believed, should have an education focusing wholly on their duties to God and family— it is said that Ryshpan went so far as to refuse to allow his third youngest child, Bertha, to marry the man she loved because, though

16. *Ibid.*, p. 289.

he was Jewish, he was insufficiently orthodox in belief and observant in practice.

Sheba Ryshpan, on the other hand, strongly believed that all her children deserved an equal opportunity to pursue as much schooling as they could obtain and fruitfully make use of. Thus, when her youngest daughters, Bertha, Mary, and Sarah, completed their years of public schooling, she encouraged them to go further and gently persuaded Solomon to permit them to attend the Normal College of the City of New York, later Hunter College—Bertha attended from 1893 to 1894, Mary, from 1897 to 1900, and Sarah, from 1898 through 1902. With a view to preparing for teaching, Mary used the opportunity to study Latin and probably Greek, English, history, mathematics, and science, essentially the equivalent of a first-class secondary education along with some college-level work. Sheba also encouraged her children to partake of the activities of the Henry Street Settlement, and it might well have been there—though it might have been virtually anywhere on the Lower East Side—that Mary became acquainted with the trade unionist and reformer Leonora O'Reilly. Ryshpan's acquaintance with O'Reilly ripened into a lifelong friendship (the Cohens would later name their daughter, Leonora, after O'Reilly), in which O'Reilly served as Ryshpan's initial guide to political and social reform (it was almost certainly O'Reilly, who had known Edward King since 1886, who persuaded Ryshpan to join the Comte Synthetic Circle at the Educational Alliance, where they both came to know Morris Cohen). Finally, like virtually every other literate Jew on the Lower East Side, Mary read the Yiddish newspapers, regularly imbibing their general reformist orientation along with their news of the East European Jewish community on both sides of the Atlantic.[17]

Ryshpan and Cohen both enrolled in Thomas Davidson's 1899 course at the Alliance. Cohen later described her at the time as "in the forefront of the struggle of those who, growing to young womanhood amidst the intellectual concerns of the immigrant East Side, helped to break the Jewish tradition that had excluded women from full participation in the highest intellectual pursuits." When Davidson, excited by the responsiveness of the young people in the course, decided to invite the most promising to Glenmore at no cost in return for occasional services, he chose Ryshpan as well as Cohen. Both thrived amid the heady intellectualism of Davidson's Summer School

17. The *Annual Reports of the Normal College* from 1893 through 1902 list the Ryshpan women as well as the required courses by grade for each of the years Mary Ryshpan attended.

of the Culture Sciences, and Davidson wrote to his class at the Alliance on July 25, 1899, "Miss Ryshpan is here and seems very happy, and I may say the same of Mr. Cohen. They are both great favorites and I am delighted to have them. I am only sorry that my health does not permit me to do as much for them as I should wish." The adoration Cohen felt for Davidson was fully shared by Ryshpan. On his death, both joined in the determination to keep his spirit alive.[18]

Upon completing her work at the Normal College, Ryshpan became a teacher at Public School 12 on the Lower East Side (at an annual salary that began at $610 in 1901 and increased to $773 in 1905), where she worked with children who were generally impoverished and from backgrounds not unlike her own. In addition, she taught a course in geography at the Alliance under the auspices of the Davidson Society. With O'Reilly, Lillian Wald, Mary Dreier, Florence Kelley, and others, she also participated in the activities of the Women's Trade Union League of New York and maintained sufficient interest in the League to be asked from time to time to serve as an honorary member of the executive committee—in many ways the League's triadic commitment to trade unionism, social reform, and feminism provided an apt vehicle for the expression of Ryshpan's social concerns. She partook of efforts to assist refugees from the pogroms in Russian Poland. And, probably through O'Reilly, who had known Felix Adler since 1894, she became active in the Ethical Culture Society, where, as a member of the women's auxiliary, she made the Manhattan Trade School for Girls (where O'Reilly taught) one of her special interests.[19]

Cohen apparently remarked to Davidson before going to Glenmore in the summer of 1899 that he was attracted to Ryshpan, but he added that he was "trying to fight it." Davidson is supposed to have replied with a twinkle in his eye, "Let me know what success you have." After the summer at Glenmore, Cohen and Ryshpan were classmates in David Saville Muzzey's course in Greek history at the Alliance. Cohen was too busy to do his homework; Ryshpan was always diligent about hers. She would coach him shortly before the class convened, and he would then hold forth. It was the sort of assistance she would frequently render over the next forty years.

18. *Dreamer's Journey*, p. 97; and Rosenfield, *Portrait of a Philosopher*, p. 50.

19. Mary Ryshpan's salary schedule is carried in the Journal of the Board of Education of the City of New York (Special Collections, Milbank Memorial Library, Teachers College, Columbia University, New York City), II, 1901–1905. For Ryshpan's service on the WTUL executive committee, see Minutes, Executive Board, June 30, 1905 (Women's Trade Union League of New York Papers, State Department of Labor Research Library, New York City).

Their relationship developed on a high intellectual plane, full of spiritual peaks and depressions; and then in 1903 Cohen proposed: "I ask you to take me—take me to your self, to your love, your sympathy, your faith—your hope and trust in humanity, to your simple womanly beauty, take me and inspire me further to my life's ideals—ideals that are one with your own—and together we will reach up to God." Ryshpan accepted, deeply believing in Cohen's intellectual promise and determined to keep him sufficiently free of "petty cares" to realize that promise. The engagement period had its own peaks and depressions, with Cohen in Cambridge and Ryshpan in New York, but she was a fount of solicitude and encouragement. By the time they were married in 1906, the pattern of their relationship had become fairly well established. Although both had been Davidson's philosophic protégés of 1899, only one would realize his philosophic potential, while the other would provide the nurturance that would make that possible.[20]

Once married, Mary Ryshpan Cohen left her position with the New York City public school system—married women were not eligible for public school teaching positions. The Cohens' first child, Felix Solomon Cohen (the Felix after Adler or Frankfurter or both), was born in 1907, and was sufficiently sickly to be tutored at home by his mother until he was eight. Leonora Davidson Cohen was born in 1909, and Victor William Cohen (the William after William James) in 1911. Putting the needs of her husband and children first, Mary Cohen created a household in which he could do his work with minimum distraction and they could develop their potential to the fullest. Both parents encouraged the youngsters to go as far as they could in their schooling and all three achieved the doctorate—Felix in philosophy (he also took a degree in law), Leonora in French civilization, and Victor in physics. Mary Cohen also continued some of her outside activities on a modified basis—she taught English for a time at the Educational Alliance and later helped to establish and lead the Organization for Rehabilitation and Training (ORT) to assist refugee Jews from Europe and Palestine to become retrained for productive careers. But it was always within the framework of family obligations.

However fulfilling Mary Cohen's life may have been in many ways, after marriage her continuing growth and autonomy were undoubtedly constrained. There was a revealing entry in Leonora O'Reilly's diary for June 7, 1924, that eloquently made the point. O'Reilly was

20. Rosenfield, *Portrait of a Philosopher*, pp. 26, 29.

a virtual shut-in at the time, owing to poor health and her own family obligations. Hence, when Mary Cohen came to see her, bringing two house dresses, the two women eagerly conversed until, as the diary noted, Cohen "left about 6: to be home in time for supper with the family." Some years later, when Mary Cohen was at the peak of her involvement with the ORT, she would leave dinner so that her husband and children could feed themselves; but the departure from custom was sufficiently significant so that it was worthy of mention. Her son-in-law, Harry N. Rosenfield, once remarked of her, "She lived with four Ph.D.'s, but she was the smartest one in the family." The observation testified to an intellect that never dimmed, even if convention and circumstance combined to preclude its development to the fullest.[21]

VI

Arthur Flegenheimer was born on August 6, 1902, on Second Avenue near 89th Street, in the Yorkville section of Manhattan. His parents, Herman and Emma Neu Flegenheimer, were German-Jewish immigrants. Herman Flegenheimer worked as a glazier, a baker, and a liveryman before he either deserted the family or died when Arthur was around eight years old. Emma Flegenheimer then moved with Arthur and his younger sister, Helen, to the south Bronx, where she became a janitor in the succession of tenements where they made their home and also worked as a laundress. Although Arthur later claimed that the family was not religious and did not attend synagogue services (he himself would be baptized as a Roman Catholic shortly before his death), there is evidence that Emma Flegenheimer regularly bought kosher food for Friday evening dinners and that she was at least privately observant.

Arthur attended public school through the sixth grade and apparently enjoyed his studies, particularly in history and composition. He also acquired a love of reading that served him in good stead in later years when he was forced from time to time to spend protracted periods in hiding. Arthur left school at the age of fourteen, ostensibly to help support his family. He claimed to have worked as an errand boy, an office boy, a newspaper boy, a feeder and pressman in a print

21. Leonora O'Reilly, Diary (25 vols.; Leonora O'Reilly Papers, Schlesinger Library, Radcliffe College, Cambridge, Mass.), XXII, June 7, 1924, A-39, by permission of the Schlesinger Library; interview with Harry N. Rosenfield, Washington, D.C., July 21–22, 1986.

shop, and, most important, a roofer—he liked to carry his roofer's union card in later years as "proof" that he was an honest workingman. However that may be, a policeman who grew up in the same neighborhood as Arthur later remembered that Arthur rarely worked in roofing or in any other gainful occupation. Instead, he apparently spent a good deal of time with a gang of "streetcorner toughs" in the Morrisania section of the Bronx. Whatever Emma Flegenheimer tried to teach her son about life, work, and how to survive in the Bronx, and whatever instruction his public school teachers tried to dispense about the values of formal education, it is clear that Arthur learned more on the streets from his fellow gang members than he did from his mother or his schoolteachers. What is more, because he was bright and dealt easily with people, he learned his lessons well.[22]

As Emma Flegenheimer moved her family from one tenement to another, always in desperate straits, it became increasingly evident to Arthur that there were various ways out of poverty and that some of the illegal ways were easier and quicker than the legal. Instead of schooling or a job, he immersed himself in the world of social clubs and pool halls. He began to spend more and more of his time with the Bergen gang, whose base of operations was the Bergen Social Club, in the neighborhood of the Yankee Stadium. One of his closest friends there was a member of the gang named Marcel Poffo, who was only about a year older than Arthur but who had already learned a good deal from his experience on the streets. Poffo was able to teach Arthur such simple ways of augmenting his income as stealing packages from delivery trucks, looting neighborhood stores, burglarizing apartments, and breaking up illegal dice games where the players had not purchased local protection. At the age of seventeen, Arthur was arrested for the first time, for breaking and entering, and was sentenced to the reformatory on Blackwell's Island, from which he escaped, only to be recaptured and returned to serve out a term of fifteen months. The experience in prison hardened Arthur at the same time that it heightened his prestige with the gang—so much so, in fact, that he was nicknamed Dutch Schultz, after a legendary member of an earlier gang in the neighborhood.

By the age of nineteen, Schultz—he soon preferred to be called by his nickname—had been arrested (but not convicted) two more times, on charges of larceny and assault. Despite that record, his name was included on a list of deputy sheriffs appointed by Sheriff Edward J.

22. Paul Sann, *Kill the Dutchman: The Story of Dutch Schultz* (New Rochelle, N.Y.: Arlington House, 1971), p. 190.

Flynn of the Bronx. Schultz had no interest whatever in law enforcement, but the deputy sheriff's badge did allow him legally to carry a gun. He began to work for Otto and Jake Gass, brothers in the trucking business, who, with the onset of Prohibition in 1920, began carrying beer from the breweries to the speakeasies where it was sold. This experience, as well as his friendship with Joey Noe, whose father was a beer pipe cleaner, taught him that there was a great deal of money to be made in the transportation and sale of bootleg beer—the brew cost some three or four dollars a keg to manufacture, went to the distributors for some eight or nine dollars a keg, and sold for some eighteen or nineteen dollars a keg in the speakeasies. Noe established a small speakeasy in their Bronx neighborhood and asked Schultz to join him as a partner. The business expanded rapidly, and they not only opened several additional speakeasies of their own but also began to acquire contracts to supply both beer and hard liquor to speakeasies owned by others. Beyond that, they soon learned that, through intimidation and occasional violence, they could fairly easily secure a monopoly on the beer running for most of the establishments in the Bronx. Their business expanded north into Yonkers and south into Manhattan, including Washington Heights, Harlem, and Yorkville; and, the more it expanded, the more they needed to add to their staff of "persuaders" and "protectors"—gangsters such as Vincent and Peter Coll, Bo Weinberg, Larry Carney, Joey Rao, and Edward McCarthy, with whom they had grown up and shared the life of the streets. As the span of control lengthened, they also needed to master the skills that every entrepreneur in an expanding business needed to learn, of assessing competence and loyalty and of selecting and training lieutenants. Noe was killed in a shootout in midtown Manhattan in 1928, and Schultz assumed sole ownership of the business. By the time Prohibition ended in 1933, he was widely known as the "Beer Baron of the Bronx."[23]

In 1930, Schultz began to diversify his interests to include the numbers games, also known as the policy racket, in Harlem. The games were largely dominated by black "bankers" at the time, and Schultz used a combination of coercion and large loans to gain entry to the operations. As his income soared into the millions, he found he required more and more protection, on the one hand, against legal threats to his illegal business, and, on the other hand, against competing gangsters who wished to take over his illegal business.

23. *Ibid.*, p. 158.

He hired Richard J. Davis, a lawyer for many of those involved in the
policy racket, who represented him in negotiations with the Harlem
bankers, who defended his henchmen against continuing charges
growing out of the policy operations, and who introduced him to
Jimmy Hines, the Democratic boss of the Eleventh Assembly District. With the support of Hines and Davis, he was able sharply to
reduce the number of arrests and prosecutions of his lieutenants,
with the result that his business proceeded virtually without inter-
ruption. He also hired the best thugs available to defend his interests against the competition.

Ultimately, Schultz faced trial for tax evasion, which was about the
only demonstrable charge the federal and New York State governments seemed able to bring against him. His first trial resulted in a
split jury—he was able to appeal to the jurors' sense of injustice by
reminding them of how many wealthy businessmen in more legitimate
fields had evaded taxes without being subjected to criminal charges.
His second trial ended in his acquittal. He was preparing to face a
third trial when he was gunned down, along with several associates,
at the Palace Chop House in Newark, New Jersey, where the group
had been in hiding to protect themselves from the wrath of other
gangsters.

Through it all, Schultz led a relatively stable domestic life—he had
at least one common law wife, Frances Maxwell, with whom he had
two children; but there is every indication that, given the illegal nature
of his business, there was a sharp separation between his home life
and his business life, with the latter clearly dominant so far as his time
and energy were concerned. Through it all, too, Schultz lived by his
wits, appraising new opportunities for profit and power, for lucrative
or fatal alliances, or for further entanglements with the law, according
to hunch and the intelligence of the underworld. However unfortunate one may find the use he made of his education, there is no
denying that the lessons he had learned on the street, at the Bergen
Social Club, and in prison had enabled him to leave behind the poverty and dreary struggles of his early years. When Schultz decided to
change his name and his persona, he took advantage of an option that
told much about the nature of metropolitan life and education. For
better or worse, people like Schultz who came of age in the metropolis
and were educated there faced a widening range of vocational
choices—illegal as well as legal; and, more than had been true earlier
or was true elsewhere, they could, as Arthur Flegenheimer did, quite
literally define the people they would be and become.

VII

William Santora was born in Jersey City, New Jersey, around 1915 to a working-class family that lived in that community's "Italian ghetto." William's father was a skilled sheet metal worker who commuted daily to his job in New York City. A proud and loyal union member, he was "a nationalist" in outlook and a political "conservative." William's mother, one of eighteen children born to an impoverished Italian family in New York City, was a deeply religious, churchgoing Roman Catholic, who had worked as a dressmaker before her marriage. A woman of strong union sympathies, she was also an ardent feminist who had been active in the women's suffrage movement. Though she devoted full time to rearing William and his two siblings, she stayed in touch with political issues and discussed them at length with the youngsters. Her biases toward liberalism, feminism, and equalitarianism surely played a role in the development of William's own deeply held commitments to decent working conditions for all people and equal compensation for men and women. Years later, he recalled with pride that his mother had taught herself Yiddish as a young woman so she could converse on an equal basis with her Jewish co-workers in the dressmaking factory where she worked.

The Santoras lived in a "modest flat" in a neighborhood where "everybody knew everybody." Santora reminisced that, even though his grandmother owned the flat, it was a "struggle" each month to meet the payments on the mortgage. The life of the neighborhood was in many ways simply an extension of the life of the Santora household. William was twelve years old before he met anyone who was neither Italian nor Catholic. The center of social and religious activity for the Santoras and most other families in the neighborhood was a church known as Our Lady of Carmel. Santora remembered that neighborhood life and activity "revolved around" Our Lady of Carmel, so much so that, when he joined the Boy Scouts and his mother learned that the troop met in the basement of a Protestant church, she expressed strong disapproval of his membership. William's continued participation in the scout troop was likely one of his first efforts self-consciously to extend his activities beyond the confines of family and church in the face of opposition from family and church; it would not be his last.[24]

24. All the quotations in this section are taken from Ruth F. Prago, Taped interview with William Santora, July 24, 1980, Series I (Oral History of the American Left, Tamiment Library, New York University, New York City).

Santora attended the William L. Dickinson High School during the early 1930's, where, as part of the standard curriculum, he took a course in "The Problems of American Democracy." The issues dealt with and the discussions of those issues proved a revelation. Having begun to use the public library in those years, Santora used the reading list from the course to direct his choice of books at the library. When he completed his studies at Dickinson in 1933, his prospects for employment were dismal. The Depression had wrought havoc in Jersey City: people were living in the city dump and the only public assistance came in the form of food that the city occasionally distributed as a charity to its poorest families. Santora therefore took a series of part-time jobs, such as helping with the landscaping of the local cemetery, and, with some additional financial support from his father, was able to spend the rest of his time being of assistance to various members of the family and studying in the public library.

During these initial years of partial unemployment, Santora scrupulously avoided working in what he thought of as "sweatshops." His mother's stories of her work as a dressmaker may well have figured in his determination, along with the fact that he seemed able to earn more money in part-time and self-created work than he might have earned in full-time employment. As part of what soon became an increasingly systematic program of self-education at the library, he undertook the study of electronics and, almost in the fashion of an apprenticeship, began to repair radios as a part-time business, becoming in the process "a fairly decent radio repairman." He eventually acquired a full-time job at the Emerson radio and television factory in New York City through a friend of one of his uncles, who introduced him to an engineer at the factory. The engineer, who served as the plant manager, was "a nice Italian guy," who set him to work soldering on the assembly line. Santora's immediate supervisor on the line was a woman who, after nine years at the factory, was receiving a lower wage than he was receiving as a beginning worker. Santora found that harsh reality of factory life "infuriating." Later, when a woman fainted on the assembly line and the foreman, rather than ministering to her needs, took her place on the line so that it would not have to be shut down, Santora came to her assistance. As he reflected on that "lack of humanity in production," on the ways in which material needs seemed to outweigh human needs, he was again infuriated. Thereafter, the process of radicalization that had in many ways begun under the influence of his mother's teaching, began to accelerate.

At about that time Santora also began to read the *Daily Worker* as he traveled between Jersey City and New York. He later recalled the *Worker,* published by the Communist Party, as a large newspaper filled with excerpts from the writings of Karl Marx and long articles by Nikolai Lenin. What Santora found valuable about the paper was that many of the articles seemed to him to "reinforce" his own thinking—they seemed to lend meaning to his daily experience. They also provided him with an intellectual framework for the union activities he initiated at the Emerson plant. When he had started at Emerson, there had been no union; the work was seasonal and every year, beginning at Christmastime, there had been a four-month layoff. There had been some talk of a union but Emerson had fought the effort; indeed the National Labor Relations Board had cited Emerson for its apparent policy of discriminating against union members in its hiring practices. That notwithstanding, Santora joined the United Electrical Workers Union (UE) and became president of its unrecognized local at Emerson. He vigorously set about organizing the plant and was promptly discharged for his effort. His co-workers came to his aid, however, and the members of his department struck until, after a long conversation with the president of the firm, Santora was restored to his job. Thereafter, he persisted in his effort and eventually organized a successful strike that led to Emerson's recognition of the union (Santora had recently married and both his wife and his brother joined him on the picket line). The workers won a wage increase and the right to have the union press grievances for any employee at the factory. The strike was not only a personal victory for Santora, it also attested to the value of his systematic effort at self-education. As he later recalled, it seemed to him to confirm his belief in the validity of Marxist ideas. Trade unionism had "helped to school" him "in socialism."

Beyond his union activities at the Emerson plant, Santora had vivid memories of the Spanish Civil War—the issues in the conflict fascinated him and he did a good deal of reading on those issues in the library (and doubtless in the *Worker*). He recalled that, when the priest of Our Lady of Carmel delivered a sermon in defense of General Francisco Franco, his "rupture" with the church began. Later, when he read Pope Pius's assessment of the conflict, the rupture deepened.

In 1940 Santora decided to leave the Emerson plant for a job as a laboratory technician at the International Telephone and Telegraph Company in New Jersey. The demands of the job made it relatively easy for him to move about the factory, and he once again began his organizing activities and once again was fired for his effort. The following year, he was hired by UE as a staff organizer. One requirement of the job was that he take employment at any plant he hoped to organize; and, characteristically, he used the opportunity to inform himself on conditions at the various factories. He quickly learned that workers had "many grievances" in common, over safety, wage rates, and enforced overtime. He also learned that many workers had read Marx and Lenin and shared with him a Marxist interpretation of the capitalist system. As a result, he organized a study group in Jersey City that later became a unit of the Communist Party, a unit whose foremost concern was the support of unions.

Santora was deferred from military service during World War II because, having helped avert a strike at a defense plant, he was considered "necessary to the national security." By the 1950's, he was no longer connected with UE; but, in the context of the McCarthyite attack on Communists and "fellow travelers," he was unable to find employment. He became a television repairman during those years, using the skills he had learned at Emerson. In 1956 the International United Electrical Workers Union hired him as a staff organizer at plants in Erie, Pennsylvania. He left that job after a year, feeling that he "couldn't stay away from home any longer." From 1958 on, he worked with the National Education Association and the New Jersey Education Association. He found those organizations far more conservative than the Union, but concluded that his view of the world and his previous experience were as relevant to "intellectual workers" as they were to factory workers. At the very least, he observed, he was no longer afraid of being fired for standing up for his belief in the importance of humane and nonexploitative working conditions. As a state union leader and a member of policymaking bodies, he continued to view Marxism as the "compass" that guided his efforts and pointed the way for "humanity's progress toward socialism." Equally fundamentally, his "compass" was his lifelong curiosity about ideas and his unusual capacity to relate theoretical arguments to the immediate here-and-now of his life—put otherwise, his own educative style.

VIII

Jacob Lawrence was born in Atlantic City, New Jersey, on September 7, 1917. His father, who was also named Jacob Lawrence, and his mother, Rose Lee Lawrence, were among the large number of blacks who had moved north during the Great Migration of World War I. The elder Jacob Lawrence worked as a cook on railway cars—a job that kept the family moving from city to city and that as a result occasioned growing strain in the family. The Lawrences separated in 1924, and Rose Lee Lawrence moved Jacob and his brother and sister, first, to Philadelphia and, then, in 1929 or 1930, to Harlem. There she obtained a job with the city Department of Welfare and resolved to educate her children as well as possible and especially to protect them from what she perceived to be the corrupting effects of the street. The family joined the Abyssinian Baptist Church on West 138th Street, which, under the vigorous leadership of the Reverend Adam Clayton Powell, could boast one of the largest Protestant congregations in the United States, with some 14,000 members. The church conducted a wide range of social and religious programs, and the Lawrence children regularly attended not only the usual Sunday services but also the Sunday school and the plays produced by the church's drama group. Years later, Jacob Lawrence vividly recalled Powell's preaching, and particularly his "dry bones" sermons. Jacob attended Public School 89; and, since Rose Lawrence did not want him playing unattended during the afternoons, she also enrolled him in Utopia House, a neighborhood settlement that provided day care along with a variety of clubs and other activities for young people.[25]

It was at Utopia House that Jacob first came under the tutelage of the black artist Charles Alston. A gifted teacher who had attended Columbia College and who was enrolled in a master's degree program at Teachers College, Alston was immediately drawn to Jacob's work with crayons, noting his intense concentration on color and his interest in repetitive geometric designs. In the progressive pedagogical tradition of the time, Alston did not try to shape Jacob's efforts, given that the youngster seemed very much self-directed. When Jacob moved into new media, however, as when he began to create reproductions of neighborhood buildings with cardboard and poster paints or when he began to work at papier-mâché mask making after seeing an article on the subject in one of the magazines that were deliberately scattered around Utopia House to interest the youngsters, Alston helped him obtain the necessary material and proffered the instruction required to help him experiment. Alston's studied restraint enabled Jacob to work out his own styles, and the dedication and discipline with which the youngster went about doing so impressed Alston

25. Carroll Greene, Interview with Jacob Lawrence, October 25 and November 26, 1969 (Archives of American Art, Smithsonian Institution, Washington, D.C.). "Dry bones" sermons, in black idiom, are sermons that hang together, that are well articulated and well connected.

to the point where he soon began to think of Jacob as a protégé and called the attention of other artists to his work.

Alston was also conducting art classes with his colleague, Henry Bannern, at the 135th Street Public Library, under a Carnegie Corporation College Art Grant. The library, which housed the famous Schomburg Collection of source materials relating to Afro-American history and culture, was a research center and gathering place for many of the artists, writers, and scholars who had contributed to the Harlem Renaissance of the 1920's; and, while the Depression had severely dampened both the exhilaration and the optimism that had been associated with the renaissance, it had not wholly stifled the creative productivity that had been at its heart. As Jacob's competence grew, Alston began to bring him to those classes, as well as to the studio he and Bannern maintained at 306 West 141st Street, which served the Harlem art community in somewhat the same fashion as Alfred Stieglitz's gallery at 291 Fifth Avenue had served the Greenwich Village art community a quarter-century before.

Jacob went on from P.S. 89 to the High School of Commerce, where he remained for two years. Rose Lawrence lost her job in 1934, and Jacob left school to enroll for a six-month tour in the Civilian Conservation Corps, where he helped build a dam near Middletown, in upstate New York. On his return to the city, his mother, somewhat skeptical of his ability to earn a living as an artist, particularly since he was black, urged him to return to school; but his real interests were in his work with Alston and Bannern, so he took a series of menial jobs by day and spent his evenings at the studio, at the public library, and at the Harlem YMCA, where he enjoyed playing pool. In addition, under the auspices of the new WPA Federal Arts Project, a Harlem Community Art Center was established at 125th Street and Lenox Avenue under the direction of the black sculptress Augusta Savage. Savage was not only an immensely talented artist in her own right, she was also particularly interested in nurturing the talent of young black artists; and, when young Lawrence began to frequent the Center, she quickly recognized his ability and took him under her wing, along with Norman Lewis, Romare Bearden, William Artis, and Ernest Crichlow. As Lawrence worked at the Community Art Center under Savage's guidance, he also became aware of other WPA arts activities, and in particular the murals program that so much reflected the commitment of contemporary Mexican muralists like Diego Rivera and José Clemente Orozco to an art that derived from, expressed, and ennobled the daily life of the Mexican people.

In 1935 Lawrence also came under the tutelage of Charles Christopher Seyfert, who was giving a course of lectures on Afro-American history and culture at the YMCA. An autodidact who made his living as a carpenter, Seyfert had gathered a rich collection of source materials not unlike the Schomburg Collection and delighted in using it to awaken in young blacks an interest in the Afro-American heritage. He took a special interest in the young artists of Harlem, thinking that they could through their art inspire in black people a dignity and pride in their history; and indeed, when the Museum of Modern Art in 1935 mounted an exhibit of West African sculpture, Seyfert personally rounded up groups of Harlem artists and took them to see the exhibit. Lawrence apparently went on his own, however, and, profoundly impressed, returned to his home to fashion his own wooden sculptures modeled on the ones he had seen at the museum. For weeks, he and his fellow artists talked about the show and what it had meant to them. Further, he began to spend hours in the Schomburg Collection at the 135th Street library, reading in the sources of Afro-American history. Schomburg himself was serving as curator of the collection in those years, and Lawrence frequently spoke with him as he worked in the materials.

The combination of populist nationalism that predominated in WPA arts circles and his own immersion in Afro-American history profoundly affected Lawrence's work during the mid-1930's; and, when he won a scholarship in 1937 to study at the American Artists School, where he worked closely with Anton Refregier, Sol Wilson, and Eugene Morely, that combination was further strengthened. Many of his early paintings of the mid-1930's pictured scenes from Harlem life, in casein on paper. In 1937, he began work on a series of small tempera on paper paintings—there would be forty-one in all—depicting the life and work of the black Haitian liberator François Dominique Toussaint L'Ouverture (he worked on the Toussaint paintings in 1937 and 1938); the series format would come to be a major part of Lawrence's work, perhaps his adaptation of the contemporary work of the Mexican and American muralists to his own needs and style. In 1938, through the good offices of Savage, he obtained a job as an easel painter in the WPA Arts Project (his obligation was to deliver two paintings every six weeks, at a salary of $28.86 per week plus materials), and he was able to complete the Toussaint series and to undertake a Frederick Douglass series (1938–39) and a Harriet Tubman series (1939–40).

Lawrence had his first one-person show in 1938 at the Harlem YMCA. Sponsored by the James Weldon Johnson Literary Guild, it consisted of the paintings he had done of street life in Harlem. Shortly thereafter, the Toussaint series was shown at the Vesey Street head-quarters of the Catholic Interracial Council. In 1939, the series was also shown at the Baltimore Museum in that institution's first exhibit of the work of black artists; and in 1940 it was shown at the American Negro Exposition in Chicago. As he gained in reputation—1940 brought the first of three prized Rosenwald Fund fellowships—Lawrence painted ever more boldly in the genre he had made his own, with the Migration series of 1940–41, depicting the Great Migration in which his own parents had participated, and the John Brown series of 1941, depicting the life and death of the abolitionist hero.

Lawrence married in 1941, a young painter named Gwendolyn Knight whom he had come to know when they worked together at the Community Art Center. She was to become his most important critic, and in that role one of his most influential teachers. They traveled for a time in the South, staying a few months first in New Orleans and then in Lenexa, Virginia; and then, when they returned to New York, Lawrence embarked upon his Harlem series (1942–43), returning thereby to the themes that had occupied him in the mid-thirties—the portrayal of the color and the drabness, the excitement and the somberness, and the hope and the despair of everyday life in Harlem. By the time it was necessary to interrupt his work to do military service in 1943, he had completed in the six series an imposing body of work that placed him in the first rank of younger American artists. As the critic Milton Brown later wrote of that oeuvre, Lawrence "had as much training as one would expect a young man of that age to have, and yet his art appeared pure, naive, original, uncontaminated by the mannerisms of the time, except that as a social art it was precisely of its time. His was a new voice with its own pitch and a distinct Black resonance." Put in educational terms, Lawrence had been taught but he had escaped any particular imprint of his teachers; he had studied but had come to his own interpretations; and he had surely learned and made what he had learned decisively his own. The product was an art that was fresh, original, and unique.[26]

Lawrence spent two years in the United States Coast Guard during World War II. He was initially a steward, the usual position for blacks in that service, until he came under the command of Captain J. S. Rosenthal, a man knowledgeable about art and especially about photography, who assigned him to the U.S.S. Sea Cloud. Lawrence described the Sea Cloud, a ship with an integrated crew, as "the best

26. Milton W. Brown, Jacob Lawrence (New York: Whitney Museum of American Art, 1974), p. 10.

democracy I've ever known." The captain of the *Sea Cloud,* Lieutenant
Commander Carlton Skinner, recognized the potential of the man
and helped him become a noncommissioned officer in public relations, where he could spend some of his time painting. His paintings
after his discharge from the service were increasingly symbolic rather
than realistic. In 1946, with a Guggenheim Fellowship, he undertook
his War series, a cycle of fourteen paintings, each embodying an
impression or an idea.[27]

In the summer of 1946, Lawrence was invited by Josef Albers,
formerly of the Bauhaus, to teach at Black Mountain College in
North Carolina. It was not only his first real experience teaching in
a formal academic setting, it also gave him the chance to attend
Albers's lectures, which were destined greatly to influence his own
teaching in later years. Albers's discussions of the "plastic elements
of painting, . . . form and shape, line, color, texture and space regardless of . . . content" came to mark Lawrence's own approaches
to student work. And, with respect to the actual business of painting, Albers taught Lawrence about "tension," about "pull," about
"organic" as against "geometric" movement, about "moving against
the edge." He showed Lawrence how to capture "tension in color"
and how to think about "the dynamics of the picture plane." In a
sense, Albers helped Lawrence to conceptualize his work in ways
that had not occurred to him before, and in so doing enabled him to
exercise even greater discipline over his work and to suffuse it with
ever greater meaning.[28]

In 1956, Lawrence began to teach regularly at Pratt Institute in
Brooklyn, and intermittently at other institutions. And, with the
emergence of the civil rights movement, he began to paint a series
of "polemical paintings" depicting the struggles that were at the
heart of the movement. In 1964, despite a lifelong opposition to
black nationalism, Lawrence and his wife spent some months in Nigeria; and his Nigeria series, full of a joyful exhilaration, resulted.
That same exhilaration marked his illustrations for the book *Harriet
and the Promised Land* (1968), a book on the life of Harriet Tubman.
Lawrence left Pratt for a full professorship at the University of
Washington in 1971, where he continued to teach and to paint during the 1980's.[29]

27. *Ibid.,* p. 13.
28. Greene, Interview; and Avis Berman, Interview of Jacob Lawrence with Gwen Lawrence, July 20, 1982, and August 4, 1983 (Archives of American Art, Smithsonian Institution, Washington, D.C.).
29. Brown, *Jacob Lawrence,* p. 25.

IX

Hop Kun Leo was born in Canton, China, in 1928. Her parents and most of her siblings emigrated to Singapore when she was a small child, but she was left in the care of her grandparents in the village of Sun Wei, Mui Gok, Canton. Hop Kun's grandparents were financially comfortable—they owned land and employed a number of household servants—and in addition they believed in the importance of at least a minimal level of literacy for children of both sexes, so that Hop Kun was sent to a local school where she learned to read and write at approximately a third-grade level. Because she was a girl, however, she was removed from that school and sent to what was called a girls' school in the village. There, under the tutelage of her "Auntie," a woman whose husband had emigrated, she was taught, with other girls, how to knit, sew, and crochet. While Hop Kun assumed she would eventually marry and rear a family, at one point, after an acrobatic troupe had passed through Sun Wei, she aspired to become an acrobat; at another point, perhaps after having been treated for some childhood illness, she aspired to study medicine.

Hop Kun's horizons broadened somewhat when her father's brother and his wife, Uncle Andy Leo and Aunt Ruth Leo, began to correspond with her from the United States. Aunt Ruth had been born in the Chinatown community of Portland, Oregon, in 1899, and had met Andy when he had come to the church there in an effort to learn the English language. When Andy's father had sent him $500 to start a business, he and Ruth had purchased a motorcycle and had ridden across the country to New York City, where they had taken up residence in the Chinatown community and had opened a laundry. They wrote regularly to Hop Kun's family about their life in New York, and took a special interest in the youngster, sending her small presents and other tokens of their affection. Hop Kun, in return, accepted the couple as her special advisers, and took Ruth in particular as her model.

One of the most important services Uncle Andy and Aunt Ruth performed for Hop Kun was to select a husband for her. Their choice was Bay Doc Chiang, a young man from a village not far from Sun Wei whom they had come to know at the First Chinese Presbyterian Church in Chinatown (New York City). He had been born in 1924 and had come to the United States in 1935 as a "paper son" of his brother, Lee Ho Chiang, in whose laundry on Staten Island he had worked while attending a public school there through the eighth grade. He had learned the laundry business in much the same way as he would later teach it to his children—through informal instruction combined with careful imitation and constant correction. First, one ironed handkerchiefs, then, doilies, then, other linens, then, underwear, and then, more complicated items like shirts and dresses. In addition, he had taken every opportunity to learn all he could about his adopted land— he had read the New York *Daily News,* listened to the radio, gone to the movies, visited museums, explored the parks, and relaxed on Coney Island—at the same time that he had continued to read a Chinese newspaper and Chinese novels, taken part in the activities of the First Chinese Presbyterian Church, and joined in the Sunday meetings of the Chiang family association in Chinatown. He had met Andy and Ruth Leo at the church and had adopted them as something of a surrogate family; and, when by 1950 he had managed to establish his own laundry in Queens and was ready for marriage, it fell to them to arrange for him to marry their niece in China, Hop Kun.[30]

Hop Kun was not yet twenty-two when she married Bay Doc Chiang in China and immigrated to the United States. Interestingly, her parents and siblings left Singapore at about the same time and settled in New York's Chinatown on Henry Street. In her own mother and in Ruth Leo, Hop Kun had two quite different role models. Her mother was a Buddhist, a strict vegetarian, and a very traditional Chinese wife and mother. Ruth Leo's life had been more cosmopolitan and less bounded by tradition, probably because she had been born in the United States and had learned to live in two cultures. Hop Kun deliberately chose Ruth Leo as her primary model. The young couple lived in Queens in the back of Bay Doc's laundry in a mixed ethnic neighborhood with few Chinese residents. Hop Kun, who had never cooked and cleaned in her life, learned how to perform household tasks from her husband, who often shared them with her. Over the next few years they had four children, three daughters, all named Fay, with different middle names according to Chinese custom, and one son. Hop Kun spent a good deal of her time caring for the youngsters, and also, from her husband, learned to tag, sort, and inventory laundry and dry cleaning to be sent to the central facility where the laundering and cleaning were done. As the children grew up and took less of her time, she used the sewing skills she had learned

30. All the quotations in this section are taken from an interview with Hop Kun Leo Chiang's daughter Fay Ping Chiang on October 21, 1986. A "paper son," in Chinese-American idiom, is a fictive son who enters the United States as a genuine son to evade the restrictive laws governing Chinese immigration.

at the girls' school in Sun Wei to take on tailoring duties at the laundry. She was both conscious and proud of her contribution to the family business.

Until the children began to attend school, Chinese was the only language spoken in the Chiang home. Once the children started school, Hop Kun found herself learning English from them, although having to deal with the customers in the laundry and with the family shopping also contributed to her facility. She eventually became quite fluent in the language, though she never learned to read English beyond what she needed to know to perform her tasks at the laundry. By contrast, she did systematically expand her reading knowledge of Chinese by using a Chinese dictionary when she read the Chinese newspaper to which her husband had a subscription.

Perhaps the most profound educative experience of Hop Kun's adulthood, one that forced her to reassess her role as a woman, came in the wake of the death of Bay Doc when she was forty-six years old. Her daughter Fay Ping Chiang assumed management of the laundry for a time after the death of her father, but she was not in a position to continue with it for more than a few months. She undertook to teach her mother all that she needed to know to run the laundry herself, from dealing with the customers, to doing the hand ironing, to managing the bills, to working with the accountant in Chinatown. At first, Hop Kun was resistant to the change from assistant to manager, but she had no alternative. Within six months, she was running the laundry and was consciously describing herself as a woman who had acquired "a new way of thinking." She learned in good time to stand up to difficult customers, defend the quality of her work, travel on her own about the city, and open and close the laundry according to her own schedule. Moreover, as the ethnic composition of her Queens neighborhood changed, she deliberately learned to speak a third language, Spanish, in order better to serve her customers. She remarried in 1981, but kept her business as her own source of income, independent of her husband's.

X

Two points should be added by way of postscript. First, there were thousands of people in the New York metropolitan region who, at least during the years before World War II, lived lives and underwent educative experiences that were essentially characteristic of rural and small-town Americans. Lewis and Mary Rowland, for example, grew up and reared their two daughters in the farming community of Dayton, New Jersey, during the early decades of the twentieth century, supplying the local truck and dairy farmers with John Deere implements and generally taking an interested part in the social and educational affairs of Dayton. Their daughters attended the Dayton public school and the consolidated high school in nearby New Brunswick. The elder Rowlands rarely visited New York City, though New Brunswick was a major station on the Pennsylvania Railroad between Philadelphia and New York. World War II transformed Dayton, as New Brunswick and its environs became suburbanized and as television made its entree into Dayton's households. The Rowlands' daughters left Dayton when they had completed their secondary education, one to live in suburban Long Island, the other to work at a New York City university. Or, to cite another instance, Dennis and Edna Williams grew up and reared eight children in the lake region of Putnam County, New York, also during the early decades of the twentieth century, eking a marginal living out of the subsistence farm in Kent Cliffs on which they settled and the odd jobs they managed to obtain in the neighborhood. All their children attended the one-room Foshay's School in Kent Cliffs, which Dennis Williams had attended as a child, and most went on to the consolidated high school in nearby Carmel, though none completed the work of the high school. Dennis Williams visited New York City only once during his lifetime, though Brewster, only a dozen miles from their home, was a major station on the Harlem Division of the New York Central Railroad. The war transformed Kent Cliffs, as the Putnam County lake region became exurbanized and as radio (there was no electricity available in Kent Cliffs until shortly before the war) and then television became part of Kent Cliffs' households. And the Williams children scattered: the eldest son went into defense work in Hartford, Connecticut; two of his younger brothers entered the armed services; and his eldest sister moved to New York City for a time. Interestingly, however, all returned to the area after the war and none settled more than twenty-five miles from Kent Cliffs.

Second, it should be noted that the educational biographies sketched above are essentially in the tradition of *The Autobiography of Benjamin Franklin,* that is, except for the instance of Arthur Flegenheimer, they tend to portray individuals with activist educative styles threading their way through educative opportunities that were more or less benign. But there were thousands of people in the New York metropolitan region who did not manifest activist educative styles and whose educative opportunities were anything but benign. Dennis Williams had three years of formal education at the Foshay's School; and, although he continued to read on his own, he did little to further his formal education. He did not partake of the social and educational activities of the Kent Cliffs township; in fact, he had limited access to individuals other than kin. Williams lived his life passively with respect to education, though not necessarily discontentedly. Beyond that, throughout the metropolitan region there were families that abused their children rather than nurtured them, schoolteachers who demeaned their students rather than encouraged them, and work situations that were viciously exploitative rather than continuously educative. And, beyond that, there was the ever present factor of chance. Alfred E. Smith, Jr., escaped from routine jobs as a bookkeeper and shipping clerk when Henry Campbell arranged for him to be a process server in the office of the commissioner of jurors; others similarly situated stayed in routine jobs all their lives. Morris Raphael Cohen worked as a teen-ager in his brother Samuel's poolroom, where he daily encountered gangsters, petty hustlers, and drug pushers; Morris read Gibbon's *The Decline and Fall of the Roman Empire;* others doubtless learned the ways of crime. And Bay Doc Chiang gambled for a time, until his wife, family, and friends in Chinatown prevailed upon him to give it up for the sake of his children and his business; others with similar proclivities fell into debt and lost everything. In the end, individuals could be activist about their education, but unlucky as well. One finds their lives poignantly portrayed in such literary works as Stephen Crane's *Maggie: A Girl of the Streets* (1892), Samuel Ornitz's *Hannah, Paunch, and Jowl* (1923), Pietro Di Donato's *Christ in Concrete* (1939), Warren Miller's *The Cool World* (1958), and Piri Thomas's *Down These Mean Streets* (1967), as well as in the records of the courts and their associated probation services.

Chapter 14

CHARACTERISTICS

Is it possible for an educational system to be conducted by a national state and yet the full social ends of the educative process not be restricted, constrained, and corrupted?

JOHN DEWEY

Popularization and multitudinousness, in tandem, remained distinguishing features of American education during the twentieth century. They manifested themselves, first, in the near universality, initially, of schooling, and later, of television viewing, along with the prevalence of churches and synagogues, colleges and universities, and newspapers and magazines; second, in the development of new and more varied forms of education in an ever more extensive range of sites and situations; third, in the continuing transformation of curricula evident in all educative agencies as they reached out to ever broader clienteles; and finally, in the community-based character of most educative institutions.

Schooling had become prevalent in the United States by the 1870's, though with considerable variation with respect to race, class, ethnicity, gender, and region; it became virtually universal over the next century. Every state had enacted compulsory schooling legislation by 1918, and most states began to enforce the requirement of compulsory schooling during the 1920's and 1930's, though again, significant segments of the population, for example, the children of migrant Chicano farm workers in the Southwest or of Native Americans in the remote regions of Florida or of transient Caribbean immigrants in the city of New York, remained outside the reach of truant officers and indeed outside the active concern of school authorities. Yet, granted such exceptions, the fact is that by 1920 over 90 percent of American children between the ages of seven and thirteen were reported as enrolled in school, by 1950 that figure had climbed to 96 percent, and by 1980 it had climbed to 98 or 99 percent. Moreover, children tended to remain in school for ever longer periods of time, to the point where by the 1970's, for every 100 pupils in the fifth grade in 1972, 99 entered the ninth grade in 1976, 89 entered the eleventh grade in 1978, and 75 were graduated from high school in 1980—again, whites had a greater chance of graduating than blacks or Hispanics, young women had a greater chance of graduating than young men, young people who lived in the northeastern, northcentral, and western states had a greater chance of graduating than those living in the South, young people living in urban areas had a greater chance of graduating than those living in rural areas, and large numbers of young people remained invisible to Census enumerators and school authorities.[1]

The vast majority of American children were enrolled in public elementary and secondary schools. Most of the elementary schools were neighborhood schools and most of the secondary schools were comprehensive schools. In rural communities and small towns outside the South—at least until the 1970's and 1980's—that meant that children of various class, ethnoreligious, and racial backgrounds would attend the same public school buildings together, however much a variety of modes of formal and informal tracking segregated them from one another during major parts of the school day. In large cities, it meant that there was a considerable degree of class, ethnoreligious, and racial segregation in elementary schools, reflecting the character of residential neighborhoods, and somewhat less segregation in the secondary schools, though in many urban secondary schools the students tended to segregate themselves informally according to ascriptive social criteria or vocational aspirations. Although in some large cities there were both comprehensive high schools and vocational high schools of various kinds, it was the comprehensive high school that stood as one of the significant innovations of American schooling. It not only leavened the educational experience of many secondary school students through social intercourse with a variety of groups, it also afforded a broader range of social, academic, and cultural opportunities to those students who were able to take advantage of them—

1. Eleanor H. Bernert, *America's Children* (New York: John Wiley & Sons, 1958), pp. 43–60; W. Vance Grant, "School Retention Rates," *American Education*, XVII (June, 1981), 37; and Harold L. Hodgkinson, *All One System: Demographics of Education, Kindergarten Through Graduate School* (Washington, D.C.: Institute for Educational Leadership, 1985), pp. 11–12.

one must always bear in mind the extent to which the experience of schooling was invariably affected by the familial education that preceded it and that ordinarily accompanied it.

Once television became prevalent during the 1960's, schooling and television viewing constituted the great common educative experiences of the American people, with television viewing as a rule beginning earlier than schooling, continuing during the years of schooling, and then extending beyond the period of schooling. Significantly, both schoolteachers and their pupils viewed television, so that schooling often proceeded within a shared context of television viewing—even those who eschewed television were touched by it, through conversations with peers and through reporting on television in other media. What is more, just as the pedagogy of schooling during the nineteenth century had been profoundly influenced by the pedagogy of the evangelical movement, so the pedagogy of schooling during the latter part of the twentieth century was profoundly influenced by the pedagogy of television. When Joan Ganz Cooney and her colleagues at the Children's Television Workshop decided during the 1960's to use the techniques of television commercials to teach the letters of the alphabet to preschool children, they were simply doing explicitly what teachers in classrooms across the country were doing with less awareness, namely, using everything from the gestures to the pacing to the colloquialisms of television entertainment in their efforts to hold the attention of their charges and instruct them.

The experience of television also overlapped with the experience of college and university instruction, attendance at church and synagogue services, and engagement with other media and institutions of culture. One could take a formal college course via television—for example, "Sunrise Semester"; one could take a popular version of a formal course—for example, "The Body in Question" or "The Faiths of Mankind"; one could view a church service on television and indeed one could participate in an extended range of church activities—for example, through the programs of the Christian Broadcasting Network; one could partake of a Shakespeare play, a Verdi opera, a Balanchine ballet, or a Mozart symphony via television on "Live from Lincoln Center"; and one could view dramatizations of the classics of English literature on "Masterpiece Theatre." No one would contend that viewing "The Body in Question" was identical with a college biology course, though at the least it might have been equivalent and possibly superior to a poorly taught biology course (of which there were many); and no one would argue that a telecast of a Verdi opera was identical to a live performance of that opera at the Metropolitan Opera House in New York City, though, again, it might have been equivalent and possibly superior to a poor performance (even at the Metropolitan). The point is that, as direct access to churches and synagogues, schools, colleges, and cultural agencies steadily broadened during the twentieth century, indirect access to the substance of their curricula also broadened via television, making that substance available to the illiterate, the homebound, the shy, the poor, the discriminated against, and the newly arrived. Such access was not always taken advantage of, and, when taken advantage of, it did not confer credentials; but, for better or worse, it did educate, however variously the substance was learned.

The development of new and more varied forms of education in an ever more extensive range of sites and situations further expanded the availability of education by making opportunities for teaching and learning more diverse in method, substance, and timing. Day care centers offered young children opportunities for learning not to be found in their households, if only by providing access to agemates and adults who were not kin. Social settlements offered English instruction to the newly arrived, music lessons to the poor, and opportunities for the collaborative pursuit of hobbies to the aged. Demonstration farms and factory and office training centers offered vocational instruction in the most realistic of situations. Printed material in a variety of formats, from comic books to technical treatises, and in every conceivable language, permitted the autodidact to seek instruction according to his or her fancy and at his or her pace. Courses in libraries, museums, zoos, planetariums, botanical gardens, historical societies, and national parks (the National Park Service of the United States Department of the Interior taught everything from paleontology at the Dinosaur National Monument in Utah to the decorative arts at the various historic houses owned and administered by the Service) supplemented the books, exhibits, and presentations that were their common fare, enabling the interested inquirer to gain knowledge and to deepen appreciation and understanding. And the simple perusal of a daily newspaper, with its columns of advice on how to cook, dress, stay healthy, find a mate, rear children, be popular, and get ahead in the world, was a vestibule to all kinds of learning, which the specialized magazines in any and all of those domains stood prepared to advance, extend, and deepen.

The sheer profusion of educational opportunity in an American community of the 1960's or 1970's, much of it advertised in the effort to gain takers, could prove bewildering to the average person, with the result that often, in the end, none was chosen. Moreover, study after study proved the Biblical injunction that "to him that hath shall be given": that it was the already better schooled, the better taught, the better read, and in a variety of other ways the better off who most frequently availed themselves of the opportunities and in the process became even better educated. Yet the injunction could cut two ways, so that as the average schooling of the population rose, the clientele for other forms of education increased. Moreover, with the remarkable extension of postsecondary education during the 1960's and 1970's, the opportunity to interrupt formal schooling and then take it up again was also substantially enlarged, so that the learning gained in a museum or through printed materials might well impel a person to return for further formal coursework. Thus, as had been the case in the nineteenth century, the forces of popularization in the several institutions tended to be mutually reinforcing, as each enlarged the potential clientele of all the others. Yet, as had also been the case in the nineteenth century, there were groups that did not or could not partake. Some remained isolated from the process by geographical distance; others were isolated by linguistic incapacity or cultural estrangement; and some isolated themselves from the process out of principle.

Granted differential use by various segments of the population, the larger and ever more diverse clienteles of educative institutions continued to transform the curricula of those institutions. The churches and synagogues altered everything from their theology to their liturgy to make their teaching more palatable to the clienteles they wished to attract—the Roman Catholic churches rendered the Mass in English and Reform Jewish temples rendered the Torah in English; fundamentalist sects set themselves firmly against "the world" on behalf of clienteles disenchanted with modernism; and ministers and rabbis of every persuasion incorporated rock music, folk songs, and contemporary dance into their devotions and celebrations. In like fashion, the schools, colleges, and universities proffered more practical, more interesting, and less intellectually demanding curricula in their effort to provide something of value for everyone who came—the schools offered courses in driver education and typing skills, the community colleges offered courses in beauty culture and cooking, the senior colleges offered courses in archery and tennis, and the universities offered courses in remedial English and how to use the library. A host of private entrepreneurial schools taught everything from how to repair radios to how to take tests. And publishers, broadcasters, libraries, museums, and zoos distributed materials and sponsored lectures, displays, programs, and events that were intended to edify while they entertained—there were the "blockbuster" shows of the Metropolitan Museum of Art, the mail-order book series on nature, art, and history of Time-Life Books, and the weekly tests concerning recent events of the *New York Times*. Groups that could not obtain a satisfactory offering from extant institutions—fundamentalists who felt ignored by the colleges or artists who felt ignored by the museums—founded their own institutions to advance what seemed to be needed, which often pressed both the extant and the newly founded institutions to broaden their offerings and hence their appeal. Not all educative institutions were popular and not all were popularized—many continued to serve specialized elite functions; but there seemed to be institutions to meet an extraordinary range of demands and there were even a few that needed to create the demands they wished to meet—where else but in the minds of aficionados would a Museum of the Piano or a Museum of Comic Art have been born?

Finally, whether public or private in the particulars of their support and control, twentieth-century educative institutions, like their nineteenth-century forebears, tended to portray themselves and in turn to be perceived as community institutions; indeed, the very fact of their being educative institutions seemed to constitute them community institutions. The churches and synagogues were surely private in support and control; yet religious institutions in general were seen as community institutions. In Muncie, Indiana, the Lynds in the 1930's and Caplow and his associates in the 1970's found the churches symbolizing permanent community values amid the conflicts and uncertainties of everyday life. Similarly, schools, colleges, and universities presented themselves as community institutions, whether or not they were controlled by and responsible to the public—most private colleges in their fund-raising drives tended to paraphrase Woodrow Wilson as president of Princeton when he spoke of Princeton as "in the nation's service." Much the same was true of libraries, museums, and other cultural agencies. In fact, the proffering or sponsorship of education became an ever more widely used device by which private, commercial organizations of every sort laid claim upon the public to be viewed as community institutions. The Metropolitan Life Insurance Company lectured the public on how to maintain good health. The Schenley Distillers Company lectured the public on the perils of driving while under the influence of alcohol. And the American Telephone and Telegraph Company boasted in newspaper advertisements that it sponsored educational programs over television without the interruptions of commercials.[2]

Popularization and multitudinousness, then, were no less characteristic of American education during the twentieth century than they had been in the nineteenth. But they were now joined by a third distinguishing feature that lent a rather different character to the enterprise, namely, politicization, meaning, as in the broad Aristotelian sense, the increasingly direct harnessing of education to social ends. Horace Mann and his contemporaries had believed that universal schooling would advance the cause of republicanism and indeed that republicanism demanded a particular level of schooling, one that would be sufficient to teach boys and girls the common values of a Christian-republican society at the same time that it equipped them to continue their education on their own. But they had stopped short of narrowly politicizing the school curriculum and indeed had preached the avoidance of controversy where possible—teach the common elements of Christianity, Mann had urged, not the precepts of any particular denomination, and the common elements of republicanism, not the precepts of any particular party.[3]

John Dewey and his contemporaries went further, viewing schooling as a reformist device that would not only teach youngsters to think clearly and independently but also imbue them with an understanding of the essential character of the new industrial society and saturate them with a commitment to serve their fellow human beings. When youngsters were taught thusly, Dewey argued, Americans would have the "deepest and best guarantee" of a larger society that would be "worthy, lovely, and harmonious." As one read further in Dewey, however, one became increasingly aware that it was ultimately a democratic socialist society that he hoped the schools would help bring into being. When Dewey's colleague George S. Counts asked in 1932, "Dare the school build a new social order?" Dewey responded that the school alone could not build a new social order but that it could certainly ally itself with the political forces in the society at large that were attempting to bring a new social order into being. Dewey was obviously not urging that American schools become socialist schools;

2. *The Public Papers of Woodrow Wilson,* edited by Ray Stannard Baker and William E. Dodd, I, 259–285.

3. *The Politics of Aristotle,* translated with notes by Ernest Barker (Oxford: Clarendon Press, 1948), pp. 366, 392.

but he was indeed urging that American schools become not only politically aware but politically reformist in orientation. So far as Dewey was concerned, that did not constitute politicization; for his critics, of course, it constituted flagrant politicization.[4]

In the end, Dewey's vision of a democratic socialist society did not triumph. American schools did not become politically reformist; in fact, they were if anything politically conservative, despite the widespread adoption of the Rugg social studies textbooks during the 1930's and despite the tendency of progressive innovations to become commonplace in the 1960's. But the Deweyan rhetoric about the schools allying themselves with the forces of reform was indicative of a widening effort on the part of various interest groups in local communities and in the society at large to harness the schools to some view, in Aristotle's phrase, of "the good life." The National Association of Manufacturers wanted schools to teach the virtues of the capitalist system. The Farmers' Alliance wanted schools to teach the true history of the laboring classes and the downtrodden. The American Legion wanted schools to teach an unquestioning patriotism and sought to cleanse classrooms of "subversive" influences. And various Christian denominations wanted schools to teach the general precepts, theological and ethical, of the Christian faith. On a more specific plane, state legislatures enacted laws requiring the schools to teach everything from the evils of alcohol to the advantages of dairy products. And associations dedicated to a variety of causes distributed teaching materials, sponsored essay contests, and organized teacher institutes to advance one point of view or another—on conservation, on nuclear energy, on electric power, on foreign imports, on farm subsidies—at the same time that they organized inquiries, launched investigations, and pressed school authorities to excise one point of view or another—on abortion, on race relations, on religion, politics, or morality.

In part, it was didacticism that underlay the effort. As Robert McClintock has pointed out, there was a tendency throughout the Western world during the nineteenth and twentieth centuries to shift from paradigms of study to paradigms of instruction, whether for social, religious, or political purposes. Certainly the enactment of compulsory schooling laws was a pivotal event in the movement. It

---

4. John Dewey, *The School and Society* [1899], in *John Dewey: The Middle Works, 1899–1924*, edited by Jo Ann Boydston (15 vols.; Carbondale: Southern Illinois University Press, 1976–83), I, 19–20; and George S. Counts, *Dare the School Build a New Social Order?* (New York: The John Day Company, 1932).

happened more rapidly in schools than in libraries and museums, partly because schools dealt principally with youngsters, partly because schools became public earlier and more decisively than libraries and museums, and partly because, historically, libraries and museums retained a different mix of edification and entertainment in their offering. When the designer Charles Eames was asked to explain the pedagogical principles underlying the superb museum exhibit entitled "The Age of Franklin and Jefferson" that he organized in celebration of the bicentennial of American independence in 1976, he replied that he had tried to create the characteristically Jeffersonian opportunity for a "found education," for the sort of education one happens upon in the course of living a varied and reflective life. As Eames himself noted, in Jefferson's time that was the dominant form of education available to Americans; in 1976, Eames was creating an island in a sea of didacticism.[5]

Well before the 1970's, didacticism had become a characteristic feature of American life. Not only did the schools press views of the good life upon their students, but a vast variety of institutions and organizations pressed views of the good life upon the American people. The National Association of Manufacturers went far beyond pressing the schools to teach the virtues of capitalism and undertook its own extensive program of public education in the advantages of government encouragement of business and the disadvantages of the closed shop. And the Farmers' Alliance went far beyond pressing the schools to teach the true history of the laboring classes and the downtrodden and became a school in its own right, instructing its members and the public at large on the historic conflict in America between the moneyed interests and the great body of producers and on the political measures that were needed properly to resolve the conflict. For these groups and a host of others, education in a forcefully didactic mode became, not merely a complement to politics, but a form of politics and increasingly a substitute for politics.

Didacticism, of course, brought with it demands for orthodoxy, and such demands, too, were a characteristic feature of American education. The antievolution legislation that led to the Scopes trial was exemplary of the phenomenon, and indeed Walter Lippmann in *American Inquisitors: A Commentary on Dayton and Chicago* (1928) explicated the ways in which the trial could be seen as a clash between

5. Robert McClintock, "Toward a Place for Study in a World of Instruction," *Teachers College Record*, LXXIII (1971–72), 161–205; and Charles Eames, "On Reducing Discontinuity," *Bulletin of the American Academy of Arts and Sciences*, XXX, No. 6 (March, 1977), 32.

the didacticism of the scientists and the didacticism of the parents, both of whom claimed to be acting in the best interests of the children. Much the same could be said of the American Legion's drive during the 1930's to rid the schools of the Rugg social studies textbooks. During the 1950's, at precisely the time that Representative Hubert B. Scudder was seeking to have Anton Refregier's murals removed from the Rincon Annex of the San Francisco Post Office, Senators Joseph R. McCarthy and Patrick A. McCarran and Representative Harold Velde were seeking to have teachers and professors dismissed from their posts for holding or being reputed to hold "subversive" political views, whether or not, incidentally, there was evidence that they had taught those views in their classrooms or urged them upon their students. During the late 1960's and early 1970's, radical student groups on college and university campuses shouted down invited lecturers whose views differed from theirs and occasionally prevented them from speaking at all. And, during the 1980's, books were removed from library shelves in scores of communities across the country—Mother Goose because it was "anti-Semitic," Huckleberry Finn because it was "racist," and a Time-Life book on Tokyo because it included a photograph of the backs of Japanese men bathing in the nude. To be sure, demands for orthodoxy had been sounded at least since the trial and death of Socrates; yet there could be no denying that, the more education became a form of politics and even a substitute for politics, the more the clash of orthodoxies was likely to remain a recurrent phenomenon on the American educational scene.[6]

II

Rising rates of literacy continued to be one of the most significant direct outcomes of the popularization of education. It was widely assumed, however, that literacy was an outcome of schooling, so direct an outcome, in fact, that the United States Bureau of the Census increasingly used years of schooling as a surrogate for literacy itself— a practice founded on assumptions that may have been reasonable but not always valid. The Bureau in 1870 asked marshals to record the number of persons ten years of age or older who were unable to write and unable to read and set the ability to write (the more stringent criterion) as evidence of the possession of literacy. That criterion remained in effect over the next three-quarters of a century, with

6. Robert P. Doyle, *Banner Books Week '85: Celebrating the Freedom to Read* (Chicago: American Library Association, 1985).

Census reports repeating the definition that illiteracy signifies "inability to write in any language, not necessarily English," and then adding, "In general, the illiterate population as shown by the census figures should be understood as comprising only those persons who have had no education whatever." According to that definition, rates of illiteracy declined steadily in the United States between 1870 and 1930, as indicated in the following table:

TABLE VIII

Year	Percent Illiterate Age 10 and Over
1870	20.0
1890	13.3
1910	7.7
1930	4.3

When one examines the data more carefully, however, the assertion that the illiterate population may be assumed to comprise "only those persons who have had no education whatever" turns out to be erroneous. For one thing, not all persons reported as illiterate lacked formal schooling. Some had attended school for one or more years but had not acquired the ability to read or to write. Others had acquired the ability to read and to write in school but had lost it after leaving school, often for lack of opportunity to make use of the ability. In addition, not all persons reported as literate had been to school. In the twentieth century as in the nineteenth, there were opportunities to learn to read and write in households, in churches and their affiliated organizations, and in various community agencies—an occasional library, for example, or an informal adult education circle.[7]

The Bureau of the Census also noted in 1920 and in 1930 that "the statistics do not show directly or definitely the proportion of the population which may be termed illiterate when the word is used to imply lack of ability to read and write with a reasonable degree of facility; but they do afford a fairly reliable measure of the effect of the improvement in educational opportunities from decade to decade." In effect, the Bureau was recognizing that the crude literacy rates

7. U.S., Bureau of the Census, *Fourteenth Census of the United States, Population: 1920* (Washington, D.C.: Government Printing Office, 1922), II, 1145, and *Illiteracy in the United States: November 1969* (Current Population Reports, Series P-20, No. 217; Washington, D.C.: Government Printing Office, 1971), pp. 5, 1.

being reported were simply surrogates for increased schooling rather than vice versa—or at best that the reasoning was circular. In any case, it was during the 1930's that the lack of ability to read and write with a reasonable degree of facility came to be called "functional illiteracy." The phrase was first used in connection with the literacy training programs of the Civilian Conservation Corps during the 1930's, when it was applied to persons who had completed fewer than three years of formal schooling. Later, it was used by the armed forces during World War II to describe individuals who could not read effectively enough to carry out basic military tasks, and was applied to persons who had completed fewer than four years of formal schooling. After World War II, the Bureau of the Census defined illiteracy as "the inability to read and write a simple message either in English or any other language"; and, though the Bureau protested that "the completion of no one particular grade of school corresponds to the attainment of literacy," it did use a fifth-grade equivalency to define persons who were functionally illiterate.

Granted these more stringent criteria—and granted too the continued circularity of using years of schooling as a surrogate for literacy and then defining literacy as an outcome of schooling and hence a measure of educational attainment, rates of illiteracy continued to decline in the United States, as indicated in the following table:

TABLE IX

Year	Percent Illiterate Age 14 and Over
1947	2.7
1959	2.2
1970	1.0
1980	.5

It is worth noting that to derive the 1970 statistic, the Bureau of the Census applied its criterion of a fifth-grade equivalency to define literacy and determined that 5 percent of the adult population (age fourteen and over) fell short of the criterion, but it also determined that four-fifths of those individuals could probably read and hence reached the conclusion that one percent of the adult population was illiterate. To derive the 1980 statistic, the Bureau used a sampling technique in which individuals were asked how many years of schooling they had completed, and if the response was fewer than five years they were also asked if they could read. The one-half of one percent figure was the result.[8]

What conclusions might one draw from these data? Two seem warranted. First, as the average number of years of formal schooling of the American population increased, crude literacy—the ability to decipher printed words and sentences—increased proportionately. Second, as the United States became a metropolitan society, printed materials became more important, more complex, and more difficult to read, with the result that the skills required for functional literacy (meaning the ability to read and write with sufficient skill to enable a person to engage in the full range of activities in which literacy was normally assumed in American society) also increased proportionately. Beyond those two general conclusions, there was considerable controversy, both over the meaning of functional literacy and the proportion of the adult population that managed to achieve it. Some argued that, given the difficulty of understanding the deductions on the stub of a pay check, or the details of a help-wanted advertisement, or the provisions of a credit-card agreement, or the warnings and antidote instructions on the packages of ordinary kitchen cleansers, functional literacy had come to imply levels of competence in reading, writing, and computing associated with the completion of ten, eleven, or twelve years of schooling. And, on this basis, they claimed that, by any measure—years of schooling completed or actual competence in reading, writing, and computing—functional illiteracy as late as the 1980's ran at rates of a third or more of the adult population. Others argued that it was the definitions that were creating the crisis, that schools had been reasonably successful in steadily extending literacy through the American population, and that, as the levels of schooling increased in the population at large, functional literacy would increase accordingly. In light of the ever more complex demands of a metropolitan civilization, one was tempted to analogize to the greyhounds chasing the mechanical rabbit in a dog race: no matter how fast they ran, they could never catch or catch up with the rabbit. Partly in response to such controversies, the Census Bureau in 1982 undertook a new study of a sample of Americans twenty years of age and older, using a basic literacy test of twenty-six multiple choice items setting

8. *Fourteenth Census of the United States, Population: 1920*, II, 1145; John K. Folger and Charles B. Nam, *Education of the American Population* (A 1960 Census Monograph; Washington, D.C.: Government Printing Office, 1967); *Illiteracy in the United States: November 1969*, p. 1; and U.S., Bureau of the Census, *Statistical Abstract of the United States: 1984* (Washington, D.C.: Government Printing Office, 1984), p. 146.

forth reading problems drawn from everyday life. Thirteen percent of those who took the test failed it, including 9 percent of those whose native language was English and 48 percent of those whose native language was not English (many of whom were literate in their own language); interestingly, 20 percent of those originally offered the test—it was given in the homes of the respondents—refused to take it, many doubtless fearing to reveal their illiteracy.[9]

Much of the discussion of literacy during the twentieth century continued to assume that literacy was a technical skill. Yet, if literacy did involve the achievement of a technical skill, its meaning also depended on what an individual did with that technical skill, on how it was used, on what sorts of material, with what frequency, and to what ends. Conceived that way, literacy became, not merely a technical skill, but an interaction between a person with a technical skill and a particular literary and cultural environment. During the national period, at the same time that schools and other agencies for conveying literacy became more popular, the American literary environment expanded rapidly, as a flood of printed materials, from daily newspapers to religious and political tracts to books intended to entertain while they instructed became widely and inexpensively available. Literacy became a useful skill in both private and public affairs, a skill increasingly worth having. Moreover, a growing number of readers stimulated an expanding publishing industry, which in turn issued growing supplies of printed materials, which in turn stimulated the motivation to read.

This process, first evident during the national period, not only continued but accelerated during the twentieth century. Ever greater percentages of the population read as ever larger supplies of printed materials became available to them. Not all people read, of course. Some remained illiterate by any definition, while others remained "aliterate," that is, they possessed the ability to read but exercised it infrequently. Yet, by the 1970's, when the Bureau of the Census was reporting literacy as nearly universal, a national survey undertaken at the Educational Testing Service indicated that "reading is a ubiquitous activity of American adults." Seventy-three percent read a newspaper every day, 39 percent read in a magazine, and 33 percent read

9. U.S., Department of Education, *Update on Adult Illiteracy* and *Adult Illiteracy Estimates for States* (April 14, 1986) and *New York Times,* April 21, 1986, p. A1. See also Irwin S. Kirsch and Ann Jungeblut, *Literacy: Profiles of America's Young Adults* (Princeton, N.J.: Educational Testing Service, 1986) and Richard Venezky, Carl F. Kaestle, and Andrew M. Sum, *The Subtle Danger: Reflections on the Literacy Abilities of America's Young Adults* (Princeton, N.J.: Educational Testing Service, 1987).

in a book. Beyond that, many spent a good deal of time reading printed matter in connection with formal course work (textbooks and other instructional materials), church activities (the Bible remained the most frequently read book), and jobs (technical manuals, employee newsletters, and communications from superiors). And many read as a purely recreational activity. People of higher socioeconomic status tended to read more than people of lower socioeconomic status; and many illiterates, most of whom were of low socioeconomic status, frequently depended on others to read to them. None of this would be incompatible with a degree of strain introduced by ever greater demands on readers deriving from ever more complicated printed materials, and none would be incompatible with a degree of concern introduced by the continuing problem of large numbers of functional illiterates, by any definition.[10]

The high rates of literacy in twentieth-century America, coupled with the wide variety of inexpensive printed materials made available by publishers operating in a relatively open market protected by the guarantees of the First and Fourteenth Amendments to the United States Constitution, created a situation of "liberating" literacy. This contrasted with the more "inert" literacy of traditional society, in which people read the Bible and other sacred texts well-known in the oral as well as the written traditions but not much else, as well as with the more "constraining" literacy of totalitarian societies, in which most people possessed the skills of literacy but were permitted to read only a limited range of printed materials. Liberating literacy in metropolitan American meant that people could read freely and widely in search of whatever information and knowledge they chose. It also meant that literacy could serve a multitude of purposes in a multitude of ways. Ambitious young men and women used the skills of literacy to find out what they needed to know to get ahead in the world; family members used the skills of literacy to correspond with one another; lovers of fiction used the skills of literacy to entertain themselves; and politically engaged citizens used the skills of literacy to find out what their elected officials were doing. Employers counted on the skills of literacy to facilitate the carrying out of company-wide policies; governments counted on the skills of literacy to facilitate the collection of personal income taxes; churches and synagogues counted on the skills of literacy to facilitate the performance of their rituals and ceremonies; and advertisers counted on the skills of literacy to facilitate

10. Amiel T. Sharon, "What Do Adults Read," *Reading Research Quarterly,* IX (1973–74), 148–170.

the sale of their products. Literacy rationalized experience, systema-
tizing it on the one hand—thus making possible new technologies of
organization—and individualizing it on the other—thereby facilitating not only reflection but also criticism. In addition, there was always
the tension between the forces leading to the standardization of print
materials, for example, the increasing concentration of newspaper
ownership after 1920, and the forces making for diversification, for
example, the resurgence of the foreign language press after 1950. In
the end, "liberating" literacy held the potential for liberation but it
could not guarantee liberation; it was a necessary but not a sufficient
condition of freedom.

With the rise of broadcasting, and particularly of television, there
was much discussion, first, of the continued need for universal literacy
in print materials, second, of the possible influence of television viewing on popular reading habits, and third, of the desirability of broadening the definition of literacy to take account of the television experience. Taking note of the ability of "illiterate" Bedouin nomads in the
Middle East to stay abreast of public affairs through cheap transistor
radios, Marshall McLuhan and his disciples talked of the outmoded
character of print literacy. Print literacy, they contended, had filled
the world with abstraction, categorization, bureaucracy, and nationalism at the same time that it had dissociated human beings from their
primal imaginative and emotional selves. They also talked of the need
for a new kind of "hot," electronic literacy in the global village that
telecommunications had brought into being.[11]

Contemporary with McLuhanite criticism, there was widespread
concern that television viewing would gradually replace reading as a
significant activity of the American people. Actually, however, it became increasingly clear during the 1960's and 1970's that television
viewing was not replacing reading so much as it was influencing what
people read, under which circumstances, and why. Books and magazines continued to circulate briskly and to be read widely, particularly
as they catered to ever more specialized audiences; but newspaper
reading did gradually decline—whereas three out of four Americans
read a newspaper on any given day during the early 1970's, that figure
had declined to two out of three Americans by the 1980's. When asked
to compare newspaper reading with television viewing, Americans
responded that television was the medium "easier to get information
from" and more "relaxing," while newspapers "got beneath the sur-

11. Marshall McLuhan, *Understanding Media: The Extensions of Man* (New York: McGraw-
Hill Book Company, 1964), chap. ii and *passim*.

face of the news" and demanded "more energy and concentration." Moreover, television was seen as the more objective medium and the one that provided the quickest overview of the news, while newspapers provided more facts and more opinion.[12]

It was the idea of television as a medium "easy to get information from" that clearly pointed to the need for a broadening of the definition of literacy; for it was clear by the 1970's that, however much and however intensively individuals continued to read, television viewing had become for all intents and purposes universal in the United States and that the ability to view television programming discerningly, intelligently, and critically was a most important dimension of literacy— "visual literacy" was the phrase widely used, though "audiovisual literacy" would appear to be more accurate. In any case, a flurry of "critical viewing" courses at the elementary- and secondary-school level appeared during the 1970's and 1980's, by way of response to the need, many of them supported by federal and foundation grants, though their success in making critical viewers of those who completed them remained inconclusive. One problem, of course, was whether the school by itself could turn a person into a critical viewer of television. The education writer John Holt addressed the question incisively in a 1971 article in the *Atlantic* entitled "Big Bird, Meet Dick and Jane." Commenting on the success of the Children's Television Workshop with its program "Sesame Street," Holt noted that the aim of the Workshop had been to provide preschool children, particularly underprivileged preschool children, with the sort of experiences with letters and numbers that would prepare them to learn more effectively when they went to school. That aim, Holt judged, was entirely admirable though insufficiently radical. What was really necessary, Holt went on to argue, was not merely a television program that would help children learn more effectively in school but a television program that would help children learn more effectively from television—a television program, in effect, that would teach television literacy, including the skills of critical viewing. The point was well made, but neither the power nor the potential of television as an educational medium had been sufficiently recognized by the early 1980's for Holt's suggestion to have been acted upon.[13]

Rising rates of literacy—whether crude or functional—were

12. Leo Bogart, *The Age of Television: A Study of Viewing Habits and the Impact of Television on American Life* (3d ed.; New York: Frederick Ungar Publishing Company, 1972), pp. 370–371.

13. John Holt, "Big Bird, Meet Dick and Jane: A Critique of Sesame Street," *Atlantic,* CCXXVII (May, 1971), 72–74, 77–78.

among the more direct outcomes of the popularization of education during the twentieth century. But the outcomes of education went far beyond literacy, and indeed literacy, once conveyed, itself became a tool of education, both for teachers seeking to instruct and for students seeking to learn on their own. What, then, can be said about the larger outcomes of American education during the twentieth century?

In the domain of knowledge, two major testing programs of the 1960's, 1970's, and 1980's revealed a variety of interesting data. The first, the International Evaluation of Educational Achievement, sought to determine the knowledge and skills achieved by ten-year-olds, fifteen-year-olds, and students in the terminal year of full-time secondary schooling, in a number of nations, including the United States. It measured knowledge and skill in science, reading comprehension, literature, French as a foreign language, and civic education (a preliminary mathematics study was done on an experimental basis during the 1960's and a more detailed mathematics study during the early 1980's). The second, the National Assessment of Educational Progress, sought to determine the knowledge and skills achieved by nine-year-olds, thirteen-year-olds, and seventeen-year-olds in the United States. It measured knowledge and skill in citizenship, literature, mathematics, reading comprehension, science, and social studies. The former study used norm-referenced tests to gather its data, that is, tests in which the various items were intended to discriminate among students who did well in the subject, students who performed at the average, and students who did poorly; the latter study used criterion-referenced tests to gather its data, that is, tests in which the various items were intended to measure absolute rather than relative achievement in the knowledge and skills that all students were expected to have achieved. Seventeen-year-olds on the National Assessment were expected to have such knowledge as the comparative differences in size between Kansas, Massachusetts, and Texas, the meaning of relative humidity, the reasons why the American colonists rebelled against Great Britain, the uses of the quadratic formula, and the major themes of *The Adventures of Huckleberry Finn* and *Moby Dick*. The items on the tests administered by the International Evaluation were not dissimilar, though they were constructed in such a way as to be equivalent for students in different countries—students in Chile were not expected to be familiar with *The Adventures of Huckleberry Finn* and *Moby Dick*.

Probably the most significant findings of the International Evaluation came in the relative performance of American students in the various subject domains that were assessed. Young Americans did rather well in literature and in civics in comparison with their counterparts in other countries, less well in science, and quite poorly in French and in mathematics, though it is important to bear in mind that the differences in performance among the various populations of school children in the well developed, industrial nations that participated were statistically fairly narrow. Probably the most significant findings of the National Assessment concerned the overall decline in the performance of American seventeen-year-olds in most subjects during the 1970's and early 1980's—a decline probably associated with the multiplication of elective options in the secondary-school curriculum, the waning of public interest in and expectation of the schools, the unstable family situations of increasing numbers of children, particularly poor and minority children, and the reduced budgets for school remedial and enrichment programs across the country. And probably the most significant criticism addressed to both studies concerned the use of test items falling within the various subject domains as ultimate measures of the outcomes of education.

Two more general studies undertaken by Herbert H. Hyman and his collaborators during the 1970's went beyond test items derived from the various subject matter domains to survey, first, information held by nationally representative samples of men and women about sports, entertainment, public affairs, and public figures, as well as about general academic knowledge, and second, value commitments and orientations held by similar samples. Hyman and his collaborators derived their data from a secondary analysis of 54 national sample surveys conducted between 1949 and 1971, involving some 77,-000 individuals. The information items ranged from "Which planet is nearest the sun?" to "Do you know the names of your two senators?" to "Do you know the site of the Olympics (1956)?"; the value items ranged from "Which three of the following values would be the most desirable for a child to learn?" (that he has good manners, tries hard to succeed, is honest, is neat and clean, has good sense and sound judgment, has self-control, acts like a boy [or she acts like a girl], gets along well with other children, obeys his parents well, is responsible, is considerate of others, is interested in how and why things happen, is a good student) to "Should an atheist be allowed to vote?" Hyman found that there was a clear and enduring correlation between the level of schooling a person had completed (elementary school, secondary school, college) and the amount of information that person possessed, general as well as specialized, current as well as traditional; and that there was a less striking but nevertheless clear and enduring correlation between the level of schooling a person had completed and the humaneness of that person's values, the person's commitment to civil liberties, freedom of information, and due process of law, and the person's readiness to grant equal opportunity to members of minority groups. Hyman and Charles R. Wright concluded *Education's Lasting Influence on Values* with a comment on the relation of the school's educative efforts to those of other institutions. In learning and maintaining knowledge in school, they observed, there may be distractions and barriers, but rarely opposition from other institutions; in learning and maintaining values, any values, there is always opposition. Given that opposition, the Hyman and Wright findings concerning the enduring effects of schooling on values were all the more impressive.[14]

The International Evaluation, the National Assessment, and the studies of Hyman and his colleagues dealt with the outcomes of the American school system with respect to the knowledge and values of the general population. The information items they used to obtain their data by no means scaled the peaks of knowledge; they concentrated rather on ordinary everyday knowledge. One might also ask a number of broader questions that involve the colleges and universities as well. How effectively did the system as a whole recruit and train talented individuals from the population at large, without regard to restrictions associated with race, class, ethnicity, or gender? How well did it prepare constructive critics of the society? How effectively did it produce scholars and artists whose work was judged outstanding by international standards? And how attractive were its advanced degrees to aspiring young men and women from other countries? On all these counts, the American school system from the elementary through the most advanced levels performed relatively well, especially during the period following World War II. It provided large numbers of highly trained individuals to fill the needs of agriculture, industry, business, government, and the professions; it drew these individuals from the general population on an increasingly nondiscriminatory basis—at least until the late 1970's; it produced and housed a major share of the nation's most articulate critics—critics of everything from the government's policies to the society's styles of life; it produced a

14. Herbert H. Hyman, Charles R. Wright, and John Shelton Reed, *The Enduring Effects of Education* (Chicago: University of Chicago Press, 1975); and Herbert H. Hyman and Charles R. Wright, *Education's Lasting Influence on Values* (Chicago: University of Chicago Press, 1979).

large share of the world's Nobel Prize winners as well as winners of such other prizes as the Balzan Award, the awards of the film festival at Cannes, and the awards of the Tchaikovsky competition at Moscow; and it attracted more candidates for advanced degrees, particularly in the sciences and engineering, from other countries than any other system in the world. To be sure, there were critics who maintained that the schools and colleges were not producing a truly educated citizenry, that their graduates were failing to demonstrate broad knowledge and humane commitments, and that as a result the intellectual and moral tone of the society was in precipitous decline—one thinks of Robert M. Hutchins and Jacques Barzun in the 1950's and of Allan Bloom and E. D. Hirsch, Jr., in the 1980's (and one must recall that the elitist charge of decline has long been a staple of American cultural controversy). However that may be, there could be no denying the considerable evidence to the effect that the formal school and university system was producing outcomes that were valuable not only to individual graduates but also to the society at large.[15]

Whatever the generalized outcomes of the formal system of schooling, there were also significant educational dissonances within that system and between that system and other educative agencies. Schools in some states taught the advantages of dairy products under legislative mandate at the same time that their health education teachers taught the dangers of cholesterol. There were doubtless social studies teachers who taught the values of fairness in schools where the football coach taught that "nice guys finish last." The researches of James S. Coleman revealed the ways in which high school student bodies often divided among those who valued academic achievement most, those who valued sociability most, and those who valued athletic prowess most, and the frequency with which given schools were dominated by the values of the second or third groups, often to the detriment of whatever the faculty was attempting to accomplish. Horace Mann Bond's studies of the origins of black Ph.D.'s indicated that an extraordinarily high percentage came from communities where a tightly knit configuration of black family and black church united with the local school to encourage academic achievement and to hold out high expectations of youngsters. The finding corroborated the more general phenomenon of continuing collaboration between the family

15. The criteria are based on Clark Kerr, "Introduction: The Evaluation of National Systems of Higher Education," in Barbara Burn *et al., Higher Education in Nine Countries: A Comparative Study of Colleges and Universities Abroad* (New York: McGraw-Hill Book Company, 1971), pp. 1–6.

and the formal school system that Benjamin Bloom found so common in the educational development of outstanding scientists, mathematicians, and musicians. Obversely, Francis A. J. Ianni's studies of the origins of delinquents indicated that an extraordinarily high percentage came from neighborhoods where impoverished families and ailing churches tried with waning influence to support the efforts of the local school while adolescent peer groups, fortified by money derived from illicit activities, taught the idiocy of study in contrast to the reality of illicit opportunity. In those instances, the variable was the continuing conflict between the peer group and the family-church-school configuration.[16]

Through it all, too, at least during the period following World War II, there was the incessant education—many would call it miseducation—via television that George Gerbner and his associates portrayed in their inquiries into the characters on prime-time programs, where males outnumbered females by a ratio of three to one, where females were most often cast as lovers and nonworking mothers, where the elderly were most often portrayed as sick, silly, or helpless, and where crime raged at a rate some ten times greater than in real life—and all this quite apart from the commercials proclaiming the nutritional values of junk food and the educational values of junk toys. It was not merely that such teaching conflicted with the teaching of the schools and colleges, as Hyman and Wright noted, it was that such teaching conflicted with the education derived from reality reflected upon—and indeed with the very notion of the commitment to reflection. For all its potential to convey knowledge, sharpen understanding, and refine taste, television was also capable of relentless vulgarization, as evidenced by grade C films revolving around adolescent fantasies, poorly made soap operas incorporating so-called soft pornography, trite situation comedies featuring scatological humor, and pseudo–sports events portraying wrestlers stumbling around in mud.[17]

Beyond the domains of knowledge and values, the outcomes of American education were less conclusive. During the national period,

16. James S. Coleman, *The Adolescent Society: The Social Life of the Teenager and Its Impact on Education* (New York: The Free Press, 1961); Horace Mann Bond, *Black American Scholars: A Study of Their Beginnings* (Detroit: Belamp Publishing, 1972); Benjamin Bloom, ed., *Developing Talent in Young People* (New York: Ballantine Books, 1985); and Francis A. J. Ianni, *Home, School, and Community in Adolescent Education* (New York: ERIC Clearinghouse on Urban Affairs, 1983), pp. 77, 78.

17. George Gerbner, Larry Gross, Nancy Signorielli, and Michael Morgan, "Aging with Television: Images on Television Drama and Conceptions of Social Reality," *Journal of Communication*, XXX (Winter, 1980), 37–47; and George Gerbner and Nancy Signorielli, "The World According to Television," *American Demographics*, IV (October, 1982), 15–17.

Alexis de Tocqueville had noted in his inimitable *Democracy in America* that much of the success of Americans in developing a democratic republic in the United States had derived from the specific combination of formal instruction, informal nurture, and individual self-reflection that had come to constitute the essential education provided by American families, to the solid foundation of common knowledge, beliefs, and values imparted by the churches and the schools, and to the extraordinarily important education conveyed by the press and by widespread participation in voluntary associations and in public affairs. A half century later, James Bryce in *The American Commonwealth* also pointed to the crucial role of public opinion in American public affairs and explained the central contribution of voluntary associations to the development of public opinion, insofar as they roused attention, excited discussion, formulated principles, submitted plans, and emboldened and stimulated their members.[18]

One might ask, then, about what had become of those important domains of "public education" during the twentieth century. Did the education provided by families, churches and synagogues, schools, colleges, and the media of popular communication lead Americans to participate in public affairs and did that participation continue to have an educative value in and of itself? Several studies carried out during the post–World War II era shed light on such questions. During the late 1950's, Gabriel Almond and Sidney Verba gathered data for a comparative study of the "political cultures" of the United States, the United Kingdom, Germany, Italy, and Mexico, part of which involved gathering data on the relationship between a sense of "civic competence"—the ability to make a difference in public affairs—and political participation in each country. Using a national sample of American adults, they found that 67 percent had a feeling that they could do something about an unjust national or local regulation, 56 percent said they would enlist the aid of an informal group or voluntary association in countering an unjust local regulation, 57 percent belonged to one or more voluntary organizations (ranging from trade unions to charity organizations to fraternal associations), and 46 percent had served as officers of one or another of the organizations to which they belonged. On all these measures, the American percentages were the highest among the five nations. Also germane, those Americans who were members of organizations had a relatively high

18. Alexis de Tocqueville, *Democracy in America*, edited by Phillips Bradley (2 vols.; New York: Alfred A. Knopf, 1945); and James Bryce, *The American Commonwealth* (3 vols.; London: Macmillan and Co., 1888), III, Part IV.

sense of "political competence" and those who were most active in organizations had the highest sense of political competence.[19]

Some years later, Verba collaborated with Norman H. Nie to carry out a study of political participation in the United States across the entire spectrum of political activities, from voting in presidential elections to membership in political clubs and organizations. They found that 72 percent of a national sample claimed to have voted in the 1960 and 1964 presidential elections, 47 percent reported that they also voted regularly in local elections, slightly under 32 percent claimed to be active members of organizations involved in community affairs, 28 percent reported that they had occasionally attempted to persuade others how to vote, 26 percent claimed to have worked actively at one time or another for a political party or candidate during an election, slightly less than 20 percent reported having initiated a contact with a local government leader about some issue or problem, and roughly 19 percent reported having attended at least one political meeting or rally during the previous three years. Verba and Nie concluded that most acts of political participation beyond the act of voting were taken by a relatively small segment of the citizenry, roughly a third, and that those most active tended to be male, to have completed higher levels of formal schooling, and to be of upper socioeconomic status.[20]

Verba, Nie, and Jae-on Kim went on to compare the American performance with the performance of citizens in Austria, India, Japan, the Netherlands, Nigeria, and Yugoslavia. They found that the Americans lagged behind Austria, the Netherlands, and Yugoslavia in percentage of citizens voting—a lag that became strikingly greater as the percentage of the eligible American electorate that voted in the presidential election of 1980 fell to 58.5 percent—but they led in the percentage of citizens working actively in organizations engaged in attempting to solve community problems. Given the rather specific definition of political participation that Verba, Nie, and Kim used, namely, acts aimed at influencing *governmental* decisions, the results were not incompatible with the earlier Almond and Verba findings. Indeed, the Gallup organization reported in 1979 that 84 percent of American adults had contributed to voluntary associations the previous year and Waldemar Neilson estimated in 1980 that there may have been as many as six or seven million voluntary groups in the

19. Gabriel A. Almond and Sidney Verba, *The Civic Culture: Political Attitudes and Democracy in Five Nations* (Princeton: Princeton University Press, 1963).

20. Sidney Verba and Norman H. Nie, *Participation in America: Political Democracy and Social Equality* (New York: Harper & Row, 1972).

United States. Clearly, participation in voluntary organizations and the education that derived from such participation continued to be an important element in the formation of the American character, though Tocqueville's observation in 1835 that the aim of education in the United States was political while the aim of education in Europe was to fit men for private life was no longer valid.[21]

What outcomes might be expected to derive from the educational opportunities associated with participation in public affairs? At the least, what one might call sociability, or the skills of getting along with people of various tastes and backgrounds, as well as what one might call intelligence, or the thoughtful pursuit of thoughtfully chosen goals. Tocqueville noted that the spirit of Americans was averse to general ideas, that neither politics nor manufactures directed Americans toward theoretical speculation; and he saw the resulting tendency toward the particular and the utilitarian as the reason why the United States had produced so few writers, poets, jurists, and intellectuals of distinction. Yet during the nineteenth century American creativity had expressed itself in a variety of significant domains—in the sparsely functional design of American clipper ships, in the assertively utilitarian organization of American factories, in the loosely woven texts of Emerson and Whitman, in effect, in American vernaculars at their best. The same clean, organic, functional simplicity that marked the giant Corliss engine that created such a sensation at the Philadelphia Centennial Exposition of 1876 and that tended to mark automobile design (the Ford Model A), architecture (Raymond M. Hood's McGraw-Hill Building), and engineering (Othmar H. Ammann's George Washington Bridge) also marked Seaman A. Knapp's demonstration farm and John Dewey's concept of intelligence. American society did produce its share of men and women of "general ideas" during the twentieth century—one thinks of a succession of Nobelists from Albert A. Michelson in physics to Rosalyn S. Yalow in medicine to Saul Bellow in literature; but it also produced millions of men and women capable of using knowledge instrumentally in the ordinary affairs of their private and public lives. And American educa-

21. Sidney Verba, Norman H. Nie, and Jae-on Kim, *Participation and Political Equality: A Seven-Nation Comparison* (Cambridge: Cambridge University Press, 1978); Walter Dean Burnham, *The Current Crisis in American Politics* (Oxford: Oxford University Press, 1982); *New York Times*, March 20, 1983, Review of the Week, p. 4E (for an alternative statistic for the United States of 55.1 percent for 1980, see Jack Beatty, "The Vanishing Voter," *New Republic*, March 21, 1983, p. 35); Stuart Langton, "The New Voluntarism," *Journal of Voluntary Action Research*, X (January–March, 1981), 7; and Tocqueville, *Democracy in America*, I, 318.

tion, in forms as different as advanced scientific study and diurnal reflection upon experience, was centrally involved in both outcomes.[22]

The attitudes, skills, and sensibilities associated with literacy, participation, and intelligence were mutually reinforcing and of a piece; and they contributed in a variety of ways to the larger education of the American public. Herbert Croly observed toward the end of *The Promise of American Life* (1909) that the nation could realize itself only through education, and he proceeded to argue his case by drawing an analogy between "individual" and "collective" education. An individual's education, Croly reasoned, consisted primarily in the discipline undergone to fit oneself both for fruitful association with one's fellows and for one's own special work. As important as the liberal and technical aspects of education might be, they were in Croly's view at best preliminary. It was a person's readiness to engage in "the persistent attempt to realize in action some kind of purpose" that provided the real opportunity for education, and it was the gain in personal discipline and insight realized from reflecting upon such attempts that brought true enlightenment. So it was also, Croly continued, with the education of society at large. "National education in its deeper aspect," he wrote, "does not differ from individual education. Its efficiency ultimately depends upon the ability of the national consciousness to draw illuminating inferences from the course of the nation's experience; and its power to draw such inferences must depend upon the persistent and disinterested sincerity with which the attempt is made to realize the national purpose—the democratic ideal of individual and social improvement. So far as Americans are true to that purpose, all the different aspects of their national experience will assume meaning and momentum; while in so far as they are false thereto, no amount of 'education' will ever be really edifying. The fundamental process of American education consists and must continue to consist precisely in the risks and experiments which the American nation will make in the service of its national ideal."[23]

Now, there was a good deal of mysticism about Croly's observations, insofar as they hypostatized the nation and reified its consciousness, its purpose, and its experience. And there can be no denying Croly's inordinate faith in charismatic leaders who would inspire a

22. Tocqueville, *Democracy in America*, I, 315.
23. Herbert Croly, *The Promise of American Life* [1909], edited by Arthur M. Schlesinger, Jr. (Cambridge, Mass.: Harvard University Press, 1965), pp. 404–405.

democratic citizenry to its finest achievements—recall that he concluded *The Promise of American Life* with a plea for "some imitator of Jesus" who would reveal to Americans the path whereby they might attain new individual and social heights "by virtue of personal regeneration." And yet there was an essential insight as well. Whatever the contribution of families, churches and synagogues, schools, colleges, and the media of popular communications to the education of Americans, it was only as Americans invested the results of that education in opportunities to learn from experience itself, individually and collectively, that their education would be a worthy one. And it was the quality of that larger education during the twentieth century, as it proceeded in myriad ways from discussions in living rooms to forums on television to campaigns for election to debates in the Congress, that remained problematical; for it demanded a level of sustained public interest and attention that was difficult to achieve and even more difficult to maintain.[24]

As early as 1922, the historian Arthur M. Schlesinger called attention to a cyclical process in American history in which reform movements came into being, flourished, and triumphed, only to be replaced by conservative and consolidating movements, which in turn were succeeded by reform movements—the agitators and visionaries who thought in terms of theories and emotions gave way to the realists who dealt in bargains and compromises; the realists in turn were displaced by a new group of agitators and visionaries. For Schlesinger the moral of the process was that both radicals and conservatives had contributed importantly to American life and thought; in effect, experimentation and opportunism had been the animating spirit of American progress, and in the process Americans had had a continuing education in public affairs. The economist Albert O. Hirschman returned to the theme sixty years later and saw a much different process at work, in which people disappointed with the quest for happiness through the accumulation of consumer goods sought the satisfactions of participation in collective action, which bred its own frustrations and disappointments, which in turn moved people to privatization. For Hirschman the moral of the process was that people were not always single-mindedly goal oriented in their behavior but rather more complex in their views and estimates of their happiness, and that they learned from their disappointments as well as from their successes. As in the Schlesinger analysis, there was a continuing edu-

24. *Ibid.*, pp. 453–454.

cation in public affairs, although in both instances it was a process undergone by individuals and not the discipline of a "nation" seeking to realize its "national purpose."[25]

In the end, of course, the question was whether the processes of public education available to Americans were sufficiently edifying to meet the demands of a metropolitan civilization. It was not merely the problem of discontinuity in the "shifting involvements" that Hirschman explicated; it was rather the more fundamental question of what was happening to the educative character of "involvement" itself, as television coverage of the day became increasingly sensational and as election campaigns turned from genuine argument to the manipulative sloganeering of thirty-second television "spots"—and all this as the issues of monetary policy, industrial policy, environmental policy, health and welfare policy, international trade policy, and defense and disarmament policy became ever more vexing and complex. One could point to the vast mobilization of public opinion against the Vietnam war during the late 1960's and early 1970's as one of the historic "involvements" of average Americans in an issue of great political moment, and one that was indisputably occasioned by public education in a variety of forms. Yet, even in light of that experience, there could be no denying the secular trends toward privatization and superficiality. Whatever Croly might have meant by the "ability of the national consciousness to draw illuminating inferences from the course of the nation's experience," one wondered whether the educational opportunities available through politics and other forms of public experience would prove sufficient to the need.[26]

Finally, as it had in the nineteenth century, American education in the large contributed in multifarious and frequently contradictory ways to the delicate balance of liberty, equality, and comity that continued to mark the American ethic during the twentieth century. The considerable variety of family-church configurations of education, extended and enhanced by successive waves of immigration from Europe, Latin America, the Middle East, and South Asia, continued the nurture of individualism that Tocqueville had noted in the 1830's. And now they were aided and abetted by school and college curricula that sought to tailor subject matter and methods to the needs of particular students, by a plethora of print materials catering to every

25. Arthur M. Schlesinger, "Radicalism and Conservatism in American History," in *New Viewpoints in American History* (New York: The Macmillan Company, 1922), chap. v; and Albert O. Hirschman, *Shifting Involvements: Private Interest and Public Action* (Princeton: Princeton University Press, 1982).

26. Croly, *Promise of American Life*, p. 405.

conceivable interest and need, by television programming that featured larger-than-life characters like Wonder Woman and Superman, and by a popular culture that lionized not only the true individuality of genuine achievers but also the bizarre individuality of entertainers who flouted public decency and of hijackers who terrorized airline passengers. At the same time that support for individualism was on the rise, the larger educative influence of a generalized Protestant evangelicism conveyed by the churches and the schools waned in favor of a secularized version of the Judeo-Christian ethic taught by the schools and colleges as a public philosophy. And that public philosophy lent support to a sense of community built around belief in the essential dignity of the individual human being, respect for law, devotion to truth, commitment to fairness, and the like.

Again reflecting a crucial tension of the age, schools became more standardized during the twentieth century, as they also became more cosmopolitan, thereby continuing their historic role of extending the range of choice for individuals. Once again, one need not deny the persistent inequalities in access to schooling and one need not deny that the same school could convey messages of encouragement to some children and messages of discouragement to others, to affirm that schooling tended to broaden the vistas of students beyond those of their households and neighborhoods. The legal philosopher Bruce A. Ackerman argued in a treatise entitled *Social Justice in the Liberal State* that schooling ought to be divided into two phases, a primary phase that essentially complemented and confirmed the values and attitudes of the child's parents, and a secondary phase in which the liberal state provided a cosmopolitan education that would afford individuals release from the constraints of geographic and social place and in so doing advance personal liberty. In fact, American secondary schools and colleges were increasingly committed to performing that second function during the latter half of the twentieth century. By advancing liberty and choice, American schools and colleges also tried to advance equality of opportunity. They did not succeed in doing so equally for everyone—family background and familial education continued to play an important part in an individual's life chances. But they were able to advance opportunity in significant ways for a significant proportion of the population, redistributing life chances and providing an important measure of intergenerational mobility. What education in general and the schools in particular did less well was to ensure any kind of equality of results. One need only recall that, when the federal government subsidized the production of "Sesame Street" in the 1960's and 1970's to give disadvantaged children the kinds of preparation with letters and numbers that middle-class children received as a matter of course in their households, the outcomes were positive, insofar as the disadvantaged children subsequently did better in school; but an equalizing of outcomes was not achieved, because the middle-class children also watched "Sesame Street" and subsequently did even better in school, thereby widening the gap.[27]

Finally, American education proffered a sense of comity, community, and common aspiration to the population at large and in so doing continued to transmit and transform the American *paideia* that had emerged during the nineteenth century. In this respect, an increasingly standardized, indeed, metropolitanized, schooling provided one important foundation of common language, common knowledge, and common values throughout the society. It was essentially that foundation on which Gunnar Myrdal based his argument in *An American Dilemma: The Negro Problem and Modern Democracy* (1944). Myrdal explicated a complex of "valuations" he called the "American creed" (recall that he summed it up as "liberty, equality, justice, and fair opportunity for everybody"). He portrayed that creed—one might substitute the term *paideia*—as a commonly held pattern of beliefs (variously arranged and variously practiced by different groups and individuals) that derived from Christianity, the Enlightenment, the English legal tradition, and American constitutionalism, and he argued that it was universally acknowledged (if not adhered to) and served as a prime moving force in American life. The "American dilemma" was the contradiction between that creed that most Americans professed and their failure to afford the most elemental civil and political rights to blacks—in Myrdal's words, "the status accorded the Negro in America represents nothing more and nothing less than a century-long lag of public morals." Not surprisingly, Myrdal saw the most important agenda of Americans as one of bringing their practices into conformity with their creed. What is more, the politics of the civil rights movement during the 1950's and 1960's rested heavily on the assumption that there was indeed an American creed and that it continued to exert sufficient influence so that it could be assigned the force of law and Americans could be expected to obey that law.[28]

After World War II, television increasingly reached the population

27. Bruce A. Ackerman, *Social Justice in the Liberal State* (New Haven: Yale University Press, 1980), chap. v; and Thomas D. Cook *et al.*, *"Sesame Street" Revisited* (New York: Russell Sage Foundation, 1975).

28. Gunnar Myrdal, *An American Dilemma: The Negro Problem and Modern Democracy* (New York: Harper & Brothers, 1944), pp. xlviii and 24.

at large—adults as well as children—with a steady flow of common teaching. That teaching was different from the kind of teaching that went on in schoolrooms, but it served as a vehicle to create a public in ways reminiscent of the McGuffey readers and the books and pamphlets of the American Tract Society during the nineteenth century. For better or worse, it furnished Americans with a common set of secular symbols, secular discourse, and indeed secular sacraments. It was a common teaching that came not so much from didactic programming like "Sesame Street," "Nova," and "America" but rather from the ceremonials (the funeral of John F. Kennedy), the rituals (the national political conventions, the national election returns), the myths ("All My Children," "Dallas"), the saints (Walter Cronkite, Mary Tyler Moore), and the icons (Crest toothpaste, Diet Pepsi) conveyed by general programming and the commercials that sustained it. The problem of that new common teaching was the problem of its superficiality and evanescence—it taught the substance and values of a consumer culture, a hedonistic culture, and a spectator culture, the very sort of culture Tocqueville had feared individualism might bring into being in the United States; and it conveyed that culture in a new language for which the public had not yet learned or been taught a critical literacy.

A growing number of commentators addressed themselves to the problems of that culture during the 1980's, seeing the challenge as one of creating an American community in which the wide range of self-conscious ethnic, religious, racial, and class subgroups that constituted the American people could freely associate and of defining an American *paideia* to which they could freely subscribe. Thus, the psychologist Daniel Yankelovich, in a study entitled *New Rules: Searching for Self-Fulfillment in a World Turned Upside Down*, described the ethos of self-fulfillment that had grown up during the affluent years of the sixties and seventies and called for a new social ethic of commitment that would channel the search for individual material gain into social enterprises involving self-help, self-government, and the breaking down of rigid racial, ethnic, class, and gender segmentation in a mutual effort to invent truly human forms of freedom and autonomy. And the sociologist Robert N. Bellah and his associates, in a study entitled *Habits of the Heart: Individualism and Commitment in American Life,* described much of the same individualistic self-seeking among middle-class individuals as Yankelovich had described more broadly, and called for a transformation of American culture that would revive the traditional idea of "public virtue" and create ways in which men and women who had slipped into privatism might again become involved in public affairs. In effect, Yankelovich and Bellah were acting very much in the role of latter-day prophets, calling upon their fellow Americans to honor the traditional values of the American *paideia* at the same time that they redefined that *paideia* in contemporary terms.[29]

III

A metropolitan civilization maintains a distinctive relationship with the rest of the world. It continues to import ideas and materials from abroad—raw materials, foodstuffs, manufactured products, luxury items, technology, literature, and systems of ideas. And, having processed those ideas and materials in myriad ways, it exports its own ideas and products and especially the styles and designs associated with those ideas and products; one characteristic of a metropolis is that its ideas and products carry a mark of superiority, they tend to command attention and become dominant. As the United States became a metropolitan civilization during the late nineteenth and twentieth centuries, its ideas and products began to exercise hegemony in far places, to the delight of some and the dismay of others. William Thomas Stead, the crusading editor of the *Review of Reviews* and something of a maverick of British journalism, was one of those who was delighted. An outspoken and enthusiastic exponent of Anglo-American unity, along with Arthur Conan Doyle, Walter Besant, James Bryce, and H. G. Wells, Stead devoted the entire 1902 annual of the *Review of Reviews* to an explication of America's rise to preeminence among nations, entitling the volume "The Americanisation of the World." He began with characteristic directness: "The advent of the United States as the greatest of world-Powers is the greatest political, social, and commercial phenomenon of our times." And he then proceeded to detail the rise of American influence in the British Empire as well as in the nations of Europe, Asia, the Middle East, and Central and South America, pointing to the special role of American religion, literature, journalism, science, art, sport, and entertainment in the Americanization process. Toward the end, Stead raised what he saw as the critical question: "What is the secret of American success?"

29. Daniel Yankelovich, *New Rules: Searching for Self-Fulfillment in a World Turned Upside Down* (New York: Random House, 1981); and Robert N. Bellah *et al., Habits of the Heart: Individualism and Commitment in American Life* (Berkeley: University of California Press, 1985), pp. 253–255.

He responded on two levels. In the large, he argued, there was no single secret of American success. It derived from a young and vigorous people let loose among the incalculable treasures of a virgin continent; it derived as well from the absence of a feudal tradition, from the "great amalgam of heterogeneous energies" released by a "new composite race," and from an extraordinarily single-minded focus on industrial pursuits. But more particularly, he continued, it derived from three American secrets he saw as eminently exportable: first, incentives to production, the willingness to invest in labor-saving machinery; second, the espousal of democracy, which gave rise to energy and ambition; and third, and most important, the commitment to universal education, by which he meant not only popular schooling but also the prevalence of colleges, universities, libraries, and technical institutes. Great Britain might well begin the much needed reform of its institutions by adopting the American commitment to universal education, Stead counseled. "Until a change comes over the spirit of our country, and society with a big S recognizes that unless our people are educated the game is up, we shall not see any material improvement."[30]

Stead's tract was addressed to his contemporaries in Great Britain and the United States, and it was intended to excite controversy and in the process sell subscriptions to both the English and the American *Review of Reviews*. That said, however, his idea of American education as an exportable American "secret" was not without a basis in fact, and indeed was fairly commonly held. In part, of course, it was but one version of the increasingly general late-nineteenth-century belief that the nation with the most efficient and effective education system would in the end dominate the world—the theme was repeatedly sounded in the great international expositions of the era. And, in the context of that belief, there was a good deal of interest in many parts of the world in the exchange of educational ideas and institutions. Not surprisingly, as the metropolitanization announced by Stead advanced, so also did the borrowing of American educational ideas and institutions. Indeed, the two processes were mutually supportive and of a piece, so that the technologies of American education, once borrowed, often themselves became elements in the further extension of metropolitan influence and as such an important domain of American education in their own right.

30. W. T. Stead, *The Americanisation of the World; or, The Trend of the Twentieth Century* (London: The "Review of Reviews" Office, 1902), pp. 5, 147, 148.

As a metropolis, the United States continued to import educational ideas and institutions from around the world. At one time or another during the twentieth century, significant numbers of Americans became enamored of Maria Montessori's ideas concerning early childhood education, Sigmund Freud's ideas concerning child rearing, and Shinichi Suzuki's ideas concerning the teaching of violin to toddlers; and one can trace the influence of a variety of educational institutions, from the informal courses of the Danish folk school to the cultural broadcasts of the British Broadcasting Company. But it was the export of educational ideas and institutions that became increasingly significant, proceeding as it did in a number of ways and at a number of levels. At its simplest, it was a process of the movement of particular individuals from the United States abroad and vice versa. The young men and women of the Protestant missionary movement during the late nineteenth and early twentieth centuries were just such individuals. To choose but one example, Sarah Luella Miner was born in 1861, to the family of Daniel and Lydia Miner of Oberlin, Ohio, both graduates of Oberlin College. She grew up in Ohio, Iowa, Kansas, and Mississippi, where her father held teaching posts, attended Oberlin Academy, the Normal Department of Tougaloo University (where her father was treasurer from 1877 to 1882 and where she was the one white student in her class), and then Oberlin College, from which she was graduated in 1884. She early felt the resolve to undertake missionary work abroad and, after teaching for a time at Fisk University in Nashville, she won an appointment in 1887 to a mission school at Tungchow, near Peking, through the American Board of Commissioners for Foreign Missions. She remained in China for forty-eight years, teaching everything from geology to history and serving in a variety of administrative posts with effectiveness and verve. There being no geology textbook in Chinese when she arrived in the 1880's, she wrote one, and for a quarter-century it was the standard work in its field. Later, she served as principal of the Bridgman Academy for girls in Peking, as president of the newly organized North China Union Women's College, and as dean of the Women's Medical Unit and then dean of women at Cheeloo University in Tsinan. An interpreter of China to her fellow Americans and a consistent supporter of an indigenous Chinese Christian church, she was also a vigorous proponent of women's education to the Chinese and in the process exemplified the ideals of equal education for women that she had imbibed in her home and at Oberlin (though interestingly, in China she resisted the absorption of the separate women's colleges into coeducational universities because of the pattern of male dominance in those universities).

In a quite different mode of influence, John Dewey visited the Far East between 1919 and 1921, lecturing at the Imperial University in Tokyo in February and March of 1919 and then going on to China in April of 1919, where he lectured at the National University, the Tsing-Hua College, and the National Teachers College in Peking, at the National Teachers College in Nanking, and in a number of the provincial capital cities. There were former students of Dewey, who had worked with him at Chicago and at Columbia, in both countries, and he made a number of converts during the course of the lectures, but his influence on Japanese and Chinese philosophy per se was neither strong nor lasting. His influence on education, however, especially in China, was profound. Indeed, his philosophy dominated Chinese educational discussion until the 1949 revolution, when it became the chief target of Maoist critics.

Luella Miner was but one of hundreds of American missionaries who spent their lives as educators, not only in China but throughout the world; and John Dewey was but one of scores of American educational theorists whose works were influential in other parts of the world. The obverse process, in which individuals from other countries came to the United States to observe American education or to be educated in American institutions and then returned to their homelands to carry on the work of education in an American style, was equally important, if not more so. The career of the African educator James E. K. Aggrey provides an excellent case in point. Born in Anomabu in the Gold Coast Colony in 1875 to the family of a Fantu gold-taker (one skilled in measuring the quantity and evaluating the quality of gold dust), Aggrey attended the Wesleyan Methodist school at Cape Coast and then embarked upon a teaching career at the age of fifteen, first at a village school at Abura Dunkiva and then at the Wesleyan Methodist school at Cape Coast, where he subsequently became the headmaster. Popular with the leaders of the Methodist community and regarded by them as a likely candidate for the ministry, he was sent to the United States for further education, completing the undergraduate classical course at Livingstone College in Salisbury, North Carolina, in 1902 and then staying on there as a teacher and administrator and also being ordained as an elder of the Zion Methodist Church. It was as a representative of Livingstone at a YMCA convention that Aggrey met Thomas Jesse Jones of Hampton

Institute, who befriended Aggrey, encouraged him to go on for further study at Teachers College, Columbia University, and subsequently persuaded him of the applicability of the Hampton-Tuskegee mix of Christianity and vocational training to the African blacks. When Jones led the Phelps-Stokes surveys of African education some years later, he arranged for Aggrey to be a member of the survey commissions, believing that it would be politic to have an African black visibly associated with the enterprise—not just any African black, though, but one committed to the Hampton-Tuskegee approach, one who had demonstrated the greatest tact in getting on with white colleagues and one who did not, like W. E. B. Du Bois, talk incessantly of rights, demands, and protests. Connected to the Phelps-Stokes work and subsequently supported by the Phelps-Stokes Fund, Aggrey became the great interpreter and proponent of the Hampton-Tuskegee approach to Africans. In 1924, he was appointed to the vice-principalship of the newly established Achimota School in the Gold Coast, which was intended to model the recommendations of the Phelps-Stokes reports; but he died unexpectedly in 1927, before the school could really exercise an influence. Yet his intellectual influence through major portions of Africa was far reaching, more extensive, perhaps, than that of any other black educator until the second half of the twentieth century.

Aggrey studied at Livingstone College and at Columbia on a combination of personal savings, church funds, and Phelps-Stokes subsidies. Subsequently, his experience would be repeated by thousands of young men and women, not only from Africa, but from throughout the world, who would study in the United States on various sorts of scholarships, increasingly sponsored by their governments, and then return home to work in the arts, the sciences, and the professions. As the United States became ever more metropolitan, the number of such individuals steadily increased (there were 30,000 such students in American colleges and universities in 1950, and 286,000, in 1979); as the number increased, the United States became ever more metropolitan—the two processes, to repeat, were mutually supportive and of a piece.[31]

The movement of individuals, then, from the United States to foreign countries and vice versa, was one mode of the extension of American influence abroad. Mention of the Phelps-Stokes Fund

31. Larry Sirowy and Alex Inkeles, "University-Level Student Exchanges: The U.S. Role in Global Perspective," in Elinor G. Barber, ed., *Foreign Student Flows: Their Significance for American Higher Education* (New York: Institute of International Education, 1985), p. 35.

brings into play another important factor in the export of American educational ideas and institutions, namely, the philanthropic foundations. Again and again during the twentieth century, American foundations—and occasionally, foreign foundations—acted programmatically to initiate, facilitate, and assist the export of American education. The role of the Phelps-Stokes Fund in the export of the Hampton-Tuskegee system of education for blacks has already been discussed. It was not only a direct export from the United States to Africa; it was also an indirect export, as the British government made the recommendations of the Phelps-Stokes commissions its official policies in its African colonies. The Carnegie Corporation of New York exported libraries—Carnegie himself contributed a library to his birthplace at Dunfermline in Scotland, and he and the Corporation later contributed libraries to other communities in the United Kingdom. And during the 1930's the Corporation under its Commonwealth Program promoted the exchange of educational researchers between the United States and Australia and New Zealand and played a crucial role in the establishment of the Australian Council for Educational Research and the New Zealand Council for Educational Research. The Rockefeller Foundation established the Peking Union Medical College in 1921 as a kind of "Johns Hopkins of China"—at the dedication ceremonies that year John D. Rockefeller, Jr., described the institution as bringing to China "the best that is known to Western civilization not only in medical science but in mental development and spiritual culture." The Commonwealth Fund, having set up experimental child guidance clinics in a number of American cities, assisted in the organization of a Child Guidance Council in London in 1927, and of a clinic staffed by American mental health specialists a year later. And the Ford Foundation during the years following World War II made enormous investments in the establishment of a wide range of educative institutions, from demonstration farms to educational broadcasting stations to advanced schools of business and management, in the countries of Africa, Central and Latin America, and South Asia. Obviously, the movement of individuals was involved in all these activities, but the transfer of expensive technology was also involved; and it was the organization of that sort of transfer that the foundations were able to support and facilitate.[32]

In this domain as in others, the foundations frequently pioneered, with governmental and quasi-governmental agencies then involving

32. *Addresses and Papers, Dedication Ceremonies and Medical Conference, Peking Union Medical College, September 15–22, 1921* (Peking: Peking Union Medical College, 1922), pp. 63–64.

themselves, first on an experimental basis and later on a larger scale. Frequently, foreign governments would establish scholarship programs that enabled promising educators to visit the United States and observe American schools, colleges, workplaces, and cultural institutions at first hand; and some visitors stayed for more extended periods of time in order to undertake advanced study at one or another of the American universities. It was but a short step from subsidizing individuals to sending prestigious commissions to investigate this or that aspect of the American education system. Indeed, there was a steady flow of such commissions during the twentieth century, from the Mosely Educational Commission in 1903 and the Royal Prussian Industrial Commission in 1904 to the plethora of delegations from the People's Republic of China during the later 1970's and 1980's. The obverse in this instance was the flow of American commissions abroad, initially to American dependencies such as Cuba, Puerto Rico, and the Philippines, where such commissions used the survey as a device for establishing American patterns of instruction, and later to nations intent upon "modernizing" or "democratizing" their education systems along American lines. Republican China went through such a phase during the 1920's, along with the Turkey of Kemal Ataturk; later in the century, Shah Mohammed Pahlevi of Iran imported any number of such American commissions in his effort rapidly to modernize the Iranian economy and social structure. Special instances of the use of such commissions to export American educational ideas and institutions, of course, occurred during the American occupations of Germany and Japan after World War II—a commission under the leadership of former United States Commissioner of Education George F. Zook performed that function in Germany, while a commission under the leadership of New York State Commissioner of Education (and president-elect of the University of Illinois) George D. Stoddard performed that function in Japan. After World War II, government sponsorship of the export of American educational ideas and institutions expanded tremendously, as the several programs of Point Four, the Peace Corps, the International Cooperation Administration, and the Agency for International Development led to the establishment of schools, colleges, agricultural demonstration programs, adult education programs, and community development programs on the American model throughout the Third World.

Finally, there was the vast range of activities under which the private entrepreneurial sector exported American educational ideas and institutions. Publishers had been circulating books and periodicals abroad for generations; and then, during the post–World War II era, the United States Information Agency lent its financial and administrative support to the translation and publication of American printed materials abroad and to the establishment of libraries of American printed materials around the world. American films circulated everywhere, as did American television programs. In fact, during the 1970's and 1980's, American television fare constituted by far the bulk of the world's television programming. The efforts of a growing number of multinational corporations to train their work forces in countries abroad represented another export of American educational technology, as men and women from Caracas to Singapore to Hong Kong mastered the techniques of the mass production of fuel, automobiles, clothing, and electronic products. And, needless to say, the products thus made available educated at the same time that they fulfilled their primary functions. Thus, the export of clothing offered protection against the elements, while also furnishing instruction in styles of life and costume; the export of automobiles provided transportation, while also teaching design and sooner or later necessitating the training of maintenance mechanics; and the export of Coca-Cola quenched thirst, while also developing new tastes and in the process creating new wants. If the advertising of American products educated people to wish for things they had not formerly needed, the presence of the products themselves only strengthened the effectiveness of the advertising.

It should be noted, of course, that the export of American educational ideas and institutions was often a highly charged issue both within the United States and in the recipient countries. At the time Stead wrote *The Americanisation of the World,* the quality of American schooling and its appropriateness as a model for Great Britain were a matter of heated debate among British intellectuals and politicians. At the time the Rockefeller Foundation was determining its mission in China, there was considerable controversy within the Foundation as well as within the American medical community as to whether a premier, research-oriented medical school on the Johns Hopkins model was what was most needed for either the health or the general welfare of the Chinese people. And at the time of the Phelps-Stokes reports during the 1920's, the appropriateness of the Hampton-Tuskegee model of education for either American or African blacks was a matter of debate, not only between James Aggrey and W. E. B. Du Bois, but also within the American and the African black communities. What is more, whether foundation-, government-, or corporation-sponsored, most exports of American educational products and technology to other countries were seen by some at least as merely another instance of American imperialism. That was certainly true through much of the twentieth century with respect to the flow of American cultural products across the Canadian border and, as has been pointed out, it was certainly the central issue in the controversy during the 1970's and 1980's over UNESCO's "new international communications order."

The issue of imperialism, of course, was inherent in the very nature of metropolitanism—those on the so-called periphery were always ambivalent at best about the products of the so-called center and often stubbornly resistant—and in the wish of peoples everywhere to be culturally autonomous. Beyond that, it had profound bearing on the nature and character of the American *paideia.* Dewey put the question in educational terms as early as 1916, in *Democracy and Education.* "Is it possible," he asked, "for an educational system to be conducted by a national state and yet the full social ends of the educative process not be restricted, constrained, and corrupted?" It was not merely a matter of teaching the horrors of war and the advantages of peace, Dewey continued; it was ultimately a matter of teaching the things that bound people together in cooperative human pursuits. And to carry on such teaching, he concluded, would demand that the "secondary and provisional character of national sovereignty in respect to the fuller, freer, and more fruitful association and intercourse of all human beings with one another" be nurtured as "a working disposition of mind." Put otherwise, he was arguing that the American *paideia* would ultimately have to be made compatible with a world *paideia*—it would have to be made transnational.[33]

It was precisely that problem that Margaret Mead was working on at the time of her death, in her effort to develop a "worldwide shared culture," in which a common world language built upon glyphs, a common core of knowledge from all peoples, and a common commitment to education across the entire life span would become the basis for civilization on "Island Earth." Interestingly, Mead insisted that the common world language always be a second language, "in order to protect and assure the diversity of thought which accompanies the use of different mother tongues" and to avoid imposing "a too common stamp." Interestingly, too, she insisted that the world-wide shared culture remain always unfinished. For no one was more aware than

33. Dewey, *Democracy and Education* [1916], in *John Dewey: The Middle Works*, IX, 104–105.

Mead of the relentless pace of change in the world of the twentieth century and no one was more conscious of the need of education to take account of it. Mead's answer to that need, in the United States and in the world at large, was her insistence upon human inclusiveness in the formulation and testing of any hopes and plans for the future. The surest guarantee that change would be the occasion for human growth rather than human ossification, she argued, was the inclusion of diverse people at every stage in the development of every significant activity. Their lives, their experience, and their continuing response—even their resistance—would suffuse any visions of the future with vitality and realism. The old would contribute sagacity; the middle-aged, continuity; and the young, novelty. Together, in their interaction, they would contribute wisdom. Not only would the American *paideia* have to be made transnational, Mead insisted, it would have to remain ever in the making, renewed by the contributions of successive generations. Hopes and plans for the future, she was fond of remarking, tend to become old even before they are lived; but the future itself is always newborn and, like any newborn thing, open to every kind of living experience.[34]

34. Margaret Mead, "The Future as the Basis for Establishing a Shared culture," *Daedalus*, XCIV (1965), 153, 154.

BIBLIOGRAPHICAL ESSAY

> To end a book with a display of the machinery by which it has been
> assembled is to stress the toil which has gone into its making, not
> the pleasure. No formal list can truly represent a lively aggregation
> of sources, or suggest the luster with which these have been
> touched in moments of discovery.
>
> CONSTANCE ROURKE

The present volume continues in the historiographical mode of *American Education: The Colonial Experience, 1607–1783* (New York: Harper & Row, 1970) and
American Education: The National Experience, 1783–1876 (New York: Harper & Row,
1980). The historiographical position it reflects is explicated in the bibliographical essays in those volumes, in my earlier monograph *The Wonderful World of
Ellwood Patterson Cubberley: An Essay on the Historiography of American Education* (New
York: Bureau of Publications, Teachers College, Columbia University, 1965), and
in the note on problematics and sources appended by my 1976 Merle Curti
Lectures, *Traditions of American Education* (New York: Basic Books, 1977).

Given the way in which I approach the study of education, certain standard
works in social and intellectual history have proved consistently valuable, among
them Herbert W. Schneider, *A History of American Philosophy* (2d ed.; New York:
Columbia University Press, 1963); Elizabeth Flower and Murray G. Murphy, *A
History of Philosophy in America* (2 vols.; New York: Capricorn Books, 1977); Robert
E. Spiller *et al.*, eds., *Literary History of the United States* (4th ed.; 2 vols.; New York:
The Macmillan Company, 1974); Merle Curti, *The Growth of American Thought* (3rd
ed.; New York: Harper & Row, 1964), and *Human Nature in American Thought: A
History* (Madison: University of Wisconsin Press, 1980); Howard Mumford Jones,
The Age of Energy: Varieties of American Experience, 1865–1915 (New York: The Viking
Press, 1971); Warren I. Susman, *Culture as History: The Transformation of American
Society in the Twentieth Century* (New York: Pantheon Books, 1984); Sydney E.
Ahlstrom, *A Religious History of the American People* (New Haven: Yale University
Press, 1972); Robert T. Handy, *A History of the Churches of the United States and
Canada* (New York: Oxford University Press, 1976); John Tebbel, *A History of Book
Publishing in the United States* (4 vols.; New York: R. R. Bowker, 1972–1981); Frank

Luther Mott, *American Journalism: A History, 1690–1960* (3d ed.; New York: The Macmillan Company, 1962), and *A History of American Magazines* (5 vols.; Cambridge, Mass.: Harvard University Press, 1930–1968); Erik Barnouw, *A History of Broadcasting in the United States* (3 vols.; New York: Oxford University Press, 1966–1970); Robert Sklar, *Movie-Made America: A Cultural History of American Movies* (New York: Random House, 1975); Alexandra Oleson and John Voss, eds., *The Organization of Knowledge in Modern America, 1860–1920* (Baltimore: Johns Hopkins University Press, 1979); Oliver W. Larkin, *Art and Life in America* (rev. ed.; New York: Holt, Rinehart and Winston, 1960); Marshall B. Davidson, *Life in America* (2 vols.; Boston: Houghton Mifflin Company, 1951); Daniel J. Boorstin, *The Americans: The Democratic Experience* (New York: Random House, 1973); Morris Janowitz, *The Last Half-Century: Societal Change and Politics in America* (Chicago: University of Chicago Press, 1978); Walter Nugent, *Structures of American Social History* (Bloomington: Indiana University Press, 1981); Robert H. Wiebe, *The Search for Order, 1877–1920* (New York: Hill and Wang, 1967); George E. Mowry, *The Urban Nation, 1920–1960* (New York: Hill and Wang, 1965); John Whiteclay Chambers II, *The Tyranny of Change: America in the Progressive Era, 1900–1917* (New York: St. Martin's Press, 1980); Ellis W. Hawley, *The Great War and the Search for a Modern Order, A History of the American People and Their Institutions, 1917–1933* (New York: St. Martin's Press, 1979); Gerald D. Nash, *The Great Depression and World War II: Organizing America, 1933–1945* (New York: St. Martin's Press, 1979); and William H. Chafe, *The Unfinished Journey: America Since World War II* (New York: Oxford University Press, 1986).

Also valuable were such reference works as U.S., Bureau of the Census, *Historical Statistics of the United States, Colonial Times to 1970* (2 vols.; Washington, D.C.: Government Printing Office, 1975); Edwin Scott Gaustad, *Historical Atlas of Religion in America* (New York: Harper & Row, 1962); Allen Johnson et al., eds., *Dictionary of American Biography* (25+ vols.; New York: Charles Scribner's Sons, 1928–); Edward T. James et al., eds., *Notable American Women, 1607–1950: A Biographical Dictionary* (3 vols.; Cambridge, Mass.: Harvard University Press, 1971); Barbara Sicherman and Carol Hurd Green, eds., *Notable American Women, The Modern Period: A Biographical Dictionary* (Cambridge, Mass.: Harvard University Press, 1980); *The International Library of Negro Life and History* (7 vols.; New York: Publishers Company, 1967–1968); Rayford W. Logan and Michael R. Winston, eds., *Dictionary of American Negro Biography* (New York: W. W. Norton & Company, 1982); *Recent Social Trends in the United States* (2 vols.; New York: McGraw-Hill Book Company, 1933); Nelson R. Burr et al., *A Critical Bibliography of Religion in America* (2 vols.; Princeton: Princeton University Press, 1961); and Stephan Thernstrom, ed., *Harvard Encyclopedia of American Ethnic Groups* (Cambridge, Mass.: Harvard University Press, 1980).

Several standard collections of documents have proved helpful, including Henry Steele Commager, ed., *Documents of American History* (9th ed.; 2 vols.; New York: Appleton-Century-Crofts, 1973); John R. Commons et al., *A Documentary History of American Industrial Society* (11 vols.; Cleveland: The Arthur H. Clark Company, 1910–1911); Richard Hofstadter and Wilson Smith, eds., *American Higher Education: A Documentary History* (2 vols.; Chicago: University of Chicago Press, 1961); Sol Cohen, ed., *Education in the United States: A Documentary History* (5 vols.; New York: Random House, 1974); Robert H. Bremner, ed., *Children and*

Youth in America: A Documentary History (3 vols.; Cambridge, Mass.: Harvard University Press, 1970–1974); Wilcomb E. Washburn, ed., *The American Indian and the United States: A Documentary History* (4 vols.; New York: Random House, 1975); and Frank J. Kahn, ed., *Documents of American Broadcasting* (New York: Appleton-Century-Crofts, 1968).

INTRODUCTION

The Philadelphia Centennial Exhibition of 1876 is depicted in Christine Hunter Donaldson, "The Centennial of 1876: The Exposition, and Culture for America" (doctoral thesis, Yale University, 1948); John Mass, *The Glorious Enterprise: The Centennial Exhibition of 1876 and H. J. Schwartzmann, Architect-in-Chief* (Watkins Glen, N.Y.: American Life Foundation, 1973); and Robert C. Post, ed., *1876: A Centennial Celebration* (Washington, D.C.: Smithsonian Institution, 1976). The American social and political context of the exhibition is sketched in Dee Brown, *The Year of the Century: 1876* (New York: Charles Scribner's Sons, 1966); Fred A. Shannon, *The Centennial Years: A Political and Economic History of America from the Late 1870s to the Early 1890s,* edited by Robert Huhn Jones (Garden City, N.Y.: Doubleday and Company, 1967); and John D. Bergamini, *The Hundredth Year: The United States in 1876* (New York: G. P. Putnam's Sons, 1976).

The land policies governing the incorporation of the trans-Mississippi West into the United States are described in Jack Ericson Eblen, *The First and Second United States Empires* (Pittsburgh: University of Pittsburgh Press, 1968). The changing character of the American population during the period following 1876 is detailed in Conrad Taeuber and Irene B. Taeuber, *The Changing Population of the United States* (New York: John Wiley and Sons, 1958); Donald J. Bogue, *The Population of the United States: Historical Trends and Future Projections* (New York: The Free Press, 1985); Maldwyn Allen Jones, *American Immigration* (Chicago: University of Chicago Press, 1960); and and David M. Reimers, *Still the Golden Door: The Third World Comes to America* (New York: Columbia University Press, 1985). The changing concepts and laws that have governed naturalization and citizenship are discussed in Reed Ueda, "Naturalization and Citizenship" in Stephen Thernstrom, ed., *Harvard Encyclopedia of American Ethnic Groups* (Cambridge, Mass.: Harvard University Press, 1980), pp. 734–748.

My conception of the phenomenon of metropolitanization has been significantly informed by R. D. McKenzie, *The Metropolitan Community* (New York: McGraw-Hill Book Company, 1933). Richard L. Meier, *A Communications Theory of Urban Growth* (Cambridge, Mass.: The M.I.T. Press, 1962) and Max A. Eckstein and Harold J. Noah, *Metropolitanism and Education: Teachers and Schools in Amsterdam, London, Paris and New York* (New York: The Institute of Philosophy and Politics of Education, Teachers College, Columbia University, 1973) have particular relevance to the metropolitan experience in education. Blake McKelvey, *The Urbanization of America, 1860–1915* (New Brunswick: Rutgers University Press, 1963), and *The Emergence of Metropolitan America, 1915–1966* (New Brunswick: Rutgers University Press, 1968) describe the history of metropolitanization in the United States; Amos H. Hawley and Vincent P. Rock, eds., *Metropolitan America in Contemporary Perspective* (New York: Sage Publications, 1975) describes the recent situation.

Michael H. Ebner, "Urban History: Retrospect and Prospect," *Journal of American History*, LXVIII (1981–82), 69–84, is an excellent review of the literature.

The political, religious, and cultural aspects of American metropolitanism beyond American borders are explicated in Albert K. Weinberg, *Manifest Destiny: A Study of Nationalist Expansionism in American History* (Baltimore: Johns Hopkins Press, 1935); Ernest R. May, *American Imperialism: A Speculative Essay* (New York: Atheneum, 1967); David Healy, *US Expansionism: The Imperialist Urge in the 1890s* (Madison: University of Wisconsin Press, 1970); John M. Dobson, *America's Ascent: The United States Becomes a World Power, 1880–1914* (DeKalb: Northern Illinois University Press, 1978); Robert T. Handy, *A Christian America: Protestant Hopes and Historical Realities* (New York: Oxford University Press, 1976); William R. Hutchison, *Errand to the World: American Protestant Thought and Foreign Missions* (Chicago: University of Chicago Press, 1987); and Emily S. Rosenberg, *Spreading the American Dream: American Economic and Cultural Expansion, 1890–1915* (New York: Hill and Wang, 1982).

INTRODUCTION TO PART I: THE MORAL COMMONWEALTH

An excellent reprint of the 1891 edition of Josiah Strong's *Our Country*, with an informative introduction by Jurgen Herbst, is available in the John Harvard Library (Cambridge, Mass.: Harvard University Press, 1963). Further information on Strong can be gleaned from Dorothea R. Muller, "Josiah Strong and the Challenge of Social Christianity" (doctoral thesis, New York University, 1955), "The Social Philosophy of Josiah Strong: Social Christianity and American Progressivism," *Church History*, XXVIII (1959), 183–201, and "Josiah Strong and American Nationalism: A Reevaluation," *Journal of American History*, LIII (1966–67), 487–503; there is a brief biography of Strong by Marvin B. Rosenberry in the *Dictionary of American Biography*. The millennial strain in Strong's thought—and in the idea of the United States as a moral community with a special mission to regenerate the world—is explicated in Robert T. Handy, *A Christian America: Protestant Hopes and Historical Realities* (New York: Oxford University Press, 1971) and Ernest Lee Tuveson, *Redeemer Nation: The Idea of America's Millennial Role* (Chicago: University of Chicago Press, 1968).

CHAPTER 1: THE CHALLENGE OF MODERNISM

The three best sources for the modernist tradition in American Protestantism are Kenneth Cauthen, *The Impact of American Religious Liberalism* (New York: Harper & Row, 1962); William R. Hutchison, *The Modernist Impulse in American Protestantism* (Cambridge, Mass.: Harvard University Press, 1976); and Martin E. Marty, *Modern American Religion: The Irony of It All, 1893–1919* (Chicago: University of Chicago Press, 1986). The standard works on the liberal Protestant response to the challenge of the city are C. Howard Hopkins, *The Rise of the Social Gospel in American Protestantism, 1865–1915* (New Haven: Yale University Press, 1940); Aaron Ignatius Abell, *The Urban Impact on American Protestantism, 1865–1900* (Cambridge, Mass.: Harvard University Press, 1943); and Henry F. May, *Protestant Churches and Industrial America* (New York: Harper & Brothers, 1949). Robert T. Handy, ed., *The Social Gospel in America, 1870–1920: Gladden, Ely, Rauschenbusch* (New York:

Oxford University Press, 1966) is a useful collection of contemporary writings with an incisive introduction. Ralph E. Luker, "The Social Gospel and the Failure of Racial Reform, 1877–1898," *Church History*, XLVI (1977), 80–99, is a discerning commentary, as are the more general discussions of American Protestantism and the question of race in David M. Reimers, *White Protestantism and the Negro* (New York: Oxford University Press, 1965) and H. Shelton Smith, *In His Image, But . . .: Racism in Southern Religion, 1780–1910* (Durham, N.C.: Duke University Press, 1972).

Jacob H. Dorn, *Washington Gladden: Prophet of the Social Gospel* (Columbus: Ohio State University Press, 1967) is the definitive biography; Richard D. Knudten, *The Systematic Thought of Washington Gladden* (New York: Humanities Press, 1968) is a useful complement. Both have comprehensive bibliographies. Washington Gladden, *Recollecting* (Boston: Houghton Mifflin Company, 1909) is an invaluable autobiographical account. Gladden's papers are at the Ohio Historical Society in Columbus and at the First Congregational Church in Columbus.

James F. Findlay, Jr., *Dwight L. Moody: American Evangelist, 1837–1899* (Chicago: University of Chicago Press, 1969) is the definitive biography; it includes a useful note on the whereabouts of the Moody papers, which are in the possession of members of the family, the Moody Bible Institute, and the Library of Congress. Wilbur M. Smith, *An Annotated Bibliography of D. L. Moody* (Chicago: Moody Press, 1948) is an excellent guide to the published sources. William G. McLoughlin, Jr., *Modern Revivalism: Charles Grandison Finney to Billy Graham* (New York: The Ronald Press Company, 1959) and *Revivals, Awakenings, and Reform: An Essay on Religious and Social Change in America, 1607–1977* (Chicago: University of Chicago Press, 1978) provide context for Moody's work. There is a brief biography of Ira D. Sankey by Harris Elwood Starr in the *Dictionary of American Biography;* it is usefully complemented by Sandra S. Sizer, *Gospel Hymns and Social Religion: The Rhetoric of Nineteenth Century Revivalism* (Philadelphia: Temple University Press, 1978) and the discussion of Sankey's contribution in McLoughlin, Jr., *Modern Revivalism.*

Two recent studies have sparked a revival of interest in fundamentalism within the context of American culture. Ernest R. Sandeen, *The Roots of Fundamentalism: British and American Millenarianism, 1800–1930* (Chicago: University of Chicago Press, 1970) traces the roots of American fundamentalism to nineteenth-century British millenarianism; George M. Marsden, *Fundamentalism and American Culture: The Shaping of Twentieth-Century Evangelicalism, 1870–1925* (New York: Oxford University Press, 1980) views fundamentalism as a more characteristically American phenomenon. Sandeen's book includes a superb critical commentary on the historiography of fundamentalism; Marsden's article "Fundamentalism as an American Phenomenon, A Comparison with English Evangelicalism," *Church History*, XLVI (1977), 215–232, explicates the differences between his interpretation and Sandeen's. In addition, Douglas E. Herman, "Flooding the Kingdom: The Intellectual Development of Fundamentalism, 1930–1941" (doctoral thesis, Ohio University, 1980) traces fundamentalist thought through the 1930's.

There is an abundance of historical writing on the Scopes trial. Ray Ginger, *Six Days or Forever? Tennessee v. John Thomas Scopes* (Boston: Beacon Press, 1958) and L. Sprague de Camp, *The Great Monkey Trial* (Garden City, N.Y.: Doubleday and Company, 1968) convey the excitement of the trial itself. *The World's Foremost*

Trial (Cincinnati: National Book Company, 1925); Leslie H. Allen, ed., *Bryan and Darrow at Dayton: The Record and Documents of the "Bible-Evolution Trial"* (New York: Arthur Lee and Company, 1925); and Sheldon Norman Grebstein, ed., *Monkey Trial: The State of Tennessee vs. John Thomas Scopes* (Boston: Houghton Mifflin Company, 1960) present records of the trial. Willard B. Gatewood, Jr., *Preachers, Pedagogues and Politicians: The Evolution Controversy in North Carolina, 1920–1927* (Chapel Hill: University of North Carolina Press, 1966); William B. Gatewood, Jr., ed., *Controversy in the Twenties: Fundamentalism, Modernism, and Evolution* (Nashville, Tenn.: Vanderbilt University Press, 1969); and Kenneth K. Bailey, *Southern White Protestantism in the Twentieth Century* (New York: Harper & Row, 1964) provide political and religious context. Lawrence W. Levine, *Defender of the Faith: William Jennings Bryan, the Last Decade, 1915–1925* (New York: Oxford University Press, 1965) is the best source for Bryan's participation; Clarence Darrow, *The Story of My Life* (New York: Holt, Rinehart and Winston, 1967) is the best source for Scopes's participation. Robert T. Handy, "Fundamentalism and Modernism in Perspective," *Religion in Life*, XXIV (1954–55), 381–394, provides a useful analysis. Shailer Mathews, *The Faith of Modernism* (New York: The Macmillan Company, 1924); Henry Fairfield Osborn, *Evolution and Religion in Education: Polemics of the Fundamentalist Controversy of 1922 to 1925* (New York: Charles Scribner's Sons, 1926); and Maynard Shipley, *The War on Modern Science: A Short History of the Fundamentalist Attacks on Evolution and Modernism* (New York: Alfred A. Knopf, 1927) present the modernist perspective. Walter Lippmann, *American Inquisitors: A Commentary on Dayton and Chicago* (New York: The Macmillan Company, 1928) sets forth some of the continuing dilemmas of public policy for public education inherent in the Scopes trial. Gregory Singleton makes an impressive case for fundamentalism as an urban as well as a rural phenomenon in "Fundamentalism and Urbanization: A Quantitative Critique of Impressionistic Interpretations," in Leo F. Schnore, ed., *The New Urban History: Quantitative Explorations by American Historians* (Princeton: Princeton University Press, 1975).

Richard Wightman Fox, *Reinhold Niebuhr: A Biography* (New York: Pantheon Books, 1985) is the definitive work; it contains a superb critical bibliography that details, *inter alia*, the various locations of Niebuhr's papers. D. B. Robertson, *Reinhold Niebuhr's Works: A Bibliography* (rev. ed.; Lanham, Md.: University Press of America, 1983) is the most complete listing of Niebuhr's published works and of published works on Niebuhr. Of the latter, Gordon Harland, *The Thought of Reinhold Niebuhr* (New York: Oxford University Press, 1960) and Charles W. Kegley, ed., *Reinhold Niebuhr: His Religious, Social, and Political Thought* (rev. ed.; New York: Pilgrim Press, 1984) are the best introductions to his ideas; the Kegley volume includes a revealing intellectual autobiography by Niebuhr as well as a response by Niebuhr to the various interpretations and criticisms therein. Donald B. Meyer, *The Protestant Search for Political Realism, 1919–1941* (Berkeley: University of California Press, 1960) and Richard H. Pells, *Radical Visions and American Dreams: Culture and Social Thought in the Depression Years* (New York: Harper & Row, 1973) provide excellent intellectual context. Timothy Wayne Rieman, "A Comparative Study of the Understanding of Man in the Writings of Reinhold Niebuhr and John Dewey and Some Implications for Education" (doctoral thesis, Northwestern University, 1959) and Harley Stump, "The Educational Philosophy of Reinhold Niebuhr" (doctoral thesis, University of Oklahoma, 1964) explicate

Niebuhr's views on education. Albert C. Outler, "H. Shelton Smith: An Appreciative Memoir," in Stuart C. Henry, ed., *A Miscellany of American Christianity: Essays in Honor of H. Shelton Smith* (Durham, N.C.: Duke University Press, 1963), pp. 3–21, is a thoughtful introduction to the life and work of Smith; H. Shelton Smith, "Christian Education," in Arnold S. Nash, ed., *Protestant Thought in the Twentieth Century: Whence and Whither?* (New York: The Macmillan Company, 1951), pp. 225–246, presents Smith's analysis and criticism of the modernist tradition in religious education, with a focus on the work of George Albert Coe. William Bean Kennedy, "The Genesis and Development of the Christian Faith and Life Series" (doctoral thesis, Yale University, 1957) includes biographical material on James D. Smart. James D. Smart, *What a Man Can Believe* (Philadelphia: The Westminster Press, 1943) and *The Teaching Ministry of the Church* (Philadelphia: The Westminster Press, 1954) present Smart's views on Christian education.

There is no satisfactory history of recent religious thought in the United States. I have gleaned the leading developments and the leading interpretations of those developments from the essays in William G. McLoughlin and Robert N. Bellah, eds., *Religion in America* (Boston: Houghton Mifflin Company, 1969), a reprint of the Winter, 1967, issue of *Daedalus;* Mary Douglas and Steven M. Tipton, eds., *Religion and America: Spirituality in a Secular Age* (Boston: Beacon Press, 1983), an expanded reprint of the Winter, 1982, issue of *Daedalus;* and Jackson W. Carroll, Douglas W. Johnson, and Martin E. Marty, *Religion in America: 1950 to the Present* (San Francisco: Harper & Row, 1979). A. Roy Eckhardt, *The Surge of Piety in America: An Appraisal* (New York: Association Press, 1958) sketches the religious revival of the 1950's. Will Herberg, *Protestant–Catholic–Jew: An Essay in American Religious Sociology* (Garden City, N.Y.: Doubleday and Company, 1955) sets forth the most influential contemporary interpretation of that revival. Harry J. Ausmus, *Will Herberg: From Right to Right* (Chapel Hill: University of North Carolina Press, 1987) is the fullest account of Herbert's life and thought, and includes an excellent bibliography of Herberg's writings. John P. Diggins, *Up from Communism: Conservative Odysseys in American Intellectual History* (New York: Harper & Row, 1975) presents an incisive analysis of Herberg's intellectual development. The papers in John Cogley, ed., *Religion in America: Original Essays on Religion in a Free Society* (New York: Meridian Books, 1958) address many of the issues raised in Herberg's treatise.

There is a brief biographical sketch of Harvey Cox in *Contemporary Authors,* LXXVII–LXXX (1979), 100–101. Harvey Cox, *The Secular City: Secularization and Urbanization in Historical Perspective* (New York: The Macmillan Company, 1965), which should be read in the context of Gibson Winter, *The New Creation as Metropolis* (New York: The Macmillan Company, 1963), elicited a wide range of responses, many of which are articulated in Daniel Callahan, ed., *The Secular City Debate* (New York: The Macmillan Company, 1966). Cox returned to many of his 1965 themes in *Religion in the Secular City: Toward a Postmodern Theology* (New York: Simon and Schuster, 1984). Gayraud S. Wilmore and James H. Cone, eds., *Black Theology: A Documentary History, 1966–1979* (Maryknoll, N.Y.: Orbis Books, 1979) is an excellent introduction to black theology during the 1960's and 1970's; Gustavo Gutierrez, *A Theology of Liberation: History, Politics and Salvation,* translated and edited by Sister Caridad Inda and John Eagleson (Maryknoll, N.Y.: Orbis Books, 1973), is an excellent introduction to the liberation theologies of the same era. There is a brief biographical sketch of Paulo Freire in *Contemporary Authors,* CXVI (1986), 157. Freire's chief works on education available in English translation are *Pedagogy of the Oppressed,* translated by Myra Bergman Ramos (New York: Herder and Herder, 1970), *Education for Critical Consciousness* (New York: The Seabury Press, 1973), and *The Politics of Education: Culture, Power, and Liberation,* translated by Donaldo Macedo (South Hadley, Mass.: Bergin and Garvey Publishers, 1985). Denis E. Collins, *Paulo Freire: His Life, Works, and Thought* (New York: Paulist Press, 1977) and Daniel S. Schipani, *Conscientization and Creativity: Paulo Freire and Christian Education* (Lanham, Md.: University Press of America, 1984) are thoughtful introductions to Freire's ideas. There is a brief biography of Ivan Illich in *Contemporary Authors,* LII–LVI (1975), 306. Illich's chief works on education available in English are *Celebration of Awareness: A Call for Institutional Revolution* (Garden City, N.Y.: Doubleday and Company, 1970), *Deschooling Society* (New York: Harper & Row, 1971), and *Tools for Conviviality* (New York: Harper & Row, 1973). John L. Elias, *Conscientization and Deschooling: Freire's and Illich's Proposals for Reshaping Society* (Philadelphia: Westminster Press, 1976) is a thoughtful introduction to Illich's ideas.

Owen Chadwick, *The Secularization of the European Mind in the Nineteenth Century* (Cambridge: Cambridge University Press, 1975) provides an indispensable context for any discussion of twentieth-century secularism; there is no comparable work for the "American mind." John Dewey, *A Common Faith* (New Haven: Yale University Press, 1934) and Horace Kallen, *Secularism Is the Will of God: An Essay on the Social Philosophy of Democracy and Religion* (New York: Twayne Publishers, 1954) present the case for secularism in the American context. Robert N. Bellah's now-classic essay "Civil Religion in America," which was the lead article in McLoughlin and Bellah, eds., *Religion in America,* set forth an interpretation of secularization that stimulated a wide-ranging and intellectually fruitful controversy among scholars of religion. The argument was carried forward by Bellah in *Beyond Belief: Essays on Religion in a Post-Traditional World* (New York: Harper & Row, 1970) and *The Broken Covenant: American Civil Religion in Time of Trial* (New York: The Seabury Press, 1979), and in Robert N. Bellah and Phillip E. Hammond, *Varieties of Civil Religion* (New York: Harper & Row, 1980); as well as in John F. Wilson, "The Status of 'Civil Religion' in America," in Elwyn A. Smith, ed., *The Religion of the Republic* (Philadelphia: Fortress Press, 1971), and *Public Religion in American Culture* (Philadelphia: Temple University Press, 1979); Russell E. Richey and Donald G. Jones, eds., *American Civil Religion* (New York: Harper & Row, 1974); and Sidney E. Mead, *The Nation with the Soul of a Church* (New York: Harper & Row, 1975). Michael W. Hughey, "The Sacred and Profane Foundations of Moral Order: A Critique of the Idea of Civil Religion" (doctoral thesis, New School for Social Research, 1981) is a thoughtful analysis of the idea of civil religion within the stream of social theory since Emile Durkheim.

CHAPTER 2: METROPOLITAN MISSIONS

Owen Chadwick, *The Victorian Church* (2 vols.; London: Adam and Charles Black, 1970) provides an indispensable context for understanding the transatlantic character of the response of the churches to urbanization. Robert D. Cross, ed., *The Church and the City, 1865–1910* (Indianapolis: The Bobbs-Merrill Company, 1967) offers a useful overview of the American experience, as do the relevant sections of Robert T. Handy, *A History of the Churches in the United States and Canada* (New York: Oxford University Press, 1977). Aaron Ignatius Abell, *The Urban Impact on American Protestantism, 1865–1900* (Cambridge, Mass.: Harvard University Press, 1943) and Henry F. May, *Protestant Churches and Industrial America* (New York: Harper & Brothers, 1949) deal with the experience of the Protestant churches in particular. Dorothea R. Muller, "Josiah Strong and the Challenge of Social Christianity" (doctoral thesis, New York University, 1955) is the definitive study of Strong's later career; Philip D. Jordan, *The Evangelical Alliance for the United States of America, 1848–1900: Ecumenicism, Identity and the Religion of the Republic* (New York: The Edwin Mellen Press, 1982) is the best source on the Alliance. The papers of the Alliance are at Union Theological Seminary in New York.

The institutional church movement is treated at length in Abell, *The Urban Impact on American Protestantism.* There is also an abundance of information on institutional church programs in W. S. Rainsford, *The Story of a Varied Life: An Autobiography* (Garden City, N.Y.: Doubleday, Page and Company, 1922); George Hodges and John Reichert, *The Administration of an Institutional Church: A Detailed Account of the Operation of St. George's Parish in the City of New York* (New York: Harper & Brothers, 1906); and Charles Stelzle, *Christianity's Storm Centre: A Study of the Modern City* (New York: Fleming Revell, 1907).

Allen F. Davis, *Spearheads for Reform: The Social Settlements and the Progressive Movement, 1890–1914* (New York: Oxford University Press, 1967) is the most comprehensive history of the early settlement movement. It is usefully complemented by John P. Rousmaniere, "Cultural Hybrid in the Slums: The College Woman and the Settlement House, 1889–1894," *American Quarterly,* XXXII (1970), 45–66; Harry P. Kraus, "The Settlement House Movement in New York City, 1886–1914" (doctoral thesis, New York University, 1970); Maureen Karen Fastenau, "Maternal Government: The Social Settlement Houses and the Politicization of Women's Sphere, 1889–1920" (doctoral thesis, Duke University, 1982); and Kathryn Kish Sklar, "Hull House in the 1890s: A Community of Women Reformers," *Signs,* X (1984–85), 658–677. Robert A. Woods and Albert J. Kennedy, *The Settlement Horizon: A National Estimate* (New York: Russell Sage Foundation, 1922) remains an invaluable source of information. Allen F. Davis, *American Heroine: The Life and Legend of Jane Addams* (New York: Oxford University Press, 1973) is the best biography of Addams. Ellen Condliffe Lagemann, ed., *Jane Addams on Education* (New York: Teachers College Press, 1985) is an excellent collection of documents, with an incisive introduction and a discriminating bibliographical commentary. Jane Addams, *Twenty Years at Hull–House* (New York: The Macmillan Company, 1910) and *Hull–House Maps and Papers* (New York: Thomas Y. Crowell and Company, 1895) are the best accounts of the early educational work at Hull House. There is a splendid archive of original sources at Hull House. Roy Lubove, *The Professional Altruist: The Emergence of Social Work as a Career* (Cambridge, Mass.: Harvard University Press, 1965) and Leslie Leighninger, *Social Work: Search for Identity* (Westport, Conn.: Greenwood Press, 1987) describe the professionalization of social work. Judith Ann Prolander, *Settlement Houses and the Great Depression* (Detroit: Wayne State University Press, 1975) describes the adaptation of social settlements to the changing conditions of the 1930's.

Roger Sandall and Arch Wiggins, *The History of the Salvation Army* (5 vols.;

London: Thomas Nelson, 1947–1968) is the standard history of the Army during its early decades. Herbert A. Wisbey, Jr., *Soldiers Without Swords: The History of the Salvation Army in the United States* (New York: The Macmillan Company, 1955); Sallie Chesham, *Born to Battle: The Salvation Army in America* (Chicago: Rand McNally and Company, 1965); and Edward H. McKinley, *Marching to Glory: The History of the Salvation Army in the United States of America, 1889–1980* (San Francisco: Harper & Row, 1980) depict the Army's work in the United States. Norman H. Murdock, "The Salvation Army: An Anglo-American Revivalist Social Mission" (doctoral thesis, University of Cincinnati, 1985) offers a critically appreciative view and includes an excellent bibliography. Norris Magnuson, *Salvation in the Slums: Evangelical Social Work, 1865–1920* (Metuchen, N.J.: The Scarecrow Press, 1977) presents the work of the Salvationists in a more general context of evangelical efforts to alleviate the ills of the urban downtrodden. The Salvation Army Archives and Research Center in New York City was generous in providing microfilm records and statistical data.

The origins of the Federal Council of Churches of Christ in America, within the context of the more general organizational movements within American Protestantism during the late nineteenth and early twentieth centuries, are discussed in John A. Hutchison, *We Are Not Divided: A Critical and Historical Study of the Federal Council of the Churches of Christ in America* (New York: Roundtable Press, 1944), Charles F. Macfarland, *Christian Unity in the Making: The First Twenty-Five Years of the Federal Council of the Churches of Christ in America, 1905–1930* (New York: Federal Council of the Churches of Christ in America, 1948), and Samuel McCrea Cavert, *Church Cooperation and Unity in America: A Historical Review, 1900–1970* (New York: Association Press, 1970). Elias B. Sanford, *Federal Council of Churches of Christ in America: Report of the First Meeting of the Federal Council, Philadelphia, 1908* (New York: The Revell Press, 1909) brings together the chief documents related to the founding of the Council.

Edwin Wilbur Rice, *The Sunday-School Movement, 1780–1917, and the American Sunday-School Union, 1817–1917* (Philadelphia: American Sunday-School Union, 1917) and Gerald E. Knoff, *The World Sunday School Movement: The Story of a Broadening Mission* (New York: The Seabury Press, 1979) are informative but essentially celebratory. Robert W. Lynn and Elliott Wright, *The Big Little School: Sunday Child of American Protestantism* (New York: Harper & Row, 1971) is more critical. John T. McFarland, Benjamin S. Winchester, R. Douglas Fraser, and J. Williams Butcher, eds., *The Encyclopedia of Sunday Schools and Religious Education* (3 vols.; New York: Thomas Nelson and Sons, 1915) is a treasure trove of useful data. The development of the system of uniform lessons is traced in Rice, *The Sunday-School Movement;* Andrew H. Mills, "A Hundred Years of Sunday School History in Illinois, 1818–1918," *Transactions of the Illinois State Historical Society for the Year 1918* (Springfield: Illinois State Journal Company, 1919), pp. 98–196; and Leon H. Vincent, *John Heyl Vincent: A Biographical Sketch* (New York: The Macmillan Company, 1925). The development of the modernist position in Sunday school education is inseparable from the development of the Religious Education Association. Stephen A. Schmidt, *A History of the Religious Education Association* (Birmingham, Ala.: Religious Education Association, 1983) is a thoughtful account; Boardman W. Kathan, ed., "Pioneers of Religious Education in the 20th Century: A Festschrift for Herman E. Wornom," *Religious Education,* LXXIII (Special Edition, September–October, 1978) contributes additional information but is wholly uncritical. William Clayton Bower, *The Curriculum of Religious Education* (New York: Charles Scribner's Sons, 1925), and *Religious Education in the Modern Church* (St. Louis: The Bethany Press, 1929); Paul H. Vieth, *The Development of a Curriculum of Religious Education* (Chicago: The International Council of Religious Education, 1928), and *Objectives in Religious Education* (New York: Harper & Brothers, 1930); and Paul H. Vieth, ed., *The Church and Christian Education* (St. Louis: The Bethany Press, 1947) all expound the modernist position. The development of the Christian Faith and Life Curriculum of the Presbyterian Church in the United States is detailed in William Bean Kennedy, "The Genesis and Development of the Christian Faith and Life Series" (doctoral thesis, Yale University, 1957). Edith Hunter draws the distinctions between the modernist and the neo-orthodox Sunday school materials in "Two Approaches to the Church School Curriculum," *Religious Education*, XLIV (1949), 195–203, "Jesus: A Unitarian and a Presbyterian Interpretation," *ibid.*, XLV (1959), 341–348, and "Neo-Orthodoxy Goes to Kindergarten," *Religion in Life*, XX (Winter, 1950–51), 3–15. There is a splendid collection of Sunday school textbooks at the Princeton Theological Seminary.

C. Howard Hopkins, *History of the Y.M.C.A. in North America* (New York: Association Press, 1951) is the standard history. It is usefully complemented by Kenneth Scott Latourette, *World Service: A History of the Foreign Work and World Service of the Young Men's Christian Association of the United States and Canada* (New York: Association Press, 1957); Alan Eddy Hugg, "Informal Adult Education in the Y.M.C.A.: A Historical Study" (doctoral thesis, Columbia University, 1950); Lillian S. Williams, "To Elevate the Race: The Michigan Avenue YMCA and the Advancement of Blacks in Buffalo, New York, 1922–1940," in Vincent P. Franklin and James D. Anderson, eds., *New Perspectives on Black Educational History* (Boston: G. K. Hall and Company, 1978), pp. 129–148; and Paul M. Limpert, *New Perspectives for the YMCA* (New York: Association Press, 1964). Ethel Josephine Dorgan, *Luther Halsey Gulick, 1865–1918* (New York: Bureau of Publications, Teachers College, Columbia University, 1934) is the chief available published source on Gulick. A comprehensive history of the YWCA as a national organization is much needed. Mary S. Sims, *The Natural History of a Social Institution—The Young Women's Christian Association* (New York: The Woman's Press, 1936) and *The Purpose Widens, 1947–1967* (n.p.: National Board of Young Women's Christian Association of the U.S.A., 1969); Grace H. Wilson, *The Religious and Educational Philosophy of the Young Women's Christian Association* (New York: Columbia University Press, 1933); and Anna W. Rice, *A History of the World's Young Women's Christian Association* (New York: The Woman's Press, 1947) are older general sources. Martin O. Robinson, *Eight Women of the YWCA* (New York: National Board of the Young Women's Christian Association of the U.S.A., 1966) and Helen Bittar, "The Y.W.C.A. of the City of New York: 1870 to 1920" (doctoral thesis, New York University, 1979) are modern works; the Bittar volume has a comprehensive bibliography. Annie Graham, *Grace H. Dodge: Merchant of Dreams* (New York: The Woman's Press, 1926) includes some relevant data on the early years of the YWCA. The YMCA Archives are at the University of Minnesota.

Ernest R. Sandeen, *The Roots of Fundamentalism: British and American Millenarianism, 1800–1930* (Chicago: University of Chicago Press, 1970); George S. Marsden, *Fundamentalism and American Culture: The Shaping of Twentieth Century Evangeli-*

calism, 1870–1925 (New York: Oxford University Press, 1980); Timothy P. Weber, *Living in the Shadow of the Second Coming* (rev. ed.; Grand Rapids, Mich.: The Zondervan Corporation, 1983); and Douglas E. Herman, "Flooding the Kingdom: The Intellectual Development of Fundamentalism, 1930–1941" (doctoral thesis, Ohio University, 1980) depict the development of the fundamentalist movement and its complex of educative agencies. *God Hath Spoken* (Philadelphia: Bible Conference Committee, 1919) presents the proceedings and documents of the organizational meeting of the World's Christian Fundamentals Association. C. Ferenc M. Szasz, "Three Fundamentalist Leaders: The Roles of William Bell Riley, John Roach Straton, and William Jennings Bryan in the Fundamentalist-Modernist Controversy" (doctoral thesis, University of Rochester, 1969); C. Allyn Russell, *Voices of American Fundamentalism: Seven Biographical Studies* (Philadelphia: The Westminster Press, 1976); William V. Trollinger, "One Response to Modernity: Northwestern Bible School and the Fundamentalist Empire of William Bell Riley" (doctoral Thesis, University of Wisconsin, 1984); and Kermit L. Staggers, "Reuben A. Torrey: American Fundamentalist, 1856–1928" (doctoral thesis, Claremont Graduate School, 1986) offer vivid portraits of the leading fundamentalists. The William Bell Riley papers at Northwestern College, Roseville, Minnesota, are a treasure trove on the fundamentalist movement. Virginia Lieson Brereton, "Protestant Fundamentalist Bible Schools, 1882–1940" (doctoral thesis, Teachers College, Columbia University, 1981) is a brilliant portrayal of fundamentalist Bible institutes within the context of contemporary intellectual, social, and educational history that significantly influenced my interpretation. It also includes a splendid critical bibliographical essay. Joel A. Carpenter, "Fundamentalist Institutions and the Rise of Evangelical Protestantism, 1929–1942," *Church History*, XLIX (1980), 62–75, and "Youth for Christ and the New Evangelicals' Place in the Life of the Nation," in Roland Sherrill, ed., *American Recoveries: Religion in the Life of the Nation* (Urbana: University of Illinois Press, 1987) are incisive analyses of the vitality of fundamentalist educative institutions. James DeForest Murch, *Cooperation Without Compromise: A History of the National Association of Evangelicals* (Grand Rapids, Mich.: William B. Eerdmans Publishing Company, 1956) describes the early activities of the NAE. Donald G. Bloesch, *The Evangelical Renaissance* (Grand Rapids, Mich.: Eerdmans Publishing Company, 1973) and David F. Wells and John D. Woodbridge, eds., *The Evangelicals* (Nashville, Tenn.: Abingdon Press, 1975) depict the neo-evangelical movements of the post–World War II era. William Stoms, "The Growth of Evangelical Schools: A Study of Parental Concerns and Other Contributing Factors" (doctoral thesis, Rutgers University, 1982); William J. Reese, "Soldiers for Christ in the Army of God: The Christian School Movement in America," *Educational Theory*, XXXV (1985), 175–194; and Alan Peshkin, *God's Choice: The Total World of a Fundamentalist Christian School* (Chicago: University of Chicago Press, 1986) suggest the motivating forces behind the increase in the number of evangelical Christian schools during the 1960's and 1970's and convey a sense of the nature and character of those schools.

The classic comprehensive history of missions is included within Kenneth Scott Latourette, *A History of the Expansion of Christianity* (7 vols.; New York: Harper & Brothers, 1937–1945). Kenneth Scott Latourette, *A History of Christian Missions in China* (New York: The Macmillan Company, 1929) and *Missions and the American*

Mind (Indianapolis: National Foundation Press, 1949) are also relevant. The classic turn-of-the-century world survey of missions is James S. Dennis, *Christian Missions and Social Progress: A Sociological Study of Foreign Missions* (3 vols.; New York: Fleming H. Revell Company, 1902). Both Latourette and Dennis saw Christian missions as essentially unmixed blessings for both the missionaries and their clients. Clarence P. Shedd, *Two Centuries of Student Christian Movements: Their Origin and Intercollegiate Life* (New York: Association Press, 1934); Robert P. Wilder, *The Student Volunteer Movement for Foreign Missions: Some Personal Reminiscences of Its Origin and Early History* (New York: The Student Volunteer Movement, 1935); C. Howard Hopkins, *History of the Y.M.C.A. in North America* (New York: Association Press, 1951); *John R. Mott, 1865–1955: A Biography* (Grand Rapids, Mich.: William B. Eerdmans Publishing Company, 1979); and James F. Findlay, Jr., *Dwight L. Moody: American Evangelist, 1837–1899* (Chicago: University of Chicago Press, 1969) provide the data on the Student Volunteer Movement. Paul A. Varg, *Missionaries, Chinese, and Diplomats: The American Protestant Missionary Movement in China, 1859–1952* (Princeton: Princeton University Press, 1958); Loren Williams Crabtree, "Christian Colleges and the Chinese Revolution, 1840–1940: A Case Study in the Impact of the West" (doctoral thesis, University of Minnesota, 1969); James C. Thomson, Jr., *While China Faced West: American Reformers in Nationalist China, 1928–1937* (Cambridge, Mass.: Harvard University Press, 1969); Jessie Gregory Lutz, *China and the Christian Colleges, 1850–1950* (Ithaca, N.Y.: Cornell University Press, 1971); John K. Fairbank, ed., *The Missionary Enterprise in China and America* (Cambridge, Mass.: Harvard University Press, 1974); Valentin H. Rabe, *The Home Base of American China Missions, 1880–1920* (Cambridge, Mass.: Harvard University Press, 1978); Janet Elaine Heininger, "The American Board in China: The Missionaries' Experiences and Attitudes, 1911–1952" (doctoral thesis, University of Wisconsin, 1981); and Jane Hunter, *The Gospel of Gentility: American Women Missionaries in Turn-of-the-Century China* (New Haven: Yale University Press, 1984) provide rich data on the missionary enterprise in China as it affected China and the United States. Harold Edward Greer, Jr., "Southern Baptists in Cuba, 1896–1916," in Eugene R. Huck and Edward H. Moseley, eds., *Militarists, Merchants, and Missionaries: United States Expansion in Middle America* (University: University of Alabama Press, 1970), pp. 63–79; Peter Buck, *American Science and Modern China, 1876–1936* (Cambridge: Cambridge University Press, 1980); Walter L. Williams, *Black Americans and the Evangelization of Africa, 1877–1900* (Madison: University of Wisconsin Press, 1982); Patricia R. Hill, *The World Their Household: The American Woman's Foreign Mission Movement and Cultural Transformation, 1870–1920* (Ann Arbor: University of Michigan Press, 1985); and Kenton J. Clymer, *Protestant Missionaries in the Philippines, 1898–1916: An Inquiry into the American Colonial Mentality* (Urbana: University of Illinois Press, 1986) are informative specialized studies. *Re-Thinking Missions: A Laymen's Inquiry after One Hundred Years* (New York: Harper & Brothers, 1932) is the report of the so-called Laymen's Foreign Missions Inquiry, under the leadership of William Ernest Hocking; Kenneth Scott Latourette, *Missions Tomorrow* (New York: Harper & Brothers, 1933) is Latourette's spirited response. Robert A. McCaughey describes the role of Latourette and other returned missionaries in the development of international studies in the United States in *International Studies and Academic Enterprise: A Chapter in the Enclosure of American Learning* (New York: Columbia University Press, 1984). The papers of the American Board of Commissioners for Foreign Missions are in the Houghton Library at Harvard University; the Day Missionary Library of the Yale Divinity School and the Missionary Research Library of the Union Theological Seminary in New York are invaluable collections.

The planning of the Interchurch World Movement after World War I and the vision of a final crusade for the Christianization of the world are depicted in Eldon G. Ernst, *Moment of Truth for Protestant America: Interchurch Campaigns Following World War One* (Missoula, Mont.: Scholars' Press, 1972). The decline of American Protestantism during the 1920's and 1930's is discussed in Robert T. Handy, "The American Religious Depression, 1925–1935," *Church History*, XXIX (1960), 3–16, and *A Christian America: Protestant Hopes and Historical Realities* (New York: Oxford University Press, 1971). The Roman Catholic embrace of a vigorous Americanism at precisely the same time is documented in Edward R. Kantowicz, "Cardinal Mundelein of Chicago and the Shaping of Twentieth-Century American Catholicism," *Journal of American History*, LXVIII (1981–82), 52–68, and Fayette Breaux Veverka, " 'For God and Country': Catholic Schooling in the 1920s" (doctoral thesis, Teachers College, Columbia University, 1984).

CHAPTER 3: PATTERNS OF DIVERSITY

The shift in American attitudes during the twentieth century from an idea of conformity to a dominant Anglo-American Protestant *paideia* to an idea of a more variegated cultural pluralism is documented in Isaac B. Berkson, *Theories of Americanization: A Critical Study, with Special Reference to the Jewish Group* (New York: Teachers College, Columbia University, 1920); Milton M. Gordon, *Assimilation in American Life: The Role of Race, Religion, and National Origins* (New York: Oxford University Press, 1964); F. H. Matthews, "The Revolt Against Americanism: Cultural Pluralism and Cultural Relativism as an Ideology of Liberation," *Canadian Review of American Studies*, I (1970), 4–31; Allan Smith, "Metaphor and Nationality in North America," *Canadian Historical Review*, LI (1970), 247–275; Timothy L. Smith, "Religion and Ethnicity in America," *American Historical Review*, LXXXIII (1978), 1155–1185; and the articles on "Pluralism" by Michael Novak and Michael Walzer in Stephan Thernstrom, ed., *Harvard Encyclopedia of American Ethnic Groups* (Cambridge, Mass.: Harvard University Press, 1980).

The case for considering black American Protestantism separately from white American Protestantism is persuasively made by Robert T. Handy in "Negro Christianity and American Church Historiography," in Jerald C. Brauer, ed., *Reinterpretation in American Church History* (Chicago: University of Chicago Press, 1968), pp. 91–112. The classic works on the development of the black churches after the Civil War are W. E. Burghardt Du Bois, *The Negro Church* (Atlanta: Atlanta University Press, 1903); Carter G. Woodson, *The History of the Negro Church* (Washington, D.C.: The Associated Publishers, 1921); and E. Franklin Frazier, *The Negro Church in America* (Liverpool: Liverpool University Press, 1963). James M. McPherson *et al.*, *Blacks in America: Bibliographical Essays* (Garden City, N.Y.: Doubleday and Company, 1971) includes a useful bibliography on the black church, 1865–1915, on pp. 153–157. Richard D. McKinney, "The Black Church: Its Development and Recent Impact," *Harvard Theological Review*, LXIV (1971), 452–481, is a thoughtful review.

Robert C. Morris, *Reading, 'Riting, and Reconstruction: The Education of Freedmen in the South, 1861–1870* (Chicago: University of Chicago Press, 1981) is the most comprehensive account of the educational programs for the freed slaves; James M. McPherson, *The Struggle for Equality: Abolitionists and the Negro in the Civil War and Reconstruction* (Princeton, N.J.: Princeton University Press, 1964) and Leon F. Litwak, *Been in the Storm So Long: The Aftermath of Slavery* (New York: Alfred A. Knopf, 1979) place those programs in a rich context of Civil War and Reconstruction history. Joe M. Richardson, *Christian Reconstruction: The American Missionary Association and Southern Blacks, 1861–1890* (Athens: University of Georgia Press, 1986) is an excellent study of the educational work of the AMA with a splendid bibliography. Jacqueline Jones, *Soldiers of Light and Love: Northern Teachers and Georgia Blacks, 1865–1873* (Chapel Hill: University of North Carolina Press, 1980); Elizabeth Jacoway, *Yankee Missionaries in the South: The Penn School Experiment* (Baton Rouge: Louisiana State University Press, 1980); and James M. McPherson, *The Abolitionist Legacy: From Reconstruction to the NAACP* (Princeton, N.J.: Princeton University Press, 1975), and "The New Puritanism: Values and Goals of Freedmen's Education in America," in Lawrence Stone, ed., *The University in Society* (2 vols.; Princeton: Princeton University Press, 1974), II, 611–639, portray the teachers, the students, and the schools themselves. McPherson, *The Abolitionist Legacy;* Dwight Oliver Wendell Holmes, *The Evolution of the Negro College* (New York: Bureau of Publications, Teachers College, Columbia University, 1934); and Thomas Jesse Jones, *Negro Education: A Study of the Private and Higher Schools for Colored People in the United States* (2 vols.; U.S., Bureau of Education, Bulletin, 1916, Nos. 38–39; Washington, D.C.: Government Printing Office, 1917) document the rise of the black colleges; W. E. Burghardt Du Bois, ed., *The College-Bred Negro* (Atlanta: Atlanta University Press, 1900) discusses the black leadership that was largely produced by the black churches and colleges. Ellen Condliffe Lagemann, *The Politics of Knowledge: A History of the Carnegie Corporation of New York* (Middletown: Wesleyan University Press, forthcoming) sketches the context of the Jones survey, its kinship with the Flexner report on medical education, and the role of the philanthropic foundations in sponsoring it; Kenneth James King, *Pan-Africanism and Education: A Study of Race Philanthropy and Education in the Southern States of America and East Africa* (Oxford: Clarendon Press, 1971) sketches the export to Africa of American black colleges on the Hampton-Tuskegee model.

James D. Anderson, "The Hampton Model of Normal School Industrial Education, 1868–1900," in Vincent P. Franklin and James D. Anderson, eds., *New Perspectives on Black Educational History* (Boston: G. K. Hall and Company, 1978), pp. 61–98, sketches the long-standing debate among blacks over the adequacy of the industrial education model typified by Hampton and Tuskegee that was in part the context of the controversy between Booker T. Washington and W. E. B. Du Bois. Louis R. Harlan, *Booker T. Washington* (2 vols.; New York: Oxford University Press, 1972–1983) is the definitive biography; Louis R. Harlan and Raymond W. Smock, eds., *The Booker T. Washington Papers* (13 vols.; Urbana: University of Illinois Press, 1972–1984) is the authoritative collection. Francis L. Broderick, *W. E. B. Du Bois, Negro Leader in a Time of Crisis* (Stanford: Stanford University Press, 1959) and Elliott M. Rudwick, *W. E. B. Du Bois: Propagandist of the Negro Protest* (2d ed.; Philadelphia: University of Pennsylvania Press, 1968) are the best available biographies; Paul G. Partington, *W. E. B. Du Bois: A Bibliography of His*

Published Writings (rev. ed.; Whittier, Cal.: Paul G. Partington, 1979) is a useful guide to Du Bois's voluminous publications; W. E. B. Du Bois, *The Education of Black People: Ten Critiques, 1906–1960,* edited by Herbert Aptheker (Amherst: University of Massachusetts Press, 1973) is an excellent collection of Du Bois's writings on education. The largest collection of Du Bois papers, which is not wholly open to the public, is at the University of Massachusetts, Amherst. Patricia Watkins Romero, "Carter G. Woodson: A Biography" (doctoral thesis, Ohio State University, 1971) is the best available biography of the eminent black historian; Alfred Young, "The Educational Philosophies of Booker T. Washington and Carter G. Woodson: A Liberating Praxis" (doctoral thesis, Syracuse University, 1977) gives particular attention to Woodson's educational ideas.

Philip M. Hauser, "Demographic Factors in the Integration of the Negro," *Daedalus,* XCIV (1965), 847–877; T. Lynn Smith, "The Redistribution of the Negro Population of the United States, 1910–1960," *Journal of Negro History,* LI (1966), 155–173; George Groh, *The Black Migration* (New York: Weybright and Talley, 1972); and Florette Henri, *Black Migration: Movement North, 1900–1920* (Garden City, N.Y.: Anchor Press/Doubleday, 1975) explicate the great migrations of American blacks during the twentieth century. Frazier, *The Negro Church in America;* Arthur H. Fauset, *Black Gods of the Metropolis* (Philadelphia: University of Pennsylvania Press, 1944); C. Eric Lincoln, *The Black Church Since Frazier* (New York: Schocken Books, 1974); and Ida Rousseau Mukenge, *The Black Church in Urban America: A Case Study in Political Economy* (Lanham, Md.: University Press of America, 1983) discuss the black churches after World War I. Stephen B. Oates, *Let the Trumpet Sound: The Life of Martin Luther King, Jr.* (New York: Harper & Row, 1982); David J. Garrow, *Bearing the Cross: Martin Luther King, Jr., and the Southern Christian Leadership Conference* (New York: William Morrow, 1986); and Adam Fairclough, *To Redeem the Soul of America: The Southern Christian Leadership Conference and Martin Luther King, Jr.* (Athens: University of Georgia Press, 1987) are the best biographical studies of King. C. Eric Lincoln, *The Black Muslims in America* (rev. ed.; Boston: Beacon Press, 1973) is a useful analysis of the Black Muslims as a mass movement. Peter Goldman, *The Death and Life of Malcolm X* (New York: Harper & Row, 1973) is an incisive biography of Malcolm X; *The Autobiography of Malcolm X* (New York: Grove Press, 1964) is an American classic. Raymond L. Hall, *Black Separatism in the United States* (Hanover, N.H.: University Press of New England, 1978) provides a useful historical context for ideologies of black separatism, including that of the Black Muslims. The special role of the Highlander Folk School in the civil rights movement of the 1950's and 1960's is explicated in Aldon D. Morris, *The Origins of the Civil Rights Movement: Black Communities Organizing for Change* (New York: The Free Press, 1984). Frank Adams, *Unearthing Seeds of Fire: The Idea of Highlander* (Winston-Salem, N.C.: John F. Blair, Publisher, 1975) and John M. Glen, "On the Cutting Edge: A History of the Highlander Folk School, 1932–1962" (doctoral thesis, Vanderbilt University, 1985) are useful introductions to the work at Highlander. Clayborne Carson, *In Struggle: SNCC and the Black Awakening of the 1960s* (Cambridge, Mass.: Harvard University Press, 1981) explicates the views and tactics of the younger black separatists during the 1960's.

The dilemmas facing the historic black colleges during the post–World War II period are discussed in Earl J. McGrath, *The Predominantly Negro Colleges and*

Universities in Transition (New York: Bureau of Publications, Teachers College, Columbia University, 1965); Henry Allen Bullock, *A History of Negro Education in the South: From 1619 to the Present* (Cambridge, Mass.: Harvard University Press, 1967); Christopher Jencks and David Riesman, "The American Negro College," *Harvard Educational Review*, XXXVII (1967), 3–60, and Stephen J. Wright, Benjamin E. Mays, Hugh M. Gloster, Albert W. Dent, Christopher Jencks, and David Riesman, " 'The American Negro College': Four Responses and a Reply," *ibid.*, 451–468; "The Future of the Black Colleges," *Daedalus*, C (1971), 539–899; Frank Bowles, *Between Two Worlds: A Profile of Negro Higher Education* (New York: McGraw-Hill Publishing Company, 1971); and Charles V. Willie and Ronald R. Edmonds, eds., *Black Colleges in America: Challenge, Development, Survival* (New York: Teachers College Press, 1978).

I found John Tracy Ellis, *American Catholicism* (2d ed., rev.; Chicago: University of Chicago Press, 1969); James Hennesey, *American Catholics: A History of the Roman Catholic Community in the United States* (New York: Oxford University Press, 1981); and Jay P. Dolan, *The American Catholic Experience: A History from Colonial Times to the Present* (Garden City, N.Y.: Doubleday and Company, 1985) the best general histories of Roman Catholics and their churches in the United States. The Ellis volume has a discriminating bibliography; and the Hennesey and Dolan volumes have rich end notes. Gerald Shaughnessy, *Has the Immigrant Kept the Faith: A Study of Immigration and Catholic Growth in the United States, 1780–1920* and Hennesey, *American Catholics* have been my sources for Roman Catholic church membership statistics over the years. Philip Gleason, "Coming to Terms with American Catholic History," *Societas*, III (1973), 283–312, explicates the historiographical problems implicit in depicting the Americanization of the Roman Catholic Church in the United States.

John Bodnar, *The Transplanted: A History of Immigrants in Urban America* (Bloomington: Indiana University Press, 1985); Mason Wade, "The French Parish and Survivance in Nineteenth-Century New England," *Catholic Historical Review*, XXXVI (1950), 163–189; Richard M. Linkh, *American Catholicism and European Immigrants (1900–1924)* (New York: Center for Migration Studies, 1975); Randall M. Miller and Thomas D. Marsik, eds., *Immigrants and Religion in Urban America* (Philadelphia: Temple University Press, 1977); Philip Gleason, *The Conservative Reformers: German-American Catholics and the Social Order* (Notre Dame, Ind.: University of Notre Dame Press, 1968); and Silvano M. Tomasi and Madeline H. Engel, eds., *The Italian Experience in the United States* (New York: Center for Migration Studies, 1970) document the variety of alternative configurations of education Roman Catholics developed in order to preserve their faith. Neil G. McCluskey, ed., *Catholic Education in America* (New York: Bureau of Publications, Teachers College, Columbia University, 1964); Edward J. Power, *A History of Catholic Higher Education in the United States* (Milwaukee: The Bruce Publishing Company, 1958); Harold A. Buetow, *Of Singular Benefit: A History of Catholic Education in the United States* (New York: The Macmillan Company, 1970); Glen E. Gabert, Jr., "A History of the Roman Catholic Parochial School System in the United States: A Documentary Interpretation" (doctoral thesis, Loyola University of Chicago, 1971); and Karl Peter Ganss, "American Catholic Education in the 1960's: A Study of the Parochial School Debate" (doctoral thesis, Loyola University of Chicago, 1979) are useful sources for the development of Roman Catholic schools and colleges. Peter Guilday, ed., *The National Pastorals of the American Hierarchy, 1792–1919* (Westminster, Md.: The Newman Press, 1954) and *A History of the Councils of Baltimore (1791–1884)* (New York: The Macmillan Company, 1932); and Francis P. Cassidy, "Catholic Education in the Third Plenary Council of Baltimore," *Catholic Historical Review*, XXXIV (1948–49), 257–305, 414–436, explicate church policy as formulated by the hierarchy.

Jay P. Dolan, *The Immigrant Church: New York's Irish and German Catholics, 1815–1865* (Baltimore: Johns Hopkins University Press, 1975), and "Philadelphia and the German Catholic Community," in Miller and Marzik, eds., *Immigrants and Religion in Urban America*, pp. 69–83; Colman Barry, *The Catholic Church and the German Americans* (Milwaukee: The Bruce Publishing Company, 1953); Silvano M. Tomasi, *Piety and Power: The Role of the Italian Parishes in the New York Metropolitan Area, 1880–1930* (New York: Center for Migration Studies, 1975); and Peter d'A. Jones and Melvin G. Holli, eds., *Ethnic Chicago* (Grand Rapids, Mich.: William B. Eerdmans Publishing Company, 1981) illuminated my understanding of the issues involved in the demand for national parishes. On the conflict over pluralism, see John J. Meng, "Cahenslyism: The First Stage, 1883–1891," *Catholic Historical Review*, XXXI (1945–46), 380–413, and "Cahenslyism: The Second Chapter, 1891–1910," *ibid.*, XXXII (1946–47), 302–340, and Barry, *The Catholic Church and the German Americans*. On the conflict over Americanism, see Daniel F. Reilly, *The School Controversy (1891–1893)* (Washington, D.C.: The Catholic University of America Press, 1943). John Tracy Ellis, *The Life of James Cardinal Gibbons: Archbishop of Baltimore, 1834–1921* (2 vols.; Milwaukee: The Bruce Publishing Company, 1952) and James H. Moynihan, *The Life of Archbishop John Ireland* (New York: Harper & Brothers, 1953) are the definitive biographies. On the conflict over modernism, I found Robert D. Cross, *The Emergence of Liberal Catholicism in America* (Cambridge, Mass.: Harvard University Press, 1958) especially helpful.

Most of my data on the development of Roman Catholic configurations of education in Chicago were derived from Jones and Holli, eds., *Ethnic Chicago;* Humbert S. Nelli, *The Italians in Chicago, 1880–1930: A Study in Ethnic Mobility* (New York: Oxford University Press, 1970); and James W. Sanders, *The Education of an Urban Minority: Catholics in Chicago, 1833–1965* (New York: Oxford University Press, 1977). I found Edward R. Kantowicz, "Cardinal Mundelein of Chicago and the Shaping of Twentieth-Century American Catholicism," *Journal of American History*, LXVIII (1981–82), 52–68, especially helpful on George Cardinal Mundelein as a "consolidating bishop" in Chicago. And, on the debate among Roman Catholics concerning the intellectual quality and achievements of American Catholic education, I found Hennesey, *American Catholics*, chap. xx; John J. Kane, *Catholic-Protestant Conflicts in America* (Chicago: Henry Regnery Company, 1955); Thomas F. O'Dea, *American Catholic Dilemma: An Inquiry into the Intellectual Life* (New York: Sheed and Ward, 1958); and Andrew W. Greeley, "Why Catholic Higher Learning Is Lower," *National Catholic Reporter*, XIX (September 23, 1983), illuminating.

Nathan Glazer, *American Judaism* (2d ed., rev.; Chicago: University of Chicago Press, 1972); Henry L. Feingold, *Zion in America: The Jewish Experience from Colonial Times to the Present* (New York: Twayne Publishers, 1974); Arthur Goren's essay on the Jews in Thernstrom, ed., *Harvard Encyclopedia of American Ethnic Groups;* and Charles E. Silberman, *A Certain People: American Jews and Their Lives Today* (New York: Summit Books, 1985) are the best general histories of the Jewish communities in the United States and their synagogues and temples. The Glazer volume has a discriminating bibliography; the Feingold and Silberman volumes have rich end notes. Marc Lee Raphael, *Profiles in American Judaism: The Reform, Conservative, Orthodox, and Reconstructionist Traditions in Historical Perspective* (San Francisco: Harper & Row, 1984) is the best brief introduction to the diverse traditions of American Judaism. The essays in Jacob Rader Marcus and Abraham J. Peck, eds., *The American Rabbinate: A Century of Continuity and Change, 1883–1983* (Hoboken, N.J.: KTAV Publishing House, 1985) discuss the evolution of the rabbinate within each of the three major branches of American Judaism. Sidney Goldstein, "Jews in the United States: Perspectives from Demography," in Milton Himmelfarb and David Singer, eds., *American Jewish Year Book 1981* (Philadelphia: The Jewish Publication Society of America, 1980), pp. 3–59, and Calvin Goldscheider, "Demography of Jewish Americans: Research Findings, Issues, and Challenges," in Marshall Sklare, ed., *Understanding American Jewry* (New Brunswick, N.J.: Transaction Books, 1982), pp. 1–55, have been my principal sources for the Jewish population in the United States over the years.

Leon A. Jick, *The Americanization of the Synagogue, 1820–1870* (Hanover, N.H.: University Press of New England, 1976) is an incisive study of the early accommodation of the synagogue and its educational programs to the American situation during the first part of the nineteenth century. S. M. Dubnow's classic *History of the Jews in Russia and Poland from the Earliest Times until the Present Day* (3 vols.; Philadelphia: The Jewish Publication Society of America, 1916–1920) remains a valuable source of information on the communities from which most of the East European Jews who migrated to the United States between 1880 and 1920 came. Simon Kuznets, "Immigration of Russian Jews to the United States: Background and Structure," *Perspectives in American History*, IX (1975), 35–124, depicts the migration itself in detail. Louis Wirth, *The Ghetto* [1928] (reprint ed.; Chicago: University of Chicago Press, 1956); Moses Rischin, *The Promised City: New York's Jews, 1870–1914* (Cambridge, Mass.: Harvard University Press, 1962); Irving Howe, *World of Our Fathers: The Journey of the East European Jews to America and the Life They Found and Made* (New York: Harcourt, Brace, Jovanovich, 1976); Jeffrey S. Gurock, *When Harlem Was Jewish, 1870–1930* (New York: Columbia University Press, 1979); Irving Cutler, "The Jews of Chicago: From Shtetl to Suburb," in Jones and Holli, eds., *Ethnic Chicago*, pp. 40–79; Morris A. Gutstein, *A Priceless Heritage: The Epic Growth of Nineteenth Century Chicago Jewry* (New York: Bloch Publishing Company, 1953); Murray Friedman, ed., *Jewish Life in Philadelphia, 1830–1940* (Philadelphia: ISHI Publications, 1983); and Stuart E. Rosenberg, *The Jewish Community in Rochester, 1843–1925* (New York: Columbia University Press, 1954) provided data on the institutions Jewish communities established in the United States.

Eduardo L. Rauch, "Jewish Education in the United States, 1840–1920" (doctoral thesis, Harvard University, 1978) is the fullest account of the educative institutions established by the German Jews in the earlier nineteenth century, of the educative institutions established by the East European Jews in the later nineteenth century, and of the educative institutions established by the German Jews to help "Americanize" the East European Jews during the later nineteenth century. It is usefully complemented by Lloyd P. Gartner, ed., *Jewish Education in the United States: A Documentary History* (New York: Teachers College Press, 1969), which has an excellent critical bibliography; Alexander M. Dushkin, *Jewish Educa-*

tion in New York City (New York: Bureau of Jewish Education, 1918); Jonathan D. Sarna, "The American Jewish Response to Nineteenth-Century Christian Missions," *Journal of American History*, LXVIII (1981–82), 35–51; Morris Isaiah Berger, "The Settlement, The Immigrant and the Public School: A Study of the Influence of the Settlement Movement and the New Migration upon Public Education, 1900–1924" (doctoral thesis, Columbia University, 1956); S. P. Rudens, "A Half Century of Community Service: The Story of the New York Educational Alliance," in Harry Schneiderman, ed., *The American Jewish Year Book*, XLVI (1944–45), 73–86; Judah Pilch, ed., *A History of Jewish Education in the United States* (New York: American Association for Jewish Education, 1969); and Stephan F. Brumberg, *Going to America, Going to School: The Jewish Immigrant Public School Encounter in Turn-of-the-Century New York City* (New York: Praeger Publishers, 1986). Cyrus Adler, ed., *The Jewish Theological Seminary of America* (New York: The Jewish Theological Seminary of America, 1939), while celebratory, is a good source of information on the founding and early years of the Seminary; Norman Bentwich, *Solomon Schechter: A Biography* (Philadelphia: The Jewish Publication Society of America, 1938) and Abraham A. Newman, *Cyrus Adler: A Biographical Sketch* (New York: The American Jewish Committee, 1942) are also useful.

Berkson, *Theories of Americanization* offers insight into the debates within the early-twentieth-century Jewish community concerning assimilation. I also relied upon Arthur A. Goren, *New York Jews and the Quest for Community: The Kehillah Experiment, 1908–1922* (New York: Columbia University Press, 1970), which is a masterful study. Norman Bentwich, *For Zion's Sake: A Biography of Judah L. Magnes* (Philadelphia: The Jewish Publication Society of America, 1954) is a useful complement, as are Nathan H. Winter, *Jewish Education in a Pluralist Society: Samson Benderley and Jewish Education in the United States* (New York: New York University Press, 1966) and the several articles in the Summer, 1949, issue of *Jewish Education;* Ira Eisenstein and Eugene Kohn, eds., *Mordecai M. Kaplan: An Evaluation* (New York: Jewish Reconstructionist Foundation, 1952); and Alexander M. Dushkin, *Living Bridges: Memoirs of an Educator* (Jerusalem: Keter Publishing House, 1975).

Deborah Dash Moore, *At Home in America: Second Generation New York Jews* (New York: Columbia University Press, 1981) and Sidney Goldstein and Calvin Goldscheider, *Jewish Americans: Three Generations in a Jewish Community* (Englewood Cliffs, N.J.: Prentice-Hall, 1968) describe the generational changes in the Jewish communities of New York City and Providence. Herbert J. Gans, "The Origin and Growth of a Jewish Community in the Suburbs: A Study of the Jews of Park Forest," in Marshall Sklare, ed., *The Jews* (Glencoe, Ill.: The Free Press, 1958) and Marshall Sklare, *Jewish Identity on the Suburban Frontier* (2nd ed.; Chicago: University of Chicago Press, 1979) describe the suburbanization of American Jewish communities in the post–World War II era. Solomon Poll, *The Hasidic Community of Williamsburg* (Glencoe, Ill.: The Free Press, 1962) is a revealing study of an ultra-orthodox Jewish community. Marshall Sklare, *America's Jews* (New York: Random House, 1971) and Silberman, *A Certain People* informed my understanding of the situation of post–World War II American Jews.

I derived the concept of the "new ethnoreligiosity" of the post–World War II era from Gerhard Lenski, *The Religious Factor: A Sociological Study of Religion's Impact on Politics, Economics, and Family Life* (Garden City, N.Y.: Doubleday and Company, 1961); Nathan Glazer and Daniel Patrick Moynihan, *Beyond the Melting*

Pot: The Negroes, Puerto Ricans, Jews, Italians, and Irish of New York City (Cambridge, Mass.: The M.I.T. Press and Harvard University Press, 1963); Nathan Glazer and Daniel P. Moynihan, eds., *Ethnicity: Theory and Experience* (Cambridge, Mass.: Harvard University Press, 1975); Smith, "Religion and Ethnicity in America"; and Thernstrom, ed., *Harvard Encyclopedia of American Ethnic Groups.*

INTRODUCTION TO PART II: THE PROGRESSIVE NATION

Rush Welter, *Popular Education and Democratic Thought in America* (New York: Columbia University Press, 1962) remains the most incisive work on the special role education has played in American politics and political thought. I dealt with Alexis de Tocqueville's understanding of the relationship between American education and American democracy in *American Education: The National Experience, 1783–1876* (New York: Harper & Row, 1980), with appropriate references in the bibliography there. H. A. L. Fisher, *James Bryce* (2 vols.; New York: The Macmillan Company, 1927), which is still the definitive biography, includes a substantial discussion of Bryce's political ideas and of his experience in the United States. Edmund Ions, *James Bryce and American Democracy* (New York: Humanities Press, 1970) provides excellent context for Bryce's *The American Commonwealth.* John L. Thomas, *Alternative America: Henry George, Edward Bellamy, Henry Demarest Lloyd, and the Adversary Tradition* (Cambridge, Mass.: Harvard University Press, 1983) is the best recent commentary on the principal American utopian thinkers of the later nineteenth century. Arthur Lipow, *Authoritarian Socialism in America: Edward Bellamy and the Nationalist Movement* (Berkeley: University of California Press, 1982) is an incisive analysis of Bellamy's writings, whether or not one wholly concurs in Lipow's mordant criticisms. Both the Thomas study and the Lipow monograph have excellent bibliographical references.

There has been an outpouring in recent years of writings reappraising the meaning and legacy of American progressivism, especially since the publication of Peter G. Filene's stimulating essay "An Obituary for 'the Progressive Movement,' " *American Quarterly*, XXII (1970), 20–34. Among those writings, I have found most illuminating in connection with my own interpretation of the progressive tradition in American education Robert H. Wiebe, *The Search for Order, 1877–1920* (New York: Hill and Wang, 1967); Clyde Griffen, "The Progressive Ethos," in Stanley Coben and Lorman Ratner, eds., *The Development of an American Culture* (Englewood Cliffs, N.J.: Prentice-Hall, 1970), pp. 120–149; John D. Buenker, John C. Burnham, and Robert M. Crunden, *Progressivism* (Cambridge, Mass.: Schenkman Publishing Company, 1977); and Robert M. Crunden, *Ministers of Reform: The Progressives' Achievement in American Civilization, 1889–1920* (New York: Basic Books, 1982). James T. Kloppenberg, *Uncertain Victory: Social Democracy and Progressivism in European and American Thought, 1870–1920* (New York: Oxford University Press, 1986) places American progressive thought in a transatlantic context.

CHAPTER 4: MODES OF PROGRESSIVISM

A modern biography of William Torrey Harris is much needed; meanwhile, Kurt F. Leidecker, *Yankee Teacher: The Life of William Torrey Harris* (New York: The Philosophical Library, 1946) is the best biography available. William H. Goetzmann, ed., *The American Hegelians: An Intellectual Episode in the History of Western America* (New York: Alfred A. Knopf, 1973) is the best recent interpretation of the St. Louis movement in philosophy and education; it profoundly affected my view of William T. Harris. Henry A. Pochmann, *German Culture in America, 1600–1900: Philosophical and Literary Influences* (Madison: University of Wisconsin Press, 1961) and *New England Transcendentalism and St. Louis Hegelianism: Phases in the History of American Idealism* (Philadelphia: Carl Schurz Memorial Foundation, 1948) are excellent complements to the Goetzmann anthology. Elizabeth Flower and Murray G. Murphy, *A History of Philosophy in America* (2 vols.; New York: Capricorn Books, 1977) includes an incisive discussion of Harris's contribution. Brian Holmes, "Some Writings of William Torrey Harris," *British Journal of Educational Studies*, V (1956–57), 47–66, remains the best general discussion of Harris's educational ideas. Henry Ridgely Evans, "A List of the Writings of William Torrey Harris," in U.S., *Report of the Commissioner of Education, 1907* (2 vols.; Washington, D.C.: Government Printing Office, 1908), I, 37–72, is comprehensive, though far from complete. The principal collection of Harris papers is at the Library of Congress.

George Dykhuizen, *The Life and Mind of John Dewey* (Carbondale: Southern Illinois University Press, 1973) is the best available biography; it is usefully complemented by Neil Coughlan, *Young John Dewey: An Essay in American Intellectual History* (Chicago: University of Chicago Press, 1975) and Willinda Savage, "The Evolution of John Dewey's Philosophy of Experimentalism as Developed at the University of Michigan" (doctoral thesis, University of Michigan, 1950). Milton Halsey Thomas, *John Dewey: A Centennial Bibliography* (Chicago: University of Chicago Press, 1962) is the most complete listing of Dewey's published writings, and includes an ample list of published writings about Dewey; with respect to the latter, it is usefully complemented by Jo Ann Boydston and Kathleen Poulos, eds., *Checklist of Writings about John Dewey, 1887–1977* (2d ed.; Carbondale: Southern Illinois University Press, 1978). Darnell Rucker, *The Chicago Pragmatists* (Minneapolis: University of Minnesota Press, 1969) places Dewey's early work in its intellectual context. I found Robert Brett Westbrook, "John Dewey and American Democracy" (doctoral thesis, Stanford University, 1980) an especially incisive analysis of Dewey's political writings. Brian Hendley, *Dewey, Russell, Whitehead: Philosophers as Educators* (Carbondale: Southern Illinois University Press, 1986) includes an excellent discussion of the theory and practice of the Laboratory School at the University of Chicago during the Dewey era there. And Steven M. Cahn, ed., *New Studies in the Philosophy of John Dewey* (Hanover, N.H.: University Press of New England, 1977) presents thoughtful critical reviews, as do the relevant essays in the Spring and Winter, 1975, issues of the *History of Education Quarterly*, and Walter Feinberg, "Progressive Education and Social Planning," *Teachers College Record*, LXXIII (1971–72), 486–505, and *Reason and Rhetoric: The Intellectual Foundations of 20th Century Liberal Educational Policy* (New York: John Wiley and Sons, 1975). The three series of Dewey's published works that have been issuing from the Southern Illinois Press since 1969, under the superb editorship of Jo Ann Boydston, have been and will continue to be the definitive editions; they also carry informed and incisive introductions. The principal collection of Dewey papers is at the Center for Dewey Studies at Southern Illinois University.

I have discussed the references on Jane Addams in the context of the social settlement movement on p. 693 *supra.*

Ronald Steel, *Walter Lippmann and the Twentieth Century* (Boston: Little, Brown and Company, 1980) is the fullest available biography. It does less with Lippmann's ideas than one might have hoped and is usefully complemented by Charles Wellborn, *Twentieth Century Pilgrimage: Walter Lippmann and the Public Philosophy* (Baton Rouge: Louisiana State University Press, 1969); Larry L. Adams, *Walter Lippmann* (Boston: Trayne Publishers, 1977); Charles Forcey, *The Crossroads of Liberalism: Croly, Weyl, Lippmann, and the Progressive Era, 1900–1925* (New York: Oxford University Press, 1961); Marquis Childs and James Reston, eds., *Walter Lippmann and His Times* (New York: Harcourt, Brace and Company, 1959); David Weingast, *Walter Lippmann: A Study in Personal Journalism* (New Brunswick, N.J.: Rutgers University Press, 1949), and David Craig Ramsay, "Community and Authority in the Political Thought of Walter Lippmann" (doctoral thesis, University of Michigan, 1979). The Steel volume includes an excellent bibliography of Lippmann's books and of books about Lippmann. The bibliography of the Ramsay thesis includes a listing of other theses about Lippmann on pp. 168–171. The principal collection of Lippmann papers is at Yale University.

C. A. Bowers, *The Progressive Educator and the Depression: The Radical Years* (New York: Random House, 1969) is the most comprehensive study of the *Social Frontier* and its leading editors and authors. There is no satisfactory biography of George S. Counts; the chapter on his life in Robert J. Havighurst, ed., *Leaders in American Education* (Chicago: University of Chicago Press, 1971), which includes an autobiographical sketch and a biographical commentary by Raymond E. Callahan, present the fullest array of data. Gerald L. Gutek, *The Educational Theory of George S. Counts* (Columbus: Ohio State University Press, 1970) and *George S. Counts and American Civilization: The Educator as Social Theorist* (Mercer, Ga.: Mercer University Press, 1984); and Bruce A. Romanish, "An Historical Analysis of the Educational Ideas and Career of George S. Counts" (doctoral thesis, Pennsylvania State University, 1980) are useful discussions of Counts's ideas. The Romanish work includes a full, but not complete, bibliography of Counts's published writings. The principal collection of Counts papers is at Southern Illinois University. Paul M. Buhle, "Marxism in the United States, 1900–1940" (doctoral thesis, University of Wisconsin-Madison, 1975) and Robert W. Iverson, *The Communists and the Schools* (New York: Harcourt, Brace and Company, 1959) provide context for the American Communist analysis of American education during the 1930's; Zalmen Slesinger, *Education and the Class Struggle: A Critical Examination of the Liberal Educator's Program for Social Reconstruction* (New York: Covici-Friede, Publishers, 1937) and Howard David Langford, *Education and the Social Conflict* (New York: The Macmillan Company, 1936) are the leading American Communist treatises. Martin Carnoy, "Education, Economy and the State," in Michael W. Apple, ed., *Cultural and Economic Reproduction in Education: Essays on Class, Ideology and the State* (London: Routledge and Kegan Paul, 1982), pp. 79–126, is an incisive review of more recent Marxian analyses of American education. Clarence Karier, "The Neo-Humanist Protest in American Education, 1890–1930" (doctoral thesis, University of Wisconsin-Madison, 1960); Michael V. Harris, *Five Counterrevolutionists in Higher Education: Irving Babbitt, Albert J. Nock, Abraham Flexner, Robert Maynard Hutchins, Alexander Meiklejohn* (Corvallis: Oregon State University Press, 1970);

Amy Apfel Kass, "Radical Conservatives for a Liberal Education" (doctoral thesis, The Johns Hopkins University, 1973); and J. David Hoeveler, Jr., *The New Humanism: A Critique of Modern America, 1900–1940* (Charlottesville: University Press of Virginia, 1977) are valuable expositions of humanist and intellectualist views on twentieth-century American culture and education. Mary Ann Dzuback, "Robert M. Hutchins, 1899–1977: Portrait of an Educator" (doctoral thesis, Columbia University, 1987) is an able study of Hutchins's educational ideas, with a comprehensive bibliography. David Tyack, Robert Lowe, and Elisabeth Hansot, *Public Schools in Hard Times: The Great Depression and Recent Years* (Cambridge, Mass.: Harvard University Press, 1984) presents in rich detail the actual predicament of the schools that Counts and his critics saw themselves as addressing.

Ellen Condliffe Lagemann, "A Philanthropic Foundation at Work: Myrdal's *American Dilemma* and the Carnegie Corporation," *Minerva*, XXXV (1987), 441–470; Walter A. Jackson, "The Making of a Social Science Classic: Gunnar Myrdal's *An American Dilemma,*" *Perspectives in American History*, n.s., II (1985), 221–267; and David W. Southern, *Gunnar Myrdal and Black-White Relations: The Use and Abuse of* An American Dilemma, *1944–1969* (Baton Rouge: Louisiana State University Press, 1987) provide excellent background for an understanding of Gunnar Myrdal, *An American Dilemma: The Negro Problem and Modern Democracy* (New York: Harper & Brothers, 1944). Charles Flint Kellogg, *NAACP: A History of the National Association for the Advancement of Colored People,* Volume I (1909–1920) (Baltimore: Johns Hopkins Press, 1967) chronicles the early years of the Association. Genna Rae McNeil, "To Meet the Group Needs: The Transformation of Howard University School of Law, 1920–1935," in Vincent P. Franklin and James D. Anderson, eds., *New Perspectives on Black Educational History* (Boston: G.K. Hall and Company, 1978), pp. 149–207; Richard Kluger, *Simple Justice: The History of* Brown v. Board of Education *and Black America's Struggle for Equality* (New York: Alfred A. Knopf, 1976); and Mark V. Tushnet, *The NAACP's Legal Strategy Against Segregated Education, 1925–1950* (Chapel Hill: University of North Carolina Press, 1987) sketch the context of the NAACP's decision to challenge the Plessy doctrine in the courts; *Simple Justice* then goes on to document the legal struggle from *Missouri ex rel. Gaines v. Canada* (1938) to *Brown v. Board of Education* (1954, 1955). J. Harvie Wilkinson III, *From Brown to Bakke: The Supreme Court and School Integration, 1954–1978* (New York: Oxford University Press, 1979) documents the legal struggle down to *Regents of the University of California v. Bakke* (1978). The articles that constitute "The Courts, Social Science, and School Desegregation" in the Winter and Spring, 1975, issues of *Law and Contemporary Problems* brilliantly explicate the role that social science data and argument played in the school desegregation cases. Randall W. Bland, *Private Pressure on Public Law: The Legal Career of Justice Thurgood Marshall* (Port Washington, N.Y.: The Kennikat Press, 1973) is a brief biography of Marshall; Nat Hentoff, "The Integrationist," *New Yorker*, LVIII (August 23, 1982), 37–73, is a brief biography of Kenneth B. Clark. Clark's treatise *Dark Ghetto: Dilemmas of Social Power* (New York: Harper & Row, 1965), appropriately, has a foreword by Gunnar Myrdal.

Jane Howard, *Margaret Mead: A Life* (New York: Simon and Schuster, 1984) is the best available biography; Mary Catherine Bateson, *With a Daughter's Eye: A Memoir of Margaret Mead and Gregory Bateson* (New York: William Morrow, 1984) is a sensitive portrayal from the special perspective of a daughter who became an anthropologist in her own right; Margaret Mead, *Blackberry Winter: My Earlier Years* (New York: Simon and Schuster, 1972) is a superb autobiography. The articles that constitute the June, 1980, issue of *American Anthropologist* provide the best overall review of Mead's contribution. Joan Gordon, ed., *Margaret Mead: The Complete Bibliography, 1925–1973* (The Hague: Mouton, 1976) is the most comprehensive bibliography of Mead's published writings; Howard includes a selective bibliography in her biography. The appearance of Derek Freeman, *Margaret Mead and Samoa: The Making and Unmaking of an Anthropological Myth* (Cambridge, Mass.: Harvard University Press, 1983) created a storm of controversy over Mead's work. Howard includes in her biography a listing of the early articles that appear in the Mead-Freeman controversy. The most incisive rebuttals to Freeman are Robert I. Levy, "The Attack on Mead," *Science*, CCXX (1983), 829–832; Bonnie A. Nardi, "The Height of Her Powers: Margaret Mead's Samoa," *Feminist Studies*, X (1984), 323–337; and Roy A. Rappaport, "Desecrating the Holy Woman: Derek Freeman's Attack on Margaret Mead," *American Scholar*, LV (1986), 313–347. Lowell D. Holmes, *Quest for the Real Samoa: Assessing the Mead-Freeman Debate* (South Hadley, Mass.: Bergin and Garvey Publishers, 1986) reviews the controversy. The principal collection of Mead papers is at the Library of Congress.

CHAPTER 5: PROGRESSIVE SCHOOL MOVEMENTS

I advanced an interpretation of the progressive school reform movement a quarter-century ago in *The Transformation of the School: Progressivism in American Education, 1876–1957* (New York: Alfred A. Knopf, 1961). Since that time the nature and character of that movement have been matters of lively inquiry and debate on the part of historians of education. Michael B. Katz pointed to the wide gaps between the rhetoric and the reality of the movement, and particularly to what he saw as the effort by Dewey, Addams, and other progressive reformers to "foster modes of social control appropriate to a complex urban environment" in *Class, Bureaucracy, and Schools: The Illusion of Educational Change in America* (New York: Praeger Publishers, 1971). Clarence J. Karier, Paul C. Violas, and Joel Spring sharpened that criticism in *Roots of Crisis: American Education in the Twentieth Century* (Chicago: Rand McNally and Company, 1973). David B. Tyack analyzed the various elements of the movement and the differences among them in *The One Best System: A History of American Urban Education* (Cambridge, Mass.: Harvard University Press, 1974), distinguishing among those he saw as "administrative progressives," "pedagogical progressives," "libertarian" progressives, and "social reconstructivist" progressives. Samuel Bowles and Herbert Gintis portrayed the movement as essentially an effort to proletarianize the new immigrants from southeastern Europe and ready them for service in the American capitalist economy in *Schooling in Capitalist America: Educational Reform and the Contradictions of Economic Life* (New York: Basic Books, 1976). More recently, Julia Wrigley, focusing on Chicago, sought to demonstrate the genuine class politics that was at the heart of the movement in *Class Politics and Public Schools: Chicago, 1900–1950* (New Brunswick, N.J.: Rutgers University Press, 1982). David John Hogan argued along many of the same lines in *Class and Reform: School and Society in Chicago, 1880–1930* (Philadelphia: University of Pennsylvania Press, 1985), contending that the school reform movement was neither liberating nor constraining at its heart but rather a series of developments that converted the schools into adjuncts of the market economy. Paul E. Peterson, drawing upon data from Chicago, Atlanta, and San Francisco, argued that the movement was dominated by class issues from 1880 to 1930 and then by racial and ethnic issues from 1950 to 1980 in *The Politics of School Reform, 1870–1940* (Chicago: University of Chicago Press, 1985). Ira Katznelson and Margaret Weir, building on the work of Wrigley and Peterson, lamented what they saw as the role of race, class, and ethnic conflict in the decline of public support for equal and universal schooling in *Schooling for All: Class, Race, and the Decline of the Democratic Ideal* (New York: Basic Books, 1985). And William J. Reese, basing his argument on comparative studies of Kansas City (Missouri), Milwaukee, Rochester, and Toledo, documented the local character of school reform and its consequent political and educational variegation in *Power and the Promise of School Reform: Grass-Roots Movements During the Progressive Era* (Boston: Routledge and Kegan Paul, 1986). I have reviewed this literature with interest, followed its leads to the primary sources, and attempted to take account of it in formulating my own interpretations. In general the recent work has made me ever more aware of the political issues and conflicts among individuals and groups who thought of themselves as progressive and who were thought of by at least some others as progressive. In addition, I have become increasingly aware of the mediating power of individual agency as people have participated in educational institutions designed for them by others; and, in this respect, the arguments advanced by Stephen Hardy and Alan G. Ingham in "Games, Structures, and Agency: Historians on the American Play Movement," *Journal of Social History,* XVII (1983–84), 285–301, while addressed explicitly to the historiography of the progressive recreation movement, have been relevant theoretically.

Eric Foner, "Reconstruction Revisited," in Stanley I. Kutler and Stanley N. Katz, eds., *The Promise of American History: Progress and Prospects* (Baltimore: Johns Hopkins University Press, 1982), pp. 82–100—the volume is a reprint of the December, 1982, issue of *Reviews in American History*—is an incisive review of the recent historiography of Reconstruction. I found John Hope Franklin, *Reconstruction after the Civil War* (Chicago: University of Chicago Press, 1961); Kenneth M. Stampp, *The Era of Reconstruction* (New York: Alfred A. Knopf, 1965); David Donald, *Charles Sumner and the Rights of Man* (New York: Alfred A. Knopf, 1970); Joe Gray Taylor, *Louisiana Reconstructed, 1863–1877* (Baton Rouge: Louisiana State University Press, 1974); Leon F. Litwak, *Been in the Storm So Long: The Aftermath of Slavery* (New York: Alfred A. Knopf, 1979); Otto H. Olsen, ed., *Reconstruction and Redemption in the South* (Baton Rouge: Louisiana State University Press, 1980); Eric Foner, *Nothing but Freedom: Emancipation and Its Legacy* (Baton Rouge: Louisiana State University Press, 1983); and Joel Williamson, *The Crucible of Race: Black-White Relations in the American South Since Emancipation* (New York: Oxford University Press, 1984) especially useful with respect to the context of Reconstruction. I found Alfred H. Kelly, "The Congressional Controversy over School Segregation, 1867–1875," *American Historical Review,* LXIV (1958–59), 537–563; Elisabeth Joan Doyle, "Nurseries of Treason: Schools in Occupied New Orleans," *Journal of Southern History,* XXVI (1960), 161–179; Louis R. Harlan, "Desegregation in New Orleans Public Schools during Reconstruction," *American Historical Review,* LXVII (1961–62), 663–675; William Preston Vaughn, *Schools for All: The Blacks and Public Education in the South, 1865–1877* (Lexington: University Press of Kentucky, 1974); Ronald E. Butchart, *Northern Schools, Southern Blacks, and*

Reconstruction: Freedmen's Education, 1862–75 (Westport, Conn.: Greenwood Press, 1980); James D. Anderson, "Ex-Slaves and the Rise of Universal Education in the New South, 1860–1880," in Ronald K. Goodenow and Arthur O. White, eds., *Education and the Rise of the New South* (Boston: G. K. Hall and Company, 1981), pp. 1–25; Robert C. Morris, *Reading, 'Riting, and Reconstruction: The Education of Freedmen in the South, 1861–1870* (Chicago: University of Chicago Press, 1981); Richard N. Current, *Northernizing the South* (Athens: University of Georgia Press, 1983); and David Tyack and Robert Lowe, "The Constitutional Moment: Reconstruction and Black Education in the South," *American Journal of Education*, XCIV (1985–86), 236–256 especially useful with respect to Reconstruction schooling.

C. Vann Woodward, *Origins of the New South, 1877–1913* (rev. ed.; Baton Rouge: Louisiana State University Press, 1971) remains the classic work; it is usefully complemented by Dewey W. Grantham, *Southern Progressivism: The Reconciliation of Progress and Tradition* (Knoxville: University of Tennessee Press, 1983). Charles William Dabney, *Universal Education in the South* (2 vols.; Chapel Hill: University of North Carolina Press, 1936), though much out of date and opaque with respect to issues of race, remains a storehouse of information. Among the more recent works on the role of progressive school reform in the program for a New South, I found Louis R. Harlan, *Separate and Unequal: Public School Campaigns and Racism in the Southern Seaboard States, 1901–1915* (Chapel Hill: University of North Carolina Carolina Press, 1958); John Hope Franklin, "Jim Crow Goes to School: The Genesis of Legal Segregation in Southern Schools," *South Atlantic Quarterly*, LVIII (1959), 225–235; and the several essays in Goodenow and White, eds., *Education and the Rise of the New South* especially valuable for my purposes. John Milton Cooper, Jr., *Walter Hines Page: The Southerner as American, 1855–1918* (Chapel Hill: University of North Carolina Press, 1977) is the best available biography of Page. H. Leon Prather, Sr., *Resurgent Politics and Educational Progressivism in the New South: North Carolina, 1890–1913* (Cranbury, N.J.: Associated University Presses, 1979) and William A. Link, *A Hard Country and a Lonely Place: Schooling, Society, and Reform in Rural Virginia, 1870–1920* (Chapel Hill: University of North Carolina Press, 1986) are excellent studies of progressive school reform in particular states. James D. Anderson, "Philanthropic Control over Private Black Higher Education," in Robert F. Arnove, ed., *Philanthropy and Cultural Imperialism: The Foundations at Home and Abroad* (Bloomington: Indiana University Press, 1982), pp. 146–177; and Kenneth James King, *Pan-Africanism and Education: A Study of Race Philanthropy and Education in the Southern States of America and East Africa* (Oxford: Clarendon Press, 1971) document the role of the philanthropic foundations in the diffusion of black education on the Hampton-Tuskegee model through the American South and abroad. Many of the references cited on pp. 699–700 *supra* are relevant here.

I dealt at length in *The Transformation of the School* with the late nineteenth- and early twentieth-century effort to vocationalize the schools and to convert them into social centers. More recently, those themes have been further developed in Marvin Lazerson, *Origins of the Urban School: Public Education in Massachusetts, 1870–1915* (Cambridge, Mass.: Harvard University Press, 1971); Marvin Lazerson and W. Norton Grubb, ed., *American Education and Vocationalism: A Documentary History* (New York: Teachers College Press, 1974); Arthur G. Wirth, *Education in the Technological Society: The Vocational-Liberal Studies Controversy in the Early Twentieth*

Century (Scranton, Pa.: Intext Educational Publishers, 1972); John Leslie Rury, "Women, Cities and Schools: Education and the Development of an Urban Female Labor Force, 1890–1930" (doctoral thesis, University of Wisconsin-Madison, 1982); Edward W. Stevens, Jr., "Social Centers, Politics, and Social Efficiency in the Progressive Era," *History of Education Quarterly,* XII (1972), 16–33; Lawrence A. Finfer, "Leisure as Social Work in the Urban Community: The Progressive Recreation Movement, 1890–1920" (doctoral thesis, Michigan State University, 1974); William L. Bowers, *The Country Life Movement in America, 1900–1920* (Port Washington, N.Y.: Kennikat Press, 1974); Joel Morton Roitman, "The Progressive Movement: Education and Americanization" (doctoral thesis, University of Cincinnati, 1981); and Reese, *Power and the Promise of School Reform.* The effort during that same era to remove the school from politics—or rather, to create a different politics of schooling—is described in William A. Bullough, *Cities and Schools in the Gilded Age: The Evolution of an Urban Institution* (Port Washington, N.Y.: Kennikat Press, 1974); Tyack, *The One Best System;* and Peterson, *The Politics of School Reform.* The effort to make schooling scientific is portrayed in Geraldine Jonçich, *The Sane Positivist: A Biography of Edward L. Thorndike* (Middletown: Wesleyan University Press, 1968); Dorothy Ross, *G. Stanley Hall: The Psychologist as Prophet* (Chicago: University of Chicago Press, 1972); and Patrick Suppes, ed., *Impact of Research on Education: Some Case Studies* (Washington, D.C.: National Academy of Education, 1978).

Leonard Glenn Smith, "A History of the United States Office of Education, 1867–1967" (doctoral thesis, University of Oklahoma, 1967) and Donald R. Warren, *To Enforce Education: A History of the Founding Years of the United States Office of Education* (Detroit: Wayne State University Press, 1974) provided context for my argument concerning the Office of Education as a disseminator of reformist ideas. I documented some of the variegation of progressive school reform in *The Transformation of the School.* That variegation has been further documented in Patricia Albjerg Graham, *Community and Class in American Education, 1865–1918* (New York: John Wiley & Sons, 1974); Diane Ravitch, *The Troubled Crusade: American Education, 1945–1980* (New York: Basic Books, 1983); Peterson, *The Politics of School Reform;* and Reese, *Power and the Promise of School Reform.* I also argued the pervasive influence of the progressive school reform movement in *The Transformation of the School.* In the period since, Arthur Zilversmit, "The Failure of Progressive Education, 1920–1940," in Lawrence Stone, ed., *Schooling and Society: Studies in the History of Education* (Baltimore: Johns Hopkins University Press, 1976); Thomas Joseph Kaplan, "From Theory to Practice in American Educational Reform, 1900–1925" (doctoral thesis, University of Wisconsin-Madison, 1979); Larry Cuban, *How Teachers Taught: Constancy and Change in American Classrooms, 1890–1980* (New York: Longman, 1984); and Michael W. Sedlak and Steven Schlossman, "The Public School and Social Services: Reassessing the Progressive Legacy," *Educational Theory,* XXXV (1985), 371–383, have argued that that influence was less profound. John M. Ralph, "Determinants of Primary and Secondary Educational Expansion in the United States, 1870–1970" (doctoral thesis, Johns Hopkins University, 1978) is an excellent documentation and discussion of the rise in school enrollments during the century following 1870; John L. Rury, "American School Enrolment in the Progressive Era: An Interpretive Inquiry," *History of Education,* XIV (1985), 49–67, concentrates on regional differences between 1890 and 1930; John W. Meyer, David Tyack, Joane Nagel, and Audri Gordon, "Public Education as Nation-Building in America: Enrollments and Bureaucratization in the American States, 1870–1930," *American Journal of Sociology*, LXXXV (1979–80), 591–613, places the school enrollment rise in a world context. Tyack, *The One Best System*, and David B. Tyack and Elisabeth Hansot, *Managers of Virtue: Public School Leadership in America, 1920–1980* (New York: Basic Books, 1982) describe the rise of systematization, and of a managerial class, in American public school affairs.

The phenomenon of curricular differentiation in relation to race, ethnicity, class, gender, and so-called intelligence is documented in George Sylvester Counts's classic study *The Selective Character of American Secondary Education* (Chicago: University of Chicago, 1922), as well as in Edward A. Krug, *The Shaping of the American High School* (New York: Harper & Row, 1964) and *The Shaping of the American High School, 1920–1941* (Madison: University of Wisconsin Press, 1972); Harlan, *Separate and Unequal;* David Martin Ment, "Racial Segregation in the Public Schools of New England and New York, 1840–1940" (doctoral thesis, Columbia University, 1975); Meyer Weinberg, *A Chance to Learn: The History of Race and Education in the United States* (Cambridge: Cambridge University Press, 1977); Judy Jolley Mohraz, *The Separate Problem: Case Studies of Black Education in the North, 1900–1930* (Westport, Conn.: Greenwood Press, 1979); Guadelupe San Miguel, Jr., "From a Dual to a Tri-Partite School System: The Origins and Development of Educational Segregation in Corpus Christi, Texas," *Integrateducation*, XVII, No. 5–6 (September–October, 1979), 27–38, and *"Let Them All Take Heed": Mexican-Americans and the Campaign for Educational Equality, 1929–1981* (Austin: University of Texas Press, 1987); and Joel Perlmann, "Curriculum and Tracking in the Transformation of the American High School: Providence, R.I., 1880–1930," *Journal of Social History*, XIX (1985–86), 29–55. Richard Rubinson, "Class Formation, Politics, and Institution: Schooling in the United States," *American Journal of Sociology*, XCLL (1986–87), 519–548, advances a thoughtful set of counterarguments concerning the equalitarianism implicit in the American system of common schools and comprehensive high schools. Philip H. Du Bois, *A History of Psychological Testing* (Boston: Allyn and Bacon, 1970) traces the development of various kinds of psychological tests; Paul Davis Chapman, "Schools as Sorters: Lewis M. Terman and the Intelligence Testing Movement, 1890–1930" (doctoral thesis, Stanford University, 1979) stresses the relationship between testing and tracking. Wrigley, *Class Politics and Public Schools;* Peterson, *The Politics of School Reform;* and Hogan, *Class and Reform* portray the conflicts between business and labor groups in the politics of public schooling. Diane Ravitch, *The Great School Wars, New York City, 1805–1973: A History of the Public Schools as Battlefield of Social Change* (New York: Basic Books, 1974) and Raymond A. Mohl, "Schools, Politics, and Riots: The Gary Plan in New York City 1914–1917," *Paedagogica Historica*, XV (1975), 39–72, portray the battle over the Gary Plan in New York City. William Joseph Maxwell, "Frances Kellor in the Progressive Era: A Case Study in the Professionalization of Reform" (doctoral thesis, Teachers College, Columbia University, 1968); Robert A. Carlson, *The Quest for Conformity: Americanization Through Education* (New York: John Wiley & Sons, 1975); and John F. McClymer, "The Federal Government and the Americanization Movement, 1915–1924," *Prologue*, X (1978), 23–41, describe the broader Americanization movement and the special role assigned to the schools. Edgar B. Wesley, *NEA: The First Hundred Years* (New York: Harper & Brothers, 1957) is the only available history of the Association; a modern history is much needed. James Earl Clarke, "The American Federation of Teachers: Origins and History from 1870 to 1952" (doctoral thesis, Cornell University, 1966) and William Edward Eaton, *The American Federation of Teachers, 1916–1961: A History of the Movement* (Carbondale: Southern Illinois University, 1975) are the best histories of that union.

I portrayed the history of the independent progressive schools in *The Transformation of the School*. Patricia Albjerg Graham, *Progressive Education: From Arcady to Academe: A History of the Progressive Education Association, 1919–1955* (New York: Teachers College Press, 1967) is a discriminating history of the Association, which for much of its early history articulated and represented the interests of the independent progressive schools. Graham explores the interrelationships between the PEA and the New Education Fellowship in *Progressive Education*, seeing the NEF as a vehicle, *inter alia*, for the export of American schooling on the progressive model; her discussion there is usefully complemented by William Boyd and Wyatt Rawson, *The Story of the New Education* (London: Heinemann, 1965). The influence of American models of schooling on European school reform is discussed in I. L. Kandel, *Comparative Education* (Boston: Houghton Mifflin Company, 1933) and *The New Era in Education: A Comparative Study* (Boston: Houghton Mifflin Company, 1955). James F. Tent, *Mission on the Rhine: Reeducation and Denazification in American-Occupied Germany* (Chicago: University of Chicago Press, 1982) and Toshio Nishi, *Unconditional Democracy: Education and Politics in Occupied Japan, 1945–1952* (Stanford, Cal.: Hoover Institution Press, 1982) describe the imposition of American educational ideas and institutions in the context of the post–World War II occupations. For the ideas of Arthur E. Bestor, Jr., Hyman G. Rickover, and James B. Conant, see Cremin, *Transformation of the School*, chap. ix.

Laurence R. Veysey, *The Emergence of the American University* (Chicago: University of Chicago Press, 1965) covers the period from 1865 to 1910 in higher education, though with a somewhat less inclusive idea of the progressive tradition in higher education than mine. It is usefully complemented by Mabel Newcomer, *A Century of Higher Education for American Women* (New York: Harper & Brothers, 1959); Barbara Miller Solomon, *In the Company of Educated Women: A History of Women and Higher Education in America* (New Haven: Yale University Press, 1985); Frederick Rudolph, *The American College and University: A History* (New York: Alfred A. Knopf, 1962) and *Curriculum: A History of the American Undergraduate Course of Study since 1636* (San Francisco: Jossey-Bass, 1977); and John S. Brubacher and Willis Rudy, *Higher Education in Transition: A History of American Colleges and Universities, 1636–1976* (3rd ed., rev. and enl.; New York: Harper & Row, 1976), which, incidentally, includes an excellent bibliography of institutional histories. Colin B. Burke, *American Collegiate Populations: A Test of the Traditional View* (New York: New York University Press, 1982) and "The Expansion of American Higher Education," in Konrad H. Jarausch, ed., *The Transformation of Higher Learning, 1860–1930: Expansion, Diversification, Social Opening, and Professionalization in England, Germany, Russia, and the United States* (Chicago: University of Chicago Press, 1983) are authoritative on enrollments and on where the students went. Roger L. Geiger, *To Advance Knowledge: The Growth of American Research Universities, 1900–*

1940 (New York: Oxford University Press, 1986) documents the rise of the research universities, though with more attention to the faculties of arts and sciences than to the so-called professional faculties. J. F. C. Harrison, *Learning and Living, 1790–1960: A Study in the History of the English Adult Education Movement* (London: Routledge and Kegan Paul, 1961) is an especially rich account. Louis E. Reber, *University Extension in the United States* (U.S., Bureau of Education, Bulletin, 1914, no. 19; Washington, D.C.: Government Printing Office, 1914); W. S. Bittner, *The University Extension Movement* (U.S., Bureau of Education, Bulletin, 1919, No. 84; Washington, D.C.: Government Printing Office, 1920); and George M. Woytanowitz, *University Extension: The Early Years in the United States, 1885–1915* (Iowa City: National University Extension Association and the American College Testing Program, 1974) trace the rise of university extension work; Richard J. Storr, *Harper's University: the Beginnings; A History of the University of Chicago* (Chicago: University of Chicago Press, 1966) discusses the arrangements Harper made at the University of Chicago. Merle Curti and Vernon Carstensen, *The University of Wisconsin: A History, 1848–1925* (2 vols.; Madison: University of Wisconsin Press, 1949) and Clifford S. Griffin, *The University of Kansas: A History* (Lawrence: University Press of Kansas, 1974) are splendid histories of those universities. Roland Lincoln Guyotte III, "Liberal Education and the American Dream: Public Attitudes and the Emergence of Mass Higher Education, 1920–1951" (doctoral thesis, Northwestern University, 1980) and David O. Levine, *The American College and the Culture of Aspiration, 1915–1940* (Ithaca, N.Y.: Cornell University Press, 1986) include informative accounts of the experience of the General College at the University of Minnesota.

Martin Trow, "The Democratization of Higher Education in America," *Archives Européennes de Sociologie*, III (1962), 231–262, and *Problems in the Transition from Elite to Mass Higher Education* (Berkeley, Cal.: Carnegie Commission on Higher Education, 1972) are thoughtful analyses of the popularization of American higher education during the period following World War II. A major study is needed of the so-called G.I. Bill of Rights and its effect on American higher education. Davis R. B. Ross, *Preparing for Ulysses: Politics and Veterans During World War II* (New York: Columbia University Press, 1969) is incisive on the legislative history of the program. Keith W. Olson, *The G.I. Bill, the Veterans, and the Colleges* (Lexington: University Press of Kentucky, 1974) and U.S., Congress, 93d Congress, 1st sess., Committee on Veterans' Affairs, *Final Report on Educational Assistance to Veterans: A Comparative Study of Three G.I. Bills* (Washington, D.C.: Government Printing Office, 1973) describe the program in operation. Guyotte III, "Liberal Education and the American Dream" and Levine, *The American College and the Culture of Aspiration* discuss the origins of the patterns of popular higher education that emerged during the post–World War II era. The publications of the Carnegie Commission on Higher Education and the Carnegie Council on Policy Studies in Higher Education, both presided over by Clark Kerr, provide the fullest account of developments in higher education during the years following 1945; those publications are summarized in *A Digest of Reports of the Carnegie Commission on Higher Education* (New York: McGraw-Hill Book Company, 1974); *Sponsored Research of the Carnegie Commission on Higher Education* (New York: McGraw-Hill Book Company, 1975); and *The Carnegie Council on Policy Studies in Higher Education: A Summary of Reports and Recommendations* (San Francisco: Jossey-

Bass Publishers, 1980). Ellen Condliffe Lagemann provides excellent context for the work of the Commission and the Council in *Private Power for the Public Good: A History of the Carnegie Foundation for the Advancement of Teaching* (Middletown: Wesleyan University Press, 1983).

The California three-tier system is described in T. R. McConnell, *A General Pattern for American Public Higher Education* (New York: McGraw-Hill Book Company, 1962). The student unrest of the 1960s and 1970s is discussed from various perspectives in Kenneth Keniston, *Young Radicals: Notes on Committed Youth* (New York: Harcourt, Brace and World, 1968); Paul Jacobs and Saul Landau, *The New Radicals: A Report with Documents* (New York: Random House, 1966); Lewis S. Feuer, *The Conflict of Generations: The Character and Significance of Student Movements* (New York: Basic Books, 1969); Steven Kelman, *Push Comes to Shove: The Escalation of Student Protest* (Boston: Houghton Mifflin Company, 1970); Seymour Martin Lipset and Gerald M. Schaflander, *Passion and Politics: Student Activism in America* (Boston: Little, Brown and Company, 1971); and Ravitch, *The Troubled Crusade*. Harold S. Wechsler, *The Qualified Student: A History of Selective College Admission in America* (New York: John Wiley & Sons, 1977) and David E. Lavin, Richard D. Alba, and Richard A. Silberstein, *Right versus Privilege: The Open Admissions Experiment at the City University of New York* (New York: The Free Press, 1983) are informative on the open admissions experiment at the City University of New York: Geoffrey Wagner, *The End of Education: The Experience of the City University of New York with Open Enrollment and the Threat to Higher Education in America* (Cranbury, N.J.: A. S. Barnes and Company, 1976) and Theodore L. Gross, *Academic Turmoil: The Reality and Promise of Open Education* (Garden City, N.Y.: Anchor Press/Doubleday, 1980) are mordant criticisms of the experiment.

Allen J. Matusow, *The Unraveling of America: A History of Liberalism in the 1960s* (New York: Harper & Row, 1984) and William H. Chafe, *The Unfinished Journey: America Since World War II* (New York: Oxford University Press, 1986) provide a context for post–World War II efforts to integrate American schools; John Frederick Martin, *Civil Rights and the Crisis of Liberalism: The Democratic Party, 1945–1976* (Boulder, Colo.: Westview Press, 1979) discusses the conflicts among liberals over questions of civil rights. All the references discussed on pp. 699–700 *supra* are relevant. In addition, the Summer, 1957, issue of the *Journal of Negro Education* describes the legal situation with respect to the schooling of black children as of 1940. Hugh Davis Graham, *The Uncertain Triumph: Federal Education Policy in the Kennedy and Johnson Years* (Chapel Hill: University of North Carolina Press, 1984) describes the development of a strong federal education presence within the Department of Health, Education and Welfare. And Julia Roy Jeffrey, *Education for the Children of the Poor: A Study of the Origins and Implementation of the Elementary and Secondary Education Act of 1965* (Columbus: Ohio State University Press, 1978) deals with many of the same people and events from a more critical perspective. I found the Graham account more accurate and persuasive.

There is a wealth of literature discussing the effects of *Brown v. Board of Education* in the three decades following 1954; among the works I found most useful were Gary Orfield, *The Reconstruction of Southern Education: The Schools and the 1964 Civil Rights Act* (New York: Wiley-Interscience, 1969) and *Must We Bus? Segregated Schools and National Policy* (Washington, D.C.: The Brookings Institution, 1978); "School Desegregation: Lessons of the First Twenty-Five Years," constituting the Summer and Autumn, 1978, issues of *Law and Contemporary Problems;* Walter G. Stephan and Joe R. Feagin, eds., *School Desegregation: Past, Present, and Future* (New York: Plenum Press, 1980); Derrick Bell, ed., *Shades of Brown: New Perspectives on School Desegregation* (New York: Teachers College Press, 1980); Laurence R. Marcus and Benjamin D. Stickney, *Race and Education: The Unending Controversy* (Springfield, Ill.: Charles C. Thomas, 1981); Gail E. Thomas, ed., *Black Students in Higher Education: Conditions and Experiences in the 1970's* (Westport, Conn.: Greenwood Press, 1981); Adam Yarmolinsky, Lance Liebman, and Carinne S. Shelling, eds., *Race and Schooling in the City* (Cambridge, Mass.: Harvard University Press, 1981); Alexander W. Astin *et al., Minorities in American Higher Education* (San Francisco: Jossey-Bass, 1982); Christine H. Rossell and Willis D. Hawley, eds., *The Consequences of School Desegregation* (Philadelphia: Temple University Press, 1983); Jennifer L. Hochschild, *The New American Dilemma: Liberal Democracy and School Desegregation* (New Haven: Yale University Press, 1984); C. Eric Lincoln, *Race, Religion, and the Continuing American Dilemma* (New York: Hill and Wang, 1984); Raymond Wolters, *The Burden of "Brown": Thirty Years of School Desegregation* (Knoxville: University of Tennessee Press, 1984); and M. Beatriz Arias, ed., "The Education of Hispanic Americans: A Challenge for the Future," *American Journal of Education* XCV (1986–87), 1–272. Ray C. Rist, ed., *Desegregated Schools: Appraisals of an American Experiment* (New York: Academic Press, 1979) and David L. Kirp, *Just Schools: The Idea of Racial Equality in American Education* (Berkeley: University of California Press, 1982) convey a vivid sense of the extent to which local conditions affect the politics and outcomes of desegregation. On the *Brown* decision and its consequences as a "second Declaration of Independence," see Marcus and Stickney, *Race and Education,* chap. ii; for the *Brown* decision and its consequences as a "second Reconstruction," see John B. Turner and Whitney M. Young, Jr., "Who Has the Revolution, or Thoughts on the Second Reconstruction," *Daedalus,* XCIV (1964–65), 1148–1163; C. Vann Woodward, "What Happened to the Civil Rights Movement?" *Harper's,* CCXXXIV (January, 1967), 29–37; and Manning Marable, *Race Reform and Rebellion: The Second Reconstruction and Black America, 1945–1982* (Jackson: University Press of Mississippi, 1984). On the inextricable ties between federal family policies and federal school policies as they affect black children, see Lee Rainwater and William L. Yancey, *The Moynihan Report and the Politics of Controversy* (Cambridge, Mass.: M.I.T. Press, 1967); Kenneth B. Clark and John Hope Franklin, eds., *A Policy Framework for Racial Justice* (Washington, D.C.: Joint Center for Political Studies, 1983); and Daniel Patrick Moynihan, *Family and Nation* (New York: Harcourt, Brace, Jovanovich, 1986).

Chapter 6: Child Saving and Social Service Agencies

Child saving was one element in the broader social justice movements of the Progressive era. Those movements are incisively explicated in Robert H. Bremner, *From the Depths: The Discovery of Poverty in the United States* (New York: New York University Press, 1956); Paul Boyer, *Urban Masses and Moral Order in America, 1820–1920* (Cambridge, Mass.: Harvard University Press, 1978); James T. Patterson, *America's Struggle Against Poverty, 1900–1980* (Cambridge, Mass.: Harvard University Press, 1980); David J. Rothman, *Conscience and Convenience: The Asylum and Its Alternatives in Progressive America* (Boston: Little, Brown and Company, 1980); Gerald N. Grob, *Mental Illness and American Society, 1875–1940* (Princeton: Princeton University Press, 1983); and Michael B. Katz, *Poverty and Policy in American History* (New York: Academic Press, 1983) and *In the Shadow of the Poorhouse: A Social History of Welfare in America* (New York: Basic Books, 1986). Katz's notes in the two volumes are especially rich in bibliographical references. Anthony M. Platt, *The Child Savers: The Invention of Delinquency* (Chicago: University of Chicago Press, 1969); Walter I. Trattner, *Crusade for the Children: A History of the National Child Labor Committee and Child Labor Reform in America* (Chicago: Quadrangle Books, 1970); Joseph M. Hawes, *Children in Urban Society: Juvenile Delinquency in Nineteenth Century America* (New York: Oxford University Press, 1971); Robert M. Mennel, *Thorns and Thistles: Juvenile Delinquents in the United States, 1825–1940* (Hanover, N.H.: University Press of New England, 1973); Steven L. Schlossman, *Love and the American Delinquent: The Theory and Practice of "Progressive" Juvenile Justice, 1825–1920* (Chicago: University of Chicago Press, 1977); Susan Tiffin, *In Whose Best Interest? Child Welfare Reform in the Progressive Era* (Westport, Conn.: Greenwood Press, 1982); Barbara M. Brenzel, *Daughters of the State: A Social Portrait of the First Reform School for Girls in North America, 1856–1905* (Cambridge, Mass.: M.I.T. Press, 1983); and Leroy Ashby, *Saving the Waifs: Reformers and Dependent Children, 1890–1917* (Philadelphia: Temple University Press, 1984) focus on the various aspects of child saving. Not surprisingly, this literature reflects many of the same differences that mark the literature on progressive school reform, with, to take but a few examples, Bremner seeing progressive child saving efforts as generally beneficial, Platt seeing them as essentially repressive, Schlossman noting the difference between the rhetorical intentions and realistic outcomes of such efforts, and Tiffin pointing to the ambivalence of the reformers with respect to familial nurture vis-à-vis institutional nurture. David Nasaw, *Children of the City, at Work and at Play* (Garden City, N.Y.: Anchor Press/Doubleday, 1985) is a colorful portrayal of the lives of urban, working-class children during the Progressive era. Robert H. Bremner *et al., Children and Youth in America: A Documentary History* (3 vols.; Cambridge, Mass.: Harvard University Press, 1970–74) is an indispensable collection of documents.

The evangelical child-rearing literature is explicated in Anne L. Kuhn, *The Mother's Role in Childhood Education: New England Concepts, 1830–1860* (New Haven: Yale University Press, 1947); Bernard Wishy, *The Child and the Republic: The Dawn of Modern Child Nurture* (Philadelphia: University of Pennsylvania Press, 1968); and Mary Patricia Ryan, "American Society and the Cult of Domesticity" (doctoral thesis, University of California, Santa Barbara, 1971). A broader literature is explicated over a longer time frame in Jane Silverman Mulligan, "The Madonna and Child in American Culture, 1830–1915" (doctoral thesis, University of California, Los Angeles, 1975). The progressive ambivalence with respect to child saving institutions is detailed in Tiffin, *In Whose Best Interest?* Charles Loring Brace's efforts are incisively placed in context in R. Richard Wohl, "The 'Country Boy' Myth and Its Place in American Culture: The Nineteenth-Century Contribution," *Perspectives in American History,* III (1969), 77–156. James R. Lane, *Jacob A. Riis and the American City* (Port Washington, N.Y.: Kennikat Press, 1974) is the best discussion of Riis as a reform leader; I also found the portrait of Riis in Roy Lubove, *The Progressives and the Slums: Tenement House Reform in New York City,*

1890–1917 (Pittsburgh: University of Pittsburgh Press, 1962) illuminating. Roy Lubove, *The Professional Altruist: The Emergence of Social Work as a Career, 1880–1930* (Cambridge, Mass.: Harvard University Press, 1965) depicts the social workers as a reform group; Trattner, *Crusade for the Children* depicts the work of the National Child Labor Committee.

The special role of women in the nineteenth-century evangelical movement is developed in many works, among them Nancy F. Cott, *The Bonds of Womanhood: "Woman's Sphere" in New England, 1780–1835* (New Haven: Yale University Press, 1977). The special role of clubwomen in the kindergarten movement is developed by Timothy L. Smith, "Progressivism in American Education, 1880–1900," *Harvard Educational Review*, XXXI (1961), 168–193; Gerda Lerner, "Early Community Work of Black Club Women," *Journal of Negro History*, LIX (1974), 158–167; William J. Reese, "Between Home and School: Organized Parents, Clubwomen, and Urban Education in the Progressive Era," *School Review*, LXXXVII (1978–79), 3–28; and Karen J. Blair, *The Clubwoman as Feminist: True Womanhood Redefined, 1868–1914* (New York: Holmes and Meier, 1980). Dorothy Ross, *G. Stanley Hall: The Psychologist as Prophet* (Chicago: University of Chicago Press, 1972) is the best biography of Hall in his relation to the child study movement; it includes an excellent bibliography. Steven L. Schlossman, "Before Home Start: Notes Toward a History of Parent Education in America, 1897–1929," *Harvard Educational Review*, XLVI (1976), 436–464, and "Philanthropy and the Gospel of Child Development," *History of Education Quarterly*, XXI (1981), 275–299, greatly informed my account of the parent education movement. Nancy Pottishman Weiss, "Save the Children: A History of the Children's Bureau, 1903–1918," (doctoral thesis, University of California, Los Angeles, 1974) did likewise for my account of the Children's Bureau; the Weiss dissertation, too, includes an excellent bibliography. Lewis J. Covotsos, "Child Welfare and Social Progress: A History of the United States Children's Bureau, 1912–1935" (doctoral thesis, University of Chicago, 1976) complements the Weiss study. Jacqueline K. Parker and Edward M. Carpenter, "Julia Lathrop and the Children's Bureau: The Emergence of an Institution," *Social Service Review*, LV (March, 1981), 60–77, depicts Lathrop's work at the Bureau; Lela B. Costin, *Two Sisters for Social Justice: A Biography of Grace and Edith Abbott* (Urbana: University of Illinois Press, 1983) depicts both Lathrop's and Grace Abbott's work there. Mary Mills West and her pamphlets are discussed in Molly Ladd-Taylor, *Raising a Baby the Government Way: Mothers' Letters to the Children's Bureau, 1915–1932* (New Brunswick: Rutgers University Press, 1986). Kathleen W. Jones, "Sentiment and Science: The Late Nineteenth-Century Pediatrician as Mother's Advisor," *Journal of Social History*, XVII (1983–84), 79–96, explicates the ideas of L. Emmett Holt. Lucille Terese Birnbaum, "Behaviorism: John Broadus Watson and American Social Thought, 1913–1933" (doctoral thesis, University of California, Berkeley, 1964) explicates the ideas of Watson. Sol Cohen, "The Mental Hygiene Movement, the Development of Personality and the School: The Medicalization of American Education," *History of Education Quarterly*, XXIII (1983), 123–149, is an informed discussion of the ideas and assumptions of the mental hygiene movement as they affected education. Michael Zuckerman, "Dr. Spock: The Confidence Man," in Charles E. Rosenberg, ed., *The Family in History* (Philadelphia: University of Pennsylvania Press, 1975), pp. 170–207; Nancy Pottishman Weiss, "Mother, the Invention of Necessity: Dr. Benjamin

Spock's *Baby and Child Care,*" *American Quarterly,* XIX (1977), 519–546; and William Graebner, "The Unstable World of Benjamin Spock: Social Engineering in a Democratic Culture, 1917–1950," *Journal of American History,* LXVII (1980–81) 612–629, explicate the ideas of Benjamin Spock. Michael Gordon reviews the literature on American child-rearing practices as derived from successive editions of *Infant Care* in "*Infant Care* Revisited," *Journal of Social History,* IX (1975–76), 49–63, and I profited from his cautions against equating the advice given mothers on child rearing with how those mothers actually reared their children.

A modern biography of Joseph Lee is much needed. Barbara Miller Solomon sketches a revealing portrait of him in *Ancestors and Immigrants: A Changing New England Tradition* (Cambridge, Mass.: Harvard University Press, 1956), styling him the "archetype of the socially conscious philanthropist." William M. Landes and Lewis C. Solmon, "Compulsory Schooling Legislation: An Economic Analysis of Law and Social Change in the Nineteenth Century," *Journal of Economic History,* XXXII (1972), 54–91, is the best review of the development of compulsory schooling. Margaret O'Brien Steinfels, *Who's Minding the Children? The History of Politics of Day Care in America* (New York: Simon and Schuster, 1973) includes an excellent historical discussion. Mark H. Leff, "Consensus for Reform: The Mothers'-Pension Movement in the Progressive Era," *Social Service Review,* XLVII (1974–75), 375–417, is an incisive account. Ilse Forest, *Preschool Education: A Historical and Critical Study* (New York: The Macmillan Company, 1927) remains a classic work; it is usefully supplemented by Alice Burnett, "Pioneer Contributions to the Nursery School" (doctoral thesis, Teachers College, Columbia University, 1964). The work of the Bureau of Educational Experiments is briefly covered in Joyce Antler, *Lucy Sprague Mitchell: The Making of a Modern Woman* (New Haven: Yale University Press, 1987), as well as in Lucy Sprague Mitchell, *Two Lives: The Story of Wesley Clair Mitchell and Myself* (New York: Simon and Schuster, 1953). The activities of the Laura Spelman Rockefeller Memorial are discussed in Schlossman, "Philanthropy and the Gospel of Child Development." The work of the WPA nursery schools is detailed in Doak S. Campbell, Frederick H. Bair, and Oswald L. Harvey, *Educational Activities of the Works Progress Administration* (U.S., Advisory Committee on Education, Staff Study No. 14; Washington, D.C.: Government Printing Office, 1939). Hamilton Cravens, *The Triumph of Evolution: American Scientists and the Heredity-Environment Controversy, 1900–1941* (Philadelphia: University of Pennsylvania Press, 1978) provides splendid intellectual context for the assumptions behind the several child saving movements.

Joseph Kett, *Rites of Passage: Adolescence in America, 1790 to the Present* (New York: Basic Books, 1977) traces the shifting definition and character of adolescence in American society. William F. Ogburn, *Progress and Uniformity in Child Labor Legislation: A Study in Statistical Measurement* (New York: Longmans, Green and Company, 1912) and Miriam E. Loughran, *The Historical Development of Child-Labor Legislation in the United States* (Washington, D.C.: Catholic University of America, 1921) remain classic compilations. Ross, *G. Stanley Hall* explicates Hall's views on adolescence. Paula Fass, *The Damned and the Beautiful: American Youth in the 1920s* (New York: Oxford University Press, 1977) portrays middle-class adolescents in and out of college. N. S. Timasheff, *One Hundred Years of Probation, 1841–1941* (New York: Fordham University Press, 1941); Rothman, *Conscience and Convenience;* and Schlossman, *Love and the American Delinquent* trace the development of the juvenile court and its associated apparatus of probation. Lawrence A. Finfer, "Leisure as Social Work in the Urban Community: The Progressive Recreation Movement, 1890–1920" (doctoral thesis, Michigan State University, 1974) and Dominick Cavallo, *Muscles and Morals: Organized Playgrounds and Urban Reform, 1880–1920* (Philadelphia: University of Pennsylvania Press, 1981) discuss the playground movement. Helen Buckler *et al.*, eds., *Wo-He-Lo: The Camp Fire History* (Kansas City, Mo.: Camp Fire Inc., 1980) and David I. MacLeod, *Building Character in the American Boy: The Boy Scouts, YMCA, and Their Forerunners, 1870–1920* (Madison: University of Wisconsin Press, 1983) convey a sense of the uses of the boys' and girls' clubs for purposes of education; M. M. Chambers, *Youth-Serving Organizations: National Nongovernmental Associations* (2d ed.; Washington, D.C.: American Council on Education, 1941) conveys a sense of their number and diversity. George Philip Rawick, "The New Deal and Youth: The Civilian Conservation Corps, the National Youth Administration and the American Youth Congress" (doctoral thesis, University of Wisconsin, 1957) and John A. Salmond, *The Civilian Conservation Corps, 1933–1942: A New Deal Case Study* (Durham, N.C.: Duke University Press, 1967) are the best studies of the NYA and the CCC for my purposes.

Sar A. Levitan, *The Great Society's Poor Law: A New Approach to Poverty* (Baltimore: Johns Hopkins University Press, 1969), and *Programs in Aid of the Poor for the 1970s* (Baltimore: Johns Hopkins Press, 1969); Sar A. Levitan and Benjamin H. Johnston, *The Job Corps: A Social Experiment That Works* (Baltimore: Johns Hopkins University Press, 1975); Frederick H. Harbison and Joseph D. Mooney, eds., *Critical Issues in Employment Policies* (Princeton, N.J.: Industrial Relations Section, Princeton University, 1966); and John C. Donovan, *The Politics of Poverty* (2d ed.; Indianapolis: The Bobbs-Merrill Company, 1973) provide an excellent introduction to the Great Society's antipoverty programs. Gilbert Y. Steiner, *The Children's Cause* (Washington, D.C.: The Brookings Institution, 1976) and Edward Zigler and Jeanette Valentine, eds., *Project Head Start: A Legacy of the War on Poverty* (New York: The Free Press, 1979) focus on child care policies and programs. Allen I. Matusow, *The Unraveling of America: A History of Liberalism in the 1960s* (New York: Harper & Row, 1984) also discusses the antipoverty effort, though with greater skepticism. Robert H. Mnookin, ed., "Children and the Law," which constituted the Summer, 1975, issue of *Law and Contemporary Problems,* presents explications of the legal conceptions and issues involved. The essays in Eli Ginzberg and Robert M. Solow, eds., "The Great Society: Lessons for the Future," which constituted the Winter, 1974, issue of the *Public Interest,* especially Ralph W. Tyler's "The Federal Role in Education," advance a cautiously optimistic assessment of the programs, as does John E. Schwarz, *America's Hidden Success: A Reassessment of Twenty Years of Public Policy* (New York: W. W. Norton and Company, 1983); Charles Murray, *Losing Ground: American Social Policy, 1950–1980* (New York: Basic Books, 1984) presents a controversial and uniformly negative assessment.

Chapter 7: Media of Popular Communication

Frank Luther Mott, *American Journalism: A History, 1690–1960* (3d ed., New York: The Macmillan Company, 1962) and *A History of American Magazines* (5 vols.; Cambridge, Mass.: Harvard University Press, 1930–1968) remain the classic histories of American journalism. They are usefully complemented by Michael

Schudson, *Discovering the News: A Social History of American Newspapers* (New York: Basic Books, 1978), which significantly informed my understanding of the "new journalism," and Theodore Peterson, *Magazines in the Twentieth Century* (2nd ed., Urbana: University of Illinois Press, 1964). Sidney Kobre, *The Yellow Press and Gilded Age Journalism* ([Tallahassee]: Florida State University, 1964); George Juergens, *Joseph Pulitzer and the New York World* (Princeton: Princeton University Press, 1966); Roy Everett Littlefield, "William Randolph Hearst: His Role in American Progressivism" (doctoral thesis, Catholic University of America, 1979); W. A. Swanberg, *Citizen Hearst* (New York: Charles Scribner's Sons, 1961); Meyer Berger, *The Story of the New York Times, 1851–1951* (New York: Simon and Schuster, 1951); and Richard Kluger, *The Paper: The Life and Death of the New York Herald Tribune* (New York: Alfred A. Knopf, 1986) provided further detail with respect to the "new journalism." Stuart Ewen, *Captains of Consciousness: Advertising and the Social Roots of the Consumer Culture* (New York: McGraw-Hill Book Company, 1976); Stuart Ewen and Elizabeth Ewen, *Channels of Desire: Mass Images and the Shaping of American Consciousness* (New York: McGraw-Hill Book Company, 1982); and Richard Wightman Fox and T. J. Jackson Lears, eds., *The Culture of Consumption: Critical Essays in American History, 1880–1980* (New York: Pantheon Books, 1983) see advertising at the heart of the creation of a consumer culture in the United States, and Roland Marchand, *Advertising the American Dream: Making Way for Modernity, 1920–1940* (Berkeley: University of California Press, 1985) sees it as having created the American self-image. Michael Schudson, "Criticizing the Critics of Advertising: Towards a Sociological View of Marketing," *Media, Culture and Society,* III (1981), 3–12, and *Advertising, the Uneasy Persuasion: Its Dubious Impact on American Society* (New York: Basic Books, 1984) are skeptical of the power of advertising to create a consumer culture, or any other culture, for that matter. Daniel Pope, *The Making of Modern Advertising* (New York: Basic Books, 1983) and Stephen Fox, *The Mirror Makers: A History of American Advertising and Its Creators* (New York: William Morrow and Company, 1984) are engaging histories of advertising.

Lewis Jacobs, *The Rise of the American Film: A Critical History* (rev. ed.; New York: Teachers College Press, 1968); Robert Sklar, *Movie-Made America: A Cultural History of American Movies* (New York: Random House, 1975); and Garth Jowett, *Film: The Democratic Art* (Boston: Little, Brown and Company, 1976) are the best histories of the American film. William K. Everson, *American Silent Film* (New York: Oxford University Press, 1978) and Lary May, *Screening Out the Past: The Birth of Mass Culture and the Motion Picture Industry* (New York: Oxford University Press, 1980) detail aspects of the early years of the film industry. Raymond Fielding, *A Technological History of Motion Pictures and Television* (Berkeley: University of California Press, 1967) reviews the underlying technical developments. Erik Barnouw, *Documentary: A History of the Non-Fiction Film* (New York: Oxford University Press, 1974) and Raymond Fielding, *The American Newsreel, 1911–1967* (Norman: University of Oklahoma Press, 1972) consider particular genres. Richard Schickel, *D. W. Griffith: An American Life* (New York: Simon and Schuster, 1984) is an incisive biography. John Hope Franklin reviews the response to *The Birth of a Nation* in " 'Birth of a Nation'—Propaganda as History," *Massachusetts Review,* XX (1979), 417–434.

Harold D. Lasswell's classic *Propaganda Techniques in the World War* (New York:

Alfred A. Knopf, 1927) and H. C. Peterson, *Propaganda for War: The Campaign Against American Neutrality, 1914–1917* (Norman: University of Oklahoma Press, 1939), which explicates the kind of propaganda Americans had experienced at the time the United States entered World War I, provide useful context for the work of the Committee on Public Information. So, too, in different ways, does David M. Kennedy, *Over Here: The First World War and American Society* (New York: Oxford University Press, 1980). Stephen Vaughn, *Holding Fast the Inner Lines: Democracy, Nationalism, and the Committee on Public Information* (Chapel Hill: University of North Carolina Press, 1980) is an excellent modern history; James R. Mock and Cedric Larson, *Words That Won the War: The Story of the Committee on Public Information, 1917–1919* (Princeton: Princeton University Press, 1939) is an informative older work. Both have full bibliographies. The papers of the CPI are in the National Archives. Richard Redlow, *Keeping the Corporate Image: Public Relations and Business, 1900–1950* (Greenwich, Conn.: JAI Press, 1979) traces the early development of public relations as an activity and a profession.

Erik Barnouw, *A History of Broadcasting in the United States* (3 vols.; New York: Oxford University Press, 1966–1970) is the premier history. Daniel J. Czitrom, *Media and the American Mind: From Morse to McLuhan* (Chapel Hill: University of North Carolina Press, 1982) and Catherine L. Covert and John D. Stevens, *Mass Media Between the Wars: Perceptions of Cultural Tension, 1918–1941* (Syracuse, N.Y.: Syracuse University Press, 1984) are more general works that include excellent material on radio broadcasting. F. Fred MacDonald, *Don't Touch That Dial: Radio Programming in American Life from 1920 to 1960* (Chicago: Nelson-Hall, 1979) deals somewhat nostalgically with radio programming; Muriel G. Cantor and Suzanne Pingree, *The Soap Opera* (Beverly Hills, Cal.: Sage Publications, 1983) and David Holbrook Culbert, *News for Everyman: Radio and Foreign Affairs in Thirties America* (Westport, Conn.: Greenwood Press, 1976) focus on particular genres. Philip T. Rosen, *The Modern Stentors: Radio Broadcasters and the Federal Government, 1920–1934* (Westport, Conn.: Greenwood Press, 1980) deals broadly with the question of regulation; Ellis W. Hawley, "Herbert Hoover, the Commerce Secretariat, and the Vision of an 'Associative State,' 1921–1928," *Journal of American History,* LXI (1974–75), 116–140, and Joan Hoff Wilson, *Herbert Hoover: Forgotten Progressive* (Boston: Little, Brown and Company, 1975) detail the political technologies Hoover used as secretary of commerce in contending with radio regulation. Hadley Cantril and Gordon Allport, *The Psychology of Radio* (New York: Harper & Brothers, 1935) is a rich gathering of data on the effects of radio broadcasting; Paul F. Lazarsfeld and Harry Field, *The People Look at Radio* (Chapel Hill: University of North Carolina Press, 1946) is similarly rich in data on the public reception and perception of radio broadcasting. Roger G. Noll, *Economic Aspects of Television Regulation* (Washington, D.C.: The Brookings Institution, 1973) is an incisive analysis of the problem. Douglass Cater and Richard Adler, eds., *Television as a Social Force: New Approaches to TV Criticism* (New York: Praeger Publishers, 1975), and *Television as a Cultural Force* (New York: Praeger Publishers, 1976) present informed essays on various aspects of the substance and effects of television broadcasting. Leo Bogart, *The Age of Television: A Study of Viewing Habits and the Impact of Television on American Life* (3d ed., New York: Frederick Ungar Publishing Company, 1972); George Comstock *et al., Television and Human Behavior* (New York: Columbia University Press, 1978); and U.S., National Institute of Mental

Health, *Television and Behavior: Ten Years of Scientific Progress and Implications for the Eighties,* Vol. I: *Summary Report* (Rockville, Md.: National Institutes of Mental Health, 1982) are incisive compendia concerning the substance and effects of television broadcasting. Robert J. Blakely, *To Serve the Public Interest: Educational Broadcasting in the United States* (Syracuse: Syracuse University Press, 1979), and *The People's Instrument: A Philosophy of Programming for Public Television* (Washington, D.C.: Public Affairs Press, 1971); Carnegie Commission on Educational Television, *Public Television: A Program for Action* (New York: Bantam Books, 1967); Carnegie Commission on the Future of Public Broadcasting, *A Public Trust* (New York: Bantam Books, 1979); Cantor and Pingree, *The Soap Opera;* Lincoln Diamant, *Television's Classic Commercials: The Golden Years, 1948–1958* (New York: Hastings House, 1971); Edward Jay Epstein, *News from Nowhere: Television and the News* (New York: Random House, 1973); Razelle Frankl, *Televangelism: The Marketing of Popular Religion* (Carbondale: Southern Illinois University Press, 1987); William Melody, *Children's Television: The Economies of Exploitation* (New Haven: Yale University Press, 1973); and Gerald S. Lesser, *Children and Television: Lessons from Sesame Street* (New York: Random House, 1974) focus on particular domains of broadcasting. Ithiel de Sola Pool, *Technologies of Freedom* (Cambridge, Mass.: Harvard University Press, 1983) and Wilson P. Dizard, *The Coming Information Age: An Overview of Technology, Economics, and Politics* (New York: Longman, 1982) raise fundamental questions concerning the relation of new technologies to human freedom. The Museum of Broadcasting in New York City is an incomparable repository of programming.

Allan M. Winkler, *The Politics of Propaganda: The Office of War Information, 1942–1945* (New Haven: Yale University Press, 1978) and Robert E. Elder, *The Information Machine: The United States Information Agency and American Foreign Policy* (Syracuse: Syracuse University Press, 1968) are incisive studies of recent American propaganda and information efforts. The literature of "media imperialism" is reviewed in Fred Fejes, "Media Imperialism: An Assessment," *Media, Culture and Society,* III (1981), 281–289, and Michael Tracey, "The Poisoned Chalice? International Television and the Idea of Dominance," *Daedalus,* CXIV (Fall, 1985), 17–56. William H. Read, *America's Mass Media Merchants* (Baltimore: Johns Hopkins University Press, 1976); Herbert I. Schiller, *Communication and Cultural Domination* (White Plains, N.Y.: International Arts and Sciences Press, 1976); Thomas H. Guback, *The International Film Industry: Europe and America Since 1945* (Bloomington: Indiana University Press, 1969), and "Film as International Business," *Journal of Communication,* XXIV (1974), 90–101; Kaarle Nordenstreng and Tapio Varis, *Television Traffic: A One Way Street: A Survey and Analysis of the International Flow of Television Programme Material* (UNESCO, Reports and Papers on Mass Communication, No. 70; Paris: UNESCO, 1974); and Tapio Varis, "Global Traffic in Television," *Journal of Communication,* XXIV (1974), 102–109, argue the thesis of "media imperialism." Elihu Katz and George Wedell, *Broadcasting in the Third World: Promise and Performance* (Cambridge, Mass.: Harvard University Press, 1977) presents data on the actual situation in the Third World. International Commission for the Study of Communication Problems, *Many Voices, One World: Towards a New, More Just, and More Efficient World Information and Communication Order* (Paris: UNESCO, 1980), often referred to as the McBride report, and Kaarle Nordenstreng, ed., *The Mass Media Declaration of UNESCO* (Norwood, N.J.: Ablex Publishing Corporation, 1984) pertain to the development of UNESCO's "new world information and communication order."

PART III: THE INFORMED SOCIETY

The rise of new intellectual and cultural elites, each claiming special expertise to rule upon what knowledge is of most worth in one domain or another, is documented in Alexandra Oleson and John Voss, eds., *The Organization of Knowledge in Modern America, 1860–1920* (Baltimore: Johns Hopkins University Press, 1979); Thomas L. Haskell, *The Emergence of Professional Social Science: The American Social Science Association and the Nineteenth Century Crisis of Authority* (Urbana: University of Illinois Press, 1977); Thomas L. Haskell, ed., *The Authority of Experts: Studies in History and Theory* (Bloomington: Indiana University Press, 1984); Mary O. Furner, *Advocacy and Objectivity: A Crisis in the Professionalization of American Social Science, 1865–1905* (Lexington: University Press of Kentucky, 1975); Burton J. Bledstein, *The Culture of Professionalism: The Middle Class and the Development of Higher Education in America* (New York: W. W. Norton & Company, 1976); and Thomas Bender, "The Cultures of Intellectual Life: The City and the Professions," in John Higham and Paul K. Conkin, eds., *New Directions in American Intellectual History* (Baltimore: Johns Hopkins University Press, 1979), pp. 181–195. The politics of knowledge is explicated in Ellen Condliffe Lagemann, "The Politics of Knowledge: The Carnegie Corporation and the Formulation of Public Policy," *History of Education Quarterly*, XXVII (1987), 205–220, and *The Politics of Knowledge: A History of the Carnegie Corporation of New York* (Middletown: Wesleyan University Press, forthcoming). The popularization of knowledge and the rise of vernaculars in the United States are discussed in Merle Curti, *The Growth of American Thought* (3d ed.; New York: Harper & Row, 1964); Daniel J. Boorstin, *The Americans: The Democratic Experience* (New York: Random House, 1973); Constance Rourke, *The Roots of American Culture and Other Essays*, edited by Van Wyck Brooks (New York: Harcourt, Brace and Company, 1942); John Kouwenhoven, *Made in America: The Arts in Modern Civilization* (Garden City, N.Y.: Doubleday and Company, 1948) and *The Beer Can by the Highway: Essays on What Is "American" about America* (Garden City, N.Y.: Doubleday and Company, 1961). Luther V. Hendricks, *James Harvey Robinson: Teacher of History* (New York: King's Crown Press, 1946) is the best biography; Robert Allen Skotheim, *American Intellectual History and Historians* (Princeton: Princeton University Press, 1966) includes an incisive discussion of Robinson's ideas. The sources on John Dewey and Jane Addams are discussed on pp. 693 and 706 *supra.* Edward P. Alexander, *Museum Masters: Their Museums and Their Influence* (Nashville, Tenn.: American Association of State and Local History, 1983) includes an excellent chapter on John Cotton Dana and the Newark Museum. Gilbert Seldes, *The Seven Lively Arts* (New York: Harper & Brothers, 1924) remains one of the classic discussions of American vernacular.

CHAPTER 8: THE NATURE AND USES OF KNOWLEDGE

Hugh Hawkins, *Between Harvard and America: The Educational Leadership of Charles W. Eliot* (New York: Oxford University Press, 1972) is the best discussion of Eliot's influence; it includes a superb bibliography. Henry James, *Charles W. Eliot: Presi-*

dent of Harvard University, 1869–1909 (2 vols.; Boston: Houghton Mifflin Company, 1930) remains the fullest life study. *Charles W. Eliot: The Man and His Beliefs,* edited by William Allan Neilson (2 vols.; New York: Harper & Brothers, 1926) is a useful collection of documents, with commentary. Laurence R. Veysey, *The Emergence of the American University* (Chicago: University of Chicago Press, 1965); Andrew L. Barlow, "Coordination and Control: The Rise of Harvard University, 1825–1910" (doctoral thesis, Harvard University, 1979); Samuel Eliot Morison, *Three Centuries of Harvard* (Cambridge, Mass.: Harvard University Press, 1936); Theodore R. Sizer, *Secondary Schools at the Turn of the Century* (New Haven: Yale University Press, 1964); and Burton R. Bledstein, *The Culture of Professionalism: The Middle Class and the Development of Higher Education in America* (New York: W. W. Norton & Company, 1976) provide useful context for Eliot's work. The Eliot papers are in the Harvard College Archives.

Richard Hofstadter, *Social Darwinism in American Thought, 1860–1915* (Philadelphia: University of Pennsylvania Press, 1945); Cynthia Eagle Russett, *Darwin in America: The Intellectual Response, 1865–1912* (San Francisco: W. H. Freeman and Company, 1976); and Robert C. Banister, *Social Darwinism: Science and Myth in Anglo-American Social Thought* (Philadelphia: Temple University Press, 1979) depict the varied manifestations of social Darwinism in American thought; all three volumes have excellent notes and bibliographies. Anthony Oberschall, ed., *The Establishment of Empirical Sociology: Studies in Continuity, Discontinuity, and Institutionalization* (New York: Harper & Row, 1972); Edward Shils, *The Calling of Sociology and Other Essays on the Pursuit of Learning* (Chicago: University of Chicago Press, 1980); Steven J. Diner, "Department and Discipline: The Department of Sociology at the University of Chicago, 1892–1920," *Minerva,* XIII (1975), 514–553, and *A City and Its Universities: Public Policy in Chicago, 1892–1919* (Chapel Hill: University of North Carolina Press, 1980); Roscoe C. Hinkle, *Founding Theory of American Sociology, 1881–1915* (Boston: Routledge and Kegan Paul, 1980); J. David Lewis and Richard L. Smith, *American Sociology and Pragmatism: Mead, Chicago Sociology, and Symbolic Interaction* (Chicago: University of Chicago Press, 1980); Robert Bierstedt, *American Sociological Theory: A Critical History* (New York: Academic Press, 1981); Ellen Fitzpatrick, "Academics and Activists: Women Social Scientists and the Impulse for Reform, 1892–1920" (doctoral thesis, Brandeis University, 1981); and Martin Bulmer, *The Chicago School of Sociology: Institutionalization, Diversity, and the Rise of Sociological Research* (Chicago: University of Chicago Press, 1984) portray the rise of American sociology, with emphasis on the Chicago school. Arthur J. Vidich and Stanford M. Lyman, *American Sociology: Worldly Rejections of Religion and Their Directions* (New Haven: Yale University Press, 1985) discusses the ways in which American Protestantism and American sociology interacted during the late-nineteenth and twentieth centuries.

J. D. Y. Peel, *Herbert Spencer: The Evolution of a Sociologist* (New York: Basic Books, 1971) and David Wiltshire, *The Social and Political Thought of Herbert Spencer* (New York: Oxford University Press, 1987) are excellent introductions to Spencer's life and thought. John Fiske, *Edward Livingston Youmans: Interpreter of Science to the People* (New York: D. Appleton and Company, 1894) remains the best general source on Youmans, though his thought is ably discussed in Bannister, *Social Darwinism.* F. A. Cavenagh, ed., *Herbert Spencer on Education* (Cambridge: Cambridge University Press, 1932) is the best modern edition of the *Education;*

Andreas M. Kazamias, ed., *Herbert Spencer on Education* (New York: Teachers College Press, 1966) is the best collection of documents, and includes a thoughtful introduction. Maurice R. Davie, *William Graham Sumner* (New York: Thomas Y. Crowell Company, 1963) and Bruce Eugene Curtis, "The Middle Class Progressivism of William Graham Sumner" (doctoral thesis, University of Iowa, 1964) are the best introductions to Sumner's life and thought. They are well complemented by the excellent discussions of Sumner in Bannister, *Social Darwinism* and Robert Garson and Richard Maidment, "Social Darwinism and the Liberal Tradition: The Case of William Graham Sumner," *South Atlantic Quarterly,* LXXX (1981), 61–86. The Sumner papers are in the Yale University Library. Samuel Chugerman, *Lester F. Ward, The American Aristotle: A Summary and Interpretation of His Sociology* (Durham: Duke University Press, 1939) remains the fullest study of Ward's life and work. It is usefully complemented by the discussions of Ward's thought in Elsa Peverly Kimball, *Sociology and Education: An Analysis of the Theories of Spencer and Ward* (New York: Columbia University Press, 1932) and Israel Gerver, *Lester Frank Ward* (New York: Thomas Y. Crowell Company, 1963). Henry Steele Commager, ed., *Lester Ward and the Welfare State* (Indianapolis: The Bobbs-Merrill Company, 1967) is a discriminating selection of documents. The Ward papers are in the Brown University Library. Vernon K. Dibble, *The Legacy of Albion Small* (Chicago: University of Chicago Press, 1975) and Bulmer, *The Chicago School of Sociology* are the best introductions to Small's life and work. Julius Weinberg, *Edward Alsworth Ross and the Sociology of Progressivism* (Madison: The State Historical Society of Wisconsin, 1972) and Edward Alsworth Ross, *Seventy Years of It: An Autobiography* (New York: D. Appleton-Century Company, 1936) are the best introductions to Ross's life and work. Mary A. Hill, *Charlotte Perkins Gilman: The Making of a Radical Feminist, 1860–1896* (Philadelphia: Temple University Press, 1980) and Charlotte Perkins Gilman, *The Living of Charlotte Perkins Gilman: An Autobiography* (New York: D. Appleton-Century Company, 1935) are the best introductions to Gilman's life and work.

Ernest R. Hilgard, *Psychology in America: A Historical Survey* (New York: Harcourt Brace Jovanovich, 1986) and Clarence J. Karier, *Scientists of the Mind: Intellectual Founders of Modern Psychology* (Urbana: University of Illinois Press, 1986) review the development of scientific psychology in the United States and the bearing of scientific psychology on educational theory and practice. Ralph Barton Perry, *The Thought and Character of William James* (2 vols.; Boston: Little, Brown and Company, 1935) remains in my judgment the pre-eminent biography; it is usefully complemented by Gay Wilson Allen, *William James: A Biography* (New York: The Viking Press, 1967) and Howard M. Feinstein, *Becoming William James* (Ithaca, N.Y.: Cornell University Press, 1984); Elizabeth Flower and Murray G. Murphy, *A History of Philosophy in America* (2 vols.; New York: Capricorn Books, 1977) provides the philosophical context for James's thought; Bruce Kuklick, *The Rise of American Philosophy: Cambridge, Massachusetts, 1860–1930* (New Haven: Yale University Press, 1977) provides the academic context. Israel Scheffler, *Four Pragmatists: A Critical Introduction to Peirce, James, Mead, and Dewey* (New York: Humanities Press, 1974); John E. Smith, *Purpose and Thought: The Meaning of Pragmatism* (New Haven: Yale University Press, 1978); David A. Hollinger, "William James and the Culture of Inquiry," *Michigan Quarterly Review,* XX (1981), 264–283; Jacques Barzun, *A Stroll with William James* (New York: Harper & Row, 1983); Daniel W.

Bjork, *The Compromised Scientist: William James in the Development of American Psychology* (New York: Columbia University Press, 1983); and Gerald E. Myers, *William James: His Life and Thought* (New Haven: Yale University Press, 1986) are useful expositions of James's thought in the context of American pragmatism. The definitive edition of James's works continues to issue from the Harvard University Press. The James papers are in the Houghton Library at Harvard. The sources for John Dewey's thought are discussed on p. 706 *supra.*

Henry F. May, *The End of American Innocence: The First Years of Our Own Time, 1912–1917* (New York: Alfred A. Knopf, 1959); Roderick Nash, *The Nervous Generation: American Thought, 1917–1930* (Chicago: Rand McNally and Company, 1970); Claire Sacks, "The Seven Arts Critics: A Study of Cultural Nationalism in America, 1910–1930" (doctoral thesis, University of Michigan, 1955); and Edward Abrahams, *The Lyrical Left: Randolph Bourne, Alfred Stieglitz, and the Origins of Cultural Radicalism in America* (Charlottesville: University Press of Virginia, 1986) are the best introductions to Van Wyck Brooks and the literary movements of the 1920's; Brooks, *An Autobiography* (New York: E. P. Dutton and Company, 1965) documents his particular role in the movements. David R. Conrad, *Education for Transformation: Implications in Lewis Mumford's Ecohumanism* (Palm Springs, Cal.: ETC Publications, 1976) is a useful introduction to Mumford's life and work and the bearing of that work on education; it is well complemented by Frank G. Novak, Jr., "Lewis Mumford as a Critic of American Culture" (doctoral thesis, University of Tennessee, 1975) and Guy J. Piccolo, "Technology, Politics, and Freedom: The Critical Perspective of Lewis Mumford" (doctoral thesis, University of California, Santa Barbara, 1979). Elmer S. Newman, *Lewis Mumford: A Bibliography, 1914–1970* (New York: Harcourt Brace Jovanovich, 1971) lists most of Mumford's published works.

A biography of Gilbert Seldes is much needed; in its absence, one is left with the brief fragmentary accounts in reference works like Max J. Herzberg, *The Reader's Encyclopedia of American Literature* (New York: Thomas Y. Crowell Company, 1962) and James D. Hart, *The Oxford Companion to American Literature* (New York: Oxford University Press, 1965) and with Arthur M. Schlesinger, Jr.'s appreciative introduction to the reprint of Seldes's *The Stammering Century* [1928] (New York: Harper & Row, 1956).

Bernard Rosenberg and David Manning White, eds., *Mass Culture: The Popular Arts in America* (Glencoe, Ill.: The Free Press, 1957), and *Mass Culture Revisited* (New York: Van Nostrand Reinhold Company, 1971); Daniel J. Czitrom, *Media and the American Mind: From Morse to McLuhan* (Chapel Hill: University of North Carolina Press, 1982); and Patrick Brantlinger, *Bread and Circuses: Theories of Mass Culture as Social Decay* (Ithaca, N.Y.: Cornell University Press, 1983) exposit the range of theories about the nature of popular culture. I found Dennis Duffy, *Marshall McLuhan* (Toronto: McClelland and Stewart, 1969) to be the best brief introduction to the ideas of McLuhan; *Current Biography Yearbook, 1967* carries a brief biography. *The Writings of Marshall McLuhan, Listed in Chronological Order from 1934 to 1975* (Fort Lauderdale, Fla.: Wake–Brook House, 1975) is the fullest bibliography of McLuhan's published works. McLuhan's papers are in the Public Archives of Canada in Ottawa. Donald Creighton, *Harold Adams Innis: Portrait of a Scholar* (Toronto: University of Toronto Press, 1957) is the best general work on Innis's life and thought. Jacob S. Dreyer, ed., *Breadth and Depth in Economics:*

Fritz Machlup—The Man and His Ideas (Lexington, Mass.: Lexington Books, 1978) is the best general consideration of Machlup's ideas. Machlup hoped to update and expand the analysis in *The Production and Distribution of Knowledge in the United States* (Princeton: Princeton University Press, 1962) in a magisterial, ten-volume series entitled *Knowledge: Its Creation, Distribution, and Economic Significance.* Fritz Machlup, *Knowledge and Knowledge Production* (Princeton: Princeton University Press, 1980) and *The Branches of Learning* (Princeton: Princeton University Press, 1982) appeared before his death in 1983; Michael Rogers Rubin and Mary Taylor Huber, *The Knowledge Industry in the United States, 1960–1980* (Princeton: Princeton University Press, 1986), completed by Machlup's associates, appeared posthumously. Machlup's papers are in the Hoover Institution on War, Revolution, and Peace, at Stanford University. Other significant works that mark the explosion of interest in the relation between education and economic development during and after the late 1950's include Theodore W. Schultz, *The Economic Value of Education* (New York: Columbia University Press, 1963), and *Investment in Human Capital: The Role of Education and of Research* (New York: The Free Press, 1971); Gary S. Becker, *Human Capital: A Theoretical and Empirical Analysis with Special Reference to Education* (New York: National Bureau of Economic Research, 1964); W. Arthur Lewis, *Education and Economic Development* (Saskatoon: University of Saskatchewan, 1964); Frederick Harbison and Charles A. Myers, *Education, Manpower, and Economic Growth: Strategies of Human Resource Development* (New York: McGraw-Hill Book Company, 1964); Jacob Mincer, "On-the-Job Training: Costs, Returns and Some Implications," *Journal of Political Economy* (supplement), LXX (October, 1962); Edward F. Denison, *The Sources of Economic Growth in the United States and the Alternatives Before Us,* Supplementary Paper No. 13 (New York: Committee for Economic Development, 1962); Robert M. Solow, "Technical Change and the Aggregate Production Function," *Review of Economics and Statistics,* XXXIV (1957), 312–330, and "Technical Progress, Capital Formation, and Economic Growth," *American Economic Review,* LII (May, 1962), 76–86; Theodore W. Schultz, ed., *Economics of the Family: Marriage, Children, and Human Capital* (Chicago: University of Chicago Press, 1974); and Gary S. Becker, *A Treatise on the Family* (Cambridge, Mass.: Harvard University Press, 1981).

CHAPTER 9: PLACES OF CULTURE

Carl F. Kaestle and his associates at the University of Wisconsin–Madison have conducted a number of pioneering studies of the American reading public. Among the reports of those studies available in draft form in 1987 were one by Kaestle and Katherine A. Tinsley on autobiographies as sources for the history of reading, one by Kaestle and Helen Damon-Moore on studies of the American reading public, 1900–1940, and one by Kaestle on standardization and diversity in American print culture, 1880–1980. Among the reports published by 1987 were Carl F. Kaestle, "The History of Literacy and the History of Readers," in Edmund W. Gordon, ed., *Review of Research in Education,* Vol. XII (Washington, D.C.: American Educational Research Association, 1985), pp. 11–53; Lawrence C. Stedman and Carl F. Kaestle, "Literacy and Reading Performance in the United States, from 1880 to the Present," *Reading Research Quarterly,* XXII (1987), 8–46; and Richard L. Venezky, Carl F. Kaestle, and Andrew M. Sum, *The Subtle*

Danger: Reflections on the Literacy Abilities of America's Young Adults (Princeton, N.J.: Educational Testing Service, 1987). John Tebbel, *A History of Book Publishing in the United States* (4 vols.; New York: R. R. Bowker, 1972–1981); Frank Luther Mott, *Golden Multitudes: The Story of Best Sellers in the United States* (New York: The Macmillan Company, 1947); James D. Hart, *The Popular Book: A History of America's Literary Taste* (New York: Oxford University Press, 1950); Alice Payne Hackett, *70 Years of Best Sellers, 1895–1965* (New York: R. R. Bowker Company, 1967); Russel B. Nye, *The Unembarrassed Muse: The Popular Arts in America* (New York: The Dial Press, 1970); and Donald Franklin Joyce, *Gatekeepers of Black Culture: Black-Owned Book Publishing in the United States, 1817–1981* (Westport, Conn.: Greenwood Press, 1983) are replete with information on books and book publishing. Frank Luther Mott, *American Journalism: A History, 1690–1960* (3d ed.; New York: The Macmillan Company, 1962) and *A History of American Magazines* (5 vols.; Cambridge, Mass.: Harvard University Press, 1930–1968) are the best general sources for newspapers and magazines. John T. Winterich, *Three Lantern Slides: Books, the Book Trade, and Some Related Phenomena in America: 1887, 1901 and 1926* (Urbana: University of Illinois Press, 1949) is filled with astute observations about books and readers. The reports of the *Publishers Weekly* contest of 1876 were carried intermittently in that serial from January 15, 1876 to April 7, 1877. Robert W. Haney, *Comstockery in America: Patterns of Censorship and Control* (Boston: Beacon Press, 1960) and Heywood Broun and Margaret Leech, *Anthony Comstock: Roundsman of the Lord* (New York: Alfred and Charles Boni, 1927) document print censorship in general and Comstock's crusade in particular. Charles Lee, *The Hidden Public: The Story of the Book-of-the-Month Club* (Garden City, N.Y.: Doubleday and Company, 1958) and Joan Shelley Rubin, "Self, Culture, and Self-Culture in Modern America: The Early History of the Book-of-the-Month Club," *Journal of American History,* LXXI (1984–85), 782–806, are the best sources for the paradigmatic book club. Henry C. Link and Harry Arthur Hoff, *People and Books: A Study of Reading and Book-Buying Habits* (New York: Book Manufacturers' Institute, 1946); the Winter, 1963, issue of *Daedalus* on "The American Reading Public"; and the Winter, 1983, issue of *Daedalus* on "Reading: Old and New" provide data on the more recent era.

Theodora Penny Martin, "Women's Study Clubs, 1860–1900: 'The Sound of Our Own Voices' " (doctoral thesis, Harvard University, 1985) explores women's clubs as vehicles of mutual education. Joseph E. Gould, *The Chautauqua Movement: An Episode in the Continuing American Revolution* (Albany: State University of New York Press, 1961) and Theodore Morrison, *Chautauqua: A Center for Education, Religion, and the Arts in America* (Chicago: University of Chicago Press, 1974) are the best recent histories of the Chautauqua movement; both have excellent bibliographies. The sources for the social settlement movement are discussed on p. 693 *supra.* Theodore Reed Mitchell, "Oppositional Education in the Southern Farmers' Alliance: 1890–1900" (doctoral thesis, Stanford University, 1983) added greatly to my understanding of the educational activities of the Farmers' Alliances; David A. Shannon, *The Socialist Party of America: A History* (New York: The Macmillan Company, 1955) and Paul Buhle, "Marxism in the United States, 1900–1940" (doctoral thesis, University of Wisconsin—Madison, 1975) were equally helpful with respect to those of the Socialist Party. Nathan Reingold, "Definitions and Speculations: The Professionalization of Science in America in the Nineteenth Century," in Alexandra Oleson and Sanborn C. Brown, eds., *The*

Pursuit of Knowledge in the Early American Republic (Baltimore: Johns Hopkins University Press, 1976) distinguished fruitfully among "cultivators," "practitioners," and "scholars" in the fields of science; the categories are useful for the arts and humanities as well. The sources for the St. Louis Movement in philosophy are discussed on pp. 705–706 *supra.* They are usefully complemented, with respect to the cultural institutions of nineteenth-century St. Louis, by Jane Allen Shikoh, "The 'Higher Life' in the American City of the 1890's: A Study of Its Leaders and Their Activities in New York, Chicago, Philadelphia, St. Louis, Boston, and Buffalo" (doctoral thesis, New York University, 1972); Walter E. Hendrickson, "Science and Culture in the Middle West," in Nathan Reingold, ed., *Science in America Since 1820* (New York: Science History Publications, 1976), pp. 33–47, and "The Western Academy of Natural Sciences of St. Louis," *Bulletin of the Missouri Historical Society,* XVI (1959–60), 114–129; Harvey Saalberg, "Dr. Emil Pretorius, Editor-in-Chief of the *Westliche Post,* 1864–1905," *ibid.,* XXIV, 103–112; and Julian S. Rammelcamp, "St. Louis in the Early 'Eighties," *ibid.,* 328–339. Helen Lefkowitz Horowitz, *Culture & the City: Cultural Philanthropy in Chicago from the 1880s to 1917* (Lexington: University Press of Kentucky, 1976) and Kathleen D. McCarthy, *Noblesse Oblige: Charity and Cultural Philanthropy in Chicago, 1849–1929* (Chicago: University of Chicago Press, 1983) are useful sources on cultural philanthropy, though the McCarthy volume tends to make insufficient distinction between the cultural philanthropy of Charles Hutchinson and the cultural philanthropy of Jane Addams. Shikoh, "The 'Higher Life' in the American City of the 1890's"; Laura Wood Roper, *FLO: A Biography of Frederick Law Olmsted* (Baltimore: Johns Hopkins University Press, 1973); Geoffrey Blodgett, "Frederick Law Olmsted: Landscape Architecture as Conservative Reform," *Journal of American History,* XLII (1975–76), 869–889; and Douglas Sloan, "Science in New York City, 1867–1907," *Isis,* LXXI (1980), 35–76, are the best sources on cultural philanthropy in New York City. J. Kirkpatrick Flack, *Desideratum in Washington: The Intellectual Community in the Capital City, 1870–1900* (Cambridge, Mass.: Schenkman Publishing Company, 1975) and Michael James Lacey, "The Mysteries of Earth-Making Dissolve: A Study of Washington's Intellectual Community and the Origins of American Environmentalism in the Late Nineteenth Century" (doctoral thesis, George Washington University, 1979) are the best sources on cultural philanthropy in Washington, D.C. And Shikoh, "The 'Higher Life' in the American City of the 1890's"; Frederick Cople Jaher, "Nineteenth-Century Elites in Boston and New York," *Journal of Social History,* VI (1972–73), 33–77; Martin Green, *The Problem of Boston: Some Readings in Cultural History* (New York: W. W. Norton & Company, 1966); Ronald Story, *The Forging of an Aristocracy: Harvard and the Boston Upper Class, 1800–1870* (Middletown: Wesleyan University Press, 1980); E. Digby Baltzell, *Philadelphia Gentlemen: The Making of a National Upper Class* (Glencoe, Ill.: The Free Press, 1958), and *Puritan Boston and Quaker Philadelphia: Two Protestant Ethics and the Spirit of Class Authority and Leadership* (New York: The Free Press, 1980) are the best sources on cultural philanthropy in Boston and Philadelphia. Daniel Walker Howe, ed., "Victorian Culture in America," which constituted the December, 1971, issue of *American Quarterly,* explicates the values and ideals of late American Victorianism; Stanley Coben, "The Assault on Victorianism in the Twentieth Century," *American Quarterly,* XXVII (1975), 604–625, explicates the intellectual assault on that culture.

John Y. Cole, "Storehouses and Workshops: American Libraries and the Uses of Knowledge," in Alexandra Oleson and John Voss, eds., *The Organization of Knowledge in Modern America, 1860–1920* (Baltimore: Johns Hopkins University Press, 1979) discusses the tension between two prevalent conceptions of the American library. Sidney Ditzion, *Arsenals of a Democratic Culture: A Social History of the American Public Library Movement in New England and the Middle Colonies from 1850 to 1900* (Chicago: American Library Association, 1947) and Dee Garrison, *Apostles of Culture: The Public Librarian and American Society, 1876–1920* (New York: The Free Press, 1979) are useful accounts of the development of American public libraries; Michael Harris, "The Purpose of the American Public Library: A Revisionist Interpretation of History," *Library Journal*, XCVIII (1973), 2509–2514, takes issue with the traditional assumptions concerning the benign, humanitarian impulse behind the public library movement; Phyllis Dain, "Ambivalence and Paradox: The Social Bonds of the Public Library," *ibid.*, C (1975), 261–266, is a response. Ellen Condliffe Lagemann, *The Politics of Knowledge: A History of the Carnegie Corporation of New York* (Middletown: Wesleyan University Press, forthcoming) discusses the critical role of the Carnegie philanthropies in the development of American public libraries.

Nathaniel Burt, *Palaces for the People: A Social History of the American Art Museum* (Boston: Little, Brown and Company, 1977) is a useful general history; Edward P. Alexander, *Museums in Motion: An Introduction to the History and Functions of Museums* (Nashville, Tenn.: American Association of State and Local History, 1979) describes the different, and often conflicting, conceptions of museums. Walter Muir Whitehill, *Museum of Fine Arts, Boston: A Centennial History* (2 vols.; Cambridge, Mass.: Harvard University Press, 1970) and Calvin Tomkins, *Merchants and Masterpieces: The Story of the Metropolitan Museum of Art* (New York: E. P. Dutton and Company, 1970) trace the history of the two great art museums founded during the 1870's. Laurence Vail Coleman, *The Museum in America: A Critical Study* (3 vols.; Washington, D.C.: The American Association of Museums, 1939) was the first great national survey of American museums undertaken under the auspices of the American Association of Museums; more recently, the Association has undertaken such surveys and reports with increasing frequency. Theodore Lewis Low, *The Educational Philosophy and Practice of Art Museums in the United States* (New York: Bureau of Publications, Teachers College, Columbia University, 1948) and Francis Henry Taylor, *Babel's Tower: The Dilemma of the Modern Museum* (New York: Columbia University Press, 1945) discuss the conflicts among curators and sponsors of museums as between conservation and education, on the one hand, and elitism and popularization, on the other. David F. Burg, *Chicago's White City of 1893* (Lexington: University Press of Kentucky, 1976) and Reid Badger, *The Great American Fair: The World's Columbian Exposition and American Culture* (Chicago: Nelson Hall, 1979) portray the 1893 fair; Joseph P. Cusker *et al., Dawn of a New Day: The New York World's Fair, 1939/40* (New York: New York University Press, 1980) portrays the 1939 fair. Stanley Appelbaum, *The Chicago World's Fair of 1893: A Photographic Record* (New York: Dover Publications, 1980) and *The New York World's Fair, 1939/1940 in 155 Photographs* (New York: Dover Publications, 1977) are valuable complementary works. There is no comparable history of the Brussels fair.

Edward P. Alexander, *Museum Masters: Their Museums and Their Influence* (Nashville, Tenn.: American Association for State and Local History, 1983) includes an excellent chapter on John Cotton Dana and the Newark Museum. Dana's *A Plan for a New Museum: The Kind It Will Profit a City to Maintain* (Woodstock, Vt.: Elm Tree Press, 1920) is the fullest mature statement of his vision. Charles C. Alexander, *Nationalism in American Thought, 1930–1945* (Chicago: Rand McNally and Company, 1969); Alfred Haworth Jones, "The Search for a Usable Past in the New Deal Era," *American Quarterly*, XXIII (1971), 710–723; Wayne Carr Willis, "A Fanfare for the Common Man: Nationalism and Democracy in the Arts of the American 1930's" (doctoral thesis, Brandeis University, 1977); and Charles C. Alexander, *Here the Country Lies: Nationalism and the Arts in Twentieth-Century America* (Bloomington: Indiana University Press, 1980) provide social and intellectual context for the New Deal arts projects; Jane De Hart Mathews, "Arts and the People: The New Deal Quest for Cultural Democracy," *Journal of American History*, LXII (1975–76), 316–339, provides an overview that was indispensable to my account. Grace Overmyer, *Government and the Arts* (New York: W. W. Norton and Company, 1939) and William F. McDonald, *Federal Relief Administration and the Arts* (Columbus: Ohio State University Press, 1973) discuss the economics and administration of the several federal arts projects. Richard D. McKinzie, *The New Deal for Artists* (Princeton: Princeton University Press, 1973) is an account of the Public Works of Art Project and the Federal Art Project. Francis V. O'Connor, ed., *Art for the Millions: Essays from the 1930's by the Artists and Administrators of the WPA Federal Art Project* (Greenwich, Conn.: New York Graphic Society, 1973) conveys the contemporary vision of the Federal Art Project. Jane De Hart Mathews, *The Federal Theatre, 1935–1939: Plays, Relief, and Politics* (Princeton: Princeton University Press, 1967) is an account of the Federal Theatre Project; Hallie Flanagan, *Arena* (New York: Duell, Sloan and Pearce, 1940) conveys the contemporary vision of the Project. Jerre Mangione, *The Dream and the Deal: The Federal Writers' Project, 1935–1943* (Boston: Little, Brown and Company, 1972) and Monty Noam Penkower, *The Federal Writers' Project: A Study in Government Patronage of the Arts* (Urbana: University of Illinois Press, 1977) are studies of the Federal Writers' Project. And Cornelius B. Canon, "The Federal Music Project of the Works Progress Administration: Music in a Democracy" (doctoral thesis, University of Minnesota, 1963) and Jannelle Jedd Warren Findley, "Of Tears and Need: The Federal Music Project, 1935–1943" (doctoral thesis, George Washington University, 1973) are accounts of the Federal Music Project. The WPA library program is discussed in Michael S. Blaney, " 'Libraries for the Millions': Adult Public Library Services and the New Deal," *Journal of Library History, Philosophy, and Comparative Librarianship*, XII (1977), 235–249.

Jane De Hart Mathews, "Art and Politics in Cold War America," *American Historical Review*, LXXXI (1976), 762–785, is an able discussion of the issues of censorship. Gary O. Larson, *The Reluctant Patron: The United States Government and the Arts, 1943–1965* (Philadelphia: University of Pennsylvania Press, 1983) is an excellent study of federal patronage before the enactment of the National Foundation on the Arts and Humanities Act of 1965. Anne Conyne Kaplan, "The National Endowment for the Humanities: Private Men and Public Causes" (doctoral thesis, Washington University, 1983) is a detailed study of the founding, organization, and early activities of the NEH. Statistics on libraries and museums are given in Filomena Simora, ed., *The Bowker Annual of Library and Book Trade*

Information, 25th Edition, 1980 (New York: R. R. Bowker Company, 1980), and *Museums for a New Century: A Report of the Commission on Museums for a New Century* (Washington, D.C.: American Association of Museums, 1984).

CHAPTER 10: PLACES OF WORK

Roy V. Scott, *The Reluctant Farmer: The Rise of Agricultural Extension to 1914* (Urbana: University of Illinois Press, 1970) and Theodore Reed Mitchell, "Oppositional Education in the Southern Farmers' Alliance, 1890–1900" (doctoral thesis, Stanford University, 1983) are excellent accounts of the educational efforts of the Grange and the Alliances; the Scott volume includes a comprehensive bibliography, including the classic works on the subject by Alfred Charles True. Edward Danforth Eddy, Jr., *Colleges for Our Land and Times: The Land-Grant Idea in American Education* (New York: Harper & Brothers, 1957); Margaret W. Rossiter, *The Emergence of Agricultural Science: Justus Liebig and the Americans, 1840–1880* (New Haven: Yale University Press, 1975) and "The Organization of Agricultural Sciences," in Alexandra Oleson and John Voss, eds., *The Organization of Knowledge in Modern America, 1860–1920* (Baltimore: Johns Hopkins University Press, 1979), pp. 211–248; the essays in Part II of Charles E. Rosenberg, *No Other Code: On Science and American Social Thought* (Baltimore: Johns Hopkins University Press, 1976); and Alan I. Marcus, *Agricultural Science and the Quest for Legitimacy: Farmers, Agricultural Colleges, and Experiment Stations, 1870–1890* (Ames: Iowa State University Press, 1985) provide the intellectual and academic context for the innovations of Seaman A. Knapp. Joseph Cannon Bailey, *Seaman A. Knapp: Schoolmaster of American Agriculture* (New York: Columbia University Press, 1945); *The General Education Board: An Account of Its Activities, 1902–1914* (New York: General Education Board, 1915); Raymond B. Fosdick, *Adventure in Giving: The Story of the General Education Board* (New York: Harper & Row, 1963); and *Century of Service: The First 100 Years of the United States Department of Agriculture* (Washington, D.C.: United States Department of Agriculture, 1963) are the best sources for Knapp's endeavors. William L. Bowers, *The Country Life Movement in America, 1900–1920* (Port Washington, N.Y.: Kennikat Press, 1974) and David B. Danbom, *The Resisted Revolution: Urban America and the Industrialization of Agriculture, 1900–1930* (Ames: Iowa State University Press, 1979) are the best accounts of the work of the Country Life Commission. Scott, *The Reluctant Farmer* and Clarence Beakan Smith and Meridith Chester Wilson, *The Agricultural Extension System of the United States* (New York: John Wiley & Sons, 1930) convey the legislative history and initial outcomes of the Smith-Lever Act; Grant McConnell, *The Decline of Agrarian Democracy* (Berkeley: University of California Press, 1953) informed my understanding of the relationship between the Smith-Lever Act, the American Farm Bureau Federation, and the increasing political power of American farmers during and after the 1930's.

Daniel Nelson, *Managers and Workers: Origins of the New Factory System in the United States, 1880–1920* (Madison: University of Wisconsin Press, 1975); Alfred D. Chandler, *The Visible Hand: The Managerial Revolution in American Business* (Cambridge, Mass.: Harvard University Press, 1977); Daniel T. Rodgers, *The Work Ethic in Industrial America, 1850–1920* (Chicago: University of Chicago Press, 1978); and Sanford M. Jacoby, *Employing Bureaucracy: Managers, Unions, and the Transformation of Work in American Industry, 1900–1945* (New York: Columbia University Press,

1985) discuss various aspects of the rise and rationalization of American industry. Herbert G. Gutman, *Work, Culture and Society in Industrializing America: Essays in American Working-Class and Social History* (New York: Alfred A. Knopf, 1976); David Montgomery, *Workers' Control in America: Studies in the History of Work, Technology, and Labor Struggles* (Cambridge: Cambridge University Press, 1979); and Richard Edwards, *Contested Terrain: The Transformation of the Workplace in the Twentieth Century* (New York: Basic Books, 1979) discuss the rationalization of industry from the vantage point of the worker. Alice Kessler-Harris, *Out to Work: A History of Wage-Earning Women in the United States* (New York: Oxford University Press, 1982); Leslie Woodcock Tentler, *Wage-Earning Women: Industrial Work and Family Life in the United States, 1900–1930* (New York: Oxford University Press, 1979); and Winifred D. Wandersee, *Women's Work and Family Values, 1920–1940* (Cambridge, Mass.: Harvard University Press, 1981) discuss industrialization from the perspective of women workers.

Paul H. Douglas, *American Apprenticeship and Industrial Education* (New York: privately printed, 1921); Roy Willmarth Kelly, *Training Industrial Workers* (New York: Ronald Press Company, 1920); John Van Liew Morris, *Employee Training: A Study of Education and Training Departments in Various Corporations* (New York: McGraw-Hill Book Company, 1921); and Nathaniel Peffer, *Educational Experiments in Industry* (New York: The Macmillan Company, 1932) document the various apprenticeship and training programs of American industry, as do the bulletins of the National Society for the Promotion of Industrial Education after its founding in 1906 and the National Association of Corporation Schools after its founding in 1913. Carroll D. Wright, *The Apprenticeship System in Its Relation to Industrial Education* (U.S., Bureau of Education, Bulletin, 1908, No. 6; Washington, D.C.: Government Printing Office, 1908) and the articles in the January, 1909, issue of the *Annals of the American Academy of Political and Social Science* are also replete with detailed information.

Samuel Haber, *Efficiency and Uplift: Scientific Management in the Progressive Era, 1890–1920* (Chicago: University of Chicago Press, 1964) and Daniel Nelson, *Frederick W. Taylor and the Rise of Scientific Management* (Madison: University of Wisconsin Press, 1980) discuss scientific management as a basis for industrial training programs. Stuart D. Brandes, *American Welfare Capitalism, 1880–1940* (Chicago: University of Chicago Press, 1976) and Gerd Korman, *Industrialization, Immigrants, and Americanizers: The View from Milwaukee, 1866–1921* (Madison: The State Historical Society of Wisconsin, 1967) discuss "welfarism" as the basis for industrial training programs. And Kendall Birr, *Pioneering in Industrial Research: The Story of the General Electric Research Laboratory* (Washington, D.C.: Public Affairs Press, 1957); Leonard S. Reich, *The Making of American Industrial Research: Science and Business at GE and Bell, 1876–1926* (Cambridge: Cambridge University Press, 1985); and David F. Noble, *America by Design: Science, Technology, and the Rise of Corporate Capitalism* (New York: Alfred A. Knopf, 1977) discuss research and development as bases for industrial training programs. Sonny Kleinfield, *The Biggest Company on Earth: A Profile of AT&T* (New York: Holt, Rinehart and Winston, 1981); Prescott C. Mabon, *Mission Communications: The Story of Bell Laboratories* (published by AT&T); and Stan Luxenberg, "Education at AT&T," *Change*, X (December–January, 1978–79), 26–36, provide details on company-sponsored education programs at AT&T before the court-ordered division of the Bell system in 1982. *Employee Training Activities of Trade Associations: Digest of Report of Conference in Chicago and Supplementary Statements* (Washington, D.C.: Trade Association Division, Chamber of Commerce of the United States, 1941) is informative on the educational programs of trade associations. Nell P. Eurich, *Corporate Classrooms: The Learning Business* (Princeton, N.J.: Carnegie Foundation for the Advancement of Teaching, 1985) is a thoughtful survey of programs during the early 1970's; it is usefully complemented by Charles R. De Carlo and Armsbee W. Robinson, *Education in Business and Industry* (New York: Center for Applied Research in Education, 1966); Suzanne Whitlock, "Education Programs in Industry: Case Studies—IBM Entry-Level Marketing Training and Rust International, Inc." (doctoral thesis, University of Alabama, 1982); Bonita L. Betters-Reed, "A History and Analysis of Three Innovative Graduate Institutions: The Arthur D. Little Management Education Institute, The Massachusetts General Hospital Institute of Health Professions and the Wang Institute of Graduate Studies" (doctoral thesis, Boston College, 1982); and Lee Frances Pitre, "Credit and Non Credit Education Opportunities Offered by Large Industrial Corporations" (doctoral thesis, University of Texas—Austin, 1980); and Jeanette Sledge Baker, "An Analysis of Degree Programs Offered by Selected Industrial Corporations" (doctoral thesis, University of Arizona, 1983). Theodore Brameld, ed., *Workers' Education in the United States* (New York: Harper & Brothers, 1941); Richard J. Altenbaugh, "Forming the Structure of a New Society within the Shell of the Old: A Study of Three Labor Colleges and Their Contribution to the American Labor Movement" (doctoral thesis, University of Pittsburgh, 1980); Rita R. Heller, "The Bryn Mawr Workers' Summer School, 1921–1938: A Surprising Alliance," *History of Higher Education Annual,* I (1981), 110–131, and "The Women of Summer: The Bryn Mawr Summer School for Women Workers, 1921–1938" (doctoral thesis, Rutgers University, 1986); Rachel Cutler Schwartz, "The Rand School of Social Science, 1906–1924: A Study of Worker Education in the Socialist Era" (doctoral thesis, State University of New York—Buffalo, 1984); and Kenneth Neil Teitelbaum, "Schooling for 'Good Rebels': Socialist Education for Children in the United States, 1900–1920" (doctoral thesis, University of Wisconsin—Madison, 1985) provide excellent accounts of educational institutions and programs conducted under Socialist, trade-union, or working-class oriented auspices; Kenneth D. Carlson, "Labor Education in America," *Review of Educational Research,* XLI (1971), 115–130, is a useful bibliographical discussion with regard to recent programs.

Donald Fleming, *William H. Welch and the Rise of Modern Medicine* (Boston: Little, Brown and Company, 1954); A. McGehee Harvey, "John Shaw Billings: Forgotten Hero of American Medicine," *Perspectives in Biology and Medicine,* XXI (1977–78), 35–57; and Kenneth M. Ludmerer, *Learning to Heal: The Development of American Medical Education* (New York: Basic Books, 1985) were the chief sources for my discussion of the transformation of American medical education toward the end of the nineteenth century. Robert Stevens, *Law School: Legal Education in America from the 1850's to the 1980's* (Chapel Hill: University of North Carolina Press, 1983) served as the basis for my account of the transformation of legal education under the leadership of Christopher Columbus Langdell at Harvard. Regina Markell Morantz-Sanchez, *Sympathy and Science: Women Physicians in American Medicine* (New York: Oxford University Press, 1985) and Karen Berger

Morello, *The Invisible Bar: The Woman Lawyer in America, 1836 to the Present* (New York: Random House, 1986) describe the unequal access of women to medical and legal education and to the professions of medicine and law. Rudolph C. Blitz, "Women in the Professions, 1870–1970," *Monthly Labor Review,* XCVII (May, 1974), 34–39, is a more general discussion of women's access to the professions. The transformation of theological education during the same era is described in Everett Hughes *et al., Education for the Professions of Medicine, Law, Theology, and Social Welfare* (New York: McGraw-Hill Book Company, 1972) and in a contemporary article by William Adams Brown in Paul Monroe, ed., *Cyclopedia of Education* (5 vols.; New York: The Macmillan Company, 1911–1913), V, 582–606. George Hunston Williams, ed., *The Harvard Divinity School: Its Place in Harvard University and in American Culture* (Boston: The Beacon Press, 1954) details the reshaping of the school during Eliot's administration. Monte A. Calvert, *The Mechanical Engineer in America, 1830–1910: Professional Cultures in Conflict* (Baltimore: Johns Hopkins Press, 1967) traces the development of professional education for engineers. Michael W. Sedlak, "The Emergence and Development of Collegiate Business Education in the United States, 1881–1974" (doctoral thesis, Northwestern University, 1977) traces the development of professional education for businesspeople. Jane E. Mottus, *New York Nightingales: The Emergence of the Nursing Profession at Bellevue and New York Hospital, 1850–1920* (Ann Arbor, Mich.: UMI Research Press, 1980) and Philip A. Kalisch and Beatrice J. Kalisch, *The Advance of American Nursing* (Boston: Little, Brown and Company, 1978) trace the development of professional education for nurses, albeit somewhat uncritically. Ellen Condliffe Lagemann, ed., *Nursing History: New Perspectives, New Possibilities* (New York: Teachers College Press, 1983) includes an excellent bibliography on nursing education.

Robert A. McCaughey, "The Transformation of American Academic Life: Harvard University, 1821–1892," *Perspectives in American History,* VIII (1974), 293–332, informed my understanding of the early development of the American academic profession. Jurgen Herbst, "Professionalization in Public Education, 1890–1920: The American High School Teacher," in Werner Conze and Jürgen Kocka, eds., *Industrielle Welt: Bildungsbürgertum im 19. Jahrhundert,* Part I (Stuttgart: Klett-Cotta Sonderdruck, 1985), pp. 495–529, did likewise for my understanding of the profession of schoolteaching. New York, University of the State of New York, College Department, *Professional Education in the United States* (3 vols.; Albany: University of the State of New York, 1899–1900) is the most detailed survey of American professional education at the end of the nineteenth century. Amitai Etzioni, *The Semi-Professions and Their Organization: Teachers, Nurses, Social Workers* (New York: The Free Press, 1969) and Nathan Glazer, "The Schools of the Minor Professions," *Minerva,* XII (1974), 346–364, discuss the educational problems of the so-called semi-professions. Ellen Condliffe Lagemann, *Private Power for the Public Good: A History of the Carnegie Foundation for the Advancement of Teaching* (Middletown: Wesleyan University Press, 1983) explicates the pivotal role of the Carnegie Foundation in the reshaping of American professional education. Paul Dickson, *Think Tanks* (New York: Atheneum, 1971) reviews the development of research institutes in the United States. Eli Ginzberg, "The Professionalization of the U.S. Labor Force," *Scientific American,* CCXL (March, 1979), 48–53, reviews the continuing professionalization of the American labor force.

Sidney Forman, *West Point: A History of the United States Military Academy* (New

York: Columbia University Press, 1960) and John P. Lovell, *Neither Athens nor Sparta? The American Service Academies in Transition* (Bloomington: Indiana University Press, 1979) provide basic historical data on the service academies. Gene M. Lyons and John W. Masland, *Education and Military Leadership: A Study of the ROTC* (Princeton: Princeton University Press, 1959) presents an account of the development of the Reserve Officers Training Corps. Amos A. Gordon, Jr., "Officer Education," in Roger W. Little, ed., *Handbook of Military Institutions* (Beverly Hills, Cal.: Sage Publications, 1970), pp. 211–245, is a general review. Rudolph Schwartz, "Non-Military Education in the United States Army and Air Force, 1900–1960" (doctoral thesis, New York University, 1963); Samuel Goldberg, *Army Training of Illiterates in World War II* (New York: Bureau of Publications, Teachers College, Columbia University, 1951); Louis H. Strehlow, "History of the Army General Educational Development Program: Origin, Significance, and Implications" (doctoral thesis, George Washington University, 1967); Harold F. Clark and Harold S. Sloan, *Classrooms in the Military: An Account of Education in the Armed Forces of the United States* (New York: Bureau of Publications, Teachers College, Columbia University, 1964); Morris Janowitz, "Basic Education and Youth Socialization in the Armed Forces," in Little, ed., *Handbook of Military Institutions*, pp. 167–210; Charles C. Moskos, Jr., *The American Enlisted Man: The Rank and File in Today's Military* (New York: Russell Sage Foundation, 1970); and Jack Edward Pulwers, "The Information and Education Programs of the Armed Forces: An Administrative and Social History, 1940–1945" (doctoral thesis, Catholic University of America, 1983) provide data on the training of enlisted personnel; Morris Janowitz and Stephen D. Westbrook, eds., *The Political Education of Soldiers* (Beverly Hills, Cal.: Sage Publications, 1983) deals incisively with one aspect of that training. Morris J. MacGregor, Jr., *Integration of the Armed Forces, 1940–1965* (Washington, D.C.: Center of Military History, United States Army, 1981); Charles C. Moskos, Jr., "Racial Integration in the Armed Forces," *American Journal of Sociology*, LXXII (1966–67), 132–148; and Warren L. Young, *Minorities and the Military: A Cross-National Study in World Perspective* (Westport, Conn.: Greenwood Press, 1962) provide rich data on the problems of race segregation and discrimination as well as racial integration in the armed services. Jeanne Holm, *Women in the Military: An Unfinished Revolution* (Novato, Cal.: Presidio Press, 1982) does likewise with respect to the problems of gender discrimination and equality in the armed services. Morris Janowitz, *The Reconstruction of Patriotism: Education for Civic Consciousness* (Chicago: University of Chicago Press, 1983) explores the relationship between conscription and civic education.

John Simmons, *The Education Dilemma: Policy Issues for Developing Countries in the 1980's* (Oxford: Pergamon Press, 1980); Michael P. Todaro, *Economic Development in the Third World* (2d ed.; New York: Longman, 1981); P. T. Bauer, *Equality, the Third World, and Economic Delusion* (Cambridge, Mass.: Harvard University Press, 1981); and Ingemar Fagerlind and Lawrence J. Saha, *Education and National Development: A Comparative Perspective* (Oxford: Pergamon Press, 1983) discuss the fundamental issues involved in aid and development programs. Merle Curti and Kendall Birr, *Prelude to Point Four: American Technical Missions Overseas, 1838–1938* (Madison: University of Wisconsin Press, 1954) and Merle Curti, *American Philanthropy Abroad: A History* (New Brunswick: Rutgers University Press, 1963) provide excellent historical data. Jacob A. Rubin, *Your Hundred Billion Dollars: The Complete History of American Foreign Aid* (Philadelphia: Chilton Books, 1964) is a comprehensive, if somewhat loosely organized, account; it is usefully complemented by the papers in William Y. Elliott, ed., *Education and Training in the Developing Countries: The Role of U.S. Foreign Aid* (New York: Frederick A. Praeger, 1966). Thomas S. Loeber, *Foreign Aid: Our Tragic Experiment* (New York: W. W. Norton Company, 1961) is highly critical of American efforts at overseas assistance. Thorsten V. Kalijarvi, "Point Four in the Contemporary Setting," *Annals of the American Academy of Political and Social Science*, CCLXVIII (March, 1950), 1–8, and Dean Acheson, *What Is Point Four?* (Washington, D.C.: Department of State, January 25, 1952) offer useful summaries of the rationale of Point Four and some of its early programs. Brent Ashbranner, *A Moment in History: The First Ten Years of the Peace Corps* (Garden City, N.Y.: Doubleday & Company, 1971) is an engaging account. Leon Weintraub, *International Manpower Development: A Role for Private Enterprise in Foreign Assistance* (New York: Frederick A. Praeger, 1969) is an informed discussion of programs and models of training under the auspices of multinational corporations; Krishna Kumar, ed., *Transnational Enterprises: Their Impact on Third World Societies and Cultures* (Boulder, Colo.: Westview Press, 1980) takes a more critical approach. *World Development Report, 1980* (New York: Oxford University Press, 1980) and *Education: Sector Policy Paper* (3d ed.; Washington, D.C.: World Bank, 1980) include incisive evaluations of transnational aid programs, undertaken by staff members of the World Bank. The addresses in Andrew Taylor, ed., *Insights into African Education: The Karl W. Bigelow Memorial Lectures* (New York: Teachers College Press, 1984) reflect some of the disenchantment of the 1980's with technical and educational assistance programs.

PART IV: A METROPOLITAN EDUCATION

The sources that describe the metropolitanization of American society are discussed on pp. 687–688 *supra*. In addition to metropolitanization itself, there is the crucial history of the perception of metropolitanization, which is depicted in a wide range of literature, including Georg Simmel, "The Metropolis and Mental Life," in *The Sociology of Georg Simmel*, translated and edited by Kurt H. Wolff (Glencoe, Ill.: The Free Press, 1950), pp. 409–424; Graham Wallas, *The Great Society: A Psychological Analysis* [1914] (reprint ed.; Lincoln: University of Nebraska Press, 1967); Walter Lippmann, *Public Opinion* (New York: Harcourt, Brace and Company, 1922); John Dewey, *The Public and Its Problems* (2d ed.; Chicago: Gateway Books, 1946); Anselm L. Strauss, *Images of the American City* (New York: The Free Press of Glencoe, 1961); Morton White and Lucia White, *The Intellectual versus the City: From Thomas Jefferson to Frank Lloyd Wright* (Cambridge, Mass.: Harvard University Press, 1962); Daniel J. Boorstin, *The Americans: The Democratic Experience* (New York: Random House, 1973); Malcolm Bradbury and James McFarlane, eds., *Modernism, 1890–1930* (New York: Penguin Books, 1976); and Patrick Brantlinger, *Bread and Circuses: Social Theories of Mass Decay* (Ithaca: Cornell University Press, 1983).

CHAPTER 11: INSTITUTIONS

Mary Jo Bane, *Here to Stay: American Families in the Twentieth Century* (New York: Basic Books, 1976); Howard Hayghe, "Marital and Family Characteristics of Workers, March 1974," *Monthly Labor Review*, XCVIII (January, 1975), 60–64, and

"Families and the Rise of Working Wives—An Overview," *ibid.*, XCIX (May, 1976), 12–19; Herbert G. Gutman, *The Black Family in Slavery and Freedom, 1750–1925* (New York: Pantheon Books, 1976); Paul C. Glick, "Marrying, Divorcing, and Living Together in the U.S. Today," *Population Studies,* XXXII (October, 1977), 3–39; John Demos and Serane Spence Boocock, eds., *Turning Points: Historical and Sociological Essays on the Family* (Chicago: University of Chicago Press, 1978); Sar A. Levitan and Richard S. Belous, *What's Happening to the American Family?* (Baltimore: Johns Hopkins University Press, 1981); Tamara K. Hareven, *Family Time and Industrial Time: The Relationship Between the Family and Work in a New England Industrial Community* (Cambridge: Cambridge University Press, 1982); Mary E. Cookingham, "Working after Childbearing in Modern America," *Journal of Interdisciplinary History,* XIV (1983–84), 773–792; and Linda J. Waite, *U.S. Women at Work* (Santa Monica, Cal.: The Rand Corporation, 1981) provide a plethora of data and interpretation concerning American families during the late nineteenth and early twentieth centuries. Lawrence A. Cremin, "The Family as Educator: Some Comments on the Recent Historiography," in Hope Jansen Leichter, ed., *The Family as Educator* (New York: Teachers College Press, 1974), pp. 76–91, and "Family Community Linkages in American Education: Some Comments on the Recent Historiography," in Hope Jensen Leichter, ed., *Families and Communities as Educators* (New York: Teachers College Press, 1979), pp. 119–140, review the literature and propose a theoretical orientation. U.S., Bureau of the Census, *Household and Family Characteristics: March 1984* (Current Population Reports, Series P-20, No. 238; Washington, D.C.: Government Printing Office, 1985) and *Marital Status and Living Arrangements: March 1984* (Current Population Reports, Series P-20, No. 399; Washington, D.C.: Government Printing Office, 1985); and Suzanne M. Bianchi and Daphne Spain, *American Women in Transition* (New York: Russell Sage Foundation, 1986) were the most recent sources of my Census data.

Robert S. Lynd and Helen Merrell Lynd, *Middletown: A Study in American Culture* (New York: Harcourt, Brace and Company, 1929), and *Middletown in Transition: A Study in Cultural Conflicts* (New York: Harcourt, Brace and Company, 1937) reported the Lynds' findings on Muncie, Indiana; Richard Jensen, "The Lynds Revisited," *Indiana Magazine of History,* LXXV (1979), 303–319, and Henry Etzkowitz, "The Americanization of Marx: *Middletown* and *Middletown in Transition,"* *Journal of the History of Sociology,* II (1979–80), 41–57, provide critical perspectives on the Lynds' studies that significantly informed my work. Theodore Caplow *et al., Middletown Families: Fifty Years of Change and Continuity* (Minneapolis: University of Minnesota Press, 1982) and "The Changing Middletown Family," *Journal of the History of Sociology,* II (1979–80), 66–98, report on the findings of Caplow's restudy of Muncie; Samuel H. Preston and John McDonald, "The Incidence of Divorce Within Cohorts of American Marriages Contracted since the Civil War," *Demography,* XVI (1979), 1–25, presents data taking issue with the claims of Caplow and his associates concerning continuity.

John Bodnar, *The Transplanted: A History of Immigrants in Urban America* (Bloomington: Indiana University Press, 1985) is an incisive synthesis of the recent literature, which conveys, *inter alia,* a sense of the rich variegation in immigrant family structures and styles. Among the recent studies of Italian-Americans, Lydio F. Tomasi, *The Italian American Family* (Staten Island, N.Y.: Center for

Migration Studies, 1972); George Enrico Pozzetta, "The Italians of New York City, 1890–1914" (doctoral thesis, University of North Carolina, 1971); Virginia Yans McLaughlin, *Family and Community Italian Immigrants in Buffalo, 1880–1930* (Ithaca: Cornell University Press, 1977); John W. Briggs, *An Italian Passage: Immigrants to Three American Cities, 1890–1930* (New Haven: Yale University Press, 1978); Patrick L. Venditta, "The Americanization of the Italian-American Immigrants in Omaha, Nebraska" (doctoral thesis, University of Nebraska, 1983); Robert Anthony Orsi, *The Madonna of 115th Street: Faith and Community in Italian Harlem, 1880–1950* (New Haven: Yale University Press, 1985); and Gary Ross Mormino, *Immigrants on the Hill: Italian-Americans in St. Louis, 1882–1982* (Urbana: University of Illinois Press, 1986) proved especially helpful. Josef J. Barton, *Peasants and Strangers: Italians, Rumanians, and Slovaks in an American City, 1890–1950* (Cambridge, Mass.: Harvard University Press, 1975) explores the interaction between familial education and schooling in Cleveland, with particular interest in the relationship between that interaction and social mobility. Among the recent studies of Mexican-Americans, Albert Camarillo, *Chicanos in a Changing Society: From Mexican Pueblos to American Barrios in Santa Barbara and Southern California, 1848–1930* (Cambridge, Mass.: Harvard University Press, 1979); Richard Griswold del Castillo, *The Los Angeles Barrio, 1850–1890* (Berkeley: University of California Press, 1979) and *La Familia: Chicano Families in the Urban Southwest, 1848 to the Present* (Notre Dame: University of Notre Dame Press, 1984); Mario T. Garcia, *Desert Immigrants: The Mexicans of El Paso, 1880–1920* (New Haven: Yale University Press, 1981); and Ricardo Romo, *East Los Angeles: History of a Barrio* (Austin: University of Texas Press, 1983) proved especially helpful. Gutman, *The Black Family in Slavery and Freedom;* Robert Aponte, Kathrynn M. Neckerman, and William Julius Wilson, "Race, Family Structure and Social Policy," *Working Paper 7: Race and Policy* (Washington, D.C.: Project on the Federal Social Role, National Conference on Social Welfare, 1985), chap. ii; Henry E. Felder, *The Changing Patterns of Black Family Income, 1960–1982* (Washington, D.C.: Joint Center for Political Studies, 1984); Suzanne Windholz Model, "Ethnic Bonds in the Workplace: Blacks, Italians, and Jews in New York City," (doctoral thesis, University of Michigan, 1985); and Bianchi and Spain, *American Women in Transition* provided the basic data for my discussion of the Afro-American family.

All the sources cited in connection with Part I are relevant to the development of the educational programs of churches and synagogues. There are three efforts in the recent literature to determine with some precision the extent of religious affiliation on the part of the American people over the past century. Edwin S. Gaustad, "America's Institutions of Faith," in Donald R. Cutler, ed., *The Religious Situation: 1968* (Boston: Beacon Press, 1968), 835–870; Milton V. Backman, Jr., *Christian Churches of America: Origins and Beliefs* (Provo: Brigham Young University Press, 1976); and Roger Kent Finke, "The Churching of America: 1850–1980" (doctoral thesis, University of Washington, 1984). They agree on the generalities, but disagree on the details. In the end, therefore, I constructed my own table from the Bureau of the Census surveys of religious bodies in 1890, 1916, 1936, and 1957, the more general Census data from U.S., Bureau of the Census, *Historical Statistics of the United States* (2 vols.; Washington, D.C.: Government Printing Office, 1975), and the more general survey data from the annual *Yearbook of American and Canadian Churches.* Dean R. Hoge and David A. Roozen, eds., *Under-*

standing Church Growth and Decline: 1950–1978 (New York: The Pilgrim Press, 1979); Jackson W. Carroll *et al.*, *Religion in America: 1950 to the Present* (San Francisco: Harper & Row, 1980); and Andrew M. Greeley and Peter H. Rossi, *The Denominational Society: A Sociological Approach to Religion in America* (Glenview, Ill.: Scott, Foresman and Company, 1972) are useful general works—the Carroll volume carries the data from the several Gallup polls on the religious beliefs of Americans in comparative perspective. Robert S. Michaelsen, "The Protestant Ministry in America: 1850 to the Present," in H. Richard Niebuhr and Daniel D. Williams, eds., *The Ministry in Historical Perspectives* (New York: Harper & Row, 1956); Charles W. Gilkey, "Preaching," in Arnold S. Nash, ed., *Protestant Thought in the Twentieth Century: Whence and Whither?* (New York: The Macmillan Company, 1951), pp. 203–221; Daniel P. Fuller, *Give the Winds a Mighty Voice: The Story of Charles E. Fuller* (Waco, Tex.: Word Books, 1972); James Morris, *The Preachers* (New York: St. Martin's Press, 1973); Jeffrey K. Haddon and Charles E. Swann, *Prime Time Preachers: The Rising Power of Televangelism* (Reading, Mass.: Addison-Wesley Publishing Company, 1981); and Razelle Frankl, *Televangelism: The Marketing of Popular Religion* (Carbondale: Southern Illinois University Press, 1987) were essential to my understanding of twentieth-century preaching and evangelical activities. Lynd and Lynd, *Middletown* and *Middletown in Transition* include data on the religious life of Muncie; Theodore Caplow *et al.*, *All Faithful People: Change and Continuity in Middletown's Religion* (Minneapolis: University of Minnesota Press, 1983) reports the findings of Caplow's restudy of Muncie. The sources on the Italian and Hispanic Roman Catholic experience have been discussed above. Barton, *Peasants and Strangers;* Marian Mark Stolarik, "Immigration and Urbanization: The Slovak Experience, 1870–1918" (doctoral thesis, University of Minnesota, 1974), and "Immigration, Education, and the Social Mobility of Slovaks, 1870–1930" in Randall M. Miller and Thomas D. Marzik, eds., *Immigrants and Religion in Urban America* (Philadelphia: Temple University Press, 1977), pp. 103–116; Howard F. Stein, "An Ethno-Historic Study of Slovak-American Identity" (doctoral thesis, University of Pittsburgh, 1972); and Sylvia June Alexander, "The Immigrant Church and Community: The Formation of Pittsburgh's Slovak Religious Institutions, 1880–1914" (doctoral thesis, University of Minnesota, 1980) are incisive sources on the Slovak religious experience. Arthur H. Fauset, *Black Gods of the Metropolis* (Philadelphia: University of Pennsylvania Press, 1944) portrays aspects of the black experience in the northern cities. In addition to many of the sources listed above, C. Luther Fry, *The U.S. Looks at Its Churches* (New York: Institute of Social and Religious Research, 1930); Robert L. Kelly, *Theological Education in America: A Study of One Hundred Sixty-One Theological Schools in the United States and Canada* (New York: George H. Doran Company, 1924); and W. A. Daniel, *The Education of Negro Ministers* (New York: George H. Doran Company, 1925) are valuable references on the education of ministers.

All the sources cited in connection with the sections on schooling in Chapter 5 are relevant to the development of schooling as an institution. The best sources for statistics of schooling are U.S., Bureau of the Census, *Historical Statistics of the United States* and the annual *Statistical Abstract of the United States;* the old United States Bureau of Education's Biennial Surveys of Education; and the more recent Department of Education's annual *Digest of Educational Statistics* and *The Condition of Education.* The data in Charles H. Judd's report on education in *Recent Social*

Trends in the United States: Report of the President's Research Committee on Social Trends (2 vols.; New York: McGraw-Hill Book Company, 1933), chap. vii, form an important benchmark study; U.S., Bureau of the Census, *Educational Attainment in the United States: March 1981 and 1980* (Current Population Reports, Series P-20, No. 390; Washington, D.C.: Government Printing Office, 1984) and the volumes on *The Condition of Education* published in the 1980's provided my latest data on schooling. Harold L. Hodgkinson, *All One System: Demographics of Education: Kindergarten through Graduate School* (Washington, D.C.: Institute for Educational Leadership, 1985) is a useful summary volume.

Edward A. Krug, *The Shaping of the American High School* (New York: Harper & Row, 1964), and *The Shaping of the American High School, 1920–1941* (Madison: University of Wisconsin Press, 1972) is the definitive work; John Elbert Stout, *The Development of High-School Curricula in the North Central States from 1860 to 1918* (Chicago: University of Chicago Press, 1921) remains a classic. Nina C. Vanderwalker, *The Kindergarten in American Education* (New York: The Macmillan Company, 1923); Evelyn Irene Weber, "The Kindergarten: Its Encounter with Educational Thought in America" (doctoral thesis, University of Wisconsin, 1966); and Agnes Snyder, *Dauntless Women in Childhood Education, 1856–1931* (Washington, D.C.: Association for Childhood Education International, 1972) are useful sources of data, though they are weak on interpretation. Lawrence J. Schweinhart, *Early Childhood Development Programs in the Eighties: The National Picture* (Ypsilanti, Mich.: High/Scope Childhood Policy Papers, 1985) presents recent enrollment data. Carole S. Ford, "The Origins of the Junior High School, 1890–1920" (doctoral thesis, Teachers College, Columbia University, 1982) is an excellent study; it is usefully complemented by Ronald Rex Barton, "A Historical Study of the Organization and Development of the Junior High and Middle School Movement, 1920–1975" (doctoral thesis, University of Arkansas, 1976). Herbert M. Kliebard, *The Struggle for the American Curriculum, 1893–1958* (Boston: Routledge and Kegan Paul, 1986) is a thoughtful study of the politics of curriculum making in the schools. David Tyack, Robert Lowe, and Elisabeth Hansot, *Public Schools in Hard Times: The Great Depression and Recent Years* (Cambridge, Mass.: Harvard University Press, 1984); John I. Goodlad, *A Place Called School: Prospects for the Future* (New York: McGraw-Hill Book Company, 1984); and Robert Hampel, *The Last Little Citadel: American High Schools since 1940* (Boston: Houghton Mifflin Company, 1986) present data on more recent developments in schooling. Morris Val Jones, ed., *Special Education Programs Within the United States* (Springfield, Ill.: Charles C. Thomas, 1968) is a series of essays on the education of exceptional children, many of which include historical data; Arch O. Heck, *Special Schools and Classes in Cities of 10,000 Population and More in the United States* (U.S., Office of Education Bulletin, 1930, No. 7; Washington, D.C.: Government Printing Office, 1930) is a useful benchmark study. James McLachlan, *American Boarding Schools: A Historical Study* (New York: Charles Scribner's Sons, 1970) and Otto F. Kraushaar, *American Nonpublic Schools: Patterns of Diversity* (Baltimore: Johns Hopkins University Press, 1972) are thoughtful studies of independent schools; the literature on religious day schools is reviewed in the bibliographies for Chapters 2 and 3. A first-class history of teachers and teaching in the United States is much needed. For the present, Lotus Delta Coffman, *The Social Composition of the Teaching Profession* (New York: Teachers College, Columbia University, 1911); Willard S.

Elsbree, *The American Teacher: Evolution of a Profession in a Democracy* (New York: American Book Company, 1939); Dan C. Lortie, *Schoolteacher: A Sociological Study* (Chicago: University of Chicago Press, 1975); and Michael Sedlak and Steven Schlossman, *Who Will Teach? Historical Perspectives on the Changing Appeal of Teaching as a Profession* (Santa Monica, Cal.: The Rand Corporation, 1986) are the best sources.

All the sources cited in connection with the sections on higher education in Chapter 5 are relevant to the development of colleges and universities in the late nineteenth and twentieth centuries; so also are the sources discussed in connection with the section on the professions and professional education in Chapter 10. In addition, those sources are usefully complemented by R. Freeman Butts, *The College Charts Its Course: Historical Conceptions and Current Properties* (New York: McGraw-Hill Book Company, 1939); Richard Hofstadter and Walter P. Metzger, *The Development of Academic Freedom in the United States* (New York: Columbia University Press, 1955), which remains a fine general history of American higher education; Edward J. Power, *A History of Catholic Higher Education in the United States* (Milwaukee: The Bruce Publishing Company, 1958); Robert Stanley Hodgman, "Shaping the Idea of the University: An Historical Analysis of the Origins and Development of the University Idea in European and American Thought" (doctoral thesis, University of Southern California, 1964); Merle Curti and Roderick Nash, *Philanthropy in the Shaping of American Higher Education* (New Brunswick: Rutgers University Press, 1965); William Clyde DeVane, *Higher Education in Twentieth-Century America* (Cambridge, Mass.: Harvard University Press, 1965); Charlotte Williams Conable, *Women at Cornell: The Myth of Equal Education* (Ithaca: Cornell University Press, 1977); Roberta A. Frankfort, *Collegiate Women: Domesticity and Career in Turn-of-the-Century America* (New York: New York University Press, 1977); Mary Roth Walsh, *"Doctors Wanted: No Women Need Apply": Social Barriers in the Medical Profession, 1835–1975* (New Haven: Yale University Press, 1977); Joan Grace Zimmerman, "College Culture in the Midwest, 1890–1930" (doctoral thesis, University of Virginia, 1978); Kenneth Bradley Orr, "The Impact of the Depression Years, 1929–39, on Faculty in American Colleges and Universities" (doctoral thesis, University of Michigan, 1978); William C. Ringenberg, *The Christian College: A History of Protestant Higher Education in America* (Grand Rapids, Mich.: William B. Eerdmans Publishing Company, 1984); and Helen Lefkowitz Horowitz, *Alma Mater: Design and Experience in the Women's Colleges from Their Nineteenth-Century Beginnings to the 1930s* (New York: Alfred A. Knopf, 1984), and *Campus Life: Undergraduate Cultures from the End of the Eighteenth Century to the Present* (New York: Alfred A. Knopf, 1987).

Hofstadter and Metzger, *The Development of Academic Freedom in the United States* includes the fullest discussion of the German influence on American higher education, along with a critical discussion of the literature; Thomas Neville Bonner, *American Doctors and German Universities: A Chapter in International Intellectual Relations, 1870–1914* (Lincoln: University of Nebraska Press, 1963) discusses the German influence in one significant academic domain. Roger L. Geiger, *To Advance Knowledge: The Growth of American Research Universities, 1900–1940* (New York: Oxford University Press, 1986) documents the rise of the research universities, though, as has been mentioned, with greater attention to faculties of arts and sciences than to so-called professional faculties. Richard J. Storr, *The Beginnings of Graduate Education in America* (Chicago: University of Chicago Press, 1953) and *The Beginning of the Future: A Historical Approach to Graduate Education in the Arts and Sciences* (New York: McGraw-Hill Book Company, 1973) detail the rise of graduate studies in the United States. Merle Curti and Vernon Carstensen, *The University of Wisconsin: A History, 1848–1925* (2 vols.; Madison: University of Wisconsin Press, 1949); Hugh Hawkins, *Pioneer: A History of the Johns Hopkins University, 1874–1889* (Ithaca: Cornell University Press, 1962); and Richard J. Storr, *Harper's University: The Beginnings* (Chicago: University of Chicago Press, 1966) portray several models of the research university. Joseph Dorfman, *Thorstein Veblen and His America* (New York: The Viking Press, 1934) and David Riesman, *Thorstein Veblen: A Critical Interpretation* (New York: Charles Scribner's Sons, 1953) provide biographical and intellectual context for Veblen's criticisms of university administrators. Ellen Condliffe Lagemann, *Private Power for the Public Good: A History of the Carnegie Foundation for the Advancement of Teaching* (Middletown: Wesleyan University Press, 1983) discusses the standardizing efforts of the foundation. George E. Peterson, *The New England College in the Age of the University* (Amherst: Amherst College Press, 1964) discusses the colleges that decided not to become universities during the late nineteenth and early twentieth centuries. Horowitz, *Alma Mater* is eloquent on the varying aims and designs of the women's colleges. Raymond Wolters, *The New Negro on Campus: Black College Rebellions of the 1920's* (Princeton: Princeton University Press, 1975) is an excellent study of student unrest in the black colleges during the 1920's. The changing character of the American professoriate is revealed, *inter alia,* in Robert A. McCaughey, "The Transformation of American Academic Life: Harvard University, 1821–1892," *Perspectives in American History,* VIII (1974), 239–332; Martin Trow, *Teachers and Students: Aspects of American Higher Education* (New York: McGraw-Hill Book Company, 1975); Patricia Albjerg Graham, "Expansion and Exclusion: A History of Women in American Higher Education," *Signs,* III (1978), 759–773; and Susan B. Carter, "Academic Women Revisited: An Empirical Study of Changing Patterns of Women's Employment as College and University Faculty, 1890–1963," *Journal of Social History,* XIV (1980–81), 675–699. My colleague Walter P. Metzger kindly shared with me his research in progress on the history of the academic profession in the United States during the late nineteenth and twentieth centuries.

John W. C. Johnstone and Ramon J. Rivera, *Volunteers for Learning: A Study of the Educational Pursuits of American Adults* (Chicago: Aldine Publishing Company, 1965) is an excellent survey undertaken under the auspices of the National Opinion Research Center. The statistics on adult education in the 1980's are taken from *The Condition of Education: 1983 Edition.* All the sources cited in the bibliography for Chapter 7 are relevant to the development of the media of popular communication as educators. My general argument about the substance presented by the media of popular communication is a version of Jeremy Tunstall's in *The Media Are American* (New York: Columbia University Press, 1977). Benjamin M. Compaine, ed., *Who Owns the Media? Concentration of Ownership in the Mass Communications Industry* (White Plains, N.Y.: Knowledge Industry Publications, 1979) is the most comprehensive work on concentration of ownership; it is usefully complemented by David Halberstam, *The Powers That Be* (New York: Alfred A. Knopf, 1979). A. M. Sperber, *Murrow: His Life and Times* (New York: Freundlich

Books, 1986) is the fullest biography of Edward R. Murrow, and provides an excellent context for his comments concerning the potential of television as an instrument of public education. Daniel Pope, *The Making of Modern Advertising* (New York: Basic Books, 1983); Stephen Fox, *The Mirror Makers: A History of American Advertising and Its Creators* (New York: William Morrow and Company, 1984); Roland Marchand, *Advertising the American Dream: Making Way for Modernity, 1920–1940* (Berkeley: University of California Press, 1985); and Michael Schudson, *Advertising, the Uneasy Persuasion: Its Dubious Impact on American Society* (New York: Basic Books, 1984) are rich sources of data on the development of American advertising—the Schudson work is surely the most skeptical and the most incisive. Michael Schudson, *Discovering the News: A Social History of American Newspapers* (New York: Basic Books, 1978); Susan Kingsbury *et al., Newspapers and the News: An Objective Measurement of Ethical and Unethical Behavior by Representative American Newspapers* (New York: G. P. Putnam's Sons, 1937); Llewellyn White, *The American Radio: A Report to the Broadcasting Industry in the United States from the Commission on Freedom of the Press* (Chicago: University of Chicago Press, 1947); and Leo Bogart, *The Age of Television: A Study of Viewing Habits and the Impact of Television on American Life* (3d ed.; New York: Frederick Ungar Publishing Company, 1972) are useful for the substance conveyed by the media of popular communication. John Tebbel and Sarah Miles Watts, *The Press and the Presidency, From George Washington to Ronald Reagan* (New York: Oxford University Press, 1985) details the ways in which twentieth-century presidents have used the media of popular communication to advertise and advance their policies. Edward J. Epstein, *News from Nowhere: Television and the News* (New York: Random House, 1973) and Herbert J. Gans, *Deciding What's News: A Study of "CBS Evening News," "NBC Nightly News," "Newsweek," and "Time"* (New York: Pantheon Books, 1979) discuss the decisions involved in what becomes the substance of the news. The essays in the Fall, 1982, issue of *Daedalus*, under the title "Print Culture and Video Culture," explore the differences in content, structure, and style of print and electronic communications. Steven J. Simmons, *The Fairness Doctrine and the Media* (Berkeley: University of California Press, 1978) and Ford Rowan, *Broadcast Fairness: Doctrine, Practice, Prospects* (New York: Longman, 1984) explicate the law and the politics of the Fairness Doctrine. Bernard A. Weisberger, *The American Newspaperman* (Chicago: University of Chicago Press, 1961); John W. C. Johnstone, Edward J. Slawski, and William W. Bowman, *The News People: A Sociological Portrait of American Journalists and Their Work* (Urbana: University of Illinois Press, 1976); Irving Fang, *Those Radio Commentators* (Ames: Iowa State University Press, 1977); and David H. Weaver and C. Cleveland Wilhoit, *The American Journalist: A Portrait of U.S. News People and Their Work* (Bloomington: Indiana University Press, 1986) are useful sources for the journalist's career in the twentieth century.

CHAPTER 12: CONFIGURATIONS

The conceptual framework for this chapter is set forth in my discussion of the configuration of education as an interrelated complex of educative institutions in *Public Education* (New York: Basic Books, 1976). The essays by Hope Jensen Leichter and J. W. Getzels in Leichter, ed., *Families and Communities as Educators* (New York: Teachers College Press, 1979) are also relevant. My conception of

New York as the "archetypical" American metropolis is derived from Ira Katznelson's early formulations of the work of the Committee on New York City of the Social Science Research Council, which he graciously shared with me; my conception of the New York metropolitan region as a "laboratory" for the study of metropolitan education is derived from Jean Gottmann, *Megalopolis: The Urbanized Northeastern Seaboard of the United States* (New York: The Twentieth Century Fund, 1961).

There is no first-class comprehensive history of New York City that would be the counterpart of Bessie L. Pierce's history of Chicago or Blake McKelvey's history of Rochester—Edward Robb Ellis's *The Epic of New York City* (New York: Coward-McCann, 1966) is a popular account with a useful bibliography. There are, however, a number of monographs touching on a variety of aspects of the city's development that, taken together, provide a useful composite social history of the city during the late nineteenth and twentieth centuries. Among the works I relied on were Moses Rischin, *The Promised City: New York's Jews, 1870–1914* (Cambridge, Mass.: Harvard University Press, 1962); Seth M. Scheiner, "The Negro in New York City, 1865–1910" (doctoral thesis, New York University, 1963); Gilbert Osofsky, *Harlem: The Making of a Ghetto: Negro New York, 1890–1930* (New York: Harper & Row, 1966); Arthur A. Goren, *New York Jews and the Quest for Community: The Kehillah Experiment, 1908–1922* (New York: Columbia University Press, 1970); Herbert G. Gutman, *The Black Family in Slavery and Freedom, 1750–1925* (New York: Pantheon Books, 1976); Thomas Kessner, *The Golden Door: Italian and Jewish Immigrant Mobility in New York City 1880–1915* (New York: Oxford University Press, 1977); Ronald H. Bayor, *Neighbors in Conflict: The Irish, Germans, Jews, and Italians of New York City, 1929–1941* (Baltimore: Johns Hopkins University Press, 1978); Jeffrey S. Gurock, *When Harlem Was Jewish, 1870–1930* (New York: Columbia University Press, 1979); David Ment, *The Shaping of a City: A Brief History of Brooklyn* (New York: The Brooklyn Educational and Cultural Alliance, 1979); Carl W. Condit, *The Port of New York: A History of the Rail and Terminal System from the Beginnings to the Pennsylvania Station* (Chicago: University of Chicago Press, 1981); Ira Katznelson, *City Trenches: Urban Politics and the Patterning of Class in the United States* (New York: Pantheon Books, 1981); and Suzanne Windholz Model, "Ethnic Bonds in the Work Place: Blacks, Italians, and Jews in New York City" (doctoral thesis, University of Michigan, 1985). Ira Rosenwaike, *Population History of New York City* (Syracuse: Syracuse University Press, 1972) and Thomas Bender, *New York Intellect: A History of Intellectual Life in New York City, from 1715 to the Beginnings of Our Own Time* (New York: Alfred A. Knopf, 1987) are superb, as are the collections of photographs in John A. Kouwenhoven, *The Columbia Historical Portrait of New York City* (Garden City, N.Y.: Doubleday and Company, 1953) and Grace M. Mayer, *Once Upon a City* (New York: The Macmillan Company, 1958). *New York City Guide* [1939] (reprint ed.; New York: Octagon Books, 1970), produced under the auspices of the Federal Writers' Project, is a treasure trove of information.

Jane Allen Shikoh, "The 'Higher Life' in the American City of the 1890's: A Study of Its Leaders and Their Activities in New York, Chicago, Philadelphia, St. Louis, Boston, and Buffalo" (doctoral thesis, New York University, 1972) and Gunther Barth, *City People: The Rise of Modern City Culture in Nineteenth-Century America* (New York: Oxford University Press, 1980) are pathbreaking works on the culture of American cities in the late nineteenth and early twentieth centuries. Diane Ravitch, *The Great School Wars, New York City, 1805–1973: A History of the Public Schools as Battlefield of Social Change* (New York: Basic Books, 1974) is an incisive history of the public school system; it is usefully complemented by Moses C. Stambler, "The Democratic Revolution in the Public High Schools of New York City, 1898–1917" (doctoral thesis, New York University, 1964); Selma Berrol, "Immigrants at School: New York City, 1898–1914" (doctoral thesis, City University of New York, 1967); Isabella J. W. Lee, "A History of the Labor Union Movement among New York City Public School Teachers" (doctoral thesis, New York University, 1971); David Martin Ment, "Racial Segregation in the Public Schools of New England and New York, 1840–1940" (doctoral thesis, Columbia University, 1975); Martin E. Dann, " 'Little Citizens': Working Class and Immigrant Childhood in New York City, 1890–1915" (doctoral thesis, City University of New York, 1978); and Stephan E. Brumberg, *Going to America, Going to School: The Jewish Immigrant Public School Encounter in Turn-of-the-Century New York City* (New York: Praeger Publishers, 1986). New York (City), Board of Education, *Fiftieth Annual Report of the Superintendent of Schools,* published under the title "The First Fifty Years: A Brief Review of Progress, 1898–1948," is an excellent source of information on the development of the public school system of Greater New York. The records and papers of the New York City Board of Education are in the Teachers College Library.

S. Willis Rudy, *The College of the City of New York: A History, 1847–1947* (New York: City College Press, 1949) and Sherry Gorelick, *City College and the Jewish Poor: Education in New York, 1880–1924* (New Brunswick: Rutgers University Press, 1981) illuminate the history of City College; Samuel White Patterson, *Hunter College: Eighty-five Years of Service* (New York: Lantern Press, 1955) is a house history. Sheila C. Gordon, "The Transformation of the City University of New York, 1945–1970" (doctoral thesis, Columbia University, 1975) and David E. Lavin, Richard D. Alba, and Richard A. Silberstein, *Right versus Privilege: The Open Admissions Experiment at the City University of New York* (New York: The Free Press, 1981) illuminate the development of the City University. *A History of Columbia University, 1754–1904* (New York: Columbia University Press, 1904) and R. Gordon Hoxie *et al., A History of the Faculty of Political Science, Columbia University* (New York: Columbia University Press, 1955) deal with aspects of the history of Columbia University; Theodore Francis Jones, ed., *New York University, 1832–1932* (New York: New York University Press, 1933) does the same for New York University. I am indebted to my colleague Douglas Sloan for sharing with me his research on the networks of artists and humanists in New York City that represent the continuation of his research published as "Science in New York City, 1867–1907," *Isis,* LXXI (1980), 35–76.

Harry P. Kraus, "The Settlement House Movement in New York City, 1886–1914" (doctoral thesis, New York University, 1970); Catherine J. Ross, "Society's Children: The Care of Indigent Youngsters in New York City, 1875–1903" (doctoral thesis, Yale University, 1977); and Helen Bittar, "The Y.M.C.A. of the City of New York, 1870 to 1920" (doctoral thesis, New York University, 1979) provide accounts of the development of welfare institutions and services. Berrol, "Immigrants at School"; Dann, " 'Little Citizens' "; and Brumberg, *Going to America, Going to School* provide data on the Americanization efforts of the schools. Nicholas John Russo, "The Religious Acculturation of the Italians in New York City" (doctoral thesis, St. John's University, 1968); George Enrico Pozzetta, "The Italians of New York City, 1890–1914" (doctoral thesis, University of North Carolina, 1971); and Silvano Tomasi, *Piety and Power: The Role of Italian Parishes in the New York Metropolitan Area* (Staten Island, N.Y.: Center for Migration Studies, 1975) discuss the larger educational experience of the Italian-Americans. Joseph P. Fitzgerald, *Puerto Rican Americans: The Meaning of Migration to the Mainland* (Englewood Cliffs, N.J.: Prentice-Hall, 1971) and Deborah Dash Moore, *At Home in America: Second Generation New York Jews* (New York: Columbia University Press, 1981) do likewise for Puerto Ricans and Jews. Miriam Cohen, "Changing Education Strategies among Immigrant Generations: New York Italians in Comparative Perspective," *Journal of Social History*, XV (1981–82), 443–466, undertakes a variety of illuminating comparisons among ethnoreligious groups and across generations. Gutman, *The Black Family in Slavery and Freedom* and Model, "Ethnic Bonds in the Work Place" explicate aspects of the larger educational experience of the blacks.

The study of the New York Metropolitan Region undertaken during the 1950's under the direction of Raymond Vernon yielded several pioneering volumes, the most important of which for my purposes were Edgar M. Hoover and Raymond Vernon, *Anatomy of a Metropolis: The Changing Distribution of People and Jobs within the New York Metropolitan Region* (Cambridge, Mass.: Harvard University Press, 1959); Oscar Handlin, *The Newcomers: Negroes and Puerto Ricans in a Changing Metropolis* (Cambridge, Mass.: Harvard University Press, 1959); and Raymond Vernon, *Metropolis 1985: An Interpretation of the Findings of the New York Regional Study* (Cambridge, Mass.: Harvard University Press, 1960). Gottmann, *Megalopolis* is also a pioneering study that proved invaluable to my work. David W. Levy, *Herbert Croly of the "New Republic": The Life and Thought of an American Progressive* (Princeton: Princeton University Press, 1985) provides context for Croly's writing on New York's metropolitan dominance. John Tebbel, *A History of Book Publishing in the United States* (4 vols.; New York: R. R. Bowker, 1972–1981) details the central role of the New York publishers in the development of the book industry in the United States. Caroline F. Ware, *Greenwich Village, 1920–1930: A Comment on American Civilization in the Post-War Years* (Boston: Houghton Mifflin Company, 1935); Henry F. May, *The End of American Innocence: The First Years of Our Own Time, 1912–1917* (New York: Alfred A. Knopf, 1959); and Kenneth S. Lynn, "The Rebels of Greenwich Village," *Perspectives in American History*, VIII (1974), 335–377, detail the role of Greenwich Village in the artistic and literary movements of the 1920's and 1930's. Nathan Irvin Huggins, *Harlem Renaissance* (New York: Oxford University Press, 1971); David L. Lewis, *When Harlem Was in Vogue* (New York: Alfred A. Knopf, 1981); and Jervis Anderson, *This Was Harlem: A Cultural Portrait, 1900–1950* (New York: Farrar, Straus and Giroux, 1982) do the same for Harlem. John Michael Kennedy, "Philanthropy and Science in New York City: The American Museum of Natural History, 1868–1968" (doctoral thesis, Yale University, 1968); Phyllis Dain, *The New York Public Library: A History of Its Founding and Early Years* (New York: New York Public Library, 1972); and Calvin Tomkins, *Merchants and Masterpieces: The Story of the Metropolitan Museum of Art* (New York: E. P. Dutton and Company, 1970) present accounts of three characteristic metropolitan cultural and educational institutions. Harold Rugg, *That Men May Understand*

(New York: Doubleday, Doran and Company, 1941), which was written in the style of a memoir, and Peter F. Carbone, Jr., *The Social and Educational Thought of Harold Rugg* (Durham: Duke University Press, 1967) provide an account of the Rugg social studies textbooks, in context.

Chapter 13: Lives

The conceptual framework for this chapter is set forth in my discussion of the educational biography as a life history prepared with educational matters uppermost in mind, in *Public Education* (New York: Basic Books, 1976). Hope Jensen Leichter, "Families and Communities as Educators: Some Concepts of Relationship," in Leichter, ed., *Families and Communities as Educators* (New York: Teachers College Press, 1979), pp. 3–94, and Ellen Condliffe Lagemann, *A Generation of Women: Education in the Lives of Progressive Reformers* (Cambridge, Mass.: Harvard University Press, 1979) are also relevant.

Oscar Handlin, *Al Smith and His America* (Boston: Little, Brown and Company, 1958) and Matthew Josephson and Hannah Josephson, *Hero of the Cities: A Political Portrait of Alfred E. Smith* (Boston: Houghton Mifflin Company, 1969) are the best biographies; they are usefully complemented by Paula Eldot, *Governor Alfred E. Smith: The Politician as Reformer* (New York: Garland Publishing, 1983) and Donn C. Neal, *The World Beyond the Hudson: Alfred E. Smith and National Politics, 1918–1928* (New York: Garland Publishing, 1983). Alfred E. Smith, *Up to Now: An Autobiography* (New York: The Viking Press, 1928) was an indispensable source for my purposes. Emily Smith Warner, *The Happy Warrior: A Biography of My Father, Alfred E. Smith* (Garden City, N.Y.: Doubleday and Company, 1956) was also helpful.

The Joy of Service: Memoirs of Elizabeth Dodge Huntington Clarke (New York: National Board of the Young Women's Christian Association, 1979) was my principal source for Clarke's life; it is usefully complemented by Mrs. George Huntington, "In Constantinople During the War," *Women's International Quarterly,* IX (1919), 6–12, and Elizabeth Dodge Clarke, Introduction, in Phoebe Clary, *When Latticed Windows Opened: Experiences of an American in Turkey* (New York: National Board of the Young Women's Christian Association, 1969), pp. 5–14. Lagemann, *A Generation of Women,* chap. i, is the best source on Grace H. Dodge. Ruth Howell, a niece of Clarke, kindly furnished information on Clarke's relationship with her mother, Grace Parish Dodge.

David A. Hollinger, *Morris R. Cohen and the Scientific Ideal* (Cambridge, Mass.: M.I.T. Press, 1975) is the most incisive biographical work on Cohen; it is usefully complemented by David Slive, "Morris Raphael Cohen as Educator" (doctoral thesis, State University of New York—Buffalo, 1984), which has a superb bibliography. *A Dreamer's Journey: The Autobiography of Morris Raphael Cohen* (Boston: The Beacon Press, 1949) was indispensable to my account, as was Leonora Cohen Rosenfield, *Portrait of a Philosopher: Morris R. Cohen in Life and Letters* (New York: Harcourt, Brace and World, 1962). The *Autobiography* includes a comprehensive bibliography of Cohen's published works. Cohen's diaries and other papers are in the University of Chicago Library.

One can glean information on the life of Mary Ryshpan Cohen from the sources listed in connection with Morris Raphael Cohen. Their son-in-law, Harry N. Rosenfield, was generous in providing reminiscences and additional data.

Paul Sann, *Kill the Dutchman: The Story of Dutch Schultz* (New Rochelle, N.Y.: Arlington House, 1971) and the essay by Alvin F. Harlow on Arthur Flegen-heimer (Dutch Schultz) in Supplement One of the *Dictionary of American Biography* were my principal sources for Flegenheimer's life.

Ruth F. Prago's taped interview of William Santora, dated July 24, 1980, in the Oral History of the American Left at the Tamiment Library, New York Univer-sity, was my principal source for Santora's life.

Ellen Harkins Wheat, *Jacob Lawrence: American Painter* (Seattle: Seattle Art Museum, 1986), and "Jacob Lawrence" (doctoral thesis, University of Washing-ton, 1986) are the best accounts of Lawrence's life. Both have rich notes and bibliographical comments; the former also includes beautiful illustrations of Law-rence's work; Carroll Greene's interviews with Lawrence on October 25, 1969 and November 26, 1969, and Avis Berman's interviews with Jacob and Gwen Lawrence on July 20, 1982 and August 4, 1983, both of which are in the Archives of American Art at the Smithsonian Institution, were invaluable for my purposes. Martin Duberman, *Black Mountain: An Exploration in Community* (New York: E. P. Dutton and Company, 1972) provides useful context for Lawrence's experience there. Lawrence currently teaches at the University of Washington.

Fay Ping Chiang was generous in providing data on Hop Kun Leo Chiang and Bay Doc Chiang, her parents. In addition, "The Eight-Pound Livelihood," a documentary videotape at the New York Chinatown History Project to which Fay Chiang contributed and in which she appeared, provided helpful context.

Chapter 14: Characteristics

John K. Folger and Charles B. Nam, *Education of the American Population* (Washing-ton, D.C.: Government Printing Office, 1967); *Children Out of School in America* (Washington, D.C.: Children's Defense Fund, 1974); U.S., Bureau of the Census, *Educational Attainment in the United States: March 1981 and 1980* (Current Popula-tion Reports, Series P-20, No. 390; Washington, D.C.: Government Printing Office, 1984); and Harold L. Hodgkinson, *All One System: Demographics of Education, Kindergarten through Graduate School* (Washington, D.C.: Institute for Educational Leadership, 1985) provide data on the schooling of the American population. Leo Bogart, *The Age of Television: A Study of Viewing Habits and the Impact of Television on American Life* (3d ed.; New York: Frederick Ungar Publishing Company, 1972); George Comstock *et al., Television and Human Behavior* (New York: Columbia University Press, 1978); and U.S., Public Health Service, *Television and Behavior: Ten Years of Scientific Progress and Implications for the Eighties* (Rockville, Md.: National Institute of Mental Health, 1982) provide data on the effects of television broad-casting. Rush Welter, *Popular Education and Democratic Thought in America* (New York: Columbia University Press, 1962) is the best general work on the politiciza-tion of American education, as I develop that concept. Robert W. Iversen, *The Communists and the Schools* (New York: Harcourt, Brace and Company, 1959) and Ellen K. Schrecker, *No Ivory Tower: McCarthyism and the Universities* (New York: Oxford University Press, 1986) discuss the congressional investigations of teach-ers and professors during the early 1950's. The literature on the student move-ments of the late 1960's and early 1970's is reviewed on p. 716 *supra*.

The recent studies of the history of literacy and the American reading public are discussed on pp. 729–730 *supra.* In addition, Folger and Nam, *Education of the American Population,* chap. iv, gathers together data provided by the Bureau of the Census; while David Harman, "Keeping Up in America," *Wilson Quarterly,* X (1986), 116–131, and *Illiteracy: A National Dilemma* (Cambridge, Mass.: Cambridge Book Company, 1987) present data on the special problems of the insufficiently literate. Herbert H. Hyman, Charles R. Wright, and John Shelton Reed, *The Enduring Effects of Education* (Chicago: University of Chicago Press, 1975); Richard M. Wolf, *Achievement in America: National Report of the United States for the International Educational Achievement Project* (New York: Teachers College Press, 1977); Herbert H. Hyman and Charles R. Wright, *Education's Lasting Influence on Values* (Chicago: University of Chicago Press, 1979); and Kenneth A. Feldman and Theodore M. Newcomb, *The Impact of College on Students* (2 vols.; San Francisco: Jossey-Bass Publishers, 1973) are the best analyses of the outcomes of American schooling. Barbara Lerner, "American Education: How Are We Doing?" *Public Interest,* No. 69 (Fall, 1982), 59–82, takes issue with Richard Wolf; Wolf replies in "American Education: The Record Is Mixed," *ibid.,* No. 72 (Summer, 1983), 124–128; Lerner's rejoinder, "Facing the Unpleasant Facts about Achievement" follows in *ibid.,* 129–132. Alex Inkeles, "The International Evaluation of Educational Achievement," in *Proceedings of the National Academy of Education,* IV (1977), 139–200; Ellis B. Page, "The Methodology of International Evaluation of Educational Achievement," in *ibid.,* V (1978), 19–48; and the several articles in the February, 1987, issue of the *Comparative Education Review* provide context and criticism for the work of the International Association for the Evaluation of Educational Achievement. William Greenbaum, *Measuring Educational Progress* (New York: McGraw-Hill Book Company, 1977) does likewise for the National Assessment of Educational Progress.

Gabriel A. Almond and Sidney Verba, *The Civic Culture: Political Attitudes and Democracy in Five Nations* (Princeton: Princeton University Press, 1963); Sidney Verba and Norman H. Nie, *Participation in America: Political Democracy and Social Equality* (New York: Harper & Row, 1972); Sidney Verba, Norman H. Nie, and Jae-on Kim, *Participation and Political Equality: A Seven-Nation Comparison* (Cambridge: Cambridge University Press, 1978); Walter Dean Burnham, *Critical Elections and the Mainsprings of American Politics* (New York: W. W. Norton & Company, 1970) and *The Current Crisis in American Politics* (Oxford: Oxford University Press, 1982) discuss the participation of Americans in political and social affairs. Herbert Croly, *The Promise of American Life* [1909], edited by Arthur M. Schlesinger, Jr. (Cambridge, Mass.: Harvard University Press, 1965); Arthur M. Schlesinger, "Radicalism and Conservatism in American History," in *New Viewpoints in American History* (New York: The Macmillan Company, 1922), chap. v; and Albert O. Hirschman, *Shifting Involvements: Private Interest and Public Action* (Princeton: Princeton University Press, 1982) put forward historically significant interpretations of the shifting involvement of Americans in political and social affairs and, explicitly in Croly's case and implicitly in Schlesinger's and Hirschman's, the bearing of those involvements on education. The relationship of schooling to social and economic mobility has been endlessly debated by American social scientists; the articles by David L. Featherman and Sidney L. Willhelm in the March/April, 1979, issue of *Society* (XVI, No. 3, 4–17) sum up the debate thoughtfully. The ceremonials, rituals, myths, and icons conveyed by television programming are incisively analyzed in Gregor T. Goethals, *The TV Ritual: Worship at the Video Altar* (Boston: Beacon Press, 1981), a work that has been too little noticed. Daniel Yankelovich, *New Rules: Searching for Self-Fulfillment in a World Turned Upside Down* (New York: Random House, 1981) and Robert N. Bellah *et al.*, *Habits of the Heart: Individualism and Commitment in American Life* (Berkeley: University of California Press, 1985) present interpretations of recent shifts in American values based on interview and survey data.

Edward Shils, *Center and Periphery: Essays in Macrosociology* (Chicago: University of Chicago Press, 1975) addresses many of the issues and problems involved in metropolitanism, particularly in Part I. Frederick Whyte, *The Life of W. T. Stead* (2 vols.; London: Jonathan Cape, 1925) and Richard Heathcote Heindel, *The American Impact on Great Britain, 1898–1914: A Study of the United States in World History* (Philadelphia: University of Pennsylvania Press, 1940) provide context for Stead's *The Americanisation of the World; or, The Trend of the Twentieth Century* (London: The "Review of Reviews" Office, 1902). Jane Hunter, *The Gospel of Gentility: American Women Missionaries in Turn-of-the-Century China* (New Haven: Yale University Press, 1984) provides context for the work of Sarah Luella Miner; there is an excellent biography of Miner by Robert E. Chandler in *Notable American Women*. John Dewey's influence abroad is explicated in William W. Brickman, "John Dewey: Educator of Nations," in William W. Brickman and Stanley Lehrer, eds., *John Dewey: Master Educator* (New York: Society for the Advancement of Education, 1959), pp. 89–100; in Thomas Berry, "Dewey's Influence in China," in John Blewett, ed., *John Dewey: His Thought and Influence* (New York: Fordham University Press, 1960), chap. viii; and in William W. Brickman, ed., *John Dewey's Impressions of Soviet Russia and the Revolutionary World, Mexico-China-Turkey, 1929* (New York: Bureau of Publications, Teachers College, Columbia University, 1964). L. H. Ofosu-Appian, *The Life of Dr. J. E. K. Aggrey* (Accra, Ghana: Waterville Publishing House, 1975) is the most recent biography. The role of the Phelps-Stokes Fund in the export of American education on the Hampton-Tuskegee model to Africa is detailed in Kenneth James King, *Pan-Africanism and Education: A Study of Race Philanthropy and Education in the Southern States of America and East Africa* (Oxford: Clarendon Press, 1971). The role of the Rockefeller Foundation in the export of medical education on the Johns Hopkins model to China is detailed in Peter Buck, *American Science and Modern China, 1876–1936* (Cambridge: Cambridge University Press, 1980). The essays in Robert F. Arnove, ed., *Philanthropy and Cultural Imperialism: The Foundations at Home and Abroad* (Bloomington: Indiana University Press, 1982) deal with similar issues. The references illuminating the more general export of American models of education during the twentieth century are discussed on pp. 714 and 738–739 *supra*.

INDEX

Lawrence A. Cremin is Frederick A. P. Barnard Professor of Education at Teachers College, Columbia University, and President of the Spencer Foundation. He has been a member of the Teachers College Faculty since 1949 and of the Columbia University Department of History since 1961; and he served as President of Teachers College from 1974 to 1984. He has also been President of the History of Education Society and of the National Academy of Education.

A historian and interpreter of education, he has been at work for a quarter-century on the comprehensive history of American education that the present volume concludes. The first volume, *American Education: The Colonial Experience, 1607–1783,* was published in 1970. The second volume, *American Education: The National Experience, 1783–1876,* was published in 1980, and was awarded the Pulitzer Prize for History in 1981. Cremin is also the author of *The Transformation of the School: Progressivism in American Education, 1876–1957* (1961), which was awarded the Bancroft Prize in American History for 1962.

Professor Cremin's other books include *The American Common School: An Historic Conception* (1951), *The Wonderful World of Ellwood Patterson Cubberley* (1965), *The Genius of American Education (1965), Public Education* (1976), and *Traditions of American Education* (1977).

Professor Cremin was born in New York City on October 31, 1925, and attended the Townsend Harris High School and the College of the City of New York. He received the Master of Arts and Doctor of Philosophy degrees from Columbia University. He is an elected member of the American Philosophical Society, the American Academy of Arts and Sciences, and the Society of American Historians, and he holds honorary doctorates from sixteen colleges and universities.